How to Examine Psychological Experts in Divorce and Other Civil Actions

Marc J. Ackerman, Ph.D.
Andrew W. Kane, Ph.D.

 LEGAL PUBLISHING™

Edited by Kristen Rasmussen
 and Jane Culbert
Graphics by Deb Lockhart

For information on this and other PESI manuals, audiotapes and videotapes, please contact:

Customer Relations
Professional Education Systems, Inc.
P.O. Box 1208
Eau Claire, WI 54702

1-800-826-7155

ISBN 1-55957-102-0

Authors

Marc J. Ackerman, Ph.D., is a licensed psychologist in Wisconsin who has testified in hundreds of custody cases in Wisconsin and throughout the United States. Dr. Ackerman recently developed the "Ackerman-Schoendorf Parent Evaluation for Custody Test" (ASPECT) which will be published in 1990. He has served as dean or director of clinical training of the Wisconsin School of Professional Psychology since 1981. He also serves as the director of North Shore Psychotherapy Associates, is a member of the Board of Governors of the Wisconsin Society of Clinical and Consulting Psychologists, past president of the Milwaukee Area Psychological Association, member of the National Register of Health Service Providers in Psychology and the American Psychological Association, and a Diplomate of the American Board of Medical Psychotherapists.

Andrew W. Kane, Ph.D., is a licensed psychologist in Wisconsin who has been involved in more than a thousand cases involving involuntary commitment, guardianship, protective placement, personal injury, juvenile court, and family court. Dr. Kane is the current president of the Division of Forensic and Correctional Psychologists of the Wisconsin Psychological Association, a member of the Board of Governors of the Wisconsin Society of Clinical and Consulting Psychologists, and a former president of the Wisconsin and Milwaukee Area psychological associations. He is a member of the senior faculty of the Wisconsin School of Professional Psychology and of the clinical faculty at the Medical College of Wisconsin and the University of Wisconsin-Milwaukee. In 1987, Dr. Kane received an award for "Distinguished Professional Contribution to the Practice of Psychology in the Public Interest" from the Wisconsin Psychological Association. He is a Fellow and Diplomate of the American Board of Medical Psychotherapists and is listed in the National Register of Health Service Providers in Psychology. This is Dr. Kane's second co-authorship of a book, and he has eighteen other professional publications. Dr. Kane is president of Andrew W. Kane & Associates, S.C., a firm providing clinical, consulting, and forensic psychological services.

Dedicated to the children of divorce.

Table of Contents

Foreword

In the past, child custody disputes arising out of divorce actions generally focused on the testimony of the parties, and occasionally the parties' friends. One parent might argue that he or she bought the clothes for the children, and the other party might respond by saying that he or she took the children to the pediatrician. Occasionally a teacher might be called as a witness. However, that testimony would not go beyond whether the children came to school on time, were dressed appropriately, and had their homework completed. The teacher was not able to compare the two parties in their roles as parents, and certainly had no ability to distinguish the psychological makeup of the parents.

In recent years a new trend has emerged. The courts now are looking to qualified psychologists to provide information for the court to utilize in determining what is in the best interests of the children. However, all too often psychologists speak a different language than lawyers and judges. Their testimony of what occurred in psychological evaluations means little if the court does not understand its implications.

As an attorney who frequently represents a party in a child custody dispute arising either in a divorce or a post divorce situation, I have often looked for sources of information regarding psychological testing. Questions that I asked included: what tests are administered in a complete psychological evaluation, why are they administered, and what do they mean? Then my focus would turn to examining—and cross-examining—the expert psychological witness.

Although a number of treatises discuss these tests, most current treatises are directed at psychologists. Until now, there has not been any book which explained psychological evaluations and testimony in a manner intended for the legal community.

Dr. Marc J. Ackerman and Dr. Andrew W. Kane, both clinical psychologists practicing in Milwaukee, have finally authored such a book. *How to Examine Psychological Experts in Divorce and Other Civil Actions* provides a comprehensive explanation that allows attorneys to understand the tests which are administered in custody disputes, and why they are administered. More than that, however, this treatise will assist attorneys and psychologists in preparing for direct and cross-examination. Each chapter includes a list of questions designed to elicit important information.

Realizing that there is more to psychological evaluations and testimony than just testing, the authors have also addressed issues such as ethical questions, how divorce affects families, and statistical concepts.

I strongly applaud Drs. Ackerman and Kane for their outstanding contribution to the legal and the psychological communities.

James J. Podell

Preface

This book was written for the purpose of aiding attorneys in the difficult task of examining and cross-examining psychological experts in court actions. A psychologist generally has an undergraduate major in psychology, a doctorate in psychology, and a clinical internship, followed by many years of experience. The training process lasts from eight to ten years. Attorneys entering into the areas of psychological expertise often find themselves confused and easily led astray. Unfortunately, as a result, much good testimony is lost because the attorney does not know what questions to ask or how or when to ask them.

This book is not written from the point of view of "how to get the expert." Instead, it is written to provide "the information that you need to know" to do an intelligent examination and cross-examination of a psychological expert.

It is important to note that each chapter of this book is a summary of information used to teach entire courses in the training of psychologists. The authors, as a result, selected the information that they felt attorneys were most likely to need in dealing with these matters rather than including all the information available. Most chapters are followed by a list of suggested questions for examination and cross-examination. The attorney is cautioned not to assume that every question will apply to every case. The questions are followed by page citations within the chapter to help the attorney understand the basis for the question. It is essential for the attorney to read the chapter to understand the basis for each question, and not merely list off the questions in court.

Although the primary focus of this book is psychologists involved in divorce actions, the vast majority of the information provided applies to psychologists involved in any court action.

Chapter One introduces the reader to the concept of expert witnesses and discusses the various types of mental health professionals to help the attorney understand whom he or she may be examining in court matters. This chapter identifies how to qualify and disqualify expert testimony.

Chapter Two discusses ethical issues that both psychologists and attorneys must be aware of when involved with court actions. The standards for administering psychological tests and reporting data are also presented in this chapter.

Chapter Three covers what constitutes a psychological evaluation. It also presents test administration, examiner effect, and research discussing the state of art in custody evaluations.

Chapter Four is presented as an informational chapter to help the reader understand the dynamics of custody actions on the family as a whole. It discusses the mediation process, how divorce affects children at different developmental milestones, and presents considerable research in the area of how divorce affects families.

Chapter Five is designed to help the reader understand basic statistical concepts. Only those statistical concepts that will be useful in interpreting data from tests used in custody evaluations are presented. Readers interested in an in-depth discussion of more sophisticated statistical procedures are referred to statistics textbooks.

Chapter Six focuses on the major intelligence tests administered within the profession. The Wechsler Scales, Stanford-Binet, the McCarthy Scales of Children's Abilities, and the Kaufman-Assessment Battery for Children are discussed in-depth in this chapter.

Chapter Seven covers the Minnesota Multiphasic Personality Inventory (MMPI). Although other personality inventory instruments are discussed at the end of the chapter, the bulk of the presentation deals with the MMPI. The reader must understand that over 12,000 articles and books have been published on the MMPI since its inception almost 50 years ago. As a result, although a lengthy chapter, it is only an overview of what the MMPI is all about. The reader is referred to books published by Graham, Greene, Dahlstrom, Welch and Dahlstrom, and Duckworth and Anderson listed in the reference section for a more in-depth discussion of the MMPI. A section on the revised MMPI (MMPI-2) discusses changes made to the MMPI because of out-of-date or objectionable items, new problem areas, and the need to develop new norms for the MMPI.

Chapter Eight discusses other forms of personality testing. The Rorschach, Thematic Apperception Test (TAT), and the Children's Apperception Test (CAT) are presented at length in this chapter. The end of the chapter includes a discussion of other minor instruments used.

Chapter Nine presents the reader with three tests that have been designed primarily for use in custody evaluations. The Ackerman-Schoendorf Parent Evaluation for Custody Test (ASPECT), the Bricklin Perceptual Scales (BPS), and the Parenting Stress Index (PSI) are discussed. Both the ASPECT and the Bricklin are relatively new instruments. The Bricklin was introduced for national distribution in 1987 and the ASPECT will be published in 1990. They both offer advances in the area of helping individuals make custody determination decisions.

Chapter Ten deals exclusively with abuse-related issues, including research and special testing considerations for physical abuse, sexual abuse, and psychological abuse.

Chapters Eleven through Fourteen present other special considerations that may arise during psychological evaluations: alcoholism, mental disorders, mental retardation, and criminal histories. The presentation in these chapters includes information that the reader should know about these areas and special testing considerations.

Chapter Fifteen presents the various coding systems that have been used in diagnosing individuals. It discusses the Diagnostic and Statistical Manual of Mental Disorders (DSM-III-R) and the International Classification of Diseases (ICD-9) in detail. It also presents an explanation of how the classification systems were devised and gives a description of their benefits and shortcomings.

Acknowledgments

There are many individuals who should be acknowledged for the support and help that they have provided during the two and one-half years of this project. First, the authors would like to acknowledge the undying support, valuable feedback, and legal expertise provided by attorneys James and Peggy Podell. Furthermore, the authors would like to acknowledge the insightful ideas and valuable probing provided by attorney Gary Bakke. Another acknowledgment goes to Stephanie S. Ackerman for her support and help in coordinating this task. Lastly, the authors would like to acknowledge the office staffs of Marc J. Ackerman, Ph.D., and Podell & Podell for the countless hours of clerical support provided throughout this entire project.

Chapter One
The Expert Witness

One of the most significant trends in litigation has been the increased reliance on testimony by expert witnesses. Divorce and custody litigation is no exception. Mental health professionals now appear routinely to express opinions in custody and visitation disputes. Thus, the selection, preparation, and presentation of an expert witness is frequently crucial to the outcome.

As a general rule, a witness who qualifies as an expert will be permitted to testify to opinions and, in some states, to hearsay; in contrast, testimony of a lay witness is generally restricted to observed facts.

The rules of evidence governing expert testimony are based on the assumption that there is a distinction between facts and opinions. Because the judge and jury are often not chosen for their expertise in any particular area, there will be some areas in which they require assistance if they are to understand the facts presented to them. Thus, people with expertise in areas such as human development, personality, psychopathology, and so forth are called on to go beyond the facts and to state opinions which may be helpful to the judge and/or jury in drawing conclusions.[1]

Furthermore, there are circumstances where expert testimony *must* be presented and those where it *may* be presented. The former are those wherein "psychiatric or psychological issues are material in a case and lay people are incapable of reaching rationally based conclusions on these issues without specialized assistance."[2] The latter occurs when the judge determines that it would be helpful to him and/or the jury to have expert testimony. Thus, Rule 702 of the Federal Rules of Evidence permits the introduction of expert testimony when "scientific, technical, or other specialized knowledge will assist the trier of fact to understand the evidence or to determine a fact in issue."[3] Seventeen states have adopted Rule 702 verbatim, while four other states have adopted modified versions of the rule.[4]

The quality of expert testimony is dependent on a number of factors. First, psychology and psychiatry are not exact sciences. "Facts" in both fields are those data which the present state of knowledge indicates are accurate, but they are always subject to displacement by information which becomes available at a later time. Many conclusions are based on the data a given expert accepts as factual, while another expert may draw conclusions from a different data base. While the weight of scientific opinion may fall on one side or the other, on a given issue there may be two or more legitimate opinions, each based on a significant data base. Each position may be widely enough held to be considered to have gained general acceptance in the field.[5]

Second, psychologists and psychiatrists have repeatedly been shown by research to be no better at predicting the future, whether with regard to dangerousness or to quality of parenting, than are laymen, with the exception of short-range predictions. In spite of this, they are frequently called upon to make long-range predictions, e.g., which parent in a custody matter will be the best parent to award custody of the children to until of legal age.[6]

Third, the quality of the opinions given by the expert depends on a number of factors. Different experts will have different levels of familiarity with the professional literature and personal experience in the area being testified about. Some experts will work much harder than others to gather data on which to base an opinion in a particular case. Up to a point, the more data the expert has, and the more diverse the sources of information (the divorcing couple, the children, teachers, other professionals, etc.), the better.[7]

Fourth, a number of factors make the interface of psychology and the law a difficult one for the mental health professional.

> First, legal decisionmaking often is bedeviling to psychologists because it seems to require testimony that *either* is artificially certain or is made to seem unreliable. As scientists, psychologists are accustomed to regarding truth as established through an objective, impersonal inquiry, yielding fully disclosed results. . . . Second, truth in science is reached only probabilistically, rests on educated hypotheses about

> what works, and is always subject to change. . . .
> Third, scientists seek consistency. But, while courts
> try to adhere to established principles of law, achiev-
> ing consistency is not itself a paramount virtue. . . .
> Fourth, in the courtroom, each participant's personality
> is shaped by the role he or she is forced to play. . . .
> Fifth, psychologists must always be aware of the dif-
> ference between being asked to testify in a 'micro' or
> experimental context, and a 'macro' or policy con-
> text. . . . Sixth, the all too frequent image is of a
> rational scientific psychologist seeking to enlighten,
> but often being rebuffed by traditional, archaic and
> irrational law. [However,] much of the psychology
> that is applied to legal issues has little in common
> with the natural sciences. . . . Seventh, psychologists
> themselves enter court with a prejudice against the
> adversary process.[8]

However, the fact that there are difficulties in translating
psychological answers into legal answers does not mean that
the attempt should not be made. These difficulties are "inherent in the adversarial process and can be found any time a
legal question requires non-legal information from experts. . . ."[9]
"Clinicians have tended to be the ones who have pointed out the
limitations on predicting behavior. But in *Barefoot v. Estelle*,[10]
the U.S. Supreme Court reasoned that the fact-finding and
adversary system would make up for the shortcomings of the
predictions."[11]

The expert can also benefit the attorney by developing both
general and specific questions for lay and expert witnesses,
including helping to anticipate the arguments and theories of
the opposition. It is also part of the expert's responsibilities to
apprise the attorney of research, testing, and trends in professional areas which may affect the attorney's theories and plan
of action. Ingenuity, creativity, and perseverance are important
qualities in an expert.[12]

CHOOSING AND QUALIFYING THE EXPERT WITNESS

The attorney must have some understanding of the nature
and meaning of the qualifications of a potential expert, so that
the best qualified expert for the given purpose may be retained.

In most forensic matters, courts have long shown a preference for psychiatrists over psychologists, in large part because
of the wide acceptance of a medical model of mental disorder,
and in part because psychology as a nonacademic profession
did not emerge until after World War II.[13] The "medical model"
indicates that

> (1) There are disease entities, which have etiology,
> course, and outcome; (2) These diseases are of
> organic origin; (3) Even if conceived as psychological
> diseases, they are viewed in analogy with physical
> ailments. There is an underlying state which is
> manifested in surface symptoms. Disease is to be
> inferred from symptoms; changing symptoms will
> not cure the disease; (4) People get these diseases
> through no fault of their own; (5) Cure depends on
> professional intervention, preferably by people with
> medical training, and (6) The diseases are in the
> person and, although they may have culturally dis-
> tinct manifestations, the essential disease process is
> universal and not culturally specific.[14]

However, in child custody cases it is psychologists who have
most of the relevant training and experience.

> Most expert testimony about relevant disordered
> behavior in a legal setting does not turn on organic
> or biological explanations for behavior, for which a
> medical school education may be important. Instead,
> psychological and behavioral theories tend to under-
> ly these explanations, subjects on which psycholo-
> gists have education and training at least equal to
> and perhaps superior to that of many
> psychiatrists."[15]

Part of the problem is that any physician may legally call
himself a psychiatrist, since physicians, like lawyers, are
licensed as generalists.[16] Since medical school and internships
provide very little training in psychiatry, some psychiatrists in
any community will be practicing

> with only an introductory course in psychiatry and a
> psychiatric clinical rotation, [which is] negligible

education in psychological theories as compared with a Ph.D. or Psy.D. clinical psychologist who has received extensive education and training in these fields. Moreover, the field of academic psychiatry has itself gradually begun to utilize its medical expertise to explore the organic and biological facets of mental disorder, leaving the psychological arena to psychologists.[17]

Thus, unless the testimony one seeks is primarily biological in nature, the expert should usually be a psychologist.

Definition of a Psychiatrist

"A *psychiatrist* is a *physician*, either allopathic (M.D.) or osteopathic (D.O.), who specializes in the study and treatment of mental disorders."[18] There are about 31,000 practicing psychiatrists in the United States.[19] After medical school and an internship, most go into a residency involving three years of seminars and colloquia and provision of clinical services under supervision in both inpatient and outpatient settings. However, the residency is not necessary in order for a physician to call himself or herself a psychiatrist. A small percentage seek certification from the American Board of Psychiatry and Neurology through oral and written examinations after several years of practice, but about two-thirds of practicing psychiatrists are not board certified.[20] A psychiatrist who is certified in psychiatry and neurology may also elect to take further examinations to become certified as well in child psychiatry. "This examination, like the one in psychiatry, is designed to test basic competence in child psychiatry, not special expertise."[21]

It is also possible for a psychiatrist to become certified by the American Board of Forensic Psychiatry on the basis of oral and written examinations testing both legal knowledge and clinical skills. "Eligibility for the examinations requires licensure in the jurisdiction in which the applicant resides, five years of residency training, and substantial experience in forensic psychiatry. There are currently about 80 diplomates in forensic psychiatry in the country."[22]

Definition of a Psychologist

"A *psychologist* is a person who is trained to study and measure mental processes, and to diagnose and treat mental disorders. The use of the title *psychologist* is regulated by state law in all 50 states."[23]

> *Licensure* is a process by which individuals are granted permission to perform a defined set of *functions*, [e.g.,] diagnosing or treating behavioral, emotional or mental disorders . . . . In contrast, *certification* focuses not on the function performed but on the use of a particular *professional title* (such as 'psychologist'), and limits its use to individuals who have met specified standards for education, experience, and examination performance.[24]

There are currently about 25 states with true licensure laws, which carefully specify what the functions of a psychologist are, while 15–20 have "permissive licensing" or certification statutes. A few states establish specialty criteria for psychologists, but most license only generically.[25] Most states permit a psychologist licensed by another state to work for about 20–30 days per year without seeking separate licensure, so it is possible for an expert to reside in one state but to do an evaluation and testify in another state.

A "psychologist" in most jurisdictions means an individual who possesses a doctoral degree in psychology, either a Ph.D. or a Psy.D. (Doctor of Psychology) degree. Some states license individuals with master's degrees through grandfathering when the law was instituted, through current statutes or administrative code, or both. The typical Ph.D. or Psy.D. clinician majored in psychology as an undergraduate, having ten or more courses in psychology and often more in related disciplines. He or she then went to graduate school, where there were 90 or more semester hours (or equivalent) in the specialty area, plus a full-time predoctoral internship for a full year, usually involving both inpatient and outpatient treatment.[26]

The individual with a Ph.D. had as part of his or her graduate training supervised experience in the conduct of research, and did a research project in partial satisfaction of the doctoral degree. The Psy.D. received advanced training in statistics as well, but may have no personal research experience. If the attorney needs someone with research experience, the Ph.D. is usually the better candidate. If the amount of predoctoral clinical experience is more important, the Psy.D. may have more than a Ph.D. with the same years of training.[27]

There are five major areas of graduate study in psychology: clinical, counseling, school, industrial/organizational, and experimental. The first, clinical, will produce most of the experts an attorney may wish to consult. Their training "prepares the future practitioner to evaluate and treat patients with severe psychological difficulties."[28] Most Ph.D.'s and virtually all Psy.D.'s are clinical psychologists, and nearly all are licensed or eligible for licensure for independent practice.

One of the more frequently asked questions is, "what is the difference between psychiatry and clinical psychology?" There is probably an 80 to 90 percent overlap between what the psychiatrist and clinical psychologist are able to do with their professional expertise. The major distinction between psychology and psychiatry is that psychiatrists can prescribe medication, while psychologists can administer, score, and interpret psychological tests. As stated earlier, psychiatry has moved more in the direction of the biological or organic aspects of mental health. This has resulted in their expertise in prescribing medications becoming a more central part of their work. There is a preliminary movement in some states to train psychologists to prescribe medications. However, it is not likely that this will occur for a number of years, if ever.

As psychologists become more independent in their ability to practice, much of their work has included hospitalizing severely disturbed individuals. Until recent years, psychologists generally did not have admitting privileges in psychiatric hospital settings. Patients generally had to be referred to psychiatrists to be hospitalized. However, in recent years psychologists have increasingly been allowed co-admitting privileges with psychiatrists, or total admitting privileges independent of any other practitioners, depending upon the state in which they practice and the hospital with which they are affiliated. The trend throughout the United States is for more and more states and hospitals to allow psychologists to admit independently. These psychologists are allowed to admit patients, be totally in charge of treatment, write orders, and perform all nonmedical tasks.

"Counseling psychology training is oriented toward preparing psychologists who intend to work with less severely disturbed individuals, usually in outpatient and higher education settings."[29] They also need an internship lasting one academic year rather than the full year required for the clinical psychologist.[30] It is also a concern that a majority of counseling psychology training programs require no course work in projective testing, leaving most counseling psychologists poorly prepared to administer or interpret these tests.[31] Thus, they will generally do well at dealing with ongoing problems in living, but less well than clinical psychologists, on the average, in assessing and treating serious psychopathology.

"School psychologists are trained to evaluate, treat, and consult in areas directly related to educational problems of children and adolescents. The training emphasis is less on severe emotional problems and more on evaluation and remediation of learning problems."[32] Their internships last one academic year.[33] Thus, one would look to a school psychologist in cases where educational problems figure prominently, and where diagnosis and treatment of psychopathology are less of a factor.

Each of the above specialty programs within psychology is evaluated by the American Psychological Association, and people coming out of an "APA-approved" training program and internship are likely to have had a quality education. The other two specialty programs, experimental and industrial/organizational, "do not require internships and are not granted APA approval."[34] The former primarily prepares psychologists for careers in teaching and research. While relatively few experimental psychologists are called upon as experts, "one study reports on a sample of experimental psychologists who had testified in more than 200 cases in the last decade alone."[35] Industrial/Organizational psychologists are trained to apply principles of psychology to business problems.

There are postdoctoral fellowships in psychology for people who wish further specialized training, but relatively few people take advantage of them.[36] Neuropsychology, for example, is an area where postdoctoral fellowships are often required.

The difficulty of becoming licensed as a psychologist varies significantly among the states. Most use a national examination,[37] but each sets its own cutoff point on that examination.[38] This national examination is used to help establish reciprocity from one state to the next. A psychologist submits the score to the state he or she is moving to, and if the score exceeds the state's cutoff, a license may be granted in the new state without additional content examinations. However, most states add additional examinations, e.g., in ethics or law.[39] Most require at least one year of postdoctoral supervised experience prior to receipt of a license for independent practice.[40]

While most licensing of psychologists is generic (i.e., no specialty designation as "clinical," "counseling," etc.), some states recognize that some psychologists meet the requirements for listing in the *National Register of Health Service Providers in Psychology*.[41] Those requirements include being

> currently licensed or certified by the State Board of Examiners of Psychology at the independent-practice level of psychology; a doctoral degree in psychology from a regionally accredited educational institution, [and] two years of supervised experience in health services in psychology, of which one year is in an organized health service training program or internship and one year is post doctoral.[42]

There are more than 15,000 psychologists listed by the National Register. Wherever "clinical" or "health" expertise is relevant, an attorney would do well to try to retain a psychologist who is National Register listed.

Diplomate status may be conferred upon psychologists by the American Board of Professional Psychology (ABPP) in the areas of clinical, counseling, school, industrial/organizational, and neuropsychology, each on the basis of four years minimum of postdoctoral experience and an examination conducted by a panel of five diplomates involving all areas of practice.[43]

Diplomate status in forensic psychology is conferred by the American Board of Forensic Psychology (ABFP). It also requires four years' postdoctoral experience, plus letters from people familiar with the candidate's work, evaluation of a forensic work sample, and an oral examination by three diplomates.[44]

A relatively new diplomate-conferring body, the American Board of Medical Psychotherapists, originated in 1982. It is interdisciplinary, permitting psychologists, psychiatrists, social workers, and other mental health professionals to apply. Certification at the diplomate level requires at least five years of supervised experience (three in medical psychotherapy), three professional letters of reference, a representative work sample, and a professional vita. The 1988–1989 *National Directory of Medical Psychotherapists* lists about 1,800 individuals who have achieved the level of "Fellow and Diplomate" or are clinical associates pursuing the former level of certification.

Social Workers

Social workers may have either a bachelor's or master's degree (M.S.W., M.S.S.W., etc.) and are trained to help the individual in the context of the social and economic milieu, e.g., to find a living setting which meets the individual's social, psychological, and physical needs.[45] Many social workers will also be competent to evaluate children's developmental needs, parental emotional and economic stability, and each parent's ability to address the child's emotional, social, and economic needs.

As of December, 1988, 45 states, Puerto Rico, and the Virgin Islands license or certify social workers at the master's level, and some states also license or certify at the bachelor's level.[46] It should be noted that many people are hired to do social work tasks who have no educational background in social work, making it necessary to ask what the "social worker's" training is.[47] There are few programs that grant Ph.D.'s in social work.

Social workers may receive certification through the Academy of Certified Social Workers, within the National Association of Social Workers, and may use "ACSW" after their names when so certified. Certification requires (1) graduation from a school of social work accredited by the Council on Social Work Education, (2) two years of full-time paid social work practice beyond a graduate social work degree, or an equivalent amount of part-time professional practice, (3) regular NASW membership, (4) submission of three professional references, and (5) successful completion of the ACSW examination.[48]

Social workers who meet the requirements for ACSW certification can be listed in the *NASW Register of Clinical Social Workers*.[49]

Skills Needed by Expert

Given the above distinctions among psychiatrists, psychologists, and social workers, and within psychology, the attorney must define the skills needed by his or her expert and choose accordingly.

If there are young children (10 years old or younger) in the custody suit, the best expert would likely be a psychologist with graduate training in child clinical psychology and substantial experience in the provision of services to this age group. A number of child psychologists are also certified or licensed as school psychologists, adding to their qualifications and usefulness.

Children aged 11–12 may be appropriately evaluated by either a clinical child psychologist or a clinical psychologist who has done substantial work with adolescents, the choice depending in part on the level of maturity of the child.

Minor children 13 years or older would appropriately be evaluated by a clinical psychologist with substantial experience with adolescents.

In each age group, if there are substantial educational issues, a counseling psychologist or school psychologist may be either the appropriate evaluator or, more likely, an adjunct to the clinical psychologist doing the primary evaluation.

If there are substantial medical issues, it would be appropriate to consider a psychiatrist who has substantial experience with the relevant age group, particularly if he or she is board certified in child psychiatry. Here, also, the primary evaluator would generally best be a clinical psychologist, since a complete evaluation will usually require use of psychological tests. It could also be advantageous if the psychologist is a board certified medical psychotherapist.

If there are questions about the quality of the living situation for the child, it may be appropriate to have an ACSW-certified social worker do an evaluation of the living situation of each parent or guardian.

While a mental health professional can do a lot to educate attorneys and the court about psychological concepts and insights that may be relevant to a case, there are a number of things he or she *cannot* do:[50]

(a) Mental health professionals are not lie detectors. While some psychological tests can address malingering, nothing guarantees that an individual could not fool any professional.

(b) While professionals can often bring out a variety of information from an individual, they cannot necessarily do any better at getting information from a reluctant individual than can his lawyer.

(c) While professionals can do fairly well at identifying current factors, they have substantial limitations in identifying past and future factors which may be relevant.

(d) People's motivations are very often ambiguous, and accurate presentation of those motivations by the professional may require that the presentation also be ambiguous.

(e) Diagnoses and many behavioral descriptions and conclusions are relative, not absolute. For the professional to be accurate, he or she may also have to be equivocal to some degree.

Professional Organizations

An essential part of the qualifications of an expert is the list of organizations to which he or she belongs, particularly if membership is based in part or entirely on a formal process of peer review, rather than simply on the payment of dues to the organization. "Fellow" status in most organizations is predicated on such a peer review.

Psychiatrists

American Psychiatric Association. Founded in 1844, the American Psychiatric Association had more than 26,000 members in 1981, representing about 70 percent of the psychiatrists in the United States. Members must be physicians with some training and experience in psychiatry who pay annual dues. Fellows must have been members of the organization for at least eight years and have made significant contributions to psychiatry and to the association.[51]

American Board of Psychiatry and Neurology. Founded in 1934, the American Board of Psychiatry and Neurology grants certification in psychiatry, neurology, and child psychiatry based on examinations.[52]

American Psychoanalytic Association. The American Psycho-analytic Association is an association of psychoanalysts who are also psychiatrists. Membership is refused to nonphysician psychoanalysts. It has about 2,700 members.[53]

American Board of Forensic Psychiatry. Founded in 1978, the American Board of Forensic Psychiatry grants certification in forensic psychiatry based on examinations. There were 80 diplomates in 1986.[54]

American Academy of Psychiatry and Law. Founded in 1969, the American Academy of Psychiatry and Law is an organization of psychiatrists interested in the practice of, and training in, legal psychiatry. It does not certify—any member of the American Psychiatric Association who is willing to pay the membership fee may join. There were about 800 members in 1986.[55]

Psychologists

American Psychological Association. Full membership in the American Psychological Association is limited to psychologists with doctoral degrees who pay the membership fee. Specialty areas are represented by separate divisions, e.g., Division 12 (Clinical Psychology) and Division 41 (Law and Psychology). There were more than 53,000 members in 1986. "Fellow" status is conferred upon those who have made "unusual and outstand-ing contributions or performance in the field of psychology." The criteria for fellow status have been continually upgraded, so that an individual recently achieving Fellow status has had to show greater competence than did someone in past years.[56]

American Board of Professional Psychology. Founded in 1947, the American Board of Professional Psychology confers diplo-mate status on psychologists in the areas of clinical, counseling, school, industrial/organizational, and neuropsychology based on examinations. There were more than 2,500 diplomates in 1986.[57]

American Board of Forensic Psychology. Founded in 1978, the American Board of Forensic Psychology (ABFP) is being acquired by the American Board of Professional Psychology. It provides certification of psychologists in forensic psychology based on examinations.[58]

American Psychology-Law Society. Founded in 1968, the American Psychology-Law Society has now become Division 41 of the American Psychological Association. Membership is open to APA members who pay the membership fee.[59]

National Register of Health Service Providers in Psychology. As indicated above, the National Register of Health Service Providers in Psychology provides certification that the individual listed in their directory has met a standard for level of training and experience.[60]

Social Workers

National Association of Social Workers. Founded in 1955, the National Association of Social Workers is the primary membership organization for social workers. Membership is open to "professional social workers" who pay the membership dues.[61] There are about 118,000 members in the NASW as of December 1988, which NASW estimates to be about half of the "qualified professional social workers" in the United States.[62]

Academy of Certified Social Workers. An administrative unit of the NASW, the Academy of Certified Social Workers certifies master's-degreed social workers who meet the criteria listed in the above section on the training of "social workers."

Other Organizations

American Board of Medical Psychotherapists. Founded in 1982, the American Board of Medical Psychotherapists certifies psychologists, psychiatrists, social workers, and others who have substantial knowledge and experience as medical psychotherapists.[63]

American Orthopsychiatric Association. Founded in 1951, the American Orthopsychiatric Association is an interdisciplinary association which has psychologists, psychiatrists, social workers, and others as members. "Fellow" status is offered to members in good standing for at least five years.[64]

Sources of Experts[65]

(a) The above professional organizations, particularly those which certify the expertise of members.

(b) The grapevine: attorneys, judges, and others in the legal system with experience with particular experts.

(c) Professional literature: authors of research or reports in the desired area of testimony. It should be noted that research quality and writing ability do not guarantee an ability to verbalize one's knowledge in a courtroom setting, so many authors' expertise should be utilized in trial preparation only.

(d) Academic institutions: faculty members at colleges, universities, psychology professional schools, medical schools, and so forth. As above, the fact that an individual does research and/or teaching does not guarantee that he or she can communicate knowledge well, so it may be necessary to utilize these people in trial preparation only.

(e) "Professional witnesses"/"expert witness services": the former work more or less full time providing expert testimony, some as, e.g., county or state hospital psychiatrists, others as independent experts. The latter advertise in legal journals and magazines and are sources of the former. The advantage of professional witnesses is that they are experienced and tested. The disadvantage is that they may be identified with one side, and their testimony in other trials may give opposing counsel substantial information about them and their probable testimony prior to a trial.[66]

The Expert's Attitude and Personality

Dr. Melvin Goldzband, in his book *Custody Cases and Expert Witnesses*, notes that the attitudes and personality of the expert are also very important. Specifically, the attorney needs to know the following:[67]

(a) whether the expert is interested in the lawyer's case;

(b) if so, whether the expert is "objective enough to be a good and convincing witness";

(c) whether the expert is "sympathetic to the judicial process" (i.e., does not dislike lawyers, does not dislike testifying, does not fear humiliation in the courtroom, is not dogmatic or defensive, does not resent cross-examination, does not become hostile when delays occur, and is able to communicate clearly in both lay and professional language with the attorney, the judge, and, if relevant, the jury).

Goldzband also suggests that whether the expert "is a teacher as well" may be important.[68] Experts who are members of the teaching faculty of a graduate or medical school are relatively likely to keep up with professional developments and research, and to have significant experience communicating ideas to other people. So are experts who lecture before professional and lay groups. Given that the task of the expert is to educate the judge and/or jury, experience as a teacher in any context may be very important.

Goldzband also notes that an attorney may want his or her expert to take notes during the trial and offer information and suggestions to the attorney regarding testimony offered by various people, but particularly the other expert(s).[69] The expert can especially help the attorney with formulating questions for cross-examination. Some experts will do so willingly, others want to be more distant from the adversarial process. The attorney needs to clearly define the role of the expert he or she retains in advance to avert a disagreement on this point during the trial.

The expert also needs to maintain an appearance of independence and objectivity to be considered credible by the judge and/or jury, even though everyone knows he or she is hired as a technical consultant to one side. As indicated above, if the expert is viewed primarily as a "hired gun," his or her credibility will suffer.[70]

PREPARATION OF THE EXPERT[71]

(a) The expert should have access to all of the attorney's files. It would be a significant problem if the expert hears of some problem or data for the first time while on the stand.

(b) The attorney should tell the expert to be candid about his or her findings, positive and negative. This increases the expert's credibility and appearance of objectivity.

(c) The expert should know that he or she must make all of his or her files accessible to the attorney(s), and that his or her statements in court must be consistent with the information in the files.

(d) The attorney and the expert should go over the expert's credentials and determine what will be presented in court.

(e) The attorney and the expert should go over the data to be presented by the expert, with an emphasis on covering all the important points without overwhelming the listener.

(f) The attorney should caution the expert to answer the questions asked succinctly, not going far beyond the question in his or her response. He or she should also be sure not to lose the listeners through excess use of technical terminology.

(g) The expert should be prepared to discuss his or her fees, and, if asked, to make the point that he or she is being paid for professional services rather than for testimony.

(h) The attorney should prepare the expert regarding what to expect on cross-examination. "The cross-examination of an expert generally addresses five areas of testimony: lack of qualifications, bias, error in the observed or assumed facts, error in conclusion or opinion, and specific impeachments, i.e., previous contradictory or inconsistent statements, writings, or general lack of credibility."[72] The attorney should remind the expert that the shortcomings of the mental health field may be emphasized as a means of discrediting expert testimony. The expert should also be aware that "well-recognized publications" or "learned treatises" may be used to discredit testimony—and that the expert should avoid lending credibility to these publications by accepting them as authoritative. Rather, the expert should state, e.g., "I accept that book as authoritative in the

field with certain reservations," thereby permitting disagreement when necessary.[73]

(i) Joseph Smith, M.D., J.D., in his book *Medical
Malpractice: Psychiatric Care*, offers several specific
suggestions regarding testimony-related behavior that
an attorney should convey to the expert:

- to answer truthfully to the best of his or her knowledge ("I don't know" is perfectly acceptable);

- to keep responses simple, comprehensible to a lay
jury;

- to keep responses on point regarding the questions
asked;

- to reflect objectivity rather than mere subjective
opinion in all responses;

- to respond to questions requiring description in that
manner and reserve interpretations and conclusions
for later;

- not to respond immediately, but to gather thoughts
and weigh the answer;

- to maintain awareness of the flow and implications
of the questions;

- to remain calm, and answer directly and confidently.[74]

- The attorney should make certain that the expert is
familiar with applicable case law, and should, if necessary, provide the expert with copies of court decisions with which the expert must be familiar.[75]

DISQUALIFYING THE EXPERT WITNESS

Evaluating Training and Experience

Being a psychologist, psychiatrist, etc., does *not* make one
an expert on any particular topic.[76] The attorney must carefully
review the individual's professional vita to identify what specific *training* and *experience* the individual has—and what
gaps in each exist:

- What training and experience does the "expert" have in
evaluating children, and what ages of children is he or
she qualified by training and experience to evaluate?

- What training and experience does the "expert" have in family law-related matters? Does the expert understand the requirements of the statutes in custody matters?

- If alcohol or other drug abuse is a question which the "expert" needs to address, what specific training and experience does he or she have in this area?

- If any central individual has been in a psychiatric hospital or on a psychiatric ward, does the "expert" have specific training and experience relevant to drawing conclusions about that hospitalization?

- If any central individual is retarded, does the "expert" have any specific training or experience in evaluating people who are retarded (developmentally disabled)?

- In general, nonphysicians should not testify about medication issues. Exceptions may be made under special circumstances for psychopharmacologists and nurses or others with specialized knowledge. Psychologists can generally testify regarding treatment methods to supplement or supplant psychotropic medications, e.g., behavior therapy, relaxation therapy, or biofeedback.

- How many times has the "expert" testified in custody matters? How many times in other family court or juvenile court matters? In other forensic matters?

- Does the "expert" have an evident bias— e.g., does he or she always testify for one side or the other? If not, what percentage of the time has he or she been court appointed, been appointed at the request of the guardian ad litem, been appointed at the joint request of the parents and their attorneys, and/or been retained by each side?

- Does the expert have the training and experience to evaluate the presence and magnitude of any psychological disorders that any party is alleged to have or have had? In general, this will mean the expert will be a clinical psychologist or a psychiatrist, as other types of mental health professionals rarely have significant training or experience in diagnosis and treatment of serious disorders.

- What evidence is there that the "expert" has undergone peer review and been found to be competent and/or meritorious? Competence may be assessed, e.g., by certification as a diplomate in any specialty, by membership in an organization where one has to do more than pay dues to belong, and by membership on the faculty of any college, university, medical school, or professional school. Professional merit may be measured, e.g., by whether the "expert" has held elected office in any professional organizations.

- Has the "expert" published articles in professional journals? Given juried or invited addresses to professional organizations? Authored or co-authored any professional books?

Nonmental Health Experts

Parents in contested custody matters and their attorneys often rely on physicians without psychiatric training, on clergy, and on other trusted individuals as if those individuals were well-trained mental health professionals. With few exceptions, they are not. As a result, parents and attorneys frequently receive inappropriate advice. Attorneys should ascertain what formal training and experience these individuals have, and caution their clients against weighing advice from nonmental health experts more heavily than advice from mental health experts.

SUMMARY

Well-chosen expert witnesses can help the attorney to evaluate the parties to a custody action, help identify and resolve issues which may arise during the litigation, and, ultimately, help assure that the best interests of the child are served.

ENDNOTES

1. D. Shuman, Psychiatric and Psychological Evidence 171–72 (1986) [hereinafter Psychiatric and Psychological Evidence].

2. *Id.* at 174.

3. *Id.* at 175.

4. *Id.*

5. *Id.* at 176–77; Clements & Ciccone, *Ethics and Expert Witnesses: The Troubled Role of Psychiatrists in Court,* 12 Bull. Am. Acad. Psychiatry L. 135–36 (1984).

6. Psychiatric and Psychological Evidence, *supra* note 1, at 181–82; J. Ziskin, Coping with Psychiatric and Psychological Testimony 13, 14, 15–21, 260 (1981).

7. Psychiatric and Psychological Evidence, *supra* note 1, at 184.

8. C. Stromberg, The Psychologist's Legal Handbook 591–92 (1988) [hereinafter The Psychologist's Legal Handbook].

9. Bales, *APA Rebuts Criticism of Clinician Witnesses,* APA Monitor 17 (Sept. 19, 1988) (quoting R. Fowler and J. Matarazzo).

10. Barefoot v. Estelle, 463 U.S. 880 (1983).

11. Bales, *APA Rebuts Criticism of Clinician Witnesses,* APA Monitor 17 (Sept. 19, 1988).

12. J. Smith, Medical Malpractice Psychiatric Care 443 (1986) [hereinafter Medical Malpractice Psychiatric Care].

13. Psychiatric and Psychological Evidence, *supra* note 1, at 189–90.

14. S. Korchin, Modern Clinical Psychology 90 (1976).

15. Psychiatric and Psychological Evidence, *supra* note 1, at 190–91.

16. *Id.* at 100.

17. *Id.* at 191.

18. *Id.* at 95.

19. *Id.*

20. *Id.* at 100.

21. *Id.* at 104.

22. *Id.* at 103.

23. *Id.* at 106.

24. The Psychologist's Legal Handbook, *supra* note 8, at 1–2.

25. *Id.* at 2.

26. Psychiatric and Psychological Evidence, *supra* note 1, at 106–08.

27. *Id.* at 108.

28. *Id.*

29. *Id.*

30. The Psychologist's Legal Handbook, *supra* note 8, at 44.

31. C. Watkins & V. Campbell, *Personality Assessment and Counseling Psychology*, 53 J. Personality Assessment 302 (1989).

32. Psychiatric and Psychological Evidence, *supra* note 1, at 108.

33. The Psychologist's Legal Handbook, *supra* note 8, at 44.

34. Psychiatric and Psychological Evidence, *supra* note 1, at 109.

35. The Psychologist's Legal Handbook, *supra* note 8, at 603.

36. Psychiatric and Psychological Evidence, *supra* note 1, at 109.

37. *Id.* at 110.

38. The Psychologist's Legal Handbook, *supra* note 8, at 7.

39. *Id.*

40. Psychiatric and Psychological Evidence, *supra* note 1, at 110.

41. *Id.* at 111.

42. National Register of Health Service Providers in Psychology xxi (1987 ed.).

43. There are more than 1,800 diplomates in clinical psychology. Psychiatric and Psychological Evidence, *supra* note 1, at 111–12.

44. There are about 100 diplomates in forensic psychology in the United States. *Id.* at 112.

45. Lytle-Vieira, *Kramer vs. Kramer Revisited: The Social Work Role in Child Custody Cases*, 32 Soc. Work 5 (1987).

46. Whiting, State Comparison of Laws Regulating Social Work (April 1988).

47. Personal communication with L. Whiting, Dec. 20, 1988.

48. The Academy of Certified Social Workers, Mark of Professional Excellence, undated.

49. Standard 10, NASW "Standards for the Practice of Clinical Social Work," 1984.

50. The Psychologist's Legal Handbook, *supra* note 8, at 611.

51. Psychiatric and Psychological Evidence, *supra* note 1, at 113.

52. *Id.* at 114.

53. *Id.*

54. *Id.*

55. *Id.*

56. *Id.* at 115.

57. *Id.*

58. *Id.* at 115–16.

59. *Id.* at 116.

60. *Id.* at 111; The Psychologist's Legal Handbook, *supra* note 8, at 41.

61. NASW Code of Ethics 11 (1980).

62. Personal communication with L. Whiting, Dec. 20, 1988.

63. American Board of Medical Psychotherapists, 1987.

64. Bylaws, American Orthopsychiatric Association.

65. Psychiatric and Psychological Evidence, *supra* note 1, at 142–47.

66. *Id.* at 145–46.

67. M. Goldzband, Custody Cases and Expert Witnesses 9–10 (1980) [hereinafter Custody Cases and Expert Witnesses].

68. *Id.* at 11–12.

69. *Id.* at 146.

70. Medical Malpractice Psychiatric Care, *supra* note 12, at 444.

71. Based in part on Custody Cases and Expert Witnesses, *supra* note 67, at 18–21, 36, 37.

72. Medical Malpractice Psychiatric Care, *supra* note 12, at 452.

73. *Id.* at 455–56.

74. *Id.* at 454.

75. T. Blau, The Psychologist as Expert Witness 335 (1984).

76. Psychiatric and Psychological Evidence, *supra* note 8, at 189, 193.

Chapter Two
Ethical Issues

Ethical guidelines are propounded by all professions and are an essential part of maintenance of the integrity and cohesiveness of a profession.[1] They are a primary ingredient in the professionalization of an occupation, in part because society accords professionals special privileges which it does not offer to commercial enterprises. People expect professionals to be more trustworthy, competent, and error free than the average businessman. This has led to professionals instituting ethical codes as mechanisms to balance the self-interest of the individual professional against the interests of the people with whom they work. These ethical codes function as moral guides to self-regulation and try to assure the appropriate use of skills and techniques.[2]

Unfortunately, the ethical codes of psychologists and attorneys will, on occasion, be in conflict. This may occur when the psychologist is addressing the "best interests of the child," while the attorney is obligated to address the wishes of his or her client. It may also occur when the psychologist attempts to keep therapy notes or specific test responses confidential, while the attorney addresses his or her obligation to try to look at all documents which may have a bearing on litigation. As indicated below, there is no simple solution to this problem. The attorney who is anticipating questioning a psychologist needs to know what these potential problems are, so that he can plan his examination of the psychologist.

The ethical code currently in use by psychologists is the *Ethical Principles of Psychologists*, last revised in 1981. About 30 states have adopted the 1981 revision of the *Ethical Principles* as part of their licensing/discipline laws, and some additional states' laws contain earlier versions of the *Ethical Principles* (see the appendix at the end of this chapter for a list of these states).[3] Thus, while technically applicable only to members of the American Psychological Association, the *Ethical Principles* in fact govern nearly all psychologists in the United States. They have been supplemented by *General Guidelines for Providers of Psychological Services* (1987), *Specialty Guidelines for the Delivery of Services by Clinical [Counseling; Industrial/Organizational; School] Psychologists* (1981), and *Standards for Educational and Psychological Tests* (1984). Like other professional ethics codes, it is the intent "to promote the welfare of consumers served, to maintain competence, to protect confidentiality and/or privacy, to act responsibly, to avoid exploitation, and to uphold the integrity of the profession through exemplary conduct."[4] Overall, "the promotion of human welfare is the primary principle guiding the professional activities of all members of the psychological service unit."[5]

The following is a description of some of the ethical problems which psychologists and/or attorneys may confront in the course of a custody evaluation and subsequent testimony.

CONCLUSIONS ON MATTERS OF LAW

Being relatively naive about the legal process, a psychologist may end up drawing conclusions on matters of law rather than solely providing data and recommendations which may be used by the judge in making the determination of what would be in the best interests of the child. While psychologists can and should provide data regarding the positive and negative aspects of parenting by each parent, the quality of the "fit" between the needs of the child and the abilities of the parents, and so forth, it goes beyond the present ability of any psychologist to predict with certainty which parent would be the better custodial parent in all circumstances. The psychologist is obligated to acknowledge in stating his or her opinions this lack of a threshold below which custodial rights should be denied. That judgment belongs to the court.[6] This does not necessarily mean that a psychologist must not render an opinion regarding type of custody arrangement, visitation, and so forth. Rather, that opinion must be so labeled. It should also be noted that some state laws oppose the stating of recommendations regarding the ultimate disposition of the case, while laws of other states require it (e.g., Wisconsin). The attorney should advise the psychologist regarding what the relevant statute in his or her state requires or permits.

LIMITS ON PREDICTIONS

While there is a substantial and growing body of research regarding the effects of divorce on children, there is a "lack of any methodologically sound empirical evidence allowing psychological predictions as to the effects of various types of custodial placements on children, or whether joint custody, in general, is a better option than single-parent custody."[7] Thus, the psychologist may use the data from his or her evaluation to make statements "to a reasonable degree of professional certainty" about the past and present, but any statements about the future must be stated as opinions, the psychologist noting the limitations of the testimony and being willing and able to identify the bases for those opinions.[8]

LIMITS ON PREDICTIONS FROM TESTS

Very few of the tests used by psychologists have been specifically validated for use in custody proceedings, making it necessary for the psychologist to report (a) what the test *does* validly address, and then (b) how that intermediate factor would be expected to impact on the ability of an individual to parent well, on the needs of a child, and so forth. For example, if a child is determined to have a very substantial need for nurturing, while a given parent is found to have a severe narcissistic personality disorder or frequent, ongoing major depressive episodes, it is reasonable to conclude that there is a poor fit between this need of the child and the ability of the parent to address the need—not because the test showed the degree of fit, but because the test yielded information which could be analyzed and addressed in drawing this conclusion.[9]

LIMITS ON CUSTODY RECOMMENDATIONS

A psychologist is to take into consideration all factors which may potentially have a major effect on his or her opinions and recommendations and to try to avoid situations wherein there is a significant potential for misuse of those opinions and recommendations.[10] One consequence is that a psychologist is potentially compromising ethical standards when he or she is hired by one parent in a custody evaluation, rather than serving as a court-appointed expert or, at the least, as an independent expert retained by both parents jointly. It would be an ethical violation to draw *any* conclusions about which parent would be the better custodial parent unless one has assessed *both* parents. Similarly, it would be an ethical

violation to indicate that *either* parent would be the better custodial parent unless one has evaluated each child for whom
that statement is to be made, since the better custodial parent
for one child may not be better for another child.

Further, the primary responsibility of the psychologist is to
the child (by virtue of the requirement that the decision ultimately made be in the best interests of the child), a fact that
may become cloudy if the psychologist is retained by only one
parent. It does not serve the best interest of the child if the
psychologist appears to be a "hired gun," and even the most
ethical psychologist may feel some pressure to shade the
results of the evaluation in the direction of the parent who is
paying the bill. "Even merely the fact of being employed by one
side or the other will create a tendency toward bias or somewhat diminished objectivity, sometimes, even without awareness on the part of the expert that such a tendency is
operating."[11]

These factors do not preclude a psychologist from being
retained by one parent in a custody matter. They *do* point out
the ethical traps inherent in doing so, and the extreme caution
a psychologist must exercise in making any statements at all
about one or some, but not all, of the parties involved in the
custody action.[12]

THE PSYCHOLOGIST'S NEED FOR DATA

A psychologist is obligated to identify all the major factors
which need to be addressed prior to stating an opinion, and to
refuse to do an evaluation (or to limit the scope of an evaluation) if those factors cannot, for whatever reason, be addressed
adequately. This would apply to the situation, above, where the
psychologist may not have access to all of the parties in the
custody action. It would also apply if any medical, school,
social service, or other records were refused. It would apply if a
low and arbitrary limit were placed on the number of hours a
psychologist could devote to the data gathering and analysis.
While there need not be a blank check, any limits on time need
to be liberal if the best interests of the child are to be served.
[Note: One author suggests that "sixteen hours can be considered a minimum amount of time for a study involving two parents and one child. For each additional child or stepparent to

be interviewed two hours could be added. These estimates do not include 'mulling it over' time but rather represent direct involvement hours."[13] Her figures also leave out time to write a report, and deposition and court time. The experience of the present authors and the research by Keilin and Bloom[14] are consistent with hers. A psychologist who cannot devote that large amount of time, or who has a client who is unwilling to retain the psychologist for enough hours to do the job right, has an obligation to refuse the task. It should be added that psychologists are ethically required to do some work pro bono,[15] so the latter is not necessarily a financial question.]

LIMITS ON GOING BEYOND THE DATA

As clinicians and scientists, psychologists are well trained to gather and interpret data, whether from observations, interviews, psychological testing, medical or school records, or other sources. The data gathered and analyzed may relate to abilities, attitudes, thoughts, feelings, behavior, relationships, and so forth. The psychologist is also trained to organize the data from disparate sources into a meaningful whole which may then be presented as part of the legal inquiry. And psychologists are trained to be able to elaborate on those aspects of functioning of each parent that relate to the unique needs of each child. Ethically, however, psychologists must limit how far beyond the data they go in speculating about the future, and must clearly distinguish between those conclusions based on hard data and those based on speculation.[16]

REQUIREMENT TO REPORT ALL THE DATA

Psychologists are ethically obligated to report *all* the data they have that relate directly to the purpose of an evaluation.

> They provide thorough discussion of the limitations of their data, especially where their work touches on social policy or might be construed to the detriment of persons in specific age, sex, ethnic, socioeconomic or other social groups. In publishing reports of their work, they never suppress disconfirming data, and they acknowledge the existence of alternative hypotheses and explanations of their findings.[17]

"If a psychologist is appointed by the court, he may feel more independent. Nevertheless, an expert is professionally obligated to state his findings and opinions truthfully and without bias—regardless of who engaged him."[18] The psychologist is also obligated to try to prevent distortion of his or her views.[19]

This point is underscored by Judge David Bazelon's statement that

> conclusory statements are bad enough when they merely propound the scientific gospel. They become positively dangerous when they verge into naked pronouncements on the ultimate issue faced by the decision maker. . . . What the public needs most from any expert, including the psychologist, is a wealth of intermediate observations and conceptual insights that are adequately explained. Only then can his or her contributions be combined with the communal sense of right and wrong to produce a decision.[20]

AVOIDING DUAL RELATIONSHIPS

Psychologists must "make every effort to avoid dual relationships"[21]—that is, to avoid situations where there is loyalty owed to more than one person or institution, or which may otherwise compromise the quality of one's judgment by involving a conflict of interest. In a custody case, the primary loyalty is owed to the "best interests of the child," but loyalty is also owed to the psychologist's other clients: the court, each person evaluated, and, unless court appointed, to one or more attorneys. The psychologist is, therefore, obligated to abide by ethical obligations regarding informed consent for those assessed, confidentiality, clarification of any matters related to fees, and so forth. "As adjuncts to the fact-finding process, psychologists must internalize the court's concern for objectivity, fairness, and the well-being of the child."[22]

There is automatically a dual relationship involved when a psychologist is both the therapist for any party to a custody action *and* an expert who is to offer information (and possibly recommendations) to the court. If either parent is the psychologist's patient/client, the psychologist may have a conflict of interest in that the best interests of the child and those of the patient/client may not be the same. If the psychologist believes the patient/client *would* be a good custodial parent, this potential conflict of interest may be avoidable. If the *child* is the patient/client, it may irreparably damage the progress of therapy if the psychologist has to testify in open court regarding his or her knowledge and opinions. Doing so could create a conflict between the role of the child as patient/client, on the one hand (including the issue of confidentiality), and the obligation of the psychologist to advocate for the best interests of the child on the other. This conflict may be resolvable only by having the psychologist meet in chambers with the judge and the attorneys, with his testimony being unavailable to the parents until therapy ends.[23]

Having pointed out in an evaluation that one or more parties to an action should have individual or conjoint psychotherapy, it is not unusual for the independent or court-appointed evaluating psychologist to be asked to be that therapist, given that he or she already knows the family members well. If the request is for therapy to begin prior to the end of the custody matter, it would be unethical (as a dual relationship problem) for the psychologist to agree. If therapy is to begin after the custody matter is settled, there would no longer be a dual relationship and therapy could proceed. However, this should be done only if all parties and attorneys agree that the psychologist's role as an independent evaluator has terminated and that he or she will no longer be required to fulfill the role of an independent expert in the case. Once the psychologist becomes a therapist, his or her independent status is relinquished. It would not be unethical for a psychologist to evaluate a single parent or child and proceed to become that person's therapist while the custody matter is still under way.

INFORMED CONSENT

Psychologists are obligated to obtain informed consent for all professional activities, including informing "consumers as to the purpose and nature of an evaluative . . . procedure."[24] The psychologist must assure that any party to the custody action old enough to understand the explanation is aware of who requested the psychologist's services, who is paying the fees, and whether the psychologist is representing one of the parents, has been appointed by the court, or has been hired by the guardian ad litem. The psychologist should inform the individual whether the report will go only to one of the attorneys, who may or may not use the information, or whether it will go directly to the court. While people are not likely to refuse to participate in an evaluation because it will give the appearance they have something to hide, once informed of the limits of confidentiality they do retain the right to disclose or not disclose any information they wish.[25]

TEST INTEGRITY

Psychologists are obligated to maintain the integrity of the tests they use, both by ethical requirements[26] and by contractual agreements with the publishers which hold the copyrights on those tests. It would be a violation of those ethical and contractual requirements for the psychologist to submit raw data, answer sheets, or other information which would compromise both the validity of the test and its utility for others to an attorney or to the court, though (with patient/client consent or a court order) it could be released to another psychologist.[27]

There is no simple solution to the dilemma posed if a psychologist's test records are subpoenaed. The ethical and contractual obligation is to refuse disclosure, while there is an obvious personal danger for the psychologist to be held in contempt of court if the records are not disclosed. It would be hoped that discussion among the psychologist, the judge, and the attorneys could resolve the matter without trying to force the psychologist to violate his or her obligations.[28] At a minimum, it may be possible for the subpoena to be narrowed sufficiently for the psychologist to be able to respond without ethical or contractual breaches.[29]

REPORTING OF CHILD ABUSE

Psychologists are mandated by most states' laws to report suspected child abuse.[30] The *Ethical Principles of Psychologists*[31] and the *General Guidelines for Providers of Psychological Services*[32] reinforce that requirement. If a psychologist who is conducting any part of a custody evaluation suspects child abuse, he or she would be obligated to report that suspicion to the designated social services agency, except in those few states which have an exemption for disclosures made in voluntary treatment sought by an abuser.[33]

REQUIREMENT FOR QUALITY SERVICES

There is a "right and responsibility of psychologists to withhold an assessment procedure when not validly applicable [and a] right and responsibility of psychologists to withhold services in specific instances in which their own limitations or user characteristics might impair the quality of the services."[34]

REQUIREMENT THAT TESTS BE CORRECTLY ADMINISTERED

Psychologists are responsible for assuring that tests are correctly administered. This includes assuring that the correct instructions are used, that the environmental conditions are appropriate, and that the patient/client personally responds to all of the test items. The "Casebook for Providers of Psychological Services"[35] indicates that

> [w]hen the psychologist does not have direct, first-hand information as to the conditions under which a test is taken, he or she is forced . . . to assume that the test responses were not distorted by the general situation in which the test was taken (e.g., whether the client consulted others about test responses). Indeed, the psychologist could have no assurance that this test was in fact completed by the client. In the instance where the test might be introduced as data in a court proceeding, it would be summarily dismissed as hearsay evidence.

Further, Standard 6.2 of the *Standards for Educational and Psychological Testing* (1985) indicates that "When a test user makes a substantial change in test format, mode of administration, instructions, language, or content, the user should revalidate the use of the test for the changed conditions or have a rationale supporting the claim that additional validation is not necessary or possible."

To be absolutely certain that tests are correctly administered, the psychologist should administer the tests personally.

This assures that correct procedures are used, that extra-test behavior (reactions, expressions, side comments, etc.) is noted, and that the entire realm of test taking behavior is considered in the interpretation done by the psychologist.[36]

PRESERVATION OF LEGAL/CIVIL RIGHTS

Forensic psychologists must "make a reasonable effort to ensure that their services and the products of their services are used in a manner consistent with the preservation of the legal rights of all parties to a legal proceeding."[37]They also "have an obligation to understand the basic civil rights of parties in legal proceedings in which they participate, and manage their professional conduct in a manner that does not diminish or threaten those rights."[38]

CONTINGENCY FEES

Forensic psychologists may not "enter into professional services with parties to a legal proceeding on the basis of 'contingent fees.'"[39] To avoid the appearance of bias, all fees owed the expert should be paid prior to the expert's furnishing a written report, and any further fees paid prior to the expert's testimony.[40]

PERSONAL NOTES

Notes taken during the course of an examination or interview for the purpose of recording relevant aspects of the individual's demeanor, verbal behavior and so forth are not considered personal notes. . . . Personal notes include only notations made for the personal use of the evaluator (e.g., hunches, speculations, areas to pursue) and which do not function as a basis, whether partial or otherwise, for the evaluator's professional product, testimony, or other evidence.[41]

HEARSAY

While hearsay or otherwise inadmissible evidence may form the partial basis of their opinion, evidence or professional product, [psychologists] actively seek to minimize their reliance upon such evidence. Where circumstances reasonably permit, forensic psychologists seek to obtain independent and personal verification of data relied upon as part of their professional services to the court or to a party to a legal proceeding. . . . When data . . . has not been corroborated, but is nevertheless utilized, the forensic psychologist has an affirmative responsibility to clarify its evidentiary status and the reasons for relying upon such data.[42]

LIMITS ON COMPETENCY OF THE PSYCHOLOGIST

"Forensic psychologists have an *affirmative duty* to present accurately to the court the boundaries of their competence, the factual bases (knowledge, skill, experience, training, or education) for their qualification as an expert, and to explain the relevance of those factual bases to their qualification as an expert." A psychologist will be in violation of Principle 3 of the *Ethical Principles of Psychologists* if he or she claims "expertise with insufficient training or experience, or by engaging in professional relationships with clients based upon insufficient training or experience which fail to adequately protect the welfare of their clients."[43]

CONCLUSION

In summary, there are a number of areas where the needs of the psychologist may limit or conflict with the needs of the attorney. It is essential that these potential or actual problems be anticipated and understood by both, so that unnecessary conflict can be avoided. The psychologist needs to find ethical ways to address the questions of the attorney. The attorney needs to find ways of obtaining important information from the psychologist without compromising the psychologist's ethical obligations. With a spirit of cooperation, it should be possible to accomplish both tasks, thereby serving the best interests of the child.

ENDNOTES

1. P. Keith-Spiegel & G. Koocher, Ethics in Psychology xiii (1985) [hereinafter Ethics in Psychology].

2. *Id.* at 1–2.

3. C. Stromberg, The Psychologist's Legal Handbook 228 (1988) [hereinafter The Psychologist's Legal Handbook].

4. Ethics in Psychology, *supra* note 1, at 3.

5. General Guidelines for Providers of Psychological Services, Guideline 3.1 (1987).

6. Weithorn & Grisso, *Psychological Evaluations in Divorce Custody: Problems, Principles, and Procedures*, Psychology and Child Custody Determinations 157–61 (1987) [hereinafter Psychological Evaluations in Divorce Custody].

7. *Id.* at 161.

8. *Ethical Principles of Psychologists*, Principle 2 Preamble (1981).

9. Psychological Evaluations in Divorce Custody, *supra* note 6, at 162–63; *Ethical Principles of Psychologists* Principle 8(c) (1981).

10. *Ethical Principles of Psychologists,* Preamble; Principle 1, Preamble; Principle 1(f); and Principle 8(c) (1981).

11. J. Ziskin, Coping with Psychiatric and Psychological Testimony 37 (1981).

12. Psychological Evaluations in Divorce Custody, *supra* note 6, at 163–64; Weithorn, *Psychological Consultation in Divorce Custody Litigation: Ethical Considerations*, Psychology and Child Custody Determinations 194–95 (1987) [hereinafter Psychological Consultation in Divorce Custody Litigation].

13. D. Skafte, Child Custody Evaluations: A Practical Guide 25–26 (1985).

14. Keilin & Bloom, *Child Custody Evaluation Practices: A Survey of Experienced Professionals*, 17 Professional Psychology: Research and Practice 338–46 (1986).

15. *Ethical Principles of Psychologists*, Principle 6(d) (1981).

16. Psychological Evaluations in Divorce Custody, *supra* note 6, at 170–71.

17. *Ethical Principles of Psychologists*, Principle 1(a) (1981).

18. The Psychologist's Legal Handbook, *supra* note 3, at 646.

19. *Id.* at 663; *Ethical Principles of Psychologists*, Principle 8(c) (1981).

20. Bazelon, *Veils, Values and Social Responsibility*, 37 Am. Psychologist 115, 116 (1982).

21. *Ethical Principles of Psychologists*, Principle 6(a) (1981).

22. Psychological Consultation in Divorce Custody Litigation, *supra* note 12, at 193.

23. *Id.* at 196–97.

24. *Ethical Principles of Psychologists*, Principle 6, Preamble (1981).

25. Psychological Consultation in Divorce Custody Litigation, *supra* note 12, at 197–98.

26. *Ethical Principles of Psychologists*, Principle 8, Preamble (1981); *Standards for Educational and Psychological Testing* , Standards 15 and 15.2 (1985).

27. The Psychologist's Legal Handbook, *supra* note 3, at 266; *General Guidelines for Providers of Psychological Services*, Guideline 2.3.7 (1987); Ethics in Psychology, *supra* note 1, at 69, 74, 103–04, 110–11.

28. Psychological Consultation in Divorce Custody Litigation, *supra* note 12, at 204–06.

29. The Psychologist's Legal Handbook, *supra* note 3, at 407.

30. *Id.* at 416.

31. *Ethical Principles of Psychologists,* Principle 3(d); Principle 5 Preamble, and Principle 5(d) (1981).

32. *General Guidelines for Providers of Psychological Services*, Guideline 2.2.4 n.26 (1987).

33. The Psychologist's Legal Handbook, *supra* note 3, at 417.

34. *General Guidelines for Providers of Psychological Services*, Guideline 3.1 (1987).

35. *Committee on Professional Standards,* 39 Am. Psychologist 663, 664 (1984).

36. Berman, *The Expert at Trial: Personality Persuades*, 9 Fam. Advoc. 11–12 (1986). *See also* Nissenbaum, *The Expert at Trial: Tests Tell All*, 9 Fam. Advoc. 14–19 (1986).

37. S. Golding, T. Grisso & D. Shapiro, *Working Draft: Specialty Guidelines for Forensic Psychologists*, 6/10/89 revision, at 4.

38. *Id.* at 5.

39. *Id.* at 6.

40. T. Blau, The Psychologist as Expert Witness 336 (1984).

41. *Id.* at 9–10.

42. *Id.* at 12.

43. *Id.* at 5.

APPENDIX*

The jurisdictions that have adopted the 1981 APA Ethics Code (often with modifications of certain sections) are as follows: Alabama, Alaska, Arkansas, Delaware, District of Columbia, Georgia, Idaho, Indiana, Kentucky, Louisiana, Maine, Maryland, Mississippi, Missouri, Montana, New Hampshire, North Carolina, North Dakota, Oklahoma, Oregon, Pennsylvania, Rhode Island, South Carolina, South Dakota, Texas, Vermont, West Virginia, Wisconsin, and Wyoming.

The jurisdictions that have adopted the 1977 or 1979 APA Ethics Code are as follows: Iowa, Massachusetts, New Mexico, Tennessee, Utah, West Virginia, and seven of the eight Canadian provinces with registration acts (Alberta, British Columbia, Manitoba, New Brunswick, Nova Scotia, Ontario, and Saskatchewan).

The jurisdictions that require adherence to the 1977 Standards for Providers of Psychological Services are as follows; Alabama, Alaska, Arkansas, Indiana, Maryland, North Dakota, British Columbia, Nova Scotia, and Ontario.

*Information is taken from C. Stromberg, The Psychologist's Legal Handbook 311 (1988).

Chapter Three

What Constitutes a Psychological Evaluation?

INTRODUCTION

There are generally three stages in a psychological evaluation performed on adults or children. The first stage involves gathering information. During this stage, it is important for the evaluator to identify the questions that he or she would like to have answered in the evaluation process. In a custody dispute, the overriding question in determining the best interest of the child is "which parent would make the appropriate custodial parent." A good evaluator will first identify the questions that need to be answered in the evaluation process. Questions asked of all parents would include, e.g.: "What do you most like to do with your child(ren)?" "What do you see as your deficiencies as a parent?" "How is your child(ren) doing in school?" When there is a known problem area for a parent, additional, specific questions would be asked, e.g.: "Will the parent's alcoholism adversely affect the child(ren)?" "Does the parent have the personality of a physical abuser?" "Although the parent has a history of psychiatric hospitalizations, is the person currently stable enough to be considered as a custodial parent?"

As part of the information-gathering stage, the evaluator decides which tests to administer, what collateral information to gather, and whom to interview. At this point, the tests are administered and scored, the individuals are interviewed, and collateral information is gathered. Collateral information could include: police reports, letters from attorneys, previous psychological evaluations, school information, and other documentation deemed appropriate.

The second step of the evaluation is the processing stage. During this process, all of the information that is gathered through interview, testing, or collateral sources is synthesized and processed by the examiner. It is the examiner's responsibility to score and interpret all of the tests administered. This information is then integrated with information obtained through

interviews and supporting documents. The examiner should separate the more important information from the extraneous irrelevant material. Then the examiner is ready to write a report.

The last stage of the evaluation involves preparing the
report. During this stage the examiner writes a report that
includes hypotheses about each individual tested, the family as
a whole, and the custody dispute outcome; makes predictions
based on the evaluation data and established research; and
makes recommendations regarding custody and related matters.

TEST ADMINISTRATION

The first step in administering the evaluation is finding an
appropriate setting. It is essential that the setting be quiet, free
from distractions, and comfortable. It is important to establish
rapport with the individual being tested. As part of this process,
a brief description of the evaluation process is given in a manner that puts the individual at ease. An experienced examiner
can usually establish rapport in a relatively short period of
time. However, it can be difficult to establish rapport with
young children who are fearful. Occasionally a parent requests
permission to sit in the evaluation room with a child during the
evaluation. This is generally not recommended, as the parent
may unknowingly provide additional stress for the child or may
inadvertently attempt to help the child. If the examiner decides
there is a significant amount of reticence on the part of the
child, the parent can be invited to accompany the child to the
testing room, and leave shortly after the child is settled.

The most important requirement for the examiner during a
psychological evaluation is that the tests be correctly administered. With tests that are standardized, it is assumed by individuals who read or interpret the results of an evaluation that
the exact instructions were followed. Whether the examiner
agrees or disagrees with the format used in instructing the individual being tested, the directions must be followed verbatim. If
examiners used their own stylized version of the directions, the
standardization would be in jeopardy and the results would
need to be interpreted with skepticism. If the examiner deviates
from the established directions for any legitimate reason, it
must be indicated in the report. Acceptable reasons for deviation include visual, auditory, physical, or mental impairment. A

discussion of the appropriate administration procedures for each test follows in Chapters Six through Nine.

Many psychologists permit individuals to take various tests home to be answered at the subject's leisure. This procedure may work when individuals are coming in merely for therapy. However, in the circumstances of a custody evaluation, it is essential to ensure that the answers were provided by the subject and were not the result of collaborative work. This can be a particular problem when both a parent and a stepparent are filling out the same instruments at home. The American Psychological Association case book for providers of psychological services addresses this issue. It states,

> When the psychologist does not have direct, first-hand information as to the conditions under which a test is taken, he or she is forced (in the above instance, unnecessarily) to assume that the test responses were not distorted by the general situation in which the test was taken (e.g., whether the client consulted others about the test responses). Indeed, the psychologist could have no assurance that this test was in fact completed by the client. In the instance where the test might be introduced as data in a court proceeding, it should be summarily dismissed as hearsay evidence. Although the psychologist should be free to exercise judgment as to the trustworthiness of the client, it is generally not a good professional practice to surrender direct monitoring of test administering.[1]

THE INTERVIEW

A complete custody evaluation must include some form of interview. This process is often referred to in the psychological report as the "clinical interview." The interview process can follow several different formats. The psychologist could spend a considerable amount of time in a question and answer format with each of the individuals. This approach is often facilitated by the use of a questionnaire to provide background information. When such a questionnaire is used, the interview time with the psychologist is often reduced. In addition, the interview material could be gained through the use of a social worker obtaining a social history.

Whatever method is used, there are many components that need to be covered in the interview process. They include: place of residence; place of employment; employment history; educational history; names and ages of the children, and whether the children are living at home; the status of the children (student, occupational, marital, other); previous psychological or psychiatric treatment; whether the treatment was inpatient or outpatient; any psychiatric medication previously taken or currently being taken; satisfaction with life (job, friends, relatives); alcohol history; problems with the law; organizations belonged to; hobbies, skills, or interests; information about the family of origin; whether the parents are living or deceased; what types of occupations or professions the parents have or had; ages, marital status, and closeness with brothers and sisters; any problems with developmental milestones; any history of sexual assault; any current medical problems; major stressors in their life; histories of previous marriages; if previously married, were there children, and, if so, who received custody; what were the reasons for divorce in the previous marriages?

In addition to these background personal-history-type questions, several questions need to be asked about the current divorce situation. They would include the following: problems with visitation or periods of physical placement; why the individual feels that he or she would make the best custodial parent; why the individual feels the other parent would not make the best custodial parent; what concerns the individual feels the other parent has about him or her; the reason for the current divorce; how much time with the child(ren) the parent is willing to allow the other parent to have; the living environment that the parent will provide for the child(ren), including place of residence, school, use of day care, use of baby sitters; what additional concerns the other parent has.

When the children are interviewed, either a direct interview technique or a diagnostic interview technique can be used. As part of the child's interview, the child should be asked: why he or she thinks the divorce is taking place; how he or she feels about it; and any questions regarding any areas of concern that have been raised (physical abuse, sexual abuse, alcoholism, psychological abuse, mental illness, criminal histories). The child should *not* be asked which parent he or she prefers to live with. Instead, the question should be framed in a format, such as: "How would you feel if the judge said you should live with your father/mother?"

A relatively new approach to interviewing children involves "structured diagnostic interviews." One of the more prominent diagnostic interview techniques developed is the Diagnostic Interview Schedule for Children (DISC) developed by the National Institute for Mental Health (NIMH). The work was performed by Dr. Barbara Herjanic, Dr. Joaquim Puig-Antizh, and Dr. Keith Conners. An outgrowth of this instrument is the Diagnostic Interview for Children and Adolescents (DICA). The other major diagnostic review instrument is popularly referred to as the Kiddie-SADS (K-SADS). It is adapted from the original Schedule for Affective Disorders and Schizophrenia. The structured diagnostic interviews hold promise for future assessment of children. However, since they are so new, considerable further research on the validity of using these instruments is necessary before they can replace other techniques.

CHARACTERISTICS OF THE EXAMINEE

There is a phenomenon in psychological testing that is referred to as "practice effect." The more frequently one takes a specific test, the more familiar one becomes with the items, and the more it could affect the outcome. One who has been through a significant number of psychological evaluations will undoubtedly benefit from practice effect on most tests. To prevent the practice effect from distorting results, intelligence tests generally should not be administered more frequently than once per year with adults and older children, or once per six months with younger children. It is the authors' contention that individuals who are more outgoing and those more likely to guess are more likely to score higher on tests of cognitive functioning than those who are more passive and introverted. Results of evaluations must be interpreted with this in mind.

FACTORS AFFECTING THE EXAMINER

There are many factors that affect the examiner during the evaluation process. They include: race, sex, and experience.

Race

It has been hypothesized that examiners of one race testing people of another race could adversely affect the results of the evaluation. This includes black subjects tested by white examiners and white subjects tested by black examiners. Jensen, a researcher,[2] reviewed 30 studies done between 1936 and 1977 which address this issue. He indicated that only 17 of the studies were adequately designed to properly measure this variable. All of the 17 studies concluded that the race of the examiner is not an important variable in determining performance on tests of cognitive functioning.

Sex

It has also been hypothesized that individuals tested by examiners of the same sex would perform better than individuals tested by examiners of the opposite sex. There have been many studies performed in this area.[3] Although some indicate that the sex of the examiner can have a small effect on the results, most conclude that there is no significant difference in results based on the sex of the examiner.[4]

Experience of the Examiner

One might expect that the evaluator with more training and more experience in assessment techniques will generate more accurate results. However, one study suggests that medium-experienced examiners have higher accuracy than high- or low-experienced examiners.[5] The most experienced examiner can become stale in his or her evaluation skills without appropriate continuing education. As a result, it is important to make sure that experienced examiners also maintain their skills through continuing education.[6]

CONFIDENTIALITY

The American Psychological Association clearly states guidelines for confidentiality in its ethical principles for psychologists (Appendix). However, when an individual is involved in a custody dispute, the aspects of confidentiality change somewhat. If the evaluation is court ordered, individuals must understand that what occurs during the evaluation may not be confidential. Generally, activity that takes place between a psychologist and a client is considered privileged communication. The information can only be supplied to others if a release of information form is signed by the parties involved. A client/patient can legally waive privilege, and, in some circumstances, a court can order the removal of privilege. Information is generally either privileged or it is not. A psychologist should be careful about release authorizations that attempt to limit disclosure to only one person.

When utilizing a "release of information" form as part of a custody dispute, it is generally a good idea to have each individual sign a release officially allowing the psychologist to talk to all three attorneys and any other evaluators. If there are other significant individuals who would need to be contacted, then releases to these individuals should also be signed. This allows the psychologist to speak to all parties involved in the custody matter, maximizing the accuracy and thoroughness of the evaluation. The release of information form should be stated in such a way that it allows for an *exchange* of information between the evaluator and the other parties. Furthermore, the "release of information" form should state if and when the release expires, and that the individual has the right to withdraw the release at any time.

When an individual is seen in psychotherapy by a therapist and chooses not to have the content of that therapy process disclosed in the custody dispute, that individual may invoke privilege, and the therapist, in most states, may invoke it on behalf of his or her patient (at least if the therapist is a psychologist or psychiatrist). Social workers seldom have privileged communication status. However, it is important for the individual to realize that privilege is an "all or none" situation. The therapist may not be allowed to disclose certain information and withhold other information. Even if no release of information form has been signed, the psychologist may have an ethical responsibility to breach confidentiality when, in his or her judgment, the individual is dangerous to himself or herself, or someone else through abuse, acts of violence, or other criminal acts. In particular, *Tarasoff v. The Regents of the University of California*[7] is considered the landmark decision by the California Supreme Court. A considerable amount of litigation has recently centered around a therapist's "failure to warn."

On December 24, 1974, the California Supreme Court issued its first *Tarasoff* ruling: "When a doctor or psychotherapist in the exercise of his professional skill and knowledge, determines or should determine, that a warning is essential to avert danger arising from the medical or psychological condition of his patient, he incurs a legal obligation to give that warning."[8] In *Bellah v. Greenson*, the California Court of Appeals refined the *Tarasoff* ruling.[9]

Mavroudic v. Superior Court for the County of San Mateo affirmed the *Tarasoff* principle on February 26, 1980.[10] *Thompson v. County of Alameda*, in front of the California Superior Court handed down the next significant decision regarding the duty to protect.[11] *Jablonski v. United States* was heard in the U.S. Court of Appeals, 9th Circuit, on August 3, 1983. The decision stated that when there was no specific threat, the clinician should have determined that the patient was a threat.[12] In *Hedlund v. Superior Court of Orange County*, on September 29, 1983, the California Superior Court handed down a decision which enlarged the scope of *Tarasoff* even further.[13]

Section 48.92 of the Civil Code of California put into law a post-*Tarasoff* decision. It states:

> There shall be no monetary liability on the part of and no cause action shall arise against any person who is a psychotherapist . . . in failing to warn of and protect from a patient's threatened violent behavior or failing to predict and warn of and protect from a patient's violent behavior, except where the patient has communicated to the psychotherapist a serious threat of physical violence against a reasonably identifiable victim or victims.[14]

The law goes on to state exactly how this duty shall be discharged: "If there is a duty to warn and protect under the limited circumstances specified above, the duty shall be discharged by the psychotherapist making reasonable efforts to communicate the threat to the victim or victims into a law enforcement agency."

Knapp and Vandecreek, experts in the area of privileged communication, pointed out many concerns that have surfaced around the issue of confidentiality and privileged communication. The laws regarding privileged communication vary from state to state. They point out,

> only doctors can practice medicine, and only lawyers can practice the law. Psychiatrists, psychologists, social workers, mental health counselors and pastoral counselors, however, all provide psychotherapy . . . Privileged communication laws often apply to psychiatrists and psychologists qualified for private practice, but less frequently for other mental health professionals who are likely to work in community mental health centers.[15]

The authors also point out that there needs to be a balance between what the court requires and what the psychotherapist requires. Both are working for the best interest of the children. However, at times attorneys and judges feel pressure to discover everything about a particular case, while psychotherapists may be reluctant to disclose certain pieces of information because of the therapeutic harm that could come to the child or family. In sensitive situations, it can be suggested that the judge screen records privately in chambers before allowing open testimony in court. This may protect individuals from being required to expose irrelevant, potentially harmful information.[16]

It is also the ethical obligation of the psychologist to inform the participants of the evaluation, the extent of the evaluation, the cost of the evaluation, the amount of time the evaluation should take, and any fee arrangements that are to be entered into, preferably in writing.[17] The psychologist should also inform the parties of what will be done with the information after the evaluation process has been completed.

COMMUNICATING RESULTS

The results of the psychological evaluation are generally communicated in report form. It is important to know that the clients have a right to receive information about the tests they have taken.[18] However, it is the psychologist's responsibility to communicate the information so that it is not misunderstood, misused, or misrepresented by the clients. As a result, it is usually important not to provide actual scores or share raw data with the individuals.

Because it is essential that the psychologists not do anything to compromise the integrity of the tests administered, they cannot share raw data with attorneys. The American Psychological Association, Guidelines for Providers of Psychological Services states, "Raw psychological data (e.g., test protocols, therapy or interview notes, or questionnaire returns), in which a user is identified or ordinarily released only with the written consent of the user or the user's legal representative, are released only to a person recognized by the psychologist as competent to interpret data."[19] Attorneys are generally not in the position to be able to fully understand the materials received, and, consequently, the information could be inappropriately used. It is far more appropriate to share the raw data with another psychologist of the attorney's choice. Then the information is likely to be used accurately and with discretion. It can be very disconcerting for a psychologist to go into a deposition or trial and find that the raw data from his or her evaluation has been shared with the attorney by another psychologist. Furthermore, it is equally disconcerting to have an attorney reading from a test manual that is supposed to be protected by the psychologist, given the ethical and contractual responsibility of the psychologist to protect the tests (see Chapter Two on Ethical Issues).

Each psychologist signs an agreement with the major test publishing companies not to share test materials with nonpsychologists. An example comes from the Psychological Corporations catalogue, the major suppliers of test materials. "Test scores and materials are to be released only to persons who are qualified to interpret and use them properly.[20] If the psychologist is put in the position of divulging specific test items or specific interpretations of various responses, the tests could be rendered invalid. Anyone in the court reading the transcript of the case could know what types of answers to give and what types to avoid. As a result, none of those individuals could ever take the tests again and obtain valid results. With all the divorce and criminal cases in the country that utilize psychologists, the test would quickly become useless and would not be available to provide the necessary information to the courts. A dilemma arises when the psychologist's need to protect conflicts with the attorney's need to discover. However, in the authors' experience, courts tend to uphold the psychologist's position.

There is no standard format for a psychological report, but there are key components that should always be present in every psychological report. The beginning of the report should include the date or dates on which the individuals were seen, the name and birth date of each individual, and a list of the tests administered. The report should also include background information or history, cognitive test results, personality test results, summary and conclusions, and recommendations. Some psychologists prefer to write a separate report for each individual accompanied by a summary cover letter. Other psychologists prefer to include all of the information in one lengthy report.

It is important to realize that a report is a summary of the finding. In a recent court case, a psychologist had to review approximately 600 pages of materials generated from previous reports and the six evaluations performed for the case. The report for the evaluation was approximately 25 to 30 pages long. However, when the psychologist testified in court, the cross-examining attorney kept asking why specific minor pieces of information were left out of the report. It is not possible to distill 600 pages of materials down to 30 pages and include every piece of relevant information.

As a result, there is much information from the evaluation process not included in the report. In most psychological evaluations, this will include both positive and negative information about an individual. If a report appears to be slanted in one direction or the other, it becomes the attorney's responsibility during cross-examination to uncover the information not included in the report. The report should not be written to include only that information which supports the examiner's conclusion. It should also include nonsupporting material and the rationale for why the supporting material was weighed more heavily than the nonsupporting material. If the psychologist has not done this, then the attorney must bring this to the court's attention on cross-examination.

There is an ethical responsibility that attorneys have upon receiving reports of psychological evaluations on their clients and their opponent's clients. It is inappropriate and potentially dangerous to share the reports with clients, if clients are likely to disseminate the information or if they may misinterpret the information given. There have been too many times that clients have taken the psychological evaluations and freely shown them to friends, neighbors, and/or relatives. They use the reports as a way of substantiating their position and demonstrating their concerns about the other parent. The best way to handle this situation may be for the attorney to have a conference with a client and provide a summary of the results and recommendations, as opposed to giving a copy of the actual report to the client. If the individual is in psychotherapy, it may be appropriate and helpful to send a copy of the report to the treating therapist, who can go over it with the individual.

CHILD CUSTODY EVALUATION PRACTICES

A 1986 study of 190 psychologists, psychiatrists, and master's degree level mental health practitioners showed that the majority of the mental health professionals were retained by the attorney for one side, but they generally preferred to be appointed by the court.[21]

In the evaluation procedures, all of the evaluators interviewed the mother and the father individually, taking approximately two hours for each individual. Almost all interviewed each child individually, taking approximately one and one-half hours for each interview. Seventy-five percent of the evaluators administered psychological tests to the parents and the children, taking approximately two and one-half hours each. Approximately 70 percent of them observed the interaction between each parent and the child for slightly less than an hour. Only half of the individuals observed the mother and father together, or had conversations with significant others (friends and relatives). Thirty percent made school visits or home visits; of those who did, the average duration was over one hour. In addition, the average report writing took 2.8 hours, the average consultation with attorneys took 1.4 hours, and the average court testimony took 2.3 hours, for a total of 18.8 hours on the average.

The most frequently used instruments in testing adults in child custody evaluations were the Minnesota Multiphasic

Personality Inventory (MMPI), the Rorschach Psychodiagnostic Series, the Thematic Apperception Test (TAT), and the Wechsler Adult Intelligence Scale-Revised (WAIS-R).

CHILD CUSTODY
TABLE 3

Frequency of Use of Psychological Testing of Adults in Child Custody Evaluations

Psychological test	% respondents using test	Mean % cases in which test is used[a]
Minnesota Multiphasic Personality Inventory	70.7	87.8
Rorschach	41.5	67.3
Thematic Apperception Test	37.8	67.3
Wechsler Adult Intelligence Scale	29.3	66.8
Bender–Gestalt	12.2	82.5
Adult Sentence Completions	12.2	76.0
Draw-a-Person	6.1	81.0
Miscellaneous Projective Drawings	6.1	80.0
Sixteen Personality Factor Questionnaire	6.1	60.0
California Psychological Inventory	4.9	86.3
Clinical Analysis Questionnaire	3.7	70.0
House-Tree-Person Projective Technique	3.7	46.7
Miscellaneous Projectives	3.7	45.0
Kinetic Family Drawings	2.4	97.5
Parent–Child Interaction Test	2.4	52.5
Personality Inventory for Children	2.4	35.0
Other tests[b]	19.5	

[a] Includes only those respondents who reported using the test.
[b] Tests used by one respondent only.

From Keilin & Bloom, "Child Custody Evaluation Practices: A Survey of Experienced Professionals," 17 (4) *Professional Psychology: Research and Practice* 341 (1986). Copyright 1986 by the American Psychological Association. Reprinted by permission.

CHILD CUSTODY
TABLE 4

Frequency of Use of Psychological Testing of Children and Adolescents in Child Custody Evaluations

Psychological test	% respondents using test	Mean % cases in which test is used[a]
Intelligence Testing (WISC, WAIS, Stanford–Binet)	45.1	85.1
Thematic Apperception Test or Children's Apperception Test	39.0	74.7
Miscellaneous Projective Drawings	32.9	85.7
Rorschach	29.2	77.9
Bender–Gestalt	23.2	81.3
Wide Range Achievement Test or other achievement test	20.7	76.0
Draw-a-Person	19.5	79.4
Children's sentence completions	12.2	70.5
House-Tree-Person Projective Technique	9.8	82.5
Kinetic Family Drawings	8.5	94.3
Peabody Picture Vocabulary Test	8.5	71.4
Roberts Apperception Test	8.5	54.3
Family Relations Test	7.3	90.0
Minnesota Multiphasic Personality Inventory [b]	7.3	48.3
Tasks of Emotional Development Test	3.7	81.7
Miscellaneous anxiety inventories	3.7	73.3
Strange Situation Test	2.4	56.0
Other	15.9	

[a] Includes only those respondents who reported using the test.
[b] Tests used by one respondent only.

From Keilin & Bloom, "Child Custody Evaluation Practices: A Survey of Experienced Professionals," 17 (4) *Professional Psychology: Research and Practice* 341 (1986). Copyright 1986 by the American Psychological Association. Reprinted by permission.

The MMPI was used by 71 percent of the evaluators, who used it 88 percent of the time; the Rorschach by 42 percent of the evaluators 68 percent of the time; the TAT by 38 percent of the evaluators 67 percent of the time; and the Wechsler Adult Intelligence Scale by 29 percent of the evaluators 67 percent of the time. All other tests were used by 12 percent or less of the evaluators.

When testing children and adolescents in child custody evaluations, there was frequently a wider range of tests used. Intelligence tests (Wechsler Intelligence Scale for Children—Revised, Wechsler Adult Intelligence Scale and Stanford-Binet) were used by 45 percent of the respondents 85 percent of the time. The Thematic Apperception Test or Children's Apperception Test was used by 39 percent of the respondents 75 percent of the time. Projective drawings were used by 33 percent of the respondents 86 percent of the time. while the Rorschach was used by 29 percent of the respondents 78 percent of the time. The Bender-Gestalt, the Wide-Range Achievement Test, and the Draw-A-Person test were used by approximately 20 percent of the respondents approximately 80 percent of the time. All the rest of the instruments were used 12 percent of the time or less.

Keilin and Bloom, the authors of the study, reached several conclusions:[22]

- Child custody evaluators generally prefer to serve in an impartial capacity.
- Child custody evaluations typically include interviews, testing, and gathering of additional information.
- Evaluators generally spend an additional 6 to 7 hours in related activities (report writing, consultation with attorneys, and court testimony).
- Evaluators spend an average of 18.8 hours in the various phases of a custody evaluation.
- The evaluator may consider requiring advanced payment of fees, particularly before court testimony.
- In the process of recommending a single custodial parent, the evaluators considered the following factors to be most important: the expressed wishes of the older child, one parent attempting to alienate the child from the other parent, the quality of the emotional bonding between the child and each parent, the psychological stability of each parent, and the parenting skills of each parent.
- Evaluators consider the following factors to be most important in deciding between joint and single-parent

custody: the wishes of the older child, the quality of the relationship the child has with each parent, the parent's willingness to enter into a joint custody agreement, the psychological stability of the parents, the ability of the parents to separate their interpersonal difficulties from their parenting decisions, and the amount of anger and bitterness between parents.

- In single-parent custody, custodial recommendations generally stipulate that all children will remain together with the same parent.

- Evaluators generally do not see joint custody as being a fantasia for all disputed custody cases.

ENDNOTES

1. American Psychological Association Case Book 664 (1984).

2. J. Graham & R. Lilly, Psychological Testing 75 (1984).

3. *Id.*

4. *Id.*

5. *Id.* at 342.

6. *Id.* at 367.

7. Tarasoff v. The Regents of the University of California, 551 P.2d 334 (Cal. 1983).

8. Pope, *Clinical and Legal Issues in Assessing and Treating the Violent Patient*, The Independent Practitioner 16, 19 (July 1986).

9. *Id.* at 19.

10. *Id.*

11. *Id.*

12. *Id.*

13. *Id.* at 20.

14. *Id.*

15. S. Knapp & L. Vandecreek, *Psychotherapy and Privileged Communications in Child Custody Cases*, 16 Professional Psychology: Research and Practice 405 (1985).

16. *Id.*

17. American Psychological Association, General Guidelines for Providers of Psychological Services 6 (1987).

18. *Id.*

19. *Id.*

20. Psychological Corporation Catalogue, at 100.

21. Keilin & Bloom, *Child Custody Evaluation Practices: A Survey of Experienced Professionals*, 17 Professional Psychology: Research and Practice 338–46 (1986).

22. *Id.* at 334.

QUESTIONS FOR CHAPTER THREE

Caution: An attorney should not expect to be able to go into court and ask all of the questions listed below. Preparation is necessary, referring to the content of the chapter to determine if the question applies to your case. The page number at the end of each question refers to where in the chapter you may read an explanation of why this question may be important.

1. Who did the psychologist interview other than those tested? (p. 43)

2. Was the client allowed to take any tests home? (p. 45)

3. Were there significant others excluded from the interview process? (p. 46)

4. What type of information was left out of the report and why? (p. 53)

5. Was the setting appropriate? If not, why not? (p. 44)

6. Was rapport easily established? If not, why not? (p. 44)

7. Did the psychologist use standardized administration procedures? If not, why not? (p. 44)

8. Did any deviation in standardized procedures affect the results of the evaluation? (p. 44)

9. Was there any practice effect? (p. 47)

10. If the evaluator has been practicing for more than 10 years, what evidence is there that the person has kept up to date? (p. 48)

11. How long did the interview process last for each individual? (p. 54)

12. How long did the whole evaluation process last? (p. 54)

13. Did the evaluator follow the standards of the profession as outlined by the Keilin and Bloom study? (p. 57)

Chapter Four
How Divorce Affects Children

The author has noticed that during the past two decades there has been a breakdown in the commitment of individuals to long-term relationships. Fewer people are staying with the same employer for the duration of their work years. People move from neighborhood to neighborhood and city to city far more frequently. There has been a steady increase in the divorce rate.

Today's laws make it relatively easy for people to obtain a divorce. Many states have "no fault" divorce laws. People are choosing to get divorced for less significant reasons today than previously. For example, the therapists this author informally surveyed report that more frequently couples are obtaining divorces because they are not good sexual partners or because their interests do not match perfectly with one another. A generation ago these were considered conflicts to be resolved within the marriage relationship, not reasons for terminating it. Unfortunately, the children of today's marriages are modeling their parents' behavior and are likely to reflect the same feelings their parents have toward interpersonal and marital relationships.

Divorce has increased significantly in the past ten to fifteen years. A recent study by L. Schwartz cited United States government data noting that the divorce rate has increased from 0.3 per thousand population in 1867 to a rate of 5.0 per thousand in 1982. The rate almost doubled between 1968 (2.9 per thousand) in 1982. Schwartz also noted that the number of children affected by divorce has increased dramatically during that same period and time, for 6.3 per thousand children under 18 years of age in 1950 to 18.7 per thousand in 1981.[1]

One of the factors noted for the rise in the divorce rate is the effect of the feminist movement on women. Many women who had previously allowed themselves to be unreasonably dominated by their husbands began to assert themselves, thus changing the rules on which the relationship was based. If one spouse's attitudes and views change, the other spouse must be willing to adjust and change as well or the marriage will be in trouble.

One question that often arises is whether a couple "should stay together for the sake of the children." Views on this issue have changed in the last decade or two. More than a generation ago, the notion was that people should remain married for the sake of the children no matter how bad the marriage was. But research has indicated that individuals who stayed together for the sake of the children often ended up with maladjusted children. As a result, more recently individuals have gotten divorced without being as concerned about how their divorce would affect the children. However, with an increase in the divorce rate, research has shown that children also suffered maladjustment as a result of their parents getting divorced.

Therefore, when is it better to stay together for the sake of the children and when is it better to get divorced for the sake of the children? When answering this question, parents must realize that divorce adversely affects children. Parents will often go to a therapist and say, "we are getting divorced and we want to do it in a way that won't upset our children." The fact remains that there is no way for parents to get divorced without initially upsetting their children and adversely affecting their children's future. The author notes that when the parents' relationship with one another is destructive, staying married would have a greater adverse effect on the children than terminating the marriage. Representative examples of destructiveness in a marriage would include verbal, physical and/or sexual abuse, frequent inappropriate expressions of anger, and continually bringing the children into unresolved conflicts. When two married people, who have "fallen out of love," can cohabitate without any of the destructiveness identified above, the breaking up of the home would have a more adverse effect on the children than staying in a home with parents who do not love each other.[2] Consequently, the parents' ability to control their feelings determines how much a divorce will or will not adversely affect their children.

ADVERSARIAL VS. COOPERATIVE DIVORCE

Once parents have decided to get divorced, many concerns must be addressed. The first concern is whether the divorce will be a cooperative or an adversarial divorce. A cooperative divorce is one in which the parties are willing to meet, discuss, and resolve the issues without requiring a court battle. Mediation is one of the methods most frequently used in cooperative divorces. In cooperative divorces, attorneys generally encourage the mediation process, facilitate reaching a stipulation, and participate in negotiations where necessary. An adversarial divorce is one which leads to a legal contest or a court battle and takes place with attorneys assuming opposite positions in court. The adversarial divorce generally occurs when the cooperative process breaks down, or with individuals who are initially unwilling to enter into a cooperative process. It is important for an attorney today to be able to participate in both cooperative and adversarial divorce processes.

DIVORCE MEDIATION

Divorce mediation is something that has become relatively popular in recent years. Since many individuals characterize themselves as divorce mediators, it is important for anyone who seeks mediation to go to an individual who is qualified to be a divorce mediator.

At this time, the Academy of Family Mediators is an organization that accredits individuals based on their training and experience as mediators. Criteria for admission to the Academy of Family Mediators includes at least 40 hours of mediation training, review of mediation agreements from at least 15 successfully completed mediations, and documentation from an already experienced mediator that the individual is qualified.

The mediation process can take place with one or two mediators. A divorce can be fully mediated including custody and placement issues, financial issues, division of property and other related issues. In other cases, it is only necessary to partially mediate one or more of these issues identified.

One advantage of the mediation process is that participants are more cooperative in resolving issues of their divorce, including custody concerns. A second advantage is that the mediation approach generally costs a fraction of what the adversarial approach costs. In addition, the mediation approach has demonstrated that it leaves far fewer scars on the family members involved than the adversarial approach.[3] Furthermore, mediated divorces are much less likely to be relitigated than adversarial divorces.[4]

It is important to note that the mediation process is not designed to exclude attorneys from the divorce process; indeed, most mediators are either attorneys or psychotherapists of some level of training. However, some attorneys perceive their role as mediators to be in violation of the Code of Professional Responsibility because they perceive it as providing legal representation to both parties.

When a mediation agreement is reached, it is taken by each parent to his or her respective attorney. The attorneys then will advise the individuals as to the legality of any of the items agreed to and will make sure that the agreement is read into the court order as agreed upon. It is still up to the court to accept the agreement.

THE ADVERSARIAL APPROACH

When the cooperative divorce process breaks down, divorce becomes more and more adversarial. When using the adversarial approach there is less and less direct communication between the parties, as time progresses. As a result, they have less direct control over the eventual outcome. Problematic to using the adversarial approach is reaching the level of going to court, when a judge, who is a relative stranger to the case and has probably known the situation for a few hours at best, is the person responsible for making a decision that will affect the divorcing couple and their children for the rest of their lives.

CUSTODY ARRANGEMENTS

Another issue that must be decided is whether the couple should enter into a joint custody agreement or allow one of the parents to be the sole custodian. In a joint custody arrangement, both parents have equal legal rights with regards to their children's education, religious upbringing, and medical treatment. Joint custody, however, does not necessarily mean that both parents will have the children live with them an equal amount of the time. It is the placement decision that addresses how much time the parents will have the child(ren) living with them. In a sole custody arrangement, the sole custodian holds all of the legal rights to decision making about the children's development and future. Joint custody is generally best for the parents and the children since it keeps both parents actively involved in the development of their children.[5] Susan Steinman, a psychological researcher, noted that joint custody arrangements done privately broke down less frequently than joint custody arrangements ordered by the court.[6] However, joint custody works most effectively when the parents can communicate with one another. Unfortunately, this presupposes that the parents are going to be able to do something outside of marriage that they were incapable of doing inside it. And if the parents could communicate effectively with one another while married, they may not have gotten divorced in the first place. When parents demonstrate that even with a considerable amount of effort and intervention they cannot communicate with each other even for the sake of their children, it becomes necessary to identify a sole custodian. Then a custody dispute usually ensues. The custody dispute, unfortunately, often involves individuals in an adversarial posture making a concerted effort to demonstrate the incompetence of the other parent and the expertise of their own parenting skills. This process is more often than not destructive and tends to leave wounds that are very difficult to heal.

Several factors need to be considered when deciding whether joint or sole custody should be sought. First, can the parents sustain the communication that is necessary to maintain joint custody? Second, what kinds of children do well in a joint custody arrangement? Joint custody generally is better for younger children, as there are more ongoing situations that need to be discussed between parents. Parents who can separate their own needs from their children's needs are much more likely to make good joint custodial parents than parents who are not able to do so. Joint custody should not be used as a compromise when no other solution can be achieved. The success or failure of joint custody will be based primarily on the parents' ability to communicate effectively with one another.[7]

PHYSICAL PLACEMENT AND VISITATION SCHEDULES

Another important issue that needs to be decided is the physical placement of the children. In most divorce situations, even when joint custody is awarded, one parent becomes the primary placement parent and the other the secondary placement parent. There are many different ways that this arrangement can take place. However, there are some situations where shared placement is arranged between the parents. Usually in shared placement the parents will have either an equal or approximately equal amount of time with their children. The traditional model of placement allows for a parent with placement and a "visiting parent." Because the term visitation has certain connotations that have become distasteful over the years, the new terminology for "visitation" is "periods of physical placement."

Periods of physical placement can vary from one situation to another. The traditional arrangement allows for an 11/3 split. This generally involves the primary parent having the child or children 11 of every 14 days and the nonprimary placement parent having the children 3 of every 14 days. Generally, the 3 days involve a Friday night and Saturday one week and Friday night to Sunday the alternate week. Placement can be on an 11/3, 10/4, 9/5, 8/6, or 7/7 basis. These decisions are generally based on the availability of parents, the input from professionals, and the desire of parents to be involved in the upbringing of their children. One of the more popular divisions recently instated is the 9/5 split, which gives the secondary placement parent one overnight one week and a four-day weekend the alternate week. The four-day weekend is generally from Thursday night to Monday morning or Friday night to Tuesday morning. This split allows the secondary placement parent to do more than visit with his or her children and to become actively involved with child rearing. It also requires active communication between parents.

When working out an arrangement for visitation schedules, the common practice is to alternate holidays. This author feels, however, that whenever possible holidays should be shared as opposed to alternated. This, of course, presupposes that the parents are living in the same city. When holidays are alternated, it requires the children to miss spending each holiday with half of the extended family. Not only are they not visiting with one of the parents, but they are also not visiting with the aunts, uncles, cousins, and grandparents on that particular side of the family.

Provided the parents are living in the same city, almost all major holidays provide an opportunity for sharing. The following plan is generally recommended for sharing holidays by the author.

Thanksgiving

One family can have Thanksgiving dinner earlier in the day, while the other family has Thanksgiving dinner later in the day. The children will spend Thanksgiving dinner with one family and have dessert with the other family. The parent having dinner can be alternated from year to year.

Christmas

The children will spend Christmas Eve with one parent, and Christmas Day with the other parent. If both parents wish to have Christmas Eve or Christmas Day, then the Christmas Eve/Christmas Day placement will be rotated annually. This allows the children to spend part of Christmas with each family.

Easter

The children can spend Easter morning and Easter brunch with one family, and Easter dinner with the other family.

4th of July

There are many activities that take place on the 4th of July, generally starting in the morning and ending with evening fireworks. The day can be split, so that the children go to the morning parade and have a picnic lunch with one family, and have dinner and fireworks with the other family. If both parents have the same preference, then this too can be rotated on an annual basis.

Other Holidays

Mother's Day should be spent with the children's mother and supersede other visitation schedules, and Father's Day should be spent with the children's father and supersede other visitation schedules. The children should also be available to each of the parents on the parent's respective birthdays, which may supersede regular visitation schedules.

Children's birthdays are rarely celebrated on the actual birth date. One parent can have a birthday celebration for the child the weekend prior to the actual birth date, and the other parent a celebration for the child the weekend following the actual birth date.

Holidays, such as Memorial Day and Labor Day, are considered minor holidays, and can either be alternated or shared, as the parents wish.

JOINT CUSTODY-SHARED PLACEMENT: THE ACKERMAN PLAN

When parents get divorced, many times they are both candidates as reasonable custodial parents, and they both want to have placement of the children. Unfortunately, all too often in making decisions about sharing placement, the judges do not take into consideration what is psychologically best for the children. Judges have issued orders requiring children to spend the first half of the week in one household and the second half of the week in the other household, alternating weeks, alternating every two weeks, alternating months, all the way up to alternating years. In addition, orders have been written where the mother would have the children Monday, Wednesday, and Friday of one week, and Sunday, Tuesday, Thursday, and Saturday of the following week, and then alternating that plan every two weeks. The problem with any of these alternating plans is that it does not provide the children with a sense of home and a secure base from which to operate. A plan has been developed to provide the parents with relatively equal time with the children throughout the year and at the same time allow a sense of security and a home base. The plan is a 9/5–10/4 flip-flop arrangement. Deciding that this was a mouthful, a judge in a recent court decision labeled it "The Ackerman Plan" after the author of the plan.

The plan allows one parent to have primary placement during school time on a 9/5 basis. The 9/5 basis is set up as described earlier. The other parent then would have the children for primary placement on a 10/4 basis during nonschool time. This would mean that the second parent would have the children 10 out of every 14 days with the first parent having the children for a three-day weekend one week and an overnight the alternate week. School time runs from September 1 to June 1. Nonschool time is defined as June 1 to September 1, a week at Thanksgiving, two weeks at Christmas, and a week at

Easter. This allows the 10/4 parent to have the children on a 10/4 basis 4 out of the 12 months of the year, and the 9/5 parent to have the children on a 9/5 basis 8 of the 12 months of the year. When all is tallied, the 9/5 parent has the children approximately 20 days per year more than the 10/4 parent. In fact, if a parent finds that the other parent having the children for 20 extra days out of the year objectionable, it is usually based on his or her need to argue and not a need to be reasonable.

One objection that has been raised is that the 10/4 parent always has the children 10/4 during holiday times. It must be noted that the 9/5 parent still has 4 days in each of these blocks of time in which to spend holiday time with the children. In addition, each parent is usually allowed two or three weeks of uninterrupted time during the course of the year to allow for vacation time.

When the decision is made as to who will have the children 9/5 during school time and who will have the children 10/4 during nonschool time, several things must be considered. Generally, the parent who is better able to academically support the children should be the 9/5 parent during school time, and the parent who is better able to provide and support recreational activities should be the 10/4 parent during nonschool time. In addition, creative arithmetic should be used to establish what support should be paid since the parents will have the children a relatively equal amount of time.

ADJUSTMENT OF THE FAMILY TO DIVORCE

The divorce process necessitates a complex adjustment for both parents and children. Parents who cannot wait until the divorce is finalized because then they think life will be much simpler are not aware that they will be required to have a relationship with the other parent as long as their children are minors. In addition, adjusting to the demands of the divorce, itself, may take six months to a year after the final decree.[8]

For the children, the adjustment period after the divorce is as important as the adjustment during the divorce process, itself. Furthermore, both parents and children must deal with such concerns as living in a new neighborhood, going to a new school or job, getting used to new relationships, and becoming familiar with the visitation schedules.

In deciding what the placement arrangements are to be, several considerations must be taken into account. This author believes that children under two years of age should generally not have overnight visitations. Linda Bird Franke states, "In visitation, a baby under two should not be moved back and forth between the homes of his divorced parents, for example, but should stay put in one place and have the parents visit him."[9]

"It's too hard for the young mind to integrate that lack of constancy." says Frank Williams at Thaliens Community Mental Health Center in Los Angeles. "A baby needs not only the familiar parent's face, but the familiar colors on the wall and the familiar shapes of the room and his own crib to make him feel secure. Not until the child is at least two years old does he or she have the maturity to tolerate spending alternate weekends or a summer stint as long as two weeks away from the familiarity of 'home.' In the interim, the baby will benefit from as much visitation as possible from the noncustodial parent."[10]

Young children need to have a home base. As a result, except in unusual situations, a 50/50 arrangement is not in the young child's best interest. A 50/50 arrangement should never be allowed when the parents live in different states. That would require the children to be continually moving and adjusting to different homes, schools and neighborhood environments.[11] This author believes the only case where a 50/50 arrangement works effectively is when both parents live within the same school district and relatively close to one another. This affords the children the opportunity to attend the same school and maintain the same neighborhood friends regardless of whose home they happen to be residing in. This arrangement, of course, presupposes that the parents can communicate effectively with one another.

Another question that is often raised regards whether the mother should work after the divorce. Undoubtedly, divorce has a financial impact on a family. Since there is no way that two individuals can live separately as cheaply as they can together, it may be necessary for the mother to work after the divorce. Research clearly demonstrates that if the mother has worked before divorce, her working after the divorce will not be negatively received by the children.[12] However, if the mother did not work prior to the divorce, her working once the divorce has occurred will be negatively received by the children.[13] They will perceive this as a second loss. First dad left, and now mom is leaving, also.

In those cases where parents cannot agree on custody and/or placement arrangements, it is often left to professionals to determine who would make the best custodial parent. Many factors go into making this decision, including psychological evaluations. Research has identified many characteristics that are important in the custodial parent.[14] Generally the parent who is able to provide a more stable environment will make a better custodial parent.[15] A stable environment is generally defined by consistency regarding the number of times a parent has moved, employment history, and the physical setting in which the children will reside.[16] The better custodial parent is one who will be more sensitive to the developmental needs of children and better able to identify current and future needs.[17] Research has further demonstrated that the custodial parent of choice is less authoritative, has a greater capacity to communicate, and generally provides appropriate intellectual stimulation in the home environment.[18]

PROBLEMS CHILDREN EXPERIENCE

Researchers have predicted what proportion of children will be affected by divorce in the future. Hetherington, one of the most prominent early divorce researchers, estimated that 40 to 50 percent of children born in the 1970s will spend some time living with a single parent.[19] Kurdek, another researcher, cites Glick's projection that by 1990 33 percent of the children in the United States will experience divorce prior to 18 years of age.[20] Current reports show that 28.5 percent, or 18 million of the 63 million children in the United States under 18 years of age, live in single-parent households.[21]

There are several distinct problems that parents must anticipate when a divorce occurs. Children of divorce will confront many other problems. While no child will experience all of the problems described below, some children may experience no problems at all. However, it is unusual for a child to go through a divorce without some degree of difficulty.

Guilt and withdrawal of affection are two of the problems that often cause children particular difficulty.[22] Children, especially those five to seven years of age, may feel they caused the divorce.[23] A child may state, "If only I had been better," or "If only I had not made Mommy or Daddy scream so much, they would not be getting divorced." Children afraid of losing their parents' love may have been told that the cause for the divorce is that Mom and Dad no longer love each other. They reason, therefore, that Mom and Dad no longer love them.

Linda Bird Franke, author of *Growing Up Divorced*, looks at the way children of different ages respond to the process of divorce. She refers to the preschool years as the age of guilt. It is during this period that children feel guilty about the fact that their parents are getting divorced. The guilt is usually associated with feeling of "If I had been a better child, my parents would not have gotten divorced." It is important for parents of preschool children to explain the process of divorce in simple terms that they can understand. In doing so, it is necessary to make sure that they understand that it was not because of their behavior that the divorce is taking place. Parents must do their best to act in an adult-like manner in the presence of their children at this time. If, as a result of their anger, they become childish in their response, it is only going to confuse their preschool-age children and make their adjustment to the divorce more difficult.[24]

Franke refers to the years between six and eight as the age of sadness. The child during this age has come to rely on the security of the family structure. This age child interprets disruption of that structure as a collapse of his or her entire protective environment. Due to his or her emotional immaturity, the child cannot protect himself against these losses. The child's survival is threatened, as "loss of one parent implies the loss of the other as well."[25] Franke states, "anger, fear, betrayal, and the disruptive post-divorce household, a deep sense of deprivation are the characteristic responses of children this age to divorce. But above all, the children feel sad, a persistent and sometimes crippling sadness that, even a year after the divorce, they have only been able to mute to resignation."[26]

An example of how this sadness pervades the child's life is also taken from Franke.

> Jacob is kicking a soccer ball around his backyard. In the garage he can see the oil stain where his father's car used to be and the hook where his father's golf bag used to hang. There are still a lot of tools on his father's workbench, but Jacob isn't allowed to touch them unless his father is there. And his father hasn't been there for six months. They were going to build a bicycle rack together, but that was before his father left. Now they probably never will. Jacob halfheartedly kicks the ball again. But it isn't fun. Nothing seems to be fun these days.[27]

Franke refers to the period from nine to twelve years of age as being the age of anger.[28] This is a particularly crucial period of time in the child's life. It is essential that the anger that is felt during this period be resolved. If it is not, it will be carried forward into later childhood and early adulthood and be extremely disruptive to interrelationships. Franke states:

> The bad news follows naturally from much of the good news. As team players, children have a very strict sense of fairness, of what is right and what is wrong . . . . Children live by a rigid code of ethics that stresses black and white definitions of loyalty and behavior. When the very parent who taught the child these rules does not abide by them, the child becomes angry—very angry. It is this deep and unrelenting anger that most characterizes the reaction to divorce of late latency-age children. Unlike younger children, who fight against feelings of anger toward a parent, these children often seek it out. Often the child chooses between the "good" and "bad," reserving so much hostility for the latter that visitation with the noncustodial parent sinks to an all-time low, especially for boys.[29]

The author believes that defusing the anger that the child feels toward the parent is extremely important. It is too tempting for the angry custodial spouse to enlist the angry feelings of the child as an ally. Although these angry feelings and alliance may make the custodial parent feel triumphant, they may only prevent the child from resolving the divorce and moving on. In adolescence, this has a tendency to backfire. The child will then become angry with the custodial parent for "causing" him or her to be so angry with the noncustodial parent during the past late latency years. He may even go as far as accusing the custodial parent of preventing a relationship with the other parent. It is during the time of these extraordinarily volatile feelings that psychotherapy is a very important alternative to consider.

Franke refers to the teenage years as the "age of false maturity."[30] She feels that the developmental tasks of adolescence are both exaggerated and blurred by the divorce process. It is "during the teens, when a child begins to act and think as an adult, that the lasting effect of a badly resolved divorce— parental abandonment, inattention, or overdependence—suddenly jump to the fore."[31] Helping teenage children through divorce is not as difficult as younger children. Fortunately, they have already started to gain their independence from the parents and have some stability on their own. It is important to be totally open and honest with the teenage children as to why the marriage has ruptured. If the divorce is related to affairs, alcoholism, mental illness, or violence, the teenagers must be told, sparing them the gruesome details. They probably have been struggling with some of these issues, themselves, and will be glad to know that their perceptions were accurate. Since teenagers will be shortly entering their adult years, and are likely to become involved in meaningful heterosexual relationships, it is extremely important to handle these issues properly at the time of divorce. If the teenager comes away from the divorce with the feeling that interpersonal relationships are not worth the effort, his or her own meaningful relationships will be disrupted. If the teenager can see that the dissolution of the parents' marriage was related only to the relationship between the two, and cannot be generalized to all relationships, he or she is more likely to be able to sustain meaningful relationships.

During the early months following the divorce, it is important that the children be reassured as often as possible that their parents still love them. Certainly, the children did not cause the divorce. Reassuring them of this may be a more difficult task than expected. A child is likely to think, "Mom and Dad got married and said they would love each other forever. Now they don't love each other anymore. Mom and Dad have said they're getting divorced but they'll love me forever. How do I know for sure that they will continue to love me?" Unfortunately, time is often the only cure for this concern.

Abandonment/Rejection

Another area of concern occurs when the children experience feelings of abandonment and/or rejection. Children often perceive that the noncustodial parent has left the home and abandoned the children.[32] A child who has relied on the noncustodial parent for certain things over time now finds that this parent is not going to be available to provide those things. Even if the child is capable of understanding that the separation may be court ordered and against the will of the noncustodial parent, from a psychological point of view the child is still going to feel abandoned and rejected.[33] This view seems to be especially true of those children between the ages of five and seven. They are more likely to perceive the divorce as abandonment/rejection because of their perception that they may have caused the divorce.

Powerlessness/Helplessness

The author notes that children may also experience feelings of powerlessness and/or helplessness. These feelings are the result of the child going through many changes in his or her life and not being able to do anything about them. For example, in a relatively short period of time, the household breaks up, the noncustodial parent must find a new dwelling, the custodial parent and the children may be required to move, the children find themselves in a new neighborhood and a new school, and there is a definite change in the financial status of the family. All of these major changes take place without the advice and/or consent of the children. In other words, these changes are forced on the children. It is these undesired major changes that leave the children feeling powerless and helpless.

During and shortly after the divorce, children may exhibit a greater need for nurturing or dependency than had been shown previously. The children have just lost the close contact with one parent and they are often concerned that the other parent may leave too. It takes children of divorce a long time to understand that just because one parent has left, the other will not leave them as well. These feelings tend to increase the need for nurturing and dependency.

Insecurity

The feelings of guilt, withdrawal of affection, abandonment/rejection, powerlessness/helplessness, and the need for nurturing/dependency can collectively lead to the larger problem of overall insecurity on the part of the children.[34] The insecurity feelings may come out in the following thought process: "All right, Mom just kicked Dad out of the house. How do I know she's not going to kick me out of the house, too?" When a custody battle is part of the divorce, the feelings of insecurity are reality based. For example, "Mom and Dad and their lawyers are arguing about which parent I'm going to live with. I don't know what school I'm going to. And I don't know what neighborhood I'm going to live in and what friends I'm going to play with." The children often feel that there is nothing left of their former life. Looking at it realistically, this may be an accurate conclusion. The children's recreation, school, peer relationships, and family relationships are all unknown for a prolonged period, possibly six months to a year, until the custody battle is resolved. All of this uncertainty leads to a noticeable basic insecurity on the part of the children.

When a court decision is reached and a child knows where and with whom he or she is going to live, there will almost certainly be insecurities that go along with that decision. The child may think, "OK, I am going to move now. How do I know if I will do well in the new school? How do I know if I'm going to find friends in the neighborhood? How do I know things are going to work out? How do I know I'm not going to have to move again in another six months?"

A court decision may only be the beginning of a child's insecurity. Many times the noncustodial parent will say, "I'm going to appeal the decision." This serves to prolong the period of insecurity for the child. In the author's experience, the more times the custody issue is taken back to court, the longer the feelings of insecurity exist in the child and the more likely there will be long-term psychological problems associated with it.

Regressive Behavior

There are many behavioral and/or psychological reactions children can have as a result of divorce. Probably the most significant reaction is referred to as regressive behavior. Generally, regressive behavior means going back to a former developmental level by doing something that had not been done for a while. Children who have stopped thumb sucking may go back to it again. Children who have stopped wetting their pants or their beds (enuresis) or soiling their pants or their beds (encopresis) may go back to these behaviors. Just about any type of behavior that occurred in earlier childhood can occur again during these regressive stages.

Several general rules should be considered when deciding whether professional intervention for regressive behavior is necessary. In many cases, children will enter into regressive behaviors when any significant life changes take place. A significant life change can include a change of school, a death in the family, a serious illness, a divorce, a marriage in the family, or a change in the composition of the household. Parents will often call a professional and say, "Johnny has just started to . . . again." In the author's experience, any regressive behavior that lasts for less than two weeks has not lasted long enough for the parent(s) to consider intervention unless it is dangerous to the child. What follows concerns only nondangerous, nonharmful types of behavior. If all of the regressive behaviors that last for less than two weeks were attended to in a therapeutic setting, children would be in and out of therapy for much of their childhood. This approach would be excessive. Generally, if a type of regressive behavior lasts for a two- to four-week period, the parent(s) should make some decisions about how to deal with that behavior. If, during this two- or four-week period the behavior continues but gradually subsides, there is little need to be concerned. However, when regressive behavior continues longer than four weeks, therapeutic intervention may be called for.

Acting Out Behavior

Acting out behavior is frequently associated with the process of divorce. The acting out behavior comes from the child's sense of frustration and anger over the changes in his or her life. It is not unusual to see children of divorce, who formerly have been fairly well behaved, suddenly become involved in vandalism, shoplifting, or drug use or abuse. Soft drugs, hard drugs, alcohol, and cigarettes are all included as drug use or abuse problems. The amount of acting out behavior tends to vary as a function of the divorce process. As the issues come closer to the surface, such as court dates or interviews with attorneys, the acting out behavior will likely increase. When a lull in the divorce process occurs, the acting out behavior tends to subside.

Repetitive Behavior

Repetitive behavior can also be observed at the time of a divorce. Repetitive behavior is an act a child does repeatedly, such as asking the same question over and over or continually playing with the same toy. A child may begin to do this as a means of maintaining or establishing some kind of control over his or her life. The child may go through the following thought process, "Okay, I can't control what the courts say I have to do. I can't control which parent I'm going to live with. I can't control what house I'm going to live in, who my friends are going to be, and what school I'm going to go to. But maybe through some repetitive behavior I can demonstrate some control over my life." While the child does not actually think things through in this manner, the process does allow a similar course. Prohibiting a child from engaging in this type of repetitive behavior at this time may be somewhat dangerous. It may be the only "glue" holding the child together during the divorce process.

Of the problems described previously, three or four appear to be deep-seated psychological problems that result from the divorce process. These problems are generally the ones that will determine whether short-term or long-term therapeutic intervention may be necessary. When talking about short-term versus long-term intervention, this author makes a simple distinction. Short-term intervention is generally treatment that takes six months or less, while long-term intervention is treatment that takes more than six months. Often, short-term intervention requires only a half dozen or fewer sessions. Usually feelings of abandonment, powerlessness/helplessness, need for nurturing/dependency, and insecurity can be dealt with in short-term intervention just by helping the child understand what is going on in his or her life.

Guilt

One problem that may require long-term intervention is guilt. Children's guilt during divorce may come from many sources. They may feel guilty because the parents are getting divorced, guilty because they cannot do anything to bring the parents back together, guilty because some action of theirs led to the divorce, or else they just have unexplained guilt feelings. As a result, children will often find a concrete example on which to blame their abstract feeling. The following illustrates this need for a concrete reason:

> A 56-year-old man had been in therapy for over a year. He was staying in a terrible marriage and a terrible job experience. It came to the point that the man and the therapist felt that there was some underlying need to punish himself that kept him in these situations. At one point, the subject of his mother's death came up. His mother had died when he was 10 years old. When talking about his mother's death, he suddenly remembered the day his mother died. He was walking home from school and saw a baseball lying on somebody's front lawn. He took the baseball and walked home with it. When he got home he found out his mother had died. That night he decided that his mother died because God was punishing him for stealing the baseball. This belief was born out of a ten-year-old's need to find a concrete reason for an abstract feeling.[35]

Unresolved Anger

Two other problems that are identified during the process of divorce are most important. They are unresolved anger and depression. In this author's experience, a child of divorce usually displays either unresolved anger or depression or both. "The hapless child's fear of being overwhelmed by the intense feelings of sorrow, anger, rejection and yearning further block the acknowledgment of the family rupture."[36] This is of such great importance because people do not like to deal with anger, either their own or other people's. In group or individual therapy, it is the most difficult problem for people to deal with and resolve.

This author notices that the anger that presents itself at the time of divorce is directed at almost everyone. Children are angry at their mother for "kicking Dad out of the house," toward Dad for doing the bad things that got him "kicked out of the house," toward themselves for doing whatever they perceived they did wrong that caused the divorce, toward the people they think should have supported them through the process and did not, and toward all of the people who are not as understanding as the children would like them to be.

In other cases, the anger is copied from that of the parents. The children may not know why they are angry, but they see their mother and father angry and they believe that is the way they are supposed to act during the process of divorce.

Anger

Anger, although related to depression, has many of its own problems associated with it. It can lead to acting out behavior or somatizing, which is turning psychological problems into bodily complaints. The following example provides an illustration of somatizing:

> A 9-year-old child was referred for therapy because of stomach pains. She was using the stomach pains as an excuse to avoid participating in all activities. The pains had reached such severity that at times she was unable to stand erect. It must be noted that the girl was not merely using these pains as an excuse, but was really feeling the pain. In the first two therapy sessions, it became apparent that she was angry about the divorce that her parents had recently gone through. The therapist merely stated that it was okay to be angry and described different ways of expressing the anger appropriately as well as inappropriately. The pain symptoms subsided rather quickly at that point and did not return.[37]

This 9-year-old girl learned that it was acceptable to express the anger which she had been suppressing. It was no longer necessary for her to have the bodily symptoms.

The author notes that, unlike younger children who fight against feelings of anger toward a parent, middle-aged children seem to seek it out. Often the child, especially a boy, chooses hostility toward the noncustodial parent when visitation with the noncustodial parent sinks to an all-time low. However, in many cases, young adults carry these unresolved feelings with them into adulthood. Then it is much more difficult to undo 20 years of repressed and unresolved feelings than it is to cope with new feelings. Often, the therapy process for young children means providing a stable, reasonable, accepting adult who is not emotionally involved in the divorce process. This is not to suggest that there is anything psychologically wrong with the parents. However, because of the stress and emotional involvement in the divorce situation and the volatility of both parents' lives at that point, it is often difficult to provide the child with an objective viewpoint. As a result, the child comes to therapy and finds out that not all adults are experiencing what his or her parents are experiencing. The child learns that it is all right to get angry without fear of reprisal.

Depression

The second important problem is depression. Depression in children is the most frequently undiagnosed problem. One reason for this is that a child's acting out behavior often masks depression. Another reason that the diagnosis is often missed is that the person doing the evaluation is often a therapist who works primarily with adults. Children do not necessarily exhibit the classic signs of depression that adults exhibit. The classic adult symptoms, for the most part, are absent in depressed children unless they happen to be severely depressed. When a child is severely depressed, the diagnosis is relatively easy. It should be pointed out that depression and unresolved anger are very closely related. Depression is often anger turned inward. Therefore, one of the ways children learn to relieve their depression is by not dealing with it directly, but by dealing with it indirectly through outbursts of anger.

Following these outbursts the depression may subside somewhat. The symptoms of depression in children can be identified relatively easily in evaluations performed by psychologists who are trained to work with children. The depressed child may be overlooked in the classroom. This child usually sits quietly in the back of the classroom and causes no problems for the teacher.

Genuine suicidal thoughts, a common characteristic in depressed adults, are relatively rare in depressed young children. Depression, as a result, is often difficult for parents and teachers to recognize.

Preoccupation with death and loss may be an indication of depression. Inability to get along with friends, when this previously was not a problem, may be another sign of depression. The desire to spend more time alone and to not participate in family, school, or neighborhood activities may also be signs of depression. Certainly obvious behavior such as increased crying, serious suicidal talk, and noticeable loss of appetite should not go ignored.[38]

Children need to be made aware that it is acceptable to be sad about what they are going through. They must be permitted to express their feelings. However, parents often will not permit their children to do so, not out of maliciousness, but more likely out of frustration. For example, the mother who, after two consecutive weeks of listening to her child cry, might yell, "Quit that damn crying already. You're driving me nuts." The message that this child is receiving is that he or she is not allowed to be sad and to express these sad feelings. As part of the divorce process, the child may actually be going through a type of grief reaction. Grief reactions occur after the loss of a pet, a loved relative, or an object of affection. It can also occur when a friend moves away or a similar loss happens. It is essential that the child have the opportunity to talk these feelings through.

ADDED PROBLEMS OF DIVORCE

This section reflects a combination of 15 years of experience by this author, Marc Ackerman, in working with divorce cases. Many of the problems reported by Ackerman are also reported by other therapists and research.

During the divorce process, it is not only the parents who are getting divorced. The child gets divorced, too, even though the legal document does not specifically record the children's names. Interest in normal childhood activities decreases at this time. It is almost as if the child is saying, "What's the use? Mom and Dad are getting divorced, so why should I worry about something as trivial as school?" The child becomes preoccupied with the divorce and, as a result, may be distracted easily. This preoccupation is manifested in feelings of anger, helplessness, and insecurity. The child's teacher may be trying to explain an important concept while the child is wondering how much longer he or she will be in that school or neighborhood. Often the school performance can be a barometer of how the divorce is affecting the child. When a former A/B student suddenly becomes a C/D student, the divorce is having a dramatic effect on the child.

Children of divorce often carry with them the magical wish that their parents are going to get back together again. In a significant number of cases, this wish is carried into adulthood. Unfortunately, it is an issue that frequently does not get attended to by parents. As a result, it remains unresolved in adulthood. When one of the parents decides to date or to remarry, this unresolved issue may cause problems. A child may try to interfere with the parent's decision, not because he or she dislikes the new person, not because he or she cannot get along with the new person, but because the new person is interfering with the fantasy that the natural parents will get back together. The child reasons, "If Mom marries this man, then she cannot remarry Dad." In this situation, children may consciously or unconsciously do many inappropriate things in an effort to sabotage the upcoming marriage.

The postdivorce adjustment period involves working out the details of visitation. It remains to be seen if the custodial and the noncustodial parents are going to be reasonable about visitation or if they are going to cause problems. Often the noncustodial parent will see the children twice a week in the beginning. However, four years hence the children may be lucky to see this parent twice a year.

With younger children, it is important for the noncustodial parent to see the children more, rather than less, frequently. It is equally important for the custodial parent to be flexible. When the custodial parent becomes too rigid in the visitation schedule, it becomes difficult for the children to handle this situation. Flexibility is important for special events or simply unexpected changes in scheduling.

Another problem associated with divorce is that the child may not have an appropriate sex role model. This tends to be a problem more often with male children than with female children. Most frequently the mother becomes the custodial parent and the female child has an appropriate sex role model. It is very important for a male child to have a strong male role model available. This is particularly true during the onset of pubescence and adolescence. An uncle, an older cousin, or an organization, like Scouts or Big Brothers, can provide this type of role model. Although the Big Brother organization can be beneficial, there is one key concern with this group. The Big Brothers only require a one-year commitment. Just as the child is becoming used to his new Big Brother, the Big Brother may leave his life. This may be interpreted as another abandonment/rejection situation that the child has to resolve.

In addition to not having an appropriate sex role model, the child may not have an appropriate heterosexual relationship model. After the divorce it can be important for children to see their parents get angry with another person and then resolve it. It is also important for children to be able to see their parents hug and kiss another adult in a meaningful relationship, or sit next to another adult on the sofa. Furthermore, it is extremely important for children to see the process of resolving any disagreement. These possibilities are often absent in a divorce situation. In the time leading up to the divorce, children may see only the arguing without the resolution. They do not have the opportunity to see their mother and father interact as husband and wife. As a result, their last male/female relationship model has been an inappropriate one.

When this type of model is absent, children may have difficulty in establishing their own relationships as they approach adulthood. They may not know how to establish heterosexual relationships because they have never witnessed one during their childhood. Typically, divorces beget divorces. Their parents got divorced and the children never saw the appropriate model for establishing a meaningful heterosexual relationship. When these children get married and have difficulties within their marriages, they see divorce as the means of resolving these difficulties rather than developing interpersonal communication skills.

There are things that parents can do at the outset of divorce to prevent some of the problems described here. Perhaps the most important thing parents can do is avoid "bad mouthing" one another in front of the children. Statements such as, "if your mother hadn't . . . then this wouldn't have happened", or "you can never trust men," are problematic for children. When children hear these kinds of statements and carry them into adulthood, they have a tremendous effect on children's ability or inability to establish meaningful relationships.

Another inappropriate indirect expression of anger can occur during visitation. If the noncustodial parent arrives for visitation or brings the children back from visitation prior to the assigned times or simply does not show up at all, then this provides an opportunity for inappropriate indirect expressions of anger.

It is also important for children to hear that they still have the love of their parents. This statement of love should be repeated probably more often than would be deemed necessary by the parents. Children need to hear that even though mother and father do not love each other any more, independently they still love the children. Not only should this be expressed to the children in words, but also in signs of love through behavior and attitudes.

When parents separate, one parent stays home and the other parent finds an alternate living situation. It is particularly important for children to see where the noncustodial parent is living as soon as possible after the separation. The children still are concerned about both parents. They want to know that the noncustodial parent still has a place to sleep, a stove to cook on, and a bathroom to use. Young children are very much at the primary needs level and want to make sure that the noncustodial parent's primary needs of eating, sleeping, and eliminating are being met. If this opportunity is not provided, children often entertain the fantasy that the noncustodial parent has been "kicked out of the house" and only has the car to live in. This process may be particularly difficult for children if the noncustodial parent is required to move from a large house to a small efficiency apartment.

Parents should avoid emphasizing the money issue in front of children. It is certainly important for the children to understand the financial status of the family. However, it is not appropriate for the mother continually to be saying such things as "We can't go to the movie tonight because we don't have enough money," or "If Dad gave us more money or paid his child support on time, we could do more things together." These kinds of comments only serve to increase the child's anger toward the father and reduce the effectiveness of the relationship between the father and the children.

It is helpful for divorced parents to continue to be involved in the children's educational and sporting events. Parents should be able to put aside their differences long enough to attend parent conferences together at school. If they attend school plays or athletic events, it is not necessary for them to sit with one another. However, it may be very important for the child to know that both parents are present. It is unfortunate when one parent states that he or she will not be present if the other parent is going to be there. If parents decide to attend parent conferences together, they should avoid using these occasions as arguing grounds or as a means of expressing anger toward one another.

POSITIVE ADJUSTMENT FOLLOWING DIVORCE

There are many factors that have been identified in literature that lead to a relatively positive adjustment to the divorce process. Researchers Wallerstein and Kelley and Stolber and Anker report that little change in financial stability leads to a positive adjustment.[39] Wallerstein and Kelley[40] and Hetherington, Cox and Cox identify several variables including the emotional adjustment of the custodial parent, low levels of conflict between parents prior to and during the divorce process, and cooperative parenting following the divorce process.[41] In addition, Wallerstein and Kelley[42] feel the approval and love from both parents and the availability of regular visitation from the noncustodial parent are also important factors. Kurdek and Berg[43] point out that children adjust better, depending upon their age at the time of the marital rupture, if they have a high level of interpersonal understanding, and if they have a high level of internal locus of control. The latter means that they are self-directed.

Neal, in his article entitled, *Children's Understanding of Their Parents' Divorces*, identified several stages that a child must go through prior to fully adjusting to the divorce.[44] They include acknowledging the reality of the marital rupture; disengaging from parental conflict and distress in assuming customary pursuits; accepting the loss; resolving anger and self-blame; accepting the permanence of the divorce, and achieving realistic hope regarding relationships.

Recent Research

There has been a considerable amount of research done recently on how divorce affects children. A very comprehensive study was done by John Guidubaldi and his associates at Kent State University entitled, "Longitudinal Effects of Divorce on Children: A Report from the National Association of School Psychologists-Kent State University Nationwide Study."[45] The study included 699 children from 38 states and was designed as a two-year longitudinal examination. All of the children were evaluated with regard to the effects of divorce at least two years after the divorce (Time 1), and two years later the same children were re-evaluated to determine their level of adjustment (Time 2). The Time 1 and Time 2 evaluations looked at intelligence scores, achievement scores, social behavior rating, school behavior rating, peer acceptance or rejection rating, and parent and teacher ratings. These variables were viewed on the basis of the child's grade, sex, race, occupation of parent, family income, and length of time in a single-parent household. Children from single-parent divorced homes were compared with children from families intact since birth.

The Time 1 study indicated that physical health of children was significantly poorer in divorced homes than in intact homes. It further found that divorced-family male children were most adversely affected by the time they reached fifth grade. These children had significantly greater anxiety, were significantly more withdrawn, had physically acting out behavior, had feelings of blame, were impulsive, talked irrelevantly, had significantly poorer reading and spelling achievement, had significantly greater referrals to the school psychologist, and had significantly greater nonregular classroom placements. Divorced-family male and female children in first grade showed the same differences between divorce and intact families. However, by fifth grade, divorced-family females were similar to intact family males and females at the same age levels. In other words, between first grade and fifth grade divorced-family female children were able to adjust, but divorced-family male children were not.[46]

Two years later (Time 2), the average time since the divorce was 6.2 years. Again the results were relatively similar. Divorced family boys achieved significantly lower on 10 of the 46 variables measured, but girls were significantly lower on only one variable. When the children's adjustment was compared with intelligence, those individuals with lower intelligence had significantly poorer adjustment. When adjustment was compared to mental health variables, male children were significantly lower on six mental health variables. These studies suggest that girls are more stable over time and that boys manifest greater variability.[47]

The children's home environment was evaluated to determine its effect on their adjustment. Higher income families had significantly better adjustment than lower income families. In addition, the quality of the relationship with the noncustodial parent predicted adjustment better than did the quality of the relationship with the custodial parent. Permissive child-rearing styles yielded better adjustment for girls, but significantly poorer adjustment for boys.[48]

The classroom setting was also evaluated. Four variables were identified as being important: (1) a safe and orderly environment, (2) high expectations, (3) the use of reinforcement practices, and (4) monitoring of progress. A classroom that provided a safe and orderly environment showed significantly better adjustment in children of divorce than a less orderly classroom. For boys, frequent monitoring of school progress was negatively correlated with adjustment. However, the use of positive reinforcement practices did provide a positive correlation for adjustment with boys.[49]

This study provides a tremendous amount of useful information in determining the effects of divorce on children. It further identifies that boys will have adjustment problems with divorce as many as six years after the divorce takes place; however, girls tend to have no more long-term adjustment problems than girls from intact families. Finally, important information is also reported on what type of home and school environment will provide the most effective adjustment for children of divorce.[50]

JUDITH WALLERSTEIN'S RESEARCH

Perhaps the most widely known research in the area of how divorce affects children has been performed by Judith Wallerstein. The following sections are a compilation of more than ten years of research that Judith Wallerstein has performed. This information is presented in a number of research journals and was also part of a week long seminar at the Cape Cod Institute in 1986.

Criticisms have been leveled against some of Wallerstein's research claiming that she has generalized too much from the data that have been presented, has used too small a sample to support her conclusions, and has not been entirely in step with the generalizations that she has made. It must be noted that Wallerstein is a pioneer in the area of longitudinal studies having presented the only information of a group of children who have been followed for more than ten years. Certainly in the future research will be performed that may demonstrate tighter research design methods. However, as a pioneer in the field, Wallerstein's conclusions are nonetheless extremely important to understanding the effects of divorce on children.[51]

Wallerstein found that the most vulnerable group at the time of separation was the preschool children. The second most vulnerable group was adolescents. At the one-year mark, the girls had recovered while many of the boys had gotten worse. At the five-year mark, the boys still were much worse with significantly higher learning problems and difficulty on playgrounds and in the environment. At the 10-year mark, this changed directions. The most psychologically vulnerable group at the entry into young adulthood was young women. These 19- to 23-year old women were suffering much more from interpersonal relationship problems than young men of comparable age.

Children who are older at the time of the marital rupture respond worse than those who are younger at the time of the marital rupture. What affects the children most is not the marital rupture itself, but the postmarital course in that family.

Young children do not see divorce as a time-limited behavior. The feeling is that it is going to last forever and that their life will be permanently changed. Young children of divorce do not use their peers for support at the beginning of the divorce process. They feel they are betraying the confidence of the family in doing so. When children reach older adolescence, they are finally able to use each other for peer support. Siblings do provide support for each other unless they identify with a different parent.

Eighty percent of preschool children are not been told that their parents are divorcing and wake up one morning to find a parent gone. The process of adjusting to divorce is more difficult when this occurs. It must also be noted that adjusting to divorce is different than adjusting to the death of a loved one. At the time of bereavement, the family rallies around and everybody comes together to support each other. However, during separation or divorce, the families tend to split apart.

Boys

The boys' relationship to their fathers is an important component of the divorce process. Studies show that boys are the saddest children initially. They also tend to worry more about whether they will be "thrown out next" and see themselves as being left with a powerful mother. Older boys worry more about whether they will find someone to love them.

Boys seek to be with fathers when they are living with a psychologically deteriorating mother, or perceive a lack of warmth from the mother; when they are looking for a more permissive home; and when the father has not yet prepared to take responsibility for rearing a child.

The psychological adjustment of boys is related to the quality of the relationship with the father and not the frequency of the visits.

Girls

As girls grow older, they experience a greater degree of anxiety, as they are concerned about repeating their parents' experiences. They have a fear that no one will love them. In one-third of the cases studied, the level of anxiety reached the point of "derailing" the girl in forming relationships, going on to school, choosing a career, being social, and forming an independent life.

One-third of the women studied approaching adulthood left home to live with a man shortly before or after high school graduation. They tended to be drifting, did not have as much interest in economic support as emotional support, and chose older men. They were afraid that they were going to end up marrying someone like their father and were concerned about the problems associated with it.

Adolescence

Wallerstein found that boys need more contact with their fathers during adolescence. This appeared to be more critical for overall psychological functioning than it was for girls. However, it is still a serious consideration for both boys and girls. She found that adolescent girls want acknowledgment from their father regarding their looks, their emerging womanhood, and their accomplishments. Rejection by the father at this critical stage of development lead to further adjustment problems later.

Birth Order

Wallerstein noted that the oldest children in the family tend to do less well than younger children. When there are two children in the family, the younger of two tends to do better. Being the oldest child in a divorced family places that child at greater risk. That child is required to take more responsibility for the absent parent's tasks. The custodial parent tends to be more dependent upon the older child than the younger children in the family. The youngest children are most frightened of being abandoned physically. The emotional abandonment of the absent parent stimulates this. Younger children are also more likely to feel like they caused the divorce.

Change of Placement to Father

Most of the research discusses placement with the mother, as today, nationally, 88 percent of the children still live with their mothers. When children want to change placement to live with their father, it is often a difficult task. There is fear of moving toward the father, as they have not lived with the father previously. Furthermore, this is a topic that is very diffi-cult to talk over with the mother. The mother is generally reluctant to enter into discussions about changing placement. Both parents are generally unaware of this fear and, as a result, cannot respond appropriately to it.

Overburdened Child

The concept of the overburdened child refers to the child who is required to deal with more, psychologically and develop-mentally, than he or she is prepared to at his or her stage of development. Wallerstein's work on the overburdened child is based on research performed on 700 individuals.

One type of overburdened child is one who is required to take too much responsibility for growing up. The parent gener-ally reneges on many of the parenting roles and leaves the child to fend for himself or herself.

A second type of overburdened child is one who is responsi-ble for maintaining the psychological functioning of the parent. The parent experiences diminished capacity to function as a result of the divorce, and the child often ends up having to par-ent the parent. Children in this category feel that it is their responsibility to ward off the parent's loneliness, depression, fear of disintegration, and other serious psychological concerns.

A third situation that leads to overburdening the child is having the parents fight over the children. This occurs when the parents fight for the children's affection, time, and alliance. It often occurs when the parent is not able to reconcile the fact that being divorced means that he or she will spend less time with the children, whether the primary placement parent or not. The overburdening remains unresolved as more litigation and relitigation occur.

Young children are more vulnerable to overburdening than older children. A child is more likely to become overburdened if he or she is from a one-child family than from one with two or more children. The parent also contributes to the child being overburdened by distorting the perception of the child by tak-ing the child to adult functions and even allowing the child to sleep with the parent.

Partly because of the experience of being overburdened, there is a 45 percent chance that children of divorce will divorce, themselves. There is a 30 percent chance that these children of divorce of divorce will remarry, and there is a 20 percent chance that they will be divorced a second time.

Grandparents

The role of grandparents in the divorce process can be very important. When grandparents are committed to helping their grandchildren, it is a tremendous support during the divorce process. However, if grandparents choose to become part of the "fight," then it has even a greater adverse effect on the children. Grandparents can help counterbalance the problems that are occurring between the parents. They can help maintain a sense of family, importance, and self-esteem. Unfortunately, in only 25 percent of divorces, grandparents are available for support.

Parents

Women who are younger at the time of divorce (less than 40 years of age) generally are happier and have greater psychological growth. One-third of men never remarry. Individuals who are in their 20s at the time of divorce are considered to be the most vulnerable. Of those, 43 percent will be still struggling financially 10 years later, 60 percent have an unstable residence, one-third have irregular employment, and greater than 40 percent have a living standard that had declined in the past five years.

At the time of divorce, there is often a massive ego regression on the part of parents. People who had previously behaved reasonably well will behave poorly at this time. A spilling of aggressive and sexual impulses, in addition to intense depression, can occur. Much of this is based on the fact that most divorces are unilateral decisions. This results in a "narcissistic injury" of being rejected. Since there is a shared identity during the marriage, there is anxiety that occurs at the rupture based upon "who am I without the marriage." This is similar to the experience that an adolescent goes through. In addition, intense loneliness and diminished capacity are experienced in conjunction with ego regression. This diminished capacity can show itself in many ways including reduced sensitivity, poorer judgment, and less awareness of the children. It is difficult to maintain discipline in a family, because the parent does not want the child to be angry at him or her and reject him or her.

Diminished Capacity of Parent

Diminished capacity goes hand in hand with the crisis in the adult. There is an unconscious feeling that because the marriage contract has been broken, the parent does not have to be as attentive to the concerns of the children. This diminished capacity occurs at the time that the children's needs are greater and much more important than previously. Diminished capacity can also lead to a wish to abandon children or a greater dependency on the children. This is one of the reasons why many separations and divorces are precipitated by the birth of a child and the unconscious need to abandon the responsibility.

Parent Anger

It is difficult to have a divorce without anger between the parents. Ten years after the divorce, 40 percent of the women are still as angry as they were at the time of the divorce, while 80 percent of the men are still as angry as they were at the time of the divorce. However, there appears to be no relationship between the persistence of anger and success in a remarriage. Therefore, it appears that the therapeutic adage that anger must be resolved prior to the commencement of a successful relationship does not appear to hold true.

Much of the anger is associated with the traditional problem that mothers have more time with children, and fathers have a greater earning capacity. Anger is perpetuated by the mother being upset over the amount of disposable income the father has and the father being upset about the amount of time the mother has with the children. Each parent then tends to manipulate the visitation or money issue which, in turn, interferes with the psychological well-being of the child.

Child Support

Since 88 percent of children live with their mother, and most fathers are required to provide child support, the research looks at fathers providing support. The continued payment of child support on the part of the father correlates with the psychological intactness of the father-child relationship, the full employment of the father, and the visiting pattern of the father. Visiting pattern does not refer to frequency as much as it does consistency. There is no correlation between the continued payment of child support and whether the father remarries. Fathers are likely to continue child support when they remarry unless they have lost contact with their children and have emotional ties with children from the second marriage.

Child support is generally not affected by decline in the mother's socioeconomic circumstances, illness of the mother, or a downward socioeconomic move on the part of the mother. However, child support is affected by an increase in the mother's socioeconomic status. It tends to go down if the mother starts making more money.

College Education

College education is something that is generally not included in the divorce agreement. There are so many issues that need to be resolved at the time of divorce that attorneys are generally reluctant to add issues that will not be relevant until the children reach adulthood. Unfortunately, as a result, college education is something that is often not planned for in divorced situations. Even though the fathers could afford to pay for college, their response is often "I have been an honorable man and paid my child support all these years and fulfilled my legal obligations. As a result, it is now the mother's responsibility to pay for the college education." This is often not possible, because the mother's earning capacity is generally significantly less than the father's earning capacity.

There were 49 children studied by Wallerstein. Only one-half of the children attended college. Forty-two percent ended their education without a 2-year degree. Only 20 percent of the children attended college with full support. The children tended to feel bitter and betrayed and a victim of their parents' divorces.

Five-Year Follow-up Study

At the five-year mark, those children who did poorly were those in families where the fighting between the parents continued as if the divorce had never occurred. This was true with one-third of the children. They also did poorly when parenting skills remained diminished, when there had been a disruptive relationship with one parent, and when the child was left in the care of a psychologically ill parent. In general, these children experienced an overall diminished quality of life.

The children who did well at the five-year mark were those where the diminished parenting had improved, where the parental fighting had significantly reduced, and where the contact with the father had been maintained. These were also children who had been separated from an emotionally disturbed parent, had grandparents who had been warmly involved, and in which the overall quality of life, including economics, had been reconstituted.

Thirty percent of the children five years after the divorce were still somewhat fixated developmentally where they were at the time of the divorce. They were still angry at their father and had established a closer relationship with their mother. Even adolescent males, who at this point would have normally moved in the direction of their father, were still fixated at the developmental age of relating more closely to the mother.

There was an increase in suicidal ideation in children at the five-year mark. Although 34 percent of the children were doing well, 37 percent of the children were clinically depressed. This was characterized by parents who continued to fight, parents who were more concerned about meeting their own needs than the needs of their children, and parents who were more concerned about developing their own interests. Furthermore, these children had parents who visited more capriciously.

Ten-Year Follow-up Study

Wallerstein's 10-year study included 131 children, mostly middle class and mostly white, in Marin County, California. At the 10-year mark, 90 percent of the children were reached for the follow-up study. The children in the 10-year study were seen at the time of separation, one year after separation, five years after separation, and 10 years after separation. The bench-mark date was separation, as opposed to divorce. This is based on the fact that the psychological impact of divorce takes place in children at the time of separation and not at the time of divorce.

At the 10-year mark, the children who were young at the time of divorce were doing better, because the postdivorce course for these children was easier. Younger children did not have vivid memories of the divorce process, whereas children who were nine years old or older at the time of divorce had vivid negative memories of the divorce and separation process.

The older group tended to feel that their entire childhood and adolescence was spent in the shadow of their parents' divorce; they felt they had sacrificed a significant part of their carefree childhood through their parents' divorce. It was also noted at the 10-year study that hardly any of the children were aligned with one parent over the other. Furthermore, very few parents were still fighting with each other. This was in part based on the fact that most of the children had reached adulthood and the issues over which they would have been fighting were no longer relevant.

Ten years after the divorce, women were generally economically worse off than their former husbands. They also were not as socially isolated as they had been previously.

Wallerstein noted at the 10-year follow-up study that there was a difference between the way boys and girls responded to divorce. A considerable amount of research has demonstrated that boy children do worse in every way after divorce than boys of intact families, whereas girls have reactions indistinguishable from intact families. However, Wallerstein's research demonstrates that when girls reach young adulthood, they have trouble trusting the reliability of their partner. They have great anxiety with regard to the relationship as a whole, with regard to the sexual aspects of the relationship, and with regard to trust. One of the implications that can be drawn from this research is that boy children act out during childhood in response to the divorce. However, in doing so, they resolve their feelings about the divorce. On the other hand, girl children tend to repress their concerns which do not emerge until young adulthood when they attempt to establish meaningful relationships with others.

In conclusion, when parents and attorneys are deciding custody issues and placement issues, there are many variables that must be considered. Most importantly, each family's specific needs must be considered. Each family is unique and will emphasize its own set of concerns identified in this chapter. There are no rules of thumb that apply to all children. What works in some situations may not work in others. The most important consideration is that the parents have the children's best interest at heart and keep the lines of communication open with all concerned.

ENDNOTES

1. L. Schwartz, The Effects of Divorce on Children at Different Ages: A Descriptive Study 261 (1985).

2. J. Wallerstein, 1986 Cape Cod Institute, Institute for Psychological Study, Inc.

3. Ellison, *Issues Concerning Parental Harmony and Children's Psychosocial Adjustment*, 53 Am. J. Orthopsychiatry 73 (Jan. 1983).

4. S. Erickson, Divorce Mediation Workshop, Wisconsin Psychological Association (Fall 1984).

5. V. Shiller, *Joint Versus Maternal Custody for Families with Latency Age Boys: Parent Characteristics and Child Adjustment*, 56 Am. J. Orthopsychiatry 486 (1986).

6. S. Steinman, *The Experience of Children in a Joint Custody Arrangement: A Report of a Study*, 51 Am. J. Orthopsychiatry 403, 412 (1981).

7. Ilfeld, Ilfeld & Alexander, *Does Joint Custody Work? A First Look at Outcome Data of Relitigation*, 139 Am. J. Psychiatry 62 (Jan. 1982).

8. J. Wallerstein, 1986 Cape Cod Institute, Institute for Psychological Study, Inc.

9. L. Franke, Growing Up Divorced 70 (1983) [hereinafter Growing Up Divorced].

10. *Id.*

11. J. Wallerstein, 1986 Cape Cod Institute, Institute for Psychological Study, Inc.

12. *Id.*

13. *Id.*

14. M. Ackerman, *Recent Psychological Research on the Effect of Divorce on Children*, Wis. J. Fam. L. 29–31 (Dec. 1984) [hereinafter *Recent Psychological Research*].

15. V. Roseby, "A Custody Evaluation Model for Pre-School Children" (paper presented at the meeting of the American Psychological Association, Toronto, Canada, Aug. 1984) in *Recent Psychological Research, supra* note 14, at 29.

16. *Recent Psychological Research, supra* note 14, at 29–31.

17. V. Bronfenbrenner, The Ecology of Human Development: Experiments by Nature and Design (1979) in *Recent Psychological Research, supra* note 14, at 30.

18. V. Roseby, "A Custody Evaluation Model for Pre-School Children" (paper presented at the meeting of the American Psychological Association, Toronto, Canada, Aug. 1984) in *Recent Psychological Research, supra* note 14, at 30.

19. E. Hetherington, *Divorce: A Child's Perspective*, 34 Am. Psychologist 851 (1979).

20. L. Kurdek, *An Integrative Perspective on Children's Divorce Adjustment*, 36 Am. Psychologist 856 (1981).

21. Newsweek Magazine, Dec. 8, 1986.

22. J. Wallerstein, 1986 Cape Cod Institute, Institute for Psychological Study, Inc.

23. *Id.*

24. Growing Up Divorced, *supra* note 9, at 73–88.

25. *Id.* at 90.

26. *Id.*

27. *Id.* at 90–91.

28. *Id.* at 112.

29. J. Kelly & J. Wallerstein, *Part-time Parent, Part-time Child: Visiting After Divorce*, J. Clinical Psychology, Summer 1987, at 51–54 in Growing Up Divorced, *supra* note 9, at 113.

30. Growing Up Divorced, *supra* note 9, at 150.

31. *Id.* at 152.

32. J. Wallerstein, 1986 Cape Cod Institute, Institute for Psychological Study, Inc.

33. *Id.*

34. A. Stolberg & J. Anker, *Cognitive and Behavioral Changes in Children Resulting from Parental Divorce and Consequent Environmental Changes*, 7 J. Divorce 23–40 (1984) in L. Kurdek, D. Blisk & A. Siesky, *Correlates of Children's Long Term Adjustment to Their Parents' Divorce*, 17 Developmental Psychology 565–79 (1981).

35. Ackerman case study, 1976.

36. Wallerstein, Children of Divorce: The Psychological Tasks of the Child, 53 Am. J. Orthopsychiatry 230, 234 (1983).

37. Ackerman case study, 1982.

38. More detailed accounts of these areas of concern can be found in child and adult psychopathology texts such as E. Mash & L. Terdel, Behavioral Assessment of Childhood Disorders (1988); American Psychiatric Association, Diagnostic and Statistical Manual of Mental Disorders (III-R ed. 1987).

39. J. Wallerstein & J. Kelly, Surviving the Breakup: How Children and Parents Cope with Divorce (1980) [hereinafter Surviving the Breakup]; A. Stolberg & J. Anker, *Cognitive and Behavioral Changes in Children Resulting from Parental Divorce and Consequent Environmental Changes*, 7 J. Divorce 23 (1984).

40. Surviving the Breakup, *supra* note 39; E. Hetherington, M. Cox & R. Cox, *The Aftermath of Divorce* in Mother-Child, Father-Child Relations (1978) [hereinafter *The Aftermath of Divorce*].

41. *The Aftermath of Divorce* , *supra* note 40.

42. Surviving the Breakup, *supra* note 39.

43. L. Kurdek & B. Berg, *Correlates of Children's Adjustment to Their Parents' Divorces*, Children and Divorce, No. 19 (1983).

44. J. Neal, *Children's Understanding of Their Parents' Divorces*, Children and Divorce, No. 19 (1983).

45. J. Guidubaldi, H. Cleminshaw, J. Perry, B. Nastasi & B. Adams, "Longitudinal Effects of Divorce on Children: A Report from the NASP-KSU Nationwide Study" (paper presented at the meeting of the American Psychological Association, Toronto, Canada, Aug. 1984) in *Recent Psychological Research, supra* note 14, at 30.

46. *Id.* at 30–31.

47. *Id.* at 31.

48. *Id.*

49. *Id.*

50. *Id.*

51. J. Wallerstein, *Children of Divorce: Preliminary Report of a Ten-Year Follow-up of Older Children and Adolescents,* 24 J. Am. Acad. Child Psychiatry 545–53 (1985).

Chapter Five
Statistical Concepts

This chapter is written in an effort to provide attorneys with some of the basic principles necessary to understand statistical concepts. It will not delve in considerable depth into theoretical underpinnings of each of the statistical concepts. Instead, it will provide the overview necessary for a basic understanding of the concepts that would be utilized in cross-examination of an expert witness.

TEST STANDARDIZATION

A standardized test is administered with a standard set of directions under uniform conditions. It is assumed that every examiner administering that test will follow the directions verbatim and the testing conditions recommended as closely as possible. This level of consistency among examiners is necessary if an individual's scores are to be compared with the normative sample. After administering the test, raw scores are obtained and converted to standard scores which can be compared with norms. The norms can be based on, e.g., grade equivalents, age equivalents, or percentile ranks. There is no choice on the part of the examiner as to which norms are selected. There is only one acceptable set of norms for each person on each test based on age, sex, developmental level or other important variables. Test manuals usually include tables of norms which provide the examiner the opportunity to convert raw scores into normative scores. Following this procedure provides the examiner the opportunity to compare one individual's scores with standardized scores based upon age, sex, grade, or other important variables.

NORMS

For test scores to be meaningful, the individual taking the test must be within the group that the norms reflect. The norms are established by the individual(s) who develops the test. For example, if there are norm tables for children ages 6 to 16 on a particular test, it would generally not be useful to test children below 6 or above 16 years of age. Doing so would not provide the examiner the opportunity to meaningfully compare the results with other individuals. A well-constructed test will use a broad-based sample. One of the most popular methods used is referred to as a "stratified sample." A well-stratified sample will include individuals from all of the age, sex, race, geographical, and socioeconomic groups that may take the test. Individuals in each stratum are included in proportion to their presence in the general population. For example, if 13 percent of the population are urban blacks, then 13 percent of the test sample should be urban blacks. If 43 percent of the population is from the northeastern quadrant of the United States, then 43 percent of the test sample should be from that area. It is easy to see that establishing norms for a test following appropriate standards can be very difficult.

The most familiar form of norming is through children's achievement scores. Whenever students take tests in school, the results are often reported as grade equivalents, age equivalents, and/or percentile ranks. Often, they are reported as national norms, local norms, and possibly independent school norms. The national norms would be comparing the student with all of the people in the country in the same norm groups (age, grade). The local norms would be comparing the student with the local population. This should be defined in the results—it could be anyone in the city or suburb, or may just be that particular school system.

MEASURES OF CENTRAL TENDENCY[1]

Measures of central tendency are designed to show a typical or average performance for a specified group on a particular test. This allows the reader to compare individuals and groups within and across tests. The most commonly used measure of central tendency is the mean.[2] To obtain the mean, all of the scores are added together and the sum divided by the number of scores. It is referred to as an arithmetic mean and is designated by an x with a line over it: "$\bar{x}$."

The second measure of central tendency is the median.[3] It is the score that falls in the middle of the distribution. For example, if there were five scores in a distribution, 9, 10, 11, 16, and 18, the median would be 11, whereas the mean would be 12.8.

The last measure of central tendency is referred to as the mode.[4] The mode is defined as the most frequently occurring score in the sample. When two scores occur with equal frequency, the distribution is referred to as a bimodal distribution. It is important to know when a bimodal distribution occurs because the interpretation of the test data will be affected. This distribution would have two modes (the most frequently occurring scores): one at the lower end of the distribution and another at the upper end of the distribution. The mean (the average score) does not really reflect the distribution. In the bimodal distribution, the mean falls between the two modes and is of little statistical significance since it reflects one of the least frequently occurring scores. The following figure reflects this. The mode in this figure is both 5 and 15, thus a bimodal distribution. The mean is 10, which is an arithmetic average of all the scores, but does not provide much meaningful data.

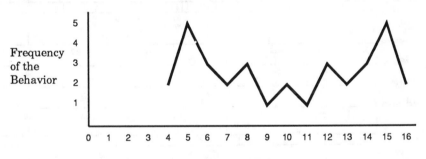

Types of Behavior

MEASURES OF VARIABILITY

Measures of variability deal with the spread of scores across the distribution. One of the most frequently used measures of variability is the range. The range represents the difference between the lowest score and the highest score. Looking at a distribution of 9, 10, 11, 16, and 18, the range would be 9 (18 minus 9). Perhaps the most widely used statistic, which also is a measure of variability, is the standard deviation.[5] The standard deviation allows an individual to understand what the average deviation or difference from the mean is. The greater the variability of scores, or the more spread out scores are, the larger the standard deviation will be. By knowing nothing more than the mean and the standard deviation of a particular set of scores, a wealth of information can be obtained.

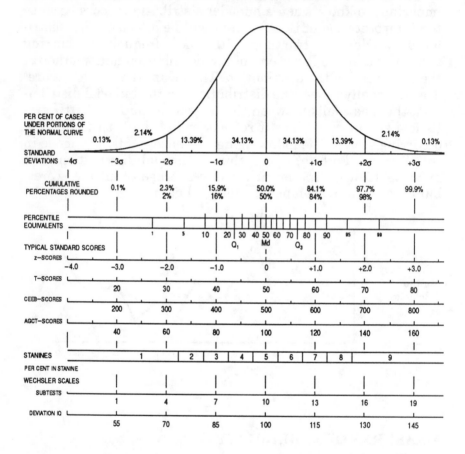

Percentile Ranks and Standard Scores Corresponding to Various Points on the Baseline of a Normal Distribution of Scores

Source: H.G. Seashore, Methods of expressing test scores, *The Psychological Corporation Test Service Bulletin* No. 48 (1985).

Looking at the top part of the above table, the Gaussian, or normal, curve is represented. It should be noted that 68.26 percent of the scores fall between plus and minus 1 standard deviation. This can be determined by adding together 34.13 between 0 and plus 1 standard deviations and the 34.13 between 0 and minus 1 standard deviations. Furthermore, approximately 96 percent of the scores fall between plus and minus 2 standard deviations. And lastly, 99.8 percent of the scores fall between plus and minus 3 standard deviations. Given the high percentage of scores that fall between plus and minus 3 standard deviations from the mean, any score that falls outside of this group is considered to be very significant. Only one out of a thousand people will score beyond 3 standard deviations above the mean and another one in a thousand below 3 standard deviations below the mean. This would indicate that the individual has set himself or herself apart from the population at one extreme or the other.

In the next section of the chart, the percentile equivalents are scored and give the reader an opportunity to look at what percentile ranks fall within the different standard deviation groups.

The next group of scores reported on the chart are standard scores—the z-scores[6] and T-scores.[7] The z-scores are not used as frequently as T-scores. However, a z-score allows the reader to understand how many standard deviations are represented. It converts standard deviation of *all* distributions into a uniform score. For example, a z-score of plus 2 means that that number falls 2 standard deviations above the mean, or a z-score of minus 1.5 would indicate that that score falls 1 1/2 standard deviations below the mean.

A z-score of plus 2 would be two standard deviations above the mean on any distribution, regardless what the standard deviations were or the variability of the distribution.

The T-scores are much more frequently reported, as they are easier to understand. A T-score is a converted standard score with a mean of 50 and a standard deviation of 10. For example, one of the most popular instruments used in psychological testing is the Minnesota Multiphasic Personality Inventory (MMPI). The MMPI has a mean of 50 and a standard deviation of 10. This corresponds with the distribution of the T-scores on the chart. Looking at the T-score of 70, which is generally the cutoff score indicative of psychopathology on the MMPI, the reader will notice on the chart that it represents a cumulative percentage of 97.7 percent. Scores above 70 show that the individual's scores are beyond more than approximately 98 percent of the population, indicating that only 2 percent of the population would fall in this area. A score of 80 on the MMPI would represent a T-score of 80, which is three standard deviations beyond the mean, and would indicate that 99.9 percent of the population would score below that score. Any time a score beyond 80 is obtained on the MMPI, it is of major concern since only 1 in 1000 individuals would have scores that extreme, indicating significant pathology. (For further discussion, see Chapter Seven.)

The next group of scores depicted on the graph are stanine scores.[8] Stanine stands for standard nines. The scores have been statistically divided into nine groups of scores that represent equal standard score units. This is true for stanines 2 through 8. However, stanine 1 and 9 are not equal to the other stanines. The stanine has a mean of 5 with a standard deviation of approximately 2. Stanines are relatively archaic and are not used with much frequency in reporting test scores except in educational tests. However, stanines of 1, 2, and 3 are generally considered low, while stanines of 4, 5, and 6 are average, and stanines of 7, 8, and 9 are considered high; high being most favorable.

Test scores can be interpreted by using the methods discussed above. For example, the College Entrance Examination Board (CEEB) or Scholastic Aptitude Tests (SAT) are shown to have a mean of 500 and a standard deviation of 100. It can be determined that the standard deviation is 100 by noticing that the score at the mean is 500, and the score at one standard deviation above the mean is 600. 600 minus 500 equals 100. Generally, SAT scores are reported from 200 to 800. Two hundred to 800 represents 99.8 percent of the population. Statistically, there could be about two out of every thousand people that would score above 800 or below 200. As a result, because of the relatively small number that would fit into this group, scores below 200 and above 800 are not reported.

The Wechsler tests are used with a great deal of frequency (see Chapter Six). Subtest scale scores generally range from 0 to 19. It can be noted in looking at the Wechsler subtest scale scores that they have a mean of 10 and a standard deviation of three. Furthermore, the intelligence quotient (I.Q.) scores on these tests are reported as deviation I.Q.'s. They have a mean of 100 and a standard deviation of 15. Therefore, an individual who has an I.Q. of 130 would be two standard deviations above the mean, scoring at the 98th percentile. An individual with a score of 55 would be three standard deviations below the mean, and would be at the .1 percentile.

For tests that are not represented on the table above, an individual needs only to find out the mean and standard deviation of a particular test and apply them to these charts to obtain useful information. For example, if a test is reported to have a mean of 80 and a standard deviation of 16, with a score of 104 reported, the table can be used. One hundred and four minus 80 (the mean) equals 24. The score is therefore 24 points above the mean. The standard deviation is 16. Twenty-four divided by 16 equals 1.5 (or 1 1/2 standard deviations above the mean). One and one-half standard deviations would be comparable to plus 1.5 z-scores. If a line is drawn up and down the point at 1.5 standard deviations above the mean, notice that the line would be approximately at the 93rd percentile and in the 8th stanine. The line would fall between the 90th and 95th percentile. By doing a visual extrapolation, it would be approximately the 93rd percentile.

The term percentiles or percentile ranks are used frequently in discussing these types of statistical analyses. A percentile score represents the percentage of the population which falls below a particular score and the percentage which falls above a particular score. For example, if an individual had a percentile rank of 65, or the 65th percentile, it would indicate that 65 out of every 100 individuals would score below that person, while 35 out of every 100 individuals would score above that person. A percentile rank of 28 would indicate that 28 out of every 100 individuals would score below that person while 72 out of 100 individuals would score above that person. When an individual achieves a percentile rank of 99.9, this indicates that 999 out of every 1,000 people score below that score while 1 out of 1,000 would exceed that score.

LEVELS OF CONFIDENCE

It is not unusual for an expert witness to include testimony about research that has been performed. Psychology is not an exact science. As a result, there is nothing that occurs 100 percent of the time on a casual relationship basis as would be true in the case of pure science. In psychology, results are reported based on levels of confidence or confidence intervals.

The measure that is used in determining the level of confidence is what is referred to as a "p" ("probability") value.[9] When psychological, educational, or sociological research is performed and results are obtained, the researcher uses tables to interpret the results in an effort to determine the "p" value. "P" values are reported anywhere from 1.0 to approaching 0.00. Generally, in research, an acceptable "p" value is one of less than .05. When an individual performs research and ends up with a "p" value of less than .05, this can be interpreted to mean that the results will have occurred 95 times out of 100 as a result of the experimental manipulations in the research and the other five times out of 100 based on chance. When a "p" value of less than .01 is reported, this would indicate that 99 times out of 100, the results were caused by the experimental manipulations generated in the research, and 1 time out of 100 would have occurred by chance. In an extraordinary case, a "p" value may be less than .0001. This would indicate that 9,999 times out of 10,000 the results would have occurred based on the research, while 1 time out of 10,000 would have occurred by chance. The smaller the "p" value, the better the results. Generally, psychology does not accept a "p" value of greater than .05 as being meaningful. The research may also report "p" values by stating that the results were "significant at the .05 level" (p is less than .05) or "significant at the .001 level" (p is less than .001). In research that is not as meaningful, a "p" value of .25 may be reported. This would indicate that 75 times out of 100 the results would occur based on the research, while 25 times out of 100 it would occur based on chance. This is not acceptable in most psychological research.

When cross-examining an expert witness on the results of research, it is important to determine the "p" value or the level of significance. Furthermore, it is also important to determine whether the research has been replicated with the same results as the original research. If the "p" value is not at least .05 or smaller, or if the research has not been replicated with the same level of success achieved in the original research, the results of the research should not carry as much weight as would the research that meets these criteria.

STANDARD ERROR OF MEASUREMENT[10]

As stated earlier, psychology is not an exact science. When results are obtained in norming a test or doing research, one of the useful statistics provided is the "standard error of measurement." The standard error of measurement enables the interpreter to estimate the limits within which the individual's true scores are expected to fall. For example, if the standard error of measurement on an intelligence test is 5, and the actual score obtained by the individual is 112, the actual true score would likely fall between plus and minus 1 standard error of measurement. As a result, many of those who interpret these tests would report the intelligence score of 112 as 107 to 117. In other words, the score is reported as a band or range as opposed to an individual number. The 107 to 117 represents plus or minus one standard error of measurement. Basically, the smaller the standard error of measurement in relation to the score, the more reliable the results will be.

If, hypothetically, an I.Q. test had a standard error of measurement of 23, and a score of 112, plus and minus one standard error of measurement would be reported as 89 to 135. It can readily be seen that this would not be a very useful test. It is also important to note that comparing test scores can be dangerous if one does not know the standard error of measurement. For example, with a standard error of measurement of 6 and scores of 112 and 115, it would be inappropriate to state that one individual was more intelligent than the other. Since the scores both fall within one standard error of measurement, they could be considered to be statistically essentially the same.

RELIABILITY[11]

When a test is constructed, the two most important factors that must be determined are the test's reliability and validity. Unfortunately, the concepts of reliability and validity are often confused by those unfamiliar with statistical concepts. A test is considered to be reliable if it consistently produces the same results under varying conditions that could produce measurement errors. The reliability of a test refers to its relative ability to be unaffected by unsystematic errors of measurement. The reliability coefficient of a test is stated with a positive decimal number ranging from .00 to 1.00. A score of 1.00 indicates perfect reliability, while a score of .00 indicates the absence of reliability. The closer to 1.0 the decimal, the more reliable the test is considered to be.

There are many different types of reliability statistics, called coefficients. Reliability coefficients are sometimes referred to as the "coefficient of stability."[12] One type is referred to as a "test-retest reliability." In test-retest reliability, the same test is administered on two separate occasions to the same group of individuals. The scores are then statistically compared with one another and a correlation coefficient is obtained.

Another means of measuring reliability is the "parallel-forms procedure."[13] In this case, parallel or equivalent forms of a test are administered to the same group of individuals. The correlation between the two sets of scores is then computed. In a situation where there is a high reliability on parallel forms, then different forms of the test can be administered at different times without concern about "practice effect." Practice effect is not something that is measured statistically. It refers to an individual's ability to perform better on the readministration of a test, when that test is given relatively shortly after the original administration. This improved performance is said to be based on "practicing" the task as part of the original administration, leading to a better performance on the second administration.

Another popular reliability measure is an internal consistency coefficient called "split-half reliability."[14] In this case, the scores on arbitrarily selected halves of the test are statistically compared with one another, and a correlation coefficient is obtained. Split-half reliability could be performed by comparing the results on the items on the first half of the measure with the items on the second half of the measure. An alternate form of split-half testing would compare the results of the odd-numbered items with the even-numbered items. This method of reliability testing can only be used when there is relative equality of items throughout the instrument. Interscorer or interrater reliability is another method to measure reliability.[15] With interrater reliability two different examiners score the same test. The scores obtained are then correlated with one another.

Any time two sets of scores are reported, they can be statistically correlated with one another. A quantitative measure of the relationship existing among two or more variables, called correlation coefficient, is obtained. Generally, correlation coefficients vary from plus 1.0 to minus 1.0. A positive correlation of 1.0 would indicate that there is a perfect relationship between the two variables being measured. In other words, every time A happens, B happens. A correlation of minus 1.0 indicates that there is a perfect inverse relationship between the two sets of scores. In other words, any time A happens, B does not happen. A correlation of 0.00 indicates that the two variables are totally unrelated to one another. Generally, the further the correlation coefficient is from 0 in either direction, the stronger the relationship between the two variables.

It is important to understand that correlation does not imply a causal relationship. It only implies the relationship between the two scores, and not necessarily that A causes B to happen. The correlation coefficient, denoted by the letter "r," can be affected by the homogeneity (how similar the variables are) of the scores. In other words, the correlation coefficient will be lower if the scores are relatively heterogeneous. The correlation coefficient can also be affected by the amount of error in the scores. The larger the amount of error, the lower the correlation coefficient.

Generally, reliability coefficients in intelligence tests need to be in the .80 range or above before a test is considered to be very useful. Some intelligence tests have reliability coefficients of less than .80 on some of the subtests or some of the subscales, but, generally, overall, the coefficients be higher than .80.

On personality tests, correlations will generally be lower. Research on the Rorschach, for example, often finds reliability coefficients of .30 to .40 (see Chapter Six). As a result, the Rorschach, standing alone, is not a very reliable instrument. However, since it is a personality test, the reliability coefficients do not need to be as high. Furthermore, as will be discussed later, the Rorschach is a much more subjective instrument. Attorneys have often asked psychologists during examination or cross-examination what the reliability of the MMPI is. It is impossible to establish a reliability coefficient for the entire MMPI, because it is not an instrument that generates just one score. The reliability coefficients can be determined for the different scales of the MMPI, but not for the instrument as a whole. It is legitimate to question the reliability of the scores on specific scales, because some scales are more reliable than others. This will be discussed in greater detail in the chapter on the MMPI (see Chapter Seven).

VALIDITY

The validity of a test is defined as how well the test measures what it is designed to measure. It is a way of stating how useful the test is. As is true of reliability, there are many different types of validity. It is important to note that a test can be reliable without being valid.[16] In other words, the first half of a test could measure the same thing as the second half of a test (split-half reliability), but the test itself may not measure what it was designed to test.

The first type of validity measure is referred to as "face validity."[17] This refers to how well the specific items appear to reflect what the test is purported to measure on their face value alone. It is not something that lends itself to statistical analysis. On a test designed to measure anxiety, a question like "do you often have butterflies in your stomach," would be face valid. Someone looking at that question would be able to state that it appears to fit the nature of the test. However, a question on the same test which states "would you like to be a mountain ranger?" would not appear to be face valid.

Content validity[18] is another type of validity that cannot be subjected to statistical analysis. Content validity applies more to achievement tests, than to personality or other psychological tests. For a test on American history to be considered content valid, it would include a wide variety of questions about all aspects of American history. If there were questions about Russian history or the periodic table, it would not be considered content valid for an American history test.

There are several forms of validity measures that are referred to as criterion-related validity.[19] An example would be comparing test scores with school grades. If the test is considered to be valid, it would be expected the higher the test scores, the higher the school grades. There are two types of validity that fit into the category of criterion-related validity. The first is concurrent validity.[20] In concurrent validity, the criterion scores are immediately available. Again, returning to the school example, the individual school grades are available and can be compared with the results on the tests.

A second form of criterion-related validity is predictive validity.[21] In this case, the criterion scores are not available at the time of testing. The criterion scores, for example the grades, become available at a later date. Predictive validity has been very useful in trying to identify individuals who potentially have problems before the problems manifest themselves. For example, if a test has high predictive validity to identify potential sexual abusers, child abusers, or criminals, intervention could be undertaken prior to the actual offense being committed.

Another form of validity is referred to as construct validity.[22] Construct validity uses information from studies of the content validity and criterion-related validity of a test. It is determined by defining the characteristic to be measured by a test and then relating this to measures of behavior in the environment where the characteristic is thought to be an important variable. It is a much more sophisticated and involved process of validity. It cannot be determined by simply providing one measure. The construct validity of a test is determined over time by gathering information from many research projects, observations, and studies.

There are many factors that can influence the validity of a test. As is true of reliability, the more homogeneous the variables, the more valid the results are likely to be. When a test is originally being developed, it should not be used for selection purposes until the predictive validity has been determined. Until concurrent and/or predictive validity of an instrument has been established, the user does not know if it measures what it is designed to measure. Therefore, unvalidated tests should not be used (except experimentally) until their validity has been demonstrated. The reliability of a test will also affect its validity. The greater the reliability, the more likely the test will be valid. Reliability is necessary, but not the only criterion for a test to have validity.

ANALYSIS OF VARIANCE[23]

The concept of analysis of variance is one that is not particularly useful to attorneys. However, it is included in this section of the book for those who may come across the concept in reading psychological research. Analysis of variance (ANOVA) has been developed for estimating the reliability of the results of a test or research. An outgrowth of analysis of variance is referred to as multivariate analysis of variance (MANOVA). Both of these are very sophisticated forms of statistical analysis. They provide the researcher with the ability to analyze what factors are most important in obtaining the results of the research. For example, a 2 by 2 by 3 analysis of variance, referred to as a 2x2x3 analysis of variance, would look at seven different variables simultaneously. For example, the first set could be whether the subjects were male or female, the second set whether they were black or white, and the third set whether they were children, adolescents, or adults. The scores are then put in the different cells (data recording areas), and the examiner can then determine statistically for which variables there are significant results, and for which variables there are not. The results would be measured by looking at the "p" values discussed earlier.

SUMMARY

Although the statistical concepts may seem confusing at first, understanding the basic concepts of mean, standard deviation, and levels of confidence can go a long way in helping an attorney understand the usefulness of the information obtained. If, under cross-examination the expert witness is talking about tests or research that are not covered in this book, then it is essential to ask about the reliability and validity of the instrument. Do not be satisfied with the psychologist simply reporting that the test is reliable or valid if you are unfamiliar with the test. Ask for reliability and validity coefficients. Ask for the mean and standard deviation of the results. Ask the psychologist how these reliability and validity coefficients compare with other tests, and how the specific individual scores fit into the distribution based on the mean and standard deviation. If the research that is being quoted does not sound familiar, ask the psychologist to tell you the "p" values or the level of significance of the research. If the psychologist states that it "approaches significance," that is not sufficient because any time the "p" value is greater than .05, the results should be considered nonsignificant.

This chapter has been written to provide attorneys with a basic overview understanding of statistical concepts. Undergraduate statistical textbooks are several hundred pages in length. This chapter should not be considered a comprehensive discussion of all statistical techniques, but only those that the attorney is likely to come across in his or her work.

ENDNOTES

1. J. Spence, J. Cotton, B. Underwood & C. Duncan, Elementary Statistics 39 (4th ed. 1983) [hereinafter Elementary Statistics]; R. Sprinthall, Basic Statistical Analysis 23 (2d ed. 1987) [hereinafter Basic Statistical Analysis]; T. Anderson & S. Sclove, An Introduction to the Statistical Analysis of Data 67 (1978) [hereinafter An Introduction to the Statistical Analysis of Data]; J. Graham & R. Lilly, Psychological Testing 14–15 (1984) [hereinafter Graham & Lilly, Psychological Testing].

2. Elementary Statistics, *supra* note 1, at 39–45; Basic Statistical Analysis, *supra* note 1, at 23; An Introduction to the Statistical Analysis of Data, *supra* note 1, at 75–78; Graham & Lilly, Psychological Testing, *supra* note 1, at 14.

3. Elementary Statistics, *supra* note 1, at 45–49; Basic Statistical Analysis, *supra* note 1, at 27–29; An Introduction to the Statistical Analysis of Data, *supra* note 1, at 71–72; Graham & Lilly, Psychological Testing, *supra* note 1, at 14–15.

4. Elementary Statistics, *supra* note 1, at 45–46; Basic Statistical Analysis, *supra* note 1, at 29–32; An Introduction to the Statistical Analysis of Data, *supra* note 1, at 67–71; Graham & Lilly, Psychological Testing, *supra* note 1, at 15.

5. Elementary Statistics, *supra* note 1, at 59–61; Basic Statistical Analysis, *supra* note 1, at 41–45; An Introduction to the Statistical Analysis of Data, *supra* note 1, at 118–19; Graham & Lilly, Psychological Testing, *supra* note 1, at 16–18.

6. Elementary Statistics, *supra* note 1, at 68–73; Basic Statistical Analysis, *supra* note 1, at 55–57; An Introduction to the Statistical Analysis of Data, *supra* note 1, at 264–69; L. Aiken, Psychological Testing and Assessment 77 (5th ed. 1985) [hereinafter Psychological Testing and Assessment]; Graham & Lilly, Psychological Testing, *supra* note 1, at 18–19.

7. Elementary Statistics, *supra* note 1, at 73; Basic Statistical Analysis, *supra* note 1, at 85–89; An Introduction to the Statistical Analysis of Data, *supra* note 1, at 326–33.

8. Psychological Testing and Assessment, *supra* note 6, at 79.

9. Elementary Statistics, *supra* note 1, at 153–55; Basic Statistical Analysis, *supra* note 1, at 151–55; An Introduction to the Statistical Analysis of Data, *supra* note 1, at 321–25; Graham & Lilly, Psychological Testing, *supra* note 1, at 26.

10. An Introduction to the Statistical Analysis of Data, *supra* note 1, at 319; Psychological Testing and Assessment, *supra* note 6, at 89–90; Graham & Lilly, Psychological Testing, *supra* note 1, at 38–39; A. Anastasi, Psychological Testing 125–27 (5th ed. 1982) [hereinafter Anastasi, Psychological Testing].

11. Psychological Testing and Assessment, *supra* note 6, at 84–92; Graham & Lilly, Psychological Testing, *supra* note 1, at 37–39; Anastasi, Psychological Testing, *supra* note 10, at 26–27.

12. Psychological Testing and Assessment, *supra* note 6, at 85–86; Anastasi, Psychological Testing, *supra* note 10, at 26.

13. Psychological Testing and Assessment, *supra* note 6, at 79–80, 86; Anastasi, Psychological Testing, *supra* note 10, at 26.

14. Psychological Testing and Assessment, *supra* note 6, at 86–88.

15. Elementary Statistics, *supra* note 1, at 80–81; Basic Statistical Analysis, *supra* note 1, at 184–86; An Introduction to the Statistical Analysis of Data, *supra* note 1, at 183; Graham & Lilly, Psychological Testing, *supra* note 1, at 21.

16. Psychological Testing and Assessment, *supra* note 6, at 93; Graham & Lilly, Psychological Testing, *supra* note 1, at 46.

17. Psychological Testing and Assessment, *supra* note 6, at 94; Graham & Lilly, Psychological Testing, *supra* note 1, at 40.

18. Psychological Testing and Assessment, *supra* note 6, at 94; Graham & Lilly, Psychological Testing, *supra* note 1, at 40–41.

19. Psychological Testing and Assessment, *supra* note 6, at 94–95; Graham & Lilly, Psychological Testing, *supra* note 1, at 41–42.

20. Psychological Testing and Assessment, *supra* note 6, at 95; Graham & Lilly, Psychological Testing, *supra* note 1, at 41–42.

21. Psychological Testing and Assessment, *supra* note 6, at 95; Graham & Lilly, Psychological Testing, *supra* note 1, at 42.

22. Psychological Testing and Assessment, *supra* note 6, at 97–98; Graham & Lilly, Psychological Testing, *supra* note 1, at 42–43.

23. Elementary Statistics, *supra* note 1, at 221–33; Basic Statistical Analysis, *supra* note 1, at 248–73; An Introduction to the Statistical Analysis of Data, *supra* note 1, at 550–54; Graham & Lilly, Psychological Testing, *supra* note 1, at 35–36.

Chapter Six
Intelligence Testing

There are probably as many different theoretical definitions of intelligence as there are individuals defining the term. When the question, "what is intelligence," has been asked, psychologists have often coyly responded "intelligence is what intelligence tests measure." What is more important for the purposes of this book than defining the concept of "intelligence" is the statistical analysis of intelligence.

There are many different classification systems for intelligence. I.Q. tests generally use one classification system. The classification system is represented in the table below.

INTELLIGENCE CLASSIFICATION

I.Q.	Classification	Percentage of Population
130 or above	very superior	2.6%
120–129	superior	6.9%
110–119	high average or above average	16.6%
90–109	average	49.1%
80–89	low average or below average	16.1%
70–79	borderline deficient or borderline retarded	6.4%
69 and below	mentally retarded or mentally deficient	2.3%

The Diagnostic and Statistical Manual (3rd edition) of the American Psychiatric Association (DSM-III-R) divides individuals into classifications of mildly, moderately, severely, or profoundly retarded.[1] Their classifications are:

	I.Q.
• mild retardation	50–55 to 70
• moderate retardation	35–40 to 50–55
• severe retardation	20–25 to 35–40
• profound retardation	less than 20 or 25

Other systems use the same labels with slightly different ranges.[2] These classifications are substitutes for the original classifications designated by Binet, the developer of the first major intelligence test, of imbecile, idiot, and moron. Unfortunately, these words had acquired such negative connotations in society that they were no longer useful.

Educational systems classify intelligence in other ways. A child with an I.Q. of 50 to 75 is often referred to as being in the EMR range or Educable Mentally Retarded.[3] This would be an individual who falls within the retarded range but is likely to be able to learn basic academic information. An individual who falls in the EMR range is likely to be able to live on his or her own in either a supervised apartment or group home setting and gain low-level meaningful employment.

The next range between and 25 and 50 is referred to as the TMR or Trainable Mentally Retarded Range. These are individuals who will not be able to acquire academic information such as reading and arithmetic skills, but can be trained to perform the activities of daily living (hygiene, nourishment, and self-care). This type of an individual is likely to be able to work only in a sheltered workshop setting and live in highly supervised structured situations.

Individuals with I.Q.'s below 25 are considered to be in the Custodial Mental Retardation range. These are individuals who are likely to be institutionalized and may not be trained to walk, talk, or carry on the activities of daily living.

The levels of adaptive behavior for mentally retarded individuals varies according to the level of retardation and the age of the individual.

Another way of looking at I.Q.'s is to examine how they relate to the general population who function in a society.

Education	I.Q
high school student	105
high school graduate	110
college student	115
college graduate	120
master's degree	125
doctorate (professional or academic)	130

STABILITY OF I.Q.

I.Q. is generally considered to be a relatively stable measure.[4] There have been many studies done which have compared I.Q. scores of young children with retests of 10 and 25 years later. A classic study by researchers Bradway, Thompson and Cravens correlated I.Q.'s with a 10-year retest and a 25-year retest. After 10 years, they found correlation coefficients of .65 with the original measures, and after 25 years, correlations of .59 with the original measures. In addition, the correlation between the 10-year retest scores and the 25-year retest scores was .85.

However, there are some studies that have indicated large upward or downward shifts in intelligence test scores. These shifts tend to be related to "drastic changes in family structure or home conditions, adoption into a foster home, severe or prolonged illness and therapeutical remedial programs . . ."[5]

HEREDITY VS. ENVIRONMENT

There is a strong hereditary component in individuals' intelligence.[6] One of the best ways of predicting the adult intelligence of a child under six years of age is to give his or her parents an intelligence test. Regarding the question of mental retardation as a hereditary factor, the retardation could be the result of nonhereditary situations such as chromosomal anomalies or phenylketonuria (PKU), other factors resulting from prenatal organic brain dysfunction, and/or primarily hereditary in causation.[7]

Even though the hereditary factor is a strong component in determining a child's intelligence, the environmental manipulations also have a great effect on an individual's measured

I.Q. In the author's experience, it is not unusual for preschool children from educationally oriented families and/or children who have been exposed to a tremendous amount of early environmental stimulation to have disproportionately high intelligence test scores. These scores tend to even out over the years when the early intervention loses its impact. Children who are born retarded will also show less of the effects of retardation with greater environmental intervention than those that have little or no environmental intervention. The I.Q. is not raised per se. The individual's capacity to function is maximized, and tested I.Q. tends to increase with these factors.

STANFORD-BINET INTELLIGENCE SCALE: FOURTH EDITION

The Stanford-Binet Intelligence Scale: Fourth Edition (SB:FE) is a revision of the 1960 Stanford-Binet Intelligence Scale: Form L-M. It was published in 1986 by Riverside Publishing Company and authored by Robert L. Thorndike, Elizabeth T. Hagen, and Jerome M. Sattler. The Stanford-Binet FE can be used with individuals two years old through adulthood. The examiner is required to determine a basal level and a ceiling level for each of the areas measured. The basal is the first age level at which all subtests are passed, while the ceiling is the first age level at which all subtests are failed. Items are grouped into 15 subtests which cover four broad cognitive ability areas as follows: verbal reasoning, abstract/visual reasoning, quantitative reasoning, and short-term memory.

The verbal reasoning area is made up of the following subtests:

- Vocabulary;
- Comprehension;
- Absurdities; and
- Verbal Relations.

The quantitative reasoning area is made up of the following subtests:

- Quantitative;
- Number Series; and
- Equation Building.

The abstract/visual reasoning is made up of the following subtests:

- Pattern Analysis;
- Copying;
- Matrices; and
- Paper Folding and Cutting.

The short-term memory area is comprised of the following subtests:

- Bead Memory;
- Memory for Sentences;
- Memory for Digits; and
- Memory for Objects.

The 15 subtests are designed to measure different aspects of cognitive functioning. The subtests include:

Test 1:   *Vocabulary.* The Vocabulary Test measures the vocabulary that is actively used by the individual, and is divided into picture and oral vocabulary items.

Test 2:   *Bead Memory.* The subject is requested to copy a bead stalk provided by the examiner.

Test 3:   *Quantitative.* This subtest measures arithmetic reasoning.

Test 4:   *Memory for Sentences.* The subject is required to repeat a sentence that has been stated by the examiner. This measures the individual's short-term auditory memory.

Test 5:   *Pattern Analysis.* In this subtest, the subject is required to duplicate a design of cubes modeled by the examiner. This measures a component of nonverbal concept formation or visual abstract reasoning.

Test 6:   *Comprehension.* This is a verbal social comprehension task and allows the examiner to measure awareness of social mores.

Test 7:   *Absurdities.* This is an abstract reasoning task
               that requires the individual to describe what is
               absurd about the statement that is being made.
               An example of this type of item would be: "Sally
               went up the hill from her house to play with her
               friend, Rebecca. She went up the hill to go home
               after she was done playing. What is absurd
               about that?"

Test 8:   *Memory for Digits.* This is another short-term
               auditory memory task that requires the individ-
               ual to repeat digits forward and reversed after
               verbally presented by the examiner.

Test 9:   *Copying.* This is another visual perceptual task
               that requires the subject to duplicate an examin-
               er's design made from blocks. This duplication is
               made with paper and pencil.

Test 10:   *Memory for Objects.* The subject is shown stimu-
               lus cards at the rate of one per second. The sub-
               ject then must identify the correct pictures in the
               correct order. This is considered a visual memory
               task.

Test 11:   *Matrices.* This is another visual perceptual task
               that requires the individual to solve the matrices
               that were presented.

Test 12:   *Number Series.* This is a quantitative reasoning
               task in which the subject is requested to indicate
               the next number or numbers in an arithmetic
               series.

Test 13:   *Paper Folding & Cutting.* This visual perceptual
               task requires the subject to duplicate a design
               that has been made by the examiner by folding
               and cutting paper.

Test 14:   *Verbal Relations.* This abstract verbal reasoning
               test requires the individual to identify relation-
               ships between verbal concepts.

Test 15:   *Equation Building.* This last subtest measures
               abstract reasoning by asking the subject to build

an equation from a given set of numbers. For example, if an individual was given the numbers 1, 2, 4, and 5, an equation of $1 + 5 - 2 = 4$ could be made using these numbers.

The Stanford-Binet FE was designed to replace a test that was over 25 years old. The Stanford-Binet Form L-M had fallen out of popularity and was used in less than five percent of intelligence test administrations. Until the Stanford-Binet FE, the Stanford-Binet Form L-M remained the best single instrument to be used with children with exceptional education needs,whether the children be gifted or retarded.[8]

The author of this book has recognized that early indications are that the Stanford-Binet FE is not being favorably received by the professional community. Criticisms indicate that it is too long, the manual is not precise enough, and the rationale is not adequate. In addition, the authors of the Stanford-Binet FE attempted to duplicate the Wechsler method of measuring cognitive ability when another test of that nature was not necessary. Further research will determine the overall usefulness of this instrument. However, at this time the author does not recommended the SB:FE for use in custody evaluations.

Limitations of the SB:FE

One of the authors of the SB:FE, Jerome Sattler, identifies several limitations of the Stanford-Binet:FE. They include the following:

- Lack of comparable battery throughout the age ranges covered by the scale.

- Variable range of scores. The SB:FE fails to provide the same range of composite scores, factor scores, or subtest scores throughout the age levels covered by this scale. This means that even if an examinee answers every item correctly, his or her score will differ by 15 points (about one standard deviation) if he or she is tested first at age 12 and again at age 18.

- Limited support for four area scores. Factory analysis does not support the four area scores throughout the age levels of the scale.

- Difficulty in interpreting norms for subtests have an estimated scaled-score value at same ages.
- Lack of description of procedure for establishing cutoff criteria.
- Overly long administration time.[9]

Summary

The Stanford-Binet Intelligence Scale: Fourth Edition, was published in 1986. It attempts to measure general cognitive ability by looking at verbal reasoning, quantitative reasoning, abstract/visual reasoning, and short-term memory. The test is too new to determine overall efficacy. However, early reports find that it is in disfavor among professionals.

MC CARTHY SCALES OF CHILDREN'S ABILITIES

A test called the McCarthy Scales of Children's Abilities was developed by Dorothea McCarthy in 1972. It can be used with children from 2 1/2 to 8 1/2 years of age. However, for seven- or eight-year-old children of above average or greater ability, it is inadvisable to use the McCarthy.[10] In that case, it is more advantageous to use the Wechsler Intelligence Scale for Children-Revised (WISC-R). The McCarthy is divided into six scales. They include the following: Verbal, Perceptual-Performance, Quantitative, Memory, and Motor. The sixth scale is an overall measure of the Verbal, Perceptual-Performance and Quantitative Scales referred to as the General Cognitive Index. The overall McCarthy consists of 18 subtests that can be administered in 45 minutes to an hour. They include:

Test 1:   *Block Building.* The block building subtest is included on the Perceptual-Performance and General Cognitive scales. It requires the subject to duplicate a model made up of six or fewer blocks. The child's spatial relations and perceptual skills are measured.

Test 2:   *Puzzle Solving.* This subtest is on the Perceptual-Performance and General Cognitive scales. It requires the subject to assemble puzzles ranging in difficulty from two to six pieces. The examiner completes the unfinished puzzle for each child before going on to the next puzzle. Poor visual motor perception, poor motor coordination, and/or low motivation can be revealed by this subtest.

Test 3: *Pictorial Memory*. This subtest appears on the Verbal, General Cognitive, and Memory scales. The child is shown a card with six pictures of familiar objects. After a 10-second exposure, the child is asked to recall from memory what was on the card. This is both a visual and auditory memory test.

Test 4: *Word Knowledge*. This subtest appears on the Verbal and General Cognitive scales. It includes both picture vocabulary and or vocabulary items. It measures the child's active language usage skills.

Test 5: *Number Questions*. This subtest appears on the Quantitative and General Cognitive scales. It indicates arithmetic reasoning skills with items of simple addition, subtraction, multiplication, and division.

Test 6: *Tapping Sequence*. This subtest appears on the Perceptual-Performance, General Cognitive, and Memory scales. It requires the child to duplicate a sequence of notes played on a four-note xylophone. It is both an auditory and visual memory task which requires perceptual motor skills. The subtest was inspired by the original Knox Cubes Test developed over 50 years ago.

Test 7: *Verbal Memory*. This subtest appears on the Verbal, General Cognitive, and Memory scales. The subject is asked to repeat a series of words on the simpler tasks, and full sentences on the more difficult tasks. It measures the individual's auditory memory skills.

Test 8: *Right-Left Orientation*. This subtest appears on the Perceptual-Performance and General Cognitive scales. It is only administered to individuals five years of age or older. Children below five years of age are not expected to be able to differentiate left from right. It will help measure for learning disabilities, perceptual difficulties, and confusion with laterality.

Test 9:   *Leg Coordination.* This subtest, along with the next three, provides an opportunity to measure gross motor abilities. It is the only test of this nature that incorporates the use of gross motor abilities with a measure of intelligence. However, it is not included on the General Cognitive Scale. The Leg Coordination subtest measures the child's ability to walk backwards, walk on tiptoe, walk a straight line, stand on one foot, and skip.

Test 10:   *Arm Coordination.* This subtest is also on the Motor Scale and measures gross motor arm movement. It measures the child's ability to bounce, catch, and throw.

Test 11:   *Imitative Action.* This subtest appears on the Motor Scale and measures four simple imitative motor abilities.

Test 12:   *Draw-a-Design.* This subtest appears on the Perceptual-Performance, General Cognitive, and Motor scales. The easier items require the subject to copy simple geometric designs, while the more difficult items require the subject to imitate complex drawings. This subtest can help assess the presence of perceptual or other neurological disabilities that may interfere with the child's ability to learn. It is a perceptual-motor task that requires eye-hand coordination.

Test 13:   *Draw-A-Child.* This subtest appears on the Perceptual-Performance, General Cognitive, and Motor scales. It is an updated version of the Goodenough Draw-a-Person Intelligence Test. It requires the child to draw a complete picture of a human figure. The greater the amount of detail, the more credit the child receives. This subtest also measures perceptual motor skills and eye-hand coordination.

Test 14:   *Numerical Memory.* This subtest appears on the Quantitative, General Cognitive, and Memory scales. On this particular subtest, the child is asked to repeat digits presented by the examiner forward and in reverse. It is considered to be a short-term auditory memory task.

Test 15:   *Verbal Fluency.* This subtest appears on the Verbal and General Cognitive scales. The child is asked to name as many things as he or she can think of that fit into a particular category. It measures the child's ability for verbal abstraction and verbal associations. In addition, it presents a measure of the individual's divergent or creative thinking.

Test 16:   *Counting and Sorting.* This subtest appears on the Quantitative and General Cognitive scales. It utilizes the blocks to help demonstrate the individual's ability for numerical sequencing. In addition, it assesses the child's ability to count and understand simple quantitative words.

Test 17:   *Opposite Analogies.* This subtest appears on the Verbal and General Cognitive scales. The examiner provides a statement, and the subject has to fill in a word having the opposite meaning. An example would be, "a hippopotamus is big and a rabbit is _____." This measures the child's relational thinking ability.

Test 18:   *Conceptual Grouping.* This subtest appears on the Perceptual-Performance and General Cognitive scales. It measures the child's understanding of size, color, and shape. Initially, the child is asked to manipulate one of these variables. However, as the tasks become more complex, the subject must be able to manipulate all three variables. ("Find the big square yellow one.")

The McCarthy Scales of Children's Abilities is probably the best test to administer to individuals between 2 1/2 and 7 years of age. It is certainly far superior to the Wechsler Preschool and Primary Scale of Intelligence (WPPSI) for this age range. The author believes the WPPSI is much too narrow in its administration and never fulfilled the expectations it would function as a downward extension of the Wechsler Intelligence Scale for Children. In plotting the profile of the six different scales discussed earlier, the examiner has an opportunity to identify whether or not there are any possible processing deficits, learning disabilities, or other actual potential educational problems.

Evaluation of the McCarthy Scales

Sattler identifies several limitations of the McCarthy. They include the following:

1. The failure to include social comprehension and judgment tasks or many abstract problem-solving tasks limits the breadth of the scales.

2. The scales may not be suitable for school-age children because of the cumbersomeness of some of the procedures.

3. GCI floor of 50 limits the scales' usefulness in assessing the abilities of severely mentally retarded children and 2 1/2 year olds with below average cognitive abilities; the low ceilings on many tests limit the scales usefulness in assessing the abilities of older gifted children.

4. The absence of norms for older children and adolescents limits the utility of the scales and follow-up evaluations.[11]

Summary

The McCarthy Scales of Children's Abilities is the test of choice for children between 2 1/2 and 7 years of age. It is used primarily for children in that age group. There are six different scales resulting in a cumulative General Cognitive Index.

Unlike the Stanford-Binet or Wechsler scales, the McCarthy does not yield an I.Q. score. The McCarthy refers to the cumulative intelligence score as a General Cognitive Index (GCI). The 18 subtests are divided to obtain the various scales. They are divided as follows:

Verbal Scale (V)
3.   Pictorial Memory
4.   Word Knowledge
7.   Verbal Memory
15. Verbal Fluency
17. Opposite Analogies

Perceptual Performance Scale (P)
1.   Block Building
2.   Puzzle Solving
6.   Tapping Sequence
8.   Right-Left Orientation
12. Draw-a-Design
13. Draw-a-Child
18. Conceptual Grouping

Quantitative Scale (Q)
5.   Number Questions
14. Numerical Memory
16. Counting and Sorting

Motor Tests (Mot)
9.   Leg Coordination
10. Arm Coordination
11. Imitative Action
12. Draw-a-Design
13. Draw-a-Child

Memory Scale (Mem)
3.   Pictorial Memory
6.   Tapping Sequence
7.   Verbal Memory
14. Numerical Memory

The GCI is comprised of the 15 subtests that make up the Verbal, Perceptual Performance, and Quantitative scales. The Motor and Memory scales are not part of the GCI.

When scoring the McCarthy, the examiner uses a very detailed scoring manual. Some value judgment is required on the part of the scorer to determine whether a particular item deserves full or partial credit.

The McCarthy is considered to be a very reliable instrument with reliability coefficients ranging from .90 to .96, depending upon the age of the child tested.[12] The reliability coefficients of the subtests range from .81 on the Quantitative Scale to .93 on the GCI. On tests/retests, the GCI has a correlation of .61. As a result, the GCI appears to be relatively stable over time.[13]

The validity studies of the McCarthy also appear to be quite promising. The McCarthy correlates well with the Stanford-Binet, the Wechsler Scales, and other tests of cognitive functioning.[14]

THE WECHSLER SCALES

A series of tests developed over a period of several decades is referred to as the Wechsler Scales. The original Wechsler Intelligence Test, the Wechsler-Bellevue, was named for the hospital at which Wechsler worked when the instrument was developed. Today there are three major Wechsler Scales in use: The Wechsler Adult Intelligence Scale Revised (WAIS-R), the Wechsler Intelligence Scale for Children-Revised (WISC-R), and the Wechsler Pre-school and Primary Scale of Intelligence (WPPSI). All of the Wechsler Scales are divided into the following categories: a Verbal Scale, which yields a verbal I.Q.; a Performance Scale, which yields a non-verbal I.Q; and a Full Scale which yields a more global full scale I.Q. Both the Verbal Scale and the Performance Scale are divided into various subtests. Each subtest yields a raw score and a scaled score. The scaled scores range from 0 to 20, with a mean of approximately 10, and a standard deviation of approximately 3.

Scale Score	Classification
0–2	severely retarded or severely deficient
3–4	retarded or deficient
5–6	borderline retarded or borderline deficient
7–8	below average or low average
9–11	average
12–13	above average or high average
14–15	superior
16–17	very superior
18–20	gifted

WECHSLER ADULT INTELLIGENCE SCALE-REVISED

The Wechsler Adult Intelligence Scale-Revised (WAIS-R) was developed in 1981 as a revision of the original Wechsler Adult Intelligence Scale which was developed in 1955. Like the other Wechsler Scales, it is divided into a Verbal Scale and a Performance Scale.

Verbal Scale

1. *Information:* The Information subtest is referred to as the general fund of knowledge subtest. It consists of 29 questions that cover a wide range of information that an individual acquires through academic experience and interaction with the environment.

2. *Digit Span:* The Digit Span subtest measures immediate rote auditory memory. It consists of progressively longer series of digits that the subject must repeat; first in the forward direction, and then in the backward direction.

3. *Vocabulary:* The Vocabulary subtest measures an individual's active language usage. It consists of 35 words which the subject is asked to define.

4. *Arithmetic:* The Arithmetic subtest measures the individual's arithmetic reasoning ability. It requires the subject to answer arithmetic questions and solve arithmetic problems without the advantage of paper and pencil.

5. *Comprehension:* The Comprehension subtest is referred to as the Verbal Social Comprehension subtest, and it correlates highly with the individual's social maturity. The subtest asks the individual questions that involve social situations.

6. *Similarities:* The Similarities subtest is referred to as the verbal concept formation task. The subject is presented with 14 pairs of words and asked to identify how they are alike.

Performance Scale

1. *Picture Completion:* The Picture Completion subtest measures the individual's ability for essential detail discrimination. Incomplete pictures are presented, and the subject is asked to identify what important part is missing. It essentially measures the subject's ability to identify details of the environment and interact with things in the environment.

2. *Picture Arrangements:* The Picture Arrangements subtest is referred to as the sequential inferences task. It requires the individual to place 10 sets of pictures of people in various social or environmental situations in the correct order. It correlates with the individual's ability to interact with people in the environment.

3. *Block Design:* The Block Design subtest is a nonverbal concept formation task that requires the individual to duplicate the design presented on a card, first with four blocks, and later with nine blocks.

4. *Object Assembly:* The Object Assembly subtest is a perceptual organization task that requires the individual to put together four puzzles to form familiar objects or things.

5. *Digit Symbol:* The Digit Symbol subtest measures the individual's efficiency in learning through visually presented material. It is sometimes also referred to as the psychomotor speed task. On this task, the individual is asked to copy symbols in the appropriate boxes based on their pairing with numbers.

After all of the subtests have been administered, a verbal I.Q. and a performance I.Q. are determined. The sum of the scale scores on both the verbal and performance I.Q. are combined to yield the full scale I.Q.

The reliability and validity coefficients on the WAIS-R are quite high. The WAIS-R correlates very well with the WAIS, the Stanford-Binet, and the WISC-R.[15] The correlation coefficients tend to be in the 80s and 90s.[16]

WECHSLER INTELLIGENCE SCALE FOR CHILDREN-REVISED

The Wechsler Intelligence Scale for Children-Revised (WISC-R) was developed in 1974 as an updated version of the original Wechsler Intelligence Scale for Children (WISC), which was developed in 1949. The purpose of the WISC was to serve as a downward extension of the Wechsler-Bellevue. The WISC-R is formatted the same as the Wechsler Adult Intelligence Scale-Revised (WAIS-R), with Verbal and Performance Scales, and it uses the same types of subtests as the WAIS-R. However, the subtests on the WISC-R are presented in a different order from the WAIS-R. The Verbal Scale presents the subtests in the following order: Information, Similarities, Arithmetic, Vocabulary, Comprehension, and Digit Span. The Performance Scale follows the order of Picture Completion, Picture Arrangement, Block Design, Object Assembly, Coding, and Mazes. The WISC-R uses both the Digit Span and Mazes subtests as supplementary subtests. It also refers to its Digit Symbol subtest as Coding. The only subtest that is unique to the WISC-R is the Mazes subtest. This is often referred to as a planning and foresight task. It requires the individual to find the way through nine paper and pencil mazes of varying difficulty without error or with a minimal number of errors.

The Information, Arithmetic, and Vocabulary subtests on the Verbal Scale are often indicators of the individual's academic achievement. From these, it is possible to determine whether the individual is an academic underachiever. The Comprehension and Similarities subtests on the Verbal Scale, along with the Block Design subtest on the Performance Scale, are the greatest indicators of abstract thinking ability.

The Arithmetic, Digit Span, and Coding subtests measure the individual's freedom from distractibility. It is also important to note that the Coding subtest is generally the lowest subtest of individuals referred for services. The Coding subtest can be affected by emotional disturbance, learning disabilities, distractibility, organicity, and attention deficit disorders.

The WISC-R is the most widely used intelligence test for the population that it is aimed to measure.[17] Its reliability coefficients (test/retest) are in the 80s and 90s.[18] The validity coefficients are equally high when comparing the WISC-R and the WISC.[19] However, they are somewhat lower in the 70s and 80s when comparing the Stanford-Binet:FE and the WISC-R.[20]

Research has been done by Alan Kaufman, one of the test's developers, in factor analyzing the subtests of the WISC-R.[21] His results suggest that there are three factors underlying WISC-R subtests. They are as follows: 1) Verbal Comprehension-Information, Similarities, Vocabulary, and Comprehension; 2) Perceptual Organization-Picture Completion, Picture Arrangement, Block Design, Object Assembly, and Mazes; and 3) Freedom from Distractibility-Arithmetic, Digit Span, and Coding.

The results of this study support Wechsler's concept of having a two-factor intelligence measure, such as "verbal" and "performance." However, Kaufman did note that some of the verbal and performance subtests broke out into a third factor which he referred to as "freedom from distractibility."[22]

Ordinarily a difference of 12 to 15 points on the Verbal and Performance Scale is necessary before the difference is considered to be significant.[23] Kaufman states that these differences could arise due to the difference between an individual's verbal and nonverbal abilities, psycholinguistic deficiencies, bilingualism, problems in coordination, time pressure, and socioeconomic influences.[24]

WECHSLER PRE-SCHOOL AND PRIMARY SCALE OF INTELLIGENCE

Like the WISC-R, the Wechsler Pre-school and Primary Scale of Intelligence (WPPSI) is divided into a verbal and a performance scale. It utilizes the same basic subtests as the WISC-R and was developed as a downward extension of the WISC-R. The WPPSI can be used with individuals between 4 and 6 1/2 years of age. In the author's experience, because of its severe limit of usability and because of the advent of the Kaufman Assessment Battery for Children (K-ABC) and McCarthy scales, the WPPSI has fallen out of favor with most examiners.

There are three subtests that are unique to the WPPSI that do not appear on any of the other Wechsler Scales. They are as follows:

1. *Sentences (Supplementary Test):* This subtest appears on the Verbal Scale and is designed to replace the Digit Span subtest on the WISC-R and WAIS-R. Ten sentences of varying difficulty are read to the child who is asked to repeat them verbatim. As a result, this also serves as a rote auditory memory task.

2. *Animal House:* This subtest is found on the Performance Scale and is used in place of the Coding subtest on the WISC-R and the Digit Symbol subtest on the WAIS-R. It requires the child to associate colored cylinders with objects in a form board. It, too, measures psychomotor speed and efficiency in learning visually presented materials.

3. *Geometric Design*: This subtest is also on the Performance Scale and is designed to replace the Block Design

subtest of the WISC-R and the WAIS-R. The child must draw designs of varying complexity.

The reliability scores on the WPPSI were relatively high in the .90 or high range.[25] However, the validity scores are not as good. The validity correlation coefficients with the Stanford-Binet were anywhere from the 60s to the 80s, depending upon the research that was performed.[26] Furthermore, the correlation coefficients between the WPPSI and the WISC and WISC-R are disappointingly low, generally in the 40s to 60s.[27] In the author's experience, based on the narrow age range of the WPPSI and the relatively low validity coefficients, the WPPSI is generally not considered the test of choice for this age range. Furthermore, since the test was published more than 20 years ago, it is considered to be somewhat outdated.

Authors Graham and Lilly evaluate the Wechsler intelligence scales as follows:

1. Each scale has been carefully developed. The content is current and appropriate for ages for which it is to be used.

2. The standardization samples for all three scales are representative of contemporary U.S. society and are completely described.

3. The WAIS-R, published in 1981, and the WISC-R, published in 1974, are both quite recent editions. The WPPSI, published in 1967, may need new normative data or more evidence that children tested in the 1980s are performing similarly to the 1967 normative sample.

4. Unlike the Stanford-Binet, which provides a single I.Q., each Wechsler Scale provides 10 to 11 subtest scores, as well as verbal, performance, and full scale I.Q.'s. Although differences among the subtest scores and between the verbal and performance I.Q. may be of clinical use, they may also be overinterpreted.

5. The verbal, performance and full scale I.Q.'s appear to be highly reliable, but the subtests are much less so. More data on the stability of I.Q.'s over longer periods of time would be desirable, although the available evidence is encouraging.

6. The manuals for all three scales report little validity information. Much of the voluminous literature on the three scales deals with their concurrent validity, mainly the correlation of the Wechsler Scales and other intelligence tests. More studies on predictive validity of the three scales are clearly needed.

7. All the Wechsler Scales measure a subject's current mental functioning and thus measure the effects of both heredity and environment.

8. Speed of responding is a factor of importance for some subtests on all the scales.

9. Taken as a package, the three Wechsler Scales provide the best available means for the individual assessment of intelligence from age 4 through old age.[28]

KAUFMAN ASSESSMENT BATTERY FOR CHILDREN (K-ABC)

The Kaufman Assessment Battery for Children (K-ABC) assesses intelligence of children between 2 1/2 and 12 1/2 years of age. This particular intelligence scale is derived from different theories of mental processing from the traditional scales of cognitive ability. The Mental Processing Scales measure the child's ability to solve problems sequentially and simultaneously. The Kaufmans were concerned that tests like the Wechsler Scales were really achievement tests. They were more concerned about emphasizing the child's ability to produce correct solutions than with the specific content of the items. To deal with the achievement aspects of cognitive ability, the K-ABC also includes an achievement scale.

The K-ABC is divided into a sequential processing scale, simultaneous processing scale, a mental processing composite, and achievement scale. Sequential processing deals with ideas linearly and temporally related to the preceding one. Sequential processing affects memorization, the learning of grammatical relationships, and associations between letters and sounds, for example.

Simultaneous processing deals with spatial analogic or organizational concepts. Input must be integrated and synthesized simultaneously to yield a solution to the problem.

Simultaneous processing is sometimes referred to as holistic problem solving. It is accomplished by processing many stimuli at once rather than feature by feature. It allows the individual to see the process as a whole by understanding main ideas, rapidly learning spatial configurations, and solving problems creatively.

The Mental Processing Composite is based on combining the Sequential and Simultaneous Processing Scales. The Achievement Scale of the K-ABC looks at vocabulary, arithmetic, reading, and general knowledge. The Kaufmans have also added a nonverbal scale. The nonverbal scale can be administered gesturally and responded to with actions by the subject. It can serve as a good estimate of mental processing for nonverbal or non-English-speaking children.

There are 16 subtests on the K-ABC, including the simultaneous, sequential, and achievement subtests.

Subtest 1: *Magic Window*. The Magic Window subtest is on the Simultaneous Processing Scale and is applicable to children 2 years 6 months through 4 years 11 months, hereinafter referred to as 2-6 through 4-11. It measures the child's ability to identify and name an object, the picture of which is only partially exposed at any one point in time. It measures the child's ability in simultaneous processing, attention to visual detail, distinguishing essential from nonessential detail, early language development, long-term memory, part-whole relationships (synthesis), short-term memory (visual), spatial ability, verbal expression, and visual perception of meaningful stimuli (people-things).

Subtest 2: *Face Recognition*. The Face Recognition subtest is on the Simultaneous Processing Scale and is applicable for children ages 2-6 through 4-11. If used as part of the nonverbal scale, it is only used for children 4-0 through 4-11 years. The subject is shown a photograph of one or two individuals. A second photograph is shown with that individual or individuals in a group photograph, and the child is asked to pick the individual(s) from the first photograph out of the second photograph. The face recognition subtest measure simultaneous processing, attention to visual detail; distinguishing essential from nonessential detail, fluid ability, short-term memory (visual), visual organization without essential motor activity, and visual perception of meaningful stimuli (people-things).

Subtest 3:   *Hand Movements.* The Hand Movement subtest is the first subtest on the Sequential Processing Scale and is given to children of all ages. The examiner produces a sequence of taps on the table with a fist, palm, or side of the hand, and the subject is asked to duplicate the sequence. The Hand Movements subtest measures sequential processing (2-6 through 12-6) and simultaneous processing (5-0 through 12-6), fluid ability, perceptual organization, reproduction of a model, short-term memory (visual), spatial ability, and visual-motor coordination.

Subtest 4:   *Gestalt Closure.* The Gestalt Closure subtest measures simultaneous processing for children of all ages. This task requires the child to mentally fill in the gaps in a partially completed drawing. The child is asked to name or describe the drawing. It measures simultaneous processing, attention to visual detail, early language development, long-term memory, part-whole relationships (synthesis), perceptual organization, spatial ability, verbal expression, and visual organization without essential motor activity.

Subtest 5:   *Number Recall.* The Number Recall subtest measures sequential processing for children of all ages. On this task, the child is asked to repeat a series of numbers presented by the examiner. The Number Recall subtest measures sequential processing, fluid ability, number facility, reproduction of a model, and short-term memory (auditory).

Subtest 6:   *Triangles.* The Triangle subtest is on both the Simultaneous Processing and Nonverbal scales for children 4-0 through 12-5. The child is asked to put together a series of abstract designs by matching a design card with yellow and blue triangles. It measures simultaneous processing, analysis, fluid ability, part-whole relationships (synthesis), perceptual organization, reasoning, reproduction of a model, spatial ability, visual motor coordination, and visual perception of abstract stimuli (design-symbols).

Subtest 7:   *Word Order.* The Word Order subtest is on the Sequential Processing Scale and is for children 4-0 through 12-5 years. The child is asked to point to silhouettes of common objects in the same crder as the objects were named by the examiner. It measures sequential processing, early language development, fluid ability, short-term memory (auditory), verbal (auditory) comprehension, and visual perception of meaningful stimuli (people-things).

Subtest 8:   *Matrix Analogies.* The Matrix Analogies subtest is on the Simultaneous Processing and Nonverbal Scales for children 5-0 to 12-5 years. On the Matrix Analogies subtest, the child is asked to select a design that best completes a visual analogy. It measures: simultaneous processing, analysis, attention to visual detail, distinguishing essential from nonessential detail, fluid ability, perceptual organization, reasoning, spatial ability, visual organization without essential motor activity, and visual perception of abstract stimuli (design symbols).

Subtest 9:   *Spatial Memory.* The Spatial Memory subtest is on the Simultaneous Processing and nonverbal scales for children ages 5-0 to 12-5. The Spatial Memory subtest measures the subject's ability to recall the locations of pictures arranged randomly on a page. The Spatial Memory subtest measures abilities in simultaneous processing, fluid ability, perceptual organization, reproduction of a model, short-term memory (visual), spatial ability, and visual organization without essential motor activity.

Subtest 10:   *Photo Series.* The Photo Series subtest is on both the Simultaneous Processing and Nonverbal Scales for children 6-0 through 12-5 years. A series of photographs is presented to the child in random display. The child is asked to put the photographs in the correct order in time sequence to make a meaningful series. This particular subtest measures simultaneous processing, analysis, attention to visual detail, distinguishing essential from nonessential detail, part-whole relationships (synthesis), perceptual organization, reasoning, spatial ability, visual organization without essential motor activity, and visual perception of meaningful stimuli (people-things).

Subtest 11:   *Expressive Vocabulary* The Expressive Vocabulary subtest is the first subtest on the Achievement Scale. It is given only to children ages 2-6 through 4-11. The child is required to correctly name the objects pictured in photographs. This subtest measures achievement, crystallized ability, early language development, fund of information (acquired facts), long-term memory, mental processing (primarily simultaneous), verbal concept formation, verbal expression, visual perception of meaningful stimuli (people-things), and word knowledge.

Subtest 12:   *Faces and Places.* The Faces and Places subtest is on the Achievement Scale and is applicable for children ages 2-6 through 12-5. The subject is shown pictures of well-known fictionalized characters, famous people, or well-known places and is asked to identify them. The Faces and Places subtest measures achievement, crystallized ability, fund of information (acquired facts), long-term memory, mental processing (primarily simultaneous), verbal expression, and visual perception of meaningful stimuli (people-things).

Subtest 13: *Arithmetic.* This Achievement subtest is for children 3-0 through 12-5 years. It measures the child's arithmetic reasoning and ability to understand mathematical concepts. The Arithmetic subtest measures achievement, applied (school-related) skills, crystallized ability, long-term memory, mental processing (sequential and simultaneous), number facility, reasoning, verbal (auditory) comprehension, visual perception of abstract stimuli (designs symbols), and visual perception of meaningful stimuli (people-things).

Subtest 14: *Riddles.* The Riddles subtest is on the Achievement Scale for children ages 3-0 through 12-5. It measures the subject's ability to identify abstract or concrete concepts when several characteristics are presented. The Riddles subtest measures achievement; crystallized ability, distinguishing essential from nonessential detail, early language development, fund of information acquired (facts), long-term memory, mental processing (primarily simultaneous), part-whole relationships (synthesis), reasoning, verbal (auditory), comprehension, verbal concept formation, verbal expression, and word knowledge.

Subtest 15: *Reading/Decoding.* The Reading/Decoding subtest is on the Achievement Scale and is used for children 5-0 to 12-5 years. It measures the child's ability to identify letters and read and printout words. The Reading/Decoding subtest identifies the following skills: achievement, applied (school-related) skills, crystallized ability, early language development, long-term memory, mental processing (sequential and simultaneous), reading ability, and verbal expression.

Subtest 16:   *Reading/Understanding.* The Reading/Under-
standing subtest is on the Achievement Scale
and is used with children ages 7-0 through 12-5.
It is essentially a reading comprehension subtest
that asks the child to act out commands given in
the sentences that are being read. For example,
the sentence might read "raise your right hand."
If the child raises his or her right hand, credit is
given. This subtest measures achievement,
applied (school-related) skills, crystallized ability, long-term memory, mental processing,
sequential and simultaneous processing, reading
ability, and verbal concept formation.

Newmark, a noted author of learned treatises about psychological testing, lists the assets and liabilities of the K-ABC.
They are as follows:

- a strong theoretical foundation on which to base measurement of children's intelligence;

- intelligence and achievement scales with completely
separate (nonoverlapping) content, normed on the same
sample of children, thereby relieving concerns about
making intelligence-achievement comparisons with
other instruments;

- sample and teaching items that allow for fair, more
accurate assessment of preschoolers, minority children,
and exceptional (e.g., retarded) populations;

- limited oral instructions on subtests and limited verbal
response again encourage a more accurate assessment
of skills of preschoolers, minority children, and other
groups as well;

- colorful items enhance rapport with and valid assessment of young children in particular;

- a 1980 census-based standardization sample which
reflects vast growth in the minority population since
1970;

- a nonverbal scale for use with children who cannot be
administered many existing intelligence tests, such as

the hearing impaired, or youngsters who do not speak or understand English;

- sociocultural norms for generating hypotheses about cultural influences on a black or white child's performance;
- a complete interpretative system offered in the test manuals;
- a framework as well as examples of materials for use in designing educational intervention programs;
- administration and scoring rules that are straightforward, allowing clinicians to spend more time observing the child and enhancing the accuracy of the scoring process;
- empirical documentation of smaller black-white, Hispanic-white, and Native American-white differences on the K-ABC than on I.Q. tests;
- results of over 40 validity studies included in the test manual.[29]

The liabilities associated with the K-ABC include:

- limits on what the K-ABC assesses. The K-ABC does not assess some of the skills assessed by existing intelligence tests and does not include some tasks that have been traditionally part of the psychologists' test battery;
- sequential processing scale—in terms of reliability and information yield—is less robust than the simultaneous processing scale. The sequential processing scale appears to measure sequential processing (as opposed to short-term memory), but would have benefited from a sequential task that did not require memory;
- a heavy dependence on visual stimuli, making the K-ABC unsuitable for visually impaired children;
- failure, perhaps, to reward adequately those bright children who adapted spontaneously expressing their thoughts and words and who excel at verbal reasoning;
- too few manipulative tasks for preschool children;

- an insufficient number of easy items on several tasks preventing adequate discrimination among 2- to 6-year olds who are below average in intelligence or achievement.

Basically, the K-ABC has yielded very high reliability and validity coefficients. The author's experience suggests it is a test today that appears to be used more frequently in educational settings than in clinical settings. However, it does provide an excellent alternative when other I.Q. tests have been previously administered.

Summary

The K-ABC is a test that was developed to separate the achievement components from the mental processing components of cognitive ability. It has successfully done so. It is used quite extensively in educational settings to help develop appropriate educational plans for children based on their simultaneous versus sequential processing abilities. In the practice of clinical psychology, the K-ABC tends to be used after the Wechsler scales and the McCarthy. It is also a valuable instrument to have available if the Wechsler scales or McCarthy have been administered recently and cannot be readministered for fear of practice effect.

WIDE RANGE ACHIEVEMENT TEST-REVISED (WRAT-R)

The Wide Range Achievement Test-Revised is an updated version of the original Wide Range Achievement Test. It is a relatively easy test to administer and provides a quick measure of achievement in the reading, spelling, and arithmetic areas. It is applicable for individuals from kindergarten age through adulthood. The WRAT-R is best used when a thorough educational diagnostic evaluation is not desired, but a quick estimate is needed. In custody evaluations, the WRAT-R will generally suffice as a measure of achievement.

RAVEN'S PROGRESSIVE MATRICES (RPM)

The Raven's Progressive Matrices was developed by Raven as a nonverbal measure of intelligence. The items consist of a set of matrices with a part missing. The subject must choose the missing piece that fills up the matrix from a variety of options. Although it has use in obtaining a general measure of intelligence, it is not widely used by clinicians today.

ENDNOTES

1. J. Sattler, Assessments of Children's Intelligence and Special Abilities 648–49 (2d ed. 1982) [hereinafter Assessment of Children's Intelligence and Special Abilities].

2. *Id.* at 648.

3. *Id.*

4. D. Wechsler, The Measurement and Appraisal of Adult Intelligence 57 (4th ed. 1958).

5. A. Anastasi, Psychological Testing 326 (6th ed. 1988).

6. *Id.* at 350.

7. *Id.*

8. Alan Kaufman personal communication, 1979.

9. Assessments of Children's Intelligence and Special Abilities, *supra* note 1, at 289–90.

10. Alan Kaufman personal communication, 1979.

11. Assessments of Children's Intelligence and Special Abilities, *supra* note 1, at 300.

12. J. Graham & R. Lilly, Psychological Testing 135 (1984).

13. *Id.* at 136.

14. *Id.* at 138–40.

15. A. Anastasi, Psychological Testing 248 (6th ed. 1988).

16. *Id.*

17. Assessments of Children's Intelligence and Special Abilities, *supra* note 1, at 143.

18. *Id.*

19. *Id.*

20. *Id.*

21. A. Kaufman, Intelligence Testing with the WISC-R (1979) in J. Sattler, Assessment of Children 130 (3d ed. 1988).

22. *Id.* at 131.

23. J. Graham & R. Lilly, Psychological Testing 118 (1984) [hereinafter Psychological Testing].

24. A. Kaufman, Intelligence Testing with the WISC-R (1979) in Psychological Testing *supra* note 23, at 118.

25. Psychological Testing *supra* note 23, at 122.

26. Id. at 123.

27. Id. at 124.

28. Id. at 12–27.

29. C. Newmark, Major Psychological Assessment Instruments 26–69 (1985).

QUESTIONS FOR CHAPTER SIX

Caution: An attorney should not expect to be able to go into court and ask all of the questions listed below. Preparation is necessary, referring to the content of the chapter to determine if the question applies to your case. The page number at the end of each question refers to where in the chapter you may read an explanation of why this question may be important.

1. If the psychologist deviated from the standard administration procedures on any of the intelligence tests, how would that affect the reliability and validity of the scores? (p. 44)

2. What classification system did the psychologist use in determining the range of performance on the I.Q. test? (p. 121)

3. Why did the psychologist select the specific intelligence test that was administered? (pp. 127, 131, 139, 148)

4. Ask the psychologist if he or she took into account the weaknesses of the selected intelligence test when making the interpretations. (pp. 127, 132, 139–40, 146–47)

5. Did the psychologist administer all of the subtests of the intelligence test administered? If not, why not? (p. 44)

6. How would the overall reliability and validity of the results be affected by those subtest that were not administered? (general, no specific page)

7. Did the psychologist address the limitations for the Stanford-Binet 4th edition discussed on page 127, the McCarthy Scales discussed on page 132, the Wechsler Scales discussed on pages 139–40, and the K-ABC discussed on pages 146–47?

8. If one of the Wechsler Scales was administered, does the full scale I.Q. accurately represent the individual's overall intelligence or is it a function of the average of the Verbal Scale and Performance Scale? (p. 138)

9. Were any of the intelligence scores adversely affected by the level of anxiety that the individual presented at testing? (p. 137)

10. If the Wechsler Preschool and Primary Scale of Intelligence was administered, why was that chosen over the WISC-R, Stanford-Binet 4th edition, or the McCarthy Scales? (pp. 138–39)

11. If there is a significant discrepancy between the child or children's I.Q. and the parent or parent's I.Q., how will that effect the custodial relationship? (p. 266)

Chapter Seven
Objective Personality Testing

MINNESOTA MULTIPHASIC PERSONALITY INVENTORY (MMPI)

Personality tests are generally classified in two broad categories: objective and projective. In reality, many tests fall more on a continuum between these poles. However, the traditional dichotomy will be observed here for organizational purposes.

The personality tests that fall in the objective category are those that demand a structured response from the subject and do not invite a free form association or a projection of the subject's feelings into the test. The most important objective personality test is the Minnesota Multiphasic Personality Inventory (MMPI).

The MMPI is a test currently comprised of 566 true-false questions. The test was designed to identify pathological personalities, but is now used to evaluate nonpathological personalities as well. It is by far the most frequently administered personality test. Its importance lies not only in its popularity, but also in the vast amount of documented research as to its reliability and validity.

The MMPI was developed by Starke R. Hathaway and J. Charnley McKinley in the early 1940s. The early form of the MMPI contained 504 true and false items. Today there are 550 true and false items, plus 16 items repeated to facilitate machine scoring. Shorter forms exist, but markedly limit the data produced. Their use is not recommended. A restandardization of the MMPI (MMPI-2) is currently being undertaken by Dahlstrom, Butcher, and Graham. (The MMPI-2 is discussed later in this chapter). The MMPI can be administered in group form, booklet form, or by computer. It is currently used with individuals 16 years of age and older who have at least a sixth-grade reading level. Individuals with a reading level below the sixth-grade level might need to respond to an oral form of the MMPI.

Examined in more than 12,000 published articles and books to date, the MMPI is the best researched of all personality tests.

Every psychologist is taught the use of the MMPI and would be expected to include it as a key part of any evaluation. Given its universal acceptance as a central part of evaluations, a psychologist who does not use it should be questioned about the omission, since reliance solely on subjective tests and interviews may permit conclusions to be drawn which would not be supported by the research base available for use with the MMPI.

Scoring

Whether hand scored or computer scored, the same profile should result on an MMPI. Differences do not come from the scoring form used, but from the various methods of interpreting the profile that are used by different individuals.

Over 125 scales have been developed for the MMPI. These scales are divided into three basic groups. The first group contains the validity scales, which help the examiner determine whether the profile is valid. The second group is referred to as the clinical scales. These scales present the information from which the traditional psychiatric diagnosis is made and are the heart of the MMPI. The remaining scales are referred to as the research or supplementary scales. They tend to look at specific personality characteristics or measure specific problem areas.

The interpretation of an MMPI test involves several steps, now frequently performed by a computer. The first step is to categorize test responses into the various scales where they are relevant. Many of the test items are scored on more than one scale.

The second step is to calculate responses and compute total scoreable responses for each scale. This step produces a raw score.

The third step involves making a correction to the raw scores. To accomplish this the K Scale was developed, which is designed to measure clinical defensiveness. (The K Scale will be discussed in more detail later.) A high score on the K Scale may indicate an attempt to maintain control and project an appearance of adequacy and effectiveness. These tendencies, indicated by a high score on the K Scale, have been shown to predictably lower the scores on certain clinical scales. Thus, this aspect of personality has the potential to distort scores on other parts of the profile. To correct this potential distortion on the clinical scales, a K factor is added to those scales. The amount to be added is different for each scale, but is always a fraction of or the total K score. The clinical scales to which a K factor is added are scales 1, 4, 7, 8, and 9. The result of this third step is to obtain a raw score adjusted to reflect K factor "loadings."

The fourth, and final, step before actual interpretation is to convert the adjusted raw scores to a standard score called T scores (see Chapter Five). The T scores have a mean value of 50 and a standard deviation of 10. Thus T scores between 30 and 70 contain two standard deviations from the mean or about 98 percent of the total. (In other words, approximately two percent of the population falls below 30 or above 70.)

Lastly, the test results are interpreted. The interpretation is a combination of comparing the results to the norms and to the many research findings published and using professional judgment to assess the subject's background and possible reasons or explanations for tendencies shown in the results.

Many of the available computer scoring systems perform the first function—that is, they compare individual test scores to the norms determined by various research publications. The computer program generates a list of characteristics, tendencies, or personality traits that the subject is likely to exhibit.

The task of the professional then is to interpret all of these data in the light of the clinical history, information from outside sources, other psychological tests administered, and the reason for the psychological evaluation.

There are a number of computer programs on the market for scoring and interpreting the MMPI. Some are usable in the psychologist's office, while others require the psychologist to mail the answer sheet to a central computer service for scoring and interpretation. While most, if not all, interpretations generated by these programs are acceptable, those to be preferred are the ones which are known to periodically update their programs in response to new research. Four which do so are the "Caldwell Report," the "Minnesota Report," and the programs from "Psychological Assessment Resources" and "Applied Innovations." Now that the MMPI-2 is published, any computer program which does not use the revised data base is open to questions.

Following is a discussion of the three groups of scales used to score the MMPI: the validity scales, the clinical scales, and the research or supplementary scales. Each group is then broken down into the various subscales that comprise each scale.

Validity Scales

? Scale (Cannot Say Scale)

The ? Scale score is the number of items left unanswered by the subject. A score of 0 to 6 is average. A score of 7 to 12 indicates the subject would prefer to avoid one or more areas. Scores of 13 to 67 are rarely seen and suggest conscious avoidance of many areas. A score exceeding 67 may indicate lack of time, indecisiveness, defensiveness, lack of reading ability, confusion, or psychological problems. In a case such as this, the validity of the results is seriously questioned.

L Scale (Lie Scale)

The L Scale is a 15-item "perfection" scale that is designed to determine how much an individual is trying to make himself or herself look positive in an obvious manner. The higher the score on the L Scale, the more the individual is attempting to appear socially appropriate. The lower the score, the more the individual is willing to admit to human weaknesses. Caldwell, the developer of one of the more popular methods of interpretation, believed this scale measures an individual's fears of shame or moral judgment. A person with these fears will deny moral fault and therefore score higher. Most people will have a T score below 50 and rarely above 60 on this scale.[1]

Colligan's research reported that the L Scale score is negatively correlated with education.[2] That is, the more education an individual has, the lower the L score. The L Scale can also be elevated if the individual has a strict religious upbringing or religious occupation, is foreign born, is of below-average intelligence, or is applying for a job and wants to look good. High L scores may also be the result of individuals being highly moralistic, having an inability to gain self insights, or having limited sophistication but attempting to look better than they really are.[3]

By summary, a T score of 50 or below on the L Scale is an indication of an individual who is willing to admit to his or her faults. A T score of 50 through 60 indicates an individual who sees himself or herself as virtuous, conforming, and self-controlled. Finally, a T score of 60 and above indicates that the individual represses or denies unfavorable traits.

F Scale (Frequency or Confusion Scale)

The higher the score on the F Scale, the more the individual is reporting confusion or unusual faults.[4] The F Scale is a 64-item scale. Scores of 75 and above on the F Scale may be a "cry for help."[5] These individuals are hurting, psychologically, and want to make sure that the examiner is aware of the extent of their pain. As a result, they are likely to overstate the unusual thoughts and experiences that may be occurring. When this score reaches 100 or more, it can be an indication that everything appears bad to the subject, and, as a result, he or she is overreacting to everything.[6]

Researcher Schenkenberg reported that younger people in the psychiatric population score higher on the F Scale than older people. Gynther reported that blacks tend to score higher on this scale than nonblacks.[7] Moderate elevations, T scores of 60 through 70, indicate that the individual has problems but is not overwhelmed by them or too worried about them.[8]

Marked elevations, T scores equaling 70 to 80, are found in individuals with an unusual and unconventional thinking style. They may be overly anxious and in high need of help, or may actually have difficulty reading the items on the MMPI.[9]

When the T scores on the F Scale are in the range of 80 through 90, according to Dahlstrom, Welsh, and Dahlstrom, authors of one of the most widely used early textbooks on the MMPI,[10] one must determine if the individual is in contact with reality, has poor reading ability, or was purposely malingering. If these criteria can be ruled out, the profile is considered valid, and a score this high usually indicates a "cry for help," a severely disturbed subject, or an adolescent who is attempting to appear unconventional.[11]

T scores in the range of 90 through 100 usually indicate a random marking of the test items. According to Carson's research, this may be the result of a person who is illiterate and does not want to admit it, someone who is confused, or someone person who has brain damage.[12]

Generally, when T scores equal 100 or above, it is an indication of error somewhere. There has either been an error in scoring the items, deliberately marking the items in an all-true, all-false or random format, or reading errors. If these are ruled out, however, the score can reflect the severity of psychopathology in the person or the degree to which the individual feels the need to look pathological.[13]

Individuals with T scores in the range of 45 or below are generally considered to be free from stress, honest, and conventional.[14]

Moderately high F Scale scores (T scores equaling 60 to 70) can indicate social protest or commitment to religious or political movements.[15]

K Scale (Correction Scale)

The K Scale (30 items) measures the individual's defensiveness or guardedness. As a result, some of the same motivation that would go into raising the L Scale score could also go into raising the K Scale score. The K Scale was developed after the other validity scales. It is called a correction scale, as "K loadings" are added to the Scales 1, 4, 7, 8, and 9. (See explanation, infra, under "Clinical Scales.") When adolescents are tested, K corrections are not used, research having shown that more accurate profiles are obtained without them.

Dahlstrom, Welsh, and Dahlstrom point out that high K scores are usually associated with lower scores on the clinical scales. The K Scale is a much more subtle scale than the L Scale, and, as a result, can detect defensiveness in even sophisticated individuals. Carson pointed out that the higher the score on the K Scale, the poorer the prognosis for therapy.[16] Average scores (T scores equaling 45 through 60) are found with people who are generally demonstrating "a balance between self-disclosure and self-protection."[17]

T scores of 60 through 70—a moderate elevation on the K Scale (T scores equaling 60 to 70)—are typical for individuals who are upper middle class or are college students. Individuals who are upper middle class and above with scores in this range are usually living well-managed and controlled lives. However, with lower socioeconomic classes, this score would reflect a greater degree of defensiveness.[18]

T scores of 70 or above usually mean that the person is impelled to present a psychologically healthy appearance to others.[19] Tromboli and Kilgore stated that elevations on this scale may be a function of repression and rationalization.[20] A very high K score in conjunction with high clinical scale scores may represent an unwillingness to look at problem areas.

There are generally two reasons why individuals have low scores, T scores of 35 to 45. Carson stated that individuals with scores in this range have problems which they are quite willing to admit.[21] On the other hand, Dahlstrom, Welsh, and Dahlstrom pointed out that these individuals believe that life has been rough for them and they are accurately perceiving their difficult background.[22]

T scores of 35 or below indicate these individuals are too willing to admit their problems and may tend to exaggerate them.[23]

L-F-K Scales

The L-F-K scales are rarely interpreted individually. A typical interpretation involves looking at combinations of these scales in pairs or taking them all together. Generally, a high F Scale score with low L and K Scale scores is an indication of a "fake bad" profile. On the other hand, high L and K Scale scores and a low F Scale score is an indication of a "fake good" profile.[24]

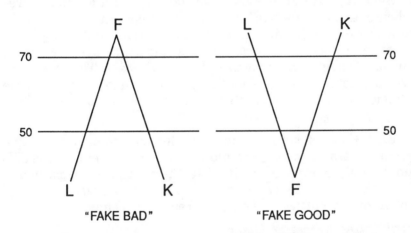

"FAKE BAD"   "FAKE GOOD"

One of the indices used in looking at the validity scales is called the F Minus K Index. This is also referred to as the "Dissimulation Index," or Gough Index. Generally a "fake bad" profile was considered if the F minus K was greater than 7, or if the F Scale score was greater than 15.[25] The Gough Index developed by Gough in 1956 is found by subtracting the raw score of the K Scale from the raw score of the F Scale. T scores should not be used for this index. Gough found that most normals on the MMPI ended up with "F minus K's" of minus 2 to minus 19.

Caldwell reports that when F Scale score is equal to or less than 16, the test is considered valid regardless of what the K Scale score is. If F is greater than 22 or 23, the test is called invalid regardless of what K is. When F is 17 through 21, and the F minus K is equal to or greater than 11, then the test is invalid.[26]

Not every researcher feels that the criteria used by Caldwell or Gough are the appropriate cutoffs. Anthony feels that a score of 19 or greater on the F Minus K Index is an indication of invalidity.[27]

Galluci performed research that concluded "elevations of the F scale and the "F - K" index do not typically indicate exaggerations of psychopathology, and compromise the validity of adolescent MMPI profiles."[28] As a result, the same F minus K concerns with adult MMPI's do not apply to adolescent MMPI's.

Elevations of L and F Scale Scores

Generally, simultaneous elevations of L and F Scale scores indicate a contradiction of problem areas. Individuals with these scores are denying inappropriate actions and thoughts as measured by the L Scale, and at the same time acknowledging unusual thoughts as measured by the F Scale. This combination may actually be the function of "poor integration of diverse behavioral trends to characterize some psychotic processes."[29]

Elevations of F and K

Elevations of both L and K Scale scores imply the same type of contradiction that would be seen by joint elevations of L and F Scale scores. In addition to the possibility of psychotic processes, these individuals may have a pervasive lack of insight or difficulties grasping the reality of situations.[30]

Invalidating Response Sets

At times, the way the individual responds on the entire MMPI can invalidate the results. If the individual chooses to respond with all true responses, all false responses, all random responses, all deviant responses, or all nondeviant responses the profile will be considered invalid. The following four profiles demonstrate these various response patterns.

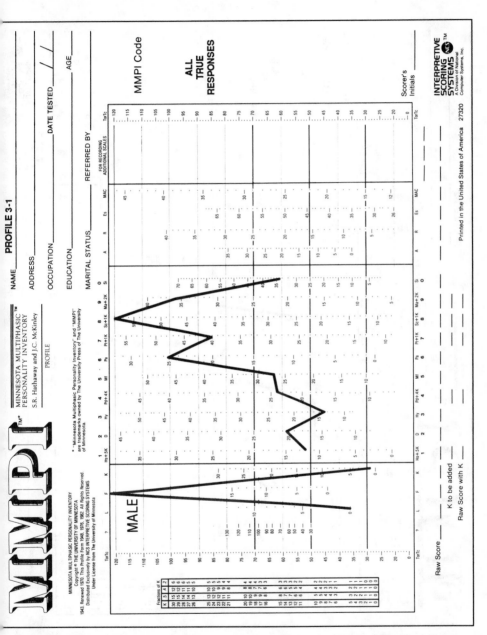

Profile 3-1. "All true" response set. Data obtained and reprinted with permission from Roger Greene, *The MMPI: An Interpretive Manual.* Copyright 1980, The Psychological Corporation. MMPI form reproduced with permission from the University of Minnesota. Copyright 1943, renewed 1970. This Profile Form 1948, 1976, 1982. All rights reserved.

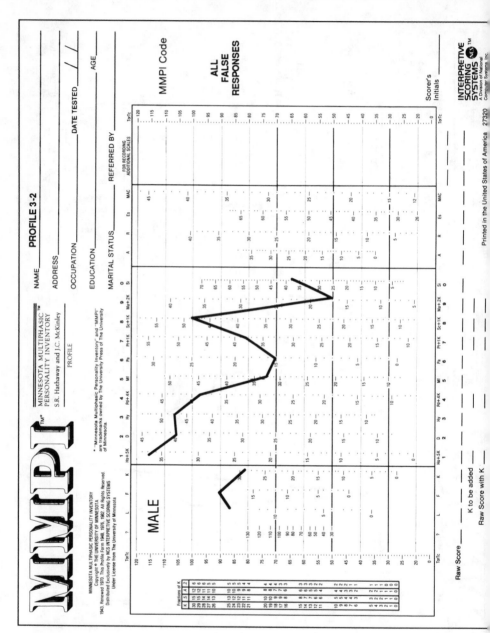

Profile 3-2. "All false" response set. Data obtained and reprinted with permission from Roger Greene, *The MMPI: An Interpretive Manual.* Copyright 1980, The Psychological Corporation. MMPI form reproduced with permission from the University of Minnesota. Copyright 1943, renewed 1970. This Profile Form 1948, 1976, 1982. All rights reserved.

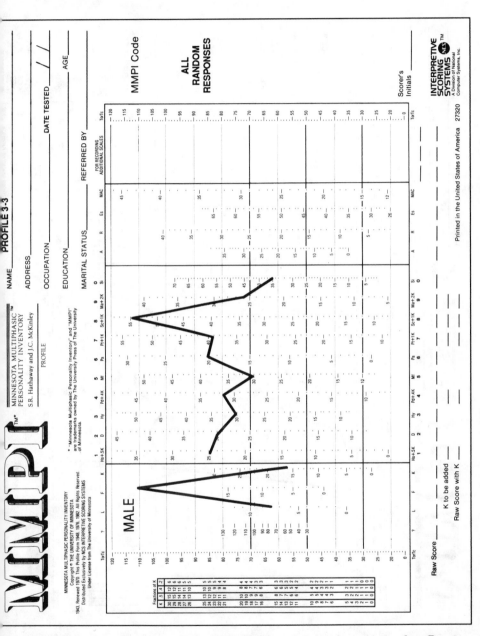

Profile 3-3. Random response set. Data obtained and reprinted with permission from Roger Greene, *The MMPI: An Interpretive Manual.* Copyright 1980, The Psychological Corporation. MMPI form reproduced with permission from the University of Minnesota. Copyright 1943, renewed 1970. This Profile Form 1948, 1976, 1982. All rights reserved.

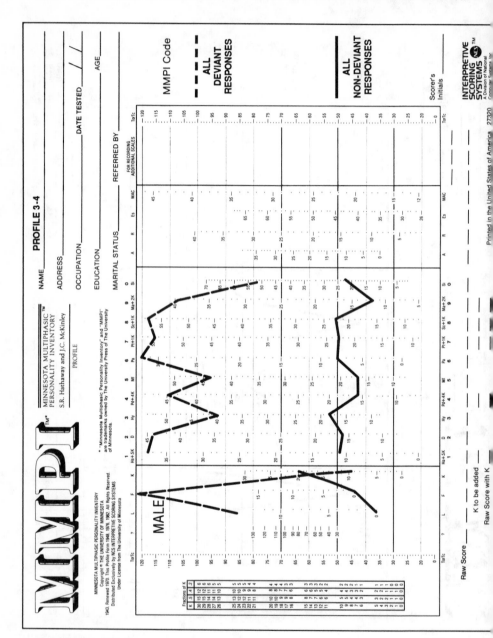

Profile 3-4. "All deviant" and "all nondeviant" response set. Data obtained and reprinted with permission from Roger Greene, *The MMPI: An Interpretive Manual*. Copyright 1980, The Psychological Corporation. MMPI form reproduced with permission from the University of Minnesota. Copyright 1943, renewed 1970. This Profile Form 1948, 1976, 1982. All rights reserved.

Clinical Scales

The clinical scales are the 10 main scales on the MMPI. Originally, there were eight basic clinical scales. In later years, two clinical scales (Masculinity-Femininity and Social Introversion) were added to reach the full complement of 10 scales used today. The 10 basic clinical scales are as follows:

Number	Abbreviation	Original Name
1	Hs	Hypochondriasis
2	D	Depression
3	Hy	Hysteria
4	Pd	Psychopathic Deviate
5	Mf	Masculinity-Femininity
6	Pa	Paranoia
7	Pt	Psychasthenia
8	Sc	Schizophrenia
9	Ma	Hypomania
0	Si	Social Introversion

Since the names of the scales do not always carry a full meaning of what the scales measure, the clinician generally refers to the scale by its number as opposed to its actual name.

Most clinicians view the basic clinical scales of the MMPI as providing an indication of the extent of problems in the basic diagnostic category areas. Different people have different opinions as to what emphasis should be placed on various scores. Generally, scores in the 60s are perceived as being moderate elevations, while scores above 70 are considered to be marked.[31] In addition, very high scale scores of greater than 80 suggest serious psychopathology, and incapacitating symptoms.[32] Scores below 45 are generally considered to be low scores. However, little research tends to be done in this area.

Scale 1: (Hs) Hypochondriasis

Scale 1 contains 33 items dealing with physical symptoms, attitudes about work, and daily activities, all which are dependent upon physical health. Individuals with scores below 45 tend to have little concern about health functioning, tend to be frustrated when in ill health, and generally seem to have a high energy level. Their medical histories generally indicate that they have positive recoveries from past illnesses and tend to react negatively to other individuals who are hypochondriacal.[33]

Individuals with scores between 50 and 69 on Scale 1 are likely to be experiencing episodes where they are concerned about their health, are generally cautious about physical risks, and will report one or two dysfunctional organ systems. Family members tend to become impatient with these individuals. Their energy level appears to be low and there is generally some history of illnesses, surgeries, or bodily traumas.[34]

Individuals with scores between 70 and 79 generally have repetitive and intense concerns about their physical health which lead to extensive worrying. They are slow to let go of their apprehensions and overprotective of their health. They are concerned about malfunctioning in several organ systems. Family members tend to respond to these individuals in a frustrated and annoyed manner. Their energy level is low and they are quick to slow down and need considerable rest. These individuals tend to have poor health histories which are usually associated with fears about bodily function and possible traumas.[35]

Individuals with scores of 80 and above on this scale usually have intense, continuous concerns about their health which lead to equally intense apprehensions and extreme overprotectiveness of their own bodily functioning. They perceive most of their organ systems as malfunctioning and leave family members chronically drained and aggravated with feelings of being grossly manipulated. These individuals have chronically low energy levels which often lead to immobilization. These scores can be the function of traumatic health histories or of having had a frightened hypochondriacal parent.[36]

Individuals with high elevations on this scale tend to use bodily complaints as a way to avoid dealing with psychological difficulties. They can also be used to manipulate others. These individuals tend to do relatively poorly in therapy because their manipulations do not work with the therapist. Therefore, they tend to "shop around" for other therapists. Elevations on this scale tend to be "characterlogical"—that is, elevations tend to reflect long-term behavior.[37]

Hibbs, et al. found that men score significantly higher than women on this scale.[38] They suggest that this may be due to sex role sanctioning of somatizing behavior. Blacks and/or people with lower socioeconomic backgrounds tend to have higher scores on this scale also.[39] Some general rules that can be applied to interpreting this scale are as follows: the more manipulative the client is with his or her physical complaints, the higher his or her score on this scale, the less he or she is able to cope with life, the more he or she has an attitude of "you must take care of me," the more the person uses his or her somatic complaints to get out of responsibility and to gratify dependency needs, the more immaturely he or /she behaves.[40]

Carson points out that this scale may measure dependency needs which are channeled into claims of physical illness. People with high scores on Scale 1 force others to take care of them. Thus, their dependency needs are met.[41]

Graham points out that individuals with high scores on this scale are characteristically pessimistic, dissatisfied, unhappy, whiny, dull, unenthusiastic, and unambitious.[42]

Scale 2: (D) Depression

Scale 2 is a 60-item scale that has some content overlap with Scales 1 and 3. Individuals with scores under 40 on this scale would generally be described as cheerful, optimistic (possibly to the point of being unrealistic), and goal oriented.[43]

Individuals with scores of 40 to 49 are cheerful individuals who are quick and spontaneous. They are seldom depressed and tend to recover relatively quickly.[44]

Cheerfulness is a trait found in individuals with scores of 50 to 59. These individuals tend to be concerned occasionally about the future and will be slow to rebound from problem areas occasionally.[45]

Individuals with scores from 60 to 69 are often serious, with occasional pessimistic feelings. Decision making can be slowed with prolonged periods of feeling depressed. These individuals will sometimes complain of low energy level, sleep disturbance, or loss of appetite.[46]

Scores of 70 to 79 suggest unhappiness, dissatisfaction, nervousness, and worry. Individuals with scores in this range are frequently pessimistic and often indecisive. They tend to stay depressed for extended periods of time. Their reduction in energy level tends to interfere with their productivity. They also start to experience recurrent sleep and appetite problems, in addition to bodily discomforts.[47]

Individuals with scores in the 80 to 89 range are described as being chronically unhappy, worrisome, and gloomy. They have a bleak outlook on the future and little hope. Chronic indecision and chronically low levels of activity and initiative are also reported. Not only do these individuals have frequent appetite and sleep problems, but they also start to report sexual dysfunctions.[48]

Scores in the 90 to 104 range are achieved by individuals who tend to be relatively incapacitated by their depression. They remain unhappy, nothing pleases them, and they see life as being essentially hopeless. They tend to be incapable of making decisions, their output is significantly reduced, and they appear to be severely depressed.[49]

Individuals with scores beyond 105 tend to feel empty, hopeless, and as if they are in a downward spiral. They generally feel that they have to force themselves to do whatever they are doing, and their output is extremely limited.[50]

Scale 2 most frequently has the highest score of all the scales used in psychiatric profiles. Carson felt that it measured people's present attitudes about themselves in relationship to others, in addition to the people's present feelings about contentment and security.[51] Caldwell perceived it as being an indication of the degree of fear of irretrievable loss that an individual experiences.[52] Tromboli and Kilgore felt that elevations on Scale 2 were the best indicator of the extent to which an individual's typical defenses have been breached.[53] Colligan, et al. noted that Scale 2 tends to be higher for older people. This may be a function of a more dysphoric emotional tone. Colligan also pointed out that the scale tends to be negatively correlated (inversely related) to education.[54]

When looking at Scale 2, one must consider suicidal risk. The suicidal risk tends to go up as the score on Scales 4 and/or 8 or 9 rise.[55] An elevation on the 2 Scale alone tends to be an uncomplicated depression.[56]

Graham points out descriptors for a high 2 Scale include pessimism, low self-esteem, crying, agitation, irritability, worrying, feelings of uselessness, inability to function, difficulty making decisions, and ability to be controlled easily.[57]

Since many of the major clinical scales have so many items on them, subscales were developed in an effort to facilitate interpretation of identical scores. The subscales help break down the major category of the clinical scale into subcategories. For example, on the Depression Scale, an analysis of the subscales would help the examiner determine what aspects of the individual's personality were contributing primarily to the depression.[58]

Harris and Lingoes developed five subscales from the Depression Scale. The five Harris and Lingoes subscales for the Depression Scale are D_1 (Subjective Depression), D_2 (Psychomotor Retardation), D_3 (Physical Malfunctioning), D_4 (Mental Dullness), and D_5 (Brooding).

The D_1 Scale (Subjective Depression) consists of 32 items. When this scale is elevated, it indicates the amount of pessimism, poor morale, and low self-esteem that the individual is feeling. When the D_2 Scale (Psychomotor Retardation) is elevated, it measures the amount of nonparticipativeness in social relations and the immobility of the individual. The D_3 (Physical Malfunctioning) Scale identifies the amount of physical malfunctioning and preoccupation with bodily functioning that the individual is demonstrating. The D_4 (Mental Dullness) Scale looks at the client's nonresponsiveness and distrustfulness of his or her own psychological functioning. The D_5 Scale (Brooding) indicates the amount of irritability and rumination the individual is experiencing.[59]

Scale 3: (Hy) Hysteria

Scale 3 is made up of 60 items. Many of the items deal with concerns about bodily functions and pain. It is generally considered to be a measure of the dimension of pain—both emotional and bodily—that the individual is experiencing. It can include fear of physical pain, pain of rejection, pain of cruelty or mistreatment, and fear of pain as a result of devaluation or criticism.[60]

Individuals with scores under 46 on this scale are generally realistic and uninhibited in expressing their dislikes. They tend to be blunt and matter-of-fact and may be perceived by others as being too direct and caustic. They, at times, appear to be indifferent to others and perceive their own illnesses as being annoying.[61]

Scores of 46 to 59 generally represent optimal functioning.

Individuals with scores of 60 to 69 tend to be hopeful and wishful and primarily see the good side of things. They lack candor and demonstrate mild denial. These individuals avoid confrontation and become protective against perceived emotional or physical pain. They, at times, tend to use repression as a primary defense.[62]

Individuals with scores of 70 to 79 tend to be unrealistic in their perceptions, with blind spots in their ability to perceive things accurately. They are quick to repress what upsets them and tend to be excessively Pollyannaish. They avoid even minimal face-to-face confrontation. They need frequent reassuring and have strong needs for nonrejection and positive attention. They are highly protective of themselves and rapidly shift from emotional to physical pain. Individuals with scores of 80 or above are using marked denial and repression and tend not to see major adversities. "Bad" feelings are almost never directly expressed, and massive repression may take place. They cannot confront individuals face-to-face, and have insatiable needs for reassurance. Their lives are dominated by overprotection against perceived physical or emotional pains.[63]

Tromboli and Kilgore point out that people with even moderate elevations of this scale tend to inhibit direct expression of anger. They are likely to express their anger indirectly through sabotaging existing plans.[64] Carson pointed out that these individuals tend to be naive and self-centered, extroverted and superficial in their relationship with others, and lack insight into their own and motivations and actions of others. They also pointed out that these individuals cannot tolerate questioning of their way of looking at the world, make inordinate demands on counselors or therapists, and tend to want concrete solutions while resisting developing insight into their problems.[65]

Graham indicated that the descriptors of high 3 scores include the following: symptoms of preoccupation with bodily functions, lack of insight, anxiety, egotism, narcissism, social involvement, a tendency to be slow to gain insight, and a tendency to have problems with authority figures.[66]

Harris and Lingoes developed five subscales for Scale 3. They include Hy_1 (Denial of Social Anxiety), Hy_2 (Need for

Affection), Hy$_3$ (Lassitude-Malaise), Hy$_4$ (Somatic Complaints), and Hy$_5$ (Inhibition of Aggression).[67]

When Hy$_1$ (Denial of Social Anxiety) is elevated, it indicates that these clients tend to be socially extroverted. Elevation of the Hy$_2$ (Need for Affection) results in clients who obtusely deny that they have a critical or resentful attitude toward others. They are seen by others as being overly optimistic. A high Hy$_3$ (Lassitude-Malaise) elevation comes from clients who complain about functioning below par physically and mentally. An elevation of Hy$_4$ (Somatic Complaints) suggests repression and conversion of affect. The Hy$_5$ (Inhibition of Aggression) is elevated for individuals who emphasize concurrence with others and disavow violence.[68]

Triad Profiles

Scales 1, 2, and 3 together are referred to as the "neurotic triad."[69] There are many different ways the triad is interpreted. Generally, the highest of the three scores is listed first, the second highest second, and the lowest of the three scores third. For example, a 1, 2, 3 profile would indicate Scale 1 being higher than Scale 2, and Scale 2 being higher than Scale 3. There are four common neurotic triads generally reported. The first triad reported is the 1, 2, 3 triad. Individuals with this profile are generally seen to be avoiding their emotional problems. They tend to see themselves as being in declining health or "over the hill." This pattern is typical with long-term alcoholics but is unusual in females.[70] These individuals also "have a long-standing somatic overconcern manifested by hypersensitivity to even the most minor dysfunction and have constant physical complaints without adequate physical pathology."[71]

A second common configuration is a 3, 1, 2 or 1, 3, 2 profile. This is generally referred to as a conversion V. Individuals with this profile tend to convert personal troubles into rational or socially acceptable problems—that is, they convert psychological problems into somatic complaints. The greater the elevation of the 1 and 3 Scales in comparison to the 2 Scale, the more severe and long standing the resistance to change on the part of these clients. These individuals tend to be poor candidates for psychological treatment.[72]

A third common neurotic triad is the 2, 1, 3 or 2, 3, 1 triad. This is an inverted V on the profile on these scales. Individuals with this profile have multiple somatic complaints, common depression, and hysteroid features. They are generally emotionally overcontrolled and report feeling bottled up. They are usually fatigued, anxious, and filled with self-doubts, which prevent them from functioning.[73]

The last neurotic triad is the 3, 2, 1 profile. This is sometimes referred to as the ascending slope. This is typically found in females with a history of gynecological complaints.[74] In both men and women, this configuration reflects a mixed pattern of depression and somaticization concerns.[75]

Scale 4: (Pd) Psychopathic Deviate

Scale 4 is made up of 50 items. It was originally designated as the "Psychopathic Deviate Scale," based on the fact that many of the original criterion groups used in establishing this scale were prison inmates or psychiatric patients with histories of habitually transgressing social standards.[76] It is important to note, though, that not only does the 4 Scale measure deviancy, but it also measures the amount of independent thinking the individual possesses. As a result, well-educated college graduates often have a high 4 Scale without demonstrating any social deviancy.[77] Furthermore, the 4 Scale also identifies family problems and the amount of anger that one may be feeling at a particular time. Caldwell points out that individuals with high 4 Scales tend to feel parental indifference during childhood.[78] They need to turn off their resting arousal and emotionality so that they will not self-destruct. These individuals tend to describe themselves as being unwanted, unprotected, and unloved. As a result, they do not demonstrate the ability or have the opportunity to bond with their parents. These individuals tend not to show anticipatory arousal when they see trouble coming.

Scale 4 is most frequently interpreted with other scales. When Scale 9 is also elevated, the diagnosis is likely to be antisocial personality disorder. These individuals are likely to be dangerous when they are upset. Individuals with both an elevated Scale 2 and an elevated Scale 4 tend to catastrophize or overexaggerate. Individuals with Scales 2 and 8 elevated along with Scale 4 tend to become suicidal when things go wrong.[79]

Individuals with scores of 45 and under generally have life styles that are highly stable over long periods of time. Family interactions are important, stable, and valued. There is not much pressure to seek change, novelty, or the excitement of danger.[80]

Individuals with scores of 46 to 54 tend to maintain many stable and enduring relationships, and show an ongoing pursuit of long-term work and life goals. They have little difficulty accepting authority figures unless they are being abused by the authority.[81]

Individuals with scores of 55 to 69 have problems that are generally area specific. For example, if an individual is having difficulties at work, the 4 Scale aspects of his or her personality would come out at work but not in other areas.[82]

When the score is 64 to 69, then more areas tend to become involved and the consequences more self-defeating. At this level, the emotional responses are less regulated, and certain self-destructive behaviors can occur. The damages at this level tend to be tangible, but the results of the damage are also usually reversible.[83]

With scores of 70 to 79, impulse control problems exist, where the individual needs to reduce stresses in his or her life by "going for" immediate excitement. At this level, long-term goals tend to be put aside and the individual tries to get out of situations he or she perceives as being difficult. "Anger overshoots into ill-judged aggression, depressions go into tailspins, ambitions become ruthless or even cold, and sexuality can become loveless fornication. Probably the central aspects are the oversurges of emotional intensity and the destructive failures to fully anticipate the consequences of momentary decisions."[84]

Individuals with scores in the 80 to 89 range are highly vulnerable to major life disruptions. Aggression tends to lack regulation, short-term goals are predominant, and relationships are unstable. Others tend to get seriously hurt by these individuals' failures. Persons in this range tend not to be able to follow through on long-term plans.[85]

When the scores on Scale 4 are 90 or above, the individual's current life circumstances are often in a shambles. Scores this high are not unusual in prisoner samples. The normal responses to anticipated future adversities and the ability to protect oneself seem to be absent in these individuals. Their ability to regulate their emotions is truncated, varying from coldness to rage or violence. What is even more difficult for these individuals who engage in repetitive self-defeating behavior is that they have no sense of how to resolve these concerns.[86]

Researchers Kunce and Anderson state that an underlying dimension of this scale is the assertiveness and ego strength of the individual. Individuals with scores in the 60 to 70 range tend to be enterprising, frank, and adventurous, and show initiative and drive.[87] The permanence of the fighting out pattern found in adolescents with high 4s reduces over time. The adolescents tend to have difficulty with family, school, and the law.

Individuals with scores of above 70 who are over the age of 40 tend to be alcoholics or involved in embezzling or other financial types of crimes. These traits probably are unchangeable.

Lachar felt that the scale measured a continuum ranging from "inhibited over conformity on the low end to rebellious, antisocial acting out of impulses on the high end."[88] These individuals tend to see others as needing change, as opposed to themselves.[89] They function with an emotional shallowness towards others[90] and an inability to profit from experience, both good and bad.[91]

Scale 4 is affected by age. Hibbs, et al. found that the 4 Scale was higher among younger people.[92] As Schenkenberg pointed out, this is also true in the psychiatric population. Individuals with elevated 4s over 40 years of age tend to reflect long-standing antisocial behavior.[93] At the same time, individuals at 65 years of age or above with an elevated 4 are likely to reflect social alienation, apathy, and lack of involvement, rather than antisocial behavior.[94]

Looking at other variables, researchers Hokanson and Calden and Mitler, Wertz, and Counts stated that blacks score higher on the 4 Scale than whites.[95] More recently, 44 percent of the cases had the 4 Scale as their highest scale.[96]

Graham listed the following characteristics of individuals with high 4 Scale scores: difficulty in incorporating values in standards of society; asocial or antisocial behavior (lying, cheating, stealing, sexual acting out); rebellion toward authority figures; stormy family relationships; blame of parents for problems; a history of underachievement in school; poor work history; marital problems; impulsiveness; impatience; poor judgment; a tendency not to profit from experience; immaturity; creation of a good first impression; shallow superficial relationships; no definite goals; sarcasm and cynicism; resentment; tendency to feel little guilt over behavior; feigned guilt and remorse when in trouble; no disabling anxiety, depression and psychotic symptoms; a poor prognosis for change in psychotherapy or counseling; intellectualization; agreement to treatment to avoid jail or other unpleasant experiences.[97]

Greene lists the Harris and Lingoes subscales that have been developed for Scale 4. (See discussion, *supra*, in "Scale 2: (D) Depression.") The 6 scales are as follows: Pd_1 (Familial Discord), Pd_2 (Authority Conflict), Pd_3 (Social Imperturbability), Pd_{4a} (Social Alienation), Pd_{4b} (Self-Alienation), Pd_4 (Alienation).[98]

The Pd_1 (Familial Discord) Scale consists of 11 items and measures the amount of struggle the individual has against familial control. The Pd_2 (Authority Conflict) Scale indicates the level of resentment that the individual has for societal demands, standards, and mores. The Pd_3 (Social Imperturbability) Scale measures the individual's denial of social anxiety and dependency needs. The Pd_{4a} (Social Alienation) Scale indicates how isolated the individual feels from others, his or her lack of feeling of belonging, and the degree to which he or she externalizes blame. The Pd_{4b} (Self-Alienation) Scale looks at the individual's level of lack of self-integration. The Pd_4 (Alienation) Scale is simply a summation of subscales Pd_{4a} and Pd_{4b}.[99]

Scale 5: (Mf) Masculinity-Femininity

Scale 5 is a 60-item scale that was not considered to be one of the original clinical scales. Hathaway and McKinley originally intended Scale 5 to be a measure of homosexuality. However, they quickly realized that the homosexual population was too heterogeneous to be measured by one scale.[100] It is also the only scale that has different norms for males and females. It is not unusual for well-educated males to score high on the 5 scale, as it acknowledges interest in things related to poetry and drama, and other cultural and aesthetic interests. Only a few items deal with overt homosexuality. As a result, this scale tends to measure interests that are considered to be stereotypically masculine or stereotypically feminine.[101]

The scoring of the scales tends to be reversed for the sexes. However, to say that a high score for a male is equivalent to a low score for a female is an oversimplification. Caldwell looks at eight different combinations of scores.

When a male scores under 40 or a female over 90, many conclusions can be drawn. Adult males with low scores often settle into jobs that are in a stereotypical male environment. They have difficulty working with individuals with complicated feelings and tend to look more for tangible goals. Females with scores over 90 tend to ignore the obvious differences between men and women in an effort to portray the equality between the two.[102]

Males who score between 40 and 50 and females who score over 80 are conscious of their rights, responsibilities, and alliances. Male-to-male companionship is very important, but tends to be limited to shared activities without much verbalization about the relationship. Females with scores over 80 have these aspects almost absent.[103]

Males scoring between 40 and 50 and females scoring between 70 and 80 show mastery in both aesthetic and verbal groups. Practicality for these individuals tends to be more important than cultural refinement. A score of over 70 is still rare among females. However, it does tend to show up in female adolescents where their interests and activities parallel males.[104]

Males and females scoring between 60 and 70 are often in conflict over whether to be practical or to consider the feelings of others. Anger is more verbal than physical; however, physical aggression is not unknown.[105]

In females scoring between 50 and 60 and males between 70 and 80, child-mother identification is usually more intense than child-father identification. Aesthetics are generally important, and anger is expressed verbally. However, physical self-defense is seen as acceptable.[106]

In females scoring 40 to 50 and males scoring 80 to 90, time spent talking about feelings is important. They are individuals who do not have the opportunity to express feelings and feel frustrated.[107]

Females scoring 30 to 40 or males scoring 90 to 100 typically are more intense in mother-child identification. Emphasis is on feelings and gentleness, including consideration of feelings of loved ones and aesthetic orientations. Individuals in this group have a disdain for violence and expressions of anger.[108]

In females scoring under 30 and males over 100, the child-mother identification is clearly predominant. An ongoing need to speak about feelings leads to intense frustration and distress when unable to do so.[109]

Kunce and Anderson see elevated 5s in males as indicating a wide range of interests. These individuals are described as being curious and tolerant. They are also unlikely to show delinquent behavior. Males with scores above 80 tend to show an appreciation for aesthetics and usually would be described as being more passive than active.[110]

In one of the most popular MMPI textbooks written, Duckworth and Anderson point out that women who score above 50 tend to be uninterested in being seen as feminine. They may or may not have masculine interests, but they are not interested in appearing or behaving as other women do.[111]

In related studies, Colligan et al. indicated that this scale is highly related to education.[112] Duckworth and Anderson pointed out that male homosexuals are able to score in the average range on this scale as they can avoid answering obvious sex-oriented items in the scoreable direction.[113]

Graham states that males who score high on the 5 Scale typically show the following descriptors. They have conflicted thoughts about their sexual identity; are insecure in a masculine role; are effeminate and have aesthetic and artistic interests; are intelligently capable; are ambitious, competitive and persevering; show good judgment and common sense; are curious; are creative, imaginative and individualistic; are social and sensitive to others; are tolerant; are capable of expressing warm feelings towards others; are passive, dependent and submissive; have good self-control, and rarely act out. Females who score high on the 5 Scale reject the traditional female role; have stereotypic masculine interests; are active, vigorous and assertive; are competitive, aggressive and dominating; are outgoing, uninhibited and self-confident; are unemotional; and are unfriendly.[114]

Greene, author of another popular MMPI textbook, reports that Serkownek developed subscales for Scale 5. The Serkownek subscales are Mf_1 (Narcissism-Hypersensitivity), Mf_2 (Stereotypic Feminine Interest), Mf_3 (Denial of Stereotypic

Masculine Interests), Mf_4 (Heterosexual Discomfort-Passivity), Mf_5 (Introspective-Critical), and Mf_6 (Social Retiring).[115]

The Mf_1 (Narcissism-Hypersensitivity) Scale measures how sensitive individuals are to others and how easily they are hurt and upset by others. The Mf_2 (Stereotypic Feminine Interests) Scale indicates how many of the interests described by the individual are seen as clearly feminine interests. The Mf_3 (Denial of Stereotypic Masculine Interests) Scale looks at how much the individual denies interests that are clearly masculine. The Mf_4 (Heterosexual Discomfort-Passivity) Scale indicates how clearly the individual admits to homosexual tendencies. The Mf_5 (Introspective-Critical) Scale looks at how much the individual looks into himself or herself with critical thinking, and avoids loud social gatherings. The Mf_6 (Social Retiring) Scale similarly looks at how the individual would avoid social activities.

Scale 6: (Pa) Paranoia

Scale 6 includes 40 items that were originally used to discriminate psychiatric from nonpsychiatric patients with paranoid symptoms.[116] This author has evaluated a number of individuals involved in custody disputes with elevated 6 Scales, even though they do not have any other characteristics that would be considered paranoid. In this author's opinion, this is based on the fact that the adversarial custody dispute engenders suspiciousness and distrust on the part of the parties. Attorneys will often indicate to their clients that certain pieces of information should not be disclosed. Furthermore, in the custody evaluation, each party is trying to demonstrate his or her own level of competence over the perceived incompetence of the other party. Individuals with high 6 Scales will be reflecting on "who is for and who is against me." It is interesting to note that in custody disputes, when Scales 6 and 3 are elevated in a woman, that mother will often adopt the attitude of "if he struck me, it is an unforgivable act and I can't let him anywhere near the children." When the 3 and 6 are elevated together and a parent adopts this posture, the interpreter must suspect the likelihood of the problem being overstated.

Caldwell identifies individuals scoring under 50 on the 6 Scale as being balanced, trustful, and self-satisfied. It is important to note that only eight items are required to yield a T score of 50, which is an unusually low number. As a result, scores below 50 may not be as statistically reliable on Scale 6 as on other scales.[117]

For the scores that are between 55 and 70, the Harris/Lingoes Scales are particularly useful. Although these scores are not considered markedly elevated, the scales will provide the interpreter with the opportunity to see specifically which aspects of the personality the paranoia comes from.[118]

Scores in the 60 to 69 range indicate significant self-righteousness and rigidity.[119]

People who score between 70 to 79 tend to be characterized as individuals who feel that what is being said or done is specifically aimed at them, who interpret criticism as if it were directed at them, and who usually feel that they are not getting what they deserve.[120] These individuals are often described as outwardly paranoid. There are very few false positives on the paranoia scale. Individuals with scores in this range tend to have child custody disputes that go on for years.[121]

Scores of 80 and above are rarely seen unless there are serious reality distortions. The paranoia is genuine and can lead to paranoid panics, in which the individual feels threatened by anyone or anything, and is usually accompanied with some delusional thinking.[122]

Graham indicated that extreme elevations on the 6 Scale (greater than 75) indicate the following descriptors: disturbed thinking; delusions of persecution; ideas of reference; anger/resentment; and feelings of being mistreated or picked on. Individuals with elevations between 60 and 75 are described as follows: sensitive; suspicious and guarded; hostile, resentful and argumentative; moralistic and rigid; overly rational; having a poor prognosis in psychotherapy; and not open in talking about emotional problems.[123]

Greene discusses the Harris and Lingoes subscales of Pa_1 (Persecutory Ideas), Pa_2 (Poignancy), and Pa_3 (Naivete). Elevations on Pa_1 (Persecutory Ideas) indicate that the individual tends to externalize blame for his or her problems and frustrations and feels persecuted. High Pa_2 (Poignancy) scale scores result in individuals who are overly subjective, appreciate sensitive feelings, and tend to be high strung. These individuals consider themselves to be different from other people. Elevated

Pa$_3$ (Naivete) Scale scores occur in individuals who affirm moral virtues, tend to be righteous about ethical matters, and display obtuse naivete. Although items on all of these scales contribute to the overall Scale 6 score, it can be seen that different types of concern will be generated depending upon which of the Harris/Lingoes Scale 6 subscales were elevated.[124]

Scale 7: (Pt) Psychasthenia

Psychasthenia is a term that is used for a variety of psychoneurotic symptoms including anxiety, excessive worrying, obsessions, and compulsions. This scale has 48 items. A few of the items overlap with Scales 1 and 2, especially those dealing with health and physical symptoms. The scale generally measures long-term neurotic symptomology. However, it can be elevated due solely to a highly stressful situation that the individual may be experiencing.[125]

Caldwell points out that individuals with scores under 50 describe themselves as being relaxed, balanced, and placid, as well as being effective, trustful, and self-confident. Furthermore, they are seen as alert, effective, and having wide interests. Others see them as being efficient, capable, and persistent. They respond to anger in an independent self-controlled manner.[126]

Scores of 50 to 59 indicate a minimal amount of vulnerability, with these individuals generally being self-confident but feeling occasionally hesitant. Concentration problems are minimal and there is minimal disruption in response to anger.[127]

Scores of 60 to 69 are achieved by individuals who have periods of worrying that come and go. When threatened, some worrying over possible lack of success may occur. The individual begins to notice some mental lapses and some difficulty in concentrating.[128]

Individuals with scores of 70 to 79 spend much of the time worrying and have feelings of lack of self-confidence, with their concentration being repeatedly disrupted. Self-initiative is uneven, and the individual is easily threatened.[129]

With scores from 80 to 89, the individual dreads many things, such as leaving home. Individuals feel useless, and are oversensitive to trivial events. People with scores in this range often feel that they have lost control of their minds because their memories are poor and undependable. Self-initiative is limited. Perceived anger in other individuals is likely to lead to outward passivity. Individuals with scores of 90 and above see life as being a constant dread, with unending feelings of fright. Memory and concentration are noticeably impaired, and rumination, internalization, and passivity abound.[130]

Researchers Cooke and Kiesler noted that college students who later receive personal adjustment counseling have elevated 7 Scales, and male mental health clients also tend to have elevated 7 Scales.[131]

Graham listed the following descriptors for high Scale 7 scorers: experience turmoil and discomfort; are anxious, tense and agitated; are worried and apprehensive; are high strung and jumpy; have difficulties in concentrating; frequently are given a diagnosis of anxiety disorders; are introspective and ruminating; are obsessive in their thinking; are compulsive; feel insecure and inferior; lack self-confidence; are rigid and moralistic; are perfectionistic and conscientious; distort importance of problems; worry about popularity; and make slow but steady progress in psychotherapy.[132] There are no separate subscales for the Pyschasthenia Scale.

Scale 8: (Sc) Schizophrenia
Scale 8 is comprised of 78 items which makes it the longest of the ten basic clinical scales. Although it is referred to as the Schizophrenia Scale, it actually measures the amount of mental confusion that an individual is experiencing at any one time, rather than diagnosing a specific disorder. The subject is essentially saying that he or she is having experiences that do not make sense at this point and time.[133] Although the Scale 8 can sometimes be elevated in individuals who are highly creative, it does not often give false positives. The confusion demonstrated on the 8 Scale can be a function of chronic disorientation or temporary disorientation. As a result, additional sophisticated interpretation is required by the examiner. Caldwell points out that individuals with scores under 50 tend to be clear in their thinking, are involved in stable relationships, and deal with conflict relatively well.[134]

Individuals with scores of 50 to 59 rarely experience confusion in adverse situations. They become somewhat irritable under pressure, and have minimal problems with attention and memory.[135]

When scores fall between 60 and 69, some confusion starts to enter along with reports of some odd sensations and feelings of unreality.[136]

Scores in the 70 to 79 range are representative of occasional episodes of confusion with feelings of unreality becoming distressing. The individuals' emotions become somewhat unpredictable, with intrusion of strange and morbid thoughts on occasion. Unrealistic thoughts under stress, inefficient learning, chronic negativism, and irritability are also noted in individuals scoring in this range.[137]

When scores reach the 80 to 89 range, individuals experience periods of interrupted awareness and recall. Studying or concentrating on anything is often unsuccessful. Individuals may have feelings of depersonalization, and experience unreality panics and confusion. Logic does not follow, and visual hallucinations are often reported in this group. These individuals demonstrate little attention to ordinary practical details. Their emotions are either flat or unpredictable and dangerous.[138]

Individuals with scores of 90 to 104 have acute episodes of confusion over their own identity. These individuals are often not oriented to time, place, or person. They tend to report emotional oversurges coming from nowhere. Thought patterns are morbid, gruesome, and decompensated. Little that is talked about is decipherably relevant. Severe aggression and childlike negativism are often noted.[139]

With scores of 105 and above, the individual is likely to be fragmented, not able to have a complete thought, and totally flooded by uncontrollable emotion. Hallucinations of all sorts abound and tend to be very morbid. Virtually all mental content appears internally generated. Individuals with scores in this range are almost completely shut down and incapable of functioning.[140]

It is important to note that scores in these ranges must be interpreted in conjunction with the validity scales. It is not unusual for scores on this scale to enter these upper level ranges when the F Scale is grossly distorted. As a result, as indicated in the F Scale discussion, the profile may actually be invalid due to faking as opposed to a genuine "schizophrenic" process. Scores in this scale may also be elevated due to "anxiety,

homosexual panic, identity crisis or sudden personal disloca-
tion such as divorce or cultural shock."[141]

Goode and Brantner, MMPI researchers, indicated that
adolescents frequently score in the 70 or above range. With
adolescents, this maybe more a function of creative thinking
and/or identity confusion than confused thinking.[142]

The 8 Scale was used to help develop the Goldberg Index.[143]
The Goldberg Index is determined by summing the T scores on
the L, 6, and 8 scales and subtracting the sum of the scores on
the 3 and 7 scales. The scores on the L, 6, and 8 scales are considered to be representative of psychosis, while the scores on
the 3 and 7 scales representative of neurosis. The higher this
difference is, the more psychopathology the individual exhibits,
while the lower it is, the less pathological the individual is.[144]
Goldberg used 45 to divide neurotic (less than 45) from psychotic (greater than 45) profiles.

Graham identifies the following descriptors in individuals
with high 8 Scales: blatant psychotic behavior; confusion, disorganization and disorientation; unusual thoughts or attitudes; delusion; hallucinations; poor judgment; feelings of not
being a part of a social environment; feelings of unacceptance;
withdrawal, seclusion, secretiveness, and inaccessibility; shyness, aloofness, and lack of involvement; inability to express
feelings; self-doubt; feelings of inferiority, incompetence and
dissatisfaction, nonconformance, unusualness, unconventional-
ity, and eccentricity.[145]

As reported in *The MMPI: An Interpretive Manual* by Greene,
Harris and Lingoes developed three subscales of Scale 8. These
subscales have been further subdivided. The Sc_{1a} is called the
Self-Alienation Scale and Sc_{1b}, the Emotional Alienation Scale.
Altogether, the Sc_1 Scale is called the Object Loss Scale. The Sc_2
(Lack of Ego Mastery, Intrapsychic Autonomy) Scale is subdivid-
ed into the Sc_{2a} (Lack of Ego Mastery, Cognitive), Sc_{2b} (Lack of
Ego Mastery, Conative) and Sc_2 (Lack of Ego Mastery, Defective
Inhibition). The last Harris and Lingoes Scale is the Sc_3 scale of
Bizarre Sensory Experiences.[146]

The Sc_{1a} (Social Alienation) Scale measures the lack of rapport that the individual feels with others and withdrawal from
meaningful relationships. The Sc_{1b} (Emotional Alienation)
Scale indicates a lack of rapport that the individual feels with

himself or herself, including experiences of seeing himself or herself as being strange and alien. The Sc_1 (Object Loss) Scale then is a summation of Sc_{1a} and Sc_{1b}.[147]

The Sc_{2a} (Lack of Ego Mastery, Cognitive) Scale indicates the degree to which the individual admits autonomous thought processes, including strange and puzzling ideas. The Sc_{2b} (Lack of Ego Mastery, Conative) Scale indicates the amount of abulia, inertia, massive inhibition, and regression demonstrated. The Sc_{2c} (Lack of Ego Mastery, Defective Inhibition) Scale measures the individual's ability to control his or her impulses. The Sc_2 (Lack of Ego Mastery, Intrapsychic Autonomy) Scale as a whole measures the amount to which the individual is in control of his or her own sensations, perceptions, and thoughts. The Sc_3 (Bizarre Sensory Experiences) Scale measures the amount of change in perception of self, feelings of depersonalization, and estrangement.[148]

Scale 9: (Ma) Hypomania

Scale 9 is made up of 46 items. It is felt that the higher the scale the more energetic the individual feels. Individuals with low 9 Scales are considered to not have enough energy to sustain their efforts.[149]

According to Caldwell, an individual with scores under 45 generally presents himself or herself as being easygoing, someone who can sit back and listen intently without feeling the need to respond. These individuals are careful not to overcommit and are realistic with their abilities. Moods tend to be very stable as they stay easily focused on their tasks. These types of individuals also tend to dislike chemical stimulation.[150]

Individuals with scores between 45 and 54 take excitement in stride. However, they will find too much excitement to be unsettling and tiring. They have a good balance between commitment and lack of commitment, and are able to complete what they start. Anger tends to be situational and in proportion to the amount of provocation. Attention stays focused, and these individuals are able to handle distractions.[151]

When scores are between 55 and 64, individuals can "wire up" for a few hours or even a day or two. They get more talkative and tend to switch away from bad feelings. These individuals also tend to show abrupt mood shifts when under stress, but are generally balanced. They also like to be involved in many things at once and demonstrate transitory periods of excitability.[152]

Individuals with scores between 65 and 74 like stimulation and look forward to excitement. Their anticipatory excitement can occur weeks before an important event. When they get "wired up," they appear to be overly talkative, interrupt others, and may occasionally be lewd and bawdy. Under mild to moderate pressure, their moods may be abruptly labile. Their emotional intensity makes others anxious. These individuals tend to set up their lives to provide extensive stimuli. They tend to become somewhat unrealistic by being overinvolved in alternatives. Their total response output rate is easily accelerated. These individuals tend to like chemical stimulants, and find that they can survive on reduced sleep for several days. The "fight" side of the "fight or flight" arousal is easily elicited.[153]

When the score is between 75 and 84, the individual is likely to seek out excitement, appear high-strung, and be "wired" for weeks on end. One who is "wired" will hardly stop talking and others find him or her to be intrusive and disruptive. This individual also tends to get disconnected from the present, with little closure, due to impossible overcommitments. Sudden and wide mood changes are noticed and others feel frightened by this emotional intensity. The rate with which topics are changed becomes very high when "wired." The total response rate can remain high for weeks on end with individuals getting by on few hours of sleep. Emotions can overshoot into intense "fight-ready" arousal.[154]

Individuals with scores above 85 have an extremely high need for excitement and adventure and must do things to keep this high level going. They have difficulty staying connected to their task or environment for long periods. Their communication can be rambling with prolonged lability out of control. Their ability to focus seems shattered along with their ability to stay on one topic. Response rates are out of control and their activities of daily living, homeostatic processes, and other bodily functions become disrupted.[155]

Carson felt that the 9 Scale could not measure classic "hypomanics" because a classic hypomanic could not sit still long enough to take the MMPI.[156] Tromboli and Kilgore felt that the 9 Scale was a scale of one's character.[157] Colligan et al.

found that older individuals tend to score lower on the 9 Scale than the general population.[158] Hibbs found that men tend to have significantly higher scores on the 9 Scale than women.[159]

Graham used the following descriptors for high 9 Scale scorers: may have manic episodes; may manifest successive purposeless activities; has accelerated speech; may have hallucinations and delusions of grandeur; is emotionally labile; may be confused; displays flight of ideas; is energetic and talkative; prefers action to thought; has a wide range of interests; does not utilize energy wisely; is creative, enterprising, and ingenious; has little interest in routine or detail; is easily bored and restless; has difficulty inhibiting expression of impulses; has episodes of irritability, hostility, and aggressive outbursts; has unrealistic and unqualified optimism; has grandiose aspirations; exaggerates self-worth and self-importance; is unable to see own limitations; is outgoing, sociable, and gregarious; creates a good first impression; is friendly, pleasant, and enthusiastic; has superficial relationships; is manipulative, deceptive, and unreliable; harbors feelings of dissatisfaction; feels upset, tense, nervous, and anxious; is agitated and prone to worry; has poor prognosis for therapy; attends therapy irregularly; may terminate psychotherapy prematurely; and becomes hostile and aggressive toward therapists.[160]

Greene points out that Harris and Lingoes have developed four subscales for the Hypomania Scale. They are the Ma_1 (Amorality) Scale, the Ma_2 (Psychomotor Acceleration) Scale, the Ma_3 (Imperturbability) Scale, and the Ma_4 (Ego Inflation) Scale.[161]

The Ma_1 (Amorality) Scale identifies the individual's callousness about his or her own motives and goals. The individual is disarmingly frank and denies guilt feelings. The Ma_2 (Psychomotor Acceleration) Scale identifies how hyperactive and labile the individual is. It also measures the amount of anxiety and pressure for action. The Ma_3 (Imperturbability) Scale measures the individual's confidence in social situations, his or her denial of sensitivity and his or her proclaimed independence from the opinions of others. The Ma_4 (Ego Inflation) Scale measures how self-important the individual feels, even to the point of unrealistic grandiosity.[162]

Scale 0: (Si) Social Introversion

Scale 0, along with Scale 5, was not one of the original clinical scales developed. There are 70 items on this scale that are identified as indicating either social extroversion or social introversion. High Si Scales scores tend to show shyness, whereas a low 0 Scale is likely to indicate an individual who shows leadership and does not tolerate being alone.[163]

With scores of 45 or below, Caldwell felt that individuals may have a certain amount of exhibitionism.[164] Carson felt that these people may also have a need to be attracted to others.[165] Drake and Oetting, early researchers on the MMPI, felt that women with scores below 45 usually show good social adjustment, including parental relationships. However, with men, the social adjustment does not necessarily indicate freedom from parental conflicts. Drake and Oetting also stated that men in this range may show social aggressiveness.[166] With scores below 30, according to Duckworth and Anderson, individuals demonstrate a certain flightiness and superficiality in their relationships. They do not tend to establish relationships of real intimacy.[167]

Graham summarizes descriptors of high 0 Scale scores as follows: socially introverted; more comfortable alone; reserved, timid, shy, and retiring; uncomfortable around members of the opposite sex; self-effacing and lacking self-confidence; hard to get to know; sensitive to what others think; overcontrolled and not likely to display feelings openly; submissive and compliant; overly accepting of authority; serious; reliable and dependable; cautious, conventional, and unoriginal; rigid and inflexible; indecisive, even for minor decisions; worrisome and irritable.[168]

With moderate elevations of 60 to 70, Cottle's research found that the individual feels more comfortable alone or in a small group rather than with a large group of people.[169] Kunce and Anderson felt that scores in this range were an indication of personal autonomy and self direction.[170] According to Carson, individuals with scores above 70 feel withdrawn and anxious and are generally shy and socially insecure. They also do not connect well with others.[171] Tromboli and Kilgore felt that elevations in this range reflect the use of avoidance and withdrawal, which may be accompanied by suspiciousness.[172]

Greene identifies the 6 Serkownek Subscales that were developed for the 0 Scale. They are as follows: the Si_1

(Inferiority-Personal Discomfort) Scale, the Si_2 (Discomfort with Others) Scale, the Si_3 (Staid-Personal Rigidity) Scale, the Si_4 (Hypersensitivity) Scale, the Si_5 (Distrust) Scale, and the Si_6 (Physical-Somatic Concerns) Scale.[173]

The Si_1 (Inferiority-Personal Discomfort) Scale measures how uncomfortable or unhappy the individual feels based on perceived lack of interpersonal skills. The Si_2 (Discomfort with Others) Scale measures how uncomfortable the individual feels with other people. The Si_3 (Staid-Personal Rigidity) Scale measures the lack of pleasure the individual gets from participating in social groups. The Si_4 (Hypersensitivity) Scale measures how sensitive the individual is to reactions of others and how likely he or she is to avoid stressful situations. The Si_5 (Distrust) Scale measures how dishonest, insincere, and selfish the individual feels others are. The Si_6 (Physical-Somatic Concerns) Scale measures how much concern the individual has about bodily functions and physical appearance.[174]

Critical Items

There are 550 unique items on the MMPI. Although the MMPI is generally interpreted through combinations of items referred to as scales, clinicians are generally unwilling to ignore the clinical information that can be derived from specific items. The original concept of critical items was to select those items that were "highly indicative of severe psychopathology." It becomes the examiner's responsibility to go over those critical items answered in the scoreable direction with each individual. The clinician then uses his or her clinical judgment to determine if the explanation for the answer is reasonable, or indeed represents severe psychopathology. When the explanation of the critical item answers is reasonable, the interpretation of elevated clinical scales should be reduced. On the other hand, if the explanation for the answers on the critical items represents severe psychopathology, the scores on the clinical scales would more likely be accurate. For example, an item like, "I believe I'm being followed," is a critical item. However, if the subject's spouse has hired a private investigator to follow the individual, it would be a legitimate concern. On the other hand, if the subject's response to this item is "no matter where I go there are people in bushes taking pictures of me, standing on rooftops drawing sketches of me, and hiding in my kitchen cupboards," this would be a representation of severe psychopathology. As a result, it is essential that the clinician identify the source of the concern resulting in the response given.

Four sets of critical items have been developed over the years. Grayson identified the 38 items in 1951. Caldwell listed 78 different items in 9 content areas in 1969. Koss and Butcher selected 73 items in 1973 to be used as critical items. The most recent list was developed by Lachar and Wrobel in 1979. Through a complicated research process, they identified 11 content areas representing 111 items. Today the Koss and Butcher and Lachar and Wrobel lists of critical items are most frequently used by clinicians.[175]

Supplementary or Research Scales

There are a group of additional scales that were developed after the original MMPI was developed that are referred to as supplementary scales, research scales, or frequently scored scales. These scales tend to identify certain aspects of an individual's personality as opposed to the global measures indicated by the clinical scales.

A Scale (First Factor-Anxiety Scale)

This 39-item scale was originally developed by Welsh and generally reflects conscious emotional upset about questions concerning thinking and thought process, negative emotional tone, lack of energy, pessimism, and personal sensitivity.[176] It is strongly related to overanxiety and measures tension, nervousness, and distress. On retests, the A Scale was considered to be somewhat unstable, implying that it fluctuates in response to differing levels of anxiety.[177]

Individuals with scores below 45 on this scale are considered to not be consciously anxious. Individuals with scores above 60 on this scale are consciously anxious, easily upset, and pessimistic.[178]

R Scale (Repression Scale)

The R Scale includes 40 items which are designed to measure "health and physical symptoms, emotionality, violence in activity, reactions to other people in social situations; social dominance, feelings of personal adequacy and personal appearance; and personal and vocational interests."[179] On this scale, the individual is consciously denying these negative traits.

Scores below 45 on the R Scale indicate that the individual is not consciously repressing feelings and attitudes, while scores above 60 on the R Scale indicate that the individual prefers to avoid unpleasant topics or situations.[180]

The A Scale and the R Scale are often interpreted in combination with one another. When an individual has a high A Scale score and a low R Scale score, the person would be considered to be anxious and open and is probably motivated to work on problem areas. However, a high R Scale score and low A Scale score indicates an individual consciously repressing information who is likely to be difficult to work with in therapy. When both A and R Scale scores are high, not only is the person consciously anxious, but he or she is also consciously attempting to repress his or her concerns. This type of individual is very difficult to work with in a therapeutic environment.[181]

Es Scale (Ego Strength Scale)

The Ego Strength Scale is comprised of 68 items reported by F. Barron in 1953.[182] The higher the score on the Ego Strength Scale, the more likely it is that the individual is to recover from problems without long-term negative effects. The lower the Ego Strength Scale, the more likely the individual is going to have difficulty coping with everyday problems and recovering from identified concerns. Individuals with high Ego Strength Scale scores tend to return to homeostasis rapidly and will succeed better in therapy. Individuals with low Ego Strength Scale scores often have sufficient difficulty functioning that they may require hospitalization.[183]

Lb Scale (Low Back Pain Functional Scale)

The Lb Scale is a 25-item scale developed by Hanvick in 1949. The scale was originally developed in an effort to differentiate between individuals with organic low back pain and functional low back pain (no organic etiology). In addition to its defined purpose, though, it also tends to measure a person's ability to maintain a friendly, calm facade while feeling frustration and discontent/anger at a preconscious level.[184] An individual with a high Lb score tends to feel that anger is not appropriate, that he or she cannot do anything about felt anger, and that his or her needs are not seen by others as important.[185]

Ca Scale (Caudality Scale)

The Caudality Scale is a 36-item scale developed by H.L. Williams in 1952.[186] The scale was originally developed to differentiate between patients with focal cerebral damage in the parietal area from individuals with focal lesions in temporal areas. However, the research has indicated that it correlates highly with anxiety levels. Williams indicated that high scores tend to indicate anxiety, depression, guilt, introversion, feelings of inadequacy, worry about the future, and somatic concern. Low scores, on the other hand, tend to indicate denial of anxiety and worry and a feeling of acceptance by other people.[187]

Dy Scale (Dependency Scale)

The Dependency Scale was developed by Navran in 1954, and contains 57 items. It is a relatively easy scale to interpret, as the higher the score, the more the individual is psychologically dependent upon others, while the lower the score, the more independent he or she is.[188]

Do Scale (Dominance Scale)

The Dominance Scale is a 28-item scale developed in 1951 by Gough, McClosky, and Meehl.[189] Like the Dependency Scale, this scale is relatively easy to interpret. The higher the score, the more the individual feels in charge of his or her life, while the lower the score, the more the individual feels not in charge. The Dy and Do Scales are often interpreted together. A low Dy and high Do Scale score indicates an individual who has leadership capabilities. On the other hand, a high Dy and low Do Scale score is indicative of a person who feels unable to take charge of his or her life and tends to feel the need to rely on others.[190]

Re Scale (Social Responsibility Scale)

The Social Responsibility Scale was developed by Gough, McClosky, and Meehl, and contains 32 items.[191] Individuals receiving high scores on this scale are generally considered to be socially responsible and willing to accept the consequences of their behavior. Low scores are indicative of lack of social responsibility. With individuals under 25 years of age, a low score may be a function of rejection of parental values as opposed to social irresponsibility.[192]

Pr Scale (Prejudice Scale)

The Prejudice Scale contains 32 items and was originally developed by Gough as a measure of anti-Semitic prejudice.[193] The scale measures much more than prejudice. It is an indication of the individual's ability to tolerate opinions of others that are different from his or her own. Individuals with low scores on the Pr Scale are generally seen as open-minded and willing to entertain opinions of others that differ from their own. Persons with scores above 55 on the Pr Scale tend to be more rigid in their belief and less able to tolerate the opinions of others.[194]

St Scale (Status Scale)

The Status Scale is a 34-item scale developed by Gough in 1949.[195] The scale was originally developed in an effort to distinguish those individuals of high socioeconomic status from those of low socioeconomic status. What it actually measures is the status level that the individual desires as opposed to his or her current level. High scores (above 55) on the St Scale generally indicate a desire for things to be better in an individual's life.[196] Low scores (below 40) are generally found in individuals who work in low status jobs, have low self-esteem, low self-confidence, and low motivation.[197]

Cn Scale (Control Scale)

The Control Scale is made up of 50 items and was developed in 1953 by Cuadra.[198] This scale measures how much control the individual has over problem areas. If clinical scales are elevated along with the Control Scale, it would suggest that the individual has the ability to control his or her problem areas in the presence of others. However, a low control score is an indication that those areas identified in the clinical scales are likely to be visibly demonstrated by the individual because he or she cannot exert control over the expression of symptoms.[199]

Mac Scale (MacAndrew Alcoholism Scale)

The scale was originally developed by MacAndrew in 1965 and contains 49 items. Although it is one of the more recently developed MMPI scales, it is used widely today in making a differential diagnosis of alcoholism or other chemical dependence.[200] A cutoff raw score of 24 is usually indicative of alcoholism or other chemical dependence, with every point higher increasing the probability the diagnosis is accurate.[201] Even alcoholics sober for years do not generally go below 24. High scores are generally predictive of opiate and/or alcohol abuse, but not necessarily predictive of smoking, or cocaine or marijuana use.[202] It is also a very difficult scale to fake, as most of the items do not directly relate to substance use or abuse. They instead relate to characteristics that alcoholics tend to indicate in answering MMPI items. Often individuals with high scores feel the "pull" of substance abuse but work hard to control this pull. Individuals with scores in the high range on this scale who are not alcoholics or substance abusers have a much greater propensity to become alcoholics or substance abusers.[203]

Researchers Preng and Klopton stated that the MacAndrew Alcoholism Scale was able to differentiate alcoholics from non-alcoholic psychiatric patients, but not able to differentiate alcoholic psychiatric patients from their nonalcoholic psychiatric counterparts. As a result, they concluded, it appears that the MacAndrew Scale may be unable to identify alcoholics among patients with combined alcoholic/psychiatric diagnoses.[204]

O-H Scale (Overcontrolled Hostility Scale)

The Overcontrolled Hostility Scale was developed in 1967 by Megargee, Cook, and Mendelsohn. The scale was used to differentiate between under-controlled and over-controlled assaultive individuals. The under-controlled individuals were felt to have failed to learn to control their aggressive impulses, whereas the over-controlled individuals rigidly defended against expression of impulsive aggressiveness. However, in those case where these over-controlled individuals did express anger, it tended to come out in extreme forms including severe physical assaults.[205] High scorers on the O-H were described as displaying excessive control of their hostile impulses and feeling socially alienated. They also tend to be reluctant to admit any psychological symptomology.

Wiggins Content Scales

In 1966, Wiggins developed 13 content scales. Greene reports the description and interpretation of high scores on the content scales as follows:

SOC—Social Maladjustment. An individual with a high SOC is socially bashful, shy, and embarrassed, while a person with a low SOC score is gregarious, confident, and assertive.

DEP—Depression. A high DEP person experiences guilt, regret, and worry, in addition to difficulty in concentrating and reduced motivation.

FEM—Feminine Interest. A high FEM scale indicates an individual who tends to appreciate stereotypically feminine interests.

MOR—Poor Morale. A high MOR person is an individual lacking in self-confidence who possesses feelings of failure and is given to despair.

REL—Religious Fundamentalism. Individuals with high scores on this scale portray themselves as being religious and fundamentalist in their beliefs.

AUT—Authority Conflict. High AUT individuals see life as problematic and are convinced that others are dishonest, hypocritical, and motivated by personal profit. These people tend to distrust others and have little respect for experts or other authorities.

PSY—Psychoticism. High PSY individuals admit a number of classic psychotic symptoms, including hallucinations, delusions, and paranoid feelings.

ORG—Organic Symptoms. The high ORG person tends to admit to a number of somatic symptoms, e.g., headaches, nausea, poor concentration, and memory-related problems.

FAM—Family Problems. A high FAM person feels that home life is unpleasant and there is a lack of love replaced by argumentativeness, anger, and tension.

HOS—Manifest Hostility. A high HOS individual tends to be uncooperative, argumentative, and retaliatory. Impulsivity may be associated with assaultive or other violent behavior.

PHO—Phobias. A high PHO admits a number of fears that would fit into phobic categories.

HYP—Hypomania. High scorers characterize themselves as feeling restless, tense, and energetic.

HEA—Poor Health. An individual with a high HEA is concerned about physical problems, especially in the gastrointestinal area.[206]

Tryon, Stein, and Chu Cluster Scales (TSC Scales)

The TSC Scales were developed in 1968. Greene[207] discusses the TSC Cluster Scales. Seven cluster scales containing 192 items were derived from their research. High scores on each of the cluster scales indicates the presence of certain behavior for which the scale is named, while low scores indicate the presence of more adaptive behavior. The following table describes the TSC clusters.

Abbreviation	Number of Items	Description
I or TSC I	26	social introversion v. interpersonal poise and outgoingness
B or TSC II	33	body symptoms v. lack of physical complaints
S or TSC III	25	suspicion and mistrust v. absence of suspicion
D or TSC IV	28	depression and apathy v. positive and optimistic outlook
R or TSC V	21	resentment and aggression v. lack of resentment and aggression
A or TSC VI	23	autism and disruptive thought v. absence of such disturbance
T or TSC VII	36	tension, worry, and fear v. absence of such complaints[208]

There has been almost no report of research on the TSC Scales since they were originally published. As a result, they tend not to be weighed as much as some of the other subscales developed for the MMPI.

Wiener-Harmon Subtle-Obvious Subscales

The Wiener-Harmon Subtle-Obvious Scales are used relatively infrequently in interpreting the MMPI. The purpose for the scales is to identify those items that, on face validity, identify obvious emotional disturbances compared to more subtle items that are relatively difficult to detect as reflecting emotional disturbance.[209]

The research done identified 110 subtle and 146 obvious items. These were then subclassified into those items which fell on Scales 2, 3, 4, 6, and 9. The Subtle-Obvious Scales have been helpful in identifying both fake good and fake bad profiles. An individual who has T scores near 70 on the Subtle Scales who also has T scores which are relatively low on the Obvious Scales is likely to be trying to exaggerate problems. The converse relationship would be indicative of "faking bad."[210] In the absence of other evidence of an attempt to "fake" in either direction, these scales should not be emphasized.

Dubinsky et al., researchers in this area, summarize this concept by stating, "when subjects attempt to manipulate MMPI scores, they tend to successfully increase or decrease their scores for obvious items, but scores for subtle items tend to move in the opposite direction from that desired."[211]

MMPI-2 (1989 REVISION)

Over 12,000 research articles and books have been written on the MMPI since its inception almost 50 years ago. The revision team of Butcher, Graham, Dahlstrom, and Tellegan decided that it was essential to not attempt to reinvent the wheel. As a result, they thought it was necessary to keep as much of the original MMPI as possible. The revision team concluded that a revision was necessary because of the following reasons: some of the original MMPI items were out of date; some were objectionable; a number of items were not scored on useful scales; there was a need to expand the item pool to address new problem areas; and there was a need to develop new norms for the MMPI.

Seventy-six items were considered objectionable based on being sexist, being bodily items, or being religious items. Fourteen percent of the original items were rewritten to eliminate double negatives, obsolete terms, and sexist language.

Some changes were made to the supplementary scales. Four new items were added to the MacAndrew Alcoholism Scale to replace four that were deleted. They were validated in the same manner as the original MacAndrew items in consultation with MacAndrew. The Anxiety and Repressions scales remained essentially the same, while the Ego Strength Scale lost 12 items with no significant difference in the outcome. The Overcontrolled Hostility Scale remained intact.

The authors of the MMPI-2 concluded that some changes in other subscales were warranted. The Harris and Lingoes Subscales remained virtually intact. However, the Serkownek Scales were eliminated. The Subtle-Obvious Scales were kept largely intact and can still be scored, although there was disagreement among the revision team as to whether they should still be used. The Wiggins Content Scales were eliminated since they included many of the previous objectionable items. However, there are a number of new content scales that were developed that measure basically the same things as some of the important previous Wiggins Scales measured. These scales include the Bizarre Mentation, Anger, Cynicism, and Antisocial Practices Scales.

Another new scale added to the MMPI is a second F Scale referred to as the "Back Page F" Scale. It utilizes items in the latter third of the test booklet in an effort to measure changes in test-taking attitude between the beginning and end of the test. In addition, Tellegan developed an MPQ scale to measure consistency of responding. With the MMPI-2 an F Scale can be as high as 100 for inpatients and 90 for outpatients and still be considered to be valid.

The two point codes can be interpreted using the same interpretation methods as on the MMPI. Using a cutoff of 65 on the MMPI-2, there is a 90 percent congruence in the two point code interpretations between the MMPI and the MMPI-2.

Although 704 items were included in the revision draft, the MMPI-2 ended up with 567 items, only one more than the original MMPI. Twenty-six hundred subjects were randomly selected for the normative sample. In addition, a number of other large groups were tested to verify the utility of the MMPI-2, but not included in the normative sample. The entire revision process took seven years. The MMPI-2 requires a sixth- to eighth-grade reading level as compared to a sixth-grade reading level for the MMPI. As was true of the MMPI, the MMPI-2 is useful for individuals 18 years and older, with an adolescent version designed for individuals 14 to 17 years of age.

There are many differences between the MMPI and the MMPI-2. The cutoff score for interpretation on the MMPI was a T score of 70. However, the cutoff score for the interpretation on the MMPI-2 is a T score of 65. In conclusion, the authors state that the MMPI scales are the same—so the existing interpretative data can be used freely. None of the 50 years of research needs to be discarded.

Variability of Scores

The Graham and McCord study on the MMPI concluded: "The results of this study can be viewed . . . that . . . MMPI scores not extremely elevated . . . tend to be indicative of relatively more negative than positive characteristics. There was little support for the Kunce and Anderson suggestion that moderately elevated scores are suggested of more positive counterparts . . ."[212]

Additional research by Hunsley et al. found that the MMPI had reliability values from .71 to .84 and stability values from .63 to .86. There was also a strong relationship between the reliability and stability of the scales. These results not only support the reliability of the instrument, but also its stability over time.[213]

Further research by Haier et al. does conclude that extreme scores on MMPI scales in nonhospitalized previously undiagnosed individuals are indicative of psychiatric disorders. This serves to further substantiate the utility of the MMPI in custody evaluations with nonpsychiatric patients.[214]

Concerns in Custody Cases

Graham reported that individuals with a "27" profile (elevation on the 2 and 7 scales) will not do well with a child who needs a lot of support to offset a poor self-concept. He also indicated that individuals with a 49 profile will not do well with children needing structure. There is no "good parent" MMPI profile that has been developed. Instead, the psychologist must look at how the parent's MMPI profile matches with the child's needs.[215]

This author has found that, in addition to the concerns that were identified by Graham, many of the research, supplementary, and subscales of the MMPI can be valuable in making a custody determination. An individual with a low Ego Strength Scale may not have the psychic energy necessary to deal with crises and problem solving in child rearing. An individual with a high MacAndrew Alcoholism Scale carries with it all of the concerns involved in dealing with alcoholics. Individuals with high Repression Scales or Overcontrolled Hostility Scales may have a considerable amount of underlying anger that is not being dealt with appropriately. As a result, these individuals may be recommended for individual psychotherapy. Individuals with low Control Scales may not have sufficient control over the problem areas in their lives. Mothers with a high 3 and 6 are likely to feel that "if he struck me, it is an unforgivable act and I can't let him near my children." If the Pa$_3$ Scale is elevated along with a high 6 Scale, there is an unforgiving aspect to that individual's personality. A parent with a high 3 Scale is likely to overreact to or overinterpret problem areas. As a result, reports of episodes and incidents possibly overstated must be weighed with these tendencies in mind.

It is very important in reading this summary not to apply the interpretations as if they were etched in concrete and irrefutable. Interpretations require sophisticated integration of data. The above information should serve as guidelines. It is not intended to be prescriptive in nature.

MILLON CLINICAL MULTIAXIAL INVENTORY (MCMI)

The Millon Clinical Multiaxial Inventory was developed by Millon and modeled after the MMPI-type inventories. It is short, with only 175 items, and is scored in a true-false manner. It is used with individuals over 17 years of age and beyond an eighth-grade reading level. Twenty scales have been developed, falling into three major categories; 1) Basic Personality Patterns; 2) Pathological Personality Disorders; 3) Clinical Symptom Syndromes. The Millon is a relatively new instrument which the author states is not considered a general personality instrument to be used for "normal populations." The MMPI is generally considered to be better suited for assessment of acute clinical problems. An MCMI-2 has recently been published with broader-based reliability and validity studies. The instrument holds promise as an adjunct to the MMPI, but is unlikely to replace the MMPI.[216]

CALIFORNIA PSYCHOLOGICAL INVENTORY (CPI)

The California Psychological Inventory (CPI) is still another instrument similar to the MMPI. Unlike the MMPI and the MCMI, it was developed for use with "normal adult populations."

There are 462 true and false items yielding scores on 20 scales. Three validity scales are followed by 17 scales that assess personality dimensions (e.g., Dominance, Sociability, Responsibility, Empathy, Independence). The last two scales were added in the 1987 revision of the CPI. Cross-validation studies have yielded significant group differences, and criterion correlations are often low. The 1987 revision allows for better descriptions of the results and the addition of a new interpretive model. This instrument is not widely used and would be of little value in custody evaluations.[217]

SIXTEEN PERSONALITY FACTOR QUESTIONNAIRE (16PF)

Through the use of a statistical process called factor analysis, Cattell developed a personality inventory referred to as the Sixteen Personality Factor Questionnaire (16PF). It is designed for use with individuals 16 years of age and older and looks at such traits as "reserved vs. outgoing, humble vs. assertive, and trusting vs. suspicious." These scales are short, information is on normative samples, and test construction is inadequate. The test never gained the acclaim that the authors had hoped.[218]

PERSONALITY INVENTORY FOR CHILDREN (PIC)

The PIC is designed primarily for children and adolescents between 6 and 16 years of age. It is often considered a downward extension of the MMPI. However, the difference between the PIC and MMPI lies in the fact that the 600 true and false items are answered not by the child, but by knowledgeable adults. It contains three validity scales, a general screening scale, and twelve clinical scales. The validity scales are similar to the MMPI validity scales. The fourth scale is a screening scale to aid in identifying children in need of psychological evaluation. The twelve clinical scales are designed to assess the child's cognitive development, academic achievement, and emotional and interpersonal problems (e.g., depression, anxiety, withdrawal, hyperactivity). Although it is a relatively new instrument, and continuing research needs to be performed, it shows great promise as a personality inventory for children.[219]

ENDNOTES

1. J. Duckworth & W. Anderson, MMPI Interpretation Manual for Counselors and Clinicians 40 (3d ed. 1986) [hereinafter MMPI Interpretation Manual for Counselors and Clinicians].

2. *Id.*

3. *Id.* at 41.

4. *Id.* at 47.

5. J. Pearson & W. Swenson, A User's Guide to the Mayo Clinic Automated MMPI Program 14 (1967) [hereinafter A User's Guide].

6. MMPI Interpretation Manual for Counselors and Clinicians, *supra* note 1, at 48.

7. *Id.*

8. *Id.*

9. *Id.* at 49.

10. *Id.* at 50.

11. *Id.*

12. *Id.*

13. *Id.* at 51.

14. *Id.* at 55.

15. *Id.* at 49.

16. *Id.* at 62.

17. *Id.*

18. *Id.* at 63.

19. *Id.*

20. *Id.* at 64.

21. *Id.* at 64–65.

22. *Id.* at 65.

23. *Id.*

24. *Id.* at 69.

25. *Id.* at 73.

26. R. Greene, The MMPI: An Interpretive Manual 50 (1980) [hereinafter R. Greene, The MMPI].

27. *Id.*

28. N. Galluci, *The Influence of the Elevated F Scales on the Validity of Adolescent MMPI Profiles*, 51 J. Personality Assessment 138 (1987).

29. W. Dahlstrom, G. Welsh & L. Dahlstrom, An MMPI Handbook, Volume I Clinical Interpretation 169 (rev. ed. 1982) [hereinafter An MMPI Handbook, Volume I Clinical Interpretation].

30. *Id.* at 170.

31. MMPI Interpretation Manual for Counselors and Clinicians, *supra* note 1, at 76.

32. J. Graham, The MMPI: A Practical Guide 37 (2d ed. 1987) [hereinafter J. Graham, The MMPI].

33. A User's Guide, *supra* note 5, at 16.

34. A. Caldwell, "Families of MMPI Code Types," paper presented at the 12th Annual Symposium on the MMPI, Tampa, Florida (1982) [hereinafter "Families of MMPI Code Types"].

35. *Id.*

36. *Id.*

37. MMPI Interpretation Manual for Counselors and Clinicians, *supra* note 1, at 80.

38. *Id.* at 81.

39. *Id.*

40. *Id.* at 82.

41. *Id.* at 83.

42. J. Graham, The MMPI, *supra* note 32, at 39–40.

43. A User's Guide, *supra* note 5, at 16.

44. "Families of MMPI Code Types," *supra* note 34.

45. *Id.*

46. *Id.*

47. *Id.*

48. *Id.*

49. *Id.*

50. *Id.*

51. MMPI Interpretation Manual for Counselors and Clinicians, *supra* note 1, at 96.

52. *Id.*

53. *Id.*

54. *Id.* at 97.

55. *Id.* at 98.

56. *Id.* at 99.

57. J. Graham, The MMPI, *supra* note 32, at 42.

58. R. Greene, The MMPI, *supra* note 26, at 74.

59. *Id.* at 75

60. A User's Guide, *supra* note 5, at 17.

61. "Families of MMPI Code Types," *supra* note 34.

62. *Id.*

63. *Id.*

64. MMPI Interpretation Manual for Counselors and Clinicians, *supra* note 1, at 121.

65. *Id.* at 123.

66. J. Graham, The MMPI, *supra* note 32, at 45.

67. R. Greene, The MMPI, *supra* note 26, at 79.

68. *Id.*

69. MMPI Interpretation Manual for Counselors and Clinicians, *supra* note 1, at 133; R. Greene, The MMPI, *supra* note 26, at 182; An MMPI Handbook, Volume I Clinical Interpretation, *supra* note 29, at 20.

70. MMPI Interpretation Manual for Counselors and Clinicians, *supra* note 1, at 134.

71. R. Greene, The MMPI, *supra* note 26, at 83.

72. J. Graham, The MMPI, *supra* note 32, at 82–83.

73. R. Greene, The MMPI, *supra* note 26, at 84.

74. MMPI Interpretation Manual for Counselors and Clinicians, *supra* note 1, at 136.

75. R. Greene, The MMPI, *supra* note 26, at 84.

76. A User's Guide, *supra* note 5, at 18.

77. *Id.*

78. "Families of MMPI Code Types," *supra* note 34.

79. *Id.*

80. *Id.*

81. *Id.*

82. *Id.*

83. *Id.*

84. *Id.*

85. *Id.*

86. *Id.*

87. Kunce & Anderson, *Normalizing the MMPI*, 32 J. Clinical Psychology 776–80 (1976) [hereinafter *Normalizing the MMPI*]; Kunce & Anderson, *Perspectives on Uses of the MMPI and Non-Psychiatric Settings*, Advances in Psychological Assessment [hereinafter *Perspectives on Uses of the MMPI* in MMPI Interpretation Manual for Counselors and Clinicians, *supra* note 1, at 139.

88. D. Lachar, The MMPI: Clinical Assessment and Automated Interpretation (1974) in MMPI Interpretation Manual for Counselors and Clinicians, *supra* note 1, at 139.

89. An MMPI Handbook, Volume I Clinical Interpretation, *supra* note 29.

90. An MMPI Handbook, Volume I Clinical Interpretation, *supra* note 29, and Volume II in MMPI Interpretation Manual for Counselors and Clinicians, *supra* note 1, at 141.

91. R. Carkhauff, L. Barnette & J. McCall, The Counselor's Handbook: Scale and Profile Interpretations of the MMPI (1965), in MMPI Interpretation Manual for Counselors and Clinicians, *supra* note 1, at 141.

92. B. Hibbs, J. Kobas & J. Gonzalez, *Effects of Ethnicity, Sex and Age on MMPI Profiles*, 45 Psychological Reports 591, 597 (1979) [hereinafter *Effects of Ethnicity, Sex and Age on MMPI Profiles*] in MMPI Interpretation Manual for Counselors and Clinicians, *supra* note 1, at 142.

93. P. Good & J. Brantner, A Practical Guide to the MMPI (1974) [hereinafter A Practical Guide to the MMPI] in MMPI Interpretation Manual for Counselors and Clinicians, *supra* note 1, at 142.

94. *Id.*

95. J. Hokanson & G. Calden, *Negro-White Differences on the MMPI*, 16 J. Clinical Psychology 32–33 (1960); and C. Mitler, C. Wertz & S. Counts, *Racial Differences on the MMPI*, 17 J. Clinical Psychology 140–59, 161 in MMPI Interpretation Manual for Counselors and Clinicians, *supra* note 1, at 143.

96. R. Craig, *A Comparison of MMPI Profiles of Heroin Addicts Based on Multiple Methods of Classification*, 48 J. Personality Assessment 115–29 in MMPI Interpretation Manual for Counselors and Clinicians, *supra* note 1, at 143.

97. J. Graham, The MMPI, *supra* note 32, at 48–49.

98. R. Greene, The MMPI, *supra* note 26, at 87.

99. *Id.*

100. A User's Guide, *supra* note 5, at 19.

101. *Id.* at 20.

102. "Families of MMPI Code Types," *supra* note 34.

103. *Id.*

104. *Id.*

105. *Id.*

106. *Id.*

107. *Id.*

108. *Id.*

109. *Id.*

110. *Normalizing the MMPI, supra* note 87, at 776–80; *Perspectives on Uses of the MMPI, supra* note 87, in MMPI Interpretation Manual for Counselors and Clinicians, *supra* note 1, at 163.

111. MMPI Interpretation Manual for Counselors and Clinicians, *supra* note 1, at 164–65.

112. Colligan, Osborn, Swenson & Offord, *Development of Contemporary Norms*, 40 J. Clinical Psychology 100–07 (1984) [hereinafter *Development of Contemporary Norms*] in MMPI Interpretation Manual for Counselors and Clinicians, *supra* note 1, at 165.

113. MMPI Interpretation Manual for Counselors and Clinicians, *supra* note 1, at 166.

114. J. Graham, The MMPI, *supra* note 32, at 53–54.

115. R. Greene, The MMPI, *supra* note 26, at 91.

116. A User's Guide, *supra* note 5, at 20.

117. "Families of MMPI Code Types," *supra* note 34.

118. *Id.*

119. *Id.*

120. R. Carson, *Interpretative Manual to the MMPI*, MMPI: Research Developments and Clinical Applications 279–96 (1969) in MMPI Interpretation Manual for Counselors and Clinicians, *supra* note 1, at 180.

121. "Families of MMPI Code Types," *supra* note 34.

122. *Id.*

123. J. Graham, The MMPI, *supra* note 32, at 57–58.

124. R. Greene, The MMPI, *supra* note 26, at 96.

125. A User's Guide, *supra* note 5, at 21.

126. "Families of MMPI Code Types," *supra* note 34.

127. *Id.*

128. *Id.*

129. *Id.*

130. *Id.*

131. Cooke & Kiester, *Prediction of College Students Who Later Require Personal Counseling*, 14 J. Counseling Psychology 346–49 (1967) in MMPI Interpretation Manual for Counselors and Clinicians, *supra* note 1, at 192.

132. J. Graham, The MMPI, *supra* note 32, at 60–61.

133. MMPI Interpretation Manual for Counselors and Clinicians, *supra* note 1, at 201.

134. "Families of MMPI Code Types," *supra* note 34.

135. *Id.*

136. *Id.*

137. *Id.*

138. *Id.*

139. *Id.*

140. *Id.*

141. MMPI Interpretation Manual for Counselors and Clinicians, *supra* note 1, at 203.

142. A Practical Guide to the MMPI, *supra* note 93, in MMPI Interpretation Manual for Counselors and Clinicians, *supra* note 1, at 205.

143. L. Goldberg, *Diagnosticians vs. Diagnostic Signs: The Diagnosis of Psychosis vs. Neurosis for the MMPI*, 79 Psychological Monographs 602 (1965).

144. *Id.*

145. J. Graham, The MMPI, *supra* note 32, at 64.

146. R. Greene, The MMPI, *supra* note 26, at 103.

147. *Id.*

148. *Id.*

149. MMPI Interpretation Manual for Counselors and Clinicians, *supra* note 1, at 217.

150. "Families of MMPI Code Types," *supra* note 34.

151. *Id.*

152. *Id.*

153. *Id.*

154. *Id.*

155. *Id.*

156. R. Carson, "MMPI Profile Interpretation," paper read at the 7th Annual Symposium on the MMPI, Mexico City (1972) in MMPI Interpretation Manual for Counselors and Clinicians, *supra* note 1, at 219.

157. R. Tromboli & R. Kilgore, *A Psychodynamic Approach to MMPI Interpretation*, 47 J. Personality Assesment 614–26 (1983) [hereinafter *A Psychodynamic Approach*] in MMPI Interpretation Manual for Counselors and Clinicians, *supra* note 1, at 219.

158. *Development of Contemporary Norms, supra* note 112, at 100–07 in MMPI Interpretation Manual for Counselors and Clinicians, *supra* note 1, at 220.

159. *Effects of Ethnicity, Sex and Age on MMPI Profiles, supra* note 92, at 591, 597 in MMPI Interpretation Manual for Counselors and Clinicians, *supra* note 1, at 220.

160. J. Graham, The MMPI, *supra* note 32, at 67–68.

161. R. Greene, The MMPI, *supra* note 26, at 108.

162. *Id.*

163. A User's Guide, *supra* note 5, at 23.

164. "Families of MMPI Code Types," *supra* note 34.

165. Carson, "The MMPI and DSM-III Diagnosis," paper presented at the Advanced Psychological Studies Institute, Los Angeles, California (1985) in MMPI Interpretation Manual for Counselors and Clinicians, *supra* note 1, at 231.

166. L. Drake & E. Oetting, An MMPI Codebook for Counselors (1959) in MMPI Interpretation Manual for Counselors and Clinicians, *supra* note 1, at 231.

167. MMPI Interpretation Manual for Counselors and Clinicians, *supra* note 1, at 231.

168. J. Graham, The MMPI, *supra* note 32, at 69–70.

169. W. Cottle, The MMPI: A Review (1953) in MMPI Interpretation Manual for Counselors and Clinicians, *supra* note 1, at 229.

170. *Normalizing the MMPI, supra* note 87, at 776–80 in MMPI Interpretation Manual for Counselors and Clinicians, *supra* note 1, at 229.

171. Carson, *Interpretative Manual to the MMPI*, MMPI: Research Developments and Clinical Applications 279–96 (1969) in MMPI Interpretation Manual for Counselors and Clinicians, *supra* note 1, at 230.

172. *A Psychodynamic Approach, supra* note 157, at 614–26 in MMPI Interpretation Manual for Counselors and Clinicians, *supra* note 1, at 230.

173. R. Greene, The MMPI, *supra* note 26, at 111.

174. *Id.*

175. *Id.* at 170–74.

176. MMPI Interpretation Manual for Counselors and Clinicians, *supra* note 1, at 241.

177. R. Jurjevick, *Short Interval Test/Retest of the MMPI, Index and Symptom Checklist*, 74 J. Gen. Psychology 201–06 (1966) in MMPI Interpretation Manual for Counselors and Clinicians, *supra* note 1, at 242.

178. MMPI Interpretation Manual for Counselors and Clinicians, *supra* note 1, at 241.

179. *Id.* at 247.

180. *Id.* at 249.

181. *Id.* at 252.

182. A User's Guide, *supra* note 5, at 25.

183. MMPI Interpretation Manual for Counselors and Clinicians, *supra* note 1, at 253.

184. A User's Guide, *supra* note 5, at 26.

185. MMPI Interpretation Manual for Counselors and Clinicians, *supra* note 1, at 262.

186. A User's Guide, *supra* note 5, at 26.

187. MMPI Interpretation Manual for Counselors and Clinicians, *supra* note 1, at 265.

188. A User's Guide, *supra* note 5, at 26.

189. *Id.*

190. MMPI Interpretation Manual for Counselors and Clinicians, *supra* note 1, at 273.

191. A User's Guide, *supra* note 5, at 27.

192. MMPI Interpretation Manual for Counselors and Clinicians, *supra* note 1, at 279.

193. A User's Guide, *supra* note 5, at 27.

194. MMPI Interpretation Manual for Counselors and Clinicians, *supra* note 1, at 288–89.

195. A User's Guide, *supra* note 5, at 27.

196. MMPI Interpretation Manual for Counselors and Clinicians, *supra* note 1, at 298.

197. *Id.* at 299.

198. A User's Guide, *supra* note 5, at 27.

199. MMPI Interpretation Manual for Counselors and Clinicians, *supra* note 1, at 303.

200. *Id.* at 309.

201. "Families of MMPI Code Types," *supra* note 34.

202. *Id.*

203. *Id.*

204. Preng & Clopton, *Application of the MacAndrew Alcoholism Scale of Alcoholics with Psychiatric Diagnosis*, 50 J. Personality Assessment 113 (1986).

205. R. Greene, The MMPI, *supra* note 26, at 166.

206. *Id.* at 180–85.

207. *Id.* at 185–86.

208. *Id.* at 186.

209. *Id.* at 60.

210. *Id.* at 61.

211. Dubinsky, Gamble & Rodgers, *A Literature Review of Subtle Obvious Items on the MMPI*, 49 J. Personality Assessment 67 (1985).

212. Graham & McCord, *Interpretation of Moderately Elevated MMPI Scores for Normal Subjects*, 49 J. Personality Assessment 483 (1985).

213. Hursley, Hanson & Parker, *A Summary of the Reliability & Stability of MMPI Scores*, 44 J. Clinical Psychology 44–46 (Jan. 1988).

214. R. Haier, R. Rieder, F. Khouri & M. Buschbaum, *Extreme MMPI Scores and The Research and Diagnostic Criteria*, 36 Archives of General Psychology 534 (1979).

215. J. Graham, The MMPI, *supra* note 32.

216. A. Anastasi, Psychological Testing 538–40 (6th ed. 1988).

217. *Id.* at 534–36.

218. *Id.* at 542–43.

219. *Id.* at 536–38.

QUESTIONS FOR CHAPTER SEVEN

Caution: An attorney should not expect to be able to go into court and ask all of the questions listed below. Preparation is necessary, referring to the content of the chapter to determine if the question applies to your case. The page number at the end of each question refers to where in the chapter you may read an explanation of why this question may be important.

1. Did the psychologist ask the subject for an explanation of the critical items on the MMPI? (p. 188)

2. Did the examiner look at the L-F-K profile? (p. 159)

3. How much did the K loadings affect the clinical scales? (p. 158)

4. Were the supplementary scales scored? If so, which ones; if not, why not? (see each scale)

5. Did the examiner look at the F-K ratio? If greater than 19, why was the profile not invalid? (p. 159)

6. If there was a high Scale 2 (Depression) and the psychologist was weighing it in his or her interpretation, what was the breakout on the Harris-Lingoes subscales? (p. 169)

7. Did the examiner look at Scale 2 in combination with 4 and/or 8 or 9? (p. 168)

8. If a high Scale 3 (Hysteria) exists, where is the pain coming from? (p. 169)

9. Does it come from real life experiences? (no specific page)

10. Did the examiner look at the Scale 1, 2, 3 triad and interpret it together? (p. 171)

11. If Scale 4 (Psychopathic Deviant) was elevated, is it anger, deviancy, or education? (p. 172)

12. Were the Harris-Lingoes Scale 4 subscales looked at to determine where the high 4 came from? (p. 175)

13. If 4 is elevated with 9, is the A (Anxiety) also elevated? (p. 172)

14. Is the 4-9 deviancy or substance abuse? (p. 172. See also Chapter Twelve.)

15. Is the psychologist able to tie the scales in with real life behavior? (no specific page)

16. If Scale 6 (Paranoia) was elevated, is it in any way related to how the custody dispute has been handled (private investigators used, funds cut off). (p. 178)

17. Did the examiner look at the Scale 6 subscales to see if the high 6 was really paranoia or naivete? (p. 179)

18. Was there a combination of high 3-6Pa$_3$ and what are the implications? (p. 199)

19. Was high 8 (Schizophrenia) due to creativity? (p. 181)

20. If the Goldberg Index was used, how valid is it? (p. 183)

21. Were the Scale 8 Harris-Lingoes subscales used? (p. 183)

22. If Scale 9 (Hypomania) is elevated due to the individual being "wired," are there other explanations that might lead to this? (p. 185)

23. Was the A Scale scored, and how does it relate to the results? (p. 189)

24. How does the R Scale relate to the clinical scales? (p. 189)

25. How does Es (Ego Strength) relate to the ability to handle events? Does the psychologist feel that this individual will be able to handle events based on the Ego Strength Scale score? (p. 190)

26. How do the Dy (Dependency) and Do (Dominance) scales relate to the individual's ability to handle events? (p. 191)

27. Cn Scale (Control): Identify the problems demonstrated on the clinical scales. Ask how the Cn indicates whether the individual will be able to handle the problems associated with the high clinical scores identified. (p. 192)

28. What Mac (MacAndrew Alcoholism Scale) cutoff score was used? What does it indicate? Ask the psychologist if it is true that a recovered alcoholic sober for 10 years will still have an elevated MacAndrew Scale, even though not an active alcoholic. (p. 192)

29. If the OH (Overcontrolled Hostility Scale) was elevated, what are the inferences? (p. 193)

30. Find out if there was a difference between the S-O (Subtle-Obvious) scores. If the S score is higher than O score, what does it mean? If the individual did not look at the Subtle-Obvious Scales, ask why. (p. 195)

Chapter Eight
Projective Personality Testing

"Projective tests" are "psychologic diagnostic tests in which the test material is unstructured so that any response will reflect a projection of some aspect of the subject's underlying personality and psychopathology."[1] Prior to the availability of projective tests, psychologists relied on personality questionnaires or inventories for information. These "tests" asked the individual to indicate "yes," "no," or "uncertain" regarding specified thoughts or feelings, e.g., "are your feelings easily hurt." Since the meaning of the items was readily apparent, it was easy for an individual to falsify his or her responses to present the picture of himself that he or she wanted to be seen. This changed with the advent of projective tests, wherein the individual had to respond to ambiguous, unstructured stimuli by providing his or her own structure. Since it is not generally obvious which responses are "normal" or "abnormal," the individual is likely to be less self-conscious while taking the test, and is much less able to manipulate the test.[2]

While there are many existing tests and instruments which would fit under this heading, three particular tests are widely used: the Rorschach inkblot test (Rorschach), the Thematic Apperception Test (TAT), and the Children's Apperception Test (CAT). In addition, many psychologists use projective drawings and sentence completion tests as additional sources of information and hypotheses.

Projective tests tend to be interpreted in two different ways. In the first, specific criteria can be applied to most tests to elicit quantitative information about the content of the individual's responses—i.e., the tests can be "scored." This is sometimes helpful in defining how common or uncommon the individual's responses are, or how much certain themes or tendencies occur in a response protocol. The quantifiability of this method has made it possible to computerize the analysis of some tests.

In the second, the psychologist uses the test as a means of generating global information and hypotheses about the individual, focusing on the content of the responses rather than the statistical criteria which could be applied. A survey of

Rorschach users,[3] for example, found that a fifth of the examiners did not score the test at all, and 75 percent of those who did score it personalized the scoring in some manner, e.g., combining elements of two or more scoring systems.

Neither approach is more correct than the other. Psychologists who score tests will nearly always also analyze the content of the tests, but the converse may not hold: many psychologists forgo scoring and use the tests entirely as sources of more global information and hypotheses through content analysis. What matters for purposes of evaluation of the psychologist's work is how accurate and reasonable the analysis is rather than whether the psychologist used one or both of these methods.

EVALUATION OF PROJECTIVE TECHNIQUES

Perhaps the best review of the validity and reliability of psychological tests is Anne Anastasi's *Psychological Testing*, now in its sixth edition.

She initially notes that

> the difference between projective techniques and standardized tests are not as large or as fundamental as may appear at first sight. . . . [I]t has been argued convincingly that projective techniques and self-report inventories differ in degree rather than in kind. . . . Individual instruments fall into a continuum; although at the extremes the differences are easily recognizable, overlapping in several features is evident at the center.[4]

Next she notes some specific, extra-test purposes for projectives. They are a good way to break the ice when beginning an evaluation, in part because there are no "wrong" answers, in part because the tasks are inherently interesting, and in part because attention is diverted away from the patient or client. She also suggests that special populations, e.g., children, illiterates, and those with language or speech handicaps, may be able to articulate things through the projective tests they could not through interviews or through more objective tests.[5]

An advantage of projective tests is that, "in general, projective instruments are less susceptible to faking than are self-report inventories," in part because the purpose, scoring, and interpretation of the projective tests is generally not evident.[6] This is furthered as the individual becomes more involved in the task. Even so, these tests are not immune to faking, and research amply demonstrates that both "faking good" and "faking bad" are possible. The examiner must be alert to the possibility of faking, and must look for it both through the individual responses and response patterns and through inconsistencies with other sources of information about the individual. The MMPI may be of particular value in making this determination, since it offers the only readily available, proven, objective means of identifying the credibility, attitude, and intent of the individual taking the test.

A potentially significant source of contamination of results is the relative lack of standardization of administration of most projective techniques, in the face of research evidence that, e.g., different instructions and the quality of examiner-examinee relationships can make a significant difference in performance. Examiners must be careful to identify any such factors which may affect the examinee's productivity, defensiveness, or other performance characteristics.[7] Anastasi indicates that meaningful interpretation is possible only when the examiner has "extensive information about the circumstances under which they were obtained and the aptitudes and experiential background of the respondent."[8]

Anastasi concludes that if seen as "tests," the projective techniques will be found wanting. If seen, however, as "clinical tools," to be used as interviewing aids and combined with other data before major conclusions are drawn, the projective techniques may have significant utility in the hands of a skilled clinician. "The special value that projective techniques may have is more likely to emerge when they are interpreted by qualitative, clinical procedures than when they are quantitatively scored and interpreted as psychometric instruments."[9] "These techniques serve best in sequential decisions, by suggesting leads for further exploration or hypotheses about the individual for subsequent verification."[10]

The general lack of objective scoring may be equally serious. Nearly all projective techniques depend, ultimately, on the skill of the examiner at interpretation. There is a real potential for the tests to be interpreted according to the personal biases (theoretical orientation, favorite hypotheses, etc.)

of the examiner rather than strictly according to the data about the examinee's personality dynamics.[11]

Many projective techniques also lack substantial normative data, forcing the clinician to fall back on his or her "general clinical experience" of whatever quality, and with whatever biases the clinician may have. There is also the potential that the clinician, whose personal data bank is primarily filled with data on psychopathology, will overinterpret the data received, or will make other errors based on selective or incomplete recall.[12]

Given these potential problems, scorer reliability becomes an important question. That reliability question extends not only to the formal scoring, where there may be a high degree of consistency among examiners, but, also, to the meaning given to the data, where research has shown much less consistency. Even skilled clinicians may interpret the same data differently, to a degree.[13]

Common tests of reliability, e.g., "split-half" or "test-retest" (see Chapter Three), don't apply well to projective tests, Anastasi indicates. In the former, reliability testing is hampered by the fact that individual items are often designed to measure different variables, so no manner of splitting will result in equivalent halves. Some tests are also designed to be progressive, with stimuli responded to in a context created in part by previous stimuli and responses, together with the natural rise and fall of behavioral tendencies throughout the administration of a test.[14]

Similarly, test-retest reliability can be a problem to assess. In the short run, the individual may recall previous responses and give them (or give something different) intentionally, rather than responding directly to the stimuli. If there has been a longer interval between tests, the test should respond to any real personality changes which have taken place—but each time it does, the reliability coefficient goes down (see Chapter Three).[15]

With regard to validity, Anastasi concludes that "the large majority of published validation studies on projective techniques are inconclusive because of procedural deficiencies in either experimental controls or statistical analysis, or both."[16] She also indicates that even clinicians carry stereotypes of various kinds and may apply these rather than sticking strictly to clinical evidence in interpreting test results. People (including clinicians) tend to notice and recall data which coincides with our expectations, and to ignore and forget data which does not.[17]

Poor experimental design will often lead to an underestimate of validity.[18] For example, the TAT has been criticized for being a poor predictor of real-life aggression on the basis of the presence or absence of aggression in the stories. The research evidence, Anastasi notes, is that "high aggression in fantasy may be associated with either high or low overt aggression. There is some evidence suggesting that if strong aggressive tendencies are accompanied by high anxiety or fear of punishment, expressions of aggression will tend to be high in fantasy and low in overt behavior; when anxiety and fear of punishment are low, high fantasy aggression is associated with overt aggression."[19] In a study of TAT predictions of aggression, some subjects' scores will be positive and some negative because of the interaction—but the appearance when scores are added together for statistical analysis will be that the test is not a valid predictor of aggressive tendencies.

Anastasi calls for sophisticated experimental designs which will take these multiple effects into account. When this has been done, she indicates, "these studies point to a common conclusion: when experienced clinicians are given an opportunity to examine and interpret in their own way respondents' protocols from such projective tests as the Rorschach and TAT, their evaluations of the respondents' personalities tend to match independent case history evaluations significantly better than chance. Insofar as can be ascertained, however, the obtained relations are low."[20]

RORSCHACH PSYCHODIAGNOSTICS TEST

History

The Rorschach inkblot test is perhaps the best-known of the projective techniques, and surveys over the years suggest that it is the most widely used projective test in clinical settings in the United States.[21] While standardized series of inkblots had been used previously in the study of imagination and other functions, Rorschach pioneered the application of inkblots to personality diagnosis and description as a whole.[22] Development of the Rorschach inkblot test was begun by Hermann Rorschach in 1911, with most of his major work having been published between 1917 and 1921. His major monograph, *Psychodiagnostik*, appeared in 1921.[23] With Rorschach's untimely death in 1922, others were left to carry on his work. While a number of interpretive systems have been developed, three stand out: those of Beck, Klopfer, and Exner. When referring to any of the interpretive and scoring systems, the last name of the author is used to identify which system is being discussed.

Samuel Beck published the first major treatise on the Rorschach in the United States in the early 1930s, and several books on the test in later years.[24] His approach was cautious and empirically oriented. Bruno Klopfer, who began publishing on the Rorschach in the mid-1930s, was at the other end of the continuum, emphasizing subjective rather than objective interpretation of responses.[25] While both systems incorporate aspects of psychoanalytic theory in their interpretation of responses, they differ in technique of administration, instructions, scoring categories, how far to go in ascertaining why an individual responded as he or she did, and how to interpret the data received.

It was not until the late 1950s that John E. Exner, Jr., published the first of a number of works that compared and contrasted the Beck, Klopfer, and other systems of Rorschach administration and interpretation and began a systematic study of the test and the means of using it designed to maximize the reliability and validity of test protocols. The result is an attempt to integrate the best aspects of the various systems into one comprehensive system.[26]

In describing his system, Exner begins with a caution against overinterpretation, saying that "the technique was never designed to answer all types of diagnostic or descriptive questions, just as it was never designed to predict all or most types of behavior. . . ."[27] Rather, he writes,

> the test gives a representative view of the person as he is behaving at the present. . . . Specifically, a description of a person based on the Rorschach data can include statements about a subject's affective world, his cognitive and response styles, how he related to his interpersonal sphere and to the rest of the environment as a whole, what motivates him and what are his response styles.[28]

While one might speculate on the etiology of the individual's condition and/or on treatability, he cautions, "it must be remembered that this is speculation only, as it tends to be inferred rather than derived directly from the data provided in the protocol, and, as such, relies on the tester's deductive powers and accumulated knowledge."[29] He cautions against making predictions about the individual's future behavior based solely on the Rorschach, since one lacks information about the subject's future environment. He also cautions against using the Rorschach as a primary source of conclusions about intelligence or organic mental disorders (organicity).

Description of the Test

The Rorschach test consists of 10 cards, each about 7 x 9 1/2 inches. On each is printed a standardized, bilaterally symmetrical inkblot. Cards I, IV, V, VI and VII are gray and black. Cards II and III add a bright red to the grays and blacks. Cards VIII, IX, and X are in pastel colors. The subject is shown each card, in numerical order. On the average, the test takes 45–60 minutes.

At this point, there may be some deviation in the manner of presentation, depending in part on the system the examiner ascribes to. Each of the major systems (Beck, Klopfer, Exner) has a different approach, and each may, therefore, yield slightly different data. For example, Beck wrote that the subject "sits in front of and with his back to" the examiner,[30] Klopfer preferred side-by-side seating,[31] and Exner[32] wrote that any position except face-to-face is acceptable, suggesting that side-by-side may be best. The purpose, in all cases, is to prevent the individual from getting visual cues of any kind from the examiner, or from concentrating on what the examiner is writing down rather than on the blots.

The introduction to the test is very general, since the subject needs nearly complete freedom to react to the cards if the test is to be meaningful. The examiner might inquire whether the subject has heard about the "Rorschach" or "the inkblot test," and might tell the subject that they are "only inkblots," so that there are no right or wrong answers. It is critically important that the subject *not* have the impression that it is a measure of intelligence or a test of imagination, since the former gives a mind set that there are right and wrong answers, and the latter that one is to associate to the inkblots rather than telling what one *sees*. "It is what [the subjects] see that constitutes the Rorschach response."[33] If a test battery is given, Exner also suggests that the Rorschach be administered at or near the end, and particularly that it never be administered before the Wechsler Adult Intelligence Scale (WAIS), on the basis of research showing that these factors are very important.[34]

The instructions to the subject also vary to some degree with the system and the examiner, though all specify that the subject is to report exactly what he or she *sees*. Beck's introduction is relatively long:

> You will be given a series of ten cards, one by one. The cards have on them designs made up out of ink blots. Look at each card, and tell the examiner what you see on each card, or anything that might be represented there. Look at each card as long as you like; only be sure to tell the examiner everything that you see on the card as you look at it. When you have finished with a card, give it to the examiner as a sign that you are through with it.[35]

The examiner may vary from that exact language, so long as the essence of the message is the same, particularly the emphasis on reporting what is *seen*.

In contrast, after the brief introduction Exner hands the subject the first card, saying "What might this be?" and not another word. "Those four words are very important and should not be altered or added to in any way," Exner indicates.[36] These four words are the same recommended by Rorschach and by Klopfer.[37] Exner's research found that Beck's instructions led to relatively long protocols, Klopfer's to relatively short ones.[38] He chose to limit his instructions to try to minimize the impact of instructional sets on an individual's responding, as well as to adhere to the rule that "the primary task of the examiner is to remain silent as much as possible so as not to contaminate the testing session with unnecessary remarks that might influence the subject."[39]

The cards are handed to the subject in numerical order, from I to X, in the standard, upright position. The examiner repeats the "what might this be" statement in handing over each card, though if the subject clearly understands the task that statement need not be repeated after the first four or five cards. Although the subject is free to turn the card if he or she wishes, the examiner may not suggest that he or she do so.

Questions from the subject, regardless of the system preferred by the examiner, are answered as briefly and generally as possible. If the subject asks about turning the card, Beck would have the examiner say that he "is free to do so,"[40] while Exner recommends answering this and similar questions with, "It's up to you."[41] Beck urges the examiner to encourage the subject to give more than one response if only one is elicited by cards I–V. Klopfer and Exner indicate that one encourages the subject only on the first card, never thereafter, so long as even a single response is made for each card. Both Beck and Exner urge the examiner not to permit the subject to reject a card (give no response at all), if possible, Beck writing that he tries to make the subject hold the card at least two minutes,[42] with both Beck and Exner making statements like "we're in no hurry" and/or "everyone can find something."[43] If the subject gives a great many responses, Beck indicates he cuts off responding after 10 minutes per card.[44] Exner, however, writes that "research . . . has shown that the interpretive yield is essentially no different if only the first five responses to each blot are used than if all answers are included."[45] However, he cautions that as soon as the subject gives fewer than five responses to any blot, the examiner should not intervene again even if more than five are later given. The intent is to preserve the spontaneity of responding as much as possible.

Responses are recorded verbatim under all systems. The intent is to record every word used by the subject in describing what he or she sees, to maximize the likelihood that the examiner can perceive the same thing, not only what parts of the inkblot were used for the percept but, also, what made it look the way it did to the subject, including the shape, shading, color, and so forth.

The examiner also records comments the subject makes, facial expressions, gestures, laughter, changes in voice, exclamations, and any other behavior which may indicate that the subject is having a special reaction to something in the test. Particularly in a protocol with a small number of responses, the

extra-test behavior may tell as much or more about the individual's perceptions than do the verbal responses to the blots.

Finally, the examiner records the time it takes the individual to give his or her first response (reaction time), and the
total time the individual holds the card (response time).

After the administration of the test (the "free association")
is completed, an "Inquiry" is conducted. The Inquiry has great
importance under all systems of interpretation, though those
examiners who do not formally score the test will conduct only
a very brief one. The purpose of the Inquiry is to try to assure
that the examiner's understanding of responses is
accurate—i.e., what the subject perceived at the time the
response was initially given. No new responses are permitted,
only clarification of responses already given. Exner suggests
the following introduction:

> Now we are going to go back through the cards
> again. It won't take very long. I want to see the
> things that you saw and make sure that I see them
> like you do. We'll do them one at a time. I'll read
> what you said and then I want you to show me
> where it is on the blot and then tell me what there is
> there that makes it look like that, so that I can see
> it too, just like you did. Understand?[46]

The examiner then reads back, verbatim, what the subject said
during the initial administration of the cards, with a request to
indicate where the percept is located and what made it look as
it did. The examiner must continue to be nondirective to
assure that he or she is learning what made the blot look the
way it did to the subject rather than putting words or ideas in
the subject's mind. Thus, one asks various questions like "what
made it look like a _____," rather than "did the
color/shading/shape help make it look like a _____?" Exner
indicates that the questions should be as brief as possible,
should seek only information essential to the scoring of the
test, should keep the Inquiry as short as possible, and should
be as nondirective as possible.[47]

Scoring

Unlike an IQ test, where scoring means counting right and
wrong answers, "scoring" on the Rorschach refers to coding the

data in various ways to facilitate understanding the categories of information, which must be considered in context to be meaningful. The examiner explores several areas, including the following: Location, Determinants, Content, and Popular Responses. As indicated above, Beck, Klopfer, and Exner score the test differently. Each system will be briefly presented, along with an interpretation of the information scored.

Beck's System

Initial consideration is given to "Location": whether the individual has used the whole inkblot, a major detail, a minor detail, and/or space (the white area around or within the blot) for each response. Whether the detail is "major" or "minor" is determined from frequency tables based on research by Beck and others.

Next, one looks at the "Determinants" of the responses— the features of the blots that led the subject to respond as he or she did. The primary determinants are "form," "color," "movement," and "shading," which may be used alone or in various combinations by the subject in his or her responses, with each scored separately to identify the determinants used and the relative importance of each.

Next, one looks at the "Content" of the responses, e.g., whether the percept is an animal, a human, part of anatomy, art, an abstraction, clothing, geography, etc. Five categories encompass the majority of percepts: "human," "human detail," "animal," "animal detail," and "anatomy," though Beck identifies a total of 34 categories.[48]

"Popular" responses are those given very commonly, with Beck listing 21 such responses.[49] These were empirically derived on the basis that they were stated at least three times more often than the next-most-common response to a particular inkblot or detail. A normal record will have seven to nine "Populars."

Finally, one looks at the total number of responses. The average record will have 20 to 30 associations.

Examiners who do not do formal scoring will still make use of the categories above, recognizing the importance of identifying gross overproduction or underproduction of any type of response determinant. Their greatest emphasis, however, is usually on the content of the responses, and hypotheses that may be generated about the individual from the types of content he or she identifies.

Klopfer's System

The Klopfer scoring system is more sophisticated than the Beck system. The first consideration is scoring the "Locations." Klopfer looks at whole responses, large details, small details, unusual details, and/or space responses.

After the Location is scored, the "determinants" are scored. There are four main categories of determinants: "form," "movement," "shading," and "color."

After the Determinants are scored, the scorer looks at the "content" of the responses. Klopfer identifies twenty-four categories as the most frequently used content areas. They include "human" responses, "animal" responses, "anatomical" responses, food, nature, geography, and "abstract concepts."

Next, "Popular" responses are recorded. Popular responses are defined as those given with relative frequency. In Klopfer's scoring system, only ten responses are scored as Popular, as compared to 21 for Beck. Klopfer also looks at "Original" responses. "By definition, an original response is one that does not appear more than once in a hundred records."[50]

Exner's Comprehensive System

In slight contrast to the 20–30 responses expected with Beck's system, Exner indicates that one expects 17–27 responses with the Comprehensive System.[51] To facilitate scoring, a standard four-page form was developed, though its use is not required.

While acknowledging that the Rorschach cannot be scored in the same way many objective tests could, Exner notes that there are four sets of data which may be derived from the test:

1. "Quantitative data which can be compared across other records . . . [which is] especially helpful when the task is one of diagnosis, because normative data comparing various types of subjects do exist. In addition, the quantitative data allow an interpretation that is free from the bias of the subject's words, which may create a particular set during interpretation."

2. "Internal comparisons among the subject's own productions. It is here where the most valuable idiographic information is obtained . . . [his] own unique style of responding, his needs and motivations, and his weaknesses and strengths."

3. "The sequence of the scores can be examined. This helps to illustrate how the subject approaches the testing situation, how a response may be related to a previous response, and how the performance varies as the test progresses."

4. "The subject's own words, which are subjected to a qualitative analysis. . . . When used with caution, this yields valuable information and allows the examiner to "flesh out" his interpretation and confirm his hypotheses with some of the unique features of the subject."[52]

Exner's Comprehensive System has two basic rules that must be followed:

1. "[O]nly what was perceived during Free Association can be scored. . . . [The Free Association and Inquiry] represent two different thought processes. . . . [Thus,] the Free Association should be read in its entirety first, and then the Inquiry."[53]

2. "[T]o make sure that all determinants given in the Free Association are scored and are given equal weight. This is different from the Klopfer system, which gives a main score and then additional scores."[54]

Like Beck, Exner scores for Location, Determinants, Content, and Popularity. To these, Exner adds Organizational Activity. The first three are always scored, the last two are scored if the content of the response permits.

Also like Beck, Exner's "Location" criteria primarily involve looking at the subject's use of the whole inkblot, of major details, of minor details, and of space. "In addition to being concerned with where on the blot the subject has seen something, how he or she has used the area is of major importance. A selection of location can be highly sophisticated and organized showing considerable cognitive integrative capacity or maturity, or it may be relatively simple and unorganized. . . . [Therefore], a 'Developmental Quality' score representing this difference has been included in this category of scoring. . . . [F]our categories of Developmental Quality . . . are scored for each location."[55]

As in Beck's system, one then looks at the Determinants, which Exner indicates are "the most complex and most important scoring category, involving the perceptual-cognitive process that the individual employs in order to select and to organize the various elements in his stimulus world."[56] Thus, one would expect an impulsive person to answer quickly, a compulsive subject to check out every aspect of the card before responding, and so forth. Exner and Clark also note that there is some filtering of responses by most individuals, citing research which found that when asked to give as many responses as they could in 60 seconds, subjects averaged six per card rather than the two which subjects average in the actual test.[57]

Exner uses seven major categories of Determinants. The first three, "Form," "Movement" and "Color," which he calls "Chromatic Color," are the same as for Beck. Beck's fourth Determinant, "Shading," Exner divides into "Achromatic Color" (blacks, whites, and grays) and "Shading" (in which the light-dark aspects of the blots are used in perceptions of texture, depth, or dimensionality). Exner's last two Determinants are unique. The sixth, "Form Dimension," was developed specifically for the Comprehensive System. It denotes a reference to dimensionality or perspective based solely on form rather than form-plus-shading, e.g., where the subject perceives himself to be looking down or up at the item on the inkblot. Finally, the seventh Determinant, "Pairs and Reflections," is scored when the symmetry of the blot is a major factor in the response.[58]

Exner also scores three final categories: "Blends," "Organizational Activity," and "Form Quality." A "Blend" is the use of two or more Determinants in a single response, and is scored much as Beck's system does. Blends occur in anywhere from 15 percent to 50 percent of normal records, according to Exner's research.[59] "Organizational Activity" refers to the subject's integration of two or more parts of a blot into a meaningful relationship, e.g., "two people bending over and talking with one another" rather than just "two people." It is also scored when the whole inkblot is used by the subject. Exner uses the same table Beck does to rate the complexity of the relationship. "Form Quality" refers to what Beck called "Good Form" and "Poor Form," and uses Beck's tables of frequency data plus other data from Exner's research as norms. Exner also adds a breakdown of "good" responses into "superior" and "ordinary" classifications, the former indicating enriched quality of a response due to the manner of articulation.

As with Beck, one next looks at the "Content" of the responses, with each coded according to a list of categories derived from Exner's research. While most are similar to those of Beck, the research indicated that 22 rather than 34 categories would be appropriate.[60]

Also like Beck, Exner identifies "Popular" responses, which he defines as those occurring in at least one-third of the protocols in the research base. This led to the identification of 13 Populars, eight fewer than were identified by Beck in his earlier research, but three more than Klopfer.[61]

Exner adds two categories of responses to those of Beck and Klopfer, identifying these as "Special Scorings." The first is "Perseveration," and is scored when an individual inappropriately persists in using the same category of response in two successive responses on a single card, or when he or she identifies an object as the same one previously seen on another card (also called "Content Perseveration").[62] The second of the "Special Scorings" is "Unusual Verbalizations," all of which indicate that a response is strange in some way. Subcategories include "Deviant Verbalizations," "Inappropriate Combinations," and "Autistic Logic." While the Special Scorings all indicate disordered thought and/or faulty cognitive integration, Exner cautions that they are never sufficient, by themselves, to permit a specific diagnosis to be made. "It must be emphasized," he indicates, "that the protocol must be interpreted in a global, configurational manner and conclusions are to be drawn only through employing this procedure."[63]

Interpretation: Beck and Klopfer

Beck and Klopfer and their followers primarily base their interpretations on clinical data, including both the personal experience of the examiner and limited research on the Rorschach protocols of people with diagnosed mental disorders.[64] It should be noted that nearly all of the research data used by Beck and Klopfer was based on responses by white, middle-class Europeans and Americans, and should not be generalized much beyond those groups. Each type of scoring yields hypotheses about the individual's functioning, to be tested against what is known about the individual's case history and information from other parts of the test battery. The following are examples of specific hypotheses generated by each type of scoring.

Location

Using the whole blot, particularly on the more complex blots, indicates an ability to integrate information. Use of major details suggests an ability to use common sense and obvious information. Too much use of major details (more than 75 percent of responses) may indicate a preoccupation with detail in everyday life, possibly including some obsessive-compulsive behavior. Too little use of major details (under 30 percent) may indicate a lack of attention to the details of everyday life. Overproduction of minor details (over 10 percent of responses) may indicate a degree of meticulousness and overconcern for detail sufficient to more strongly suggest obsessive-compulsive personality problems.[65] Similarly, Klopfer notes that

> about two thirds of all responses of an intelligent adult should be usual details. . . . Their use in approximately two-thirds of a subject's responses simply means that he has enough common sense to use the most obvious materials before he starts seeking the unusual. This obvious material corresponds in the actual life situation to the routing problems of daily life, which cannot be overlooked without endangering the smooth flow of life.[66]

Determinants

Determinants are the features of the blots that lead the subject (test taker) to respond as he or she did. Form, color, movement, and shading are the primary Determinants:

- *Form*: In a normal record, 30 to 50 percent of responses will be based exclusively on form, indicative of an ability to deal with things in a logical and objective manner. Where form is used well over 50 percent of the time as the sole determinant, though, it's likely to indicate concrete, stereotyped thinking. Where the percent is below 30, it's likely the individual is much more motivated by emotional than intellectual factors.[67]

  One may also compare the individual's responses with statistical norms regarding accuracy of perceptions, to get a rating for "Good Form" and "Poor Form" in the individual's response protocol. Research by Beck and others established a table[68] which identifies form quality as good or poor based on the frequency with which each percept was given in the normative samples. A normal record will show at least 70 percent of the form responses to be accurate based on that comparison, indicative of realistic perceptions of the environment and good ego-strength. If the percentage of statistically accurate form responses exceeds 90 percent, however, there is a suggestion of intellectual rigidity.[69]

- *Color*: The color responses reveal a person's emotional relationship with the environment. "Pure" color responses, those without reference to form, usually suggest intense rage or a general lack of emotional control. Where both color and form are used, if color is the weightier factor it suggests some difficulty with emotional control, while if form is the heavier factor a more socialized emotional state is suggested. In a record where form and color are used together a number of times, but form always or nearly always dominates, there is a suggestion of overcontrol of emotionality.[70]

- *Movement*: One scores "movement" when the subject describes people engaged in some activity, e.g., "people bowling," or when animals are seen in a human-like activity, e.g., "bears dancing." Form is necessarily implied by "movement" responses. A normal record will have two to four movement responses,[71] and indicates use of creative imagination. A larger number of movement responses suggests the individual has adequate inner resources and is more cognitively than physically oriented, and vice-versa for a small number.[72] Marked overproduction suggests obsessive-compulsive or paranoid ideation, while a total lack of movement responses suggests low intelligence and/or an absence of empathy.[73]

- *Shading*: "Shading" refers to use of the gray areas of the blots, which seldom occurs more than once in normal records. More shading responses than this suggests feelings of inadequacy, depression, and/or anxiety.[74]

Content

As indicated above, there are 34 categories of percepts in Beck's system, though five cover the majority of them ("human,"

"human detail," "animal," "animal detail," and "anatomy"). The subject who gives responses from many areas is usually seen as relatively intellectual and/or having broad experience. When responses are limited to a few areas, it suggests a preoccupation with certain kinds of thoughts or behaviors, as suggested by the nature of the content, or may be an attempt at being evasive or defensive. It could also be a sign of being nonintellectual or of relatively low intelligence.[75]

As with the other categories of information, hypotheses are formed about subjects on the basis of how their responses compare with normative data collected on people who have taken the test. Some hypotheses are very strong because of the consistent association of the response with a personality type.[76] Other hypotheses are weaker because of less-consistent, though still substantial, association with personality types.[77]

Of particular interest in custody evaluations are those Rorschach indicators of difficulty with interpersonal relationships.

> One of the best single indicators of the person's basic interest in and relation to other people is contained in the Rorschach human responses, particularly when combined with movement that is appropriate to the form of the blot area and is in the context of an activity appropriate to reality as experienced by others.[78]

The ambiguity of the Rorschach sometimes allows one to detect psychotic processes which the individual can keep under control during other parts of the psychological evaluation. The schizophrenic or schizotypal individual, for example, is relatively likely to have bizarre and idiosyncratic themes (blurred boundaries, fused body parts, distorted images, etc.), confused sexual identification, and/or disturbed logic, as well as those characteristics cited above for interpersonal relationship problems.[79] Exner particularly cautions against drawing strong conclusions from individual responses. Rather, "it is the classes of projected material that generate the greatest interpretive yield. Some responses that appear to have projected features may be nothing more than straightforward translations of the blot stimuli."[80]

A given individual may have responses covering a range of personality descriptions. These are likely to be to some degree inconsistent with one another, since individuals are not generally narrow, unitary creatures. One identifies the primary hypotheses on the bases of (1) how frequently a given type of content is given during the test, (2) whether an individual exhibited "shock" on particular cards, (3) whether the individual's responses to certain blots are of unusually poor quality compared with his or her other responses, and/or (4) whether the response to a particular blot is unique. One also compares the hypotheses with what is known about the individual, looking for evidence that the hypothesis is or is not supported by other data.

Populars

As indicated above, Beck identifies 21 responses considered "Populars" because they are particularly commonly given. A normal record will have seven to nine Populars. More than this may indicate an individual who is overly conforming, or is being evasive or defensive. Fewer suggests difficulty with conventional ideas.[81]

Total Number of Responses

A higher score may indicate high intelligence and/or creativity—so long as the form of the responses is good overall, and responses do not primarily focus on minor details (which would suggest obsessive-compulsive behavior). A low number of responses may suggest low intellect, or evasiveness or defensiveness, unless the responses are well-organized.[82]

Exner[83] indicates that "four of every five protocols containing 13 or less responses will not be reliable for most and possibly all variables," and should therefore be interpreted with caution. He suggests that, when this occurs, the examiner should either discard the Rorschach and rely solely on other data, or that the examiner immediately (during the same session, if possible) retest the individual, instructing the subject to give more answers than he or she did on the first administration.

Unusual Responses

Anything unusual about the individual's responses is taken into consideration, including, e.g., how the cards were handled, response time, perseverations, excessive qualification of responses, and so forth. Everything an individual does has some potential to give insight into his or her personality, so no data is excluded from that available for forming hypotheses.

Interpretation: Exner

Exner's interpretations are based on the same types of data as those cited above for Beck and Klopfer, but with far greater research support for the conclusions offered. It is of particular note that most of the development of the Rorschach has been through the study of abnormal personalities, which has biased interpretation in the direction of maladjustment.[84] To offset this, Exner includes a table of "Descriptive Statistics for 69 Rorschach Variables for 600 Nonpatient Adults"[85] and for 1,580 nonpatient children and adolescents by age[86] in his 1985 *Workbook*, to permit analysis of responses of a given subject in the context of normal subjects as well as abnormal ones.

Validity and Reliability

The Rorschach and other projective tests have been frequently criticized on such bases as the lack of predictive ability of the test, the fact that it is common for different examiners to administer the test with minor and not-so-minor differences in approach, the many studies showing poor validity of the test, and the problems engendered by having numerous systems for scoring the tests. It is also often noted that the test is substantially more subjective than, e.g., the Minnesota Multiphasic Personality Inventory (MMPI), and validity and reliability are therefore harder to demonstrate.[87]

By the mid-1970s, many of the negative arguments were themselves no longer valid. One major reason was that psychologists increasingly looked to the Rorschach as an information source, in effect a structured interview, rather than as a stand-alone diagnostic instrument.[88] "Whenever the Rorschach is used as an information resource per se, the resultant psychological reports are useful and valuable," Richard Dana, Ph.D., University of Arkansas psychology professor, concludes.[89]

Dana cautions that taking the Rorschach test is a stressful experience for most people, and that research continues to indicate that the examiner's behavior can have a significant effect on the outcome of the test.[90] He also indicates that one must consider in the content analysis that both examiner and examinee will have specific, unique meanings for various symbols, so that interpretation must proceed cautiously. Without consideration of these variables, he indicates, there is a danger of over-interpretation of the data.[91]

Finally, Dana lauds the publishing of Exner's textbook on the Rorschach, calling it "clearly a definitive textbook incorporation of contemporary Rorschach usage. . . . [I]t is likely that conventional and more narrow textbooks will be gradually replaced as a consequence."[92] With Exner's and others' research, he writes, "a relevant validation literature with theoretical underpinnings and careful design characteristics is emerging."[93]

To address the validity question, researchers collected a sample of Rorschach validation studies from every fifth year of *Psychological Abstracts* between 1930 and 1980, totaling 120 studies.[94] They found that

> the success of conceptual research demonstrates both criterion validity, insofar as scores correlate with some concurrent or predicted aspect of behavior, and construct validity, insofar as the theoretical formulation accounts for the relationship between the Rorschach scores(s) and some condition or behavior. . . . This study suggests that inadequate research methodology, rather than the Rorschach itself, is at least partly culpable for condemnation of the technique.[95]

To address the question of reliability, researchers identified a method of computing all possible split-half correlations for a given scoring variable in order to determine how a test may best be split in half in order to assess the reliability of the test.[96] Using two samples of 100 students, they found that using usual methods led to a correlation coefficient in the low to mid-.60s, while using their method the correlations increased to the high .70s. They also determined that, for some populations, the least accurate split-half method is "odd-even," which is also among the most common methods used in research. They also found that the students in their two different samples required different split halves in order to accurately conduct the research. They conclude that "it would appear that projective techniques are probably more reliable than previous studies have indicated. . . ."[97]

In his section on "Diagnosis" in *Psychiatric and Psychological Evidence*, law professor Daniel W. Shuman writes that

> the development of the Exner system of administration and scoring represented a substantial improvement in the reliability and validity of the Rorschach technique. . . . Consequently, using this system it is now possible to compare an individual's Rorschach performance to that of normal people as well as those with mental disorders. Therefore, although still a projective technique, these improvements in its psychometric characteristics have increased its utility.[98]

Since not all psychologists use the Exner system, however, he cautions that

> the multiplicity of scoring systems and differences in reliability and validity among systems make it imperative that any challenge to Rorschach testing testimony be specific, as general attacks on the Rorschach may be irrelevant to the scoring system used. Given the sophistication necessary to mount this challenge properly, consultation with a forensic or clinical psychologist may be necessary.[99]

Fordham University professor of psychology, Anne Anastasi, Ph.D., concurs, writing that "a major contribution of Exner's work is the provision of a uniform Rorschach system that permits comparability among the research findings of different investigators. The availability of this system, together with the research completed thus far, has injected new life into the Rorschach as a potential psychometric instrument."[100]

Finally, J. Exner, E. Thomas, and B. Mason caution that the Rorschach does *not* have long-term reliability for children until at least the age of 14.[101] "Even an interval of nine months is sufficient to find very significant structural changes in the re-tests of seven-year-olds," they indicate.[102]

In sum, recent research has substantially improved the evidence that the Rorschach is both valid and reliable, particularly when it is used as part of a test battery and in the context of a complete evaluation of the individual. In the hands of a skilled clinician, it can provide data and hypotheses which few other tests or interviews can.

Intended Audience

According to *The Eight Mental Measurement Yearbook*, the Rorschach is appropriate for "ages 3 and over."[103] Exner provides data on children's responses starting with age 5.[104] However, Siegel writes that

> The very young child does not find the Rorschach an appealing task; he does not differentiate it from the structured tasks of the intelligence test. Like the disorganized hyperactive school-age child, he cannot submit to formal methods of testing. He lacks the patience and memory to go through the procedure a second time, and he cannot point out with certainty the specific location or qualities of the blot that determined his association.[105]

Even so, Siegel continues, "although the scoring of his responses may lack finesse, the experienced examiner can usually catch the drift of things. The administration of the Rorschach to the school-age child can usually be conducted along traditional procedures used with adolescents and adults."[106]

Acceptance by Mental Health Professionals

Nearly all clinical psychologists receive training in the use of the Rorschach. A 1982 survey of psychologists found that the Rorschach was the fourth-most-used psychological test.[107] This was a drop from 1969, when it was the second most used, and 1959 when it was the first. The authors note that the Rorschach is one of only two tests that have been among the top 20 tests since the initial survey in 1935.

A recent survey found that the Rorschach was used in evaluations of adults by 41.5 percent of reporting psychologists (who used it in 67.3 percent of their evaluations) and in evaluations of children by 29.2 percent of reporting psychologists (who used it in 77.9 percent of their evaluations).[108]

While usage has obviously decreased, the Rorschach remains a widely used psychological instrument.

THEMATIC APPERCEPTION TEST

History

While clinicians and researchers published various reports of use of free associations and stories as adjuncts to psychotherapy and/or personality research, there was no widely used method prior to the publication in 1935 of "A Method for Investigating Fantasies: The Thematic Apperception Test," by C.D. Morgan and H.A. Murray in the *Archives of Neurology and Psychiatry*.[109] This was followed in 1938 by the publication, by Murray and the staff of the Harvard Psychological Clinic, of *Explorations in Personality*.[110] Today, the Thematic Apperception Test (TAT) is one of the most widely used and researched projective tests.[111]

According to the manual for the test, the TAT

> is a method of revealing to the trained interpreter some of the dominant drives, emotions, sentiments, complexes and conflicts of a personality. Special value resides in its power to expose the underlying inhibited tendencies which the subject, or patient, is not willing to admit, or can not admit because he is unconscious of them. . . . The technique is especially recommended as a preface to a series of psychotherapeutic interviews or to a short psychoanalysis.[112]

Description of the Test

The TAT consists of 31 cards, of which 30 are pictures in black and white and one is blank. Each is approximately nine and a quarter by eleven inches. There are cards especially for men or women, and cards especially for boys or girls (4–14 years of age), as the test was originally structured.[113] The cards currently being used constitute the third revision of the test, each revision based on research regarding the contribution it made to the final case diagnosis involving the TAT and other psychological tests.[114]

The original instructions for the test called for the examiner to administer two series of ten cards each, at least one day apart, with the cards chosen on the basis of the individual's sex and age. The examiner was to sit in back of the subject or patient, and to note all verbalizations of the subject/patient. Each of the two sessions was to last about one hour.[115] However, clinicians commonly use fewer than 20 cards, and administer the test in a single one-hour session.[116] The examiner selects those cards most likely to provide information germane to the purpose of the examination[117] or which "elicit themes that are thought to be pertinent to a given examinee's conflicts or concerns."[118]

Psychology Professor Richard Ryan, Ph.D., writes that

> the single most important consideration in TAT administration is the creation of a psychological atmosphere in which the examinee feels relaxed, comfortable, and freely available to respond to the situation. Examiner rigidity or lack of friendliness or evaluative attitude is likely to result in constriction or discouragement of the subject, an unwanted situational contribution to the results. A quiet, comfortable physical setting is most suitable for the session.[119]

The instructions in the manual are as follows:

> This is a test of imagination, one form of intelligence. I am going to show you some pictures, one at a time; and your task will be to make up as dramatic a story as you can for each. Tell what has led up to the event shown in the picture, describe what is happening at the moment, what the characters are feeling and thinking; and then give the outcome. Speak your thoughts as they come to your mind. Do you understand? Since you have fifty minutes for ten pictures, you can devote about five minutes to each story.[120]

A parallel but simpler set of instructions, "suitable for children, for adults of little education or intelligence, and for psychotics" is also offered in the manual.

Henry Murray, Ph.D., who worked with the staff of the Harvard Psychological Clinic, adds that the exact words of the instructions "may be altered to suit the age, intelligence, personality, and circumstances of the subject."[121] He also cautions against using terms like "free imagination," since this could lead the subject/patient to assume responses will be interpreted, which "may severely check the spontaneity of his thought. He should believe that the examiner is solely interested in his literary or creative ability."[122] After the first story, the examiner is to commend the subject/patient, if possible, and ask questions to bring out any of the key elements which are lacking (i.e., what is happening, what led up to what is happening, what is the person (are the people) thinking and feeling, and what is the outcome). Thereafter, the examiner speaks only to note if the subject/patient is well ahead of or behind the 5-minutes-per-story-average schedule, to provide some encouragement, and/or to bring out any of the key elements which is missing or inadequate. The examiner does not discuss the story at all. If a story is too long or rambling, the examiner may ask, e.g., "How does it turn out?" Inquiries about details by the subject/patient are to be answered "You may make it anything you please." One is permitted to offer a prize to "extremely reticent children" if necessary to get them to tell stories. The average story length is about 300 words for adults and 150 words for 10-year-olds.

Since Murray's 1943 Manual was written, much research has been done on test-related variables. For example, Morris Stein, Ph.D., of the New York University Department of Psychology, notes that "there is no research evidence as to the effect of any [seating] position on TAT responses. The position selected has to suit the individual subject, the examiner, and the conditions of the examination."[123] In contrast, research has suggested "that Murray's instructions [re: "imagination"] result in stories of sadder emotional tone and outcome than is true of instructions designed specifically to be mental or intellectual."[124] Stein also cites two studies which indicate that, "even without specific instructions to do so, subjects seem to be generally predisposed to appear at their best when telling TAT stories."[125] Research has supported Murray's statement that average story length is 300 words for adults and 150 words for children, except that in clinical situations the average is about 100 words.[126]

Some examiners conduct an "Inquiry" at the end of the test to try to obtain additional information about the thoughts, feelings, and interactions of characters in particular stories. This is reserved for the end, so that the subject/patient will not be cued as to what might be a desirable story.[127]

There are pros and cons to each of several methods of recording the stories. If the examiner can write quickly enough, he or she may write everything down himself or herself, taking note of both what is said by the subject/patient and his or her own questions and observations. If he or she writes slowly, or has to ask the individual to repeat something, however, it can interfere with rapport and cause the subject to feel frustrated. Many examiners, therefore, tape record the stories, transcribing them later. This also allows the examiner to note facial expressions, "body language," and other nonverbal information during the test. The potential problem with this method is the loss of the material if the recorder fails for any reason. The examiner may, as a third alternative, ask the subject/patient to write down his or her own stories. This is the only possible method when the TAT is administered in a group (and slides of the pictures are available for that purpose). There is a potential, however, for the stories to be more formal, more controlled, and less spontaneous than verbalized stories, as well as the obvious lack of data in the form of pauses, changes in tone of voice, and so forth. No research indicates which method is best.[128]

Analysis/Interpretation

"Unlike the Rorschach, there are no generally accepted systems of TAT scoring and interpretation."[129] While several psychologists have attempted to formulate such a system, with cataloguing of major theme, feelings expressed, the nature of the outcomes, and so forth, most clinicians proceed to analyze the results impressionistically, as Murray did.[130]

> The data from the TAT can be scored according to a variety of existing quantitative systems. However, more commonly in clinical use the stories are interpreted in accord with general principles of inference derived from psychodynamic theory. Its use in clinical assessment is generally part of a larger battery of tests and interview data, which provide the background and convergent information necessary for appropriate interpretation. . . . (T)he strength of the "test" is no better than the . . . interpretive skills of the examiner in dealing with the material. . . . In this sense the TAT is more a method than a "test."[131]

In the manual Murray indicates that, first, one must have basic facts about the subject: "the sex and age . . . whether his parents are dead or separated, the ages and sexes of his siblings, his vocation and his marital status."[132] The TAT was not meant to reveal those details, and analysis without basic background information, he suggests, is a "stunt" rather than acceptable clinical practice.

The interpreter reads and rereads the stories, looking for significant elements. Murray recommends that the interpreter analyze each story into "the force or forces emanating from the hero, and . . . the force or forces emanating from the environment."[133] The "hero" is the character in each story with whom the subject/patient has identified himself or herself, usually the leading character in the story. Next, one looks at the "motives, trends, and feelings of the heroes" in each story, hypothesizing that these are projections of the thoughts and feelings of the subject/patient. One may categorize these in various ways, e.g., such variables as "achievement," "aggression," "social," "dominance," "nurturance," and so forth. One especially looks for evidence of "uniqueness, intensity, and frequency" for each variable.

Next, one looks at the "forces of the hero's environment."[134] One notes what elements of the pictures are emphasized, and which are ignored, as well as elements not shown in the picture which are included in the stories. One evaluates how the hero relates to people and other aspects of the environment, and particularly relationships with, e.g., members of the opposite sex, parent-like figures, and so forth. As above, increasing importance is hypothesized on the basis of uniqueness, intensity, and frequency.

Fourth, one looks at "outcomes."[135] What are the successes and failures of the heroes? How hard do the heroes fight? Do the heroes make things happen or have things happen to them? Does punishment follow transgression?

Psychology Professor Sheldon J. Korchin, of the University of California at Berkeley, adds that "the accuracy with which the picture elements is [sic] described is of considerable importance and parallels conceptually the form level of Rorschach responses."[136] On one or more pictures the subject may misperceive significant elements, e.g., misidentifying the sex of the characters or missing objects which most subjects/patients include in their stories. In many cases, this data indicates that the picture evokes particularly significant feelings.

Finally one combines all the elements to look at the "themas" (themes) in the stories—the interactions among the heroes, the environments, and the outcomes. The interpreter hypothesizes about things the subject/patient has done or wishes to do, aspects of his or her personality, his or her feelings and desires, possible future behavior, relationships with people in general and significant people in particular, and so forth. One also notes test-related behavior which may be significant—which stories were hardest to begin or resolve, which involved the greatest intensity of voice or other clear signs of emotion, and so forth.[137] Ryan notes that "response latency," the time it takes the subject to begin telling a story, may yield information about which cards the subject responds to most strongly, emotionally, since those are likely to have response times which are significantly longer or shorter than the average for that individual.[138]

Ryan indicates that "TAT stories are, before all else, samples of the subject's verbal behavior. As such, they can be used to assess aspects of the subject's language fluency, degree of concreteness versus abstractness, coherence of thought, and intellectual capacities."[139]

Murray again cautions that "the conclusions that are reached by an analysis of TAT stories must be regarded as good 'leads' or working hypotheses to be verified by other methods, rather than as proved facts."[140]

Psychology Professor Jon D. Swartz, of the University of Texas at Odessa, notes that "almost any dynamic theory of personality, particularly psychoanalysis and its various derivations, can be used as a basis for analysis of stories."[141] Thus, the crucial element is that the interpreter have an appropriate structure with which to analyze the stories, rather than which particular structure the interpreter utilizes.

Reliability and Validity

Because of the lack of a generally-agreed-upon scoring and analysis system, the reliability and validity of the TAT are harder to demonstrate than for the Rorschach.

> Reliability and validity seem especially hard to establish for the TAT due to the open-ended free response nature of the task, the high degree of interaction

between situational factors and personality, the great difficulty in obtaining suitable independent criteria against which to validate inferences about unconscious aspects of personality, and the problems encountered in trying to develop meaningful, quantitative measures from stories.[142]

Even so, Swartz concludes that "despite its shortcomings, the TAT remains a viable assessment tool."[143] Similarly, Ryan indicates that, "used in theoretically appropriate contexts and with regard to relevant criteria, the TAT can demonstrate remarkable sensitivity and utility. Nonetheless, when subjected to the criteria developed for and appropriate to many objective test instruments, the TAT provides little firm ground upon which the traditional psychometrician could stand."[144]

Ryan particularly cautions, as did Murray, against predictions of behavior based solely on the TAT. "The TAT is most appropriate for looking at psychological processes that may or may not have direct behavior correlates,"[145] he indicates, making it necessary to find convergent data from other sources before drawing conclusions. Used properly, he indicates "that the TAT method can be used for special purposes and can provide credible, sometimes impressive, results."[146] He cautions, however, that "summary conclusions about *the* reliability or *the* validity of the TAT are necessarily overgeneralizations."[147]

Professor of Law Daniel Shuman, in *Psychiatric and Psychological Evidence*, concludes that "the TAT is designed to be used for diagnosis of mental disorders as well as for understanding the patient's attitudes. This information may be useful, even crucial, to diagnosis and treatment planning when combined with other test data and the history."[148]

A series of studies by Allan Lundy, Ph.D., of the Marshall University Psychology Department, have found that the conditions of administration are significantly related to the results one gets. A 1984 study he presented to the American Psychological Association indicated that results were less accurate if the experimenter came on as an authority figure, if students were tested in their classrooms, or if the TAT was presented as a "test."[149] A 1985 study found that reliability was markedly higher when the TAT was given as a first test rather than later in a test battery, and that a test-retest method indicated reliability coefficients about the level of those for the MMPI and 16PF.[150] In a 1988 study, Lundy used four sets of instructions, one set designed to be neutral, according to Murray's criteria, and the other three to be more stressful. He found that the neutral instructions produced a substantial validity coefficient, while the other instructions produced zero or negative validity coefficients.[151] Lundy suggests that the "best way to give the TAT is in as relaxed, friendly, and approving a manner as one can manage. Also, a TAT should never follow an objective test or cognitive task, as these evoke a verbal, task-oriented approach which is likely to persist and spoil the TAT."[152]

In sum, while reliable and valid scoring systems exist for the TAT, there is no widely used system at present. Most clinicians use the TAT as part of a test battery and as a form of structured clinical interview to gather data which can be combined in an attempt to fully understand the individual. Used in this manner, the reliability and validity of the interpretation are dependent on the ability of the interpreter in the context of the other information available about the individual. To maximize the validity and reliability of the instrument, it should be administered at the beginning of a battery of tests, in a relaxed, positive environment.

Intended Audience

"Appropriate subjects are those who range in age from 4 through adult. However, since projective story tasks more pertinent to childhood issues are available, the TAT is most widely used for subjects who are late adolescents or older."[153]

Acceptance by Mental Health Professionals

In a report presented at the meeting of the American Psychological Association in 1983, psychologists B. Luben, R. Larsen, and J. Matarazzo indicate that the TAT was the fifth-most-frequently-mentioned psychological test in their survey of psychologists.[154] This is a small drop from ratings of 3.5, 2.5, and 3.5, respectively, in 1969, 1959, and 1946 surveys.

Keilin and Bloom indicate that, for adults in custody evaluations, the TAT was used by 37.8 percent of psychologist-respondents, who used it in 67.3 percent of their evaluations.[155] These are very similar to the figures for the Rorschach in their survey. Separate figures for children and adolescents for the

TAT and the Children's Apperception Test were not cited. One or the other was used by 39 percent of respondents, who used them in 74.7 percent of their evaluations.

CHILDREN'S APPERCEPTION TEST (CAT)

History

Bellak and Bellak developed the Children's Apperception Test (CAT) in 1949. They used anthropomorphic animals instead of human beings. These animals were presented in pictures that paralleled human activities that the child may experience in everyday life. Originally, the CAT was developed to look at specific problem areas such as "feeding problems," "oral problems," "about acceptance in the adult world," and "problems related to loneliness, toilet behavior and masturbation." Animals were chosen because research supports the theory that children identify more readily with animals.[156]

Description of the Test

The CAT employs 10 cards approximately 8 1/2 x 11 inches. Each picture is a black and white cartoon-like depiction of anthropomorphic animals. The cards are used for children 3 to 10 years of age, or older, developmentally delayed children.

The original instructions suggested by Bellak and Bellak stated:

> For actual instruction, it may be best to tell the child that we are going to engage in a game in which he has to tell a story about pictures; that he should tell what is going on, what the animals are doing. At suitable points, the child may be asked what went on in the story before and what will happen later.[157]

Bellak and Bellak suggest that encouragement may be necessary. However, it is important for the examiner not to be suggestive in his or her prompting. As part of the process, an inquiry takes place for each of the cards to determine why people were performing certain tasks, how they felt, what they were thinking about, or other related important variables.

During the course of the administration, all extraneous activities and comments should be recorded. The pictures are to be kept out of sight except for the one that is being utilized at the moment. The authors suggest that all 10 cards be administered in the same order in which they are numbered.

After the general administration, some examiners prefer to do an additional inquiry. The instructions for this additional inquiry would be, "now I would like you to go back through the cards and put them in two piles. Put all of the cards that you like in this pile and all of the cards that you didn't like in this pile." After the separation is made, the examiner states, "now look through the pile of cards that you liked, and choose the one that you liked the most. After that, look through the pile of cards that you didn't like and choose the one that you liked the least." An inquiry follows asking the child why he or she chose each of the cards.

Analysis/Interpretation

During the interpretation of the CAT, Bellak and Bellak suggest looking at 10 different variables. They are as follows: 1) the main theme; 2) the main hero (the center of the story). In addition, the self-image of the main hero is evaluated; 3) the main needs of the hero (what needs of the hero are being demonstrated by the content of the story?); 4) the conception of the environment (is the environment seen as hostile, friendly, dangerous, and so on); 5) the figures are seen as . . . (how does the child see figures around him or her?); 6) significant conflicts (conflicts that occur within the story); 7) the nature of anxieties; 8) the main defenses (how does the child defend against conflicts within the environment?); 9) severity of superego (what is the relationship of the punishment to the nature of the offense?); 10) integration of the ego (what is the child's general level of functioning?).

These variables are evaluated for each of the stories given on each of the 10 cards. The examiner then looks for a pattern or consistency across the stories to further the interpretation.

Reliability and Validity

As is true of the TAT, due to the lack of a consistent scoring system for the CAT, the reliability and validity are much more difficult to demonstrate than on other tests. In the section of Bellak's book on the CAT, there is no report of any reliability or validity studies.[158] Hatt, in the *Ninth Mental Measurements Yearbook*, states, "there is little, if any normative data available, poor coefficients of internal consistency and retest reliability, and inconclusive validation. In sum, the CAT is psychometrically inadequate."[159]

Intended Audience

The CAT is for use with verbal children 3 to 10 years of age. It can be used with children beyond 10 years of age who are developmentally delayed, but function at the 3- to 10-year-old level.

Acceptance by Mental Health Professionals

Shaffer, in The Ninth Mental Measurements Yearbook, states "like most projective techniques, it provides dubious psychometric data, but rich information regarding the unique emotional reactions of an individual child . . . Despite the shortcomings mentioned above, the CAT remains what it has been for decades, "a classic of its genre."[160] Stein states, "the CAT may be superior for use with disturbed children with respect to the problems specifically tested for in the CAT . . ."[161] As reported in Chapter One, in the Keilin and Bloom study, the CAT is the most widely used children's projective technique in custody evaluations. Hatt also points out that considerable training and skill are required in the administration and interpretation of the CAT.[162]

PROJECTIVE DRAWINGS

As long as psychologists have been doing assessments, there has been the recognition that not all the information desired can be gained through verbal interactions.

> Children, by nature, do not possess the ability to express themselves fully in a verbal manner. Developmentally, children lack the vocabulary and the communication skills to which adults have access. In order to present thoughts and feelings about their experiences, children need to be provided with a suitable means of expression. Self-expression through drawing offers children a familiar, non-threatening way to talk.[163]

Since children start drawing before they learn to talk, drawing techniques can be very useful in assessing children's intellectual and personality functioning.

Many researchers have asserted that for children drawing is a language. Koppitz, developer of research in drawings, identified 30 characteristics of human figure drawing as important emotional indicators. He looked at the quality of drawings, omitted features, and included features that were not typically present.

Wohl and Kaufman pointed out that there are limitations to using drawings for children. "Drawings uncover what children *will* not tell us or what they *cannot* tell us because they dare not reveal certain feelings even to themselves."[164]

Drawings have been used for the past century as projective techniques. However, it was not until the 1920s that a standardized measure of drawings was developed by Goodenough.

Draw-A-Man Test

Goodenough developed the Draw-A-Man Test in 1926. It was initially developed for children between 3 and 15 years of age as a quick estimate of the child's intellectual development. Goodenough developed a 50-item scoring scale.

The Goodenough-Harris Drawing Test

In 1963, Harris updated the Goodenough Draw-A-Man Test to include a drawing of the self and of a woman. Scoring criteria were presented for each of the drawings. Harris added 22 items to Goodenough's original criteria.

Sattler, one of the foremost experts in intelligence testing, points out the "the Goodenough drawing test is an acceptable screening instrument for use as a non-verbal measure of cognitive ability, particularly with children under 10 or 11 years of age."[165] However, Sattler felt that the drawing test should not be used as the only measure of intelligence due to reduced validity.

The House-Tree-Person Drawing Test

In working with noncompliant children, Buck, out of desperation, requested subjects to draw a house, a tree, and a person. He chose these three items, as they represented the items most frequently spontaneously drawn by children. The subject is asked to draw a house, a tree, and a person on separate pages. After the drawing of a person has been completed, the subject is asked to draw a person of the opposite sex.

Although a thorough discussion of the interpretation of the House-Tree-Person is not possible in a manuscript of this nature, "the house is thought to represent the environment, the tree depicts growth, and the person represents the integration of the subject's personality."[166]

Draw-A-Family Test

The Draw-A-Family Test was originally developed by Appel and later elaborated on by Wolff.[167] There are generally two acceptable methods of presenting this test. One method requires the subject to "draw a picture of your whole family," and the other requests the subject to "draw a picture of *a* family." Some examiners prefer the more ambiguous request to draw *a* family, as it provides the examiner with the opportunity to measure the subjects' identification with their own families. Family constellation, placement of individuals in the family, relative sizes of the family members, and other variables are used in interpreting the Draw-A-Family Test.

Kinetic Family Drawings

The Kinetic Family Drawings (KFD) test was developed by Burns and Kaufman in 1970. "The Approach of Using Kinetic (Action) instructions—i.e., asking the child to produce a drawing of figures *moving* or doing something—has been found to produce much more valid and dynamic material in the attempt to understand the psychopathology of children in a family setting."[168]

The instructions given by the examiner state "I would like you to draw a picture of everybody in your family doing something." Of particular note in the interpretation of this picture is whether the family is doing something together, or each individual is doing something separately.

Other Drawing Techniques

There are many minor drawing techniques that have been developed for use in interpreting specific kinds of personality concerns. The number of drawing techniques developed is limited only by the creativity of the examiner. Examples include: 1) the Draw-A-Person-In-The-Rain Task to measure how the individual deals with unpleasant environmental stress; 2) the Draw-A-Dream Test was designed to depict a dream that the child actually has had or one that the child would like to have;

3) the representational family drawing which was developed by Oaklander in an effort to measure how the child representationally perceives each family member. The instruction of "draw a picture of something that represents each member of your family," is given.

Bender Visual Motor Gestalt Test

The Bender Visual Motor Gestalt Test is commonly referred to as the Bender-Gestalt Test. It is widely used by clinical psychologists for the detection of brain damage. Nine simple designs are shown to the subject, one at a time, and the subject is instructed to copy each design. Many clinicians still interpret the Bender-Gestalt subjectively. However, several objective scoring systems have been developed by matching drawing errors resulting from reproducing the simple design. Koppitz developed the most extensive scoring system for use of the Bender-Gestalt with children. Although fairly reliable for children under 10 years of age, the Bender-Gestalt does not correlate significantly with intelligence test scores or age for individuals beyond 10 years of age. As a screening test for detection of brain damage, the Bender-Gestalt has proved to be one of the most successful. Some clinicians use the Bender-Gestalt as a subjective personality test. As a personality test it has questionable validity.[169]

Roberts Apperception Test for Children (RATC)

The Roberts Apperception Test for Children is a more recently developed personality test. It includes 27 stimulus cards for boys and girls. The pictures generally depict familiar interpersonal situations involving children in their relationships with each other and adults. Although it has been criticized for "pulling" for certain kinds of stories, the Roberts Apperception Test represents a serious effort to combine the flexibility of projective techniques with a valid scoring system. Further research and clinical use will determine how valid an instrument this will become over time.[170]

Vineland Social Maturity Scale

The Vineland Social Maturity Scale was originally developed by Doll, and more recently revised by American Guidance Service. The Vineland focuses on what the person usually or habitually does. Four major "domains" are explored by the Vineland. They are as follows: 1) communication; 2) daily living skills; 3) socialization; and 4) motor skills. These domains allow the examiner to compare at what level a child is functioning with reference to the general population. Supplementary norms have been established for retarded, emotionally disturbed, visually handicapped, and hearing impaired individuals.[171]

ENDNOTES

1. American Psychiatric Glossary 132 (E. Stone ed. 1988).

2. Bernstein, *Psychological Testing: II. The Rorschach Test*, 1 J. Children's Asthma Res. Inst. & Hosp. (Sept. 1961) [hereinafter *Psychological Testing:II*].

3. J. Exner, Jr. & D. Exner, *How Clinicians Use the Rorschach*, 36 J. Personality Assessment 403–08 (1972).

4. A. Anastasi, Psychological Testing 612 (6th ed. 1988).

5. *Id.* at 613.

6. *Id.*

7. *Id.* at 614.

8. *Id.* at 620.

9. *Id.* at 622.

10. *Id.* at 623.

11. *Id.* at 614.

12. *Id.* at 614–15.

13. *Id.* at 615.

14. *Id.* at 616.

15. *Id.*

16. *Id.* at 617.

17. *Id.* at 618.

18. *Id.* at 619.

19. *Id.*

20. *Id.* at 620.

21. Carr, *Psychological Testing of Personality* in H. Kaplan & B. Sadock, Comprehensive Textbook of Psychiatry/IV 522 (1985) [hereinafter *Psychological Testing of Personality*]; Lubin, Larsen & Matarazzo, *Patterns of Psychological Test Usage in the United States: 1935–1982*, 39 Am. Psychologist 451–54 (1984) [hereinafter *Patterns of Psychological Test Usage in the United States: 1935–1982*]; Keilin & Bloom, Child Custody Evaluation Practices: A Survey of Experienced Professionals, 17 Professional Psychology: Research and Practice 338–46 (1986) [hereinafter *Child Custody Evaluation Practices*].

22. A. Anastasi, Psychological Testing 565 (5th ed. 1982).

23. J. Exner, Jr. & B. Clark, The Rorschach in Clinical Diagnosis of Mental Disorders 148 (B. Wolman ed. 1978) [hereinafter Clinical Diagnosis of Mental Disorders].

24. *Id.* at 149.

25. *Id.*

26. *Id.* at 153–54.

27. *Id.* at 154.

28. *Id.*

29. *Id.*

30. S. Beck, A. Beck, E. Levitt & H. Molish, Rorschach's Test 2 (3d ed. 1961) [hereinafter Rorschach's Test].

31. Clinical Diagnosis of Mental Disorders, *supra* note 23, at 155.

32. J. Exner, Jr., A Rorschach Workbook for the Comprehensive System 1 (2d ed. 1985) [hereinafter A Rorschach Workbook for the Comprehensive System].

33. *Id.* at 2.

34. Clinical Diagnosis of Mental Disorders, *supra* note 23, at 155.

35. Rorschach's Test, *supra* note 30, at 2.

36. A Rorschach Workbook for the Comprehensive System, *supra* note 32, at 3.

37. Clinical Diagnosis of Mental Disorders, *supra* note 23, at 157.

38. *Id.*

39. *Id.* at 158.

40. Rorschach's Test, *supra* note 30, at 4.

41. A Rorschach Workbook for the Comprehensive System, *supra* note 32, at 30.

42. Rorschach's Test, *supra* note 30, at 4.

43. A Rorschach Workbook for the Comprehensive System, *supra* note 32, at 4.

44. Rorschach's Test, *supra* note 30, at 4.
45. A Rorschach Workbook for the Comprehensive System, *supra* note 32, at 6.
46. A Rorschach Workbook for the Comprehensive System, *supra* note 32, at 7.
47. Clinical Diagnosis of Mental Disorders, *supra* note 23, at 159.
48. Rorschach's Test, *supra* note 30, at 217–21.
49. *Id.* at 208–11.
50. B. Klopfer, M. Ainsworth, W. Klopfer & R. Holt, 2 Developments in the Rorschach Technique and Theory 205 (1954).
51. Clinical Diagnosis of Mental Disorders, *supra* note 23, at 160.
52. *Id.* at 163–64.
53. *Id.* at 164.
54. *Id.* at 165.
55. *Id.* at 166.
56. *Id.*
57. *Id.* at 167.
58. *Id.* at 166–68.
59. *Id.* at 169.
60. *Id.* at 170–71.
61. *Id.* at 171.
62. *Id.*
63. *Id.* at 171–72.
64. L. Phillips & J. Smith, Rorschach Interpretation: Advanced Techniques v–vii (1953) [hereinafter Rorschach Interpretation].
65. *Psychological Testing: II, supra* note 2, at 4–5.
66. B. Klopfer & D. Kelley, The Rorschach Technique 260 (1942).
67. *Psychological Testing: II, supra* note 2, at 5.
68. Rorschach's Test, *supra* note 30, at 134–207.

69. *Psychological Testing: II, supra* note 2, at 5.

70. *Id.*

71. *Id.* at 6; Rorschach Interpretation, *supra* note 64, at 81.

72. *Psychological Testing: II, supra* note 2, at 6.

73. Rorschach Interpretation, *supra* note 64, at 82.

74. *Psychological Testing: II, supra* note 2, at 6.

75. *Id.*

76. Rorschach Interpretation, *supra* note 64, at 109–10.

77. *Id.* at 115.

78. *Psychological Testing of Personality, supra* note 21, at 525.

79. *Id.* at 524–25.

80. J. Exner, Jr., *Searching for Projection in the Rorschach*, 53 J. Personality Assessment 530 (1989).

81. *Psychological Testing: II, supra* note 2, at 6.

82. *Id.* at 7.

83. J. Exner, Jr., *Problems with Brief Rorschach Protocols*, 52 J. Personality Assessment 645–46 (1988).

84. *Psychological Testing: II, supra* note 2, at 13.

85. A Rorschach Workbook, *supra* note 46, at 66.

86. *Id.* at 130–54.

87. For a fairly complete discussion of the negatives, *see, e.g.*, J. Ziskin, Coping with Psychiatric and Psychological Testimony (1981).

88. R. Dana, Rorschach, The Eighth Mental Measurements Yearbook 1040 (1978) [hereinafter The Eighth Mental Measurements Yearbook]; H. Lerner & P. Lerner, *Rorschach Inkblot Test*, IV Test Critiques 525 (1984).

89. The Eighth Mental Measurements Yearbook, *supra* note 88, at 1040–41.

90. *Id.* at 1041.

91. *Id.* at 1041–42. In the same volume of the Yearbook, R.A. Peterson cautions against using the Rorschach to make predictions about future behavior, questioning the predictive validity of the test.

92. The Eighth Mental Measurements Yearbook, *supra* note 88, at 1042.

93. *Id.*

94. L. Atkinson, B. Quarrington, I. Alp & J. Cyr, *Rorschach Validity: An Empirical Approach to Literature*, 42 J. Clinical Psychology 360–62 (1986).

95. *Id.* at 361–62.

96. Wagner, Alexander, Roos & Adair, *Optimum Split-Half Reliabilities for the Rorschach: Projective Techniques Are More Reliable Than We Think*, 50 J. Personality Assessment 107–12 (1986).

97. *Id.* at 110.

98. D. Shuman, Psychiatric and Psychological Evidence 52 (1986).

99. *Id.* at 53.

100. A. Anastasi, Psychological Testing 599 (6th ed. 1988).

101. Exner, Jr., Thomas & Mason, *Children's Rorschachs: Description and Prediction*, 49 J. Personality Assessment 13–20 (1985).

102. *Id.* at 13.

103. The Eighth Mental Measurements Yearbook, *supra* note 88, at 1033.

104. A Rorschach Workbook, *supra* note 46, at 130–55.

105. Siegel in Handbook of Clinical Assessment of Children and Adolescents 74 (C. Kestenbaum & D. Williams eds. 1988).

106. *Id.*

107. *Patterns of Psychological Test Usage in the United States: 1935–1982*, *supra* note 21, at 451–54.

108. Child Custody Evaluation Practices, *supra* note 21, at 338–46.

109. Morgan & Murray, *A Method for Investigating Fantasies: The Thematic Apperception Test*, 34 Archives of Neurology and Psychiatry 289–306 (1935).

110. H. Murray, Explorations in Personality (1938).

111. Ryan, *Thematic Apperception Test* in D. Keyser & R. Sweetland, 2 Test Critiques 799 (1984) [hereinafter Ryan, *Thematic Apperception Test*].

112. H. Murray, Thematic Apperception Test Manual 1 (1943) [hereinafter Murray, Thematic Apperception Test Manual].

113. Stein, *Thematic Apperception Test and Related Methods* in Clinical Diagnosis of Mental Disorders 179–235 (B. Wolman ed. 1978) [hereinafter Stein, *Thematic Apperception Test and Related Methods*]; S. Korchin, Modern Clinical Psychology 241–47 (1976) [hereinafter Korchin, Modern Clinical Psychology].

114. Murray, Thematic Apperception Test Manual, *supra* note 112, at 2; Stein, *Thematic Apperception Test and Related Methods*, *supra* note 113, at 183–84.

115. Murray, Thematic Apperception Test Manual, *supra* note 112, at 2–3.

116. Korchin, Modern Clinical Psychology, *supra* note 113, at 242.

117. Stein, *Thematic Apperception Test and Related Methods*, *supra* note 113, at 190.

118. Ryan, *Thematic Apperception Test, supra* note 111, at 801.

119. *Id.* at 804.

120. Murray, Thematic Apperception Test Manual, *supra* note 112, at 3.

121. *Id.* at 4.

122. *Id.*

123. Stein, *Thematic Apperception Test and Related Methods*, *supra* note 113, at 185–86.

124. *Id.* at 186.

125. *Id.*

126. *Id.* at 187.

127. *Id.*

128. *Id.* at 188.

129. Korchin, Modern Clinical Psychology, *supra* note 113, at 242.

130. *Id.*

131. Ryan, *Thematic Apperception Test, supra* note 111, at 799–800.

132. Murray, Thematic Apperception Test Manual, *supra* note 112, at 6.

133. *Id.* at 7–10.

134. *Id.* at 10–12.

135. *Id.* at 12–13.

136. Korchin, Modern Clinical Psychology, *supra* note 113, at 244.

137. Murray, Thematic Apperception Test Manual, *supra* note 112, at 6.

138. Ryan, *Thematic Apperception Test, supra* note 111, at 805.

139. *Id.* at 808.

140. Murray, Thematic Apperception Test Manual, *supra* note 112, at 14.

141. J. Swartz, Thematic Apperception Test, The Eighth Mental Measurements Yearbook 1128 (1978).

142. *Id.*

143. *Id.* at 1130.

144. Ryan, *Thematic Apperception Test, supra* note 111, at 799.

145. *Id.* at 810.

146. *Id.* at 812.

147. *Id.*

148. D. Shuman, Psychiatric and Psychological Evidence 53 (1986).

149. A. Lundy, "Testing Conditions and TAT Validity: Meta-Analysis of the Literature Through 1983," paper presented at the meeting of the American Psychological Association, August 1984, Toronto.

150. Lundy, *The Reliability of the Thematic Apperception Test*, 49 J. Personality Assessment 141–45 (1985).

151. Lundy, Instructional Set and Thematic Apperception Test Validity, 52 J. Personality Assessment 309–20 (1988).

152. *Id.* at 318.

153. Ryan, *Thematic Apperception Test, supra* note 111, at 804.

154. *Patterns of Psychological Test Usage in the United States: 1935–1982, supra* note 21, at 452.

155. *Child Custody Evaluation Practices, supra* note 21, at 338–46.

156. L. Bellak, T.A.T., C.A.T. and S.A.T. in Clinical Use 242 (4th ed. 1986) [hereinafter T.A.T., C.A.T. and S.A.T. in Clinical Use].

157. L. Bellak & S. Bellak, Children's Apperception Test 2 (1949).

158. T.A.T., C.A.T. and S.A.T. in Clinical Use, *supra* note 174.

159. *Id.* at 315.

160. *Id.* at 316–17.

161. *Id.* at 214.

162. *Id.* at 316.

163. S. Tritell, *Diagnostic and Therapeutic Uses of Drawings of Children Who Have Been Sexually Abused, A Review of the Literature*, Unpublished Doctrinal Dissertation, Wisconsin School of Professional Psychology 12 (1988) [hereinafter *Diagnostic and Therapeutic Uses of Drawings of Children Who Have Been Sexually Abused*].

164. *Id.*

165. J. Sattler, Assessments of Children's Intelligence and Special Abilities 250 (2d ed. 1982).

166. J. diLeo, *Children's Drawings as Diagnostic Aids* in *Diagnostic and Therapeutic Uses of Drawings of Children Who Have Been Sexually Abused, supra* note 163, at 35.

167. Wolfe, Edwards, Manion & Koverola, *Early Intervention for Parents at Risk of Child Abuse and Neglect: A Preliminary Investigation*, 6 J. Consulting and Clinical Psychology, February 1988, at 40–47 in *Diagnostic and Therapeutic Uses of Drawings of Children Who Have Been Sexually Abused, supra* note 163, at 35.

168. R. Burns & S. Kaufman, Kinetic Family Drawings (KFD): An Introduction to Understanding Children Through Kinetic Drawings 17–18 (1970), in *Diagnostic and Therapeutic Uses of Drawings of Children Who Have Been Sexually Abused, supra* note 163, at 36.

169. A. Anastasi, Psychological Testing 486–89 (6th ed. 1988).

170. *Id.* at 605.

171. *Id.* at 287–90.

QUESTIONS FOR CHAPTER EIGHT

Caution: An attorney should not expect to be able to go into court and ask all of the questions listed below. Preparation is necessary, referring to the content of the chapter to determine if the question applies to your case. The page number at the end of each question refers to where in the chapter you may read an explanation of why this question may be important.

1. What projective techniques were administered? (p. 215)

2. Ask the psychologist to produce evidence of reliability and validity of any test that is not discussed fully in this book. (Use the criteria in Chapter Five to determine whether the test is reliable or valid.)

3. If the psychologist only used projective methods for testing, why? This would especially be an important question if the MMPI or intelligence test were not administered.

4. Were the instructions for the specific projective tests followed according to the manual? Ask the examiner to repeat the instructions that were given. If the instructions varied from those indicated in this chapter, ask the psychologist why.

5. Were the projective instruments administered prior to objective instruments? If not, why not? (pp. 216, 222, 245)

6. If the individual used an experimental test, find out if the test used follows the APA guidelines for psychological tests. (See Appendix C, *Ethical Principles of Psychologists*, Principle 8. See also *Standards for Educational and Psychological Testing* in References.)

7. If the Rorschach was administered, what was the seating arrangement? (p. 221)

8. On the Rorschach, determine if both a free association and inquiry were used. If an inquiry was not used, ask why. (p. 224)

9. On the Rorschach, what scoring method was used, if any? If a scoring method was not used, ask why. (pp. 224–29)

10. If a psychologist identifies the scoring method, other than those discussed in this chapter, ask for professional

literature that substantiates the usage of that other scoring method.

11. Were the Rorschach cards administered in order? If not, why not?

12. How many TAT cards were administered? If less than 10, why? (pp. 238–39)

13. Did the examiner use any philosophical system or psychological theory when interpreting the TAT? (p. 243)

14. Were all 10 cards of the CAT administered? If not, why not? (pp. 246–47)

15. Were any of the additional practices in administering the CAT used? (p. 247)

16. What projective drawings were used? (pp. 248–51)

17. If no projective drawings were used, why not?

18. Ask the psychologist how the interpretations of the projective drawings tie into the results of the other instruments administered.

19. If any drawings other than those identified in this chapter were used, ask the psychologist to explain the purpose for the drawing and how those interpretations apply to the overall results.

Chapter Nine
Other Tests Used in Psychological Evaluations

Most psychological tests are designed to provide information for a psychological evaluation that may be used in a variety of contexts. There are tests that are designed specifically to provide information for a custody evaluation.

HISTORY

The decision-making process in custody disputes was not always a difficult and challenging one. Prior to the 1900s, custody of children was automatically given to the father, since he was in a better position to support them financially. If the mother gained custody, the father was no longer financially responsible for their support. With the Industrial Revolution came an increasing awareness of the mother's role in caring for her children, and this gave rise to the "tender years" doctrine which assumed that the children fared better in their mother's care, particularly younger children. This led to an almost automatic favoring of the mother in custody disputes. The Woman's Movement in the 1960s called attention to the inequity of custody decision making based solely on the gender of the parent, and focus began to shift to the "best interest of the child."[1]

In the early 1970s the Uniform Marriage and Divorce Act (UMDA) was developed and subsequently adopted by most states. The UMDA focuses on the "best interest of the child" and offers several factors that may be considered in establishing those "interests." These factors include: the wishes of the parents regarding custody; the wishes of the child; the interaction and interrelationships of the child with the parents, siblings, and anyone else who significantly affects the child's best interest; the child's adjustment to home, school, and community; the mental and physical health of the parties; and other factors that may be deemed relevant to each individual case.[2] Clearly, the above factors are not criteria, but merely areas of the child's life that are deemed important when establishing what the child's "best interest" might be. Thus, officials and mental health professionals are left with a "best interests" test that is maddeningly vague and ambiguous.[3] While this vagueness forces the court to focus on each individual case and to take into consideration any specific or special needs of the family in question, it also opens the door to personal bias in decision making.

IMPORTANT PARENTAL CHARACTERISTICS

In an effort to clarify the "best interests" tests, numerous psychologists have attempted to define specific environmental and parental characteristics that best serve the interest of the child. Goldstein, Freud, and Solnit suggested that the child should be placed with a "psychological parent," defined as the parent or other person who provides continued companionship in a stable environment.[4] They focused on the "least detrimental alternative" and stressed the need for continuity in the child's life. Chasin and Gruenebaum attempted to further specify precisely what characteristics the custodial parent should possess.[5] They emphasize a favorable attitude toward the noncustodial parent; ability to maintain continuity in the child's relationship to peers, school, and relatives; skilled parenting (empathy, knowledge of the child's daily routine, appreciation of developmental levels, ability to communicate, competent guidance, and discipline); humane, flexible, but consistent child management; and attachment to the child that is not based on the parent's own needs.

Barnard and Jenson added to this already lengthy list, focusing on the emotional security and mental stability of the parent, and the parent's ability to realistically perceive future problems and to solve them effectively. The parent's awareness of and access to community supports and services, and insights into their children, themselves, and the noncustodial parent is important.[6]

Other variables deemed to be important by various researchers include affection, ability to stimulate, parent's ability to maintain good relationships with their own parents, appreciation of the effects of divorce on the children, and ability to encourage positive character traits and good health habits.[7]

Clearly, the above list of variables considered to be important when determining the child's best interest is so lengthy as to be unmanageable. Not only are some of these variables as vague as the initial "psychological parent" concept, but they are also difficult to test. For example, how does one measure "appearance" and "ability to encourage good character traits" or the "ability to solve problems" in the future? A further difficulty with this list of variables is that they do not come directly from research on the effects of divorce and various custody arrangements on children, but, rather, from either theoretical models of parenting or research in the general area of child development. While these concepts may be helpful, it has been argued that when trying to determine the best interests of the child in a custody dispute, one should stay close to findings from empirical studies on children of divorce.

Two major long-term studies have been done with children of divorce. These are the Virginia Longitudinal Study of Divorce[8] and the California children of divorce project.[9] The results of these two studies indicate that family disorganization, anger, conflict between parents, and impaired coping ability of the custodial parent negatively affected the child's adjustment to the divorce. Positive outcome was related to availability of the noncustodial parent in a conflict-free parental relationship. The results offer some support for children doing better if in the custody of the same-sex parent.[10] However, both studies emphasize that overall adjustment of the children of divorce is a highly individual phenomenon. It may be more closely related to the developmental level of the child, the child's previous coping strategies, and successes in other idiosyncratic variables within the individual family, than to any overriding characteristics of the parents or the environment. Thus, we come full circle, back to the notion of examining each individual family, case by case, within the vague framework of "best interest of the child" to determine what custody arrangement is best in each particular case. We are a long way from being able to approach custody decision making equipped with empirically derived guidelines that can be used across cases.

The reader is referred back to Chapter Three of this book to review the typical procedure used in custody disputes reported by Keilin and Bloom. Besides the psychological tests recommended in the Keilin and Bloom study, other pertinent information for making custody decisions must be gleaned from interviews and observations.

Interviews, psychological testing, and observation of interactions between parent and child can provide needed information about the members of the family and the relationships
between them. Still needed, however, is information regarding
the social support system of each parent. Although this aspect
of parenting is often overlooked, researchers Belsky, Robins,
and Gamble suggest that the social support system of the parent often makes the difference between good competent child
development. They propose a theoretical model, referred to as
the "buffered" system, wherein parental competence includes
not only the personal characteristics of the parent, but also the
characteristics of the child and the social support system of the
parent. They suggest that personal resources of the parent are
not enough, in some cases, to assure good development.

The review of the current psychological literature leaves us
with a seemingly lengthy and unmanageable number of variables deemed important by researchers, and a wide range of
methods used to assess these variables. Clearly, what is needed is a clinical tool that assesses all variables deemed important, provides a measure that can be used to compare one
parent to another, and can compare parents across studies.

ASPECT*

The Ackerman-Schoendorf Parent Evaluation for Custody
Test (ASPECT) is a test designed to directly indicate appropriateness for custody. This test attempts to identify those characteristics that are reported in psychological literature as being
determinative of fitness for custody.

The first step in developing the ASPECT was to review the
literature in an effort to determine what criteria were being used
to make custody recommendations by mental health professionals and how custody evaluations were currently being conducted.

Sixty variables were reported in the literature and incorporated into the ASPECT. The ASPECT is divided into three subscales referred to as the Observational Scale, the Social Scale,
and the Emotional/Cognitive Scale. The total of these three
scales yields the Parental Custody Index (PCI). Furthermore,

---

*Portions of the manual for the ASPECT have been reprinted by permission
of the publisher, Western Psychological Services, 12031 Wilshire Boulevard,
Los Angeles, California 90025.

the total of Observational and Social scales is considered to be an overt measure of the individual's fitness as a custodial parent, while the Emotional/Cognitive Scale is considered to be a covert measure.

The Observational Scale measures how well the individual presents himself or herself during the evaluation process. The Social Scale identifies various interpersonal relationship, societal, and intrafamilial concerns. The Emotional/Cognitive Scale measures the individual's emotional stability and cognitive ability as indicated by the psychological evaluation process.

Construction of the ASPECT

The variables and issues that have been defined in the psychological literature as important and meaningful when doing custody evaluations were used to form the basis of the ASPECT. Instead of asking who would be the better custodial parent, or what custody arrangement would be in the best interest of the child, specific questions were generated that reflected each of the issues raised by researchers and other mental health professionals in the literature.

Each question was then examined to determine how it could best be answered. Some questions were best answered by using other test data gathered during a typical custody study (MMPI, TAT, Rorschach, Bricklin, intelligence tests, Draw-A-Family). Other questions could best be answered through observation of the parent alone, and of the parents' interaction with the child. And, finally, there were those questions that could best be answered by asking the parent directly. This last group of questions was incorporated into the ASPECT Parent Questionnaire and Personal History Forms. Thus, "data gathering" during the evaluation was organized in such a way that all issues raised in the current literature could be addressed by the examiner upon completion of the custody evaluation.

After data were gathered, they were put into a form useful to the examiner. Questions generated by the literature were then incorporated into the Examiner's Questionnaire, a 60-question test to be completed by the examiner for each parent. Each item is answered either yes, no, or DNA (does not apply). Questions were formulated so a yes answer would always be in the favorable direction. For example, the question would be phrased, "Is there an absence of a history of substance abuse" instead of "Is there a history of substance abuse." Yes responses would be tallied, and a percentage of yes responses for both parents would then be compared to determine whether one parent scored significantly better than the other.

Once the Examiner Questionnaire was developed, it became clear that the items fell quite naturally into subareas that reflected the literature as well as provisions of the UMDA Act. Since the UMDA forms the basis of most state laws regarding child custody, it seemed appropriate to utilize these subareas as subscales when reporting results, as well as using a "global score."

Subscales of the ASPECT

The ASPECT is divided into three subscales: the Observational Scale; the Social Scale; and the Emotional/ Cognitive Scale.

Observational Scale

The Observational Scale measures the parents' self-presentation. It attempts to capture the initial impression that the parent gives and measures how the parent appears, on a superficial level, to others. This outward appearance is important to the child and affects the child's life both directly and indirectly. Directly, the parent's initial impression and outward appearance can be the source of either pride or embarrassment to the child. Indirectly, the parent's self-presentation affects his or her interactions with important people in the child's life, such as teachers, clergy, other parents, and friends of the child.

It is assumed that when a parent comes to an office for a custody evaluation, he or she is aware of being observed carefully, and thus, is on best behavior. It is also assumed that the self-presentation that is seen is similar to what teachers, lawyers, the guardian ad litem, and the judge will see. Frequently, extreme first impressions, either positive or negative, bias the observer in future judgments of an individual. By including self-presentation as a separate scale in the overall evaluation of the parents, two things are accomplished. First, the importance of self-presentation is recognized and measured. Second, by measuring it separately, self-presentation is thus minimized as a possible bias when measuring other characteristics of the parents.

Information used to score the items in the Observational Scale is obtained primarily from the observation of the parent, and, to a lesser degree, from the parents' responses to specific items on the Parent Questionnaire.

Social Scale

While the Observational and Emotional/Cognitive Scales measure personal qualities of the parent, the Social Scale measures the parent's interaction with others. Personal qualities are certainly important to the task of parenting. How the parent utilizes these qualities when interacting with others determines the quality of the child's environment and the general tone of family life. Parenting is never done in isolation; rather, it involves interaction with extended family, friends, school, and community, as well as between the two parents, and between the parents and the children.

The Social Scale was developed to assess the parent's interaction with his or her family of origin, with the child, with the other parent, and with the community. Since the interaction between parent and child is the single most important area to be assessed on the Social Scale, it is afforded the most items. This interaction is further subdivided into the direct interaction between parent and child, the child's perception of the parent, and the social environment provided for the child by the parent. In addition to other areas measured, the parent's stability in the community and the parent's ability to gain support from the community are also assessed. As part of the Social Scale, the parent's legal history, as well as issues related to alcoholism, physical abuse, sexual abuse, and other legal difficulties are addressed.

Emotional/Cognitive Scale

Researchers and mental health professionals agree that the psychological health and emotional maturity of the parent is an important variable when evaluating parents in custody cases. Severe psychopathology in a parent may, and often does, negatively affect the child. Fortunately, however, mental health professionals and courts have moved away from the notion of the "psychologically fit" parent as the only criterion upon which to recommend or grant custody. Clearly, other characteristics of the parent which are important in psychological difficulties, especially past problems, are no longer viewed as reason enough to deny custody. Additionally, the cognitive abilities of the parent also need to be evaluated. Since one of the main tasks of childhood, academic competence, often requires the help and support of the parent, some minimum standard of cognitive functioning must be considered when making custody recommendations.

The Emotional/Cognitive Scale of the ASPECT includes items that reflect current psychological functioning, past psychiatric history, current stress, and overall cognitive functioning. Rather than develop new measures to assess these characteristics, the ASPECT utilizes specific measures from other tests, often already used when doing custody evaluations, to quantify and specify the parents' emotional and cognitive functioning. These tests include the Minnesota Multiphasic Personality Inventory, the Rorschach, the Wechsler Adult Intelligence Scale-Revised, and the Wide Range Achievement Test-Revised. These individual measures are weighted equally to eliminate examiner bias by preventing the examiner from becoming overly concerned with one or two negative characteristics that may emerge on psychological tests. The items are meant to reflect a minimum standard of functioning, and to serve as a quantitative, rather than qualitative, comparison.

Administration

The ASPECT is an individually administered test. There are two initial components to the ASPECT. They are the Personal History Form and the ASPECT Parent Questionnaire. They are given to an individual to fill out independently. The instructions should include statements like the following: "Here are some questions that I would like you to answer pertaining to the custody/visitation evaluation. Answer the questions as completely as possible. If you run out of room in the answer blanks, please use the back of the sheets. It is assumed that all of the questions are being answered honestly. If it is determined at a later date that the questions were intentionally answered dishonestly, it is likely to be weighed against you."

The ASPECT forms do not need to be filled out in the sight of the examiner. However, the forms *must* be filled out in the examiner's office. It cannot be taken home by the parent. If the parent is allowed to take the forms home, he or she will have an opportunity to look up some of the answers to certain questions, and thus have an artificially inflated score.

The ASPECT forms should be filled out in a quiet area away from other individuals. The mother and father should not be sitting in the same room as they fill out the forms. Parents sitting in the same room may positively or negatively affect the results of the test.

As is true of many other psychological tests, the ASPECT is a protected instrument. The questionnaires or the examiner answer sheets are not to be shared with anyone other than qualified mental health professionals. If the content of the ASPECT becomes public knowledge, it will be too easy for individuals to prepare for the ASPECT. In addition, questions need to be answered from the individual's memory and not from advance preparation.

The scoring of the ASPECT relies on all portions of the custody evaluation. As a result, many other tests besides the ASPECT forms need to be administered in an effort to score the ASPECT. Typically, parents are given the Minnesota Multiphasic Personality Inventory, the Rorschach Psychodiagnostic Series, the Thematic Apperception Test, an intelligence test such as the Wechsler Adult Intelligence Scale-Revised, and an achievement test such as the Wide Range Achievement Test-Revised. Children will receive an age-appropriate intelligence test, such as Wechsler Intelligence Scale for Children-Revised, and personality tests including the Children's Apperception Test, the Draw-A-Family Test, and/or the Projective Questions Test during an interview. The results of these tests are used in scoring the Emotional/Cognitive Scale of the ASPECT.

Scoring

The scoring portion of the ASPECT manual is divided into three sections. These sections coincide with the scales of the ASPECT, itself. For each of the 60 questions, criteria are included for what constitutes a yes answer, a no answer, and DNA (does not apply) answer. The total number of yes answers is then tallied and compared with the total number of yes answers of the other parent.

Interpretation

As is true in any test that is part of a complete psychological evaluation, recommendation should not be based on the results of the ASPECT alone. The ASPECT is a compilation of many different components that have been reported in the literature to help identify who makes the best custodial parent. The Parental Custody Index (PCI) serves as a summary of all those components in the ASPECT. However, the results of the ASPECT should not be the single criterion used to determine who should be the custodial parent. There are situations where the results of the ASPECT would be irrelevant. For example, in a situation where the father has been found guilty in court of sexually abusing his children, it is likely that the mother would be awarded custody regardless of the ASPECT scores. Since there are only two items on the Social Scale of the ASPECT that refer to sexual abuse, it is possible that the other areas would not indicate problems disqualifying the abusive parent as a custodial parent. However, it is likely that a sexually abusing parent would have pathology that would show up in other areas of the ASPECT. In other situations, such as an acute ongoing substance abuse, active psychoses, or other blatantly disqualifying situations, the results of the ASPECT would be more of interest than necessary to determine who the custodial parent should be.

Interpretation of the ASPECT, at this point in the research, only involves looking at the PCI. At a later date, with a larger sample size, it may be possible to do more sophisticated interpretations on the subscales themselves. Interpretation begins by comparing the PCI's of the two individuals. With a standard deviation on the PCI of 10, a difference in scores of 10 points or more between the mother and the father is considered to be significant. When a significant difference occurs, the examiner can report "based on the results of the ASPECT, the mother/father would make a better custodial parent." However, before reaching this conclusion, the examiner must evaluate the significant difference based on cutoff score interpretation (scores above or below predetermined numbers).

It is assumed that the custody evaluation is performed in an effort not only to determine who would make the best custodial parent, but also to make this determination based on what is in the "best interests" of the children. When no significant differences are reported on the PCI, the results of the ASPECT would suggest that neither parent would be a better custodial parent than the other. If the criterion of what is in the best interest of the child is being used, then it does not make a substantial difference which parent the child resides with, if the ASPECT PCI's are relatively close. In these situations, it may be best not to make a recommendation for placement, but instead to recommend that the parents try to mediate their differences. When mediation is successful, it saves the entire family the added financial and psychological burden of a custody dispute. Furthermore, the wounds heal much faster, there is less likelihood of relitigation, and the individuals have put their decision-making power into their own hands instead of the hands of a relative stranger—the judge. The results of the psychological evaluation and ASPECT can always be used to make a recommendation if the mediation process breaks down.

There are situations where the scores can be significantly different, but of no particular value. For example, if both scores fall above 85, which is the 80th percentile, both parents would make appropriate custodial parents, even if their scores are more than 10 points apart. When both scores fall below 65, which is the 12th percentile, it is likely that neither parent would make an appropriate custodial parent. As a result, interventions that include parenting classes, supervision, or even, in extreme cases, foster placement, must be considered.

When a significant difference occurs, it can be helpful to look at the actual items to determine which ones are scored "no" for each individual. Although they occur infrequently, there are situations where significant differences could occur in the PCI that do not result in practical differences for the purposes of interpretation. For example, one parent could be one or two points above the cutoff scores for various measures on the Emotional/Cognitive Scale, while the other parent is one or two points below the cutoff scores. A three- or four-point difference in the MMPI, WAIS-R, and/or WRAT-R does not constitute a clinically interpretable difference. For example, if one parent scores 69 and the other 71 or 72 on the MMPI, it would result in the difference between a yes or no score on the ASPECT. However, again, it would not be a clinically interpretable difference, even though one parent would score a yes and one a no on the ASPECT.

If the 10-point difference is a result of variables of lesser importance, then less weight would be given to the significant difference in PCI's.

Research

A standardization sample of the ASPECT included 200 individuals who had received the ASPECT as part of an original custody evaluation or a postjudgment dispute. The individuals had been married for an average of 8.77 years, had an average education of 1.5 years of college, had an average of three siblings, and were terminating their first marriage 82 percent of the time. During the development of the ASPECT, a number of reliability, validity, and statistical studies were completed involving a sample of 200 subjects. Means, standard deviations, and standard errors of measurement were obtained for each scale. Percentile ranks were determined for the PCI. Interrater reliability studies yielded coefficients of .90 or greater on all of the scales and the PCI for the pilot project. The intercorrelation matrix was computed in order to examine the interrelationship between subscales, and the relationship between subscales and the PCI. The results indicated that the subscales did not correlate well with each other, indicating they measure different variables, but did correlate well with the total score as would be desired. Analyses of variance were calculated to ensure that the ASPECT was measuring "parenting" and not "mothering" or "fathering." No gender difference was found on the PCI, the Observational Scale, or the Emotional/Cognitive Scale. A gender difference was found on the Social Scale, with females scoring higher than males. (The gender difference should be kept in mind when interpreting the Social Scale.) However, since there is no gender difference on the PCI, and it is the total score that is used in making custody recommendations, it can be assumed that the ASPECT is not biased in favor of the mother. It is entirely possible that as the sample using the ASPECT increases, separate norms may be established for males and females.

With regards to validity, the ASPECT is considered to be content valid, since the questions were derived from the literature on custody issues. The gender study, as well as the intercorrelation matrix, give evidence of construct validity. Predictive validity is measured in two separate ways. The first involves other psychologists administering the ASPECT, but not tallying the results until after they have already formulated to make custody recommendations. Their recommendations are compared with the ASPECT predictions to gain a measure of predictive validity.

A second predictive validity study involves comparing judges' custody decisions with the prediction made by the ASPECT. An outcome study of 56 cases compared the results of the ASPECT with the eventual outcome of the case, whether the outcome was the result of a stipulation or a judge's order. In 59 percent of the cases the outcome was the result of a judge's order, while in 41 percent of the cases it was a result of a stipulation. The study compared results in cases where there was a 10-point or greater difference in ASPECT scores between the parents and cases where there was less than a 10-point difference. As mentioned earlier, a 10-point or greater difference is considered a significant difference and should be viewed as being predictive. Less than a 10-point difference is not significant, and, as a result, the ASPECT does not predict who would make the best custodial parent. In 30 of the cases there was a 10-point or greater difference. In 28 of those 30 cases, or 90.3 percent of the time, the ASPECT results agree with the judge's final order. In those 26 cases where there was less than a 10-point difference in the ASPECT scores, the ASPECT results agreed with the judge's decision 14 times and did not agree with the judge's decision 12 times. As a result, the 10-point difference cutoff was demonstrated as an accurate predictor of who would make the best custodial parent based on the judge's eventual recommendations. Furthermore, the results substantiate the fact that a less than 10-point difference is not interpretable in making a recommendation, as it represented close to an even split with the judge's ultimate decision.

The preliminary research performed on the ASPECT demonstrates a high level of reliability and validity. Many studies will be performed by various researchers over time which will add to the reliability and validity data for the instrument.

BRICKLIN PERCEPTUAL SCALES (BPS)

History

The Bricklin Perceptual Scales (BPS) were developed by Barry Bricklin, Ph.D., a clinical psychologist, for the purpose of identifying a child's "unconscious or nonverbal perception of each parent in the areas of competence, supportiveness, follow-up consistency, and possession of admirable traits."[11] It was Dr. Bricklin's attempt to operationally define the "best interests of the child" criterion, as well as to offer an objective means of assessing that criterion by identifying which parent, in the child's perception, would make the best primary caretaking parent. This would maximize the child's involvement in the ultimate custody decision. Dr. Bricklin also wished to address his experience that parents tend to accept nonbiased test data as inherently more fair than decisions which are made solely through adversarial testimony.[12]

Bricklin also identifies three particular reasons why a test like this is a necessary part of custody evaluations:

> (1) Even parents *not* engaged in adversary battles often misrepresent themselves when observed, while parents actively engaged in custody battles *almost always* do; (2) Even if one could secretly observe competing parents there is no clear way to recognize behavior in a child's best interests, since what is most important is not what parents do but how a particular child at a particular time *utilizes* what the parents do; and (3) Children often reveal their reactions to parental behavior unconsciously, in *nonverbal* behaviors, rather than in what they say.[13]

The BPS was used as a research instrument from the early 1960s until its publication in 1984 as a test for use in custody evaluations.

Description of the Test

The BPS consists of 64 questions, half pertaining to the child's perceptions of his or her mother and half to the perceptions of his or her father. Two responses are given by the child to each item: a verbal response, which is recorded; and then a nonverbal response which the child supplies by making a hole on a continuous line at one end of which is printed "VERY WELL" and at the other end of which is printed "NOT SO WELL."

The examiner sits across a table from the child. On the table is a "card holder," a box (part of the equipment purchased with the test) approximately 8 3/4 inches long, 3 3/4 inches wide, and 1 1/4 inches deep. In the box is a rigid styrofoam pad slightly smaller than the box. The box is aligned with a dot placed on the table, so it will always be in the same place when the child makes a response. If the child moves it, the examiner replaces it at the mark.

The examiner holds a pack of 64 cards, which are about 8 1/2 inches long and 3 1/2 inches wide. Each card has on its back the statements the examiner makes to the child, together with small rectangular boxes numbered "1" to "60," so that a numerical score can readily be assigned to each nonverbal "statement" by the child. On the front of each card is a heavy black line approximately 7 1/2 inches long, at the left of which is printed "NOT SO WELL" and at the right is printed "VERY WELL."

The examiner states to the child, for Card 1:

> We are going to do something where all you have to do is answer some questions and make a pinhole with this. [Hand child the stylus.] For example, if you were having a fight with someone, say some friends or your brothers or sisters over some toys, how well would Dad do at solving this in a way that would be fair to everyone?[14]

The examiner records the verbal response verbatim, then holds the card so that its long edge rests on the card holder, with the front facing the child, and says:

> If this [point to Very Well side] is Dad doing very well at solving a fight over toys, and this [point to Not So Well side] is Dad doing not so well at solving a fight over toys, where on this line would Dad be?[15]

The examiner then immediately places this card in the card holder, so that the child may make a hole in the black line with the stylus. That hole shows up on the opposite side as a numerical score. Without looking at the numerical score, the examiner places that card aside and proceeds to the next one.

Each question is repeated for the parent of the opposite sex 32 questions later—e.g., question 33 asks the same about Mom as question 1 did about Dad. The questions alternate, so that the first is about Dad, the second about Mom, and so forth.

Bricklin cautions that the examiner must clarify whom the child calls "mom" and "dad," since each title could refer to more than one individual in a given child's environment.[16] He also notes that young children tend to respond at the extremes, and that a small proportion of children at any age give only very positive responses to a particular parent. The latter case Bricklin refers to as "the child with the mind-made-up, or as we abbreviate it, MMU. The child with the MMU is the child who perhaps has been programmed or bribed."[17] These children tend to give verbal answers which seem rehearsed, volunteer unasked information, answer very quickly (often before the question has been fully asked and before gut-level responses have a chance to proceed to consciousness), give nonverbal responses which are almost all at the "very well" end of the line, fail to relax as the testing session proceeds, avoid eye contact, and resist overtures of friendliness. For these MMU children, Bricklin indicates that the examiner may as well ask directly who the child prefers be the primary custodian, write it down, and then tell the child something to the effect of: "You have told me who you want to be with and that is very, very important information. This (the BPS) is simply designed to give us *more* information."[18] This is designed to free up the child to some degree, his or her choice now being openly expressed and less necessary to indicate indirectly via test responses. The examiner may also challenge responses felt to be suspect by, e.g., asking for concrete examples (which won't be readily available), and may watch for involuntary hand movements as the child starts to indicate one part of the black line but makes himself or herself alter the unconscious response and indicate another, better, part.

The test normally proceeds without a break through the 64 cards. Depending on the speed with which the child responds, administration takes about 20 to 30 minutes.

Scoring

As indicated, each parent ends up with scores on 32 variables within the categories of "Perception of Competency,"

"Perception of Supportiveness," "Perception of Follow-Up Consistency," and "Perception of Admirable Traits." The parent with higher scores on the largest number of the 32 paired cards is the "winner,"—"the parent more frequently able to serve the child's vital needs."[19] Bricklin's data indicate that the greater the disparity of scores for the parents, the more definite the preference of the child for the "winner." Bricklin now prefers to call the parent whom the child sees as better able to parent in a given area "the parent of choice" rather than the "winner," to reduce the negative impression given terms like "winner" and "loser." Bricklin feels strongly that test data should never serve the purpose of making parents feel bad about themselves. Hence, parental *strengths* should be emphasized. Bricklin currently labels his approach "Access to Parental Strengths," and the purpose of the evaluation is explained to the parents as a quest to make available to the child the best of what each parent has to offer.[20]

The psychologist-authors of the present text have added one scoring procedure, to try to assure optimal validity: while Bricklin scores a "win" when either parent has a score even a point higher than the other, we don't score a "win" if the disparity is less than three points. While this is a small deviation from the official instructions, it has not led to a change in direction for any custody evaluations performed by the present authors, and has increased the strength of the conclusions we could draw about the child's preferences.

The range of numbers of items by which a "winner" beat a "loser" in Bricklin's research was from two to 18 items, with a mean of six (eight in adversary cases).[21] The theoretical range is from zero to 32.

With each parent getting from zero to 60 points per card, a given parent can range from zero to 1,920 points (60 points x 32 cards). Bricklin found that a difference of 40 or more is rare on a single card, and that it is likely to signal an area of particular importance for the child when it occurs. He also recommends that an item-by-item comparison be done for the entire test, to try to find areas of particular significance for the child, particularly when the point score difference for the parents is 300 or more.[22]

Validity and Reliability

Bricklin, in dealing with reliability, notes that "there are no reasons to expect the measurements reported here to exhibit any particular degree of stability, since they should vary in accordance with changes in the child's perceptions."[23] A particular change in a particular parent may lead to a change in the child's responses, or it may not. And a given parental behavior may elicit a change in the child's perception of that parent one time and similar behavior have minimal impact another time. "What matters," he indicates, "is how these parental behaviors impact a given child at a given time."[24]

Bricklin does offer some data on the reliability of the test. In one study, 12 children in custody cases were retested on the BPS within a seven-month span of the original testing. None changed significantly. In another study, six children in a nonadversary population were retested. The only change was for a child who was in family therapy, an expressed purpose of which was to increase the quality of parenting of the new "winner."[25]

Validity has been tested in several ways.[26] One involved validation against another, previously validated instrument, the Perception of Relationships Test (PORT). This is another instrument developed to facilitate custody evaluations. In 40 of 45 cases, or 89 percent, the judge picked as best primary caretaker the same parent who was chosen by the PORT.[27] Of 23 cases in which the BPS and PORT were given within a three-month time span, 19 (83 percent) identified the same winner. In two of the four where the tests disagreed, the item difference scores were less than two points apart.[28]

A second validity measure involved two kinds of child questionnaires. The first child questionnaire asked each child to "name the parent more likely to lend assistance, support or control in a wide variety of circumstances."[29] The questionnaire agreed with the BPS 70 percent of the time—consistent with the contention that consciously generated data is *less* accurate than the nonverbal responses of the BPS. The second child questionnaire described both practical and fantasy situations (e.g., a shipwreck on a desert island), and asked what each parent would do in the situation. It was anticipated that these "would" questions would access a less-conscious part of the child's personality than the other questionnaire. The results confirm this: the "Would" questionnaire agreed with the BPS 87 percent of the time.[30]

A third validity measure was a "Parent Questionnaire," which asked questions about whom the child would go to for various kinds of information or help, which parent goes to school conferences, and so forth. Tested on "normal" families in nonadversarial situations, it was found that concordance with their children's perceptions (as measured by the BPS) was 76 percent for mothers and 88 percent for fathers. Since adversary parents don't respond honestly to questionnaires, it was not also tested on an adversary population.[31]

A fourth method involved having two mental health professionals independently rate family clinical and life-history data generated over a two- to seven-year period. The raters reviewed the massive amount of data and indicated which parent would make a better primary caretaking parent for the tested child. The raters agreed with each other on 20 of 21 cases. The magnitude of their judgment (close, considerable, or overwhelming) was highly correlated with the magnitude of the Item Difference Scores from the BPS.[32]

Bricklin also offers data on the outcome of adversarial cases which went to court. Of 29 cases that went to court in his initial sample, in 27 (94 percent) the judge, who used life histories, vocational data, school and medical records, testimony, etc., chose the winner as predicted by the BPS.[33] In a recent sample of 27 psychologists who offered data on 141 cases, "the agreement rate between the parent selected by the BPS as better able to be the primary caretaking parent (PCP) and the choice arrived at by a judge in a formal hearing" was 89 percent.[34] The same source indicated that

> the agreement rate between the choice arrived at by the psychologist's interpretation of other psychological tests and the BPS . . . was again 89%. The agreement rate between the BPS choice and the psychologist's interpretations of clinical/life history data was 91%. . . . The agreement rate between the PCP selected by the BPS and the psychologist's choices as arrived at based on all information available (tests, clinical and/or life-history data) was 97%.[35]

Thus, five methods of validating the BPS yielded measures which indicate that the BPS is a valid measure of the best interests of the child—as perceived by the child, by nonadversarial parents, and by independent psychologists and jurists. "There is some debate about the wisdom of asking a child for a parental preference directly, but the use of family drawings and a recently developed projective psychological test, the Bricklin Perceptual Scale, are helpful in determining the person the child considers to be the psychological parent."[36]

Intended Audience

The Bricklin Perceptual Scales are appropriate for children aged six and older.[37]

Acceptance by Mental Health Professionals

Since the test has been marketed only since 1984, its use is still limited. Given substantial and growing evidence of its validity and reliability, and the urgent need for increasingly objective measures of the "best interests of the child," we anticipate that its use will grow at a rapid rate. Until 1987, the test was marketed by a small Pennsylvania publishing company. One of the largest marketers of psychological tests, Psychological Assessment Resources of Odessa, Florida, added the BPS to its catalogues in 1987, markedly raising its visibility and making the test readily available to a national market for the first time.

SENTENCE COMPLETION TESTS

There are a great many tests of this type, each of which uses a format wherein individuals are asked to make sentences by completing sentence stems which are presented to them. In effect, they are a special type of projective technique, since it is expected that the individual will project into his or her responses deeply personal statements about needs, fantasies, and so forth. Examples of sentence stems could include: "I want . . . ," "Lawyers are . . . ," "Children make me . . . ," and so forth. While some examiners will make up sentence stems for a particular use, most will use one of the existing formats.

History

The use of the sentence completion technique as a psychological test is considered to have its origin with the work of Ebbinghaus (1897) in his studies of mental abilities. Binet and Simon (1905) found the method to be useful for measuring intellectual abilities and included sentence stems as one of the tests in their first battery. . . . [However,] the sentence completion method is primarily thought of as a technique for assessing personality and attitudes [today]. In terms of the use for personality assessment, the heritage of the test can be traced to the word association technique, which originated with the work of Jung in 1904 and 1906. . . . While valuable material can be gathered through the word association technique, it was soon realized that there are limitations to this method and that longer and possibly more structured stimuli and responses would be useful for the investigation of personality.[38]

First use of a sentence completion test for personality assessment is attributed to psychologist A.F. Payne in 1928.[39] Others began to use similar instruments, but not until World War II did the sentence completion method become popular. There was a need for quick, easily administered psychological tests which could be given to large groups of people, and "the sentence completion method soon became a part of psychological batteries in military settings. It was used in the Air Corps as a screening device . . . but was probably best known for its use in the Office of Strategic Service (OSS)."[40] In nearly all settings, a sentence completion test was part of a battery of tests and/or part of a larger set of data about a person, and it often served as an aid in subsequent interviews. In military hospitals, it was used as a screening device to help decide who should be given more thorough psychological testing.

One such test, developed to be used in Air Force hospitals, was adopted for civilian use after the war: the Rotter Incomplete Sentences Blank (RISB),[41] one of the most widely used sentence completion tests,[42] in part because it is one of the few which allows both qualitative and quantitative assessment of responses.[43] The RISB will be used herein as an example of sentence completion tests, with the understanding that most, but not all, comments about it can be generalized to other similar tests.

Rotter Incomplete Sentences Blank

It was Rotter's intent to use the Incomplete Sentences Blank as an alternative to a lengthy structured interview. While the test was not seen as exposing extremely deep levels of personality, it was anticipated that information not readily available during an interview would often be brought out.[44] By placing some distance between the examiner and the examinee via use of the test, it allows the examinee to respond more freely than he or she might in a face-to-face interview. The examiner can take the information at face value, yielding a quick overview of some of the issues for the given individual. This ease of administration and initial interpretation are among the reasons for the popularity of the test.[45]

Description of the Test

The Rotter Incomplete Sentences Blank (RISB) consists of 40 sentence stems which examinees are asked to complete to create statements which reflect their feelings about themselves and others. There are three similar RISB forms—for examinees of high school age, of college age, or for "adults."

The RISB can be administered to any size group. Little experience or training is required. The instructions simply involve the examiner asking the examinees to respond to all the items, to express their real feelings, and to make complete sentences. The examiner is not to embellish these instructions, as some kinds of changes in instructions or format have been found to affect the outcome of the test. For example, differences have been found if the length of the line on which the examinee responds is altered, and the tone of the instructions can have an effect on responses. Emphasizing speed or administering items verbally, however, has not been found to have a significant outcome.[46] There is no time limit, but most examinees complete the test in about 30 minutes.

M. Cosden, Ph.D., of the University of California-Santa Barbara, suggests that the RISB is probably most effective in the early part of assessments, in part to give the examinees some distance from the examiners to facilitate their expressing themselves more openly. This permits the formation of hypotheses early in the process about areas in which the individuals feel stressed, as well as providing data on the general extent of problems and level of adjustment.[47]

Scoring and Interpretation

The scoring systems for all three forms of the test are based on the scaled responses of college freshmen in the development of the College Form of the RISB. This form was adapted to create the High School and Adult Forms through modifications of the wording of some items, but new normative data was not collected. The manual indicates that "competent clinical workers" are to make the necessary transitions to appropriately use the College Form norms with the other populations.[48]

Each of the 40 items receives an "adjustment score." Each item is assigned one of four possible codes: (1) omission (no response or too short a response to be meaningful), (2) conflict response (reflecting hostility or unhappiness), (3) positive response (reflecting positive or hopeful attitudes), or (4) neutral response (no significant positive or negative affect). Both "conflict" and "positive" responses are given a weighting from 1–3 to reflect the degree of sentiment expressed. The manual provides examples for each scoring category, with men's and women's responses listed separately.

Next, each conflict response is given a score from 0 to 6 to reflect the degree of negativity, with 6 being the most negative, producing a range of possible scores from 0 to 240. The average adjustment score noted in the manual is 127, and 135 is generally used to differentiate those subjects who are "maladjusted" (and likely in need of psychotherapy) from those who are not.[49]

Most analyses of the RISB (and sentence completion tests in general) are not objective, however, but subjective, relying on the clinical expertise of the evaluator.[50] The manual suggests that content analysis of the RISB be similar to that done with the TAT, involving the formation of hypotheses about the individual which are to be compared with other data prior to drawing conclusions.

There is empirical evidence that people respond qualitatively differently to this type of projective instrument than to less-structured instruments like the Rorschach or TAT. One study, for example, found that subjects showed significantly greater levels of state anxiety after unstructured tests, e.g., the Rorschach or TAT, than after more-structured ones like the RISB or MMPI. Another study suggested that, at least for normal subjects, one would expect less psychopathology to be shown on the RISB than on unstructured projective tests, while psychotic subjects were found to project as much pathological material on the RISB and similar tests as on other projective instruments.[51]

> It may be that just those tests that offer a middle range of structure are the best aids to differential diagnosis, in that they allow normal individuals to follow the structure of the stimuli and thereby give less pathological responses while at the same time giving less forceful cues to disturbed subjects, who then project more of their dynamic issues onto the moderately structured stimuli of the test.[52]

Reliability and Validity

Interrater reliabilities using the objective scoring method in several studies have been reported to be .88 or above, very high. Split-half reliability coefficients were found to be .83–.84, also high. Given the range of responses necessary, high interrater coefficients require reliance on the manual and its examples.[53]

Using a cutting score of 135 points correctly identified nearly two-thirds of independently judged "maladjusted" individuals and screened out about 80 percent of the "adjusted" individuals in the original research sample.[54] That cutoff score has also been found to correctly identify delinquent youths 60 percent of the time, while screening out nondelinquent youths 73 percent of the time; to identify students low in use of manifest anxiety defenses 86 percent of the time and those high in it 75 percent of the time; and to identify severe drug users 80–100 percent of the time (but not to identify nonsevere drug users well). The RISB has also been successful at identifying people who are depressed, who are anxious, and/or who have a poor self-image.[55] There is, thus, significant evidence that use of a cutoff score of 135 will identify most people in crisis, but not without missing a significant number of people in need of help. Also, the RISB has *not* been found to be especially effective as assessing changes in psychological adjustment over the short term via pre- and post-test differences.[56] It should be noted that validity data are largely based on formal scoring of the RISB, while in clinical practice formal scoring is rarely done. This raises a question about the validity of a particular interpretation, since it is based on the skill of the clinician doing the interpretation for the most part.[57]

An obvious question is the degree to which responses reflect the individual's conscious or unconscious processes and the degree to which the individual can control what is revealed about himself or herself. Several studies criticize the RISB on the basis that people may give socially desirable responses rather than honest ones, while other studies have found that the relationship between social desirability and adjustment scores is low to moderate.[58] While no one doubts that one *can* be dishonest on any sentence completion test, most people who take it in clinical situations do not attempt to markedly skew the results by doing so. In custody evaluations, however, it is well-known that individuals try to place themselves in the most positive light. It should therefore be assumed that examinees will be trying to do so, both through telling the examiner what he or she wants the examiner to know and through giving socially desirable responses. Even so, it can be a valuable adjunct to the clinical interview, providing hypotheses for the interviewer and adding documentation to other sources of information about the individual.

"As the range of psychological investigations undertaken with the sentence completion method has broadened, its reputation as a useful, valid testing technique has also grown."[59] "While all of the existing sentence completion tests are considered to be more structured than the other projective tests, and material from them is therefore closer to the patient's awareness, this does not preclude the patient's indicating many important diagnostic issues on the test. . . . The test can be a useful addition to a test battery and can add meaningful information on a variety of clinical questions."[60]

Intended Audience

The RISB has three forms, one each for those in 9th–12th grades, for those in college, and for adults.

Other Sentence Completion Tests

While the RISB is the most widely used form of these tests, many others exist. Among them, the most popular include the following:

The Rohde Sentence Completion Method

The Rohde Sentence Completion Method (SCM) consists of 65 items plus an open-ended question at the end of the test. Rohde tried to choose each stem with great care, including comparing them with stems from other tests. She also arranged the order of the stems to try to lead the individual away from everyday life toward the more inaccessible areas of personality. The open-ended question is the request to "Write below anything that seems important to you." There is no formal scoring system; each response is to be evaluated in the context of psychodynamic formulations and categories of needs.[61]

The Sacks Sentence Completion Test

The Sacks Sentence Completion Test (SSCT) consists of 60 items which are relatively structured compared to most sentence completion tests. Sacks also suggests that an inquiry be conducted at the end to maximize understanding of the responses. The test is organized around 15 attitudes, with four stems per attitude—e.g., attitude toward women, toward mother, toward colleagues, and so forth. The degree of disturbance regarding each attitude is rated on a three-point scale, from none to severely disturbed.[62]

The Forer Structured Sentence Completion Test

The Forer Structured Sentence Completion Test (Forer) consists of 100 items with instructions which emphasize speed. The stems are structured to try to force the respondent to offer material useful for diagnosis, e.g., to indicate when he or she was most depressed. There are separate male and female forms. While the sentences are not formally scored, Forer suggests organizing them into seven major areas, and offers a checklist for that purpose.[63]

The Miale-Holsopple Sentence Completion Test

The Miale-Holsopple Sentence Completion Test consists of 73 items and is designed to be minimally structured. The stems consist of relatively general items, rather than obviously personal ones, with the intent of minimizing the degree to which people feel threatened or exposed. The instructions are also more general than most, asking the individual to "complete each sentence in whatever way you wish." There is no formal scoring system. Instead, the authors urge the clinician to form hypotheses sentence by sentence, and to combine them into a global description after all sentences are read. To facilitate identification of unusual responses, numerous examples of characteristic responses are given for each stem. "Overall, the Miale-Holsopple is the least structured of the sentence completion tests and depends on the subjective interpretive skills of the clinician more than any of the other tests.[64]

Acceptance by Mental Health Professionals

In a report presented at the meeting of the American Psychological Association in 1983, psychologists B. Luben, R. Larsen and J. Matarazzo[65] indicate that "sentence completion tests (all kinds)" ranked 7.5 among psychological tests in their survey of psychologists. The RISB by itself ranked 12th, and is the only sentence completion test mentioned by name in their survey. Sentence completion tests also ranked 7.5 in a 1982 survey, up from 8.5 in a 1969 survey. The RISB also ranked 12th in the 1982 survey, down from 10th in the 1969 survey but up from 61st in a 1959 survey.

In a 1986 article, psychologists Keilin and Bloom indicate that, for adults in custody evaluations, sentence completion tests were used by 12.2 percent of psychologist-respondents, who used them in 76 percent of their evaluations. For children, sentence completion tests were used by 12.2 percent of psychologist-respondents, who used them in 70.5 percent of their evaluations.[66]

"The sentence completion test (SCT) is another projective test ranked in the top 10 most used tests in surveys of practicing clinical psychologists."[67]

PARENTING STRESS INDEX

History

The Parenting Stress Index (PSI) was designed by Richard Abidin, Ed.D., as a self-report instrument which parents could fill out to offer a measure of the level and type of stress in a parent-child relationship. It is Abidin's belief that "stress in the parenting system during the first three years of life is especially critical in relation to the child's emotional/behavioral development and to the developing parent-child relationship."[68] The PSI addresses three major areas of stressors: child characteristics, mother characteristics, and situational/demographic life stress. It is designed to identify parents experiencing stress related to dysfunctional parenting.

The PSI was initially made up of items specifically based on research findings regarding dysfunctional parenting, including child abuse and stress research. "This procedure resulted in over 95% of the items included on the PSI being directly related to specific research findings."[69] The test went through five revisions, yielding the form presently used, Form 6.[70] The normative sample for the current form was 534 people, consisting of "predominantly of white mothers."[71] Of them, 92 percent were white and 6 percent black, 25 percent of the families had incomes under $10,000 and 25 percent over $20,000, about one-third were college graduates, their ages ranged from 18–61 with a mean of 29.8, and the children who were the focus of the PSI ranged from one month to 19 years with a mean age of 14 months and a median age of 9 months.[72]

Description of the Test

The PSI is a self-report questionnaire with 120 questions. The directions ask the subject to think about the child he or she is most concerned about and to indicate, for questions 1–101, the answer which is closest to describing his or her feelings along a continuum from 1 (strongly agree) to 5 (strongly disagree). Items 102–120 are optional and ask the subject to mark those life events which have occurred in the past 12 months. Abidin reports that the language of the test is understood by parents with at least a fifth-grade reading ability.[73]

The PSI items are divided into three main sources of stressors. In the Child Characteristics Domain, the six subscales are as follows: Child Adaptability/Plasticity; Acceptability of Child to Parent; Child Demandingness; Child Mood; Child Distractibility/Activity; and Child Reinforces Parent. The Parent Characteristics Domain has seven subscales: Parent Depression; Parent Attachment; Restrictions Imposed by Parental Role; Parent's Sense of Competence; Social Isolation; Relationship with Spouse; and Parental Health. The Life Stress Domain looks directly at the amount of stress the parent is experiencing outside of the parent-child relationship.

Raw scores are readily converted to percentiles on a profile sheet, allowing comparison with the normative group. Neither the administration nor the interpretation need be done by a psychologist, as they are simple and straightforward. The administrator should assure that each individual understands the directions, especially if the parents lack formal education or are inexperienced with answer sheets. Most parents complete the answer form in 30 minutes or less.

Scoring and Interpretation

The PSI form is multipage. The top page is the answer sheet, while underneath are pages on which answers are grouped according to subscales, and subscales grouped into domains. Each subscale is scored by adding the weights of the numbers above the answer selected. The domain scores are obtained by adding the subscale scores for a given domain. Scoring takes a few minutes to learn, and about five minutes to do.

Interpretation involves use of the Clinical Interpretation part of the manual. It is suggested that interpretations be seen as working hypotheses, requiring additional information prior to acceptance as factual.

The PSI has a normal range from the 15th to the 75th percentiles, with scores outside these boundaries considered interpretable for total scores, domain scores, and subscale scores. Cutoff scores are also suggested for particular actions or interpretations.

The interpretations suggested are relatively superficial and need to be seen in the light of the whole body of clinical data for the individual. "Detailed interpretation should be made by a clinician."[74]

Reliability and Validity

Reliability and validity data for the PSI are primarily from unpublished research which is presented in the manual. Test-retest reliability correlations are reported to be from .55 to .82 for the Child Domain, .69 to .91 for the Parent Domain, and .65 to .96 for the total stress score. "Generally, the test-retest stability of the PSI appears sufficiently high to assume the test provides stable measurement and can be used to assess change. Additionally, internal consistency of items and factors appears adequate based on correlational and factor analytic data reported in the manual."[75]

Validity data comes primarily from three sources:

> correlation of PSI scores with other child problem
> checklists and/or measures of parental anxiety;
> effects of intervention on PSI scores; and compari-
> son of parent groups expected to have a high fre-
> quency of stressors . . . with norm groups. The
> results from all three of these sources of validity
> information suggest the PSI is measuring an impor-
> tant aspect of parent perceptions which are related
> to child characteristics, parent stress, and child
> rearing problems. Additionally, the PSI appears to
> be a useful tool for the study of stressors and possi-
> ble stress reactions on parent and child behavior. . . .
> For clinical purposes, a high total stress score
> appears to represent a system with both excessive
> stressors and stress.[76]

> It needs to be noted that the cut-off scores are not
> validated for level of correct classification and/or
> interpretation. . . . The total score cut-off, like the
> domain score cut-offs, needs to be further evaluated
> to determine frequency of correct prediction.
> However, for the time being the cut-off does serve to
> suggest the need for further assessment. . . ."[77]

Intended Audience

> The PSI is appropriate for all parents with the abili-
> ty to read English at a minimum fifth-grade level.
> Although the norm group includes only mothers, the
> current form of the PSI is appropriately worded for
> fathers and has been given to fathers in some
> research studies . . . Based on the normative sample
> the PSI is most applicable for use with mothers of a
> target child aged three and under. Use with parents
> of a target child over three are not well represented
> in the norms and thus should be used with caution
> and preferably with the development of more appro-
> priate norms and/or comparison groups.[78]

However, the manual and the Ninth *Mental Measurements
Yearbook*[79] indicate the test is applicable to both parents of

children below 10 years of age. Since most of the research has been on mothers and on children under 3, however, increased caution is appropriate when addressing results for fathers and for children between 3 and 10. It should especially be noted that "fathers earn significantly low stress scores on all components of the PSI when compared to mothers."[80]

Acceptance by Mental Health Professionals

The PSI is more often used by physicians, especially pediatricians, than by mental health professionals, though it has been used by many psychologists as a diagnostic tool and in research since 1979.[81]

ENDNOTES

1. Thompson, *The Father's Case in Child Custody Disputes*, in M. Lamb & A. Sagi, Fatherhood and Family Policy 83 (1983) [hereinafter *The Father's Case in Child Custody Disputes*]; Howell & Toepke, *Summary of the Child Custody Laws for the Fifty States*, 12(2) Am. J. Family Therapy 56–60 (1984).

2. T. Barland, "The Role of the Guardian Ad Litem as Viewed by the Judiciary," State Bar Spring Convention, Wisconsin (1983).

3. C. Lowery, *Parents and Divorce: Identifying the Support Network for Decisions About Custody*, 12(3) Am. J. Family Therapy 26–32 (1984).

4. J. Goldstein, A. Freud & A. Solnit, Beyond the Best Interests of the Child (1973).

5. Chasin & Gruenebaum, *A Model for Evaluation in Custody Disputes*, 9(3) Am. J. Family Therapy 43–47 (1981).

6. Barnard & Jenson, *Child Custody Evaluations: A Rational Process for an Emotion-Laden Event*, 12(2) Am. J. Family Therapy 61–67 (1984).

7. *Id.*

8. Hetherington, *Divorce: A Child's Perspective*, 34 American Psychologist 851–58 (1979).

9. Wallerstein, *Children of Divorce: The Psychological Tasks of the Child*, 53 Am. J. Orthopsychiatry 230–45 (1983); J. Wallerstein & J. Kelly, Surviving the Breakup: How Children and Parents Cope with Divorce (1980).

10. *The Father's Case in Child Custody Disputes*, supra note 1.

11. B. Bricklin, Bricklin Perceptual Scales 6 (1984) [hereinafter Bricklin Perceptual Scales].

12. *Id.* at 7–10.

13. *Id.* at 11.

14. *Id.* at 22.

15. *Id.*
16. *Id.*
17. Bricklin Perceptual Scales Test Manual Supplement No. 6, at 1 (June 30, 1988).
18. *Id.* at 5.
19. Bricklin Perceptual Scales, *supra* note 11, at 46.
20. B. Bricklin, personal communication, September 27, 1988.
21. Bricklin Perceptual Scales, *supra* note 11, at 47.
22. *Id.*
23. *Id.* at 36.
24. Bricklin Perceptual Scales Test Manual Supplement No. 3, at 1 (March 28, 1986).
25. Bricklin Perceptual Scales, *supra* note 11, at 37.
26. *Id.* at 37–46.
27. *Id.* at 40.
28. *Id.* at 42.
29. *Id.* at 43.
30. *Id.*
31. *Id.* at 44–45.
32. *Id.* at 45.
33. *Id.* at 46.
34. Bricklin Perceptual Scales Test Manual Supplement No. 5, at 1 (Feb. 15, 1988).
35. *Id.*
36. D. Shuman, Psychiatric and Psychological Evidence 307 (1986) [hereinafter Psychiatric and Psychological Evidence].
37. Bricklin Perceptual Scales, *supra* note 11, at 6.
38. Watson, *The Sentence Completion Method*, in B. Wolman, Clinical Diagnosis of Mental Disorders 256 (1978) [hereinafter *The Sentence Completion Method*].
39. *Id.*

40. *Id.*

41. J. Rotter & J. Rafferty, Manual of The Rotter Incomplete Sentences Blank (1950) [hereinafter Manual The Rotter Incomplete Sentences Blank].

42. *The Sentence Completion Method, supra* note 38, at 257.

43. Cosden, *Rotter Incomplete Sentences Blank*, in D. Keyser & R. Sweetland, Test Critiques, Vol. II, 658 (1984) [hereinafter Cosden, *Rotter Incomplete Sentences Blank*].

44. *Id.* at 653.

45. *Id.* at 654.

46. *Id.* at 654–55.

47. *Id.* at 658.

48. Manual The Rotter Incomplete Sentences Blank, *supra* note 41, at 12; Cosden, *Rotter Incomplete Sentences Blank, supra* note 43, at 655.

49. Cosden, *Rotter Incomplete Sentences Blank, supra* note 43, at 655.

50. *Id.* at 656; Psychiatric and Psychological Evidence, *supra* note 36, at 54.

51. Cosden, *Rotter Incomplete Sentences Blank, supra* note 43, at 654.

52. *The Sentence Completion Method, supra* note 38, at 260.

53. Cosden, *Rotter Incomplete Sentences Blank, supra* note 43, at 656–57.

54. *Id.* at 657.

55. *Id.*

56. *Id.*

57. Psychiatric and Psychological Evidence, *supra* note 36, at 54.

58. Cosden, *Rotter Incomplete Sentences Blank, supra* note 43, at 657–58.

59. *The Sentence Completion Method, supra* note 38, at 258.

60. *Id.* at 264.

61. *Id.* at 271–72.

62. *Id.* at 272–73.

63. *Id.* at 273–74.

64. *Id.* at 274–75.

65. Lubin, Larsen, & Matarazzo, *Patterns of Psychological Test Usage in the United States: 1935–1982*, 39 Am. Psychologist 452–53 (1984).

66. Keilin & Bloom, *Child Custody Evaluation Practices: A Survey of Experienced Professionals*, 17 Professional Psychology: Research & Practice 338–46 (1986).

67. Psychiatric and Psychological Evidence, *supra* note 36, at 54.

68. R. Abidin, Parenting Stress Index 1 (2d ed. 1986) [hereinafter Abidin, Parenting Stress Index].

69. *Id.* at 4; McKinney & Peterson, *Parenting Stress Index*, in D. Keyser & R. Sweetland, Test Critiques, Vol. I, 504 (1984) [hereinafter McKinney & Peterson, *Parenting Stress Index*].

70. Abidin, Parenting Stress Index, *supra* note 68, at 5; McKinney & Peterson, *Parenting Stress Index*, *supra* note 69, at 505.

71. Abidin, Parenting Stress Index, *supra* note 68, at 13.

72. *Id.*

73. McKinney & Peterson, *Parenting Stress Index*, *supra* note 69, at 505.

74. *Id.* at 508.

75. *Id.* at 509.

76. *Id.*

77. *Id.* at 508.

78. *Id.* at 507.

79. The Ninth Mental Measurements Yearbook 920 (1985).

80. Abidin, Parenting Stress Index, *supra* note 68, at 13.

81. McKinney & Peterson, *Parenting Stress Index*, *supra* note 69, at 507.

Chapter Ten
Abuse-Related Issues

In the legal context, a psychological evaluation or the history presented frequently gives rise to specific concerns that must be addressed. The presence of any form of physical, sexual, or psychological abuse or victimization calls for a special emphasis in the evaluation.

PHYSICAL ABUSE

The reports of physical abuse have shown a dramatic increase for the past two decades. "Each year since national statistics have been published on the number of child maltreatment reports, there has been the disturbing news that the number is greater than the year before. From 1983 to 1984 alone, there was an estimated 17 percent increase in reports involving 1,727,000 children in over one million families."[1] This is partly a function of more cases being reported, due to increased public awareness, and not just an increase in incidence. One of the problems associated with reporting is attempting to define what constitutes "physical abuse." Most definitions of physical abuse include behaviors that, in the past, were considered acceptable punishment. Basically, any type of physical intervention that causes injury or harm to the victim is considered physical abuse. Punishments involving the use of paddles, "switches," and belts that leave bruises or other marks are considered physical abuse today. Abusiveness in the family does not take place just between parents and children. It also takes place among other family members.

One of the most startling pieces of information reported at the 1973 American Psychological Association Convention in New Orleans was from results of a 10-year follow-up study that looked at families in which the parents had been threatened with removal of the children 10 years previously. They found that, 10 years later, 40 percent of the children had died of neglect or abuse. Studies of this nature helped increase the awareness of the problem and foster public intervention.

One of the problems facing those individuals dealing with the physical abuse issue is the substantiation of child abuse and neglect reports. As stated earlier, the number of abuse reports made has increased steadily. However, "the percentage of those reports that have been substantiated following investigation has decreased."[2] Eckenrode's research reports that over half of the cases reported in 1974 were substantiated, and only 25 percent of those reported in 1984 were substantiated. This study points out that one of the reasons for the lower rate of substantiation is the fact that funding for social service agencies has not increased at the same rate as has the number of reports. In addition, there is concern about the stress that families go through during the abuse investigation, only to have approximately two-thirds of the cases remain unsubstantiated. Eckenrode, a researcher, studied the factors related to substantiated reports. He found that for physical abuse reports, those involving Black and Hispanic children were much more likely to be substantiated than those involving white children. For sexual abuse reports with female victims, the size of the household and the number of adults and children in the family influenced substantiation. In child neglect cases, a higher substantiation rate among younger children may reflect the fact that neglect in the youngest age groups tends to be physical.[3]

In general, a previous history of abuse or neglect in the accused family increases the probability of substantiation. Also, when reports are made by professionals mandated by the law to report, there is a greater likelihood of substantiation. Reports from nonprofessionals are least likely to be substantiated. Other significant factors included the number of contacts with the subjects of the report, the length of the investigation, and the effects of the court action.

Over and over again through the decades, research has demonstrated that the best single predictor of whether an individual will be abusive is whether that individual was abused as a child. Many researchers have attempted to develop child abuse risk assessments. Researchers Daniel, Newberger, Reed, and Kotelchuck "examine the usefulness of child abuse risk assessment and concluded that the advantages of such risk assessment did not outweigh the cost of the procedures."[4] The authors concluded that "if preventive services were delivered only to those persons who were considered 'at risk' for abuse, program efficiency would increase."[5] A considerable amount of MMPI research has been performed, only to find investigators unable to replicate specific subscale patterns to distinguish abusers from nonabusers. Caldwell et al. report that the current methods to assess maltreatment potential are encouraging, but still limited. They point out that one of the difficulties in predicting child abuse is the varying definitions of what constitutes abuse. The authors conclude, "given that current risk assessment procedures provide a relatively small increase in program efficiency, the cost of using that must be evaluated carefully."[6] "At the present, and most likely for the future, the assessment of child abuse potential is *not* a powerful aid to the efforts to prevent child abuse and neglect."[7]

Even though it is difficult to predict the at-risk families for abuse potential, it has been demonstrated that early intervention for parents at risk is beneficial. Wolfe et al. report that "case worker ratings of clients, risk of maltreatment and abilities to manage their families at a one year follow-up significantly favored the families who received parent training in addition to information."[8] They conclude, "early intervention for child abuse and neglect is in its infancy, and selection of the most beneficial treatment modalities will require ongoing evolvement. We must learn how to measure a reduction in the risk of maltreatment, and must gain an understanding of the appropriate timing and selection of intervention targets."[9]

Physical aggressiveness in the family does not always occur between the parents and the children. Majuro et al. performed a study reported in 1988 looking at the differences among anger, hostility, and depression in domestically violent men as compared to generally assaultive men. They found that

> the anger and hostility scores were very similar in the domestically violent and the generally assaultive men. However, the domestically violent men were more likely to be significantly depressed. The findings support the idea that anger dyscontrol is a key issue in the psychological profile of domestically violent men and indicates a need for clinical attention to depression as well as anger.[10]

One of the most prominent researchers in this area, Finkelhor, reported many abuse-related factors. In homicide, wives are more likely to attack husbands. In aggravated assault, the opposite is true. Intergenerational prevalence of familial violence is not as likely as would have been thought. Transition across generations is not inevitable according to his research. He also reports that alcoholics do not become violent when they drink—they drink to become violent. Alcohol is related to, but not predictive of, intrafamilial abuse.

Other researchers, Bolton and Bolton, report many factors that contribute to the likelihood to family violence. They include repeated exposure to crises; the poverty level of individuals; reduced amount of support available; absence of the nuclear family working together in a crisis; a lower level of education; problematic employment patterns; overreliance and physical punishment; rigidity and inflexibility; and lack of involvement of extended family members.[11]

Bolton and Bolton also identified those factors that contribute to appropriate family functioning. They include: a willingness to nurture and protect family members; the ability to make needs known; absence of obvious mental illness; children's ability to elicit caregiving from parents; reciprocal relationships in the family; manageable levels of competition within the family; a supportive environment; lack of a totally dominant family member; and no nagging sense that something is wrong with the family interaction.[12] Further research performed by Hershorn and Rosenbaum studied the effect of marital violence on children. They conclude,

> the results of the . . . investigation are supportive of the hypothesis that parental marital discord and violence are associated with conduct problems in witnessing children. . . The result supported the hypothesis that increased exposure to discord/violence and punitive maternal parenting were both associated with childhood problems. . . These results suggest that exposure to marital discord/violence has a more generalized affect on the behavioral and emotional health of the child than does parenting style, which seems to relate more specifically to conduct disorder . . . The results of the present investigations

suggest that marital violence be added to the list of factors enumerated by Emery, which merit consideration in studying the relationship between marital turmoil and child problems.[13]

THE PSYCHOLOGICALLY BATTERED CHILD

Behaviors on the part of parents that "jeopardize the development of self-esteem, of social competence, of the capacity for intimacy, and positive healthy interpersonal relationship"[14] are all aspects of psychological maltreatment. Garbarino et al. give five examples of psychological maltreatment. They are:

1. Each morning a mother threatens her 4-year-old son with abandonment: "Maybe today is the day I go away and leave you alone. You better be good today, boy, or you'll never see me again."[15]

2. A father restricts his 7-year-old daughter to her room every day after school: "I don't want you getting involved with any other kids; they're not good enough for you."[16]

3. Each time a 10-year-old boy brings home his report card from school, his parents look it over with expressions of disgust: "No son of ours could be such a dummy; we wish you weren't around all the time reminding us of the mistake we made."[17]

4. A 3-year-old boy's father suspects that he's not the boy's father, that the boy's mother had an affair while he was away on business. Now he refuses to speak to the boy: "He's not mine; I don't want anything to do with him."[18]

5. A mother persuades her 13-year-old daughter to earn some money by having sex with the mother's "extra" boy friends: "You're a little slut anyway, and I might as well get something out of being your mother."[19]

The accepted definition of child maltreatment reported in Garbarino came from the *Interdisciplinary Glossary on Child Abuse and Neglect*. "The definitions of emotional abuse include verbal or emotional assault, close confinement and threatened harm. The definitions of emotional neglect include inadequate nurturance/affection, knowingly permitting maladaptive behavior (for example, delinquency) and other refusal to provide essential care."[20]

Parental Factors Related to Maltreatment

Garbarino identifies the parental factors related to maltreatment. They include the following:

- the parents' unavailability to respond to the children's needs. Such parents mainly ignore and reject their children. When they are unavailable to meet their children's physical needs, they fail to feed the children appropriately, to dress them as needed, or to enable them to get enough sleep or health care.[21]

- when parents give partial and inappropriate responses to the children's needs, mainly rejecting or corrupting the children. For example, the parents try to meet the child's physical and psychological needs, yet they lack sufficient resources, knowledge, and skills for doing so effectively.[22] Another inappropriate response is infantilization. Instead of placing excessively high demands on the children, the parents underestimate the children's physical abilities and mental capabilities and consistently prevent the children from actualizing their potentials.[23] A third type of inappropriate response, corrupting or missocializing, occurs when parents teach the children values that deviate from normative community values. In some instances, children are raised on values that differ markedly from those of the community—for example, values favoring drug abuse, sexual misconduct, or delinquent activity—and therefore place the children in jeopardy.[24]

- when parents make harsh and destructive responses to the needs of their children, mainly terrorizing, but also degrading, threatening, and exploiting their children.[25]

Garbarino et al. also examine four "personal characteristics" of the parents who psychologically maltreat their children:

1. the parent, himself or herself, has been psychologically maltreated as a child;

2. the parent is addicted to drugs or alcohol;

3. the parent creates an "interactional stress environment"; and/or

4. the parent is mentally ill or mentally retarded.[26]

The Psychologically Maltreated Child

Garbarino et al. conclude,

> the psychologically maltreated child is often identified by personal characteristics, perceptions, and behaviors that convey low self-esteem, a negative view of the world, and internalized or externalized anxieties and aggressions. Whether the child clings to adults or avoids them, his or her social behavior and responses are inappropriate and exceptional.[27]

Infants are usually psychologically maltreated in the form of rejection, unavailability, malnourishment, or inconsistency. Children are psychologically maltreated by feeling unloved, unwanted, inferior, inadequate, and unrelated to any social system. Adolescents who are psychologically maltreated tend to exhibit patterns similar to those exhibited by children, except these patterns are often stronger and more elaborated, and perhaps less linked to their parents.[28]

Treatment

Considerable research has been done on how to treat psychological maltreatment within families. Interventions that reduce environmental stresses on the family, resolve problems among family members, and mobilize community resources are the most likely to be effective.

CHILD SEXUAL ABUSE

What Is Sexual Abuse?

Finkelhor states that "child sexual abuse is most commonly used in reference to sexual activity involving a child that has at least one of two characteristics. It occurs within a relationship where it is deemed exploitive by virtue of an age difference or caretaking relationship that exists with the child; it occurs as a result of threat or force."[29] The number of cases of child sexual abuse has increased dramatically in the last decade. There were 123,000 estimated cases reported in 1985, as compared to 7,559 in 1976.[30]

Profile of Abuser and Abused

Finkelhor points out that,

> although good research is scarce, there is some rea-
> sonable empirical support for propositions that are
> consistent with some of these theories: (1) Some
> groups of abusers do have an unusual need for
> power and domination which may be related to their
> offender behavior; (2) most groups of offenders who
> have been tested using physiological monitors do
> show unusual levels of deviant sexual arousal to
> children; (3) many offenders have histories of being
> victims of sexual abuse themselves; (4) many offend-
> ers have conflict over adult heterosexual relation-
> ships or are experiencing disruption in normal adult
> heterosexual partnerships at the time of the offense;
> and (5) alcohol is connected to the commission of the
> acts in a large number of the offenses.[31]

He also states,

> according to recent community studies, the following
> factors are consistently associated with higher risk
> of abuse: (1) a child who is living without one of the
> biological parents; (2) a child whose mother is
> unavailable either as a result of employment outside
> of the home, disability or illness; (3) a child who
> reports that the parents' marriage is unhappy or
> conflictful; (4) a child who reports a poor relation-
> ship with the parents or being subject to extremely
> punitive discipline or child abuse; (5) a child who
> reports having a stepfather.[32]

Issues regarding the long-term effects of sexual victimization have been addressed in two studies. Researcher Herman et
al. studied 205 women who had histories of incest. They stated
that patients frequently complained of chronic depression,
anhedonia, and innerdeadness and may be driven periodically
to seek relief in alcohol or other drug abuse, self-mutilization,
and suicide attempts.[33] They conclude,

with the more severe degrees of sexual abuse, however, few women were able to escape without long-
term sequelae. Victims who had experienced forceful
and repeated, prolonged abuse or severe physical
violation, and especially those abused by much older
men, especially by their fathers or stepfathers, were
very likely to report persistent difficulties in their
adult lives.[34]

Gold studied the relationship between childhood sexual victimization and adult functioning. One hundred three women
ranging in age from 18 to 57 were studied. Complete psychological evaluations were administered with results that provided important information in the area. Erica Gold reports,

for the first time, aspects of the woman's victimization
experience, attributional style, and social support network were related to her adult functioning. . . . The
victimized woman's present perception of the abusive
experience and her perception of her mother's
response to it were the only aspects of the victimization experience that were significantly related to her
adult functioning. . . . The quality of the support
reported by these women may reflect their ability to
have close relationships with others, including sexual
relationships.[35]

This study provides support to the notion that the mother's
response to the sexual abuse allegations can have a greater
long-term negative effect on the child's resolution of the problems than the actual sexual abuse.

Scott and Stone examined the effects of father-daughter
incest through use of the Minnesota Multiphasic Personality
Inventory (MMPI). They found that elevations on the 4 and 8
scale were most frequent with victims of father and daughter
incest. An elevated 7-8 and 6-8 were the next highest frequently
scoring profiles. MMPI researchers Scott and Stone conclude,

these findings suggest that father-daughter incest
victimization results in lower psychological adjustment for both age groups (adults and adolescents)
and indicate the probability that the adjustment

problems of child victims do, indeed, persist over time. . . . There is also evidence of "schizoid process" with deficits in ego strength (psychic energy) and serious identity confusion, as well as possible sexual preoccupation with concerns of vulnerability and inadequacy. . . . [36]

A summary of these striking similarities and differences between the two groups leads to the speculation that being sexually victimized by the father produces an arrestment of ego development and related identity confusion at the core of the personality. However, the variable (amount) of time since the molestation seems to determine how this core disturbance is expressed. Shorter time and less development, is exemplified by the adolescent victim and seem to produce more of an identity crisis, while the long-term effects from living for years with the core damage may result in a more chronically depressed and "an at odds with the environment" resignation.[37]

In another study, Scott and Stone examined the personality characteristics of father and stepfather perpetrators. They state that "approximately one-third of the stepfather group obtained 4-9/9-4 MMPI codes, indicating deficits in moral conscience with energized, narcissistic and rationalized behaviors. The natural fathers tended to show a more passive-aggressive style, including immaturity, unrecognized dependency needs, and egocentrism with respect to their adult sexuality."[38]

Hall et al. studied 406 sex offenders who had sexually abused children. They found that the 4-8 profile on the MMPI was the most common profile.[39]

Bona Fide vs. Fabricated Abuse Allegations

With an increase in concerns about child sexual abuse, there has also been an increase in concern about whether the sexual abuse allegations that are being made are bona fide or fabricated.

The number of allegations of child sexual abuse is increasing at an alarming rate. Unfortunately, when a custody/visitation dispute is in process, one parent only has to claim that the other parent has sexually abused one of the children, and the process comes to a dramatic halt. Generally, the accused parent is forbidden contact with the children until the issue is resolved.

In the past, evaluators relied on the amount of detail that the child was able to provide and the description of the abuse as an indicator of whether the allegation was bona fide or fabricated. Richard Gardner, M.D., points out that this past practice is no longer the case.[40] Children today have access to much more information about sex and sexuality than in the past. A child watching the six o'clock news can hear stories about day-care workers who have been charged with sexual abuse. Premium cable channels such as HBO, Showtime, The Movie Channel, and The Playboy Channel all show explicit sexual behavior as early as seven o'clock in the evening. X-rated home videos are much more available to children. Even long-favored soap operas have become sexual showcases during the daytime. Both general sex education and sexual abuse education occur in the schools starting as early as the preschool years. In the past, the only source of information that a child may have had about sexual abuse was when he or she had actually been abused. However, this information could now come from being abused or from any of the above-identified sources.

Gardner has developed criteria that he uses for differentiating fabrication from bona fide sexual abuse. He states that in bona fide sexual abuse, the mother will generally be upset, secretive, and embarrassed. However, in fabricated sexual abuse, the mother has the need to "tell the whole world" and expresses no shame. In bona fide sexual abuse, the child will generally be fearful and timid in the presence of the abusing parent. On the other hand, in fabricated sexual abuse, the child will also want to "tell the whole world," will be comfortable in the presence of the accused, and may even scream the accusations in the face of the accused parent. The description of the abuse in bona fide situations will be consistent, real, and serious; however, in fabricated situations, the scenarios are often preposterous.

These criteria were successfully used in a recent case where a 5-year-old girl accused her father of sexually abusing her. The girl at different times reported that the father, the mother, the mother's boyfriend, the father's therapist, and the mother's therapist had sexually abused her. Many of these accusations were made while sitting on the lap of her father. She appeared to be willing to tell anyone who would listen her preposterous story and added new details on each occasion. Furthermore, her mother was equally interested in telling the story of the alleged sexual abuse to anyone who would listen. In this particular situation, there was also reason to believe that the girl may have seen her mother masturbate on one occasion and have intercourse with her boyfriend on another occasion. This situation certainly suggested that sexual information may have been available to the child without sexual abuse. In this particular matter, the author pointed out these criteria to the judge during testimony, and the father was eventually awarded custody.

Barbara Mara, of the Child Protection Team of Central Florida, also addresses this issue.[41] At the 1986 Southeastern Psychological Association Conference in Orlando, Florida, she pointed out some of the concerns that are raised when children four to seven years of age are involved in sexual abuse allegations. Children from ages four to seven tend to overgeneralize from information they are given. They will fabricate in an effort to fill in the blanks if the facts are not there. Children in this age group, who are repeatedly interviewed, will begin to believe what they have said whether it is true or not. Mara also supported Gardner's contention that sexually abused children suppress their concerns about the sexual abuse after it has been disclosed, as opposed to continuing to talk about it.

Patricia Bresee, Geoffrey Stearns, Bruce Bess, and Leslie Packer reported in the *American Journal of Orthopsychiatry* on allegations of sexual abuse in child custody disputes.[42] These authors have developed a plan to evaluate whether the allegations are fabricated or bona fide. The plan includes interviewing both parents and their attorneys to explain the procedures to be involved. Two therapists are used, one primarily for the child, and the other for the parents. The authors of the journal article point out that either way the child is being mistreated, as a victim of sexual abuse or a pawn of malicious slander. The parents are evaluated with instruments, including the Minnesota Multiphasic Personality Inventory (MMPI) and the Rorschach. Although no single profile exists for a child molester, there are two essential aspects of parent-child sexual abuse. They are a reversal of the parent-child roles and a failure of the parent to control sexual impulses toward the child. The most common findings among those individuals involved in parent-child sexual abuse include:

1. impulse control problems;
2. difficulty monitoring or directing emotional reactions;
3. excessive self-centeredness;
4. strong dependency needs; and
5. poor judgment.[43]

Researchers Bresee et al. state divorced women who falsely accuse their spouses of incest are usually overzealous and dishonest. They may be histrionic or combative and often aggressively demand the decision makers to act quickly. Bresee et al. state that women who have influenced their children to make a false report of sexual abuse are easily recognizable. When they are questioned for specific details, such women can provide little information and are reluctant to have their children interviewed alone. There is also a need to differentiate between the mother's fabrication and a possible overreaction to marginal evidence by the mother. Such women become so interested in proving their point that they overlook the impact of this process on the child.

Bresee et al. describe five components that are found in mothers who are child focused and *not* fabricating or exaggerating the stories of sexual abuse. They are as follows:

1. They expressed remorse for not protecting the child sufficiently to prevent the abuse;
2. They are willing to consider other possible explanations for the behavior or statements that arouse their suspicions;
3. They are willing to have the child interviewed without being present;
4. They are concerned about the impact on the child if he or she has to testify; and
5. If the allegations cannot be verified, they are willing to let go of the investigatory process as long as the child's well-being can be monitored through therapy or some other process.

They also point out that mothers who are primarily interested in attacking the fathers and whose reports are more suspect may

1. insist on being present when the child is interviewed and prompt him/her when he/she is questioned about the abuse;

2. be unwilling to consider any other explanations for the child's statements, behavior or symptoms;

3. be eager for the child to testify at all costs;

4. shop for other professionals who will verify her suspicions and involve the child in multiple examinations;

5. demand that the investigation continue, irrespective of the impact the process is having on the child.[44]

In assessing the child, Bresee et al. state that three different types of data must be considered. They include the child's verbalizations, the child's test responses and play interview, and the observations and reports of parents, teachers, and others who know the child. Bresee et al. state the following:

> In order for a probable child molestation diagnosis to be made, we believe the confirming data must be found in: 1) The child's statements to someone other than the reporting parent; 2) Positive test or play interview findings that are consistent with the syndrome of a child who has been sexually abused; 3) Positive physical findings; or 4) Any combination of these factors.[45]

Bresee et al. also talk about the difference between a child who has been molested on one occasion and a child who has experienced long-term chronic molestation. A child who has been assaulted only once is likely to demonstrate increased clinging to parents, refusal to leave home, social withdrawal, sleep disturbances, and crying. However, a child who has been the victim of chronic molestation has a greater tendency to identify with the aggressor. These children typically show symptoms including pseudomaturity, role reversal with adults, acting-out behavior, depression, precocious sexual knowledge, and sexual advances toward adults and other children.[46]

In spite of this well-thought-out set of differentiating criteria, Bresee et al. identify four patterns which can complicate the diagnostic process. Children who demonstrate an underlying psychotic process may have sexual perceptions that could sound like sexual abuse. Children who have been sexually overstimulated in the manner identified by Gardner may show some of the same symptoms as victims of molestation. Children who name more than one adult perpetrator may get factual information perceptually confused. The last pattern concerns children who have been "coached" or otherwise influenced to describe the molestation. Bresee et al. found that, in an effort to deal with these four areas of concern, ongoing therapeutic sessions following the initial diagnostic period were very helpful in differentiating the bona fide from the fabricated abuse.

The last thing that Bresee et al. point out is that whether or not the sexual abuse has occurred, counseling is necessary. If the allegations are unverified, the counseling is necessary to deal with the aftermath of the allegations. If the allegations are verified, the child needs to be in therapy to deal with the abuse. The perpetrator needs to be in therapy to deal with whatever is wrong with him or her, and the nonperpetrating parent needs to be in therapy to help the child.

Mary de Young reports about a conceptual model for judging the truthfulness of a young child's allegation of sexual abuse.[47] She states that one must look for clarity, celerity, certainty, and consistency in the child's story. She points out that even though an allegation of sexual abuse may lack these four factors, the allegation should still be taken seriously until further evaluation has occurred. Ms. de Young's conceptual model includes asking the child to describe the specific sexual action in words, drawings, or with anatomically correct dolls; the context in which the sexual abuse occurred; any pressure for secrecy placed upon him or her by the alleged perpetrator; and affective details regarding how the child felt about the sexual abuse and the perpetrator.

Ms. de Young points out that there are several traumagenic factors that are present in children who have been sexually abused. The first traumagenic factor is traumatic sexualization. Due to the trauma of being sexually abused, these individuals often become sexually aggressive, engage in repetitious sexual play, or demonstrate age-inappropriate sexual knowledge or interest. Betrayal of the child's trust and dependency by the offending adult is a second traumagenic factor. This betrayal often leads to grief, depression, and dependency. A third traumagenic factor is the feeling of disempowerment. This feeling leads to symptoms of anxiety, fears, and hypervigilance. The final traumagenic factor is stigmatization. A child may often receive messages of shame, guilt, or blame for the activity. These feelings can lead to low self-esteem, suicidal ideation, and self-destructive behavior.

Ms. de Young also points out that a young child who is being pressured to lie experiences stress just as a child who is being coerced into secrecy by a sexual abuser. However, she points out that a young child coerced into lying is probably unable to give elaborate details of the abuse or demonstrate the kinds of vulnerabilities documented about abused individuals.

The area of sexual abuse allegations has received increasing attention in recent years in litigated custody or visitation disputes. Increasing attention has been placed on this area by mental health professionals in an effort to help determine whether the allegations are fabricated or bona fide. Gardner, Mara, Bresee et al., and de Young have all addressed this issue in recent literature. As a result, it is much easier for the mental health professionals, the advocate attorneys, guardians ad litem, and the courts to differentiate fabricated sexual abuse from bona fide sexual abuse.

The effects of father-daughter incest were studied by researchers Swanson and Biaggio. They report that the oldest daughter in the family is most likely to be the first victim of incestuous assault. The pressure for secrecy is generally a component of the incestuous relationship and adds to the burden placed on the child. This results in fear and guilt on the part of the child. When the child reports the incest, the delicate balance in the family is generally disrupted. In a treatment setting, the first job of the therapist is to listen to the child in a believing manner and reassure her that she will be protected from the perpetrator. Once the victim has disclosed the incest, she generally feels a deep sense of having betrayed her parents and feels increasing ambivalence about her father. Swanson and Biaggio report, "the incest victim often expresses a desire to confront her parents, hoping that they will accept the responsibility for the incest and acknowledge that they have harmed her . . . The incest secret is not fully laid to rest until the victim is able to talk about the incest with someone other than her therapist."[48]

Kluft reports,

> one-fifth to one-third of all women have experienced some form of childhood sexual encounter with an adult male, that between 4 and 12 percent have had some sort of sexual experience with a male relative, and that 1 in 100 have had a sexual experience with her father or stepfather . . . A high incidence of incest victims among psychiatric patients ranging from 8 percent to 33 percent is reported.[49]

This group of individuals demonstrates an ongoing vulnerability to exploitation and inappropriate relationships. They learn to be victims during childhood and look for continued relationships that will perpetuate their victimization. Kluft refers to this as the "sitting duck syndrome."[50]

Based on this research, when involved in a custody evaluation that involves father-daughter incest, it is essential that therapeutic intervention address the victimization issue in an effort to prevent the child from continuing to live out the role of the victim in her adult life.

Gary Melton and Susan Limber examined the appropriate roles for psychologists in child maltreatment cases. They referred to physical, sexual, and psychological abuse cases. They raise concerns about psychologists overstepping their bounds by becoming involved in the investigatory process. This was particularly true in cases investigating sexual abuse. The authors state, "whether the defendant shares characteristics of abusers or the victim shares characteristics of abused children tells little about whether the defendant perpetrated the specific offense of which he or she is accused."[51] The authors also point out that psychologists must be ever cognizant of the American Psychological Association Code of Ethics in pursuing these matters, stating that psychologists should not overstep the bounds of their professional role, must be careful to avoid intrusions of the due process rights of defendants, and should be sensitive to the ethical interests of victims. [52] As an example, the authors state, "intrusions on the privacy of victims should be no greater than necessary to meet the demands of justice."[53]

Melton and Limber also feel that it is important to continue to inform the children of the progress of the case. They perceive that this increases the child's trust in the legal process and tends to make them a more credible witness. In dealing with children, the authors also feel that psychologists must be honest about their limits of role and expertise. They specifically state that the particular violation in mixing roles involves the psychotherapy process as a "prosecutorial investigative tool."[54]

In further investigating psychologists overstepping their bounds Melton and Limber state that "under no circumstances should a court admit the opinion of an expert about whether the particular child has been abused or has told the truth . . ."[55] They believe that whenever experts are asked to render opinions on the ultimate issue experts are imposing their expertise in an area that should be left to the trier of fact.

These authors also discuss the use of sexually anatomically correct (SAC) dolls in sexual abuse allegation investigations. They state,

> use of SAC dolls has been mischaracterized as a "test" for sexual abuse, rather than a means for children to clarify their verbalizations through demonstration. The former conceptualization, which is based on a misunderstanding of the proper role of the clinicians in the fact-finding process, leads to exclusion of interview material altogether because of reliance on a scientifically unproven technique.[56]

The authors quote research which has been performed by Goodman and Aman that points out that "in an interview using dolls, young children frequently do explore the dolls genitalia visually and manually. However, young children not known to have been sexually abused infrequently engage in simulations of sexual activity with the dolls, although such play does occur occasionally, especially among the older preschoolers."[57] In addition, Melton and Limber state that the dolls can actually interfere with the child's ability to recall and describe the incident of maltreatment by being distracting or eliciting distorted accounts of the events. [58] Even though tests like the Child Abuse Potential (CAP) inventory have been developed and demonstrated a high hit rate in discriminating abusers from nonabusers, care should be given to not using such tests exclusively in attempting to substantiate abuse allegations.

The authors conclude by saying, "No matter what the role, though, psychologists must keep in mind the compelling purposes of the legal process. They must show respect for the participants in the process and the authorities charged with decision making. Doing so is fully consistent with the high professional and personal duties of psychologists to promote human dignity."[59]

ENDNOTES

1. Eckenrode, Powers, Doris, Munsch & Bolger, *Substantiation of Child Abuse and Neglect Reports*, 6 J. Consulting and Clinical Psychology 9 (Feb. 1988).

2. *Id.*

3. *Id.* at 15.

4. A. Caldwell & C. O'Hare, A Handbook of MMPI Personality Types (1986) (quoting Daniel, Newberger, Reid & Kotelchuck).

5. *Id.* at 8.

6. A. Caldwell, "Families of MMPI Code Types," paper presented at the 12th Annual Symposium on the MMPI, Tampa, Florida, 1982.

7. *Id.* at 21.

8. Wolfe, Edwards, Manion & Koverola, *Early Intervention for Parents at Risk of Child Abuse and Neglect: A Preliminary Investigation*, 6 J. Consulting and Clinical Psychology 40 (February 1988).

9. *Id.* at 46.

10. Majuro, Kahn, Vitaliano, Wagner & Zegree, *Anger, Hostility and Depression in Domestically Violent Versus Generally Assaultive Men and Nonviolent Control Subjects*, 6 J. Consulting and Clinical Psychology 17 (February 1988).

11. F. Bolton & S. Bolton, A Guide for Clinical and Legal Practitioners, Working with the Violent Family 34 (1987).

12. *Id.* at 33.

13. Hershorn & Rosenbaum, Children of Marital Violence: A Closer Look at the Unintended Victims, 52 Am. J. Orthopsychiatry 264–65 (1985).

14. J. Garbarino, E. Guttman & J. Seeley, The Psychologically Battered Child 1 (1987) [hereinafter The Psychologically Battered Child].

15. *Id.*

16. *Id.*

17. *Id.*

18. *Id.*

19. *Id.*

20. *Id.* at 4–5.

21. *Id.* at 53.

22. *Id.* at 54.

23. *Id.*

24. *Id.* at 55.

25. *Id.* at 56.

26. *Id.* at 57–59.

27. *Id.* at 62–64.

28. *Id.*

29. Finkelhor, *The Sexual Abuse of Children: Current Research Reviewed*, 17 Psychiatric Annals 233 (April 1987).

30. *Id.*

31. *Id.* at 234–35.

32. *Id.* at 235.

33. Herman, Russell & Trocki, *Long-Term Effects of Incestuous Abuse in Childhood*, 143 Am. J. Psychiatry 1293 (1988).

34. *Id.* at 1296.

35. Gold, *Long-Term Effects of Sexual Victimization in Childhood: An Attributional Approach*, 54 J. Consulting & Clinical Psychology 474 (1986).

36. Scott & Stone, MMPI Measures of Psychological Disturbance in Adolescent and Adult Victims of Father-Daughter Incest, 42 J. Clinical Psychology 257 (March 1986).

37. *Id.* at 258.

38. *Id.* at 367.

39. Hall, Majuro, Vitaliano & Proctor, *The Utility of the MMPI with Men Who Have Sexually Assaulted Children*, 54 J. Consulting & Clinical Psychology 493–96 (1986).

40. R. Gardner, "Issues in Child and Adolescent Therapy in Divorce," Fifth Annual Intervention for the Child and Family at Risk Workshop, Milwaukee, Wisconsin, April 1986.

41. B. Mara, "Child Sexual Abuse," A Workshop Presented at the Southeastern Psychological Association Convention, Orlando, Florida, March 1986.

42. Bresee, Stearns, Bess & Pecker, *Allegations of Child Sexual Abuse in Child Custody Disputes: A Therapeutic Assessment Model*, 56 Am. J. Orthopsychiatry 550–59 (1986).

43. *Id.* at 560–69.

44. *Id.* at 563.

45. *Id.* at 564.

46. *Id.* at 566.

47. de Young, *A Conceptual Model for Judging the Truthfulness of a Young Child's Allegation of Sexual Abuse*, 56 Am. J. Orthopsychiatry 550 (1986).

48. Swanson & Baiggio, *Therapeutic Perspectives on Father-Daughter Incest*, 142 Am. J. Psychiatry 673 (1985).

49. Kluft, *Incest and Adult Psychopathology: An Overview and A Study of the "Sitting Duck Syndrome,"* The Institute of the Pennsylvania Hospital 3 (1988).

50. *Id.* at 4.

51. Melton & Limber, *Psychologists Involvement in Cases of Maltreatment: Limits of Role and Expertise*, 44 Am. Psychologist 1225 (1989).

52. *Id.* at 1226.

53. *Id.*

54. *Id.* at 1228.

55. *Id.* at 1230.

56. *Id.* at 1231.
57. *Id.*
58. *Id.*
59. *Id.* at 1232.

QUESTIONS FOR CHAPTER TEN

Caution: An attorney should not expect to be able to go into court and ask all of the questions listed below. Preparation is necessary, referring to the content of the chapter to determine if the question applies to your case. The page number at the end of each question refers to where in the chapter you may read an explanation of why this question may be important.

1. Did the examiner determine if physical abuse took place during the marriage in any combination (parent to parent, parent to child)? (p. 303)

2. Did the examiner determine if physical abuse took place during any of the parents' childhoods? (p. 304)

3. Ask the same questions for sexual abuse. (no specific page)

4. Ask the same questions for psychological abuse. (no specific page)

5. If physical abuse, sexual abuse, and/or psychological abuse took place during the childhood of either of the parents, what therapeutic steps have taken place to resolve the conflicts associated with experiencing such trauma during childhood? (p. 307)

6. If the parent has experienced any of these kinds of abuse and has not undergone extensive psychotherapy, how does the psychologist performing the evaluation justify considering this parent as an appropriate custodial parent? (no specific page)

7. If the parent or child reports any form of abuse, make sure the psychologist has obtained detailed descriptions of the abuse in an effort to determine if the allegations are overstated or exaggerated. (no specific page)

8. If sexual abuse allegations have been made against one of the parents toward one of the children, were the criteria discussed in this chapter used to discriminate bona fide from fabricated sexual abuse allegations used? (pp. 311, 313, 314)

9. If allegations of physical and/or sexual abuse have been made, is there any official documentation from an objective third party (police department, social service agency, or other professional)? (no specific page)

10. Ask the psychologist if there is any evidence that the child who is the alleged victim of sexual and/or physical abuse has been coached by either parent, any other adult, or a sibling. (no specific page)

11. If one of the parents was a victim of abuse during childhood, does he or she still act as a victim during adulthood? If so, how will this affect his or her ability to be an effective custodial parent? (no specific page)

12. If there have been abuse allegations, has the mother handled them appropriately? Has the mother been able to put the issue to rest at an appropriate time? (pp. 308–09)

Chapter Eleven
Special Concerns: Mental Retardation

There are four levels of mental retardation: mild, moderate, severe, and profound. These categories have been designated by the American Association of Mental Deficiency (AAMD).

MILD RETARDATION

This is educationally referred to as the educable range for individuals with I.Q.'s between the low 50s and upper 60s, and a mental age of 8 years 3 months (8-3) to 10 years 9 months (10-9). During the first five years of life, mildly retarded individuals can develop social and communication skills. During the school age years, they can achieve academic skills up to approximately sixth grade. Mildly retarded individuals generally cannot learn high school subjects and require special education. During adult years, they are capable of social and vocational adequacy. They need frequent guidance during stressful situations.

MODERATE RETARDATION

Individuals who are moderately retarded are considered trainable, have I.Q.'s from the low 40s to the middle 50s, and generally function at the 5-7 to 8-2 range. During the preschool years, they learn to talk and communicate, have poor social awareness, and have only fair motor development. During the school age years, they can function academically to approximately the fourth-grade level by the time they reach their late teens. They will require special education all the way through school. In adulthood, they are capable of maintaining themselves in unskilled or semi-skilled occupations. They will, however, need continued supervision and guidance.

SEVERE MENTAL RETARDATION

Individuals considered to be dependent trainables with I.Q.'s from the low 20s to the middle 30s who function at the 3-2 to 5-6 age range are considered to be severely mentally retarded. During the preschool years, their motor development is poor, their speech is minimal, and they are unable to profit from training in the self-help areas. During the school age years, they do learn to talk and communicate, and can be trained to perform the activities of daily living. During adulthood, they can contribute partially to self-support under complete supervision.

PROFOUND MENTAL RETARDATION

Profoundly retarded individuals fit into the category of custodial retardates. These individuals have I.Q.'s of less than 25 with a mental age development of less than 3 years. During the preschool years, they require constant care and demonstrate minimal capacity for functioning. During the school age years, they continue to require total care with some motor development emerging. However, during their adult years, they are totally incapable of maintaining themselves, and will continue to require complete care and supervision throughout their lives.[1]

It is important to note that retarded individuals who possess the same I.Q. can demonstrate a much wider variety of development than individuals of average or above intelligence who possess the same I.Q. For example, if, on an intelligence test, it only takes one-third of the items correct to obtain an I.Q. of 60, three different individuals could obtain three different thirds of the questions correct and still have an I.Q. of 60. As a result, all three individuals would be very different while obtaining the same I.Q.

MENTAL RETARDATION AND INTELLIGENCE TESTING

"Mentally retarded persons tend to show less change in I.Q. when retested than do persons who are not mentally retarded."[2] The same instruments that have been developed for assessing nonretarded individuals are used with retarded individuals. However, the norms established are often not useful with retarded individuals. As a result, it may be necessary to only utilize age equivalent scores with this group. For example, a 14-year-old severely retarded individual could be given the McCarthy Scales of Children's Abilities which is usually administered to children under age 8 1/2. However, since this test's norms only go as high as 8 1/2 years of age, an I.Q. could not be determined. However, the 14-year-old retarded individual's scores could be compared with the age equivalent tables and an estimated age I.Q. could be determined. Although the Stanford-Binet Intelligence Scale: 4th Edition, the Wechsler Intelligence Scale for Children Revised, and the McCarthy Scales of Children's Abilities are used for evaluating mentally retarded children, they are not designed to be used with severely and profoundly retarded individuals. As is true of other groups, more than one test should be utilized in measuring retardation. It is often helpful to give two of the major intelligence tests mentioned above in addition to the Kaufman Assessment Battery for Children (K-ABC).

Assessing severely and profoundly retarded individuals is a much more difficult task. These individuals often have other areas of deficit, including hearing, speech, vision, and/or motor integration.[3]

> Profoundly retarded children, in particular, have a high incidence of devastating motoric, sensory, and physical handicaps. Their mortality rate is high. Compared to severely retarded children, they tend to have a higher incidence of delayed puberty, institutionalization, seizures and enuresis, poor communication, pika (a strong craving to eat non-nutritive objects, such as paint, gravel or hair), self-biting, fecal smearing, mutism, echopraxia (a tendency toward autonomic imitation of the movements and gestures of others), lack of self-recognition, rumination, abnormal EEGs, and encopresis (involuntary defecation not due to local organic defect or illness), lack of socialization skills and high-pain thresholds.[4]

Sattler points out that

> standardized norm-referenced tests are of limited use in the assessment of severely and profoundly handicapped children. These children have difficulty in following instructions, administrative procedures may be too inflexible to permit them to display the knowledge by unconventional means, and the small number of items at the extreme ranges of ability may restrict the sampling of their abilities. Extrapolated test scores are not appropriate for individual diagnosis because

their reliability is unknown. . . . Criterion-referenced tests, which usually follow standard curriculum guidelines, may not be appropriate for severely and profoundly handicapped children, because these children are rarely candidates for instruction and the school's standard curriculum. These tests fail to take into account the children's handicapping condition, as the standardization group for most criterion-referenced tests are composed of normal children. . . . The use of normal developmental scales with severely and profoundly handicapped children is also fraught with problems. These scales fail to take into account the limited opportunities that severely and profoundly handicapped children have to develop and refine concepts. . . . Although standardized norm-referenced, criterion-referenced and developmentally based tests and scales have potentially shortcomings, they still have a role to play in the assessment of severely and profoundly retarded youngsters. Mental ages, test ages, and developmental ages from these scales provide useful indices which place the child's performance at an approximate developmental level.[5]

In addition to the above-identified methods, task analysis, systematic observation, diagnostic teaching, informal assessment of communication, adaptive behavior questionnaires, checklists, and interviews can be used to evaluate severely and profoundly retarded individuals.

CURRENT TRENDS

Society has become much more tolerant and understanding of retarded individuals. There has been a much greater effort to integrate retarded individuals into society. The media have made a greater effort to present retardation to the public in an acceptable manner as exemplified by the character role of "Bennie" on the 1987 "L.A. Law" series. Sattler points out that the reasons for this include

1) An emphasis on the similarities between retarded and non-retarded people rather than on their differences. 2) A recognition that retarded people can

improve their level of functioning if they are given a proper opportunity. 3) A questioning of the concept of mental retardation. 4) A deemphasis on labeling. 5) Increased individualization. 6) Expansion of legal rights for the mentally retarded. 7) An increased tolerance of deviance. 8) A recognition that some mental retardation arises out of conditions in society. 9) An emphasis on prevention. 10) Planning and coordination of services.[6]

The difference between mental retardation and developmental delay must be understood. Generally, a mentally retarded individual is one who exhibits pervasive significant deficits in intellectual functioning and adaptive behavior.

A diagnosis of developmental delay alerts readers of the psychological report to the possibility that (a) the basis of the cognitive deficit is ambiguous; (b) the deficiency may be transitory; (c) the reduced functioning and adaptive behavior may not be sufficient to warrant a diagnosis of mental retardation; or (d) the problems of adaptive behavior may be temporary.[7]

ENDNOTES

1. J. Sattler, Assessment of Children 649 (3d ed. 1988).
2. *Id.* at 655.
3. *Id.*
4. *Id.* at 556, quoting Switzky, Haywood, and Rotatori.
5. J. Sattler, Assessment of Children 657 (3d ed. 1988).
6. *Id.* at 656.
7. *Id.*

QUESTIONS FOR CHAPTER ELEVEN

Caution: An attorney should not expect to be able to go into court and ask all of the questions listed below. Preparation is necessary, referring to the content of the chapter to determine if the question applies to the case. The page number at the end of each question refers to where in the chapter you may read an explanation of why this question may be important.

1. With a child who has been diagnosed as being mentally retarded, what evidence is there to support that the parent of choice will be able to provide the appropriate academic support for the child? (no specific page)

2. Does the parent have a full appreciation of the effects of mental retardation, or any other exceptional educational needs problems for that matter? (pp. 327–28)

3. If the child has been diagnosed as mentally retarded, did the psychologist use appropriate tests to measure the level of retardation? If the child is retarded or hyperactive, was the parenting stress index administered as one of the tests? (pp. 328–30)

4. If the child is severely or profoundly retarded, what plans has the parent made for the care of the child when the child reaches adulthood? (pp. 327–28)

5. Ask the psychologist at what level the parent participates in the child's exceptional educational needs programming. (no specific page)

Chapter Twelve

Special Concerns: Alcohol and Other Drug Abuse (AODA)

While alcohol and other psychoactive drugs are widely used in our culture for social, recreational, and medical purposes, there is a point where use becomes abuse because of "maladaptive behavior associated with more or less regular use of the substances,"[1] in spite of "a persistent or recurrent social, occupational, psychological, or physical problem that the person knows may be exacerbated by that use. . . ."[2] Alcohol and other drug abuse can have both an immediate and a long-term deleterious effect on children, and assessment of problems in this area is therefore a necessary part of a custody evaluation.

CLINICAL DIAGNOSIS

The *Diagnostic and Statistical Manual of Mental Disorders, Third Edition, Revised* (DSM-III-R)* (discussed in Chapter Fifteen), indicates the following diagnostic criteria for "Psychoactive Substance Dependence":

A. At least three of the following:

(1) Substance often taken in larger amounts or over a longer period than the person intended

(2) Persistent desire or one or more unsuccessful efforts to cut down or control substance use

(3) A great deal of time spent in activities necessary to get the substance (e.g., theft), taking the substance (e.g., chain smoking), or recovering from its effects

(4) Frequent intoxication or withdrawal symptoms when expected to fulfill major role obligations at work, school, or home . . . or when substance use is physically hazardous (e.g., drives when intoxicated)

---

*Reprinted with permission from the *Diagnostic and Statistical Manual of Mental Disorders, Third Edition, Revised.* Copyright 1987 American Psychiatric Association.

(5) Important social, occupational, or recreational activities given up or reduced because of substance use

(6) Continued substance use despite knowledge of having a persistent or recurrent social, psychological, or physical problem that is caused or exacerbated by the use of the substance (e.g., keeps using heroin despite family arguments about it, cocaine-induced depression, or having an ulcer made worse by drinking)

(7) Marked tolerance: need for markedly increased amounts of the substance (i.e., at least a 50% increase) in order to achieve intoxication or desired effect, or markedly diminished effect with continued use of the same amount

Note: The following items may not apply to cannabis, hallucinogens, or phencyclidine (PCP):

(8) Characteristic withdrawal symptoms. . .

(9) Substance often taken to relieve or avoid withdrawal symptoms

B. Some symptoms of the disturbance have persisted for at least one month, or have occurred repeatedly over a longer period of time.[3]

The severity of Psychoactive Substance Dependence is rated "mild," "moderate," or severe," based on the degree of dysfunction associated with abuse.[4]

If symptoms of alcohol or other drug abuse are not severe enough to meet the diagnostic criteria for Psychoactive Substance Dependence, but there is still evidence that there is "a persistent or recurrent social, occupational, psychological or physical problem that is caused or exacerbated by use of the psychoactive substance"[5] and "recurrent use in situations in which use is physically hazardous (e.g., driving while intoxicated),"[6] and "some symptoms . . . have persisted for at least one month, or have occurred repeatedly over a longer period of time,"[7] the diagnosis would then be Psychoactive Substance Abuse.[8] The distinction between "dependence" and "abuse" is an artificial one in that one diagnoses "abuse" only if presently available data are insufficient to meet the requirements for a diagnosis of "dependence."

PSYCHOLOGICAL TESTING

Minnesota Multiphasic Personality Inventory (MMPI)

The MMPI contains the MacAndrew Alcoholism Scale (MAC), which was developed to differentiate alcoholic from nonalcoholic psychiatric patients.[9] The test has high reliability according to a number of studies, even over a span of 13 years.[10] MacAndrew reported that a cutoff score of 24 correctly classified 82 percent of the alcoholics and nonalcoholics in his research. "Most subsequent research has indicated that the MAC effectively differentiates alcoholic from nonalcoholic patients in a variety of settings . . . . There also are data suggesting that drug addicts score higher than other psychiatric patients but not differently from alcoholics on the MAC."[11] "Research has indicated that the scale is a very useful one for identifying substance abuse problems of various kinds for men and women in a variety of settings."[12] Caution should be used when giving the MAC to black individuals, according to several studies, because nonalcoholic black psychiatric patients also tend to score high on the MAC.[13] G. Jacobson, Ph.D., psychologist and researcher, indicates that it appears to be "the best test of its kind,"[14] and is a promising instrument.

Psychologist J. Graham, Ph.D., indicates that when the MAC score is less than 24, one may be confident that the individual is *not* a substance abuser, since there are few false negatives with this instrument. When the MAC is 28 or greater, he indicates, one may be confident that the individual *is* a substance abuser.[15]

A study of V.A. inpatients indicated that the stability of the MAC precludes its being used as a measure of change as a result of treatment, since it is heavily weighted with historical information which does not change as a result of abstinence or treatment. They found the same for ten other substance abuse scales as well (Alcoholism or AL, Alcoholism or ALX, Institutionalized Chronic Alcoholism or ICAS, Composite Alcoholism Key or CAK, Alcoholism or AM, Alcohol or AH, Heroin Addiction or HE, Drug Abuse or DAS, Revised Alcoholism or AREV, Unitary Alcoholism Factor or UAF). They also note that validity and clinical scale scores on the MMPI *do* decrease with inpatient substance abuse treatment, particularly scales L, F, K, 1, 2, and 7.[16]

"When MMPI scores of alcoholics were examined and/or compared with scores of nonalcoholics, the most consistent finding was that alcoholics scored relatively high on Scale 4 . . . . Scale 4 elevations have been found for both male and female alcoholics. . . . Both younger and older alcoholics tend to produce elevated Scale 4 scores. . . Scale 4 elevations of alcoholics tend to be quite stable over time."[17] However, for psychiatric patients, Scale 4 does *not* consistently differentiate between alcoholic and nonalcoholic individuals.[18] Graham indicates that Scale 4 will be high for nearly all substance abusers.[19]

"Very consistent data have suggested that the mean profile for groups of alcoholics is characterized" by elevations of the fourth and second scales together.[20] However, Graham cautions, only one quarter of alcoholics have this profile, and many people with elevations on Scales 2 and 4 are *not* alcoholics.[21]

Graham reports that Goldstein and Linden have identified four basic types of alcoholics in their 1969 cluster analysis.[22] Since that time, Eshbach, Tosi, and Hoyt identified a Type V alcoholic, and Bean and Karasievich have identified a Type VI alcoholic.[23]

- Type I alcoholics typically have a primary elevation on Scale 4 of the MMPI, secondary on Scale 2, and no other scales significantly elevated. They generally have some type of personality disorder diagnosis. They are not likely to have a previous psychiatric history, although they may have prior alcoholism treatment. Their problems are not as severe as other types, even though they may be longstanding. Frequency and quantity of alcohol consumed are not as severe as other types. Anger and acting out, along with poor marital and vocational adjustment are followed by guilt and remorse. These individuals generally have a negative response to treatment, since they are generally denying their disorders. However, they will usually agree to treatment to avoid unpleasant consequences such as jail or divorce.[24]

- Type II alcoholics also have an elevated Scale 4. However, the 2, 7, and 8 Scales are generally higher than Scale 4. These individuals often fall in a "dual diagnosis" category, which includes alcoholism plus a separate diagnosis of a personality problem. They have a wide variety of symptoms, including depression, despondency, social withdrawal, feelings of inadequacy, and job instability. They tend to get angry when drinking and are more likely to get in trouble when they have been drinking. These individuals tend to drink to self-medicate, and do respond well to treatment. They show a greater likelihood of staying in treatment, although progress is slow. Alcoholics in this group demonstrate a very high alcohol use.[25]

- Type III alcoholics have a primary elevation on Scale 4 and secondary elevations on Scales 2 and/or 9. Their validity scales do not show a defensive pattern. Generally, the elevations on Scales 2 and 4 are within normal limits.[26] More than any other groups, these individuals receive a diagnosis of alcoholism. The next more frequent diagnosis for this group would be a personality disorder, an anxiety disorder, and/or a depressive disorder. They tend to have long histories of alcohol abuse with periodic acute episodes. Many of them have had brief hospitalizations for alcoholism. They are seen as being impulsive and narcissistic. They tend to act insensitively toward others, then feel guilt and remorse. These individuals tend to respond poorly to treatment, because they do not see themselves as needing treatment. As as result, they tend to be uncooperative and terminate treatment prematurely.[27]

- Type IV alcoholics have an elevation on Scales 4 and 9 and no other significant elevations. The most frequent diagnoses are "alcohol abuse" or "alcohol dependence," co-existing with an antisocial personality disorder. They are often in trouble with the authorities, and are narcissistic and impulsive. Their relationships tend to be shallow and superficial. They typically have low frustration tolerance, and frequent emotional outbursts. These individuals tend not to have had previous psychological treatment, and can achieve long periods of abstinence followed by periods of abuse. Since they do not perceive themselves as having problems, they are not likely to respond well to treatment.[28]

- Type V alcoholics have elevations on Scales 1, 2, and 3, and sometimes on 4 as well. They are likely to have had previous outpatient treatment and use alcohol as self-treatment for symptoms of anxiety and depression. Gastrointestinal symptoms are the most common presenting complaint for these individuals. They tend to see their problems as being more medical than psychological, and do not perceive themselves as being alcoholics.[29]

- Type VI alcoholics have significant elevations on Scales 8 and F, and may have several other scales elevated as well. A typical dual-diagnosis for this group is "schizophrenia" together with alcoholism. Their psychological history is likely to include inpatient treatment for a psychosis, often with major tranquilizers being prescribed. They have poor judgment, inappropriate affect, and difficulty coping with everyday life. They often become belligerent. They are likely to require inpatient treatment, and do not do well in psychotherapy.[30]

Graham points out that alcoholics who have Scale 4 elevated in conjunction with other scales are more likely to be "characterological alcoholics," while those with the 1, 2, and/or 3 Scale elevations (with or without other scale elevations) are more likely to be "neurotic alcoholics." The characterological alcoholics are much less likely to be able to benefit from treatment than are the neurotic alcoholics.[31]

Psychologists L. Morey, W. Roberts, and W. Penk found that "a large proportion of cluster analysis studies have identified an MMPI profile that is characteristic of this alcohol dependence syndrome, namely, a profile characterized by a 2-8-7-4 configuration. Furthermore, the absolute elevation of this profile may be a useful estimate of the degree of alcohol dependence manifest in a particular individual." These people are "characterized by depression, alienation, anxiety, and impulsiveness."[32] Graham indicates that Scale 8 is rarely high for alcoholics, while it is often high for heroin addicts.[33]

The Michigan Alcoholism Screening Test (MAST)

Quoting M.L. Selzer, the author of the test, in a review article, Hedlund and Vieweg indicate that it was designed "to provide a consistent, quantifiable, structured interview instrument for the detection of alcoholism that could be rapidly administered by non-professional as well as professional personnel."[34]

The MAST consists of 25 "face valid" questions about the
individual's drinking behavior and any problems which may
have been associated with it. Each item requires only a yes or
no answer, and administration takes only about 15 minutes.
Individual items are scored 0, 1, 2, or 5 points, and the total
score is the sum of the individual item scores. A score of 3 or
less is considered an indication of the absence of alcoholism, a
score of 4 represents a suspicion or suggestion of possible alcoholism, and a score of 5 or more is presumptive evidence of
alcoholism.[35]

Reliability coefficients re: internal consistency for the
MAST range from .83 to .95 in six studies cited by Hedlund
and Vieweg.[36] Most of the test-retest reliability coefficients
were in the .80 to .96 range. While the items on the test have
face validity (i.e., one can tell what the test is getting at by
looking at what it asks), there is evidence that most alcoholics
will admit enough about themselves to achieve a significant
score on the test, as did 92 percent in the normative sample.[37]
Twenty of 21 studies of the test's accuracy in identifying diagnosed alcoholics found success rates of 79 percent to 100 percent. One study was lower (57 percent). In 15 studies of
accuracy of diagnosis of nonalcoholics, rates ranged from 36
percent to 95 percent, with a median in the upper 80s.[38] There
is some indication that the MAST produces as many as 13 percent false positives (nonalcoholics identified as alcoholics)
among psychiatric patients,[39] so caution must be used when
diagnosing psychiatric patients using the MAST.

Validity coefficients for the original alcoholic vs. control
group study were from .79 to .90. It should be noted that the
MAST does not distinguish between current substance abuse
problems and past problems which have been resolved, so follow-up questioning must address this issue.[40]

A study by psychologists Otto and Hall found that the
MAST is relatively easy to fake when the individual is so motivated. When alcoholics answered honestly, they found, all were
correctly identified by the test. When instructed to answer as if
they wanted to make a good impression, however, only two of
the 20 alcoholics in the study were identified by the test. Otto

and Hall therefore caution against using the MAST in situations where people may be motivated to "fake good," which would certainly include nearly all forensic situations.[41]

Hedlund and Vieweg conclude by indicating that "its internal consistency and test-retest reliability appear to be satisfactory, it is significantly related to a number of other measures of alcoholism, and it has been demonstrated to be moderately effective in identifying alcoholics from among a variety of other clinical and non-clinical groups."[42] Jacobson also notes the wide applicability of the test to special populations, though indicating that it may be less accurate with young drinkers because many of the questions are based on certain drinking behaviors and their consequences, while younger drinkers have not yet developed the social, medical, and legal problems which would label them as alcoholics.[43] Jacobson concludes that "the MAST can be used as a reasonable screening instrument if one will take into consideration the pertinent issues that remain unresolved."[44]

Alcohol Use Inventory (AUI)

The Alcohol Use Inventory was initially developed by K.W. Wanberg, J.L. Horn and F.M. Foster as the "Alcohol Use Questionnaire," but renamed when it was revised slightly, and it retains the latter name. It contains 161 questions that can be answered objectively by checking one or more specified alternative responses. The last 20 test items relate to marriage, with individuals who have not been married or living in a marriage-type relationship within the past six months invited to skip those items. The test can be administered individually or in groups, and takes about 30 minutes to complete. Scoring can be done by a trained paraprofessional.[45]

There are 16 first-order scales produced by the AUI: (1) Social Benefit Drinking; (2) Mental Benefit Drinking; (3) Gregarious Drinking Style; (4) Obsessive-Compulsive Drinking; (5) Sustained Pattern Drinking; (6) Post-Drinking Worry, Guilt, Fear; (7) Drinking to Change Mood, (8) Prior Use of External Help to Stop; (9) Loss of Control When Drinking; (10) Social Role Maladaptation; (11) Psychoperceptual Withdrawal (DTs); (12) Psychophysical Withdrawal (Hangover); (13) Nonalcoholic Usage; (14) Derived Scale, Daily Quantity of Drinking; (15) Drinking Followed Marital

Problems; (16) Drinking Provokes Marital Conflict. There are also five second-order scales: (A) Self-Enhancing Drinking; (B) Obsessive-Sustaining Drinking; (C) Anxiety Related to Drinking; (D-l) Alcoholic Deterioration; (D-2) Adjunct, Alcoholic Deterioration. A single third-order scale is labeled "(G) general alcoholism."[46]

The test authors' major premise is that alcoholism is probably not a unitary entity; rather, there are a number of "alcoholisms."[47]

There is a high degree of face validity for most of the variables.[48] This is no problem with individuals who are willing to be open and honest, but may be a problem with people who are trying to hide or deny negative behavior—as one would expect of people in a custody dispute. The "D" scores are a built-in validity measure, with a correlation between D-l and D-2 of .75, and an expectation that D scores will be within one standard deviation of one another. If they are farther apart, the validity of the test should be questioned by the clinician.[49]

"Data on reliability measured as internal consistency suggests strong support" for the test, Jacobson indicates. Test-retest coefficients ranged from .66 to .94, with most in the .80s.[50]

Jacobson concludes that "users of this test are likely to find a valuable instrument for differential diagnosis."[51] He also notes that the test appears applicable to most special populations, and, "in fact, this may be the test of choice for use with females because of the existence of separate norms for men and women and the identification of sex-specific factors or patterns."[52] He does, however, indicate that it may be unwise to use the test "with populations having something at risk if identification of an alcoholism pattern is established, because of the high face validity of most of the items and the strong possibility of dishonest responding in such cases."[53] In custody evaluations, then, the AUI is likely to produce many false-negatives—but, at the same time, when it does indicate that alcoholism is present that result may be taken in context as an indication of unusual openness and honesty.

Conclusion

The MMPI, including the MacAndrew Alcoholism Scale, provides a valid and reliable measure of alcohol and other drug abuse which is usable with nearly all populations. Unlike the MAST and the AUI, the items do not largely have face validity —i.e., one cannot tell just by looking at most of the items that they could be used to diagnose alcohol or other drug abuse. This makes the MMPI (and the MacAndrew) the test of choice in custody evaluations, where people are likely to at least "put their best foot forward," if not outright lie in order to influence the outcome.[54]

THE EFFECT OF ALCOHOL AND OTHER DRUG ABUSE ON CHILDREN

The MMPI factor analytic and cluster analysis studies describe the alcoholic (and most other drug abusers) as depressed, anxious, alienated, and impulsive,[55] as well as having "a tendency to . . . resent authority, to have low frustration tolerance, and to have poorly controlled anger."[56] In addition, the fact that they are not meaningfully available to their families during periods of acute intoxication, during hangovers and other consequences of intoxication, and while spending time obtaining drugs worsens the picture.

It should be emphasized that it is not the drinking, per se, which is the problem—it "becomes a 'problem' when it interferes with functioning in significant areas of life, e.g., work, family relationships, social relationships, etc."[57]

A. Berkowitz and H.W. Perkins, of Hobart and William Smith Colleges, Geneva, New York, note that,

> in a comprehensive review of the literature on children of alcoholics (COAs), Russell, Henderson and Blume (1985) concluded that such children are at a particularly high risk for alcoholism and other emotional and behavioral problems, including difficult social adjustment and substance abuse. They also cited studies in which COAs were found to possess distinctive personality characteristics, including lower self-esteem . . . .[58]

Berkowitz and Perkins used eight personality measures with a group of self-identified COAs who were not in treatment. They found that the late-adolescent/young adult COAs in their study reported significantly greater self-depreciation than non-COAs, and that the difference was greater for women than men. They also note a greater propensity for depression among the women.[59] They also found that some COAs showed little or no difference from their peers, indicating that some COAs are resilient enough to cope with the situation successfully.

R. Ackerman emphasizes that one cannot understand the situation of any family member without looking at the degree of alcoholism, the type of alcoholic, and the nonalcoholic's individual perception of the situation.[60] The possible problems for the children, he indicates, include deprivation of emotional and physical support; avoidance of peer activities (especially in the home out of fear and shame); learning destructive and negative ways of dealing with problems and getting attention; lacking trust in anyone; losing sight of values, standards and goals because of the absence of consistent, strong parenting; and suffering a diminished sense of self-worth as a significant member of the family.[61]

Ackerman goes on to indicate that

> children of alcoholic parents are more affected by the disharmony and rejection in the home life than by the drinking. They see that drinking stops once in a while, though the fighting and tension continue. This constant state of agitation affects personality development. More particularly, children observe the use of alcohol as a method of dealing with uncomfortable situations, [which] may give way to use of drinking [themselves] as a means of escape during real or perceived crises in later life. The two-parent family in which alcoholism affects one or both partners cannot provide a healthy parental relationship. A single, non-alcoholic parent can give children a healthier atmosphere.[62]

> When such children discuss their parents to counselors, parental role inconsistency is a major theme. . . . In essence, these children constantly monitor their own behavior, frequently at the expense of creating feelings of conflict, resentment, anxiety, and anger within themselves. . . . Children see parental behavior as a reflection of their own worth. Children

of alcoholics tend to feel that because there is something wrong in their family, there is something wrong with them. . . . Too often the thoughts and emotions of such children remain unshared with friends, because on the one hand they may be under orders from their nonalcoholic parent to say nothing or to pretend; on the other hand they may feel embarrassed and fearful that friends cannot understand their predicament. Worse yet, they may fear ridicule or rejection from friends. Even within the home, siblings may isolate themselves, instead of sharing feelings of mutual endurance.[63]

"Another effect on attitudes of children of alcoholics derives from emotional abuse in the home. . . . The domination of parental alcoholism deprives them of the opportunity to cope with their emotions. . . . Alcoholics may move beyond emotional abuse to physical abuse as their involvement with drinking increases."[64]

Similarly, J.G. Woititz, another author, identifies 13 problems which children of alcoholics are likely to experience to some degree, and which can pose lifelong problems. They

guess what normal behavior is; have difficulty following a project through from beginning to end; lie when it would be just as easy to tell the truth; judge themselves without mercy; have difficulty having fun; take themselves very seriously; have difficulty with intimate relationships; overreact to changes over which they have no control; constantly seek approval and affirmation; feel that they are different from other people; are super-responsible or super-irresponsible; are extremely loyal, even in the face of evidence that the loyalty is undeserved; tend to lock themselves into a course of action without giving consideration to consequences.[65]

CONCLUSION

Living with an alcoholic or other drug-abusing parent is not healthy for children, and is likely to have a deleterious effect on most children in most families. While most of the hard data concerns families of alcoholics, the conclusions for nonalcoholic substance abusers should be essentially the same. All things being equal, it would usually be better for the child to live with a single parent who is not a substance abuser than in a home with two parents one of whom is a substance abuser.

ENDNOTES

1. American Psychiatric Association, Diagnostic and Statistical Manual of Mental Disorders, Third Edition, Revised (DSM-III-R) 165–66 (1987).

2. *Id.* at 165.

3. *Id.* at 167–68.

4. *Id.* at 168.

5. *Id.* at 169.

6. *Id.*

7. *Id.*

8. *Id.* at 169.

9. J. Graham, The MMPI: A Practical Guide 170 (2d ed. 1987).

10. *Id.* at 170.

11. *Id.* at 170–71.

12. *Id.* at 89.

13. *Id.* at 171; J. Graham & V. Strenger, *MMPI Characteristics of Alcoholics: A Review*, 56 J. Consulting & Clinical Psychology 201 (1988) [hereinafter *MMPI Characteristics of Alcoholics: A Review*].

14. G. Jacobson, The Alcoholisms: Detection, Assessment, and Diagnosis 237 (1976) [hereinafter The Alcoholisms].

15. J. Graham, MMPI Workshop, June 1987, Minneapolis, Minnesota.

16. Gallucci, Kay & Thornby, *The Sensitivity of 11 Substance Abuse Scales from the MMPI to Change in Clinical Status*, 3 Psychology of Addicitve Behaviors 29–33 (1989).

17. *MMPI Characteristics of Alcoholics: A Review, supra* note 13, at 197.

18. *Id.* at 198.

19. J. Graham, MMPI Workshop, June 1987, Minneapolis, Minnesota.

20. *MMPI Characteristics of Alcoholics: A Review, supra* note 13, at 198.

21. J. Graham, MMPI Workshop, June 1987, Minneapolis, Minnesota.

22. *MMPI Characteristics of Alcoholics: A Review, supra* note 13, at 198.

23. *Id.* at 200.

24. *Id.* at 198–99.

25. *Id.* at 199.

26. MMPI Workshop, April 1988, Oconomowoc, Wisconsin.

27. *MMPI Characteristics of Alcoholics: A Review, supra* note 13, at 199.

28. *Id.* at 198–99.

29. *Id.* at 200.

30. *Id.*

31. MMPI Workshop, April 1988, Oconomowoc, Wisconsin.

32. Morey, Roberts & Penk, *MMPI Alcoholic Subtypes: Replicability and Validity of the 2-7-8-4 Subtype,* 96 J. Abnormal Psychology 165, 166 (1987) [hereinafter *MMPI Alcoholic Subtypes*].

33. J. Graham, MMPI Workshop, June 1987, Minneapolis, Minnesota.

34. Hedlund & Vieweg, *The Michigan Alcoholism Screening Test (MAST): A Comprehensive Review,* 15 J. Operational Psychiatry 55 (1984) [hereinafter *The Michigan Alcoholism Screening Test (MAST)*].

35. The Alcoholisms, *supra* note 14, at 264–65.

36. *The Michigan Alcoholism Screening Test (MAST) supra* note 34, at 57.

37. *Id.* at 58.

38. *Id.*

39. The Alcoholisms, *supra* note 14, at 277–78.

40. *The Michigan Alcoholism Screening Test (MAST), supra* note 34, at 59–61.

41. Otto & Hall, The Utility of the Michigan Alcoholism Screening Test in Detection of Alcoholics and Problem Drinkers, 52 J. Personality Assessment 499–505 (1988).

42. *The Michigan Alcoholism Screening Test (MAST), supra* note 34, at 62.

43. The Alcoholisms, *supra* note 14, at 284.

44. *Id.* at 285.

45. The Alcoholisms, *supra* note 14, at 75–78.

46. *Id.* at 79–80.

47. *Id.* at 80.

48. *Id.* at 98–99.

49. *Id.* at 99.

50. Id. at 101.

51. The Alcoholisms, *supra* note 14, at 107.

52. *Id.* at 111.

53. *Id.* at 111–12.

54. The reader interested in the psychopharmacology of drugs of abuse should consult the chapter on "Substance Use Disorders" by Grinspoon and Balakar in The New Harvard Guide to Psychiatry (1988).

55. *MMPI Alcoholic Subtypes, supra,* note 32, at 166.

56. *MMPI Characteristics of Alcoholics: A Review, supra* note 13, at 202.

57. R. Gardner, Family Evaluation in Child Custody Litigation 257 (1982).

58. Berkowitz & Perkins, *Personality Characteristics of Children of Alcoholics*, 56 J. Consulting & Clinical Psychology 206, 206 (1988).

59. *Id.* at 209.

60. R. Ackerman, Children of Alcoholics 8 (2d ed. 1983).

61. *Id.* at 27.

62. *Id.* at 44.

63. *Id.* at 49–51.

64. *Id.* at 56–57.

65. Woititz, "Adult Children of Alcoholics," quoted in 5 The Medical Psychotherapist 9 (1989).

QUESTIONS FOR CHAPTER TWELVE

Caution: An attorney should not expect to be able to go into court and ask all of the questions listed below. Preparation is necessary, referring to the content of the chapter to determine if the question applies to your case. The page number at the end of each question refers to where in the chapter you may read an explanation of why this question may be important.

1. If the individual carries a diagnosis of alcoholism, determine in detail what type of treatment the individual has undergone for the alcoholism.

2. Is the individual still involved in any outpatient programming?

3. If the substance abused is other than alcohol, have urine screens been used as a method of determining compliance with programming?

4. Has the psychologist discriminated between whether the alcoholism is more a characterological defect as evidenced by Type I to Type IV alcoholics, or less characterological as evidenced by Type V or VI alcoholism? (pp. 338–40)

5. If the individual carries a diagnosis of alcoholism, what special alcoholism tests were administered either by the examiner or a specialized alcoholism diagnostician? (pp. 337–44)

6. Was the MMPI used in addition to other alcoholism tests in an effort to make sure that faking was not the cause of the results? (pp. 343–44. See also "Validity Scales" in Chapter Seven.)

Chapter Thirteen
Special Concerns: Mental Disorders

In a "normal" family, there are two parents, both of whom are in adequate touch with themselves and with the external world, and who can consistently and accurately perceive what is going on in each realm and cope adequately with their own needs and the needs of their children. When a psychological disorder is present, however, these abilities will be impaired to some degree. Those who have a severe impairment will usually be considered "psychotic," while those with less impairment will be considered "neurotic," or to have a "personality" or "character" disorder. This chapter will address the need of children for "normal" parenting, and the potential results if they do not receive it.

CHILDREN'S NEEDS

Children need a number of things from their parents if they are to develop normally. Among these "parental affection, protection, and guidance are necessary to promote the child's development of social and learning skills, self-control, socially oriented values, positive self-esteem, and a coherent sense of self."[1] Children need to feel valued and cared for, according to a Task Force on the Clinical Assessment in Child Custody of the American Psychiatric Association and they need parents who can set limits and model coping techniques.[2] "Children need parents to model and teach a value system which accommodates self-interest to social realities. . . . Parental awareness and acceptance of the child as a unique person is essential to the development of positive self-esteem and a sense of autonomy."[3]

Law professor J. Goldstein and psychoanalysts A. Freud and A. Solnit indicate that

> unlike adults, children have no psychological conception of relationship by blood-tie until quite late in their development. . . . What registers in their minds are the day-to-day interchanges with the adults who take care of them and who, on the

strength of these, become the parent figures to whom they are attached.[4]

They indicate that dysfunctional families may provide too little or too great attention to the physical care of the child, in both cases paying too little attention to the substantial psychological and emotional needs of the child, whether the family is intact or not. One result is that the child may not have appropriate models for identification.[5] When the parent has an "impoverished" or "unstable" personality, and may therefore not be able to provide adequate parenting, "unbroken closeness to them, and especially identification with them, may cease to be a benefit and become a threat. In extreme cases this necessitates state interference."[6]

Finally, they propose that the "best interests of the child" doctrine be replaced with a new standard, "the least detrimental available alternative for safeguarding the child's growth and development. . . . The least detrimental alternative, then, is that specific placement and procedure for placement which maximizes . . . his or her opportunity for being wanted and for maintaining on a continuous basis a relationship with at least one adult who is or will become his psychological parent."[7] On the basis of this book and another by the same authors, "much custody litigation now seeks to ascertain and turns upon the identity of the psychological parent."[8]

Maccoby discusses research on "child rearing and the growth of competence."[9] Among the findings of that research are the following:

- "The children who were happy, self-reliant, and able to meet challenging situations directly . . . had parents who exercised a good deal of control over their children and demanded responsible, independent behavior from them but who also explained, listened, and provided emotional support. . . . The parents of the immature children were moderately nurturant but conspicuously low in exercising control."[10]

- "When parents consistently enforce their rules and demands and do not let their children's noncompliance or resistance divert them, their children have been found to be: (1) Able to control aggressive impulses and not coercive toward parents . . . (2) Adequately controlled (as distinct from undercontrolled or overcontrolled) . . . (3) High in self-esteem at age ten or eleven . . . (4) Competent . . . that is, able to approach new situations with confidence, to take initiative and persist in tasks once begun—generally positive in mood and not withdrawn or immaturely impulsive. . . . An important element in enforcement of demands and rules is parental vigilance: Parents must notice whether children have complied. . . . Only the reasonably vigilant parent can enforce rules firmly and consistently."[11]

- While parents need to be in charge, "children must also be able to exercise some degree of control over the events impinging on them. . . . Apparently, a responsive environment—especially a responsive *human* environment—is one of the first requisites for a sense of control. . . ."[12] If the parents are unable, for whatever reason, to pay attention to and respond to the child's needs, the child is likely to "suffer a sense of loss of control—what Seligman . . . has called 'learned helplessness.' If this situation occurs consistently, the child is likely to become increasingly apathetic, passive, and even depressed."[13]

Social worker F. Givelber, ACSW, LICSW, identifies five parental tasks which he deems crucial to the evolution of self-esteem:

- "Winnicott's term, *'good enough' mothering* . . . describes a quality of parenting that responds to the basic physiological and emotional needs of the infant. These essential features of mothering include acceptance, responsiveness, sensitivity, and tolerance of the infant and his particular needs."

- "*Separateness* describes the parent's ability to differentiate a child's needs and feelings from his own and to acknowledge and support the child as a separate person."

- "*Anxiety mastery* refers to the parent's capacity to teach the child that anxiety can be tolerated. A parent, given his own ability to handle anxiety, empathically encourages the child to meet and triumph over new and frightening experiences."

- *"Mirroring of affect and achievement* reflects the parent's understanding of the child's feelings and pleasurable responsiveness to his achievements. . . ."

- *"Promotion of growth and maturation* refers to the parent's effort to guide the child toward an increasingly realistic sense of himself and the world. . . ."[14]

Givelber considers these five parenting tasks to be necessary for the development of an ability to regulate self-esteem, which he defines as "a highly sophisticated evaluative function that develops in the context of a successful reciprocity between parent and child."[15] If the parent cannot adequately address these tasks due to the presence of a psychological disorder, the child's development will suffer substantially.

THE NATURE OF "MENTAL ILLNESS"

Psychosis

When most people refer to "mental illness," they're referring to an individual who is *psychotic*, i.e., one who has

> gross impairment in reality testing and the creation of a new reality. . . . When a person is psychotic, he or she incorrectly evaluates the accuracy of his or her perceptions and thoughts and makes incorrect inferences about external reality, even in the face of contrary evidence. The term *psychotic* does not apply to minor distortions of reality that involve matters of relative judgment. For example, a depressed person who underestimates his achievements would not be described as psychotic, whereas one who believes he has caused a natural catastrophe would be so described.

> Direct evidence of psychotic behavior is the presence of either delusions or hallucinations (without insight into their pathological nature). The term *psychotic* is sometimes appropriate when a person's behavior is so grossly disorganized that a reasonable inference can be made that reality testing is markedly disturbed. . . .

> In DSM-III-R the psychotic disorders include Schizophrenia, Delusional Disorders, Psychotic

Disorders Not Elsewhere Classified, some Organic Mental Disorders, and some Mood Disorders.[16]

The *Psychiatric Dictionary* adds that

in general . . . the disorders labelled psychoses differ from the other groups of psychiatric disorders in one or more of the following: (1) severity—the psychoses are 'major' disorders that are more severe, intense, and disruptive; they tend to affect all areas of the patient's life. (2) degree of withdrawal—the psychotic patient is less able to maintain effective object relationships; external, objective reality has less meaning for the patient or is perceived in a distorted way. (3) affectivity—the emotions are often qualitatively different from the normal, at other times are so exaggerated quantitatively that they constitute the whole existence of the patient. (4) intellect—intellectual functioning may be directly involved by the psychotic process so that language and thinking are disturbed; judgment often fails; hallucinations and delusions may appear. (5) regression—there may be generalized failure of functioning and a falling back to very early behavioral levels; such regression is more than a temporary lapse in maturity and may include a return to early and even primitive patterns.[17]

The definition of "mental illness for purposes of involuntary commitment" in most state laws is similar to the above definitions of "psychosis." In Wisconsin, the definition is: "A substantial disorder of thought, mood, perception, orientation, or memory which grossly impairs judgment, behavior, capacity to recognize reality, or ability to meet the ordinary demands of life. . . ."[18]

Other Mental Disorders

A further distinction needs to be made among types of mental disorders. The most serious and severe disorders are the psychoses, as defined above. When the mental disorder is less serious and severe, but still significant, it may be classified as a "neurosis," or as a "personality" or "character" disorder.

Neurosis

According to the *American Psychiatric Glossary*, a "neurosis" is "in common usage, emotional disturbances of all kinds other than *psychosis*. It implies subjective psychological pain or discomfort beyond what is appropriate in the conditions of one's life. . . . In DSM-III-R, the term signifies a limited number of specific diagnostic categories, all of which are attributed to maladaptive ways of dealing with anxiety or internal conflict. . . . Common neuroses [include] . . . anxiety neurosis . . . depersonalization neurosis . . . depressive neurosis . . . hysterical neurosis . . . obsessive compulsive neurosis . . . [and] phobic neurosis. . . ."[19]

Similarly, a "neurotic disorder" is

> a mental disorder in which the predominant disturbance is a distressing symptom or group of symptoms which one considers unacceptable and alien to one's personality. There is no marked loss of reality testing; behavior does not actively violate gross social norms although it may be quite disabling. The disturbance is relatively enduring or recurrent without treatment and is not limited to a mild transitory reaction to stress. There is no demonstrable organic etiology. In DSM-III-R, the neurotic disorders are included in affective, anxiety, somatoform, dissociative, and psychosexual disorders.[20]

Because the neurotic individual has distressing symptoms which he or she considers "alien to one's personality," these people are relatively likely to seek treatment, and therefore to improve.

Personality or Character Disorders

"Personality disorders" or "character disorders" are

> deeply ingrained, inflexible, maladaptive patterns of relating, perceiving, and thinking of sufficient severity to cause other impairment, functioning, or distress. Personality disorders are generally recognizable by adolescence or earlier, continue through adulthood, and become less obvious in middle or old age. Some personality disorders cited in DSM-III-R are: antisocial . . . borderline . . . compulsive . . . dependent . . . histrionic . . . narcissistic . . .

paranoid . . . passive-aggressive . . . schizoid . . . [and] schizotypal.[21]

W. M. Meissner adds that

a particular character pattern or type becomes pathological when its manifestations are exaggerated to the point that behavior destructive to the individual or to others is the result or when the functioning of the person becomes so disturbed or restricted that it becomes a source of distress to the person or to others. Characterological traits tend to be nearly lifelong and are usually deeply embedded in the organization of the individual's personality.[22]

It is only when personality traits are inflexible and maladaptive and cause either significant functional impairment or subjective distress that they constitute *personality disorders*.. . . The constellation of behaviors or traits causes either significant impairment in social or occupational functioning or subjective distress.[23]

DSM-III-R groups personality disorders into three clusters.

Cluster A includes Paranoid, Schizoid, and Schizotypal Personality Disorders. People with these disorders often appear odd or eccentric. Cluster B includes Antisocial, Borderline, Histrionic, and Narcissistic Personality Disorders. People with these disorders often appear dramatic, emotional, or erratic. Cluster C includes Avoidant, Dependent, Obsessive Compulsive, and Passive Aggressive Personality Disorders. People with these disorders often appear anxious or fearful.[24]

There is also a residual category, "Personality Disorder Not Otherwise Specified," to be used when diagnostic criteria for one of the listed specific disorders do not apply, or there is a mixed disorder in which many criteria apply.

COMPETENCY

An individual's ability to make knowing and voluntary decisions is obviously related to his or her capacity to parent.

The Uniform Probate Code (adopted by Alaska, Arizona, Colorado, Hawaii, Idaho, Montana, Nebraska, New Mexico, North Dakota, Oregon, and Utah, as of 1986) requires that the person alleged to be incompetent

> is impaired by reason of mental illness, mental deficiency or disability, advanced age, chronic use of drug, chronic intoxication or other cause (except minority) to the extent that he lacks sufficient understanding or capacity to make or communicate responsible decisions concerning his person.[25]

> The standard for civil commitment to a mental hospital, a mental disorder plus dangerousness [and/] or a need for treatment, does not address the same elements required for a finding of incompetence. Thus, those committed are not thereby rendered incompetent to act in their own behalf unless a finding of incompetence accompanies the order of commitment.[26]

The concept of "competence" is further delineated by statutes and case law. For example, Wisconsin Statute § 51.61(1)(g) states that

> an individual is not competent to refuse medication if because of mental illness, developmental disability, alcoholism or drug dependence, the individual is incapable of expressing an understanding of the advantages and disadvantages of accepting treatment, and the alternatives to accepting the particular treatment offered, after the advantages, disadvantages and alternatives have been explained to the individual.

The Wisconsin Supreme Court in its 1987 ruling in the matter of *Jones v. Gerhardstein* indicated that

> the fact an individual has been committed . . . as a proper subject for treatment is not the same as finding the individual to be incompetent under sec. 51.61(1)(g). . . . In Massachusetts the supreme court held in Rogers v. Comm'r of Dept. of Mental Health[27] that under Massachusetts common law, because involuntary commitment is not a determination that

the committed individual is incompetent to make treatment decisions, such determination must be made by a judge before a committed individual can be forcibly administered psychotropic drugs in nonemergency situations.[28]

As indicated above, the definition of "psychosis" and the definition of "mental illness for purposes of involuntary commitment" are very similar. It is a fact that individuals who are psychotic *and* have been involuntarily committed (including a finding of dangerousness) *still* are not considered incompetent solely by virtue of their psychosis and commitment status. It readily follows that individuals who are psychotic but *not* involuntarily committed are also not automatically incompetent by virtue of their disorders.

Therefore, in a custody matter there must be a specific decision regarding whether each parent has the capacity to make knowing and voluntary choices. This will seldom be a significant question when a parent is diagnosed as having a neurosis or a personality or character disorder. It becomes a significant question when there is a diagnosed psychosis—but there is no automatic answer. The psychologist or psychiatrist will have to do a formal evaluation in order to make a recommendation to the court in this regard.

THE EFFECT OF PARENTAL MENTAL DISORDERS ON CHILDREN

There is relatively little research on the direct effect of mental illnesses on children, so most conclusions have to be drawn from the nature of the disorders and the expected consequences for the children.

One possible exception is with regard to the effect of Bipolar Disorder (previously known as "manic-depressive disorder"). A six-year study by D. McKnew, M.D., of seven children, one or both of whose parents had that recurrent disorder, and who were compared with a control group of children whose parents had no diagnosable mental disorder, found that significant differences could be observed as early as 12 months of age. At that age, all children became upset when their mothers left the room briefly—but only the children of parents with Bipolar Disorder remained upset once their mothers returned.

At two years of age, the children of parents with Bipolar
Disorder showed increased aggression. At six years,

> the children of parents with bipolar illness were
> more withdrawn and hyperactive, and somewhat
> more aggressive than the other children. Each child
> with an affected parent had at least one psychiatric
> diagnosis; five children had multiple diagnoses. . . .
> Of the children of normal parents, three had minor
> disorders at age six: separation anxiety and fear of
> the dark.[29]

Specific needs of children were addressed above. Those
needs include:

- parental affection, protection, and guidance;
- to feel valued and cared for;
- parents who can set limits and model coping techniques;
- a value system which accommodates self-interest to social realities;
- parental awareness and acceptance of the child as a unique person;
- physical care which is individualized and sensitive;
- sufficient parental involvement so that the child's emotional needs are fulfilled;
- parents who are suitable models for identification;
- parents who *want* the child;
- parents who will exercise the proper amount of control over their children, neither too much nor too little;
- parents who demand responsible, independent behavior but who also explain, listen, and provide emotional support;
- parents who consistently enforce their rules and demands;
- vigilant parents who notice whether their children have complied with demands;
- parents who are responsive to their children;

- parents who can differentiate the child's needs and feelings from their own and who acknowledge and support the child as a separate person;
- parents who can teach the child that anxiety can be tolerated, in part based on the parent's own ability to handle stress and anxiety;
- understanding of the child's feelings and pleasurable responsiveness to his or her achievements;
- parental efforts to guide the child toward an increasingly realistic sense of himself or herself and the world; and
- successful reciprocity between parent and child.

The parent who has no diagnosable mental disorder is likely to adequately address the above needs. So is the parent who has a short-lived mental disorder which is primarily or exclusively stress related, including the person who has a single, stress-induced acute psychotic episode but had no diagnosable disorder prior to that episode and who receives good treatment during the episode.

The situation is different for the parent who has a series of psychotic episodes or who is chronically psychotic (the disorder waxing and waning but never absent), as well as for any parent *during* an acute psychotic episode. During an acute psychotic episode, by definition, reality testing is grossly impaired. Many perceptions and thoughts are incorrectly evaluated, leading to a variety of incorrect actions. There is likely to be withdrawal from what most of us know as "reality." Emotions may be exaggerated, and may be labile. The quality of judgment and insight may be minimal. Behavior may be regressed. Thus, during any period when a parent is acutely psychotic, parenting ability is likely to be minimal, the parent focusing on his or her own needs much more than those of others, dealing with his or her own reality rather than external reality, and using all available psychic energy to maintain personal control, with little or none left over for the child.

Between acute psychotic episodes the parent will do better —with a psychological or psychiatric evaluation necessary to assess how much better. Particularly with ongoing psychotherapy or counseling, many people can be much more than adequate parents in spite of a history of psychoses. As indicated above, people do not automatically become incompetent as a result of having a mental disorder. Nor do they automatically become inadequate parents, though during the period of acute psychosis parenting ability will be at a minimum.

Various court decisions have affirmed the conclusion that parenting may be adequate in spite of a serious mental disorder. For example,

> the Oklahoma Supreme Court held that a mere showing of mental illness is not a statutory ground for terminating parental rights. Moreover, the fact that the parents were confined to an institution did not establish that the parents were unfit. *In re J.N.M., 665 P.2d 1032* (Okla Sup. Ct. 1982).[30]

In another case,

> the Missouri Court of Appeals held that termination of parental rights due to mental illness can only be justified if there is clear, cogent, and convincing proof that the children are being harmed or are likely to be harmed in the future if the parental relationship is allowed to continue. . . . In re C.P.B. and K.A.B., 641 S.W.2d 456 (Mo. Ct. App. 1982). . . . [T]he court pointed out that . . . "unlike neglect, abandonment, abuse, or nonsupport, the mental illness of a parent is not per se harmful to a child."[31]

With regard to the "neurotic" conditions, one again has to look at the extent of the disorder at any point in time to draw a conclusion about parenting ability. People who are neurotic don't lose touch with reality, so they will generally be at least adequate in dealing with their own real-world needs and those of their children. Under stress, however, these individuals will also demonstrate some loss of parenting ability, though generally not nearly to the degree of someone who has a history of psychotic episodes. It is the task of the psychologist or psychiatrist to assess the individual's functional ability at periods of both high and low stress, and to make recommendations to the court which address that range of parenting ability. As part of this process, the evaluator must determine if the problems were a function of stress induced by the dysfunctional relationship with the spouse, or a long-standing underlying neurotic process. Many parents have presented themselves as quite psychologically unstable when in a dysfunctional relationship and perceiving no solution, only to become substantially more stable when out of the destructive relationship. In others, the symptoms did not disappear at termination of the relationship. It may not be possible for the evaluator to determine which of these is occurring through the time-limited evaluation process. As a result, a reasonable approach when there is a significant question about the stability of a parent might be to hold the matter open for six months, to see whether the parent or parents become more stable with time. Even though a six-month wait would add to the stress of the entire divorce matter, this is outweighed by the importance of making sure that the correct decision is made in choosing a custodial parent.

As indicated above, the neurotic individual feels distressed by his or her symptoms and feels they are alien to his or her personality. This motivates the neurotic individual to seek treatment. In contrast, the individual with a personality or character disorder may or may not feel distress from his or her symptoms, and finds those symptoms to be "ego-syntonic," i.e., to be acceptable and consistent with the total personality.[32] He or she is relatively unlikely, therefore, to seek treatment voluntarily. Since the individual does not find the disorder to be unacceptable or inconsistent with his or her personality, he or she has no feelings of significant distress. People with personality or character disorders tend to be highly resistant to treatment. Even if these people are required to attend therapy as part of a court order, they are likely to manipulate the process, terminate early, and, in any event, derive little long-term benefit from the therapeutic process.

ENDNOTES

1. A. Derdeyn, A. Levy, J. Looney, D. Schetky, J. Westman, E. Scott & J. Spurlock, Child Custody Consultation, Report of the Task Force on Clinical Assessment in Child Custody, American Psychiatric Association, Washington, D.C., 1981, p. 21.

2. *Id.* at 21-22.

3. *Id.* at 22.

4. J. Goldstein, A. Freud & A. Solnit, Beyond the Best Interests of the Child 12–13 (1973).

5. *Id.* at 15.

6. *Id.* at 19-20.

7. *Id.* at 53.

8. D. Schuman, Psychiatric and Psychological Evidence 303 (1986) [hereinafter Psychiatric and Psychological Evidence].

9. E. Maccoby, Social Development: Psychological Growth and the Parent-Child Relationship 368 (1980).

10. *Id.* at 374–75.

11. *Id.* at 381–82.

12. *Id.* at 386–87.

13. *Id.*

14. F. Givelber, *The Parent-Child Relationship and the Development of Self-Esteem*, The Development and Sustenance of Self-Esteem in Children 163–64 (1983).

15. *Id.* at 164.

16. Diagnostic and Statistical Manual of Mental Disorders, Third Edition, Revised (DSM-III-R) 404–05 (1987) [hereinafter DSM-III-R].

17. R. Campbell, Psychiatric Dictionary 510 (5th Ed. 1981).

18. Wis. Stat. § 51.01(13)(b).

19. American Psychiatric Glossary 109–10 (E. Stone ed. 1988) [hereinafter American Psychiatric Glossary].

20. DSM-III-R, *supra* note 16, at 111.

21. American Psychiatric Glossary, *supra* note 19, at 120–23.

22. W. Meissner, *Theories of Personality and Psychopathology* in H. Kaplan & B. Saddock, Comprehensive Textbook of Psychiatry/IV 402 (1985).

23. DSM-III-R, *supra* note 16, at 355.

24. *Id.* at 337.

25. Psychiatric and Psychological Evidence, *supra* note 8, at 351.

26. *Id.* at 351–52.

27. Rogers v. Comm'r of Dept. of Mental Health, 390 Mass. 489, 458 N.E.2d 308 (1983).

28. Jones v. Gerhardstein, Wisconsin Supreme Court No. 85-1718 (December 1987) at 31–32.

29. *Precursors of Affective Ill May Be Detectable in Infants 12–15 Months*, 15 Clinical Psychiatry News 1 (Feb. 1987).

30. 7 Mental Disability Law Reporter 111 (1983).

31. *Id.* at 111–12.

32. American Psychiatric Glossary, *supra* note 19, at 32, 59.

QUESTIONS FOR CHAPTER THIRTEEN

Caution: An attorney should not expect to be able to go into court and ask all of the questions listed below. Preparation is necessary, referring to the content of the chapter to determine if the question applies to your case. The page number at the end of each question refers to where in the chapter you may read an explanation of why this question may be important.

1. Can the psychologist demonstrate that the parent has the qualities of good mothering, separateness, anxiety mastery, mirroring of affect, and achievement and promotion of growth and maturation described in this chapter? (pp. 355–56)

2. Does the parent have a history of mental illness?

3. If the parent has been hospitalized, obtain hospital records.

4. If the parent has carried a psychiatric diagnosis, have a psychologist determine if that diagnosis is still current. If not, why not?

5. If the parent is psychotic or was psychotic, what evidence can the psychologist provide that similar episodes will not occur in the future?

6. Ask the psychologist how the type of mental illness that the parent has experienced will affect typical development of children in general and the children specifically involved in this custody matter. (pp. 354–56, 361–64)

7. If the individual has taken psychiatric medication, determine how cooperative the individual was in taking the medication.

8. If the individual is currently on medication, determine if the individual is likely to be taken off the medication and what effect that will have on the individual's overall stability.

9. If the individual has been treated by a number of inpatient and/or outpatient facilities, ask the psychologist why so many changes have taken place in treatment, and what the implications of a large number of changes would be on the parents' continued emotional stability.

10. Is there any evidence of diminished capacity (discussed in Chapter Four) that would affect the parents availability to address the needs of the children? (pp. 359–61)

11. Ask the psychologist if the child has been overburdened by being required to take on too much responsibility for growing up, maintaining the psychological functioning of the parent, being caught in the middle of the parents' fights, or by the parent distorting the perception of the child's abilities. (pp. 354–56, pp. 361–65)

12. If the parent is currently in treatment, ask if the psychologist has contacted the current treating therapist. If the parent has invoked privilege, ask the psychologist how this would be interpreted.

13. If the parent carries a diagnosis of a character or personality disorder, ask the psychologist to identify the likelihood of therapy being successful. (p. 365)

14. If the individual has previously been diagnosed as psychotic, determine if the individual has ever been found incompetent or had a guardian appointed. (p. 359–61)

15. If the parent has a history of mental illness, is the parent currently able to address the needs described in this chapter?

16. If the psychologist has not felt it necessary to emphasize the mental illness of the individual, make sure that it occurred long enough ago as not to be relevant.

17. If the individual has experienced recent hospitalizations or extensive psychotherapy, has it been the result of the distress and trauma within the relationship as opposed to underlying emotional instability?

Chapter Fourteen
Special Concerns: Criminal History

If one or both of the parents has a criminal record, careful analysis needs to be done of the nature of that record and the reasons for its occurrence. Relevant factors include the seriousness of the offense(s); contributing factors from the environment, personality, and mental state of the offender; recency of the offense(s); and evidence of rehabilitation.

SERIOUSNESS OF THE OFFENSE(S)

Was the offense a felony or a misdemeanor? A crime against person or property? Was it a single occurrence of criminal behavior? Obviously, the more serious the offense, the more one worries about this parent having custody.

CONTRIBUTING FACTORS FROM THE ENVIRONMENT

Was the person caught shoplifting food because he or she was hungry? Was money embezzled because of urgent personal or family needs, e.g., for food or medical treatment? Was there pressure from the spouse to come up with money or goods "no matter what?" How responsible was the individual for the altercation that led to a disorderly conduct charge? While extraneous factors don't excuse the criminal behavior, they may make it possible to understand the cause and to better weigh the relevance of the criminal act to the custody decision. Police and court documents may shed significant light on this factor, as may interviews with family members and other significant people.

CONTRIBUTING FACTORS FROM THE PERSONALITY

Not all antisocial *behavior* is due to an antisocial *personality*. The former may range from something many people do on occasion, e.g., speeding, accepting too much change from a clerk, or not reporting all one's income on tax forms, to serious crimes involving major loss of money or goods, physical harm to others, and so forth. Thus, many people display antisocial behavior at some time, while relatively few would be diagnosed as having an Antisocial Personality Disorder.[1]

The *Diagnostic and Statistical Manual of Mental Disorders, Third Edition, Revised* (DSM-III-R) indicates that

> the essential feature [of an Antisocial Personality Disorder] is a pattern of irresponsible and antisocial behavior beginning in childhood or early adolescence and continuing into adulthood. For this diagnosis to be given, the person must be at least 18 years of age and have a history of Conduct Disorder before the age of 15. Lying, stealing, truancy, vandalism, initiating fights, running away from home, and physical cruelty are typical childhood signs. In adulthood . . . these people fail to conform to social norms and repeatedly perform antisocial acts that are grounds for arrest, such as destroying property, harassing others, stealing, and having an illegal occupation. [They] tend to be irritable and aggressive and get repeatedly into physical fights and assaults, including spouse- or child-beating. Reckless behavior without regard to personal safety is common. . . . Finally, they generally have no remorse about the effects of their behavior on others; they may even feel justified in having hurt or mistreated others. . . .[2]

"Predisposing factors," DSM-III-R continues, "are Attention-deficit Disorder and Conduct Disorder during prepuberty. *The absence of consistent parental discipline apparently increases the likelihood that Conduct Disorder will develop into Antisocial Personality Disorder.* Other predisposing factors include abuse as a child, removal from the home, and growing up without parental figures of both sexes."[3]

DSM-III-R lists nearly two pages of diagnostic criteria for Antisocial Personality Disorder:[4] the individual must be at least 18, must have shown evidence of Conduct Disorder before the age of 15 (as shown by a history of at least 3 of 12 antisocial behaviors listed), must have shown "a pattern of irresponsible and antisocial behavior since the age of 15 as indicated by at least four"[5] antisocial behaviors from a list of 10, and must not have shown antisocial behavior exclusively during a schizophrenic or manic episode. Where there is a question regarding whether an individual meets these criteria, the examiner must ask questions which will yield the necessary data. One way would be to make up a questionnaire which addresses the relevant questions to the individual verbally or on paper. Interviews with family members may shed light on some of the diagnostic questions.[6]

Another way would be to utilize the MMPI. A large body of research has shown that individuals with high scores on Scales 4 and 9 evidence

> a marked disregard for social standards and values. They frequently get into trouble with the authorities because of antisocial behavior. They have poorly developed consciences, easy morals, and fluctuating ethical values. . . . [They] are narcissistic, selfish, and self-indulgent. They are quite impulsive and are unable to delay gratification of their impulses. They show poor judgment, often acting without consider- ing the consequences of their acts, and they fail to learn from experience. . . . They seem to be inca- pable of deep emotional ties, and they keep others at an emotional distance. . . .[7]

There are five subscales for Scale 4 of the MMPI, developed by Harris and Lingoes. Those subscales address "familial dis- cord," "authority problems," "social imperturbability," "social alienation," and "self-alienation."[8] They can be a valuable adjunct to the major scale information in determining why an individual has a high score on Scale 4. Someone in a divorce and/or custody matter will obviously have "familial discord," which can contribute substantially to the overall score for scale 4. It is therefore important to look at these subscales prior to drawing conclusions about the meaning of a "high 4."

Numerous studies have shown that, in mean profiles of groups of prisoners in correctional institutions, Scale 4 usually is the most elevated scale.

> The 4-2 and 4-9 profiles are the most frequently occurring two-point codes for prisoners. . . . A com- prehensive and useful system of classifying criminal

offenders based on the MMPI was developed by
Megargee and his associates. . . . These investigators used hierarchical profile analysis to identify
clusters among the MMPIs of offenders . . . [yield-
ing] ten types of offender MMPIs and explicit rules
for classifying offenders into the type to which they
are most similar.[9]

Another useful instrument is the *Carlson Psychological
Survey*.[10] The test assesses Antisocial Tendencies, Thought
Disturbance, Chemical Abuse, and Self-Depreciation. There is
also a brief validity scale. Reliability and validity data are adequate. The test was standardized on an older and more criminal population than the MMPI, with all of Carlson's subjects
being adult male offenders serving prison sentences.[11] Carlson
includes 18 offender profiles with which an individual's scores
can be compared.

An individual who is diagnosable as having an Antisocial
Personality Disorder would rarely be a good candidate for a custodial parent. This individual would likely be self-centered,
would fail to honor commitments or to plan ahead, would be
unable to sustain consistent work behavior, would fail to conform to social norms, would be irritable and aggressive—all
qualities which virtually preclude successfully addressing a
child's needs. Q. Patterson, B. DeBaryshe, and E. Ramsey, of the
Oregon Social Learning Center, Eugene, Oregon, report that

as a predictor of adult antisocial personality, having
an antisocial parent places the child at significant risk
for antisocial behavior; having two antisocial parents
puts the child at even higher risk. . . . There is considerable evidence that parental discipline practices may
be an important mediating mechanism in this transmission. Our set of findings shows that antisocial parents are at significant risk for ineffective discipline
practices. Ineffective discipline is significantly related
to risk of having an antisocial child.[12]

These same qualities, plus the poor superego (conscience)
development, make psychotherapy with these individuals very
difficult. Where an individual's criminal history is in question,
use of the DSM-III-R criteria, the MMPI data, and the Carlson

data should yield a good estimate of the likelihood that an individual has an Antisocial Personality Disorder.

MENTAL STATE OF THE OFFENDER

What kind of stress was the individual experiencing at the time of the offense? How well does the individual handle stress when it is experienced? Was there any evidence of a major mental illness (psychosis) at the time of the offense? Was "not guilty by reason of insanity" (or "by reason of mental disease or defect") part of the defense? If so, was the individual found not guilty on that basis? Did the individual spend any time in a psychiatric hospital after the offense? After the trial? Again, the mental state of the offender doesn't excuse the offense, but it may provide important data for the present custody evaluation.

RECENCY OF THE OFFENSE(S)

It could make a great deal of difference whether the offense was last year or ten or more years ago. Given the maxim that "the best predictor of the future is the past," the longer it has been since the offense and the better the individual's behavior since the offense, the less likely the offense is to have a significant bearing on the present custody decision.

EVIDENCE OF REHABILITATION

Does the individual appear to be honestly remorseful? Was there any attempt to make restitution in any meaningful sense, and how voluntary was that attempt? While there is no specific form of treatment which has shown to be especially effective, nearly every form of treatment will be effective for some people.[13] It is relevant whether the individual was in psychotherapy at any time since the offense, and how that contributes to his or her understanding of the causes of the offense and the likelihood that there will not be another offense. Has the individual gone out of his or her way to make a contribution to society since the offense (volunteering for charities, becoming a civic leader, helping other offenders, etc.)? While not a specific response to the question of rehabilitation, it should be noted that criminal behavior naturally seems to decrease at about age 40, so that is one more factor to take into

consideration.[14] Is there any other evidence that the individual
has been rehabilitated and will not commit another offense?

Psychological testing may be of some limited assistance
here, too. The MMPI and the Carlson Psychological Survey
will give some insight into the present status of antisocial
beliefs and actions, as described above. The tests must be read
with the awareness that one cannot erase the past experiences
and behavior which will lead to substantial scores on the relevant scales, but changes in subsequent beliefs and actions can
lower the scores to some degree. The validity scales on the
MMPI also provide a direct assessment of the individual's attitude—is he or she being honest and forthright in his or her
approach to the test, or trying to present an image which is
markedly different from reality? As indicated in the chapter on
the MMPI, this test provides the only well-researched, highly
valid information about an individual's openness, honesty, and
forthrightness.

While no mental health professional or jurist can be
omniscient, consideration of the above data will maximize the
likelihood that past criminality is seen in proper context, permitting it to be weighed with other evidence in the process of
investigation and decision making.

ENDNOTES

1. D. Lewis, *Adult Antisocial Behavior and Criminality* in Kaplan & Saddock: Comprehensive Textbook of Psychiatry/IV 1865–70 (1985) [hereinafter *Adult Antisocial Behavior and Criminality*].

2. Diagnostic and Statistical Manual of Mental Disorders, Third Edition, Revised 342 (1987).

3. *Id.* at 343 (emphasis added).

4. *Id.* at 344–46.

5. *Id.* at 345.

6. *Adult Antisocial Behavior and Criminality, supra* note 1, at 1869.

7. J. Graham, The MMPI: A Practical Guide 109–10 (2d ed. 1987).

8. *Id.* at 128–30.

9. *Id.* at 92

10. K. Carlson, Carlson Psychological Survey (1982).

11. *Id.* at 7.

12. Patterson, DeBaryshe, & Ramsey, *A Developmental Perspective on Antisocial Behavior*, 44 Am. Psychologist 329, 332 (1989).

13. *Adult Antisocial Behavior and Criminality, supra* note 1, at 1869.

14. *Id.*

QUESTIONS FOR CHAPTER FOURTEEN

Caution: An attorney should not expect to be able to go into court and ask all of the questions listed below. Preparation is necessary, referring to the content of the chapter to determine if the question applies to your case. The page number at the end of each question refers to where in the chapter you may read an explanation of why this question may be important.

1. If the individual has been convicted of a felony crime, ask the psychologist how the type of personality components that would contribute to said crime would affect the parent's child rearing capabilities. (p. 374)

2. It is important to determine what the original charges were if a conviction took place, in an effort to identify whether plea bargaining led to a lesser charge.

3. Was the crime a crime against a person or a crime against property? Ask the psychologist what the difference between these types of criminals means with regard to child rearing capabilities.

4. Determine the recency of the events. There are parents in their 30s or 40s that may have been convicted of crimes that occurred in their late teens or early 20s that may not be particularly relevant issues.

5. What evidence is there of rehabilitation? (pp. 375–76)

6. Has the psychologist identified whether the individual has demonstrated antisocial behavior or has an underlying antisocial personality? (pp. 371–75)

Chapter Fifteen
Classification Systems

The "medical model" is used for diagnosing mental disorders both in the United States and by the World Health Organization. The "medical model" indicates that

(1) There are disease entities, which have etiology, course, and outcome; (2) These diseases are of organic origin; (3) Even if conceived as psychological diseases, they are viewed in analogy with physical ailments. There is an underlying state which is manifested in surface symptoms. Disease is to be inferred from symptoms; changing symptoms will not cure the disease; (4) People get these diseases through no fault of their own; (5) Cure depends on professional intervention, preferably by people with medical training; and (6) The diseases are in the person and, although they may have culturally distinct manifestations, the essential disease process is universal and not culturally specific.[1]

Unlike most other "medical" diagnoses, however, psychiatric diagnoses carry a social stigma. There have been direct legal consequences of the development of a psychiatric diagnostic system, complicated by different classification systems and different terminology at the interface of law and psychiatry, as, for example, "insanity" has no unequivocal translation into any diagnostic classification.[2]

As in any science, classification, called diagnosis in psychiatry, relies on the observations of a trained observer. What distinguishes psychiatry and psychology from the natural sciences is that what is being observed may be profoundly affected by the actions of the observer. In addition, no biologist has to cope with a leaf capable of hiding its shape or color because it does not want to be observed. Furthermore, few biologists have such strong feelings about pines or oaks that those feelings are likely to affect substantially their perceptions or memories of their observation of a tree. However, that is precisely what can happen to a diagnostician, and these individual variations in perception and memory can introduce uncertainty into classification systems. . . Uncertainty therefore makes psychiatry a probabilistic science. While the apple will always drop from the tree, a drop in mood is not always depression; but a drop in mood increases the odds that the individual is depressed.[3]

There are presently two diagnostic classification systems widely used in the United States: the *Diagnostic and Statistical Manual of Mental Disorders, Third Edition, Revised* (DSM-III-R),[4] and the *Manual of the International Statistical Classification of Diseases, Injuries, and Causes of Death* (ICD-9-CM).[5] Both suffer from a significant shortcoming: they use broad criteria for the diagnosis of mental disorders rather than any specific tests, and the reliability and validity of diagnoses are relatively open to criticism on this basis. Further, diagnoses in both were formulated by learned individuals discussing diagnoses and the criteria for them and coming to a consensus about what those diagnoses and criteria would be. As a result, the diagnostic manuals contain thousands of diagnostic criteria with virtually no citation of supportive research or references. DSM-III-R is published by the American Psychiatric Association. ICD-9 is published by the World Health Organization.

DSM-III-R

The first edition of the *Diagnostic and Statistical Manual of Mental Disorders* (DSM-I) of the American Psychiatric Association was published in 1952. The second edition, DSM-II, was published in 1968, and, unlike DSM-I, was based on the mental disorders section of the eighth *International Classification of Diseases* (ICD-8), published the same year. The third edition, DSM-III, was published in 1980. While originally planned to go into effect along with ICD-9, in 1979, there was a substantial feeling that ICD-9 was not specific enough for clinical or research use in the United States. While the major classifications were kept the same as ICD-9 for all practical purposes, publication of DSM-III was postponed until

1980 so that greater specificity could be added.[6] In addition, "a decision was made to modify the ICD-9 for use in the United States by expanding the four-digit ICD-9 codes to five-digit ICD-9-CM (for Clinical Modification) codes whenever greater specificity was required."[7] "All DSM-III-R codes are legitimate ICD-9-CM codes."[8]

In 1983, work began on a revision of DSM-III, based on a felt need to update the manual as often as necessary to keep up with advances in knowledge. Where new research pointed a direction, that direction was taken. Where it did not—which was usually the case—such factors as clinical experience and/or a belief that a change would increase the reliability and/or validity of a diagnosis was paramount.[9] The result was DSM-III-R, published in 1987. DSM-IV is scheduled for publication in 1993, in conjunction with ICD-10.[10] "The United States is under a treaty obligation with the World Health Organization to maintain a coding and terminological consistency with the ICD."[11] Unfortunately,

> the DSM and ICD have different constituencies and purposes. For example, the DSM need not be quite as concerned as is the ICD with the applicability of criteria sets across all cultures around the world. To meet this latter need, the ICD-10 requires the use of separate diagnostic criteria for clinicians and for researchers, whereas the DSM-IV will continue using the same system of diagnosis for both purposes.[12]

The authors indicate that in DSM-III-R

> each of the mental disorders is conceptualized as a clinically significant behavioral or psychological syndrome or pattern that occurs in a person and that is associated with present distress (a painful symptom) or disability (impairment in one or more important areas of functioning) or with a significantly increased risk of suffering death, pain, disability, or an important loss of freedom. In addition, this syndrome or pattern must not be merely an expectable response to a particular event, e.g., the death of a loved one. Whatever its original cause, it must currently be considered a manifestation of a behavioral,

psychological, or biological dysfunction in the person. Neither deviant behavior, e.g., political, religious, or sexual, nor conflicts that are primarily between the individual and society are mental disorders unless the deviance or conflict is a symptom of a dysfunction in the person, as described above.[13]

The next statement offers a measure each of good news and bad: "There is no assumption that each mental disorder is a discrete entity with sharp boundaries (discontinuity) between it and other mental disorders, or between it and no mental disorder."[14] The good news is for the clinician, who has a workable diagnostic manual because it takes into consideration the limited ability we presently have to make discrete diagnoses. The bad news is that, in spite of great research effort, it is rarely possible to make a highly specific, highly reliable, highly valid diagnosis using the manual. Instead, we have labels which may be applied to mental conditions of individuals to facilitate understanding of and communication about those disorders among clinicians. There is a side benefit in that insurance companies will pay for services to people who have certain diagnoses. One consequence of this lack of precision is that mental health professionals who are comparing diagnostic conclusions, whether in court or any other arena, may come to different conclusions.

A social-psychological advance in DSM-III, carried forward in DSM-III-R, is the affirmation that

> a common misconception is that a classification of mental disorders classifies people, when actually what are being classified are disorders that people have. For this reason, the text . . . avoids the use of such expressions as "a schizophrenic" or "an alcoholic," and instead uses the more accurate, but admittedly more cumbersome, "a person with Schizophrenia" or "a person with Alcohol Dependence."[15]

Unfortunately, mental health professionals seldom observe these verbal niceties, the shorthand form being used in virtually all discussions.

It is acknowledged that for most of the DSM-III-R disorders the etiology is unknown. Therefore, it is necessary to be descriptive, i.e., to limit definitions to descriptions of the clinical features of the disorders. The characteristic features consist of easily identifiable behavioral signs or symptoms, such as disorientation, mood disturbance, or psychomotor agitation, which require a minimal amount of inference on the part of the observer. For some disorders, however, particularly the Personality Disorders, the criteria require much more inference on the part of the observer.[16]

Similarly, it is noted, mental disorders are grouped into diagnostic classes on the basis of shared clinical features, e.g., disturbances of mood, rather than degree of dysfunction (e.g., "neurosis" vs. "psychosis"). The psychotic/neurotic split was a useful dichotomy until the 1960s, when research clearly indicated that the presumed etiology of psychotic conditions (constitutional and biological forces) and of neurotic conditions (developmental, psychosocial, or personality factors) was not supported by the data available.[17] "DSM-III is atheoretical with regard to the etiology of individual conditions other than those listed in the category of organic disorders."[18]

DSM-III-R is organized on a hierarchical basis, with organic conditions, psychoses, and neuroses, in that order. A diagnosis early in the series preempts emphasis on later diagnoses —for example, a person diagnosed to have a schizophrenic disorder may also have anxiety and/or depression, but the latter are not emphasized.[19]

A major innovation in DSM-III is the separation of the personality disorders into an independent axis. *Personality* refers to relatively enduring patterns of relating to, perceiving, and thinking about the self, significant others, and the environment. All individuals have such patterns. Personality *disorder* occurs only when the patterns become inflexible and maladaptive and/or significantly impair the individual's social or occupational functioning. Patients with personality disorder often do not experience subjective distress, but their behavior may generate distress and discomfort in others, particularly the immediate family.[20]

To enhance reliability, both DSM-III and DSM-III-R provide fairly specific diagnostic criteria, though many diagnoses are made by choosing from a list of symptoms those which apply in a given case, with a certain number required in order for the diagnosis to be made. Unfortunately, "for most of the categories the diagnostic criteria are based on clinical judgment, and have not yet been fully validated by data about such important correlates as clinical course, outcome, family history, and treatment response."[21]

The fact that diagnoses are based on votes taken by committees of clinicians who are using their "clinical judgments" has led to the problem that

> it is a temptation for a task force or a work group member to argue for the inclusion of changes that express his or her theoretical or empirical perspective. We have noticed many such instances in the past and present effort. Revisions made in this way are less reflective of the totality of the research evidence in the field than of the forces determining membership and influence on a particular committee.[22]

An attempt is being made to utilize research data more in DSM-IV, "to minimize the occurrence of arbitrary and whimsical revision."[23]

DSM-III and DSM-III-R use a "multiaxial system" to provide a complete description. Axis I is "major clinical syndromes" and "V codes" ("conditions not attributable to a mental disorder that are a focus of attention or treatment"). Axis II is "developmental disorders" and "personality disorders." Axis III is "physical disorders and conditions." Axis IV is "severity of psychosocial stressors." Axis V is a "global assessment of functioning."[24] "Multiple diagnoses should be made [on Axes I and II] when necessary to describe the current condition. This applies particularly to Axis I, on which, for example, a person may have both a Psychoactive Substance Use Disorder and a Mood Disorder."[25] Axis IV, Severity of Psychosocial Stressors, uses a scale from 1 (none) to 6 (catastrophic), with examples provided.[26] Axis V uses the Global Assessment of Functioning Scale, which ranges from 90 (absent or minimal symptoms, good functioning in all areas) down to 1 ("persistent danger of severely hurting self or others, OR persistent inability to maintain minimal personal hygiene OR serious suicidal act with clear expectation of death"[27]).

Axis I Major Clinical Syndromes*

The Axis I major clinical syndromes include the following:

- Disorders Usually First Evident in Infancy, Childhood, or Adolescence
  — Disruptive Behavior Disorders
  — Anxiety Disorders of Childhood or Adolescence
  — Eating Disorders
  — Gender Identity Disorders
  — Tic Disorders
  — Elimination Disorders
  — Speech Disorders Not Elsewhere Classified
  — Other Disorders of Infancy, Childhood or Adolescence
- Organic Mental Disorders
  — Dementias Arising in the Senium and Presenium
  — Psychoactive Substance-Induced Organic Mental Disorders
  — Organic Mental Disorders Associated with Axis III
  — Physical Disorders or Conditions, or Whose Etiology Is Unknown
- Psychoactive Substance Use Disorders
- Schizophrenia
- Delusional (Paranoid) Disorders
- Psychotic Disorders Not Elsewhere Classified
- Mood Disorders
  — Bipolar Disorders
  — Depressive Disorders

---

*Reprinted with permission from the *Diagnostic and Statistical Manual of Mental Disorders, Third Edition, Revised.* Copyright 1987 American Psychiatric Association.

- Anxiety Disorders (or Anxiety and Phobic Neuroses)
  — Panic Disorder
  — Agoraphobia
  — Social Phobia
  — Simple Phobia
  — Obsessive Compulsive Disorder
  — Post-traumatic Stress Disorder
  — Generalized Anxiety Disorder
  — Anxiety Disorder Not Otherwise Specified
- Somatoform Disorders
  — Body Dysmorphic Disorder
  — Conversion Disorder (or Hysterical Neurosis, Conversion Type)
  — Hypochondriasis
  — Somatization Disorder
- Dissociative Disorders
- Sexual Disorders
- Sleep Disorders
- Factitious Disorders
- Impulse Disorders Not Elsewhere Classified
- Adjustment Disorder
- Psychological Factors Affecting Physical Condition[28]

Axis II Disorders*

The Axis II disorders include the following:

- Developmental Disorders
  — Mental Retardation
  — Pervasive Developmental Disorders
  — Specific Developmental Disorders
  — Other Developmental Disorders

---

*Reprinted with permission from the *Diagnostic and Statistical Manual of Mental Disorders, Third Edition, Revised.* Copyright 1987 American Psychiatric Association.

- Personality Disorders
  - Paranoid
  - Schizoid
  - Schizotypal
  - Antisocial
  - Borderline
  - Histrionic
  - Narcissistic
  - Avoidant
  - Dependent
  - Obsessive Compulsive
  - Passive Aggressive
  - Personality Disorder Not Otherwise Specified[29]

DSM-III-R Cautionary Statement

DSM-III-R offers a cautionary statement immediately prior to the major text. That statement indicates that the diagnostic criteria "are offered as guidelines for making diagnoses," to improve reliability, and that "proper use of these criteria requires specialized clinical training. . . ." Further, they note, not all "conditions that may be legitimate objects of treatment or research efforts" are included. Finally, they indicate,

> the purpose of DSM-III-R is to provide clear descriptions of diagnostic categories. . . . It is to be understood that inclusion here . . . of a diagnostic category such as Pathological Gambling or Pedophilia does not imply that the condition meets legal or other nonmedical criteria for what constitutes mental disease, mental disorder, or mental disability. The clinical and scientific considerations involved in categorization of these conditions as mental disorders may not be wholly relevant to legal judgments, for example, that take into account such issues as individual responsibility, disability determination, and competency.[30]

Criticisms of DSM-III-R

Several criticisms have been made of DSM-III-R (or of DSM-III which still apply). The following list includes those made by Professor of Law Daniel Shuman in his book, *Psychiatric and Psychological Evidence*:

1. That it emphasizes reliability at the expense of validity.[31]

2. That a specific diagnosis should lead to a specific treatment, as it generally does in medicine.[32]

3. That it makes it appear diagnostic classifications are discrete, "ignoring the reality of continua in psychological phenomena."[33]

4. That it "emphasizes current symptoms at the expense of long-term clinical course."[34] For example, an individual who enters the hospital with a Brief Reactive Psychosis may be rediagnosed to have a Schizophreniform Disorder after a month (the limit for the BRP diagnosis) and again rediagnosed to have Schizophrenia after six months (the limit for SD), all with no change in symptoms.

5. That its "attempts to improve reliability confuses symptoms with diseases and fails to acknowledge the role of psychodynamics in the development of symptoms."[35]

6. That "it ignores the significance of symptoms as attempts at communication, particularly within the family context."[36]

7. That, "when presenting an individual's story in litigating a case, the DSM-III diagnosis is not likely to communicate much in the way of understandable human pathos. It does not help to explain the *why* the individual is suffering, only the *what*."[37]

8. That it "is not equally reliable across the diagnostic spectrum, and this must be recognized when presenting or impeaching psychiatric testimony."[38] Thus, greatest reliability was shown in the DSM-III field trials for affective disorders, followed by schizophrenia, followed by substance use disorders, then personality disorders, and, ultimately, dissociative disorders, reliability being very low.[39] Overall, interrater reliability for Axis I was

.78 when two psychiatrists interviewed jointly and .66 after separate interviews. For Axis II (Personality Disorders), the ratings were .61 for joint assessment and .54 for separate interviews.[40]

9. Diagnosis in psychiatry substantially relies on the openness and honesty of the patient, and only secondarily on observable signs and symptoms except in the most major disorders.[41] Whether conscious or unconscious, distortions, omissions, and lies may preclude accurate diagnosis. Psychological testing will improve the accuracy of diagnosis somewhat, but its use is far from universal (see Chapters 7 through 9 of this book for specific discussion regarding psychological testing).

Gary Tischler, M.D.,[42] offers the following criticisms:

1. DSM-III eliminated the term "neurosis" and most descriptions of the neuroses, in spite of the "important role that psychodynamic thinking has played, and continues to play, in American psychiatry."[43] There was strong feeling among many psychiatrists that clinical usefulness was sacrificed for statistical reliability.

2. There is a varying "extent to which the typologies reflect the 'real world' experience of the practitioner."[44]

3. There is an apparent lack of appreciation of "the value of informed clinical judgment and [an] overestimating [of] the extent to which a precise diagnosis will inform clinical decisionmaking given the current state of the art."[45] Treatment decisions will be made in part on non-DSM criteria, e.g., "the extent to which individuals represent a threat to themselves or others, their ability to care for themselves, the availability of social supports or alternative treatment resources, and prior response to treatment. . . ."[46]

June Sprock, M.S., and Roger Blashfield, Ph.D.,[47] have additional criticisms to make. They include the following:

1. "Despite the emphasis on research, the criteria were developed intuitively by experts based on their knowledge and experience with psychopathology, rather than

on empirical determination of which symptoms are most informative."[48]

2. "Not all criteria for diagnoses are explicit."[49] For example, the first criterion for "Psychogenic Amnesia" in DSM-III-R is "an episode of sudden inability to recall important personal information that is too extensive to be explained by ordinary forgetfulness."[50] Neither the precise extent nor the period of time involved are stated, and two clinicians may interpret the requirements differently.

3. "Problems of measurement have not been resolved for the new axes. For instance, Axes IV and V are measured through crude ordinal scales."[51]

4. "Although Axis II would have made the most sense if it covered the range of normal personality styles, only categories of personality *disorders* were included, and these categories have been shown to have low reliability."[52]

5. "Despite the use of multiple axes to avoid the problems of multiple diagnoses with the DSM-II, multiple diagnoses are still allowed on Axis I."[53]

6. "No references are cited: thus, the factual claims cannot be evaluated."[54]

7. "Increasing the number of categories allows for finer differentiation of clinical pictures, courses, and treatments. . . . However, evidence from research has demonstrated that reliability decreases as increasingly fine distinctions are required."[55]

8. Several research-based factors are not represented in DSM-III or III-R. "DSM-III [and III-R] has no categories for depressive disorders of childhood, yet [research has] noted at least seven factoring studies that discovered a depressive syndrome in children. . . . The DSM-III uses the same diagnostic criteria for childhood depression as for adults, qualified only by a statement that the associated features may differ and vary according to age. . . . [I]t is likely that children do not experience depression as adults do, and that research should aim at identifying symptom clusters to allow differential diagnosis and to modify these criteria."[56]

Comment: As accurate as these comments may be, for all practical purposes DSM-III-R is the only show in town. It is necessary for any mental health practitioner to be familiar with it and to make the best of what is sometimes a bad situation. Diagnoses are "explanatory fictions"—intangible, inexact, but necessary for dialogue regarding psychological states.

THE INTERNATIONAL CLASSIFICATION OF DISEASES, INJURIES, AND CAUSES OF DEATH (ICD-9, ICD-9-CM)

The ICD was begun by the World Health Organization toward the end of the last century as the International List of Causes of Death, changing to the ICD name only with the sixth revision, in 1948.[57] It was not until the fifth revision, in 1938, that a separate section for mental disorders was included—as a single category with four subcategories: mental deficiency, schizophrenia, manic depressive psychosis, and "all other mental disorders."[58] The sixth revision, in 1948, contained the first section on mental disorders, which was included in ICD-7 (1955) without major revisions. It wasn't until ICD-8, however, adopted in 1965, that the classification was sufficiently broad and inclusive to be useful to most psychiatrists. Part of its usefulness was due to the development of a "Glossary of Mental Disorders and Guide to Their Classification," for use in conjunction with ICD-8.[59]

ICD-9 was adopted in 1975, with the glossary as an integral part of the mental disorders section, the only section of ICD-9 which includes such a glossary. The reason for its inclusion, according to the World Health Organization, is that "diagnosis of many of the most important mental disorders still relies largely upon descriptions of abnormal experience and behavior, and without some guidance in the form of a glossary that can serve as a common frame of reference, psychiatric communications easily became unsatisfactory at both clinical and statistical levels."[60]

The ICD is a statistical classification of diseases and many other sources of morbidity and mortality. It has also been adapted as a nomenclature of diseases for indexing medical records. As a statistical classification system, designed to indicate the relationship between diagnostic categories but not to

facilitate the description and recording of clinical and pathological observations, it is relatively static and not well suited to
daily use by clinicians.[61]

The ICD is organized into 17 major sections, the fifth of
which is "Mental Disorders." All mental disorders must be
assigned a three-digit code, from 290–319. A fourth digit, from
.0 to .9, may be used for greater specificity within a given
code.[62] Even so, clinicians in the United States wished greater
specificity, and ICD-9-CM, the "Clinical Modification of the
World Health Organization's International Classification of
Diseases, 9th Revision" was developed. While highly similar to
ICD-9, it contains a fifth digit for many categories, and a small
number of fourth digit codes not in ICD-9. The largest disparity between ICD-9 and ICD-9-CM is in the classification of
affective psychoses (code 296). In some instances, the same
four-digit code in the two sources refers to different conditions:
e.g., 296.2 in ICD-9 is "Manic-Depressive Psychosis, circular
type but currently manic," while in ICD-9-CM it is "Major
Depressive Disorder, Single Episode."[63]

While most DSM-III three-digit codes were the same as
ICD-9-CM codes, some were different. "In contrast, all DSM-
III-R codes are legitimate ICD-9-CM codes."[64]

In general, then, ICD-9-CM and DSM-III-R are comparable
texts, but with sufficient differences that it should not be
assumed that a given category is identical in the two. At the
least, DSM-III-R is likely to be more detailed than ICD-9-CM
for any given category, and, per the above example, the content
may in fact be substantially different.

The criticisms of DSM-III and DSM-III-R would apply as
well to ICD-9-CM, only more so. The lack of specificity of the
ICD is much greater than that of the DSMs, and it is much
less in touch with current research. While there are problems
with the DSM-III-R in clinical use and in the courtroom, those
problems multiply with the ICD-9-CM.

CPT-4

The *Physicians' Current Procedural Terminology, Fourth
Edition* (1977) is published by the American Medical
Association. It

is a listing of descriptive terms and identifying codes for reporting medical services and procedures performed by physicians. The purpose of the terminology is to provide a uniform language that will accurately designate medical, surgical, and diagnostic services, and will thereby provide an effective means for reliable, nationwide communication among physicians, patients, and third parties. The present revision is the fourth edition of a work that first appeared in 1966.

... "Procedural Terminology for Psychiatrists (PTP)" is a selection of those services and procedures most commonly performed by psychiatrists using the terms, definitions and coding from the fourth edition of CPT. . . .[65]

Each procedure in CPT/PTP has a unique five-digit code. The physician is to select that code which most closely describes his or her professional activity and use it (and the terminology which accompanies it) to identify services he or she performs. Levels of service are broken down into "brief (no code)," "limited (90600)," "intermediate (90605)," "extended (90610)," and "comprehensive (90620),"[66] with "complex (90630)" being added for special circumstances.[67] Most codes are an indication of both the procedure (service) and the time involved. For example, 90841 is "individual medical psychotherapy . . . time unspecified," 90843 is "approximately 20 to 30 minutes," and 90844 is "approximately 45 or 50 minutes."[68]

EXAMINATION OF THE MENTAL HEALTH PROFESSIONAL REGARDING DIAGNOSIS

As indicated above, neither DSM-III-R nor ICD-9-CM are precise documents, raising significant questions about both validity and reliability. In the example re: Brief Reactive Psychosis vs. Schizophreniform Disorder vs. Schizophrenia, identical clinical features lead to different diagnoses over time. It becomes important to find out what criteria the expert used to make a diagnosis—and what criteria permitted a differential diagnosis between two similar disorders. Since there is no mental disorder which automatically renders an individual incompetent, it is also necessary to question the expert about competence and other issues directly related to parenting. It will normally be necessary for the attorney to retain a psychologist to assist with this part of the examination of the expert.

For example, if the expert indicates that Dad has a diagnosis of "Bipolar Disorder," the attorney may want to ask:

1. Which of the criteria in DSM-III-R on pp. 217-218 for "Manic Episode," on pp. 222-224 for "Major Depressive Episode," and on pp. 225-226 for "Bipolar Disorder" does Dad meet, and which doesn't he? What specific behavior or symptoms meet the required criteria for the diagnosis?

2. If Dad's mood does cycle into "manic" and "depressed" stages at times, is Dad's reality testing so poor that he clearly qualifies for the psychotic label of "Bipolar Disorder," or would he more accurately be characterized as having "Cyclothymia,"[69] a nonpsychotic disorder? It is obviously a more positive indicator of Dad's ability to parent if he has not been psychotic.

3. If Dad has only been depressed (no "manic" periods) in recent years, does he more likely suffer from a "Major Depression"[70] or "Dysthymia"[71] than a "Bipolar Disorder" at this time? The person with a Bipolar Disorder is relatively more likely to be a problem for the children, particularly during "manic" periods when he feels exceptionally competent and powerful and may directly inflict harm, than is an individual who is depressed. For the depressed person, the primary concern would be neglect of the children, rather than direct infliction of harm, with that neglect being much more significant, on the average, for the person with a Major Depression than for one with Dysthymia.

As is evident from the above discussion, most diagnoses are open to some degree of questioning, and it is not uncommon for small changes in data (e.g., regarding time a disorder has been present) to lead to a substantial change in diagnosis. Where there may be an issue, it may be helpful for the attorney to have a photocopy of relevant sections of DSM-III-R to hand to the psychologist who is testifying, so that he may be questioned regarding precisely which diagnostic indicators are present and why one diagnosis was preferred over another similar one.

EXAMPLE OF DIAGNOSTIC CRITERIA FROM DSM-III-R

Diagnostic criteria for Major Depressive Episode*

Note: A "Major Depressive Syndrome" is defined as criterion A below.

A. At least five of the following symptoms have been present during the same two-week period and represent a change from previous functioning; at least one of the symptoms is either (1) depressed mood, or (2) loss of interest or pleasure. (Do not include symptoms that are clearly due to a physical condition, mood-incongruent delusions or hallucinations, incoherence, or marked loosening of associations.)

   (1) depressed mood (or can be irritable mood in children and adolescents) most of the day, nearly every day, as indicated either by subjective account or observation by others

   (2) markedly diminished interest or pleasure in all, or almost all, activities most of the day, nearly every day (as indicated either by subjective account or observation by others of apathy most of the time)

   (3) significant weight loss or weight gain when not dieting (e.g., more than 5% of body weight in a month), or decrease or increase in appetite nearly every day (in children, consider failure to make expected weight gains)

   (4) insomnia or hypersomnia nearly every day

   (5) psychomotor agitation or retardation nearly every day (observable by others, not merely subjective feelings of restlessness or being slowed down)

   (6) fatigue or loss of energy nearly every day

   (7) feelings of worthlessness or excessive or inappropriate guilt (which may be delusional) nearly every day (not merely self-reproach or guilt about being sick)

---

*Reprinted with permission from the *Diagnostic and Statistical Manual of Mental Disorders, Third Edition, Revised.* Copyright 1987 American Psychiatric Association.

(8) diminished ability to think or concentrate, or indecisiveness, nearly every day (either by subjective account or as observed by others)

(9) recurrent thoughts of death (not just fear of dying), recurrent suicidal ideation without a specific plan, or a suicide attempt or a specific plan for committing suicide

B. (1) It cannot be established that an organic factor initiated and maintained the disturbance

(2) The disturbance is not a normal reaction to the death of a loved one (Uncomplicated Bereavement)

Note: Morbid preoccupation with worthlessness, suicidal ideation, marked functional impairment or psychomotor retardation, or prolonged duration suggest bereavement complicated by Major Depression.

C. At no time during the disturbance have there been delusions or hallucinations for as long as two weeks in the absence of prominent mood symptoms (i.e., before the mood symptoms developed or after they have remitted).

D. Not superimposed on Schizophrenia, Schizophreniform Disorder, Delusional Disorder, Psychotic Disorder NOS.

Major Depressive Episode codes: fifth-digit code numbers and criteria for severity of current state of Bipolar Disorder, Depressed, or Major Depression:

1- **Mild:** Few, if any, symptoms in excess of those required to make the diagnosis, **and** symptoms result in only minor impairment in occupational functioning or in usual social activities or relationships with others.

2- **Moderate:** Symptoms or functional impairment between "mild" and "severe."

3- **Severe, without Psychotic Features:** Several symptoms in excess of those required to make the diagnosis, **and** symptoms markedly interfere with occupational functioning or with usual social activities or relationships with others.

4- **With Psychotic Features:** Delusions or hallucinations. If possible, **specify** whether the psychotic features are *mood-congruent* or *mood-incongruent*.

Mood-congruent psychotic features: Delusions or hallucinations whose content is entirely consistent with the typical depressive themes of personal inadequacy, guilt, disease, death, nihilism, or deserved punishment.

Mood-incongruent psychotic features: Delusions or hallucinations whose content does *not* involve typical depressive themes of personal inadequacy, guilt, disease, death, nihilism, or deserved punishment. Included here are such symptoms as persecutory delusions (not directly related to depressive themes), thought insertion, thought broadcasting, and delusions of control.

5- **In Partial Remission:** Intermediate between "In Full Remission" and "Mild," and no previous Dysthymia. (If Major Depressive Episode was superimposed on Dysthymia, the diagnosis of Dysthymia alone is given once the full criteria for a Major Depressive Episode are no longer met.)

6- **In Full Remission:** During the past six months no significant signs or symptoms of the disturbance.

0- **Unspecified.**

Specify chronic if current episode has lasted two consecutive years without a period of two months or longer during which there were no significant depressive symptoms.

Specify if current episode is **Melancholic Type**.

Diagnostic criteria for Melancholic Type

The presence of at least five of the following:

    (1) loss of interest or pleasure in all, or almost all, activities

    (2) lack of reactivity to usually pleasurable stimuli (does not feel much better, even temporarily, when something good happens)

    (3) depression regularly worse in the morning

(4) early morning awakening (at least two hours before usual time of awakening)

(5) psychomotor retardation or agitation (not merely subjective complaints)

(6) significant anorexia or weight loss (e.g., more than 5% of body weight in a month)

(7) no significant personality disturbance before first Major Depressive Episode

(8) one or more previous Major Depressive Episodes followed by complete, or nearly complete, recovery

(9) previous good response to specific and adequate somatic antidepressant therapy, e.g., tricyclics, ECT, MAOI, lithium

Diagnostic criteria for seasonal pattern

A. There has been a regular temporal relationship between the onset of an episode of Bipolar Disorder (including Bipolar Disorder NOS) or Recurrent Major Depression (including Depressive Disorder NOS) and a particular 60-day period of the year (e.g., regular appearance of depression between the beginning of October and the end of November).

Note: Do not include cases in which there is an obvious effect of seasonally related psychosocial stressors, e.g., regularly being unemployed every winter.

B. Full remissions (or a change from depression to mania or hypomania) also occurred within a particular 60-day period of the year (e.g., depression disappears from mid-February to mid-April).

C. There have been at least three episodes of mood disturbance in three separate years that demonstrated the temporal seasonal relationship defined in A and B; at least two of the years were consecutive.

D. Seasonal episodes of mood disturbance, as described above, outnumbered any nonseasonal episodes of such disturbance that may have occurred by more than three to one.

ENDNOTES

1. S. Korchin, Modern Clinical Psychology 90 (1976).
2. D. Shuman, Psychiatric and Psychological Evidence 20–21 (1986) [hereinafter Psychiatric and Psychological Evidence].
3. *Id.* at 29.
4. Diagnostic and Statistical Manual of Mental Disorders, Third Edition, Revised (DSM-III-R) (1987) [hereinafter DSM-III-R).
5. Manual of the International Statistical Classification of Diseases, Injuries, and Causes of Death, Clinical Modification (ICD-9-CM) (9th ed. 1977).
6. DSM-III-R, *supra* note 4, at xviii–xix.
7. *Id.* at xix.
8. *Id.* at xxv.
9. *Id.* at xix–xxi.
10. Spitzer & Williams, *Classification of Mental Disorders* in H. Kaplan & B. Sadock: Comprehensive Textbook of Psychiatry/IV 613 (1985) [hereinafter *Classification of Mental Disorders]*; Frances, Widiger & Pincus, *The Development of DSM-IV,* 46 Archives of General Psychiatry 373–75 (1989) [hereinafter *The Development of DSM-IV*].
11. *The Development of DSM-IV, supra* note 10, at 373.
12. *Id.* at 374.
13. DSM-III-R, *supra* note 4, at xxii.
14. *Id.* at xxii.
15. *Id.* at xxiii.
16. *Id.*
17. Klerman, *Classification and DSM-III-R,* The New Harvard Guide to Psychiatry 77 (1988).
18. *Id.* at 78.
19. *Id.*
20. *Id.* at 79.

21. DSM-III-R, *supra* note 4, at xxiv.

22. *The Development of DSM-IV*, *supra* note 10, at 374.

23. *Id.*

24. DSM-III-R, *supra* note 4, at 15–16.

25. *Id.* at 16.

26. *Id.* at 11.

27. *Id.* at 12.

28. *Id.* at 3–10.

29. *Id.* at 3–4, 9.

30. *Id.* at xxix.

31. Psychiatric and Psychological Evidence, *supra* note 2, at 39.

32. *Id.*

33. *Id.*

34. *Id.* at 40.

35. *Id.*

36. *Id.*

37. *Id.*

38. *Id.*

39. *Id.*

40. *Classification of Mental Disorders*, *supra* note 10, at 611.

41. Psychiatric and Psychological Evidence, *supra* note 2, at 41.

42. Tischler, *Evaluation of DSM-III*, in H. Kaplan & B. Sadock, Comprehensive Textbook of Psychiatry/IV 617–621 (1985).

43. *Id.* at 617.

44. *Id.* at 619.

45. *Id.* at 619–20.

46. *Id.* at 620.

47. J. Sprock & R. Blashfield, *Classification and Nosology*, in M. Hersen, A. Kazdin & A. Bellack, The Clinical Psychology Handbook, 289–307 (1983) [hereinafter *Classification and Nosology*].

48. *Id.* at 298.

49. *Id.*

50. DSM-III-R, *supra* note 4, at 275.

51. *Classification and Nosology, supra* note 47, at 298.

52. *Id.*

53. *Id.*

54. *Id.*

55. *Id.* at 299.

56. *Id.*

57. *Classification of Mental Disorders, supra* note 10, at 598.

58. DSM-III-R, *supra* note 4, at 435.

59. *Id.*

60. *Id.* at 437.

61. *Id.* at 433–34.

62. *Id.* at 434.

63. *Id.* at 440–41.

64. *Id.* at xxv.

65. Procedural Terminology for Psychiatrists (PTP), iv (1980).

66. *Id.* at 2–4.

67. *Id.* at 8.

68. *Id.* at 9.

69. DSM-III-R, *supra* note 4, at 226–28.

70. *Id.* at 228–30.

71. *Id.* at 230–33.

Appendix A

Organizations That Make Up Organized Psychology*

---

*"Organizations That Make Up Organized Psychology," 44 (7) *American Psychologist* 982 (July 1989). Copyright 1989 by the American Psychological Association. Reprinted by permission.

Organizations That Make Up Organized Psychology (an Illustrative Sampling)

CANADIAN PSYCHOLOGICAL ASSOCIATION

Psychological Asn. of Alberta
British Columbia Psychological Asn.
Manitoba Psych. Soc., Inc.
Psychological Asn. of Manitoba
Coll. of Psychologists of New Brunswick
Psych. Asn. of Nova Scotia
Asn. of Psychologists of Nova Scotia

Asn. of Psychologists of the NW Terr.
Ontario Psychological Asn.
Corp. Prof. des Psychologues du Quebec
Saskatchewan Psychological Asn.
Psych. Soc. of Saskatchewan
Asn. of New Foundland Psychologists
Psych. Asn. of Prince Edward Is.

AFFILIATED REGIONAL PSYCHOLOGICAL ASSOCIATIONS

Eastern Psychological Asn.
Midwestern Psychological Asn.
New England Psychological Asn.
Rocky Mountain Psychological Asn.
Southeastern Psychological Asn.
Southwestern Psychological Asn.
Western Psychological Asn.

AFFILIATED STATE PSYCHOLOGICAL ASSOCIATIONS

Alabama	Louisiana	Oklahoma
Alaska	Maine	Oregon
Arizona	Maryland	Pennsylvania
Arkansas	Massachusetts	Puerto Rico
California	Michigan	Rhode Island
Colorado	Minnesota	South Carolina
Connecticut	Mississippi	South Dakota
Delaware	Missouri	Tennessee
District of Columbia	Montana	Texas
Florida	Nebraska	Utah
Georgia	Nevada	Vermont
Hawaii	New Hampshire	Virginia
Idaho	New Jersey	Washington
Illinois	New Mexico	West Virginia
Indiana	New York	Wisconsin
Iowa	North Carolina	Wyoming
Kansas	North Dakota	
Kentucky	Ohio	

INTERNATIONAL PSYCHOLOGICAL ASSOCIATIONS

Intl. Union of Psychological Science (IUPsyS)
Intl. Asn. of Applied Psychology (IAAP)
European Federation of Professional Psychologists Asn. (EFPPA)
Interamerican Soc. of Psychology (ISP)
Intl. Council of Psychologists (ICP)

INTERDISCIPLINARY GROUPS WITH STRONG PSYCHOLOGICAL INTERFACE

Amer. Asn. for the Advancement of Science (AAAS)
Amer. Education Research Asn. (AERA)
Soc. for Research in Child Development (SRCD)
Gerontological Soc. of America (GSA)
Cognitive Science Soc.
Soc. for Neuroscience
Human Factors Soc.
Intl. Neuropsych. Asn. (INSA)
World Federation for Mental Health (WFMH)
Soc. for Psychotherapy Research

Acoustical Soc. of America
Amer. Pain Society
Behavior Genetics Asn.
Intl. Soc. of Hypnosis
Amer. Correctional Asn.
Asn. for Behavior Analysis
Intl. Brain Research Org.
Amer. Psychopathological Asn.
Amer. Orthopsychiatric Asn.
Amer. Evaluation Asn.

Academy of Management
Soc. for Clinical and Experimental Hypnosis
Amer. Asn. for Marriage & Family Therapy
Asn. for the Psychophysiological Study of Sleep
Soc. for the Advancement of Field Theory
Amer. Soc. of Group Psychotherapy & Psychodrama
Asn. for Humanistic Simulation & Experiential Learning
Asn. of Mental Health Administrators
Biofeedback Soc. of America
Comm. on Rehabilitation Counselor Certification

AMERICAN PSYCHOLOGICAL ASSOCIATION

1. General Psychology
2. Teaching of Psychology
3. Experimental Psychology
4. Evaluation, Measurement and Statistics
5. Physiological and Comparative
6. Developmental Psychology
7. Personality and Social
8. Study of Social Issues (SPSSI)
9. Psychology and the Arts
10. Clinical Psychology
11. Consulting Psychology
12. Industrial and Organizational
13. Educational Psychology
14. School Psychology
15. Counseling Psychology

18. Psychologists in Public Service
19. Military Psychology
20. Adult Development and Aging
21. Applied Experimental & Engr. Psy.
22. Rehabilitation Psychology
23. Consumer Psychology
24. Theoretical and Philosophical Psy.
25. Experimental Analysis of Behavior
26. History of Psychology
27. Community Psychology
28. Psychopharmacology
29. Psychotherapy
30. Psychological Hypnosis
31. State Psychological Asn. Affairs
32. Humanistic Psychology

33. Mental Retardation & Develop. Disabilities
34. Population and Environmental Psychology
35. Psychology of Women
36. Psychologists in Religious Issues (PIRI)
37. Child, Youth and Family Services
38. Health Psychology
39. Psychoanalysis
40. Clinical Neuropsychology
41. Psychology-Law
42. Psychologists in Independent Practice
43. Family Psychology
44. Psy. Study of Lesbian and Gay Issues
45. Psy. Study of Ethnic Minority Issues
46. Media Psychology
47. Exercise and Sports Psychology

OTHER PSYCHOLOGICAL ASSOCIATIONS

Psychonomic Soc., Inc.
Soc. of Experimental Psychologists
Soc. for Multivariate Experimental Psychology
Soc. for Computers in Psychology
Soc. for Mathematical Psychology
Amer. Psychological Society (APS)
Psychometric Soc.
Ntl. Academy of Practice in Psychology
Ntl. Asn. for School Psychologists (NASP)
Amer. Asn. of Correctional Psychologists
Asn. of Practicing Psychologists
Soc. of Psychologists in Addictive Behaviors
Amer. Academy of Forensic Psychology
Natl. Organization of VA Psychologists (NOVA Psi.)
Soc. of Psychologists in Substance Abuse
Psychologists in Long-Term Care
Soc. of Air Force Clinical Psychologists
Asn. for Jungian Psychology
North Amer. Soc. of Adlerian Psychology
Soc. of Psychologists in Management
Asn. for the Advancement of Applied Sports Psychology
Psychologists for Social Responsibility
Asn. of Women in Psychology
Asn. of Lesbian and Gay Psychologists
Soc. of Experimental Social Psychology

STUDENT ORGANIZATIONS

Amer. Psychological Asn. of Graduate Students (APAGS)
Psi Chi
Psi Beta

EDUCATION AND TRAINING GROUPS

Council of Graduate Departments of Psychology (COGDOP)
National Council of Schools of Professional Psychology (NCSPP)
Asn. of Psychology Internship Centers (APIC)
Council of Training Directors (CTD)
Council of University Psychology Programs (CUPP)
Asn. of Medical School Professors of Psychology (AMSPP)
Council of Teachers of Undergraduate Psychology (CTUP)
Joint Council on Professional Education in Psychology (JCPEP)

CREDENTIALING AND LICENSING ORGANIZATIONS

Amer. Asn. of State Psychological Boards (AASPB)
Amer. Board of Professional Psychology (ABPP)
National Register of Health Service Providers in Psychology

ETHNIC MINORITY PSYCHOLOGICAL ASSOCIATIONS

Asian Amer. Psychological Asn.
Asn. of Black Psychologists
National Hispanic Psychological Asn.
Soc. of Indian Psychologists

Appendix B
Professional Organizations

Academy of Certified Social Workers, see National Association of Social Workers.

American Academy of Psychiatry and Law, 1211 Cathedral Street, Baltimore, MD 21201. Phone: 301-539-0379.

American Board of Forensic Psychiatry, 1211 Cathedral Street, Baltimore, MD 21201. Phone: 301-539-0872.

American Board of Forensic Psychology, 2100 E. Broadway, Suite 313, Columbia, MO 65201. Phone: 314-875-1267.

American Board of Medical Psychotherapists, Physicians' Park, Suite 11, 300 25th Avenue North, Nashville, TN 37203. Phone: 615-327-2984.

American Board of Professional Psychology, 2100 E. Broadway, Suite 313, Columbia, MO 65201. Phone: 314-875-1267.

American Board of Psychiatry and Neurology, 500 Lake Cook Road, Suite 335, Deerfield, IL 60015. Phone: 708-945-7900.

American College of Forensic Psychiatry, 26701 Quail Creek, Laguna Hills, CA 92656. Phone: 714-831-0236.

American Medical Association, 535 N. Dearborn Street, Chicago, IL 60610. Phone: 312-751-6000.

American Orthopsychiatric Association, 19 W. 44th Street, Suite 1616, New York, NY 10036. Phone: 212-354-5770.

American Psychiatric Association, 1400 K Street, N.W., Washington, D.C. 20005. Phone: 202-682-6000.

American Psychoanalytic Association, 309 East 49th Street, New York, NY 10017. Phone: 212-752-0450.

American Psychological Association, 1200 17th Street, N.W., Washington, D.C. 20036. Phone: 202-955-7600.

American Psychology-Law Society, 1200 17th Street, N.W., Washington, D.C. 20036. Phone: 202-955-7600.

National Association of Social Workers, 7981 Eastern Avenue, Silver Spring, MD 20910. Phone: 301-565-0333.

National Register of Health Service Providers in Psychology, 1730 Rhode Island Avenue, N.W., Washington, D.C. 20036. Phone: 202-833-2377.

For information on other organizations, consult the *Encyclopedia of Associations* (20th ed. 1990).

Appendix C
Ethical Principles of Psychologists*

*"Ethical Principles of Psychologists," 36 (6) *American Psychologist* 633–638 (June 1981). Copyright 1981 by the American Psychological Association. Reprinted by permission.

Ethical Principles of Psychologists
(Amended June 2, 1989. See back page.)

PREAMBLE

Psychologists respect the dignity and worth of the individual and strive for the preservation and protection of fundamental human rights. They are committed to increasing knowledge of human behavior and of people's understanding of themselves and others and to the utilization of such knowledge for the promotion of human welfare. While pursuing these objectives, they make every effort to protect the welfare of those who seek their services and of the research participants that may be the object of study. They use their skills only for purposes consistent with these values and do not knowingly permit their misuse by others. While demanding for themselves freedom of inquiry and communication, psychologists accept the responsibility this freedom requires: competence, objectivity in the application of skills, and concern for the best interests of clients, colleagues, students, research participants, and society. In the pursuit of these ideals, psychologists subscribe to principles in the following areas: 1. Responsibility, 2. Competence, 3. Moral and Legal Standards, 4. Public Statements, 5. Confidentiality, 6. Welfare of the Consumer, 7. Professional Relationships, 8. Assessment Techniques, 9. Research With Human Participants, and 10. Care and Use of Animals.

Acceptance of membership in the American Psychological Association commits the member to adherence to these principles.

Psychologists cooperate with duly constituted committees of the American Psychological Association, in particular, the Committee on Scientific and Professional Ethics and Conduct, by responding to inquiries promptly and completely. Members also respond promptly and completely to inquiries from duly constituted state association ethics committees and professional standards review committees.

Principle 1
RESPONSIBILITY

In providing services, psychologists maintain the highest standards of their profession. They accept responsibility for the consequences of their acts and make every effort to ensure that their services are used appropriately.

a. As scientists, psychologists accept responsibility for the selection of their research topics and the methods used in investigation, analysis, and reporting. They plan their research in ways to minimize the possibility that their findings will be misleading. They provide thorough discussion of the limitations of their data, especially where their work touches on social policy or might be construed to the detriment of persons in specific age, sex,

ethnic, socioeconomic, or other social groups. In publishing reports of their work, they never suppress disconfirming data, and they acknowledge the existence of alternative hypotheses and explanations of their findings. Psychologists take credit only for work they have actually done.

b. Psychologists clarify in advance with all appropriate persons and agencies the expectations for sharing and utilizing research data. They avoid relationships that may limit their objectivity or create a conflict of interest. Interference with the milieu in which data are collected is kept to a minimum.

c. Psychologists have the responsibility to attempt to prevent distortion, misuse, or suppression of psychological findings by the institution or agency of which they are employees.

d. As members of governmental or other organizational bodies, psychologists remain accountable as individuals to the highest standards of their profession.

e. As teachers, psychologists recognize their primary obligation to help others acquire knowledge and skill. They maintain high standards of scholarship by presenting psychological information objectively, fully, and accurately.

f. As practitioners, psychologists know that they bear a heavy social responsibility because their recommendations and professional actions may alter the lives of others. They are alert to personal, social, organizational, financial, or political situations and pressures that might lead to misuse of their influence.

This version of the Ethical Principles of Psychologists (formerly entitled Ethical Standards of Psychologists) was adopted by the American Psychological Association's Council of Representatives on January 24, 1981. The revised Ethical Principles contain both substantive and grammatical changes in each of the nine ethical principles constituting the Ethical Standards of Psychologists previously adopted by the Council of Representatives in 1979, plus a new tenth principle entitled Care and Use of Animals. Inquiries concerning the Ethical Principles of Psychologists should be addressed to the Administrative Officer for Ethics, American Psychological Association, 1200 Seventeenth Street, N.W., Washington, D.C. 20036.

These revised Ethical Principles apply to psychologists, to students of psychology, and to others who do work of a psychological nature under the supervision of a psychologist. They are also intended for the guidance of nonmembers of the Association who are engaged in psychological research or practice.

Any complaints of unethical conduct filed after January 24, 1981, shall be governed by this 1981 revision. However, conduct (a) complained about after January 24, 1981, but which occurred prior to that date, and (b) not considered unethical under prior versions of the principles but considered unethical under the 1981 revision, shall not be deemed a violation of ethical principles. Any complaints pending as of January 24, 1981, shall be governed either by the 1979 or by the 1981 version of the Ethical Principles, at the sound discretion of the Committee on Scientific and Professional Ethics and Conduct.

Principle 2
COMPETENCE

The maintenance of high standards of competence is a responsibility shared by all psychologists in the interest of the public and the profession as a whole. Psychologists recognize the boundaries of their competence and the limitations of their techniques. They only provide services and only use techniques for which they are qualified by training and experience. In those areas in which recognized standards do not yet exist, psychologists take whatever precautions are necessary to protect the welfare of their clients. They maintain knowledge of current scientific and professional information related to the services they render.

a. Psychologists accurately represent their competence, education, training, and experience. They claim as evidence of educational qualifications only those degrees obtained from institutions acceptable under the Bylaws and Rules of Council of the American Psychological Association.

b. As teachers, psychologists perform their duties on the basis of careful preparation so that their instruction is accurate, current, and scholarly.

c. Psychologists recognize the need for continuing education and are open to new procedures and changes in expectations and values over time.

d. Psychologists recognize differences among people, such as those that may be associated with age, sex, socioeconomic, and ethnic backgrounds. When necessary, they obtain training, experience, or counsel to assure competent service or research relating to such persons.

e. Psychologists responsible for decisions involving individuals or policies based on test results have an understanding of psychological or educational measurement, validation problems, and test research.

f. Psychologists recognize that personal problems and conflicts may interfere with professional effectiveness. Accordingly, they refrain from undertaking any activity in which their personal problems are likely to lead to inadequate performance or harm to a client, colleague, student, or research participant. If engaged in such activity when they become aware of their personal problems, they seek competent professional assistance to determine whether they should suspend, terminate, or limit the scope of their professional and/or scientific activities.

Principle 3
MORAL AND LEGAL STANDARDS

Psychologists' moral and ethical standards of behavior are a personal matter to the same degree as they are for any other citizen, except as these may compromise the fulfillment of their professional responsibilities or reduce the public trust in psychology and psychologists. Regarding their own behavior, psychologists are sensi-

tive to prevailing community standards and to the possible impact that conformity to or deviation from these standards may have upon the quality of their performance as psychologists. Psychologists are also aware of the possible impact of their public behavior upon the ability of colleagues to perform their professional duties.

a. As teachers, psychologists are aware of the fact that their personal values may affect the selection and presentation of instructional materials. When dealing with topics that may give offense, they recognize and respect the diverse attitudes that students may have toward such materials.

b. As employees or employers, psychologists do not engage in or condone practices that are inhumane or that result in illegal or unjustifiable actions. Such practices include, but are not limited to, those based on considerations of race, handicap, age, gender, sexual preference, religion, or national origin in hiring, promotion, or training.

c. In their professional roles, psychologists avoid any action that will violate or diminish the legal and civil rights of clients or of others who may be affected by their actions.

d. As practitioners and researchers, psychologists act in accord with Association standards and guidelines related to practice and to the conduct of research with human beings and animals. In the ordinary course of events, psychologists adhere to relevant governmental laws and institutional regulations. When federal, state, provincial, organizational, or institutional laws, regulations, or practices are in conflict with Association standards and guidelines, psychologists make known their commitment to Association standards and guidelines and, wherever possible, work toward a resolution of the conflict. Both practitioners and researchers are concerned with the development of such legal and quasi-legal regulations as best serve the public interest, and they work toward changing existing regulations that are not beneficial to the public interest.

Principle 4
PUBLIC STATEMENTS

Public statements, announcements of services, advertising, and promotional activities of psychologists serve the purpose of helping the public make informed judgments and choices. Psychologists represent accurately and objectively their professional qualifications, affiliations, and functions, as well as those of the institutions or organizations with which they or the statements may be associated. In public statements providing psychological information or professional opinions or providing information about the availability of psychological products, publications, and services, psychologists base their statements on scientifically acceptable psycholog-

ical findings and techniques with full recognition of the limits and uncertainties of such evidence.

a. When announcing or advertising professional services, psychologists may list the following information to describe the provider and services provided: name, highest relevant academic degree earned from a regionally accredited institution, date, type, and level of certification or licensure, diplomate status, APA membership status, address, telephone number, office hours, a brief listing of the type of psychological services offered, an appropriate presentation of fee information, foreign languages spoken, and policy with regard to third-party payments. Additional relevant or important consumer information may be included if not prohibited by other sections of these Ethical Principles.

b. In announcing or advertising the availability of psychological products, publications, or services, psychologists do not present their affiliation with any organization in a manner that falsely implies sponsorship or certification by that organization. In particular and for example, psychologists do not state APA membership or fellow status in a way to suggest that such status implies specialized professional competence or qualifications. Public statements include, but are not limited to, communication by means of periodical, book, list, directory, television, radio, or motion picture. They do not contain (i) a false, fraudulent, misleading, deceptive, or unfair statement; (ii) a misinterpretation of fact or a statement likely to mislead or deceive because in context it makes only a partial disclosure of relevant facts; (iii) a testimonial from a patient regarding the quality of a psychologists' services or products; (iv) a statement intended or likely to create false or unjustified expectations of favorable results; (v) a statement implying unusual, unique, or one-of-a-kind abilities; (vi) a statement intended or likely to appeal to a client's fears, anxieties, for emotions concerning the possible results of failure to obtain the offered services; (vii) a statement concerning the comparative desirability of offered services; (viii) a statement of direct solicitation of individual clients.

c. Psychologists do not compensate or give anything of value to a representative of the press, radio, television, or other communication medium in anticipation of or in return for professional publicity in a news item. A paid advertisement must be identified as such, unless it is apparent from the context that it is a paid advertisement. If communicated to the public by use of radio or television, an advertisement is prerecorded and approved for broadcast by the psychologist, and a recording of the actual transmission is retained by the psychologist.

d. Announcements or advertisements of "personal growth groups," clinics, and agencies give a clear statement of purpose and a clear description of the experiences to be provided. The education, training, and experience of the staff members are appropriately specified.

e. Psychologists associated with the development or promotion of psychological devices, books, or other products offered for commercial sale make reasonable efforts

to ensure that announcements and advertisements are presented in a professional, scientifically acceptable, and factually informative manner.

f. Psychologists do not participate for personal gain in commercial announcements or advertisements recommending to the public the purchase or use of proprietary or single-source products or services when that participation is based solely upon their identification as psychologists.

g. Psychologists present the science of psychology and offer their services, products, and publications fairly and accurately, avoiding misrepresentation through sensationalism, exaggeration, or superficiality. Psychologists are guided by the primary obligation to aid the public in developing informed judgments, opinions, and choices.

h. As teachers, psychologists ensure that statements in catalogs and course outlines are accurate and not misleading, particularly in terms of subject matter to be covered, bases for evaluating progress, and the nature of course experiences. Announcements, brochures, or advertisements describing workshops, seminars, or other educational programs accurately describe the audience for which the program is intended as well as eligibility requirements, educational objectives, and nature of the materials to be covered. These announcements also accurately represent the education, training, and experience of the psychologists presenting the programs and any fees involved.

i. Public announcements or advertisements soliciting research participants in which clinical services or other professional services are offered as an inducement make clear the nature of the services as well as the costs and other obligations to be accepted by participants in the research.

j. A psychologist accepts the obligation to correct others who represent the psychologist's professional qualifications, or associations with products or services, in a manner incompatible with these guidelines.

k. Individual diagnostic and therapeutic services are provided only in the context of a professional psychological relationship. When personal advice is given by means of public lectures or demonstrations, newspaper or magazine articles, radio or television programs, mail, or similar media, the psychologist utilizes the most current relevant data and exercises the highest level of professional judgment.

l. Products that are described or presented by means of public lectures or demonstrations, newspaper or magazine articles, radio or television programs, or similar media meet the same recognized standards as exist for products used in the context of a professional relationship.

Principle 5
CONFIDENTIALITY

Psychologists have a primary obligation to respect the confidentiality of information obtained from persons in the course of their work as psychologists. They reveal such information to others only with the consent of the person or the person's legal representative, except in those unusual circumstances in which not to do so would result in clear danger to the person or to others. Where appropriate, psychologists inform their clients of the legal limits of confidentiality.

a. Information obtained in clinical or consulting relationships, or evaluative data concerning children, students, employees, and others, is discussed only for professional purposes and only with persons clearly concerned with the case. Written and oral reports present only data germane to the purposes of the evaluation, and every effort is made to avoid undue invasion of privacy.

b. Psychologists who present personal information obtained during the course of professional work in writings, lectures, or other public forums either obtain adequate prior consent to do so or adequately disguise all identifying information.

c. Psychologists make provisions for maintaining confidentiality in the storage and disposal of records.

d. When working with minors or other persons who are unable to give voluntary, informed consent, psychologists take special care to protect these persons' best interests.

Principle 6
WELFARE OF THE CONSUMER

Psychologists respect the integrity and protect the welfare of the people and groups with whom they work. When conflicts of interest arise between clients and psychologists' employing institutions, psychologists clarify the nature and direction of their loyalties and responsibilities and keep all parties informed of their commitments. Psychologists fully inform consumers as to the purpose and nature of an evaluative, treatment, educational, or training procedure, and they freely acknowledge that clients, students, or participants in research have freedom of choice with regard to participation.

a. Psychologists are continually cognizant of their own needs and of their potentially influential position vis-à-vis persons such as clients, students, and subordinates. They avoid exploiting the trust and dependency of such persons. Psychologists make every effort to avoid dual relationships that could impair their professional judgment or increase the risk of exploitation. Examples of such dual relationships include, but are not limited to, research with and treatment of employees, students, supervisees, close friends, or relatives. Sexual intimacies with clients are unethical.

b. When a psychologist agrees to provide services to a client at the request of a third party, the psychologist assumes the responsibility of clarifying the nature of the relationships to all parties concerned.

c. Where the demands of an organization require psy-

chologists to violate these Ethical Principles, psychologists clarify the nature of the conflict between the demands and these principles. They inform all parties of psychologists' ethical responsibilities and take appropriate action.

d. Psychologists make advance financial arrangements that safeguard the best interests of and are clearly understood by their clients. They neither give nor receive any remuneration for referring clients for professional services. They contribute a portion of their services to work for which they receive little or no financial return.

e. Psychologists terminate a clinical or consulting relationship when it is reasonably clear that the consumer is not benefiting from it. They offer to help the consumer locate alternative sources of assistance.

Principle 7
PROFESSIONAL RELATIONSHIPS

Psychologists act with due regard for the needs, special competencies, and obligations of their colleagues in psychology and other professions. They respect the prerogatives and obligations of the institutions or organizations with which these other colleagues are associated.

a. Psychologists understand the areas of competence of related professions. They make full use of all the professional, technical, and administrative resources that serve the best interests of consumers. The absence of formal relationships with other professional workers does not relieve psychologists of the responsibility of securing for their clients the best possible professional service, nor does it relieve them of the obligation to exercise foresight, diligence, and tact in obtaining the complementary or alternative assistance needed by clients.

b. Psychologists know and take into account the traditions and practices of other professional groups with whom they work and cooperate fully with such groups. If a person is receiving similar services from another professional, psychologists do not offer their own services directly to such a person. If a psychologist is contacted by a person who is already receiving similar services from another professional, the psychologist carefully considers that professional relationship and proceeds with caution and sensitivity to the therapeutic issues as well as the client's welfare. The psychologist discusses these issues with the client so as to minimize the risk of confusion and conflict.

c. Psychologists who employ or supervise other professionals or professionals in training accept the obligation to facilitate the further professional development of these individuals. They provide appropriate working conditions, timely evaluations, constructive consultation, and experience opportunities.

d. Psychologists do not exploit their professional relationships with clients, supervisees, students, employees, or research participants sexually or otherwise. Psychologists do not condone or engage in sexual harassment. Sexual harassment is defined as deliberate or repeated comments, gestures, or physical contacts of a sexual nature that are unwanted by the recipient.

e. In conducting research in institutions or organizations, psychologists secure appropriate authorization to conduct such research. They are aware of their obligations to future research workers and ensure that host institutions receive adequate information about the research and proper acknowledgment of their contributions.

f. Publication credit is assigned to those who have contributed to a publication in proportion to their professional contributions. Major contributions of a professional character made by several persons to a common project are recognized by joint authorship, with the individual who made the principal contribution listed first. Minor contributions of a professional character and extensive clerical or similar nonprofessional assistance may be acknowledged in footnotes or in an introductory statement. Acknowledgment through specific citations is made for unpublished as well as published material that has directly influenced the research or writing. Psychologists who compile and edit material of others for publication publish the material in the name of the originating group, if appropriate, with their own name appearing as chairperson or editor. All contributors are to be acknowledged and named.

g. When psychologists know of an ethical violation by another psychologist, and it seems appropriate, they informally attempt to resolve the issue by bringing the behavior to the attention of the psychologist. If the misconduct is of a minor nature and/or appears to be due to lack of sensitivity, knowledge, or experience, such an informal solution is usually appropriate. Such informal corrective efforts are made with sensitivity to any rights to confidentiality involved. If the violation does not seem amenable to an informal solution, or is of a more serious nature, psychologists bring it to the attention of the appropriate local, state, and/or national committee on professional ethics and conduct.

Principle 8
ASSESSMENT TECHNIQUES

In the development, publication, and utilization of psychological assessment techniques, psychologists make every effort to promote the welfare and best interests of the client. They guard against the misuse of assessment results. They respect the client's right to know the results, the interpretations made, and the bases for their conclusions and recommendations. Psychologists make every effort to maintain the security of tests and other assessment techniques within limits of legal mandates. They strive to ensure the appropriate use of assessment techniques by others.

a. In using assessment techniques, psychologists respect the right of clients to have full explanations of the nature and purpose of the techniques in language the clients can understand, unless an explicit exception to this right has been agreed upon in advance. When the explanations are to be provided by others, psychologists establish procedures for ensuring the adequacy of these explanations.

b. Psychologists responsible for the development and standardization of psychological tests and other assessment techniques utilize established scientific procedures and observe the relevant APA standards.

c. In reporting assessment results, psychologists indicate any reservations that exist regarding validity or reliability because of the circumstances of the assessment or the inappropriateness of the norms for the person tested. Psychologists strive to ensure that the results of assessments and their interpretations are not misused by others.

d. Psychologists recognize that assessment results may become obsolete. They make every effort to avoid and prevent the misuse of obsolete measures.

e. Psychologists offering scoring and interpretation services are able to produce appropriate evidence for the validity of the programs and procedures used in arriving at interpretations. The public offering of an automated interpretation service is considered a professional-to-professional consultation. Psychologists make every effort to avoid misuse of assessment reports.

f. Psychologists do not encourage or promote the use of psychological assessment techniques by inappropriately trained or otherwise unqualified persons through teaching, sponsorship, or supervision.

Principle 9
RESEARCH WITH HUMAN PARTICIPANTS

The decision to undertake research rests upon a considered judgment by the individual psychologist about how best to contribute to psychological science and human welfare. Having made the decision to conduct research, the psychologist considers alternative directions in which research energies and resources might be invested. On the basis of this consideration, the psychologist carries out the investigation with respect and concern for the dignity and welfare of the people who participate and with cognizance of federal and state regulations and professional standards governing the conduct of research with human participants.

a. In planning a study, the investigator has the responsibility to make a careful evaluation of its ethical acceptability. To the extent that the weighing of scientific and human values suggests a compromise of any principle, the investigator incurs a correspondingly serious obligation to seek ethical advice and to observe stringent safeguards to protect the rights of human participants.

b. Considering whether a participant in a planned

study will be a "subject at risk" or a "subject at minimal risk," according to recognized standards, is of primary ethical concern to the investigator.

c. The investigator always retains the responsibility for ensuring ethical practice in research. The investigator is also responsible for the ethical treatment of research participants by collaborators, assistants, students, and employees, all of whom, however, incur similar obligations.

d. Except in minimal-risk research, the investigator establishes a clear and fair agreement with research participants, prior to their participation, that clarifies the obligations and responsibilities of each. The investigator has the obligation to honor all promises and commitments included in that agreement. The investigator informs the participants of all aspects of the research that might reasonably be expected to influence willingness to participate and explains all other aspects of the research about which the participants inquire. Failure to make full disclosure prior to obtaining informed consent requires additional safeguards to protect the welfare and dignity of the research participants. Research with children or with participants who have impairments that would limit understanding and/or communication requires special safeguarding procedures.

e. Methodological requirements of a study may make the use of concealment or deception necessary. Before conducting such a study, the investigator has a special responsibility to (i) determine whether the use of such techniques is justified by the study's prospective scientific, educational, or applied value; (ii) determine whether alternative procedures are available that do not use concealment or deception; and (iii) ensure that the participants are provided with sufficient explanation as soon as possible.

f. The investigator respects the individual's freedom to decline to participate in or to withdraw from the research at any time. The obligation to protect this freedom requires careful thought and consideration when the investigator is in a position of authority or influence over the participant. Such positions of authority include, but are not limited to, situations in which research participation is required as part of employment or in which the participant is a student, client, or employee of the investigator.

g. The investigator protects the participant from physical and mental discomfort, harm, and danger that may arise from research procedures. If risks of such consequences exist, the investigator informs the participant of that fact. Research procedures likely to cause serious or lasting harm to a participant are not used unless the failure to use these procedures might expose the participant to risk of greater harm, or unless the research has great potential benefit and fully informed and voluntary consent is obtained from each participant. The participant should be informed of procedures for contacting the investigator within a reasonable time period following participation should stress, potential harm, or related questions or concerns arise.

h. After the data are collected, the investigator provides the participant with information about the nature of the study and attempts to remove any misconceptions that may have arisen. Where scientific or humane values justify delaying or withholding this information, the investigator incurs a special responsibility to monitor the research and to ensure that there are no damaging consequences for the participant.

i. Where research procedures result in undesirable consequences for the individual participant, the investigator has the responsibility to detect and remove or correct these consequences, including long-term effects.

j. Information obtained about a research participant during the course of an investigation is confidential unless otherwise agreed upon in advance. When the possibility exists that others may obtain access to such information, this possibility, together with the plans for protecting confidentiality, is explained to the participant as part of the procedure for obtaining informed consent.

Principle 10
CARE AND USE OF ANIMALS

An investigator of animal behavior strives to advance understanding of basic behavioral principles and/or to contribute to the improvement of human health and welfare. In seeking these ends, the investigator ensures the welfare of animals and treats them humanely. Laws and regulations notwithstanding, an animal's immediate protection depends upon the scientist's own conscience.

a. The acquisition, care, use, and disposal of all animals are in compliance with current federal, state or provincial, and local laws and regulations.

b. A psychologist trained in research methods and experienced in the care of laboratory animals closely supervises all procedures involving animals and is responsible for ensuring appropriate consideration of their comfort, health, and humane treatment.

c. Psychologists ensure that all individuals using animals under their supervision have received explicit instruction in experimental methods and in the care, maintenance, and handling of the species being used. Responsibilities and activities of individuals participating in a research project are consistent with their respective competencies.

d. Psychologists make every effort to minimize discomfort, illness, and pain of animals. A procedure subjecting animals to pain, stress, or privation is used only when an alternative procedure is unavailable and the goal is justified by its prospective scientific, educational, or applied value. Surgical procedures are performed under appropriate anesthesia; techniques to avoid infection and minimize pain are followed during and after surgery.

e. When it is appropriate that the animal's life be terminated, it is done rapidly and painlessly.

Ethical Principles of Psychologists: Amendments June 2, 1989

The Board of Directors of the American Psychological Association, on June 2, 1989, rescinded and will no longer enforce the following sections of APA's Ethical Principles:

Rescinded June 1989: Principle 4.b.iii
Principle 4.b.v.
Principle 4.b.vi
Principle 4.b.vii
Principle 4.b.viii

The following portions of Principle 6.d. and Principle 7.b. have also been rescinded:

Principle 6.d.: "They neither give nor receive any remuneration for referring clients for professional services."

Principle 7.b.: "If a person is receiving similar services from another professional, psychologists do not offer their own services directly to such a person."

Appendix D

General Guidelines for Providers of Psychological Services*

*"General Guidelines for Providers of Psychological Services," 42 (7) *American Psychologist* (July 1987). Copyright 1987 by the American Psychological Association. Reprinted by permission.

General Guidelines for Providers of
Psychological Services

Board of Professional Affairs, Committee on Professional Standards

Preamble

A set of practices and implicitly recognized principles of conduct evolves over the history of every profession. Such principles guide the relationships of the members of the profession to their users, to each other, and to the community of which both professionals and users are members. Making such guiding principles and practices explicit is a sign of the profession's maturity and serves the best interests of the profession, its users, and the community at large.

Because psychology is a continually evolving science and profession, guidelines for practice are living documents that require periodic review and revision. The *General Guidelines for Providers of Psychological Services*[1,2] represents an important milestone in the evolutionary development of professional psychology.

These General Guidelines are a set of aspirational statements for psychologists that encourage continual improvement in the quality of practice and service. Some of these General Guidelines have been derived from specific APA Ethical Principles (APA, 1981a).[3] Providers of psychological services have the same responsibility to uphold these specific General Guidelines as they would the corresponding Ethical Principles. The language of the other General Guidelines must at all times be interpreted in light of their aspirational intent.

These General Guidelines are general in nature and, as such, are intended for use by all providers of psychological services; they are supplemented by the *Specialty Guidelines for the Delivery of Services by Clinical (Counseling, Industrial/Organizational, and School) Psychologists* (APA, 1981b).

Introduction

This version of the *General Guidelines* is the second revision of the principles originally adopted by the American Psychological Association on September 4, 1974, and first revised in 1977.[4] The *General Guidelines* are intended to improve the quality, effectiveness, and accessibility of psychological services.

Since 1970, the American Psychological Association has worked to develop and codify a uniform set of guidelines for psychological practice that would serve the respective needs of users, providers, third-party purchasers, and other sanctioners of psychological services. In addition, the APA has established a Committee on Professional Standards, which is charged with keeping the General Guidelines responsive to the needs of these groups and with upgrading and extending them as the profession and science of psychology continue to develop knowledge, improved methods, and additional modes of psychological service. These General Guidelines have been established by organized psychology as a means of self-regulation in the public interest.

When providing any of the covered psychological service functions at any time and in any setting, whether public or private, profit or nonprofit, any persons representing themselves as psychologists are expected, where feasible, to observe these General Guidelines of practice to promote the best interests and welfare of the users of such services. Functions and activities related to the teaching of psychology, the writing or editing of scholarly or scientific manuscripts, and the conduct of scientific research do not fall within the purview of the present *General Guidelines.*[5]

Underlying Principles

Six basic principles have guided the development of these General Guidelines:

1. These General Guidelines apply to psychological service functions offered by psychologists, regardless of their specialty, of the setting, or of the form of remuneration given to them. Professional psychology has a uniform set of guidelines just as it has a common code of ethics (APA, 1981a). These General Guidelines apply equally to individual practitioners and to those who work in a group practice, an institutional agency, or another organizational setting.

2. Guidelines describe levels of quality for covered psychological services that providers strive to attain, regardless of the nature of the users, purchasers, or sanctioners of such covered services.

3. Those people who provide psychological services

These General Guidelines were revised by the Committee on Professional Standards (COPS) in consultation with the Board of Professional Affairs (BPA) and providers of psychological services from throughout the American Psychological Association (APA). The assistance of APA staff is gratefully acknowledged. The names of members and staff who supported this effort are included in Footnote 4. This document was approved by the APA Council of Representatives in February 1987.

Comments or questions on these General Guidelines should be addressed to the Committee on Professional Standards, American Psychological Association, 1200 Seventeenth Street, NW, Washington, DC 20036.

1

meet acceptable levels of education, training, and experience that are consistent and appropriate to the functions they perform. The final responsibility and accountability for defining qualifications and supervision requirements for service rest with a professional psychologist[6] (see Definitions).

4. Guidelines do not constrain psychologists from employing new methods (see Guideline 1.8) or from making flexible use of support personnel in staffing the delivery of services. The General Guidelines illuminate potential weaknesses in the delivery of psychological services and point to their correction. Some settings may require additional guidelines for specific areas of service delivery than those herein proposed. There is no intent to diminish the scope or quality of psychological services that exceed these General Guidelines. Systematically applied, these General Guidelines serve to establish desirable levels of psychological service. They serve to establish a more effective and consistent basis for evaluating the performance of individual service providers, and they serve to guide the organizing of psychological service units in human service settings.

5. It is recognized that there are significant differences among the established fields of professional psychology in regard to education and training, technical methodology, user populations served, and methods and settings of service delivery. The *Specialty Guidelines for the Delivery of Services* (APA, 1981b) provides acknowledgment of these differences while conforming to the guiding principles delineated by the General Guidelines.

6. These General Guidelines have been developed with the understanding that psychological services must be planned and implemented so that they are sensitive to factors related to life in a pluralistic society such as age, gender, affectional orientation, culture, and ethnicity.

Implications of Guidelines

The General Guidelines presented here have broad implications both for members of the public who use psychological services and for providers of such services.

1. The Guidelines furnish a basis for a mutual understanding between providers and users. Further, they facilitate improved quality of services and more effective evaluation of these services and their outcomes.

2. The Guidelines are an important step toward greater uniformity in legislative and regulatory actions involving providers of psychological services, and provide a model for the development of accreditation procedures for service facilities.

3. The Guidelines give specific content to the profession's concept of ethical practice as reflected in the APA *Ethical Principles of Psychologists* (1981a).

4. The Guidelines have significant impact on training models for both professional and support personnel in psychology.

5. Guidelines for the provision of psychological services influence what is considered desirable organizational structure, budgeting, and staffing patterns in these facilities.

Definitions

Providers of Psychological Services

This term subsumes two categories of providers of psychological services. The two categories are as follows:

A. Professional psychologists. Psychologists have a doctoral degree in psychology from an organized, sequential program in a regionally accredited university or professional school.[6,7,8] Specific definitions of professional psychologists by each of the recognized specialties are provided in the *Specialty Guidelines for the Delivery of Services* (APA, 1981b).

B. Other persons who provide psychological services. Qualifications and supervision for these persons are commensurate with their responsibilities and are further delineated in these policies[9] and in the *Specialty Guidelines for the Delivery of Services.*

Psychological Services

This term refers to one or more of the following:[10]

A. Evaluation, diagnosis,[11] and assessment of the functioning of individuals, groups, and organizations.

B. Interventions, preventive and ameliorative, that facilitate the functioning of individuals, groups, and organizations.[12]

C. Consultation relating to A and B.

D. Program development services in the areas of A, B, and C.[13]

E. Administration and supervision of psychological services.[14]

F. Evaluation of all psychological services.

Psychological Service Unit

This is the functional unit through which psychological services are provided:

A. A psychological service unit is a unit that provides predominantly psychological services and is composed of one or more professional psychologists and support staff.

B. A psychological service unit may operate as a functional or geographic component of a larger governmental, educational, correctional, health, training, industrial, or commercial organizational unit, or as an independent professional service unit.[15]

C. A psychological service unit may take the form of one or more psychologists providing professional services in a multidisciplinary setting.

D. A psychological service unit also may be an individual or group of individuals in a private practice or a psychological consulting firm.

Users

Users include the following:

A. Direct users or recipients of psychological services.

B. Public and private institutions, facilities, or organizations receiving psychological services.

Sanctioners

Sanctioners include the following:

    A. Direct users or recipients of psychological services.

    B. Public and private institutions, facilities, or organizations receiving psychological services.

    C. Any other individual, group, organization, institution, or governing body having legitimate interaction with a psychologist functioning in a professional capacity.

General Guideline 1: Providers

1.1 Each psychological service unit offering psychological services has available at least one professional psychologist and as many more professional psychologists as are necessary to assure the quality of services offered.[16]

ILLUSTRATIVE STATEMENT:[17] The intent of this General Guideline is that one or more providers of psychological services in any psychological service unit meet the levels of training and experience of professional psychologists as specified in the preceding definitions.[18] When a professional psychologist is not available on a full-time basis, the facility retains the services of one or more professional psychologists on a regular part-time basis to supervise the psychological services provided. The psychologist who is so retained has authority and participates sufficiently to enable him or her to assess the needs for services, to review the content of services provided, and to assume professional responsibility and accountability for them.

1.2 Providers of psychological services who do not meet the requirements for professional psychologists are supervised, directed, and evaluated by a professional psychologist to the extent required by the tasks assigned (see Definitions and the *Specialty Guidelines for the Delivery of Services*. APA, 1981b). Tasks assigned to these providers are in keeping with their demonstrated areas of competence. The level and extent of supervision may vary from task to task, as long as the professional psychologist retains a close relationship that is sufficient to meet this General Guideline. In situations in which those providers work in a fair, autonomous fashion, they maintain an appropriate level of consultation and supervisory support from a professional psychologist. (See Ethical Principles 2, 7c, and 8f.)

ILLUSTRATIVE STATEMENT: For example, in health care settings, support personnel may be assigned varying levels of responsibility for providing designated functions within their demonstrated areas of competence. Support personnel are considered to be responsible for their functions and behavior when assisting in the provision of psychological services and are accountable to a professional psychologist. Ultimate professional responsibility and accountability for the services provided require that the supervisor review reports and test protocols and review and discuss intervention plans, strategies, and outcomes. In these settings, the nature and extent of supervision is determined by the professional psychologist to assure the adequacy of psychological services provided.

    To facilitate the effectiveness of the psychological service unit, the nature of the supervisory relationship is clearly and explicitly communicated to support personnel, preferably in writing. Such communications describe and delineate the duties of the employees, such as the range and type of services to be provided. The limits of independent action and decision making are defined. Descriptions of responsibilities specify the means by which employees will contact the professional psychologist in the event of emergency or crisis situations.

1.3 Wherever a psychological service unit exists, a professional psychologist is responsible for planning, directing, and reviewing the provision of psychological services.

ILLUSTRATIVE STATEMENT: The psychologist who directs or coordinates the unit maintains an ongoing or periodic review of the adequacy of services and plans in accordance with the results of such evaluation. This psychologist coordinates the activities of the psychological service unit with other professional, administrative, and technical groups, both within and outside the facility. This psychologist, who may be the director, chief, or coordinator of the psychological service unit, has related responsibilities including, but not limited to, recruiting qualified staff, directing training and research activities of the service, maintaining a high level of professional and ethical practice, and assuring that staff members function only within the areas of their competence.

    To facilitate the effectiveness of services by increasing the level of staff sensitivity and professional skills, the psychologist who is designated as director participates in the selection of professional and support personnel whose qualifications include sensitivity and consideration for the language, cultural and experiential background, affectional orientation, ethnic identification, age, and gender of the users, and whose professional skills are directly relevant to the needs and characteristics of these users. Additionally, the director ensures that professional and support personnel do not provide services in any manner that is discriminatory or exploitative to users.

    In other institutional and organizational settings, psychologists may be administratively responsible to individuals from disciplines other than psychology. In these instances, the psychologist should seek to sensitize the administrator to the need to allow participation of the psychologist in planning, directing, and reviewing the provision of psychological services.

1.4 When functioning within an organizational setting, professional psychologists seek, whenever appropriate and feasible, to bring their education, training, experience, and skills to bear upon the goals of the organization by participating in the planning and development of overall operations. (See Ethical Principle 1d.)

ILLUSTRATIVE STATEMENT: One way psychologists maintain high professional standards is by being active representatives on boards and committees concerned with service delivery and overall operation of their facility. These activities may include but are not limited to active

3

participation as voting and as office-holding members, on the governance staff as well as on executive, planning, and evaluation boards and committees.

1.5 All providers of psychological services attempt to maintain and apply current knowledge of scientific and professional developments that are directly related to the services they render. This includes knowledge relating to special populations (such as ethnic or other minorities) that may compose a part of their practice. (See Ethical Principles 2, 2c, and 2d.)

ILLUSTRATIVE STATEMENT: Methods through which knowledge of scientific and professional developments may be gained include, but are not limited to, continuing education, attendance at workshops, participation in staff development programs, formal and informal on-the-job training, and reading scientific and professional publications. All providers have access to reference material related to the provision of psychological services. All providers are prepared to show evidence periodically that they are staying abreast of and utilizing current knowledge and practices.

1.6 Professional psychologists limit their practice, including supervision, to their demonstrated areas of professional competence. Special proficiency supervision of psychologists may be provided by professionals from other disciplines whose competence in the given area has been demonstrated by previous education, training, and experience. (See Ethical Principles 2 and 2d.)

ILLUSTRATIVE STATEMENT: Psychological services are offered in accordance with the providers' areas of competence as defined by verifiable education, training, and experience. Before offering professional services beyond the range of their experience and usual practice (e.g., providing services to culturally/linguistically diverse populations), psychologists strive to obtain pertinent knowledge through such means as education, training, reading, and appropriate professional consultation.

1.7 Psychologists who change or add a specialty meet the same requirements with respect to subject matter and professional skills that apply to doctoral education, training, and experience in the new specialty.[19]

ILLUSTRATIVE STATEMENT: Retraining psychologists to qualify them for a change in specialty must be under the auspices of a program in a regionally accredited university or professional school that offers the doctoral degree in that specialty. Such education and training are individualized, due credit being given for relevant coursework or requirements that have previously been satisfied. Merely taking an internship or acquiring experience in a practicum setting or in an employment setting is not considered adequate preparation for becoming a clinical, counseling, industrial/organizational, or school psychologist. Fulfillment of such an individualized training program is attested to by official certification by the supervising department or professional school indicating the successful completion of educational preparation in the

particular specialty. Specific requirements for retraining in each of the recognized specialties are detailed in the *Specialty Guidelines for the Delivery of Services* (APA, 1981b).

1.8 Psychologists are encouraged to develop and/or apply and evaluate innovative theories and procedures, to provide appropriate theoretical or empirical support for their innovations, and to disseminate their results to others. (See Ethical Principles 2 and 2c.)

ILLUSTRATIVE STATEMENT: A profession rooted in a science continually explores, studies, conducts, and evaluates applications of theories and procedures with a view toward developing, verifying, and documenting new and improved ways of serving users.

General Guideline 2: Programs

2.1 Composition and organization of a psychological service unit

2.1.1 The composition and programs of a psychological service unit strive to be responsive to the needs of the people and settings served.

ILLUSTRATIVE STATEMENT: A psychological service unit is structured to facilitate effective and economical delivery of services. For example, a psychological service unit serving a predominantly low-income or ethnic minority group has a staffing pattern and service program adapted to the linguistic, experiential, attitudinal, and financial characteristics of the user population.

2.1.2 A psychological service unit strives to include sufficient numbers of professional psychologists and support personnel to achieve its goals, objectives, and purposes.

ILLUSTRATIVE STATEMENT: The workload, diversity of the psychological services required, and the specific goals and objectives of the setting determine the numbers and qualifications of professional psychologists and support personnel in the psychological service unit. Where shortages in personnel exist, so that psychological services cannot be rendered in a professional manner, the director of the psychological service unit initiates action to modify appropriately the specific goals, objectives, and timetables of the service. If necessary, the director appropriately modifies the scope or workload of the unit to maintain the quality of the services and, at the same time, makes continued efforts to devise alternative systems for delivery of services.

2.2 Policies

2.2.1 A written description of roles, objectives, and scope of services is developed by multi-provider psychological service units as well as by psychological service units that are a component of an organization, unless the unit has a specific alternative approach. The written description or alternative ap-

4

proach is reviewed annually and is available to the staff of the unit and to users and sanctioners upon request.

ILLUSTRATIVE STATEMENT: The psychological service unit reviews its objectives and scope of services annually and makes revisions as necessary to ensure that the psychological services offered are consistent with staff competencies and current psychological knowledge and practice. This statement is discussed with staff, reviewed by the appropriate administrator, and distributed to users and sanctioners upon request and whenever appropriate. Psychologists strive to be aware of management theories and practices that will aid in the delivery of psychological services.

2.2.2 Providers of psychological services avoid any action that will violate or diminish the legal and civil rights of users or of others who may be affected by their actions.[20] (See Ethical Principles 3b, 3c, 5, 6, and 9.)

ILLUSTRATIVE STATEMENT: Providers of psychological services are continually sensitive to the issue of confidentiality of information; they strive to be sensitive to the potential impact of their decisions and recommendations, and to other matters pertaining to individual, legal, and civil rights. Providers of psychological services strive to be aware of issues such as self-incrimination in judicial proceedings, involuntary commitment to hospitals, protection of minors, protection of legal incompetents, discriminatory practices in employment selection procedures, recommendations for special education provisions, information relative to adverse personnel actions in the armed services, and adjudication of domestic relations disputes in divorce and custodial proceedings. Providers of psychological services are encouraged to make themselves available to local committees, review boards, and similar advisory groups established to safeguard the human, civil, and legal rights of service users.

2.2.3 Providers of psychological services are familiar with and abide by the American Psychological Association's *Ethical Principles of Psychologists* (1981a), *Specialty Guidelines for the Delivery of Services* (1981b), *Standards for Educational and Psychological Testing* (1985), *Ethical Principles in the Conduct of Research with Human Participants* (1982), *Guidelines for Computer-Based Tests and Interpretations* (1986), "Guidelines for Psychologists Conducting Growth Groups" (1973), and other APA policy statements relevant to guidelines for professional services issued by the Association.[21] (See Ethical Principle 3d.)

ILLUSTRATIVE STATEMENT: Psychological service units have available a copy of each of these documents, and providers maintain current knowledge of relevant APA guidelines and principles.

2.2.4 Providers of psychological services seek to conform to relevant statutes established by federal, state, and local governments. At times psychologists may seek to challenge legal constraints that they reasonably and honestly believe unduly infringe on the rights of their users or on the right of psychologists to practice their profession; however, any such challenges should conform to appropriate legal procedures. (See Ethical Principle 3d.)

ILLUSTRATIVE STATEMENT: All providers of psychological services seek to be familiar with and practice in conformity with relevant statutes that relate directly to the practice of psychology. They also endeavor to be informed about governmental agency regulations that have the force of law and that relate to the delivery of psychological services (e.g., evaluation for disability retirement or for special education placements). In addition, all providers seek to be aware that federal agencies such as the Veterans Administration, the Department of Education, and the Department of Health and Human Services have policy statements regarding psychological services. Providers of psychological services attempt to be familiar with other statutes and regulations, including those addressed to the civil and legal rights of users (e.g., those promulgated by the federal Equal Employment Opportunity Commission) that are pertinent to their scope of practice.

2.2.5 In recognizing the matrix of personal and societal problems, providers make available, when appropriate, information regarding additional human services, such as specialized psychological services, legal aid societies, social services, employment agencies, health resources, and educational and recreational facilities. (See Ethical Principle 7a.)

ILLUSTRATIVE STATEMENT: Psychologists and support personnel are sensitive to the broader context of human needs. They refer to such resources and are encouraged, when appropriate, to intervene actively on behalf of the users. Providers make appropriate use of other professional, research, technical, and administrative resources whenever these serve the best interests of the users, and they establish and maintain cooperative or collaborative arrangements with such other resources as are required to meet the needs of users.

2.2.6 In the best interest of the users, providers of psychological services endeavor to consult and collaborate with professional colleagues in the planning and delivery of services when such consultation is deemed appropriate. (See Ethical Principles 7 and 7a.)

ILLUSTRATIVE STATEMENT: Psychologists recognize the areas of special competence of other psychologists and of other professionals for consultation and referral purposes.

2.3 Procedures

2.3.1 Each psychological service unit is guided by a set of procedural guidelines for the delivery of psychological services.

ILLUSTRATIVE STATEMENT: Depending on the nature of the setting, and whenever feasible, providers are prepared to provide a statement of procedural guidelines in oral and/or written form that can be understood by users as well as sanctioners. This statement may describe the current methods, forms, procedures, and techniques being used to achieve the objectives and goals for psychological services.

5

This statement is communicated to staff and, when appropriate, to users and sanctioners. The psychological service unit provides for the annual review of its procedures for the delivery of psychological services.

2.3.2 Psychologists develop plans for psychological services appropriate to the problems presented by the users.

ILLUSTRATIVE STATEMENT: Ideally, a plan for intervention or consultation is in written form and serves as a basis for accountability. Regardless of the type of setting or users involved, a plan that describes the psychological services indicated and the manner in which they will be provided is developed and agreed upon by the providers and users.[22] A psychologist who provides services as one member of a collaborative effort participates in the development and implementation of the overall service plan and provides for its periodic review.

2.3.3 There is a mutually acceptable understanding between a provider and a user or that user's responsible agent regarding the delivery of service. (See Ethical Principles 6 and 6b.)

ILLUSTRATIVE STATEMENT: A psychologist discusses the plan for the provision of psychological services with the user, noting procedures that will be used and respective responsibilities of provider and user. This interaction is repeated whenever major changes occur in the plan for service. This understanding may be oral or written, but in any event, the psychologist documents the nature of the understanding.[23]

2.3.4 Professional psychologists clarify early on to users and sanctioners the exact fee structure or financial arrangements and payment schedule when providing services for a fee. (See Ethical Principle 6d.)

ILLUSTRATIVE STATEMENT: Psychologists inform users of their payment policies and of their willingness to assist users in obtaining reimbursement. Those who accept reimbursement from a third party are acquainted with the appropriate statutes and regulations, instruct their users on proper procedures for submitting claims, and inform them of limits on confidentiality of claims information, in accordance with pertinent statutes.

2.3.5 Accurate, current, and pertinent records of essential psychological services are maintained.

ILLUSTRATIVE STATEMENT: At a minimum, records kept of psychological services should include identifying data, dates of services, and types of services, and where appropriate, may include a record of significant actions taken.[24] Providers make all reasonable efforts to record essential information concerning psychological services within a reasonable time of their completion.

2.3.6 Each psychological service unit follows an established policy for the retention and disposition of records.[25] (See Ethical Principle 5c.)

ILLUSTRATIVE STATEMENT: Such a policy conforms to government statutes and regulations, or to organizational or institutional regulations, policies, or practices where such are applicable.

2.3.7 Psychologists establish and maintain a system that protects the confidentiality of their users' records. (See Ethical Principles 5, 5a, 5c, and 5d.)[26]

ILLUSTRATIVE STATEMENT: Psychologists establish and maintain the confidentiality of information about the users of services, whether obtained by themselves or by those they supervise. If directed otherwise by statute, by regulations with the force of law, or by court order, psychologists seek a resolution that is both ethically and legally feasible and appropriate; for example, psychologists might request in camera (judge's chambers) hearings when they are required by the court to produce records. All people who are supervised by psychologists, including nonprofessional personnel and students, and who have access to records of psychological services are also expected to maintain this confidentiality of information. Psychologists do not release confidential information, except with the written consent of the user involved, or of his or her legal representative, guardian, or other holder of the privilege on behalf of the user, and only after being assured by whatever means may be required that the user has been assisted in understanding the implications of the release. Even after the consent has been obtained for release, psychologists clearly identify such information as confidential for the recipient of the information.

Users are informed in advance of any limits in the setting for maintaining the confidentiality of psychological information. For instance, psychologists in hospital settings inform their patients that psychological information in a patient's clinical record may be available to other hospital personnel without the patient's written consent. Similar limitations on confidentiality of psychological information may be present in certain school, industrial, business, government, or military settings or in instances where the user has waived confidentiality for purposes of third-party payment. When the user's intention to waive confidentiality is judged by a professional psychologist to be contrary to the user's best interest or to be in conflict with that person's legal or civil rights, it is the responsibility of the psychologist to discuss the implications of releasing the psychological information and to assist the user in limiting disclosure by specifying the nature of the information, the recipients, and the time period during which the release is in effect, recognizing, however, that the ultimate decision concerning release of information is that of the user. Providers of psychological services are sensitive to both the benefits and the possible misuse of information regarding individuals that is stored in computerized data banks. Providers take necessary measures to ensure that such information is used in a socially responsible manner.

Users have the right to information in their agency

records and to be informed as to any regulations that govern the release of such information. However, the records are the property of the psychologist or of the facility in which the psychologist works and are, therefore, under the control of the psychologist or of the facility. Users have the right to examine such psychological records. Preferably such examination should be in the presence of a psychologist who judges how best to explain the material in a meaningful and useful manner.

In school settings, parents have the legal right to examine such psychological records, preferably in the presence of a psychologist. In the event that a family moves to another school system, the parents have the legal right to examine a copy of such records from the former school in the new school setting. In either circumstance, the rationale for allowing parents to examine such records is to assure that parents are not in a disadvantaged position if they choose to challenge a school's decision regarding the child. Disclosure of such psychological information in the records from a former school is conducted under secure conditions; such records have been transmitted to the new school to a psychologist under whose supervision the records may be examined. Psychologists and the institutions in which they work have written policy regarding the storage and access of pupils' records. Parents are informed of the results of a psychological assessment of their child in a form most meaningful and useful to the parents.

Raw psychological data (e.g., test protocols, therapy or interview notes, or questionnaire returns) in which a user is identified are ordinarily released only with the written consent of the user or of the user's legal representative, and are released only to a person recognized by the psychologist as competent to interpret the data. Any use made of psychological reports, records, or data for research or training purposes is consistent with this General Guideline. Additionally, providers of psychological services comply with statutory confidentiality requirements and with those embodied in the *Ethical Principles of Psychologists* (APA, 1981a).

2.3.8 Providers of psychological services do not use privileged information received in the course of their work for competitive advantage or personal gain. (See Ethical Principle 5.)

ILLUSTRATIVE STATEMENT: Providers of psychological services often obtain privileged information through their work with users, or while reviewing the proposals of competing practitioners or agencies. Such information may include but not be limited to users' or user associates' business interests, or the interests of competing colleagues or practitioners. When providers acquire such information and it is protected by applicable law or through agreement, it is held confidential and shall not be used for competitive advantage. Further, information that is potentially harmful to users or their associates, or to professional colleagues, should not be used for personal advantage.

2.4 Environment

2.4.1 Providers of psychological services promote the development of a physical, organizational, and social environment in the service setting that facilitates optimal human functioning.

ILLUSTRATIVE STATEMENT: As providers of services, professional psychologists are concerned with the environment of their service unit, especially as it affects the quality of service, but also as it impinges on human functioning in the larger unit of an organization when the service unit is included in such a larger context. Attention is given to the comfort and, where relevant, to the privacy of providers and users. Federal, state, and local requirements for safety, health, and sanitation are observed. Physical arrangements and organizational policies and procedures are conducive to the human dignity, self-respect, and optimal functioning of users and to the effective delivery of service. The atmosphere in which psychological services are rendered is appropriate to the service and to the users, whether in an office, clinic, school, college, university, industrial setting, or other organizational or institutional setting.

General Guideline 3: Accountability

3.1 The promotion of human welfare is the primary principle guiding the professional activities of all members of the psychological service unit. (See Preamble of Ethical Principles.)

ILLUSTRATIVE STATEMENT: Providers of psychological services are expected to interact with users in a manner that is considerate, effective, economical, and humane; to be mindful of their accountability to the sanctioners of psychological services and to the general public; and to see that appropriate steps are taken to protect the confidentiality of the service relationship.

The psychological service unit does not withhold services to a potential user on the basis of that user's national or ethnic origin, religion, gender, affectional orientation, or age; nor does it provide services in a discriminatory or exploitative fashion. However, this does not preclude psychologists from serving agencies whose publicly declared policy restricts users to membership of a particular religious, ethnic, or other specified group, as long as that policy does not constitute unlawful discrimination.[27] Professional psychologists who find that psychological services are being provided in a manner that is discriminatory or exploitative of users or that is contrary to these General Guidelines or to government statutes or regulations take appropriate corrective actions, which may include the refusal to provide services. When conflicts of interest arise, psychologists are guided in the resolution of differences by the principles set forth in the *Ethical Principles of Psychologists* (APA, 1981a).

Recognition is given to the following considerations in regard to the withholding of services: (1) the professional right of psychologists to limit their practice to a specific category of users with whom they have achieved demonstrated competence (e.g., individuals, families,

7

groups, ethnic minorities, or organizations); (2) the right and responsibility of psychologists to withhold an assessment procedure when not validly applicable; (3) the right and responsibility of psychologists to withhold services in specific instances in which their own limitations or user characteristics might impair the quality of the services; (4) the obligation of psychologists to seek to ameliorate through peer review, consultation, therapeutic procedures, or other procedures those factors that inhibit the provision of services to particular individuals, families, groups, ethnic minorities, or organizations; and (5) the obligation of psychologists who withhold services to assist the users in obtaining services from another source.

3.2 Psychologists pursue their activities as members of the independent, autonomous profession of psychology.

ILLUSTRATIVE STATEMENT: Psychologists, as members of an independent profession, are responsible both to the public and to their peers through established review mechanisms. Psychologists are aware of the implications of their activities for the profession as a whole. They seek to eliminate discriminatory practices instituted for self-serving purposes that are not in the interest of the users (e.g., arbitrary requirements for referral and supervision or sign-off by another profession). They are cognizant of their responsibilities for the development of the profession. They participate where possible in the training and career development of students and other providers, participate as appropriate in the training of support personnel or other professionals, and integrate their contributions within the structure established for delivering psychological services. They facilitate the development of and participate in professional standards review mechanisms and seek to work with other professionals in a cooperative manner for the good of the users and for the benefit of the general public.

Psychologists recognize that it is their responsibility to keep supervisors, administrators, and other agency personnel informed of APA guidelines, principles, standards, policies, and other criteria related to their professional functioning. This information is imparted at times that are appropriate in the individual setting. This may include statements of policy procedures, disclaimers, and so forth. Psychologists are responsible for defining and developing their profession, consistent with the general canons of science and with the public welfare.[28]

3.3 There are periodic, systematic, and effective evaluations of psychological services.

ILLUSTRATIVE STATEMENT: When the psychological service unit is a component of a larger organization, regular assessment of progress in achieving goals is provided in the service delivery plan. Such evaluation could include consideration of the effectiveness of psychological services relative to costs in terms of time, money, and the availability of professional and support personnel. Evaluation of the psychological service delivery system could be con-

ducted both internally and, when possible, under independent auspices. Descriptions of therapeutic procedures and other services as well as outcome measures should be as detailed as possible. This evaluation might include an assessment of effectiveness (to determine what the service accomplished), costs, continuity (to ensure that the services are appropriately linked to other human services), availability (to determine appropriate levels and distribution of services and personnel), accessibility (to ensure that the services are barrier-free to users), and adequacy (to determine whether the services meet the identified needs of users). In such evaluations, care is taken to maintain confidentiality of records and privacy of users. It is highly desirable that there be a periodic reexamination of review mechanisms to ensure that these attempts at public safeguards are effective and cost-efficient and do not place unnecessary encumbrances on providers or unnecessary additional expenses on users or sanctioners for services rendered.

3.4 Professional psychologists are accountable for all aspects of the services they provide and are appropriately responsive to those people who are concerned with these services.

ILLUSTRATIVE STATEMENT: Depending upon the settings, accurate and full information is made available to prospective individual or organizational users regarding the qualifications of providers, the nature and extent of services offered, and, where appropriate, financial costs and potential risks. In recognizing their responsibilities to users, sanctioners, third-party purchasers, and other providers, wherever appropriate and consistent with the users' legal rights and privileged communications, professional psychologists make available information about initiation, continuation, modification, termination, and evaluation of psychological services and provide counsel to users regarding their decisions about such issues.

3.5 In the public interest, professional psychologists may wish to provide some services to individuals or organizations for little or no financial return. (See Ethical Principle 6d.)

ILLUSTRATIVE STATEMENT: Professional psychologists are encouraged to contribute a portion of their services and work for which they receive little or no financial return, according to the *Ethical Principles of Psychologists* (APA, 1981a), and to encourage those they supervise to perform services on a similar basis.

FOOTNOTES

[1] The footnotes to these General Guidelines represent an attempt to provide a coherent context of other policy statements of the APA regarding professional practice. The General Guidelines extend these previous policy statements where necessary to reflect current concerns of the public and of the profession.

[2] Note that the title and emphasis of these General Guidelines have been changed from the 1977 version of the *Standards for Providers of Psychological Services*. This has been done to reflect the development and adoption of the *Specialty Guidelines for the Delivery of Services* by the APA in 1980. The profession continues to grow in a variety of areas

in which specific guidelines are not yet necessary. These General Guidelines are intended to support practitioners in these areas.

As stated later in the Preamble, the General Guidelines are aspirational in nature. The change in title is meant to signify that the professional practice of psychology is constantly changing. No collection of principles can adequately direct these changes, and there is no intent to limit future development even though this collection represents the consensus of the profession at this time.

³ The Ethical Principles from which the General Guidelines have been derived are noted in parentheses at the end of the corresponding General Guidelines.

⁴ Early in 1970, acting at the direction of the APA's Council of Representatives, the Board of Professional Affairs (BPA) appointed a task force composed of practicing psychologists with specialized knowledge in at least one of every major class of human service facility and with experience relevant to the setting of standards. The task force's charge was to develop a set of standards for psychological practice. Soon thereafter, partial support for this activity was obtained through a grant from the National Institute of Mental Health (NIMH Grant MH 21696).

The task force promptly established liaison. with national groups already active in setting and accrediting standards. It was therefore able to influence two groups of the Joint Commission on Accreditation of Hospitals (JCAH), the Accreditation Council for Facilities for the Mentally Retarded (JCAH, 1971) and the Accreditation Council for Psychiatric Facilities (JCAH, 1972), in their adoption of certain basic principles and in their wording of their standards for psychological services. It also contributed substantially to the "constitutionally required minimum standards for adequate treatment of the mentally ill" ordered by the U.S. District Court in Alabama in the case of *Wyatt v. Stickney* (1972). In concert with other APA committees, the task force also represented the APA in national-level deliberations with government groups and insurance carriers that defined the qualifications necessary for psychologists involved in providing health services.

These interim outcomes involved influence by the APA on actions by groups of nonpsychologists that directly affected the manner in which psychological services were employed, particularly in health and rehabilitation settings. However, these measures did not relieve the Association from exercising its responsibility to speak out directly and authoritatively on what standards for psychological practice should be throughout a broad range of human service settings.

In September 1974, after more than four years of study and broad consultations, the task force completed the APA's first edition of the *Standards for Providers of Psychological Services* (1974). The task of collecting, analyzing, and synthesizing reactions to the original Standards fell to two successive committees. They were charged similarly to review and revise the Standards and to suggest means to implement them, including their acceptance by relevant government and private accreditation groups. The dedicated work of the psychologists who served on both of those committees is gratefully acknowledged. Also recognized with thanks are the several hundred comments received from scores of interested persons representing professional, academic, and scientific psychology; from consumer groups; from administrators of facilities; and from others.

Members of the Task Force on Standards for Service Facilities, which submitted the original Standards in September 1974, were Milton L. Blum, Jacqueline C. Bouhoutsos, Jerry H. Clark, Harold A. Edgerton, Marian D. Hall, Durand F. Jacobs (1972–1974 Chair), Floyd H. Martinez, John E. Muthard, Asher R. Pacht, William D. Pierce, Sue A. Warren, and Alfred M. Wellner (1970–1971 Chair). Staff liaisons from the APA Office of Professional Affairs were John J. McMillan (1970–1971), Gottlieb Simon (1971–1973), and Arthur Centor (1973–1974).

In January 1975, the APA Council of Representatives created the original Committee on Standards for Providers of Psychological Services. The Committee was charged with updating and revising the Standards adopted in September 1974. Members of the Committee were Jacqueline C. Bouhoutsos, Leon Hall, Marian D. Hall, Mary Henle, Durand F. Jacobs (Chair), Abel Ossorio, and Wayne Sorenson. The task force liaison was Jerry H. Clark, and the APA Central Office liaison was Arthur Centor.

In January 1976, the Council modified its charge to the Committee to review the Standards and to recommend revisions needed to reflect the varying needs of only those psychologists engaged in the activities

of clinical psychology, counseling psychology, industrial/organizational psychology, and school psychology. The Committee was reconstituted with one member representing each of the four applied activities, plus one member representing institutional practice and one representing the public interest. Members were Jules Barron (later replaced by Morris Goodman), clinical; Barbara A. Kirk (later replaced by Milton Schwebel), counseling; Virginia Schein (later replaced by Frank Friedlander), industrial/organizational; Durand F. Jacobs (Chair), institutional practice; M. Brewster Smith (later replaced by Pearl Mayo Dansby), public interest; Marian D. Hall (later replaced by Jack I. Bardon and Nadine M. Lambert), school. Arthur Centor and Richard Kilburg were the APA Central Office liaisons. The revised *Standards for Providers of Psychological Services* was approved by the APA Council of Representatives in January 1977 (APA, 1977).

In January 1980, the APA Council of Representatives instructed the Board of Professional Affairs to amend the 1977 Standards in keeping with the principles enunciated by the Council in connection with its action approving the four sets of *Specialty Guidelines for the Delivery of Services* (APA, 1981b). The BPA referred the task of revising the 1977 Standards to the newly created Committee on Professional Standards, composed of Juanita Braddock, public member; Judy E. Hall, experimental/mental retardation; Nadine M. Lambert, school; David Mills (Chair, January–April 1981), clinical/counseling; Milton Schwebel, counseling; Gilfred Tanabe (1980 Chair), clinical; and Murphy Thomas (Chair, May–December 1981), clinical. Subsequent members of the Committee on Professional Standards included William Chestnut, counseling; Lorraine D. Eyde, industrial/ organizational; Morris Goodman (1982–1983 Chair), clinical; John H. Jackson, school; Caroline Miller, public member; William Schofield (1984 Chair), clinical; and Barbara Wand, social. These past members of the Committee on Professional Standards were responsible for completing the 1984 revision of the Standards. Central Office staff assistance was provided by Richard Kilburg and Joy Burke (1980), Sharon Shueman and Pam Juhl (1980–1982), Jutta N. Hagner (1982–1984), and Patricia J. Aletky (1982–1985).

The 1985 draft revision was prepared by Committee on Professional Standards members Susan Robbins Berger, school; LaMaurice Gardner, clinical; Jo-Ida Hansen, counseling; Marlene Muse, public member; Lyle Schoenfeldt, industrial/organizational; William Schofield (1985 Chair), clinical; and Barbara Wand (1985 Vice-Chair), social. Central Office staff assistance was provided by Patricia J. Aletky, Patricia Brown, and Rizalina Mendiola. Between March 1985 and June 1985, a BPA work group on the Standards (composed of John H. Jackson, Chair; Morris Goodman; and William Schofield) reviewed and modified the 1985 draft revision. Central Office staff assistance was provided by Patricia J. Aletky, Patricia Brown, and Rizalina Mendiola.

In November 1985, BPA approved a revised effort that involved Committee on Professional Standards members and work groups representing each of the recognized specialties. The Committee on Professional Standards members participating were Lyle Schoenfeldt (1986 Chair), industrial/organizational; Susan Robbins Berger (1986 Vice-Chair), school; LaMaurice Gardner, clinical; Jo-Ida Hansen, counseling; Richard Kilburg, clinical; and Alan Malyon, clinical. Work group participants, by specialty area and Division, were as follows: Clinical: Robert Weitz (Division 12); Patricia Hannigan and Gerald Koocher (Division 29); Donna Copeland, Marlene Eisen, and Billie S. Strauss (Division 30); Arthur Bodin (Divisions 31, 38, 39, 42, 43); Ronald Kurz (Division 38); and Florence Kaslow (Divisions 41 and 43); Counseling: Ricki Bander, John Corrigan, Thomas Dowd, David Fago, and Milton Schwebel (Division 17); Industrial/Organizational: Hannah R. Hirsh and Manuel London (Division 14); School: Judith Alpert, John H. Jackson, and Ralph D. Wenger (Division 16); and Milton Shore (Division 37). Central Office assistance was provided by Pam Juhl, Sheila Lane Forsyth, Russell Newman, and Mary Lisa Debraggio.

⁵ These General Guidelines are designed to be consistent with existing APA policies. One APA policy governing this issue is the 1987 Model Act for State Licensure of Psychologists, prepared by a subcommittee of APA's Committee on Professional Practice and adopted by the APA Council of Representatives in February 1987.

⁶ People who met the following criteria on or before the date of adoption of the original Standards on September 4, 1974, shall also be considered professional psychologists: (a) a master's degree in a program

9

primarily psychological in content from a regionally accredited university or professional school; (b) appropriate education, training, and experience in the area of service offered; (c) a license or certificate in the state in which they practice, conferred by a state board of psychological examiners; or, in the absence of statutory regulation, the endorsement of the state psychological association through voluntary certification; or, for practice in primary and secondary schools, a state department of education certificate as a school psychologist provided that the certificate required at least two graduate years. Wherever the term *psychologist* is used in these General Guidelines, it refers to *professional psychologist.*

Within the specialty of school psychology, those persons who met the following criteria on or before, but not beyond, January 31, 1985, are also recognized as professional school psychologists: (a) a master's or higher degree, requiring at least two years of full-time graduate study in school psychology, from a regionally accredited university or professional school; (b) at least three additional years of training and experience in school psychological services, including a minimum of 1,200 hours in school settings; and (c) a license or certificate conferred by a state board of psychological examiners or a state educational agency for practice in elementary or secondary schools.

[7] Some federal and state legislation uses the term *clinical psychologist* to identify a set of service providers that is not limited to clinical psychologists as defined by the APA in the *Specialty Guidelines for the Delivery of Services by Clinical Psychologists* (APA, 1981b). APA defines the term *clinical psychologist* in health service delivery legislation in a generic sense to include all qualified professional psychologists who provide relevant services. Intraprofessionally, as represented by its *Specialty Guidelines,* APA currently supports specific and meaningful differentiation in the education, training, and practices of the specialties of clinical psychology, counseling psychology, industrial/organizational psychology, and school psychology.

[8] This definition is similar to the recommended statutory language in the "Requirements for Licensure" section of the 1987 APA Model Act for State Licensure of Psychologists (APA, 1987b), a policy statement setting forth model state legislation affecting the practice of psychology and recognizing the doctorate as the minimum educational requirement for entry into professional practice as a psychologist:

Applicants for licensure shall possess a doctoral degree in psychology from an institution of higher education. The degree shall be obtained from a recognized program of graduate study in psychology as defined by the rules and regulations of the Board.

By 1995 applicants for licensure shall have completed a doctoral program in psychology that is accredited by the American Psychological Association (APA). In areas where no accreditation exists, applicants for licensure shall have completed a doctoral program in psychology that meets recognized acceptable professional standards as determined by the Board. When a new specialty of professional psychology is recognized as being within the accreditation scope of the APA, doctoral programs within that specialty will be afforded a transition period of eight years from their first class of students to the time of their accreditation. During that transition period, graduates of such programs may sit for licensure examination whether or not the program has been accredited. The same principle applies as well to new doctoral programs of specialties previously recognized within the scope of APA accreditation.

Applicants trained in institutions outside the United States shall meet requirements established by the Board. (APA, 1987b, p. 698)

In addition to the above educational requirements, the following experience requirements also appear in the 1987 APA Model Act for State Licensure of Psychologists:

For admission to the licensure examination, applicants shall demonstrate that they have completed two years of supervised professional experience, one year of which shall be postdoctoral. The criteria for appropriate supervision shall be in accordance with regulations to be promulgated by the Board. Postdoctoral experience shall be compatible with the knowledge and skills acquired during formal doctoral or postdoctoral education in accordance with professional requirements and relevant to the intended area of practice. Applicants shall be required to show evidence of good character, that is, that they have not been

convicted of a criminal offense that bears directly on the fitness of the individual to be licensed. (APA, 1987b, p. 698)

[9] With regard to the roles, responsibilities, and supervision process for other persons who provide psychological services, a professional psychologist should consider the following issues and suggestions:

(a) A professional psychologist is identified as the ethically responsible agent in all advertising, public announcements, and billings for supervised psychological services.

(b) A supervising psychologist reviews and is responsible for all reports prepared by the assistant.

(c) Professional psychologists set a reasonable limit on the number of assistants who are employed and supervised by a single supervisor.

(d) Professional psychologists must be sufficiently available to ensure adequate evaluation or assessment, intervention planning, direction, and consultation.

(e) Assistants provide services or carry out activities at the direction of the psychologist employer/supervisor who is responsible for those services or activities.

(f) Assistants work in reasonably close physical proximity to the supervising psychologist so as to have available regular and continuing supervision.

[10] As was noted in the opening section of the General Guidelines, functions and activities of psychologists relating to the teaching of psychology, the writing or editing of scholarly or scientific manuscripts, the conduct of scientific research, and the activities of members of other professions do not fall within the purview of the General Guidelines.

[11] For the purposes of these General Guidelines and consistent with the 1987 APA Model Act for State Licensure of Psychologists, the term *diagnosis* may include the diagnosis of mental, emotional, nervous, or behavioral disorders or conditions of individuals and groups by professionals trained to do so, such as clinical, counseling, school, rehabilitation, and health psychologists (see Footnote 13).

[12] Consistent with the 1987 APA Model Act for State Licensure of Psychologists, such interventions include, but are not limited to, psychotherapy and counseling (see Footnote 13), and other interventions may include vocational development, cognitive rehabilitation, process consultation, psychological skills training, techniques of health psychology, selection and placement of personnel, and organizational development.

Specific definitions of interventions by each of the recognized specialties are provided in the *Specialty Guidelines for the Delivery of Services* (APA, 1981b).

[13] These definitions should be compared to the 1987 APA Model Act for State Licensure of Psychologists (APA, 1987b, p. 697), which includes definitions of *psychologist* and *practice of psychology* as follows:

Psychologist: A person represents himself or herself to be a psychologist if that person uses any title or description of services incorporating the words *psychology, psychological,* or *psychologist,* or if he or she possesses expert qualification in any area of psychology or if that person offers to the public or renders to individuals or to groups of individuals services defined as the practice of psychology in this Act.

Practice of Psychology is defined as the observation, description, evaluation, interpretation, and modification of human behavior by the application of psychological principles, methods, and procedures, for the purpose of preventing or eliminating symptomatic, maladaptive, or undesired behavior and of enhancing interpersonal relationships, work and life adjustment, personal effectiveness, behavioral health, and mental health. The practice of psychology includes, but is not limited to, psychological testing and the evaluation or assessment of personal characteristics such as intelligence, personality, abilities, interests, aptitudes, and neuropsychological functioning; counseling, psychoanalysis, psychotherapy, hypnosis, biofeedback, and behavior analysis and therapy; diagnosis and treatment of mental and emotional disorder or disability, alcoholism and substance abuse, disorders of habit or conduct, as well as of the psychological aspects of physical illness, accident, injury or disability; and psychoeducational evaluation, therapy, remediation and consultation. Psychological services may be rendered to individuals, families, groups, and the public. The practice of psychology shall be construed within the meaning of this definition without regard to whether payment is received for services rendered. (See Section J for exemptions.)

[14] As indicated in the *Ethical Principles of Psychologists* (APA, 1981a), especially Principle 1 (Responsibility) and Principle 3 (Moral and Legal Guidelines), when functioning as an administrator or manager in an organization or unit that is not a psychological services unit, psychologists apply their knowledge, skills, and abilities in furtherance of the objectives of that organization while remaining aware of the requirements of their profession's ethics and guidelines.

[15] The relation of a psychological service unit to a larger facility or institution is also addressed indirectly in the APA *Guidelines for Conditions of Employment of Psychologists* (APA, 1987a), which emphasizes the roles, responsibilities, and prerogatives of the psychologist when he or she is employed by or provides services for another agency, institution, or business.

[16] At the time of the adoption of these General Guidelines, there were four state statutes that did not require a doctoral degree for unsupervised provision of psychological services. Therefore, the goal of having the highest level of training for psychological practitioners is not, at the current time, fully achievable. (See Footnote 18 and Guideline 2.2.4.)

In addition to the small minority of states that recognize nondoctoral psychologists as independent providers of psychological services, almost all states recognize nondoctoral school psychologists who meet the requisite education, training, and experience prescribed by state departments of education as independent practitioners within local, regional, and state school systems.

[17] These illustrative statements have been selected to clarify how these General Guidelines might be implemented or apply in particular situations, and/or the importance of particular implications of the General Guidelines. The APA recognizes that there may be a variety of implications of and methods for implementing a specific General Guideline depending on the situation in a given setting.

[18] This General Guideline reflects changes in the 1987 revision of the Model Act for State Licensure of Psychologists adopted by the APA Council of Representatives in February 1987 (APA, 1987b). Guideline 1.1 expresses the goal of the APA that psychological service units in all organizations have at least one professional psychologist available to assure the quality of services offered.

[19] This General Guideline follows closely the statement regarding "Policy on Training for Psychologists Wishing to Change Their Specialty" adopted by the APA Council of Representatives in January 1976 and revised by the Council in January 1982. Included therein is the implementing provision that "this policy statement shall be incorporated in the guidelines of the Committee on Accreditation so that appropriate sanctions can be brought to bear on university and internship training programs which violate [it]" (Conger, 1976, p. 424).

[20] See also *Ethical Principles in the Conduct of Research with Human Participants* (APA, 1982) and *Principles Concerning the Counseling and Therapy of Women* (APA, 1978).

[21] These documents are available from the American Psychological Association, 1200 Seventeenth Street, NW, Washington, DC 20036.

[22] Another example of a specific application of this principle is found in Guideline 2 in "Guidelines for Psychologists Conducting Growth Groups" (APA, 1973):

2. The following information should be made available in writing to all prospective participants:

(*a*) An explicit statement of the purpose of the group;
(*b*) Types of techniques that may be employed;
(*c*) The education, training, and experience of the leader or leaders;
(*d*) The fee and any additional expense that may be incurred;
(*e*) A statement as to whether or not a follow-up service is included in the fee;
(*f*) Goals of the group experience and techniques to be used;
(*g*) Amounts and kinds of responsibility to be assumed by the leader and by the participants. For example, (i) the degree to which a participant is free not to follow suggestions and prescriptions of the group leader

and other group members; (ii) any restrictions on a participant's freedom to leave the group at any time; and
(*h*) Issues of confidentiality. (p. 933)

[23] When the user of the service is a child, it is desirable that both parent (or legal guardian) and child, to the extent possible, be involved in this understanding.

[24] Health care providers hold widely varying views about the wisdom of written records relating to the content of the psychotherapeutic relationship.

[25] In the absence of such, the policy is as follows:

1. Retain the full record intact for a specified period of time, if not in perpetuity. Some records need to be retained during the lifetime of an individual, either by the provider or by some other agency through arrangement by the provider. These records are necessary in special circumstances, such as in the case of handicapped individuals who need to comply with requests from the Social Security Administration for information on documented disabilities during their childhood years.
2. If a full record is not retained following completion of service delivery, a summary of the record is maintained for a specified period of time.
3. A record or the summary of a record may be disposed of only after a specified period of time following completion of planned services or the date of last contact, whichever comes later. (See the relevant sections of the *Specialty Guidelines for the Delivery of Services*, APA, 1981b, for specific retention and disposition guidelines. These are Guidelines 2.3.4 for clinical, counseling, and school psychologists.)

In the event of the death of or the incapacity of a psychologist in independent practice, special procedures are necessary to assure the continuity of active service to the user and the safeguarding of records in accordance with this Guideline. For this reason, with the approval of the affected user, it is appropriate for another psychologist, acting under the auspices of the Professional Standards Review Committee (PSRC) or the Ethics Committee of the state, where such a committee is available, to review the record with that user and recommend a course of action for continuing professional service, if needed. Depending on local circumstances, appropriate arrangements for record retention and disposal are also recommended by the reviewing psychologist. This General Guideline has been developed to address a variety of circumstances that may arise, often years after a set of psychological services has been completed. Increasingly, records are being utilized in forensic matters, for peer review, for investigation of ethical complaints, and in response to requests from users, other professionals, or other legitimate parties requiring accurate information about the exact dates, nature, course, and outcome of a set of psychological services.

[26] Support for the principle of privileged communication is found in the Model Act for State Licensure of Psychologists (APA, 1987b):

In judicial proceedings, whether civil, criminal, or juvenile; in legislative and administrative proceedings; and in proceedings preliminary and ancillary thereto, a patient or client, or his or her guardian or personal representative, may refuse to disclose or prevent the disclosure of confidential information, including information contained in administrative records, communicated to a psychologist licensed or otherwise authorized to practice psychology under the laws of this jurisdiction, or to persons reasonably believed by the patient or client to be so licensed, and their agents, for the purpose of diagnosis, evaluation, or treatment of any mental or emotional condition or disorder. In the absence of evidence to the contrary, the psychologist is presumed authorized to claim the privilege on the patient's or client's behalf.

This privilege may not be claimed by the patient or client, or on his or her behalf by authorized persons, in the following circumstances:

1. where abuse or harmful neglect of children, the elderly, or disabled or incompetent individuals is known or reasonably suspected;
2. where the validity of a will of a former patient or client is contested;
3. where such information is necessary for the psychologist to defend against a malpractice action brought by the patient or client;
4. where an immediate threat of physical violence against a readily identifiable victim is disclosed to the psychologist;
5. in the context of civil commitment proceedings, where an immediate threat of self-inflicted damage is disclosed to the psychologist;

11

6. where the patient or client, by alleging mental or emotional damages in litigation, puts his or her mental state at issue;

7. where the patient or client is examined pursuant to court order; or

8. in the context of investigations and hearings brought by the patient or client and conducted by the Board, where violations of this Act are at issue. (pp. 702–703)

Specific provisions for the maintenance of confidentiality are spelled out in each of the *Specialty Guidelines for the Delivery of Services* (APA, 1981b).

[27] Examples of such agencies are clinics for battered women, clinics for Spanish-speaking users, and clinics for members of a specific religious faith or church.

[28] The APA is prepared to provide appropriate assistance to responsible members who are subjected to unreasonable limitations upon their opportunities to function as practitioners, administrators, or consultants. The APA is prepared to cooperate with any responsible professional psychological organization in opposing any unreasonable limitations on the professional functions of the members of that organization. This insistence upon professional autonomy has been upheld over the years by the affirmative actions of the courts and of other public and private bodies in support of the right of psychologists to pursue those functions that they are trained and qualified to perform. Psychologists recognize that other professions and other groups will, from time to time, seek to define the roles and responsibilities of psychologists. The APA opposes such attempts.

REFERENCES

American Psychological Association. (1973). Guidelines for psychologists conducting growth groups. *American Psychologist, 28,* 933.

American Psychological Association. (1974). *Standards for providers of psychological services.* Washington, DC: Author.

American Psychological Association. (1977). Standards for providers of psychological services. *American Psychologist, 32,* 495–505.

American Psychological Association. (1978). Principles concerning the counseling and therapy of women. *Counseling Psychologist, 7*(4), 74–76.

American Psychological Association. (1981a). Ethical principles of psychologists. *American Psychologist, 36,* 633–638.

American Psychological Association. (1981b). Specialty guidelines for the delivery of services by clinical (counseling, industrial/organizational, and school) psychologists. *American Psychologist, 36,* 639–681.

American Psychological Association. (1982). *Ethical principles in the conduct of research with human participants.* Washington, DC: Author.

American Psychological Association. (1986). *Guidelines for computer-based tests and interpretations.* Washington, DC: Author.

American Psychological Association. (1987a). Guidelines for conditions of employment of psychologists. *American Psychologist, 42,* 724–729.

American Psychological Association. (1987b). Model act for state licensure of psychologists. *American Psychologist, 42,* 696–703.

Conger, J. J. (1976). Proceedings of the American Psychological Association, Incorporated, for the year 1975: Minutes of the annual meeting of the Council of Representatives. *American Psychologist, 31,* 406–434.

Joint Commission on Accreditation of Hospitals, Accreditation Council for Psychiatric Facilities. (1972). *Accreditation manual for psychiatric facilities: 1972.* Chicago, IL: Author.

Joint Commission on Accreditation of Hospitals, Accreditation Council for Facilities for the Mentally Retarded. (1971). *Standards for residential facilities for the mentally retarded.* Chicago, IL: Author.

Standards for educational and psychological testing. (1985). Washington, DC: American Psychological Association.

Wyatt v. Stickney, 325 F. Supp. (M.D. Ala. 1971), 334 F. Supp. 1341 (M.D. Ala.), 344 F. Supp. 373 (M.D. Ala. 1972), aff'd sub nom. Wyatt v. Aderholt, 503 F.2d 1305 (5th Cir. 1974).

Appendix E
Specialty Guidelines for the Delivery of Services*

*"Specialty Guidelines for the Delivery of Services," 36 (6) *American Psychologist* 640–681 (June 1981). Copyright 1981 by the American Psychological Association. Reprinted by permission.

Introduction

In September 1976, the APA Council of Representatives reviewed and commented on the draft revisions of the *Standards for Providers of Psychological Services* prepared by the Committee on Standards for Providers of Psychological Services. During that discussion, the Council acknowledged the need for standards in certain specialty areas in addition to the generic *Standards* covered by the draft revision. The Council authorized the committee to hold additional meetings to develop multiple standards in all specialty areas of psychology.

Following the adoption of the revised generic *Standards* in January 1977, the committee, working with psychologists in the four recognized specialty areas of psychology, spent the next three years modifying the generic *Standards* to meet the needs of clinical, counseling, industrial/organizational, and school psychologists. The four documents produced by the committee went through extensive revisions. Convention programs discussing these developments were held every year. Comments were solicited from all major constituencies in psychology and from thousands of individuals. The comments received and reviewed by the committee were varied and numerous.

In January 1980, following this extensive process and after making several additional modifications, the Council of Representatives adopted as APA policy the *Specialty Guidelines for the Delivery of Services by Clinical (Counseling, Industrial/Organizational, School) Psychologists*. As stated in the introductions of these four documents, the intent of the *Specialty Guidelines* is "to educate the public, the profession, and other interested parties regarding specialty professional practices...and to facilitate the continued systematic development of the profession."

At the same meeting, the Council also approved a reorganization of the Board of Professional Affairs' committee structure, which included the establishment of the Committee on Professional Standards to succeed the Committee on Standards for Providers of Psychological Services. The Committee on Professional Standards has been directed to review all comments on the *Specialty Guidelines* when considering its revisions. APA members and other interested individuals or groups with comments or suggestions are requested to send them to the American Psychological Association, Committee on Professional Standards, 1200 Seventeenth Street, N.W., Washington, D.C. 20036.

The members of the Committee on Standards for Providers of Psychological Services (1977-1980) who developed the *Specialty Guidelines* were Jack I. Bardon, school; Jules Barron, clinical; Frank Friedlander, industrial/organizational; Morris Goodman, clinical; Durand F. Jacobs (Chair), institutional practice; Barbara A. Kirk, counseling; Nadine M. Lambert, school; Virginia Ellen Schein, industrial/organizational; and Milton Schwebel, counseling. Arthur Centor and Richard Kilburg were the Central Office liaisons.

The members of the Committee on Professional Standards (1980-1981) who made the final changes to the *Specialty Guidelines* and were charged with future revisions were Juanita Braddock, public member; Lorraine Eyde, industrial/organizational; Morris Goodman, clinical; Judy Hall, experimental/mental retardation; John H. Jackson, school; Nadine M. Lambert, school; Dave Mills (1981 Chair, partial), clinical/counseling; Milton Schwebel, counseling; Gilfred Tanabe (1980 Chair), clinical; and Murphy Thomas (1981 Chair, partial), clinical. The Central Office liaisons were Joy Burke, Sharon A. Shueman, and Pam Arnold.

1

Specialty Guidelines for the Delivery of Services by Clinical Psychologists

The Specialty Guidelines that follow are based on the generic *Standards for Providers of Psychological Services* originally adopted by the American Psychological Association (APA) in September 1974 and revised in January 1977 (APA, 1974b, 1977b). Together with the generic *Standards*, these Specialty Guidelines state the official policy of the Association regarding delivery of services by clinical psychologists. Admission to the practice of psychology is regulated by state statute. It is the position of the Association that licensing be based on generic, and not on specialty, qualifications. Specialty guidelines serve the additional purpose of providing potential users and other interested groups with essential information about particular services available from the several specialties in professional psychology.

Professional psychology specialties have evolved from generic practice in psychology and are supported by university training programs. There are now at least four recognized professional specialties—clinical, counseling, school, and industrial/organizational psychology.

The knowledge base in each of these specialty areas has increased, refining the state of the art to the point that a set of uniform specialty guidelines is now possible and desirable. The present Guidelines are intended to educate the public, the profession, and other interested parties regarding specialty professional practices. They are also intended to facilitate the continued systematic development of the profession.

The content of each Specialty Guideline reflects a consensus of university faculty and public and private practitioners regarding the knowledge base, services provided, problems addressed, and clients served.

Traditionally, all learned disciplines have treated the designation of specialty practice as a reflection of preparation in greater depth in a particular subject matter, together with a voluntary limiting of focus to a more restricted area of practice by the professional. Lack of specialty designation does not preclude general providers of psychological services from using the methods or dealing with the populations of any specialty, except insofar as psychologists voluntarily refrain from providing services they are not trained to render. It is the intent of these Guidelines, however, that after the grandparenting period, psychologists not put themselves forward as *specialists* in a given area of practice unless they meet the qualifications noted in the Guidelines (see Definitions). Therefore, these Guidelines are meant to apply only to those psychologists who voluntarily wish to be designated as *clinical psychologists*. They do not apply to other psychologists.

These Guidelines represent the profession's best judg-

ment of the conditions, credentials, and experience that contribute to competent professional practice. The APA strongly encourages, and plans to participate in, efforts to identify professional practitioner behaviors and job functions and to validate the relation between these and desired client outcomes. Thus, future revisions of these Guidelines will increasingly reflect the results of such efforts.

These Guidelines follow the format and, wherever applicable, the wording of the generic *Standards*.[1] (Note: Footnotes appear at the end of the Specialty Guidelines. See pp. 648–651.) The intent of these Guidelines is to improve the quality, effectiveness, and accessibility of psychological services. They are meant to provide guidance to providers, users, and sanctioners regarding the best judgment of the profession on these matters. Although the Specialty Guidelines have been derived from and are consistent with the generic *Standards*, they may be used as separate documents. However, *Standards for Providers of Psychological Services* (APA, 1977b) shall remain the basic policy statement and shall take precedence where there are questions of interpretation.

Professional psychology in general and clinical psychology as a specialty have labored long and diligently to codify a uniform set of guidelines for the delivery of services by clinical psychologists that would serve the respective needs of users, providers, third-party purchasers, and sanctioners of psychological services.

The Committee on Professional Standards, established by the APA in January 1980, is charged with keeping the generic *Standards* and the Specialty Guidelines responsive to the needs of the public and the profession. It is also charged with continually reviewing, modifying, and extending them progressively as the profession and the science of psychology develop new knowledge, improved methods, and additional modes of psychological services.

The Specialty Guidelines for the Delivery of Services by Clinical Psychologists that follow have been established by the APA as a means of self-regulation to protect the public interest. They guide the specialty practice of

These Specialty Guidelines were prepared through the cooperative efforts of the APA Committee on Standards for Providers of Psychological Services (COSPOPS) and many professional clinical psychologists from the divisions of APA, including those involved in education and training programs and in public and private practice. Jules Barron, succeeded by Morris Goodman, served as the clinical psychology representative on COSPOPS. The committee was chaired by Durand F. Jacobs; the Central Office liaisons were Arthur Centor and Richard Kilburg.

3

clinical psychology by specifying important areas of quality assurance and performance that contribute to the goal of facilitating more effective human functioning.

Principles and Implications of the Specialty Guidelines

These Specialty Guidelines have emerged from and reaffirm the same basic principles that guided the development of the generic *Standards for Providers of Psychological Services* (APA, 1977b):

1. These Guidelines recognize that admission to the practice of psychology is regulated by state statute.

2. It is the intention of the APA that the generic *Standards* provide appropriate guidelines for statutory licensing of psychologists. In addition, although it is the position of the APA that licensing be generic and not in specialty areas, these Specialty Guidelines in clinical psychology provide an authoritative reference for use in credentialing specialty providers of clinical psychological services by such groups as divisions of the APA and state associations and by boards and agencies that find such criteria useful for quality assurance.

3. A uniform set of Specialty Guidelines governs the quality of services to all users of clinical psychological services in both the private and the public sectors. Those receiving clinical psychological services are protected by the same kinds of safeguards, irrespective of sector; these include constitutional guarantees, statutory regulation, peer review, consultation, record review, and supervision.

4. A uniform set of Specialty Guidelines governs clinical psychological service functions offered by clinical psychologists, regardless of setting or form of remuneration. All clinical psychologists in professional practice recognize and are responsive to a uniform set of Specialty Guidelines, just as they are guided by a common code of ethics.

5. Clinical psychology Guidelines establish clearly articulated levels of quality for covered clinical psychological service functions, regardless of the nature of the users, purchasers, or sanctioners of such covered services.

6. All persons providing clinical psychological services meet specified levels of training and experience that are consistent with, and appropriate to, the functions they perform. Clinical psychological services provided by persons who do not meet the APA qualifications for a professional clinical psychologist (see Definitions) are supervised by a professional clinical psychologist. Final responsibility and accountability for services provided rest with professional clinical psychologists.

7. When providing any of the covered clinical psychological service functions at any time and in any setting, whether public or private, profit or nonprofit, clinical psychologists observe these Guidelines in order to promote the best interests and welfare of the users of such services. The extent to which clinical psychologists observe these Guidelines is judged by peers.

8. These Guidelines, while assuring the user of the clinical psychologist's accountability for the nature and quality of services specified in this document, do not preclude the clinical psychologist from using new methods or developing innovative procedures in the delivery of clinical services.

These Specialty Guidelines have broad implications both for users of clinical psychological services and for providers of such services:

1. Guidelines for clinical psychological services provide a foundation for mutual understanding between provider and user and facilitate more effective evaluation of services provided and outcomes achieved.

2. Guidelines for clinical psychologists are essential for uniformity in specialty credentialing of clinical psychologists.

3. Guidelines give specific content to the profession's concept of ethical practice as it applies to the functions of clinical psychologists.

4. Guidelines for clinical psychological services may have significant impact on tomorrow's education and training models for both professional and support personnel in clinical psychology.

5. Guidelines for the provision of clinical psychological services in human service facilities influence the determination of acceptable structure, budgeting, and staffing patterns in these facilities.

6. Guidelines for clinical psychological services require continual review and revision.

The Specialty Guidelines here presented are intended to improve the quality and delivery of clinical psychological services by specifying criteria for key aspects of the practice setting. Some settings may require additional and/or more stringent criteria for specific areas of service delivery.

Systematically applied, these Guidelines serve to establish a more effective and consistent basis for evaluating the performance of individual service providers as well as to guide the organization of clinical psychological service units in human service settings.

Definitions

Providers of clinical psychological services refers to two categories of persons who provide clinical psychological services:

A. Professional clinical psychologists.[2] Professional clinical psychologists have a doctoral degree from a regionally accredited university or professional school providing an organized, sequential clinical psychology program in a department of psychology in a university or college, or in an appropriate department or unit of a professional school. Clinical psychology programs that are accredited by the American Psychological Association are recognized as meeting the definition of a clinical psychology program. Clinical psychology programs that are not accredited by the American Psychological Association meet the definition of a clinical psychology program if they satisfy the following criteria:

1. The program is primarily psychological in nature and stands as a recognizable, coherent 'organizational entity within the institution.

2. The program provides an integrated, organized sequence of study.

3. The program has an identifiable body of students who are matriculated in that program for a degree.

4. There is a clear authority with primary responsibility for the core and specialty areas, whether or not the program cuts across administrative lines.

5. There is an identifiable psychology faculty, and a psychologist is responsible for the program.

In addition to a doctoral education, clinical psychologists acquire doctoral and postdoctoral training. Patterns of education and training in clinical psychology[3] are consistent with the functions to be performed and the services to be provided, in accordance with the ages, populations, and problems encountered in various settings.

B. All other persons who are not professional clinical psychologists and who participate in the delivery of clinical psychological services under the supervision of a professional clinical psychologist. Although there may be variations in the titles of such persons, they are not referred to as clinical psychologists. Their functions may be indicated by use of the adjective *psychological* preceding the noun, for example, *psychological associate, psychological assistant, psychological technician,* or *psychological aide*. Their services are rendered under the supervision of a professional clinical psychologist, who is responsible for the designation given them and for quality control. To be assigned such a designation, a person has the background, training, or experience that is appropriate to the functions performed.

Clinical psychological services refers to the application of principles, methods, and procedures for understanding, predicting, and alleviating intellectual, emotional, psychological, and behavioral disability and discomfort. Direct services are provided in a variety of health settings, and direct and supportive services are provided in the entire range of social, organizational, and academic institutions and agencies.[4] Clinical psychological services include the following:[5]

A. Assessment directed toward diagnosing the nature and causes, and predicting the effects, of subjective distress; of personal, social, and work dysfunction; and of the psychological and emotional factors involved in, and consequent to, physical disease and disability. Procedures may include, but are not limited to, interviewing, and administering and interpreting tests of intellectual abilities, attitudes, emotions, motivations, personality characteristics, psychoneurological status, and other aspects of human experience and behavior relevant to the disturbance.

B. Interventions directed at identifying and correcting the emotional conflicts, personality disturbances, and skill deficits underlying a person's distress and/or dysfunction. Interventions may reflect a variety of theoretical orientations, techniques, and modalities. These may include, but are not limited to, psychotherapy, psychoanalysis, behavior therapy, marital and family therapy, group psychotherapy, hypnotherapy, social-learning approaches, biofeedback techniques, and environmental consultation and design.

C. Professional consultation in relation to A and B above.

D. Program development services in the areas of A, B, and C above.

E. Supervision of clinical psychological services.

F. Evaluation of all services noted in A through E above.

A *clinical psychological service unit* is the functional unit through which clinical psychological services are provided; such a unit may be part of a larger psychological service organization comprising psychologists of more than one specialty and headed by a professional psychologist:

A. A clinical psychological service unit provides predominantly clinical psychological services and is composed of one or more professional clinical psychologists and supporting staff.

B. A clinical psychological service unit may operate as a professional service or as a functional or geographic component of a larger multipsychological service unit or of a governmental, educational, correctional, health, training, industrial, or commercial organizational unit.[6]

C. One or more clinical psychologists providing professional services in a multidisciplinary setting constitute a clinical psychological service unit.

D. A clinical psychological service unit may also be one or more clinical psychologists in a private practice or a psychological consulting firm.

Users of clinical psychological services include:

A. Direct users or recipients of clinical psychological services.

B. Public and private institutions, facilities, or organizations receiving clinical psychological services.

C. Third-party purchasers—those who pay for the delivery of services but who are not the recipients of services.

D. Sanctioners—those who have a legitimate concern with the accessibility, timeliness, efficacy, and standards of quality attending the provision of clinical psychological services. Sanctioners may include members of the user's family, the court, the probation officer, the school administrator, the employer, the union representative, the facility director, and so on. Sanctioners may also include various governmental, peer review, and accreditation bodies concerned with the assurance of quality.

5

Guideline 1
PROVIDERS

1.1 *Each clinical psychological service unit offering psychological services has available at least one professional clinical psychologist and as many more professional clinical psychologists as are necessary to assure the adequacy and quality of services offered.*

INTERPRETATION: The intent of this Guideline is that one or more providers of psychological services in any clinical psychological service unit meet the levels of training and experience of the professional clinical psychologist as specified in the preceding definitions.[7]

When a facility offering clinical psychological services does not have a full-time professional clinical psychologist available, the facility retains the services of one or more professional clinical psychologists on a regular part-time basis. The clinical psychologist so retained directs and supervises the psychological services provided, participates sufficiently to be able to assess the need for services, reviews the content of services provided, and has the authority to assume professional responsibility and accountability for them.

The psychologist directing the service unit is responsible for determining and justifying appropriate ratios of psychologists to users and psychologists to support staff, in order to ensure proper scope, accessibility, and quality of services provided in that setting.

1.2 *Providers of clinical psychological services who do not meet the requirements for the professional clinical psychologist are supervised directly by a professional clinical psychologist who assumes professional responsibility and accountability for the services provided. The level and extent of supervision may vary from task to task so long as the supervising psychologist retains a sufficiently close supervisory relationship to meet this Guideline. Special proficiency training or supervision may be provided by a professional psychologist of another specialty or by a professional from another discipline whose competence in the given area has been demonstrated by previous training and experience.*

INTERPRETATION: In each clinical psychological service unit there may be varying levels of responsibility with respect to the nature and quality of services provided. Support personnel are considered to be responsible for their functions and behavior when assisting in the provision of clinical psychological services and are accountable to the professional clinical psychologist. Ultimate professional responsibility and accountability for the services provided require that the supervisor review and approve reports and test protocols, review and approve intervention plans and strategies, and review outcomes. Therefore, the supervision of all clinical psychological services is provided directly by a professional clinical psychologist in individual and/or group face-to-face meetings.

In order to meet this Guideline, an appropriate number of hours per week are devoted to direct face-to-face supervision of each clinical psychological service unit staff member. In no event is such supervision less than 1 hour per week. The more comprehensive the psychological services are, the more supervision is needed. A plan or formula for relating increasing amounts of supervisory time to the complexity of professional responsibilities is to be developed. The amount and nature of supervision is made known to all parties concerned.

Such communications are in writing and describe and delineate the duties of the employee with respect to range and type of services to be provided. The limits of independent action and decision making are defined. The description of responsibility also specifies the means by which the employee will contact the professional clinical psychologist in the event of emergency or crisis situations.

1.3 *Wherever a clinical psychological service unit exists, a professional clinical psychologist is responsible for planning, directing, and reviewing the provision of clinical psychological services. Whenever the clinical psychological service unit is part of a larger professional psychological service encompassing various psychological specialties, a professional psychologist is the administrative head of the service.*

INTERPRETATION: The clinical psychologist coordinates the activities of the clinical psychological service unit with other professional, administrative, and technical groups, both within and outside the facility. This clinical psychologist, who may be the director, chief, or coordinator of the clinical psychological service unit, has related responsibilities including, but not limited to, recruiting qualified staff, directing training and research activities of the service, maintaining a high level of professional and ethical practice, and ensuring that staff members function only within the areas of their competency.

To facilitate the effectiveness of clinical services by raising the level of staff sensitivity and professional skills, the clinical psychologist designated as director is responsible for participating in the selection of staff and support personnel whose qualifications and skills (e.g., language, cultural and experiential background, race, sex, and age) are directly relevant to the needs and characteristics of the users served.

1.4 *When functioning as part of an organizational setting, professional clinical psychologists bring their backgrounds and skills to bear on the goals of the organization, whenever appropriate, by participation in the planning and development of overall services.*[8]

INTERPRETATION: Professional clinical psychologists participate in the maintenance of high professional stan-

6

dards by representation on committees concerned with service delivery.

As appropriate to the setting, their activities may include active participation, as voting and as office-holding members, on the professional staffs of hospitals and other facilities and on other executive, planning, and evaluation boards and committees.

1.5 *Clinical psychologists maintain current knowledge of scientific and professional developments to preserve and enhance their professional competence.*[9]

INTERPRETATION: Methods through which knowledge of scientific and professional developments may be gained include, but are not limited to, reading scientific and professional publications, attendance at workshops, participation in staff development programs, and other forms of continuing education. The clinical psychologist has ready access to reference material related to the provision of psychological services. Clinical psychologists are prepared to show evidence periodically that they are staying abreast of current knowledge and practices in the field of clinical psychology through continuing education.

1.6 *Clinical psychologists limit their practice to their demonstrated areas of professional competence.*

INTERPRETATION: Clinical psychological services are offered in accordance with the providers' areas of competence as defined by verifiable training and experience. When extending services beyond the range of their usual practice, psychologists obtain pertinent training or appropriate professional supervision. Such training or supervision is consistent with the extension of functions performed and services provided. An extension of services may involve a change in the theoretical orientation of the clinical psychologist, a change in modality or technique, or a change in the type of client and/or the kinds of problems or disorders for which services are to be provided (e.g., children, elderly persons, mental retardation, neurological impairment).

1.7 *Professional psychologists who wish to qualify as clinical psychologists meet the same requirements with respect to subject matter and professional skills that apply to doctoral and postdoctoral education and training in clinical psychology.*[10]

INTERPRETATION: Education of doctoral-level psychologists to qualify them for specialty practice in clinical psychology is under the auspices of a department in a regionally accredited university or of a professional school that offers the doctoral degree in clinical psychology. Such education is individualized, with due credit being given for relevant course work and other requirements that have previously been satisfied. In addition, doctoral-level training plus 1 year of postdoctoral experience supervised by a clinical psychologist is re-

quired. Merely taking an internship in clinical psychology or acquiring experience in a practicum setting is not adequate preparation for becoming a clinical psychologist when prior education has not been in that area. Fulfillment of such an individualized educational program is attested to by the awarding of a certificate by the supervising department or professional school that indicates the successful completion of preparation in clinical psychology.

1.8 *Professional clinical psychologists are encouraged to develop innovative theories and procedures and to provide appropriate theoretical and/or empirical support for their innovations.*

INTERPRETATION: A specialty of a profession rooted in a science intends continually to explore and experiment with a view to developing and verifying new and improved methods of serving the public in ways that can be documented.

Guideline 2
PROGRAMS

2.1 *Composition and organization of a clinical psychological service unit:*

2.1.1 *The composition and programs of a clinical psychological service unit are responsive to the needs of the persons or settings served.*

INTERPRETATION: A clinical psychological service unit is structured so as to facilitate effective and economical delivery of services. For example, a clinical psychological service unit serving predominantly a low-income, ethnic, or racial minority group has a staffing pattern and service programs that are adapted to the linguistic, experiential, and attitudinal characteristics of the users.

2.1.2 *A description of the organization of the clinical psychological service unit and its lines of responsibility and accountability for the delivery of psychological services is available in written form to staff of the unit and to users and sanctioners upon request.*

INTERPRETATION: The description includes lines of responsibility, supervisory relationships, and the level and extent of accountability for each person who provides psychological services.

2.1.3 *A clinical psychological service unit includes sufficient numbers of professional and support personnel to achieve its goals, objectives, and purposes.*

INTERPRETATION: The work load and diversity of psychological services required and the specific goals and objectives of the setting determine the numbers and qualifications of professional and support personnel in the clinical psychological service unit. Where shortages in personnel exist, so that psychological services cannot be rendered in a professional manner, the director of the clinical psychological service unit initiates action to remedy such shortages. When this fails, the director appropriately modifies the scope or work load of the unit to maintain the quality of the services rendered.

2.2 Policies:

2.2.1 *When the clinical psychological service unit is composed of more than one person or is a component of a larger organization, a written statement of its objectives and scope of services is developed, maintained, and reviewed.*

INTERPRETATION The clinical psychological service unit reviews its objectives and scope of services annually and revises them as necessary to ensure that the psychological services offered are consistent with staff competencies and current psychological knowledge and practice. This statement is discussed with staff, reviewed with the appropriate administrator, and distributed to users and sanctioners upon request, whenever appropriate.

2.2.2 *All providers within a clinical psychological service unit support the legal and civil rights of the users.*[11]

INTERPRETATION: Providers of clinical psychological services safeguard the interests of the users with regard to personal, legal, and civil rights. They are continually sensitive to the issue of confidentiality of information, the short-term and long-term impacts of their decisions and recommendations, and other matters pertaining to individual, legal, and civil rights. Concerns regarding the safeguarding of individual rights of users include, but are not limited to, problems of self-incrimination in judicial proceedings, involuntary commitment to hospitals, protection of minors or legal incompetents, discriminatory practices in employment selection procedures, recommendation for special education provisions, information relative to adverse personnel actions in the armed services, and adjudication of domestic relations disputes in divorce and custodial proceedings. Providers of clinical psychological services take affirmative action by making themselves available to local committees, review boards, and similar advisory groups established to safeguard the human, civil, and legal rights of service users.

2.2.3 *All providers within a clinical psychological service unit are familiar with and adhere to the American Psychological Association's Standards for Providers of Psychological Services, Ethical Principles of Psychologists, Standards for Educational and Psychological Tests, Ethical Principles in the Conduct of Research With Human Participants, and other official policy statements relevant to standards for professional services issued by the Association.*

INTERPRETATION Providers of clinical psychological services maintain up-to-date knowledge of the relevant standards of the American Psychological Association.

2.2.4 *All providers within a clinical psychological service unit conform to relevant statutes established by federal, state, and local governments.*

INTERPRETATION: All providers of clinical psychological services are familiar with appropriate statutes regulating the practice of psychology. They observe agency regulations that have the force of law and that relate to the delivery of psychological services (e.g., evaluation for disability retirement and special education placements). In addition, all providers are cognizant that federal agencies such as the Veterans Administration, the Department of Education, and the Department of Health and Human Services have policy statements regarding psychological services, and where relevant, providers conform to them. Providers of clinical psychological services are also familiar with other statutes and regulations, including those addressed to the civil and legal rights of users (e.g., those promulgated by the federal Equal Employment Opportunity Commission), that are pertinent to their scope of practice.

It is the responsibility of the American Psychological Association to maintain current files of those federal policies, statutes, and regulations relating to this section and to assist its members in obtaining them. The state psychological associations and the state licensing boards periodically publish and distribute appropriate state statutes and regulations.

2.2.5 *All providers within a clinical psychological service unit inform themselves about and use the network of human services in their communities in order to link users with relevant services and resources.*

INTERPRETATION: Clinical psychologists and support staff are sensitive to the broader context of human needs. In recognizing the matrix of personal and societal problems, providers make available to users information regarding human services such as legal aid societies, social services, employment agencies, health resources, and educational and recreational facilities. Providers of clinical psychological services refer to such community resources and, when indicated, actively intervene on behalf of the users.

Community resources include the private as well as the public sectors. Private resources include private agencies and centers and psychologists in independent private practice. Consultation is sought or referral made within the public or private network of services whenever required in the best interest of the users. Clinical psychologists, in either the private or the public setting, utilize other resources in the community whenever indicated because of limitations within the psychological service unit providing the services. Professional clinical psychologists in private practice are familiar with the types of services offered through local community mental health clinics and centers, including alternatives to hospitalization, and know the costs and eligibility requirements for those services.

2.2.6 *In the delivery of clinical psychological services, the providers maintain a cooperative relationship with colleagues and co-workers in the best interest of the users.*[12]

INTERPRETATION Clinical psychologists recognize the areas of special competence of other professional psychologists and of professionals in other fields for either consultation or referral purposes. Providers of clinical psychological services make appropriate use of other professional, research, technical, and administrative resources to serve the best interests of users and establish and maintain cooperative arrangements with such other resources as required to meet the needs of users.

2.3 *Procedures:*

2.3.1 *Each clinical psychological service unit follows a set of procedural guidelines for the delivery of psychological services.*

INTERPRETATION: Providers are prepared to provide a statement of procedural guidelines, in either oral or written form, in terms that can be understood by users, including sanctioners and local administrators. This statement describes the current methods, forms, procedures, and techniques being used to achieve the objectives and goals for psychological services.

2.3.2 *Providers of clinical psychological services develop plans appropriate to the providers' professional practices and to the problems presented by the users.*

INTERPRETATION A clinical psychologist develops a plan that describes the psychological services, their objectives, and the manner in which they will be provided.[13,14] This plan is in written form; it serves as a basis for obtaining understanding and concurrence from the user and provides a mechanism for subsequent peer review. This plan is, of course, modified as new needs or information develops.

A clinical psychologist who provides services as one member of a collaborative effort participates in the development and implementation of the overall service plan and provides for its periodic review.

2.3.3 *Accurate, current, and pertinent documentation of essential clinical psychological services provided is maintained.*

INTERPRETATION: Records kept of clinical psychological services may include, but are not limited to, identifying data, dates of services, types of services, significant actions taken, and outcome at termination. Providers of clinical psychological services ensure that essential information concerning services rendered is recorded within a reasonable time following their completion.

2.3.4 *Each clinical psychological service unit follows an established record retention and disposition policy.*

INTERPRETATION The policy on record retention and disposition conforms to federal or state statutes or administrative regulations where such are applicable. In the absence of such regulations, the policy is (a) that the full record be retained intact for 3 years after the completion of planned services or after the date of last contact with the user, whichever is later; (b) that a full record or summary of the record be maintained for an additional 12 years; and (c) that the record may be disposed of no sooner than 15 years after the completion of planned services or after the date of the last contact, whichever is later. These temporal guides are consistent with procedures currently in use by federal record centers.

In the event of the death or incapacity of a clinical psychologist in independent practice, special procedures are necessary to ensure the continuity of active services to users and the proper safeguarding of inactive records being retained to meet this Guideline. Following approval by the affected user, it is appropriate for another clinical psychologist, acting under the auspices of the local professional standards review committee (PSRC), to review the records with the user and recommend a course of action for continuing professional service, if needed. Depending on local circumstances, the reviewing psychologist may also recommend appropriate arrangements for the balance of the record retention and disposition period.

This Guideline has been designed to meet a variety of circumstances that may arise, often years after a set of psychological services has been completed. More and more records are being used in forensic matters, for peer review, and in response to requests from users, other professionals, or other legitimate parties requiring accurate information about the exact dates, nature, course, and outcome of a set of psychological services. These record retention procedures also provide valuable baseline data for the original psychologist-provider when a previous user returns for additional services.

2.3.5 *Providers of clinical psychological services maintain a system to protect confidentiality of their records.*[15]

INTERPRETATION: Clinical psychologists are responsible for maintaining the confidentiality of information about users of services, from whatever source derived. All persons supervised by clinical psychologists, including nonprofessional personnel and students, who have access to records of psychological services are required to maintain this confidentiality as a condition of employment.

The clinical psychologist does not release confidential information, except with the written consent of the user directly involved or his or her legal representative. Even after consent for release has been obtained, the clinical psychologist clearly identifies such information as confidential to the recipient of the information.[16] If directed otherwise by statute or regulations with the force of law or by court order, the psychologist may seek a resolution to the conflict that is both ethically and legally feasible and appropriate.

Users are informed in advance of any limits in the setting for maintenance of confidentiality of psychological information. For instance, clinical psychologists in hospital, clinic, or agency settings inform their patients that psychological information in a patient's clinical record may be available without the patient's written consent to other members of the professional staff associated with the patient's treatment or rehabilitation. Similar limitations on confidentiality of psychological information may be present in certain school, industrial, military, or other institutional settings, or in instances in which the user has waived confidentiality for purposes of third-party payment.

Users have the right to obtain information from their psychological records. However, the records are the property of the psychologist or the facility in which the psychologist works and are, therefore, the responsibility of the psychologist and subject to his or her control.

When the user's intention to waive confidentiality is judged by the professional clinical psychologist to be contrary to the user's best interests or to be in conflict with the user's civil and legal rights, it is the responsibility of the clinical psychologist to discuss the implications of releasing psychological information and to assist the user in limiting disclosure only to information required by the present circumstance.

Raw psychological data (e.g., questionnaire returns or test protocols) in which a user is identified are released only with the written consent of the user or his or her legal representative and released only to a person recognized by the clinical psychologist as qualified and competent to use the data.

Any use made of psychological reports, records, or data for research or training purposes is consistent with this Guideline. Additionally, providers of clinical psychological services comply with statutory confidentiality requirements and those embodied in the American Psychological Association's *Ethical Principles of Psychologists* (APA, 1981b).

Providers of clinical psychological services remain sensitive to both the benefits and the possible misuse of information regarding individuals that is stored in large computerized data banks. Providers use their influence to ensure that such information is used in a socially responsible manner.

Guideline 3
ACCOUNTABILITY

3.1 *The clinical psychologist's professional activity is guided primarily by the principle of promoting human welfare.*

INTERPRETATION: Clinical psychologists provide services to users in a manner that is considerate, effective, economical, and humane. Clinical psychologists make their services readily accessible to users in a manner that facilitates the users' freedom of choice.

Clinical psychologists are mindful of their accountability to the sanctioners of clinical psychological services and to the general public, provided that appropriate steps are taken to protect the confidentiality of the service relationship. In the pursuit of their professional activities, they aid in the conservation of human, material, and financial resources.

The clinical psychological service unit does not withhold services to a potential client on the basis of that user's race, color, religion, gender, sexual orientation, age, or national origin. Recognition is given, however, to the following considerations: the professional right of clinical psychologists to limit their practice to a specific category of users (e.g., children, adolescents, women); the right and responsibility of clinical psychologists to withhold an assessment procedure when not validly applicable; and the right and responsibility of clinical psychologists to withhold evaluative, psychotherapeutic, counseling, or other services in specific instances in which their own limitations or client characteristics might impair the effectiveness of the relationship.[17,18] Clinical psychologists seek to ameliorate through peer review, consultation, or other personal therapeutic procedures those factors that inhibit the provision of services to particular users. When indicated services are not available, clinical psychologists take whatever action is appropriate to inform responsible persons and agencies of the lack of such services.

Clinical psychologists who find that psychological services are being provided in a manner that is discriminatory or exploitative to users and/or contrary to these Guidelines or to state or federal statutes take appropriate corrective action, which may include the refusal to provide services. When conflicts of interest arise, the clinical psychologist is guided in the resolution of differences by the principles set forth in the American Psychological Association's *Ethical Principles of Psychologists* (APA, 1981b) and "Guidelines for Conditions of Employment of Psychologists" (APA, 1972).

3.2 *Clinical psychologists pursue their activities as members of the independent, autonomous profession of psychology.*[19]

INTERPRETATION: Clinical psychologists, as members of an independent profession, are responsible both to the public and to their peers through established review mechanisms. Clinical psychologists are aware of the implications of their activities for the profession as a whole. They seek to eliminate discriminatory practices instituted for self-serving purposes that are not in the interest of the users (e.g., arbitrary requirements for referral and supervision by another profession). They are cognizant of their responsibilities for the development of the profession. They participate where possible in the training and career development of students and other providers, participate as appropriate in the training of paraprofessionals or other professionals, and integrate and supervise the implementation of their contributions within the structure established for delivering psychological services. Clinical psychologists facilitate the development of, and participate in, professional standards review mechanisms.[20]

Clinical psychologists seek to work with other professionals in a cooperative manner for the good of the users and the benefit of the general public. Clinical psychologists associated with multidisciplinary settings support the principle that members of each participating profession have equal rights and opportunities to share all privileges and responsibilities of full membership in hospital facilities or other human service facilities and to administer service programs in their respective areas of competence.

3.3 *There are periodic, systematic, and effective evaluations of clinical psychological services.*[21]

INTERPRETATION: When the clinical psychological service unit is a component of a larger organization, regular evaluation of progress in achieving goals is provided for in the service delivery plan, including consideration of the effectiveness of clinical psychological services relative to costs in terms of use of time and money and the availability of professional and support personnel.

Evaluation of the clinical psychological service delivery system is conducted internally and, when possible, under independent auspices as well. This evaluation includes an assessment of effectiveness (to determine what the service unit accomplished), efficiency (to determine the total costs of providing the services), continuity (to ensure that the services are appropriately linked to other human services), availability (to determine appropriate levels and distribution of services and personnel), accessibility (to ensure that the services are barrier free to users), and adequacy (to determine whether the services meet the identified needs for such services).

There is a periodic reexamination of review mechanisms to ensure that these attempts at public safeguards are effective and cost efficient and do not place unnecessary encumbrances on the providers or impose unnecessary additional expenses on users or sanctioners for services rendered.

3.4 *Clinical psychologists are accountable for all aspects of the services they provide and are responsive to those concerned with these services.*[22]

INTERPRETATION: In recognizing their responsibilities to users, and where appropriate and consistent with the users' legal rights and privileged communications, clinical psychologists make available information about, and provide opportunity to participate in, decisions concerning such issues as initiation, termination, continuation,

modification, and evaluation of clinical psychological services.

Depending on the settings, accurate and full information is made available to prospective individual or organizational users regarding the qualifications of providers, the nature and extent of services offered, and where appropriate, financial and social costs.

Where appropriate, clinical psychologists inform users of their payment policies and their willingness to assist in obtaining reimbursement. Those who accept reimbursement from a third party are acquainted with the appropriate statutes and regulations and assist their users in understanding procedures for submitting claims and limits on confidentiality of claims information, in accordance with pertinent statutes.

Guideline 4
ENVIRONMENT

4.1 *Providers of clinical psychological services promote the development in the service setting of a physical, organizational, and social environment that facilitates optimal human functioning.*

INTERPRETATION: Federal, state, and local requirements for safety, health, and sanitation are observed.

As providers of services, clinical psychologists are concerned with the environment of their service unit, especially as it affects the quality of service, but also as it impinges on human functioning when the service unit is included in a larger context. Physical arrangements and organizational policies and procedures are conducive to the human dignity, self-respect, and optimal functioning of users and to the effective delivery of service. Attention is given to the comfort and the privacy of users. The atmosphere in which clinical psychological services are rendered is appropriate to the service and to the users, whether in an office, clinic, school, industrial organization, or other institutional setting.

FOOTNOTES

[1] The footnotes appended to these Specialty Guidelines represent an attempt to provide a coherent context of other policy statements of the Association regarding professional practice. The Guidelines extend these previous policy statements where necessary to reflect current concerns of the public and the profession.

[2] The following two categories of professional psychologists who met the criteria indicated below on or before the adoption of these Specialty Guidelines on January 31, 1980, are also considered clinical psychologists: Category 1—persons who completed (a) a doctoral degree program primarily psychological in content at a regionally accredited university or professional school and (b) 3 postdoctoral years of appropriate education, training, and experience in providing clinical psychological services as defined herein, including a minimum of 1 year in a clinical setting; Category 2—persons who on or before September 4, 1974, (a) completed a master's degree from a program primarily psychological in content at a regionally accredited

university or professional school and (b) held a license or certificate in the state in which they practiced, conferred by a state board of psychological examiners, or the endorsement of the state psychological association through voluntary certification, and who, in addition, prior to January 31, 1980, (c) obtained 5 post-master's years of appropriate education, training, and experience in providing clinical psychological services as defined herein, including a minimum of 2 years in a clinical setting.

After January 31, 1980, professional psychologists who wish to be recognized as professional clinical psychologists are referred to Guideline 1.7.

The definition of the professional clinical psychologist in these Guidelines does not contradict or supersede in any way the broader definition accorded the term *clinical psychologist* in the Federal Employees Health Benefits Program (see *Access to Psychologists and Optometrists Under Federal Health Benefits Program*, U.S. Senate Report No. 93-961, June 25, 1974).

[3] The areas of knowledge and training that are a part of the educational program for all professional psychologists have been presented in two APA documents, *Education and Credentialing in Psychology II* (APA, 1977a) and *Criteria for Accreditation of Doctoral Training Programs and Internships in Professional Psychology* (APA, 1979). There is consistency in the presentation of core areas in the education and training of all professional psychologists. The description of education and training in these Guidelines is based primarily on the document *Education and Credentialing in Psychology II*. It is intended to indicate broad areas of required curriculum, with the expectation that training programs will undoubtedly want to interpret the specific content of these areas in different ways depending on the nature, philosophy, and intent of the programs.

[4] Functions and activities of psychologists relating to the teaching of psychology, the writing or editing of scholarly or scientific manuscripts, and the conduct of scientific research do not fall within the purview of these Guidelines.

[5] The definitions should be compared with the APA (1967) guidelines for state legislation (hereinafter referred to as state guidelines), which define *psychologist* and the *practice of psychology* as follows:

A person represents himself [or herself] to be a psychologist when he [or she] holds himself [or herself] out to the public by any title or description of services incorporating the words "psychology," "psychological," "psychologist," and/or offers to render or renders services as defined below to individuals, groups, organizations, or the public for a fee, monetary or otherwise.

The practice of psychology within the meaning of this act is defined as rendering to individuals, groups, organizations, or the public any psychological service involving the application of principles, methods, and procedures of understanding, predicting, and influencing behavior, such as the principles pertaining to learning, perception, motivation, thinking, emotions and interpersonal relationships; the methods and procedures of interviewing, counseling, and psychotherapy; of constructing, administering, and interpreting tests of mental abilities, aptitudes, interests, attitudes, personality characteristics, emotion, and motivation; and of assessing public opinion.

The application of said principles and methods includes, but is not restricted to: diagnosis, prevention, and amelioration of adjustment problems and emotional and mental disorders of individuals and groups; hypnosis; educational and vocational counseling; personnel selection and management; the evaluation and planning for effective work and learning situations; advertising and market research; and the resolution of interpersonal and social conflicts.

Psychotherapy within the meaning of this act means the use of learning, conditioning methods, and emotional reac-

tions, in a professional relationship, to assist a person or persons to modify feelings, attitudes, and behavior which are intellectually, socially, or emotionally maladjustive or ineffectual.

The practice of psychology shall be as defined above, any existing statute in the state of _____ to the contrary notwithstanding. (APA, 1967, pp. 1098–1099)

[6] The relation of a psychological service unit to a larger facility or institution is also addressed indirectly in the APA (1972) "Guidelines for Conditions of Employment of Psychologists" (hereinafter referred to as CEP Guidelines), which emphasizes the roles, responsibilities, and prerogatives of the psychologist when he or she is employed by or provides services for another agency, institution, or business.

[7] This Guideline replaces earlier recommendations in the 1967 state guidelines concerning exemption of psychologists from licensure. Recommendations 8 and 9 of those guidelines read as follows:

Persons employed as psychologists by accredited academic institutions, governmental agencies, research laboratories, and business corporations should be exempted, provided such employees are performing those duties for which they are employed by such organizations, and within the confines of such organizations.

Persons employed as psychologists by accredited academic institutions, governmental agencies, research laboratories, and business corporations consulting or offering their research findings or providing scientific information to like organizations for a fee should be exempted. (APA, 1967, p. 1100)

On the other hand, the 1967 state guidelines specifically denied exemptions under certain conditions, as noted in Recommendations 10 and 11:

Persons employed as psychologists who offer or provide psychological services to the public for a fee, over and above the salary that they receive for the performance of their regular duties, should not be exempted.

Persons employed as psychologists by organizations that sell psychological services to the public should not be exempted. (APA, 1967, pp. 1100–1101)

The present APA policy, as reflected in this Guideline, establishes a single code of practice for psychologists providing covered services to users in any setting. The present position is that a psychologist providing any covered service meets local statutory requirements for licensure or certification. See the section entitled Principles and Implications of the Specialty Guidelines for an elaboration of this position.

[8] A closely related principle is found in the APA (1972) CEP Guidelines:

It is the policy of APA that psychology as an independent profession is entitled to parity with other health and human service professions in institutional practices and before the law. Psychologists in interdisciplinary settings such as colleges and universities, medical schools, clinics, private practice groups, and other agencies expect parity with other professions in such matters as academic rank, board status, salaries, fringe benefits, fees, participation in administrative decisions, and all other conditions of employment, private contractual arrangements, and status before the law and legal institutions. (APA, 1972, p. 333)

[9] See CEP Guidelines (section entitled Career Development) for a closely related statement:

Psychologists are expected to encourage institutions and agencies which employ them to sponsor or conduct career development programs. The purpose to these programs would be to enable psychologists to engage in study for professional advancement and to keep abreast of developments in their field. (APA, 1972, p. 332)

[10] This Guideline follows closely the statement regarding "Policy on Training for Psychologists Wishing to Change Their Specialty" adopted by the APA Council of Representatives in January 1976. Included therein was the implementing provision that "this policy statement shall be incorporated in the guidelines of the Committee on Accreditation so that appropriate sanctions can be brought to bear on university and internship training programs that violate [it]" (Conger, 1976, p. 424).

[11] See also APA's (1981b) *Ethical Principles of Psychologists*, especially Principles 5 (Confidentiality), 6 (Welfare of the Consumer), and 9 (Research with Human Participants); and see *Ethical Principles in the Conduct of Research With Human Participants* (APA, 1973a). Also, in 1978 Division 17 approved in principle a statement on "Principles for Counseling and Psychotherapy With Women," which was designed to protect the interests of female users of clinical psychological services.

[12] Support for this position is found in *Psychology as a Profession* in the section on relations with other professions:

Professional persons have an obligation to know and take into account the traditions and practices of other professional groups with whom they work and to cooperate fully with members of such groups with whom research, service, and other functions are shared. (APA, 1968, p. 5)

[13] One example of a specific application of this principle is found in Guideline 2 in APA's (1973b) "Guidelines for Psychologists Conducting Growth Groups":

The following information should be made available *in writing* [italics added] to all prospective participants:
(a) An explicit statement of the purpose of the group;
(b) Types of techniques that may be employed;
(c) The education, training, and experience of the leader or leaders;
(d) The fee and any additional expense that may be incurred;
(e) A statement as to whether or not a follow-up service is included in the fee;
(f) Goals of the group experience and techniques to be used;
(g) Amounts and kinds of responsibility to be assumed by the leader and by the participants. For example, (i) the degree to which a participant is free not to follow suggestions and prescriptions of the group leader and other group members; (ii) any restrictions on a participant's freedom to leave the group at any time; and
(h) Issues of confidentiality. (p. 933)

[14] See APA's (1981a) *APA/CHAMPUS Outpatient Psychological Provider Manual.*

[15] See Principle 5 (Confidentiality) in *Ethical Principles of Psychologists* (APA, 1981b).

[16] Support for the principle of privileged communication is found in at least two policy statements of the Association:

In the interest of both the public and the client and in accordance with the requirements of good professional practice, the profession of psychology seeks recognition of the privileged nature of confidential communications with clients, preferably through statutory enactment or by administrative policy where more appropriate. (APA, 1968, p. 8)

Wherever possible, a clause protecting the privileged nature of the psychologist–client relationship be included.

When appropriate, psychologists assist in obtaining general

"across the board" legislation for such privileged communications. (APA, 1967, p. 1103)

[17] This paragraph is directly adapted from the CEP Guidelines (APA, 1972, p. 333).

[18] The CEP Guidelines also include the following:

It is recognized that under certain circumstances, the interests and goals of a particular community or segment of interest in the population may be in conflict with the general welfare. Under such circumstances, the psychologist's professional activity must be primarily guided by the principle of "promoting human welfare." (APA, 1972, p. 334)

[19] Support for the principle of the independence of psychology as a profession is found in the following:

As a member of an autonomous profession, a psychologist rejects limitations upon his [or her] freedom of thought and action other than those imposed by his [or her] moral, legal, and social responsibilities. The Association is always prepared to provide appropriate assistance to any responsible member who becomes subjected to unreasonable limitations upon his [or her] opportunity to function as a practitioner, teacher, researcher, administrator, or consultant. The Association is always prepared to cooperate with any responsible professional organization in opposing any unreasonable limitations on the professional functions of the members of that organization.

This insistence upon professional autonomy has been upheld over the years by the affirmative actions of the courts and other public and private bodies in support of the right of the psychologist—and other professionals—to pursue those functions for which he [or she] is trained and qualified to perform. (APA, 1968, p. 9)

Organized psychology has the responsibility to define and develop its own profession, consistent with the general canons of science and with the public welfare.

Psychologists recognize that other professions and other groups will, from time to time, seek to define the roles and responsibilities of psychologists. The APA opposes such developments on the same principle that it is opposed to the psychological profession taking positions which would define the work and scope of responsibility of other duly recognized professions. (APA, 1972, p. 333)

[20] APA support for peer review is detailed in the following excerpt from the APA (1971) statement entitled "Psychology and National Health Care":

All professions participating in a national health plan should be directed to establish review mechanisms (or performance evaluations) that include not only peer review but active participation by persons representing the consumer. In situations where there are fiscal agents, they should also have representation when appropriate. (p. 1026)

[21] This Guideline on program evaluation is based directly on the following excerpts from two APA position papers:

The quality and availability of health services should be evaluated continuously by both consumers and health professionals. Research into the efficiency and effectiveness of the system should be conducted both internally and under independent auspices. (APA, 1971, p. 1025)

The comprehensive community mental health center should devote an explicit portion of its budget to program evaluation. All centers should inculcate in their staff attention to and respect for research findings; the larger centers have an obligation to set a high priority on basic research and to give formal recognition to research as a legitimate part of the duties of staff members.

. . . Only through explicit appraisal of program effects can worthy approaches be retained and refined, ineffective ones dropped. Evaluative monitoring of program achievements may vary, of course, from the relatively informal to the systematic and quantitative, depending on the importance of the issue, the availablity of resources, and the willingness of those responsible to take risks of substituting informed judgment for evidence. (Smith & Hobbs, 1966, pp. 21–22)

⁵² See also the CEP Guidelines for the following statement: "A psychologist recognizes that . . . he [or she] alone is accountable for the consequences and effects of his [or her] services, whether as teacher, researcher, or practitioner. This responsibility cannot be shared, delegated, or reduced" (APA, 1972, p. 334).

REFERENCES

American Psychological Association, Committee on Legislation. A model for state legislation affecting the practice of psychology. *American Psychologist*, 1967, 22, 1095–1103.

American Psychological Association. *Psychology as a profession*. Washington, D.C.: Author, 1968.

American Psychological Association. Psychology and national health care. *American Psychologist*, 1971, 26, 1025–1026.

American Psychological Association. Guidelines for conditions of employment of psychologists. *American Psychologist*, 1972, 27, 331–334.

American Psychological Association. *Ethical principles in the conduct of research with human participants*. Washington, D.C.: Author, 1973. (a)

American Psychological Association. Guidelines for psychologists conducting growth groups. *American Psychologist*, 1973, 28, 933. (b)

American Psychological Association. *Standards for educational and psychological tests*. Washington, D.C.: Author, 1974. (a)

American Psychological Association. *Standards for providers of psychological services*. Washington, D.C.: Author, 1974. (b)

American Psychological Association. *Education and credentialing in psychology II*. Report of a meeting, June 4–5, 1977. Washington, D.C.: Author, 1977. (a)

American Psychological Association. *Standards for providers of psychological services* (Rev. ed.). Washington, D.C.: Author, 1977. (b)

American Psychological Association. *Criteria for accreditation of doctoral training programs and internships in professional psychology*. Washington, D.C.: Author, 1979 (amended 1980).

American Psychological Association. *APA/CHAMPUS outpatient psychological provider manual* (Rev. ed.). Washington, D.C.: Author, 1981 (a)

American Psychological Association. *Ethical principles of psychologists* (Rev. ed.). Washington, D.C.: Author, 1981. (b)

Conger, J. J. Proceedings of the American Psychological Association, Incorporated, for the year 1975: Minutes of the annual meeting of the Council of Representatives. *American Psychologist*, 1976, 31, 406–434.

Smith, M. B., & Hobbs, N. *The community and the community mental health center*. Washington, D.C.: American Psychological Association, 1966.

Specialty Guidelines for the Delivery
of Services by Counseling Psychologists

The Specialty Guidelines that follow are based on the generic *Standards for Providers of Psychological Services* originally adopted by the American Psychological Association (APA) in September 1974 and revised in January 1977 (APA, 1974b, 1977b). Together with the generic *Standards*, these Specialty Guidelines state the official policy of the Association regarding delivery of services by counseling psychologists. Admission to the practice of psychology is regulated by state statute. It is the position of the Association that licensing be based on generic, and not on specialty, qualifications. Specialty guidelines serve the additional purpose of providing potential users and other interested groups with essential information about particular services available from the several specialties in professional psychology.

Professional psychology specialties have evolved from generic practice in psychology and are supported by university training programs. There are now at least four recognized professional specialties—clinical, counseling, school, and industrial/organizational psychology.

The knowledge base in each of these specialty areas has increased, refining the state of the art to the point that a set of uniform specialty guidelines is now possible and desirable. The present Guidelines are intended to educate the public, the profession, and other interested parties regarding specialty professional practices. They are also intended to facilitate the continued systematic development of the profession.

The content of each Specialty Guideline reflects a consensus of university faculty and public and private practitioners regarding the knowledge base, services provided, problems addressed, and clients served.

Traditionally, all learned disciplines have treated the designation of specialty practice as a reflection of preparation in greater depth in a particular subject matter, together with a voluntary limiting of focus to a more restricted area of practice by the professional. Lack of specialty designation does not preclude general providers of psychological services from using the methods or dealing with the populations of any specialty, except insofar as psychologists voluntarily refrain from providing services they are not trained to render. It is the intent of these guidelines, however, that after the grandparenting period, psychologists not put themselves forward as *specialists* in a given area of practice unless they meet the qualifications noted in the Guidelines (see Definitions). Therefore, these Guidelines are meant to apply only to those psychologists who voluntarily wish to be designated as *counseling psychologists*. They do not apply to other psychologists.

These Guidelines represent the profession's best judg-

ment of the conditions, credentials, and experience that contribute to competent professional practice. The APA strongly encourages, and plans to participate in, efforts to identify professional practitioner behaviors and job functions and to validate the relation between these and desired client outcomes. Thus, future revisions of these Guidelines will increasingly reflect the results of such efforts.

These Guidelines follow the format and, wherever applicable, the wording of the generic *Standards*.[1] (Note: Footnotes appear at the end of the Specialty Guidelines. See pp. 661–663.) The intent of these Guidelines is to improve the quality, effectiveness, and accessibility of psychological services. They are meant to provide guidance to providers, users, and sanctioners regarding the best judgment of the profession on these matters. Although the Specialty Guidelines have been derived from and are consistent with the generic *Standards*, they may be used as separate documents. However, *Standards for Providers of Psychological Services* (APA, 1977b) shall remain the basic policy statement and shall take precedence where there are questions of interpretation.

Professional psychology in general and counseling psychology as a specialty have labored long and diligently to codify a uniform set of guidelines for the delivery of services by counseling psychologists that would serve the respective needs of users, providers, third-party purchasers, and sanctioners of psychological services.

The Committee on Professional Standards, established by the APA in January 1980, is charged with keeping the generic *Standards* and the Specialty Guidelines responsive to the needs of the public and the profession. It is also charged with continually reviewing, modifying, and extending them progressively as the profession and the science of psychology develop new knowledge, improved methods, and additional modes of psychological services.

The Specialty Guidelines for the Delivery of Services by Counseling Psychologists that follow have been established by the APA as a means of self-regulation to protect the public interest. They guide the specialty prac-

---

These Specialty Guidelines were prepared by the APA Committee on Standards for Providers of Psychological Services (COSPOPS), chaired by Durand F. Jacobs, with the advice of the officers and committee chairpersons of the Division of Counseling Psychology (Division 17). Barbara A. Kirk and Milton Schwebel served successively as the counseling psychology representative of COSPOPS, and Arthur Centor and Richard Kilburg were the Central Office liaisons to the committee. Norman Kagan, Samuel H. Osipow, Carl E. Thoresen, and Allen E. Ivey served successively as Division 17 presidents.

tice of counseling psychology by specifying important areas of quality assurance and performance that contribute to the goal of facilitating more effective human functioning.

Principles and Implications of the Specialty Guidelines

These Specialty Guidelines emerged from and reaffirm the same basic principles that guided the development of the generic *Standards for Providers of Psychological Services* (APA, 1977b):

1. These Guidelines recognize that admission to the practice of psychology is regulated by state statute.

2. It is the intention of the APA that the generic *Standards* provide appropriate guidelines for statutory licensing of psychologists. In addition, although it is the position of the APA that licensing be generic and not in specialty areas, these Specialty Guidelines in counseling psychology provide an authoritative reference for use in credentialing specialty providers of counseling psychological services by such groups as divisions of the APA and state associations and by boards and agencies that find such criteria useful for quality assurance.

3. A uniform set of Specialty Guidelines governs the quality of services to all users of counseling psychological services in both the private and the public sectors. Those receiving counseling psychological services are protected by the same kinds of safeguards, irrespective of sector; these include constitutional guarantees, statutory regulation, peer review, consultation, record review, and supervision.

4. A uniform set of Specialty Guidelines governs counseling psychological service functions offered by counseling psychologists, regardless of setting or form of remuneration. All counseling psychologists in professional practice recognize and are responsive to a uniform set of Specialty Guidelines, just as they are guided by a common code of ethics.

5. Counseling psychology Guidelines establish clear, minimally acceptable levels of quality for covered counseling psychological service functions, regardless of the nature of the users, purchasers, or sanctioners of such covered services.

6. All persons providing counseling psychological services meet specified levels of training and experience that are consistent with, and appropriate to, the functions they perform. Counseling psychological services provided by persons who do not meet the APA qualifications for a professional counseling psychologist (see Definitions) are supervised by a professional counseling psychologist. Final responsibility and accountability for services provided rest with professional counseling psychologists.

7. When providing any of the covered counseling psychological service functions at any time and in any setting, whether public or private, profit or nonprofit, counseling psychologists observe these Guidelines in order to promote the best interests and welfare of the users

of such services. The extent to which counseling psychologists observe these Guidelines is judged by peers.

8. These Guidelines, while assuring the user of the counseling psychologist's accountability for the nature and quality of services specified in this document, do not preclude the counseling psychologist from using new methods or developing innovative procedures in the delivery of counseling services.

These Specialty Guidelines have broad implications both for users of counseling psychological services and for providers of such services:

1. Guidelines for counseling psychological services provide a foundation for mutual understanding between provider and user and facilitate more effective evaluation of services provided and outcomes achieved.

2. Guidelines for counseling psychologists are essential for uniformity in specialty credentialing of counseling psychologists.

3. Guidelines give specific content to the profession's concept of ethical practice as it applies to the functions of counseling psychologists.

4. Guidelines for counseling psychological services may have significant impact on tomorrow's education and training models for both professional and support personnel in counseling psychology.

5. Guidelines for the provision of counseling psychological services in human service facilities influence the determination of acceptable structure, budgeting, and staffing patterns in these facilities.

6. Guidelines for counseling psychological services require continual review and revision.

The Specialty Guidelines here presented are intended to improve the quality and delivery of counseling psychological services by specifying criteria for key aspects of the practice setting. Some settings may require additional and/or more stringent criteria for specific areas of service delivery.

Systematically applied, these Guidelines serve to establish a more effective and consistent basis for evaluating the performance of individual service providers as well as to guide the organization of counseling psychological service units in human service settings.

Definitions

Providers of counseling psychological services refers to two categories of persons who provide counseling psychological services:

A. Professional counseling psychologists.[2] Professional counseling psychologists have a doctoral degree from a regionally accredited university or professional school providing an organized, sequential counseling psychology program in an appropriate academic department in a university or college, or in an appropriate department or unit of a professional school. Counseling psychology programs that are accredited by the American Psychological Association are recognized as meeting the defi-

16

nition of a counseling psychology program. Counseling psychology programs that are not accredited by the American Psychological Association meet the definition of a counseling psychology program if they satisfy the following criteria:

1. The program is primarily psychological in nature and stands as a recognizable, coherent organizational entity within the institution.

2. The program provides an integrated, organized sequence of study.

3. The program has an identifiable body of students who are matriculated in that program for a degree.

4. There is a clear authority with primary responsibility for the core and specialty areas, whether or not the program cuts across administrative lines.

5. There is an identifiable psychology faculty, and a psychologist is responsible for the program.

The professional counseling psychologist's doctoral education and training experience[3] is defined by the institution offering the program. Only counseling psychologists, that is, those who meet the appropriate education and training requirements, have the minimum professional qualifications to provide unsupervised counseling psychological services. A professional counseling psychologist and others providing counseling psychological services under supervision (described below) form an integral part of a multilevel counseling psychological service delivery system.

B. All other persons who provide counseling psychological services under the supervision of a professional counseling psychologist. Although there may be variations in the titles of such persons, they are not referred to as counseling psychologists. Their functions may be indicated by use of the adjective *psychological* preceding the noun, for example, *psychological associate, psychological assistant, psychological technician,* or *psychological aide.*

Counseling psychological services refers to services provided by counseling psychologists that apply principles, methods, and procedures for facilitating effective functioning during the life-span developmental process.[4,5] In providing such services, counseling psychologists approach practice with a significant emphasis on positive aspects of growth and adjustment and with a developmental orientation. These services are intended to help persons acquire or alter personal–social skills, improve adaptability to changing life demands, enhance environmental coping skills, and develop a variety of problem-solving and decision-making capabilities. Counseling psychological services are used by individuals, couples, and families of all age groups to cope with problems connected with education, career choice, work, sex, marriage, family, other social relations, health, aging, and handicaps of a social or physical nature. The services are offered in such organizations as educational, rehabilitation, and health institutions and in a variety of other public and private agencies committed to service in one or more of the problem areas cited above. Counseling psychological services include the following:

A. Assessment, evaluation, and diagnosis. Procedures may include, but are not limited to, behavioral observation, interviewing, and administering and interpreting instruments for the assessment of educational achievement, academic skills, aptitudes, interests, cognitive abilities, attitudes, emotions, motivations, psychoneurological status, personality characteristics, or any other aspect of human experience and behavior that may contribute to understanding and helping the user.

B. Interventions with individuals and groups. Procedures include individual and group psychological counseling (e.g., education, career, couples, and family counseling) and may use a therapeutic, group process, or social-learning approach, or any other deemed to be appropriate. Interventions are used for purposes of prevention, remediation, and rehabilitation; they may incorporate a variety of psychological modalities, such as psychotherapy, behavior therapy, marital and family therapy, biofeedback techniques, and environmental design.

C. Professional consultation relating to A and B above, for example, in connection with developing in-service training for staff or assisting an educational institution or organization to design a plan to cope with persistent problems of its students.

D. Program development services in the areas of A, B, and C above, such as assisting a rehabilitation center to design a career-counseling program.

E. Supervision of all counseling psychological services, such as the review of assessment and intervention activities of staff.

F. Evaluation of all services noted in A through E above and research for the purpose of their improvement.

A *counseling psychological service unit* is the functional unit through which counseling psychological services are provided; such a unit may be part of a larger psychological service organization comprising psychologists of more than one specialty and headed by a professional psychologist:

A. A counseling psychological service unit provides predominantly counseling psychological services and is composed of one or more professional counseling psychologists and supporting staff.

B. A counseling psychological service unit may operate as a functional or geographic component of a larger multipsychological service unit or of a governmental, educational, correctional, health, training, industrial, or commercial organizational unit, or it may operate as an independent professional service.[6]

C. A counseling psychological service unit may take the form of one or more counseling psychologists providing professional services in a multidisciplinary setting.

D. A counseling psychological service unit may also take the form of a private practice, composed of one or more counseling psychologists serving individuals or groups, or the form of a psychological consulting firm serving organizations and institutions.

Users of counseling psychological services include:

A. Direct users or recipients of counseling psychological services.

B. Public and private institutions, facilities, or organizations receiving counseling psychological services.

C. Third-party purchasers—those who pay for the delivery of services but who are not the recipients of services.

D. Sanctioners—those who have a legitimate concern with the accessibility, timeliness, efficacy, and standards of quality attending the provision of counseling psychological services. Sanctioners may include members of the user's family, the court, the probation officer, the school administrator, the employer, the union representative, the facility director, and so on. Sanctioners may also include various governmental, peer review, and accreditation bodies concerned with the assurance of quality.

Guideline 1
PROVIDERS

1.1 *Each counseling psychological service unit offering psychological services has available at least one professional counseling psychologist and as many more professional counseling psychologists as are necessary to assure the adequacy and quality of services offered.*

INTERPRETATION: The intent of this Guideline is that one or more providers of psychological services in any counseling psychological service unit meet the levels of training and experience of the professional counseling psychologist as specified in the preceding definitions.[7]

When a professional counseling psychologist is not available on a full-time basis, the facility retains the services of one or more professional counseling psychologists on a regular part-time basis. The counseling psychologist so retained directs the psychological services, including supervision of the support staff, has the authority and participates sufficiently to assess the need for services, reviews the content of services provided, and assumes professional responsibility and accountability for them.

The psychologist directing the service unit is responsible for determining and justifying appropriate ratios of psychologists to users and psychologists to support staff, in order to ensure proper scope, accessibility, and quality of services provided in that setting.

1.2 *Providers of counseling psychological services who do not meet the requirements for the professional counseling psychologist are supervised directly by a professional counseling psychologist who assumes professional responsibility and accountability for the services provided. The level and extent of supervision may vary from task to task so long as the supervising psychologist retains a sufficiently close supervisory relationship to meet this Guideline. Special proficiency training or supervision may be provided by a professional psycholo-*

gist of another specialty or by a professional from another discipline whose competence in the given area has been demonstrated by previous training and experience.

INTERPRETATION In each counseling psychological service unit there may be varying levels of responsibility with respect to the nature and quality of services provided. Support personnel are considered to be responsible for their functions and behavior when assisting in the provision of counseling psychological services and are accountable to the professional counseling psychologist. Ultimate professional responsibility and accountability for the services provided require that the supervisor review reports and test protocols, and review and discuss intervention plans, strategies, and outcomes. Therefore, the supervision of all counseling psychological services is provided directly by a professional counseling psychologist in a face-to-face arrangement involving individual and/or group supervision. The extent of supervision is determined by the needs of the providers, but in no event is it less than 1 hour per week for each support staff member providing counseling psychological services.

To facilitate the effectiveness of the psychological service unit, the nature of the supervisory relationship is communicated to support personnel in writing. Such communications delineate the duties of the employees, describing the range and type of services to be provided. The limits of independent action and decision making are defined. The description of responsibility specifies the means by which the employee will contact the professional counseling psychologist in the event of emergency or crisis situations.

1.3 *Wherever a counseling psychological service unit exists, a professional counseling psychologist is responsible for planning, directing, and reviewing the provision of counseling psychological services. Whenever the counseling psychological service unit is part of a larger professional psychological service encompassing various psychological specialties, a professional psychologist shall be the administrative head of the service.*

INTERPRETATION: The counseling psychologist who directs or coordinates the unit is expected to maintain an ongoing or periodic review of the adequacy of services and to formulate plans in accordance with the results of such evaluation. He or she coordinates the activities of the counseling psychology unit with other professional, administrative, and technical groups, both within and outside the institution or agency. The counseling psychologist has related responsibilities including, but not limited to, directing the training and research activities of the service, maintaining a high level of professional and ethical practice, and ensuring that staff members function only within the areas of their competency.

To facilitate the effectiveness of counseling services by raising the level of staff sensitivity and professional

18

skills, the counseling psychologist designated as director is responsible for participating in the selection of staff and support personnel whose qualifications and skills (e.g., language, cultural and experiential background, race, sex, and age) are relevant to the needs and characteristics of the users served.

1.4 *When functioning as part of an organizational setting, professional counseling psychologists bring their backgrounds and skills to bear on the goals of the organization, whenever appropriate, by participation in the planning and development of overall services.*[8]

INTERPRETATION: Professional counseling psychologists participate in the maintenance of high professional standards by representation on committees concerned with service delivery.

As appropriate to the setting, their activities may include active participation, as voting and as office-holding members, on the facility's professional staff and on other executive, planning, and evaluation boards and committees.

1.5 *Counseling psychologists maintain current knowledge of scientific and professional developments to preserve and enhance their professional competence.*

INTERPRETATION: Methods through which knowledge of scientific and professional developments may be gained include, but are not limited to, reading scientific and professional publications, attendance at professional workshops and meetings, participation in staff development programs, and other forms of continuing education.[9] The counseling psychologist has ready access to reference material related to the provision of psychological services. Counseling psychologists are prepared to show evidence periodically that they are staying abreast of current knowledge and practices in the field of counseling psychology through continuing education.

1.6 *Counseling psychologists limit their practice to their demonstrated areas of professional competence.*

INTERPRETATION: Counseling psychological services are offered in accordance with the providers' areas of competence as defined by verifiable training and experience. When extending services beyond the range of their usual practice, counseling psychologists obtain pertinent training or appropriate professional supervision. Such training or supervision is consistent with the extension of functions performed and services provided. An extension of services may involve a change in the theoretical orientation of the counseling psychologist, in the modality or techniques used, in the type of client, or in the kinds of problems or disorders for which services are to be provided.

1.7 *Professional psychologists who wish to qualify as counseling psychologists meet the same requirements with respect to subject matter and professional skills that apply to doctoral education and training in counseling psychology.*[10]

INTERPRETATION: Education of doctoral-level psychologists to qualify them for specialty practice in counseling psychology is under the auspices of a department in a regionally accredited university or of a professional school that offers the doctoral degree in counseling psychology. Such education is individualized, with due credit being given for relevant course work and other requirements that have previously been satisfied. In addition, doctoral-level training supervised by a counseling psychologist is required. Merely taking an internship in counseling psychology or acquiring experience in a practicum setting is not adequate preparation for becoming a counseling psychologist when prior education has not been in that area. Fulfillment of such an individualized educational program is attested to by the awarding of a certificate by the supervising department or professional school that indicates the successful completion of preparation in counseling psychology.

1.8 *Professional counseling psychologists are encouraged to develop innovative theories and procedures and to provide appropriate theoretical and/or empirical support for their innovations.*

INTERPRETATION: A specialty of a profession rooted in a science intends continually to explore and experiment with a view to developing and verifying new and improved ways of serving the public and documents the innovations.

Guideline 2
PROGRAMS

2.1 *Composition and organization of a counseling psychological service unit:*

2.1.1 *The composition and programs of a counseling psychological service unit are responsive to the needs of the persons or settings served.*

INTERPRETATION: A counseling psychological service unit is structured so as to facilitate effective and economical delivery of services. For example, a counseling psychological service unit serving predominantly a low-income, ethnic, or racial minority group has a staffing pattern and service programs that are adapted to the linguistic, experiential, and attitudinal characteristics of the users.

2.1.2 *A description of the organization of the counseling psychological service unit and its lines of responsibility and accountability for the delivery of psychological services is available in written form to staff of the unit and to users and sanctioners upon request.*

INTERPRETATION: The description includes lines of responsibility, supervisory relationships, and the level and extent of accountability for each person who provides psychological services.

2.1.3 *A counseling psychological service unit includes sufficient numbers of professional and support personnel to achieve its goals, objectives, and purposes.*

INTERPRETATION: The work load and diversity of psychological services required and the specific goals and objectives of the setting determine the numbers and qualifications of professional and support personnel in the counseling psychological service unit. Where shortages in personnel exist, so that psychological services cannot be rendered in a professional manner, the director of the counseling psychological service unit initiates action to remedy such shortages. When this fails, the director appropriately modifies the scope or work load of the unit to maintain the quality of the services rendered and, at the same time, makes continued efforts to devise alternative systems for delivery of services.

2.2 *Policies:*

2.2.1 *When the counseling psychological service unit is composed of more than one person or is a component of a larger organization, a written statement of its objectives and scope of services is developed, maintained, and reviewed.*

INTERPRETATION: The counseling psychological service unit reviews its objectives and scope of services annually and revises them as necessary to ensure that the psychological services offered are consistent with staff competencies and current psychological knowledge and practice. This statement is discussed with staff, reviewed with the appropriate administrator, and distributed to users and sanctioners upon request, whenever appropriate.

2.2.2 *All providers within a counseling psychological service unit support the legal and civil rights of the users.*[11]

INTERPRETATION: Providers of counseling psychological services safeguard the interests of the users with regard to personal, legal, and civil rights. They are continually sensitive to the issue of confidentiality of information, the short-term and long-term impacts of their decisions and recommendations, and other matters pertaining to individual, legal, and civil rights. Concerns regarding the safeguarding of individual rights of users include, but are not limited to, problems of access to professional records in educational institutions, self-incrimination in judicial proceedings, involuntary commitment to hos-

pitals, protection of minors or legal incompetents, discriminatory practices in employment selection procedures, recommendation for special education provisions, information relative to adverse personnel actions in the armed services, and adjudication of domestic relations disputes in divorce and custodial proceedings. Providers of counseling psychological services take affirmative action by making themselves available to local committees, review boards, and similar advisory groups established to safeguard the human, civil, and legal rights of service users.

2.2.3 *All providers within a counseling psychological service unit are familiar with and adhere to the American Psychological Association's Standards for Providers of Psychological Services, Ethical Principles of Psychologists, Standards for Educational and Psychological Tests, Ethical Principles in the Conduct of Research With Human Participants, and other official policy statements relevant to standards for professional services issued by the Association.*

INTERPRETATION: Providers of counseling psychological services maintain current knowledge of relevant standards of the American Psychological Association.

2.2.4 *All providers within a counseling psychological service unit conform to relevant statutes established by federal, state, and local governments.*

INTERPRETATION: All providers of counseling psychological services are familiar with and conform to appropriate statutes regulating the practice of psychology. They also observe agency regulations that have the force of law and that relate to the delivery of psychological services (e.g., evaluation for disability retirement and special education placements). In addition, all providers are cognizant that federal agencies such as the Veterans Administration, the Department of Education, and the Department of Health and Human Services have policy statements regarding psychological services. Providers are familiar as well with other statutes and regulations, including those addressed to the civil and legal rights of users (e.g., those promulgated by the federal Equal Employment Opportunity Commission), that are pertinent to their scope of practice.

It is the responsibility of the American Psychological Association to maintain current files of those federal policies, statutes, and regulations relating to this section and to assist its members in obtaining them. The state psychological associations and the state licensing boards periodically publish and distribute appropriate state statutes and regulations, and these are on file in the counseling psychological service unit or the larger multipsychological service unit of which it is a part.

2.2.5 *All providers within a counseling psychological service unit inform themselves about and use the* *network of human services in their communities in order to link users with relevant services and resources.*

INTERPRETATION: Counseling psychologists and support staff are sensitive to the broader context of human needs. In recognizing the matrix of personal and social problems, providers make available to clients information regarding human services such as legal aid societies, social services, employment agencies, health resources, and educational and recreational facilities. Providers of counseling psychological services refer to such community resources and, when indicated, actively intervene on behalf of the users.

Community resources include the private as well as the public sectors. Consultation is sought or referral made within the public or private network of services whenever required in the best interest of the users. Counseling psychologists, in either the private or the public setting, utilize other resources in the community whenever indicated because of limitations within the psychological service unit providing the services. Professional counseling psychologists in private practice know the types of services offered through local community mental health clinics and centers, through family-service, career, and placement agencies, and through reading and other educational improvement centers and know the costs and the eligibility requirements for those services.

2.2.6 *In the delivery of counseling psychological services, the providers maintain a cooperative relationship with colleagues and co-workers in the best interest of the users.*[12]

INTERPRETATION: Counseling psychologists recognize the areas of special competence of other professional psychologists and of professionals in other fields for either consultation or referral purposes. Providers of counseling psychological services make appropriate use of other professional, research, technical, and administrative resources to serve the best interests of users and establish and maintain cooperative arrangements with such other resources as required to meet the needs of users.

2.3 *Procedures:*

2.3.1 *Each counseling psychological service unit is guided by a set of procedural guidelines for the delivery of psychological services.*

INTERPRETATION: Providers are prepared to provide a statement of procedural guidelines, in either oral or written form, in terms that can be understood by users, including sanctioners and local administrators. This statement describes the current methods, forms, procedures, and techniques being used to achieve the objectives and goals for psychological services.

2.3.2 *Providers of counseling psychological services develop plans appropriate to the providers' profes-*

sional practices and to the problems presented by the users.

INTERPRETATION: A counseling psychologist, after initial assessment, develops a plan describing the objectives of the psychological services and the manner in which they will be provided.[13] To illustrate, the agreement spells out the objective (e.g., a career decision), the method (e.g., short-term counseling), the roles (e.g., active participation by the user as well as the provider), and the cost. This plan is in written form. It serves as a basis for obtaining understanding and concurrence from the user and for establishing accountability and provides a mechanism for subsequent peer review. This plan is, of course, modified as changing needs dictate.

A counseling psychologist who provides services as one member of a collaborative effort participates in the development, modification (if needed), and implementation of the overall service plan and provides for its periodic review.

2.3.3 *Accurate, current, and pertinent documentation of essential counseling psychological services provided is maintained.*

INTERPRETATION: Records kept of counseling psychological services include, but are not limited to, identifying data, dates of services, types of services, significant actions taken, and outcome at termination. Providers of counseling psychological services ensure that essential information concerning services rendered is recorded within a reasonable time following their completion.

2.3.4 *Each counseling psychological service unit follows an established record retention and disposition policy.*

INTERPRETATION: The policy on record retention and disposition conforms to state statutes or federal regulations where such are applicable. In the absence of such regulations, the policy is (a) that the full record be maintained intact for at least 4 years after the completion of planned services or after the date of last contact with the user, whichever is later; (b) that if a full record is not retained, a summary of the record be maintained for an additional 3 years; and (c) that the record may be disposed of no sooner than 7 years after the completion of planned services or after the date of last contact, whichever is later.

In the event of the death or incapacity of a counseling psychologist in independent practice, special procedures are necessary to ensure the continuity of active service to users and the proper safeguarding of records in accordance with this Guideline. Following approval by the affected user, it is appropriate for another counseling psychologist, acting under the auspices of the professional standards review committee (PSRC) of the state, to review the record with the user and recommend a

21

course of action for continuing professional service, if needed. Depending on local circumstances, appropriate arrangements for record retention and disposition may also be recommended by the reviewing psychologist.

This Guideline has been designed to meet a variety of circumstances that may arise, often years after a set of psychological services has been completed. Increasingly, psychological records are being used in forensic matters, for peer review, and in response to requests from users, other professionals, and other legitimate parties requiring accurate information about the exact dates, nature, course, and outcome of a set of psychological services. The 4-year period for retention of the full record covers the period of either undergraduate or graduate study of most students in postsecondary educational institutions, and the 7-year period for retention of at least a summary of the record covers the period during which a previous user is most likely to return for counseling psychological services in an educational institution or other organization or agency.

2.3.5 *Providers of counseling psychological services maintain a system to protect confidentiality of their records.*[14]

INTERPRETATION: Counseling psychologists are responsible for maintaining the confidentiality of information about users of services, from whatever source derived. All persons supervised by counseling psychologists, including nonprofessional personnel and students, who have access to records of psychological services maintain this confidentiality as a condition of employment and/or supervision.

The counseling psychologist does not release confidential information, except with the written consent of the user directly involved or his or her legal representative. The only deviation from this rule is in the event of clear and imminent danger to, or involving, the user. Even after consent for release has been obtained, the counseling psychologist clearly identifies such information as confidential to the recipient of the information.[15] If directed otherwise by statute or regulations with the force of law or by court order, the psychologist seeks a resolution to the conflict that is both ethically and legally feasible and appropriate.

Users are informed in advance of any limits in the setting for maintenance of confidentiality of psychological information. For instance, counseling psychologists in agency, clinic, or hospital settings inform their clients that psychological information in a client's record may be available without the client's written consent to other members of the professional staff associated with service to the client. Similar limitations on confidentiality of psychological information may be present in certain educational, industrial, military, or other institutional settings, or in instances in which the user has waived confidentiality for purposes of third-party payment.

Users have the right to obtain information from their psychological records. However, the records are the property of the psychologist or the facility in which the psychologist works and are, therefore, the responsibility of the psychologist and subject to his or her control.

When the user's intention to waive confidentiality is judged by the professional counseling psychologist to be contrary to the user's best interests or to be in conflict with the user's civil and legal rights, it is the responsibility of the counseling psychologist to discuss the implications of releasing psychological information and to assist the user in limiting disclosure only to information required by the present circumstance.

Raw psychological data (e.g., questionnaire returns or test protocols) in which a user is identified are released only with the written consent of the user or his or her legal representative and released only to a person recognized by the counseling psychologist as qualified and competent to use the data.

Any use made of psychological reports, records, or data for research or training purposes is consistent with this Guideline. Additionally, providers of counseling psychological services comply with statutory confidentiality requirements and those embodied in the American Psychological Association's *Ethical Principles of Psychologists* (APA, 1981b).

Providers of counseling psychological services who use information about individuals that is stored in large computerized data banks are aware of the possible misuse of such data as well as the benefits and take necessary measures to ensure that such information is used in a socially responsible manner.

Guideline 3
ACCOUNTABILITY

3.1 *The promotion of human welfare is the primary principle guiding the professional activity of the counseling psychologist and the counseling psychological service unit.*

INTERPRETATION: Counseling psychologists provide services to users in a manner that is considerate, effective, economical, and humane. Counseling psychologists are responsible for making their services readily accessible to users in a manner that facilitates the users' freedom of choice.

Counseling psychologists are mindful of their accountability to the sanctioners of counseling psychological services and to the general public, provided that appropriate steps are taken to protect the confidentiality of the service relationship. In the pursuit of their professional activities, they aid in the conservation of human, material, and financial resources.

The counseling psychological service unit does not withhold services to a potential client on the basis of that user's race, color, religion, gender, sexual orientation, age, or national origin; nor does it provide services in a discriminatory or exploitative fashion. Counseling psychologists who find that psychological services are being provided in a manner that is discriminatory or exploitative to users and/or contrary to these Guidelines or to state or federal statutes take appropriate corrective action, which may include the refusal to provide services. When conflicts of interest arise, the counseling psychologist is guided in the resolution of differences by the principles set forth in the American Psychological Association's *Ethical Principles of Psychologists* (APA, 1981b) and "Guidelines for Conditions of Employment of Psychologists" (APA, 1972).[1b]

Recognition is given to the following considerations in regard to the withholding of service: (a) the professional right of counseling psychologists to limit their practice to a specific category of users with whom they have achieved demonstrated competence (e.g., adolescents or families); (b) the right and responsibility of counseling psychologists to withhold an assessment procedure when not validly applicable; (c) the right and responsibility of counseling psychologists to withhold services in specific instances in which their own limitations or client characteristics might impair the quality of the services; (d) the obligation of counseling psychologists to seek to ameliorate through peer review, consultation, or other personal therapeutic procedures those factors that inhibit the provision of services to particular individuals; and (e) the obligation of counseling psychologists who withhold services to assist clients in obtaining services from other sources.[17]

3.2 *Counseling psychologists pursue their activities as members of the independent, autonomous profession of psychology.*[18]

INTERPRETATION: Counseling psychologists, as members of an independent profession, are responsible both to the public and to their peers through established review mechanisms. Counseling psychologists are aware of the implications of their activities for the profession as a whole. They seek to eliminate discriminatory practices instituted for self-serving purposes that are not in the interest of the users (e.g., arbitrary requirements for referral and supervision by another profession). They are cognizant of their responsibilities for the development of the profession, participate where possible in the training and career development of students and other providers, participate as appropriate in the training of paraprofessionals or other professionals, and integrate and supervise the implementation of their contributions within the structure established for delivering psychological services. Counseling psychologists facilitate the development of, and participate in, professional standards review mechanisms.[19]

Counseling psychologists seek to work with other professionals in a cooperative manner for the good of the users and the benefit of the general public. Counseling psychologists associated with multidisciplinary settings support the principle that members of each participating profession have equal rights and opportunities to share all privileges and responsibilities of full membership in human service facilities and to administer service programs in their respective areas of competence.

3.3 *There are periodic, systematic, and effective evaluations of counseling psychological services.*[20]

INTERPRETATION: When the counseling psychological service unit is a component of a larger organization, regular evaluation of progress in achieving goals is provided for in the service delivery plan, including consideration of the effectiveness of counseling psychological services relative to costs in terms of use of time and money and the availability of professional and support personnel.

Evaluation of the counseling psychological service delivery system is conducted internally and, when possible, under independent auspices as well. This evaluation includes an assessment of effectiveness (to determine what the service unit accomplished), efficiency (to determine the total costs of providing the services), continuity (to ensure that the services are appropriately linked to other human services), availability (to determine appropriate levels and distribution of services and personnel), accessibility (to ensure that the services are barrier free to users), and adequacy (to determine whether the services meet the identified needs for such services).

There is a periodic reexamination of review mechanisms to ensure that these attempts at public safeguards are effective and cost efficient and do not place unnecessary encumbrances on the providers or impose unnecessary additional expenses on users or sanctioners for services rendered.

3.4 *Counseling psychologists are accountable for all aspects of the services they provide and are responsive to those concerned with these services.*[21]

INTERPRETATION: In recognizing their responsibilities to users, sanctioners, third-party purchasers, and other providers, and where appropriate and consistent with the users' legal rights and privileged communications, counseling psychologists make available information about, and provide opportunity to participate in, decisions concerning such issues as initiation, termination, continuation, modification, and evaluation of counseling psychological services.

Depending on the settings, accurate and full information is made available to prospective individual or organizational users regarding the qualifications of providers, the nature and extent of services offered, and where appropriate, financial and social costs.

Where appropriate, counseling psychologists inform users of their payment policies and their willingness to assist in obtaining reimbursement. To assist their users, those who accept reimbursement from a third party are acquainted with the appropriate statutes and regulations, the procedures for submitting claims, and the limits on confidentiality of claims information, in accordance with pertinent statutes.

Guideline 4
ENVIRONMENT

4.1 *Providers of counseling psychological services promote the development in the service setting of a physical, organizational, and social environment that facilitates optimal human functioning.*

INTERPRETATION: Federal, state, and local requirements for safety, health, and sanitation are observed.

As providers of services, counseling psychologists are concerned with the environment of their service unit, especially as it affects the quality of service, but also as it impinges on human functioning in the larger context. Physical arrangements and organizational policies and procedures are conducive to the human dignity, self-respect, and optimal functioning of users and to the effective delivery of service. Attention is given to the comfort and the privacy of providers and users. The atmosphere in which counseling psychological services are rendered is appropriate to the service and to the users, whether in an office, clinic, school, college, university, hospital, industrial organization, or other institutional setting.

FOOTNOTES

[1] The footnotes appended to these Specialty Guidelines represent an attempt to provide a coherent context of other policy statements of the Association regarding professional practice. The Guidelines extend these previous policy statements where necessary to reflect current concerns of the public and the profession.

[2] The following two categories of professional psychologists who met the criteria indicated below on or before the adoption of these Specialty Guidelines on January 31, 1980, are also considered counseling psychologists: Category 1—persons who completed (a) a doctoral degree program primarily psychological in content at a regionally accredited university or professional school and (b) 3 postdoctoral years of appropriate education, training, and experience in providing counseling psychological services as defined herein, including a minimum of 1 year in a counseling setting; Category 2—persons who on or before September 4, 1974, (a) completed a master's degree from a program primarily psychological in content at a regionally accredited university or professional school and (b) held a license or certificate in the state in which they practiced, conferred by a state board of psychological examiners, or the endorsement of the state psychological association through voluntary certification, and who, in addition, prior to January 31, 1980, (c) obtained 5 post-master's years of appropriate education, training, and experience in providing counseling psychological services as defined herein, including a minimum of 2 years in a counseling setting.

After January 31, 1980, professional psychologists who wish to be recognized as professional counseling psychologists are referred to Guideline 1.7

[3] The areas of knowledge and training that are a part of the educational program for all professional psychologists have been presented in two APA documents, *Education and Credentialing in Psychology II* (APA, 1977a) and *Criteria for Accreditation of Doctoral Training Programs and Internships in Professional Psychology* (APA, 1979). There is consistency in the presentation of core areas in the education and training of all professional psychologists. The description of education and training in these Guidelines is based primarily on the document *Education and Credentialing in Psychology II*. It is intended to indicate broad areas of required curriculum, with the expectation that training programs will undoubtedly want to interpret the specific content of these areas in different ways depending on the nature, philosophy, and intent of the programs.

[4] Functions and activities of counseling psychologists relating to the teaching of psychology, the writing or editing of scholarly or scientific manuscripts, and the conduct of scientific research do not fall within the purview of these Guidelines.

[5] These definitions should be compared with the APA (1967) guidelines for state legislation (hereinafter referred to as state guidelines), which define *psychologist* (i.e., the generic professional psychologist, not the specialist counseling psychologist) and the *practice of psychology* as follows:

A person represents himself [or herself] to be a psychologist when he [or she] holds himself [or herself] out to the public by any title or description of services incorporating the words "psychology," "psychological," "psychologist," and/or offers to render or renders services as defined below to individuals, groups, organizations, or the public for a fee, monetary or otherwise.

The practice of psychology within the meaning of this act is defined as rendering to individuals, groups, organizations, or the public any psychological service involving the application of principles, methods, and procedures of understanding, predicting, and influencing behavior, such as the principles pertaining to learning, perception, motivation, thinking, emotions, and interpersonal relationships; the methods and procedures of interviewing, counseling, and psychotherapy; of constructing, administering, and interpreting tests of mental abilities, aptitudes, interests, attitudes, personality characteristics, emotion, and motivation; and of assessing public opinion.

The application of said principles and methods includes, but is not restricted to: diagnosis, prevention, and amelioration of adjustment problems and emotional and mental disorders of individuals and groups; hypnosis; educational and vocational counseling; personnel selection and management; the evaluation and planning for effective work and learning situations; advertising and market research; and the resolution of interpersonal and social conflicts.

Psychotherapy within the meaning of this act means the use of learning, conditioning methods, and emotional reactions, in a professional relationship, to assist a person or persons to modify feelings, attitudes, and behavior which are intellectually, socially, or emotionally maladjustive or ineffectual.

The practice of psychology shall be as defined above, any existing statute in the state of _____ to the contrary notwithstanding. (APA, 1967, pp. 1098–1099)

[6] The relation of a psychological service unit to a larger facility or institution is also addressed indirectly in the APA (1972)

"Guidelines for Conditions of Employment of Psychologists" (hereinafter referred to as CEP Guidelines), which emphasize the roles, responsibilities, and prerogatives of the psychologist when he or she is employed by or provides services for another agency, institution, or business.

[7] This Guideline replaces earlier recommendations in the 1967 state guidelines concerning exemption of psychologists from licensure. Recommendations 8 and 9 of those guidelines read as follows:

Persons employed as psychologists by accredited academic institutions, governmental agencies, research laboratories, and business corporations should be exempted, provided such employees are performing those duties for which they are employed by such organizations, and within the confines of such organizations.

Persons employed as psychologists by accredited academic institutions, governmental agencies, research laboratories, and business corporations consulting or offering their research findings or providing scientific information *to like organizations* for a fee should be exempted. (APA, 1967, p. 1100)

On the other hand, the 1967 state guidelines specifically denied exemptions under certain conditions, as noted in Recommendations 10 and 11:

Persons employed as psychologists who offer or provide psychological services to the public for a fee, over and above the salary that they receive for the performance of their regular duties, should not be exempted.

Persons employed as psychologists by organizations that sell psychological services to the public should not be exempted. (APA, 1967, pp. 1100–1101)

The present APA policy, as reflected in this Guideline, establishes a single code of practice for psychologists providing covered services to users in any setting. The present position is that a psychologist providing any covered service meets local statutory requirements for licensure or certification. See the section entitled Principles and Implications of the Specialty Guidelines for further elaboration of this point.

[8] A closely related principle is found in the APA (1972) CEP Guidelines:

It is the policy of APA that psychology as an independent profession is entitled to parity with other health and human service professions in institutional practices and before the law. Psychologists in interdisciplinary settings such as colleges and universities, medical schools, clinics, private practice groups, and other agencies expect parity with other professions in such matters as academic rank, board status, salaries, fringe benefits, fees, participation in administrative decisions, and all other conditions of employment, private contractual arrangements, and status before the law and legal institutions. (APA, 1972, p. 333)

[9] See CEP Guidelines (section entitled Career Development) for a closely related statement:

Psychologists are expected to encourage institutions and agencies which employ them to sponsor or conduct career development programs. The purpose of these programs would be to enable psychologists to engage in study for professional advancement and to keep abreast of developments in their field. (APA, 1972, p. 332)

[10] This Guideline follows closely the statement regarding "Policy on Training for Psychologists Wishing to Change Their Specialty" adopted by the APA Council of Representatives in January 1976. Included therein was the implementing provision

that "this policy statement shall be incorporated in the guidelines of the Committee on Accreditation so that appropriate sanctions can be brought to bear on university and internship training programs that violate [it]" (Conger, 1976, p. 424).

[11] See also APA's (1981b) *Ethical Principles of Psychologists*, especially Principles 5 (Confidentiality), 6 (Welfare of the Consumer), and 9 (Research With Human Participants); and see *Ethical Principles in the Conduct of Research With Human Participants* (APA, 1973a). Also, in 1978 Division 17 approved in principle a statement on "Principles for Counseling and Psychotherapy With Women," which was designed to protect the interests of female users of counseling psychological services.

[12] Support for this position is found in the section on relations with other professions in *Psychology as a Profession*:

Professional persons have an obligation to know and take into account the traditions and practices of other professional groups with whom they work and to cooperate fully with members of such groups with whom research, service, and other functions are shared. (APA, 1968, p. 5)

[13] One example of a specific application of this principle is found in APA's (1981a) revised *APA/CHAMPUS Outpatient Psychological Provider Manual*. Another example, quoted below, is found in Guideline 2 in APA's (1973b) "Guidelines for Psychologists Conducting Growth Groups":

The following information should be made available *in writing* [italics added] to all prospective participants:

(a) An explicit statement of the purpose of the group;

(b) Types of techniques that may be employed;

(c) The education, training, and experience of the leader or leaders;

(d) The fee and any additional expense that may be incurred;

(e) A statement as to whether or not a follow-up service is included in the fee;

(f) Goals of the group experience and techniques to be used;

(g) Amounts and kinds of responsibility to be assumed by the leader and by the participants. For example, (i) the degree to which a participant is free not to follow suggestions and prescriptions of the group leader and other group members; (ii) any restrictions on a participant's freedom to leave the group at any time; and

(h) Issues of confidentiality. (p. 933)

[14] See Principle 5 (Confidentiality) in *Ethical Principles of Psychologists* (APA, 1981b).

[15] Support for the principles of privileged communication is found in at least two policy statements of the Association:

In the interest of both the public and the client and in accordance with the requirements of good professional practice, the profession of psychology seeks recognition of the privileged nature of confidential communications with clients, preferably through statutory enactment or by administrative policy where more appropriate. (APA, 1968, p. 8)

Wherever possible, a clause protecting the privileged nature of the psychologist–client relationship be included. When appropriate, psychologists assist in obtaining general "across the board" legislation for such privileged communications. (APA, 1967, p. 1103)

[16] The CEP Guidelines include the following:

It is recognized that under certain circumstances, the interests and goals of a particular community or segment of interest in the population may be in conflict with the general welfare. Under such circumstances, the psychologist's professional activity must be primarily guided by the principle of "promoting human welfare." (APA, 1972, p. 334)

[17] This paragraph is adapted in part from the CEP Guidelines (APA, 1972, p. 333).

[18] Support for the principle of the independence of psychology as a profession is found in the following:

As a member of an autonomous profession, a psychologist rejects limitations upon his [or her] freedom of thought and action other than those imposed by his [or her] moral, legal, and social responsibilities. The Association is always prepared to provide appropriate assistance to any responsible member who becomes subjected to unreasonable limitations upon his [or her] opportunity to function as a practitioner, teacher, researcher, administrator, or consultant. The Association is always prepared to cooperate with any responsible professional organization in opposing any unreasonable limitations on the professional functions of the members of that organization.

This insistence upon professional autonomy has been upheld over the years by the affirmative actions of the courts and other public and private bodies in support of the right of the psychologist—and other professionals—to pursue those functions for which he [or she] is trained and qualified to perform. (APA, 1968, p. 9)

Organized psychology has the responsibility to define and develop its own profession, consistent with the general canons of science and with the public welfare.

Psychologists recognize that other professions and other groups will, from time to time, seek to define the roles and responsibilities of psychologists. The APA opposes such developments on the same principle that it is opposed to the psychological profession taking positions which would define the work and scope of responsibility of other duly recognized professions. (APA, 1972, p. 333)

[19] APA support for peer review is detailed in the following excerpt from the APA (1971) statement entitled "Psychology and National Health Care":

All professions participating in a national health plan should be directed to establish review mechanisms (or performance evaluations) that include not only peer review but active participation by persons representing the consumer. In situations where there are fiscal agents, they should also have representation when appropriate. (p. 1026)

[20] This Guideline on program evaluation is based directly on the following excerpts from two APA position papers:

The quality and availability of health services should be evaluated continuously by both consumers and health professionals. Research into the efficiency and effectiveness of the system should be conducted both internally and under independent auspices. (APA, 1971, p. 1025)

The comprehensive community mental health center should devote an explicit portion of its budget to program evaluation. All centers should inculcate in their staff attention to and respect for research findings; the larger centers have an obligation to set a high priority on basic research and to

give formal recognition to research as a legitimate part of the duties of staff members.

. . . Only through explicit appraisal of program effects can worthy approaches be retained and refined, ineffective ones dropped. Evaluative monitoring of program achievements may vary, of course, from the relatively informal to the systematic and quantitative, depending on the importance of the issue, the availability of resources, and the willingness of those responsible to take risks of substituting informed judgment for evidence. (Smith & Hobbs, 1966, pp. 21–22)

[21] See also the CEP Guidelines for the following statement "A psychologist recognizes that . . . he [or she] alone is accountable for the consequences and effects of his [or her] services, whether as teacher, researcher, or practitioner. This responsibility cannot be shared, delegated, or reduced" (APA, 1972, p. 334)

REFERENCES

American Psychological Association, Committee on Legislation. A model for state legislation affecting the practice of psychology. *American Psychologist*, 1967, *22*, 1095–1103.

American Psychological Association. *Psychology as a profession*. Washington, D.C.: Author, 1968.

American Psychological Association. Psychology and national health care. *American Psychologist*, 1971, *26*, 1025–1026

American Psychological Association. Guidelines for conditions of employment of psychologists. *American Psychologist*, 1972, *27*, 331–334.

American Psychological Association. *Ethical principles in the conduct of research with human participants*. Washington, D.C.: Author, 1973. (a)

American Psychological Association. Guidelines for psychologists conducting growth groups. *American Psychologist*, 1973, *28*, 933. (b)

American Psychological Association. *Standards for educational and psychological tests*. Washington, D.C.: Author, 1974. (a)

American Psychological Association. *Standards for providers of psychological services*. Washington, D.C.: Author, 1974. (b)

American Psychological Association. *Education and credentialing in psychology II*. Report of a meeting, June 4–5, 1977. Washington, D.C.: Author, 1977. (a)

American Psychological Association. *Standards for providers of psychological services* (Rev. ed.). Washington, D.C.: Author, 1977. (b)

American Psychological Association. *Criteria for accreditation of doctoral training programs and internships in professional psychology*. Washington, D.C.: Author, 1979 (amended 1980).

American Psychological Association. *APA/CHAMPUS outpatient psychological provider manual* (Rev. ed.). Washington, D.C.: Author, 1981. (a)

American Psychological Association. *Ethical principles of psychologists* (Rev. ed.). Washington, D.C.: Author, 1981. (b)

Conger, J. J. Proceedings of the American Psychological Association, Incorporated, for the year 1975: Minutes of the annual meeting of the Council of Representatives. *American Psychologist*, 1976, *31*, 406–434.

Smith, M. B., & Hobbs, N. *The community and the community mental health center*. Washington, D.C.: American Psychological Association, 1966.

Specialty Guidelines
for the Delivery of Services by
Industrial/Organizational Psychologists

The Specialty Guidelines that follow are supplements to the generic *Standards for Providers of Psychological Services*, originally adopted by the American Psychological Association (APA) in September 1974 and revised in January 1977 (APA, 1974b, 1977). Admission to the practice of psychology is regulated by state statute. It is the position of the Association that licensing be based on generic, and not on specialty, qualifications. Specialty guidelines serve the additional purpose of providing potential users and other interested groups with essential information about particular services available from the several specialties in professional psychology. Although the original APA *Standards* were designed to fill the needs of several classes of psychological practitioners and a wide variety of users, the diversity of professional practice and the use of psychological services require specialty guidelines to clarify the special nature of both practitioners and users. These Specialty Guidelines for the Delivery of Services by Industrial/Organizational (I/O) Psychologists are designed to define the roles of I/O psychologists and the particular needs of users of I/O psychological services.

Professional psychology specialties have evolved from generic practice in psychology and are supported by university training programs. There are now at least four recognized professional specialties—clinical, counseling, school, and industrial/organizational psychology.

The knowledge base in each of these specialty areas has increased, refining the state of the art to the point that a set of uniform specialty guidelines is now possible and desirable. The present Guidelines are intended to educate the public, the profession, and other interested parties regarding specialty professional practices. They are also intended to facilitate the continued systematic development of the profession.

The content of each specialty guideline reflects a consensus of university faculty and public and private practitioners regarding the knowledge base, services provided, problems addressed, and clients served.

Traditionally, all learned disciplines have treated the designation of specialty practice as a reflection of preparation in greater depth in a particular subject matter, together with a voluntary limiting of focus to a more restricted area of practice by the professional. Lack of specialty designation does not preclude general providers of psychological services from using the methods or dealing with the populations of any specialty, except insofar as psychologists voluntarily refrain from providing services they are not trained to render. It is the intent of these Guidelines, however, that after the grandparenting period, psychologists not put themselves forward as *specialists* in a given area of practice unless they meet the qualifications noted in the Guidelines (see Definitions). Therefore, these Guidelines are meant to apply only to those psychologists who voluntarily wish to be designated as *industrial/organizational psychologists*. They do not apply to other psychologists.

These Guidelines represent the profession's best judgment of the conditions, credentials, and experience that contribute to competent professional practice. The APA strongly encourages, and plans to participate in, efforts to identify professional practitioner behaviors and job functions and to validate the relation between these and desired client outcomes. Thus, future revisions of these Guidelines will increasingly reflect the results of such efforts.

Like the APA generic *Standards*, the I/O Specialty Guidelines are concerned with improving the quality, effectiveness, and accessibility of psychological services for all who require benefit from them. These Specialty Guidelines are intended to clarify questions of interpretation of the APA generic *Standards* as they are applied to I/O psychology.

This document presents the APA's position on I/O practice. Ethical standards applicable to I/O psychologists are already in effect,[1] as are other documents that provide guidance to I/O practitioners in specific applications of I/O psychology.[2] (Note: Footnotes appear at the end of the Specialty Guidelines. See p. 669.)

The Committee on Professional Standards established by the APA in January 1980 is charged with keeping the generic *Standards* and the Specialty Guidelines responsive to the needs of the public and the profession. It is also charged with continually reviewing, modifying, and

These Specialty Guidelines were prepared through the cooperative efforts of the APA Committee on Standards for Providers of Psychological Services (COSPOPS), chaired by Durand F. Jacobs, and the APA Division of Industrial and Organizational Psychology (Division 14). Virginia Ellen Schein and Frank Friedlander served as the I/O representatives on COSPOPS, and Arthur Centor and Richard Kilburg served as the Central Office liaisons to the committee. Thomas E. Tice and C. J. Bartlett were the key liaison persons from the Division 14 Professional Affairs Committee. Drafts of these Guidelines were reviewed and commented on by members of the Division 14 Executive Committee.

extending them progressively as the profession and the science of psychology develop new knowledge, improved methods, and additional modes of psychological services.

The Specialty Guidelines for the Delivery of Services by Industrial/Organizational Psychologists that follow have been established by the APA as a means of self-regulation to protect the public interest. They guide the specialty practice of I/O psychology by specifying important areas of quality assurance and performance that contribute to the goal of facilitating more effective human functioning.

Principles and Implications of the Specialty Guidelines

These Specialty Guidelines have emerged from and re-affirm the same basic principles that guided the development of the generic *Standards for Providers of Psychological Services* (APA, 1977):

1. These Guidelines recognize that where the practice of I/O psychology is regulated by federal, state, or local statutes, all providers of I/O psychological services conform to such statutes.

2. A uniform set of Specialty Guidelines governs I/O psychological service functions offered by I/O psychologists, regardless of setting or form of remuneration. All I/O psychologists in professional practice recognize and are responsive to a uniform set of Specialty Guidelines, just as they are guided by a common code of ethics.

3. The I/O Specialty Guidelines establish clearly articulated levels of quality for covered I/O psychological service functions, regardless of the nature of the users, purchasers, or sanctioners of such covered services.

4. All persons providing I/O psychological services meet specified levels of training and experience that are consistent with, and appropriate to, the functions they perform. Persons providing such services who do not meet the APA qualifications for a professional I/O psychologist (see Definitions) are supervised by a psychologist with the requisite training. This level of qualification is necessary to ensure that the public receives services of high quality. Final responsibility and accountability for services provided rest with professional I/O psychologists.

5. These Specialty Guidelines for I/O psychologists are intended to present the APA's position on levels for training and professional practice and to provide clarification of the APA generic *Standards*.

6. A uniform set of Specialty Guidelines governs the quality of I/O psychological services in both the private and the public sectors. Those receiving I/O psychological services are protected by the same kinds of safeguards, irrespective of sector.

7. All persons representing themselves as I/O psychologists at any time and in any setting, whether public or private, profit or nonprofit, observe these Guidelines in order to promote the interests and welfare of the users of I/O psychological services. Judgment of the degree to which these Guidelines are observed take into consideration the capabilities for evaluation and the circumstances that prevail in the setting at the time the program or service is evaluated.

8. These Guidelines, while assuring the user of the I/O psychologist's accountability for the nature and quality of services rendered, do not preclude the providers of I/O psychological services from using new methods or developing innovative procedures in the delivery of such services.

These Specialty Guidelines have broad implications both for users of I/O psychological services and for providers of such services:

1. Guidelines for I/O psychological services provide a basis for a mutual understanding between provider and user and facilitate effective evaluation of services provided and outcomes achieved.

2. Guidelines for I/O psychological services make an important contribution toward greater uniformity in legislative and regulatory actions involving I/O psychologists. Guidelines for providers of I/O psychological services may be useful for uniformity in specialty credentialing of I/O psychologists, if such specialty credentialing is required.

3. Although guidelines for I/O psychological services may have an impact on tomorrow's training models for both professional and support personnel in I/O psychology, they are not intended to interfere with innovations in the training of I/O psychologists.

4. Guidelines for I/O psychological services require continual review and revision.

The Specialty Guidelines here presented are intended to improve the quality and delivery of I/O psychological services by specifying criteria for key aspects of the practice setting. Some settings may require additional and/or more stringent criteria for specific areas of service delivery.

Definitions

A fully qualified *I/O psychologist* has a doctoral degree earned in a program primarily psychological in nature. This degree may be from a department of psychology or from a school of business, management, or administrative science in a regionally accredited university. Consistent with the commitment of I/O psychology to the scientist–professional model, I/O psychologists are thoroughly prepared in basic scientific methods as well as in psychological science; therefore, programs that do not include training in basic scientific methods and research are not considered appropriate educational and training models for I/O psychologists. The I/O psychology doctoral program provides training in (a) scientific and professional ethics, (b) general psychological science, (c) research design and methodology, (d) quantitative and qualitative methodology, and (e) psychological measurement, as well as (f) a supervised practicum or laboratory experience in an area of I/O psychology, (g) a field ex-

28

perience in the application and delivery of I/O services, (h) practice in the conduct of applied research, (i) training in other areas of psychology, in business, and in the social and behavioral sciences, as appropriate, and (j) preparation of a doctoral research dissertation.[3]

Although persons who do not meet all of the above qualifications may provide I/O psychological services, such services are performed under the supervision of a fully qualified I/O psychologist. The supervising I/O psychologist may be a full-time member of the same organization or may be retained on a part-time basis. Psychologists so retained have the authority and participate sufficiently to assess the need for services, to review the services provided, and to ensure professional responsibility and accountability for them. Special proficiency training or supervision may be provided by professional psychologists of other specialties or by professionals of other disciplines whose competencies in the given area have been demonstrated by previous training and experience.

Industrial/organizational psychological services involve the development and application of psychological theory and methodology to problems of organizations and problems of individuals and groups in organizational settings. The purpose of such applications to the assessment, development, or evaluation of individuals, groups, or organizations is to enhance the effectiveness of these individuals, groups, or organizations. The following areas represent some examples of such applications:

A. Selection and placement of employees. Services include development of selection programs, optimal placement of key personnel, and early identification of management potential.

B. Organization development. Services include analyzing organizational structure, formulating corporate personnel strategies, maximizing the effectiveness and satisfaction of individuals and work groups, effecting organizational change, and counseling employees for purposes of improving employee relations, personal and career development, and superior–subordinate relations.

C. Training and development of employees. Services include identifying training and development needs; formulating and implementing programs for technical training, management training, and organizational development; and evaluating the effectiveness of training and development programs in relation to productivity and satisfaction criteria.

D. Personnel research. Services include continuing development of assessment tools for selection, placement, classification, and promotion of employees; validating test instruments; and measuring the effect of cultural factors on test performance.

E. Improving employee motivation. Services include enhancing the productive output of employees, identifying and improving factors associated with job satisfaction, and redesigning jobs to make them more meaningful.

F. Design and optimization of work environments. Services include designing work environments and optimizing person–machine effectiveness.

Guideline 1
PROVIDERS

Staffing and Qualifications of Staff

1.1 *Professional I/O psychologists maintain current knowledge of scientific and professional developments that are related to the services they render.*

INTERPRETATION Methods through which knowledge of scientific and professional development may be gained include, but are not limited to, continuing education, attendance at workshops, participation in staff development, and reading scientific publications.

The I/O psychologist has ready access to reference material related to the provision of psychological services.

1.2 *Professional I/O psychologists limit their practice to their demonstrated areas of professional competence.*

INTERPRETATION I/O psychological services are offered in accordance with the providers' areas of competence as defined by verifiable training and experience.

When extending services beyond the range of their usual practice, professional I/O psychologists obtain pertinent training or appropriate professional supervision.

1.3 *Professional psychologists who wish to change their specialty to I/O areas meet the same requirements with respect to subject matter and professional skills that apply to doctoral training in the new specialty.*

INTERPRETATION Education and training of doctoral-level psychologists, when prior preparation has not been in the I/O area, includes education and training in the content, methodology, and practice of I/O psychology. Such preparation is individualized and may be acquired in a number of ways. Formal education in I/O psychology under the auspices of university departments that offer the doctoral degree in I/O psychology, with certification by the supervising department indicating competency in I/O psychology, is recommended. However, continuing education courses and workshops in I/O psychology, combined with supervised experience as an I/O psychologist, may also be acceptable.

1.4 *Professional I/O psychologists are encouraged to develop innovative procedures and theory.*

INTERPRETATION Although these Guidelines give examples of I/O psychologist activities, such activities are not limited to those provided. I/O psychologists are encouraged to develop innovative ways of approaching problems

Guideline 2
PROFESSIONAL CONSIDERATIONS

Protecting the User

2.1 *I/O psychological practice supports the legal and civil rights of the user.*

INTERPRETATION Providers of I/O psychological services safeguard the interests of the user with regard to legal and civil rights. I/O psychologists are especially sensitive to issues of confidentiality of information. In the case of dual users (e.g., individuals and organizations). I/O psychologists, insofar as possible, anticipate possible conflicts of interest and clarify with both users how such conflicts might be resolved. In addition, I/O service providers make every effort to safeguard documents and files containing confidential information.

2.2 *All providers of I/O psychological services abide by policies of the American Psychological Association that are relevant to I/O psychologists.*

INTERPRETATION: While many official APA policies are relevant to I/O psychology, such as those embodied in the *Ethical Principles of Psychologists* (APA, 1981) and the *Standards of Educational and Psychological Tests* (APA, 1974a), it is recognized that some specific policies which apply only to certain subspecialties (e.g., health care providers) may not be applicable to I/O psychologists.

2.3 *All providers within an I/O psychological service unit are familiar with relevant statutes, regulations, and legal precedents established by federal, state, and local governmental groups.*

INTERPRETATION Insofar as statutes exist relevant to the practice of the I/O psychological service provider, the provider is familiar with them and conforms to the law. In addition, the provider is familiar with statutes that may govern activities of the user as they relate to services provided. For example, an I/O psychologist who establishes selection systems for a user is aware of and conforms to the statutes governing selection systems for that user. This guideline does not imply that inappropriate statutes, regulations, and legal precedents cannot be opposed through legal processes.

Although I/O psychologists may be required by law to be licensed or certified, most I/O psychological services can be provided by persons who are not licensed or certified. Examples of such services are the administration of standardized group tests of mental abilities, aptitudes, personality characteristics, and so on for in-

structional or personnel screening uses; interviews, such as employment or curriculum advisory interviews, that do not involve the assessment of individual personality characteristics; the design, administration, and interpretation of opinion surveys; the design and evaluation of person–machine systems; the conduct of employee development programs; the counseling of employees by supervisors regarding job performance and working relationships; and the teaching of psychological principles or techniques that do not involve ameliorative services to individuals or groups

Planning Organizational Goals

2.4 *Providers of I/O psychological services state explicitly what can and cannot reasonably be expected from the services.*

INTERPRETATION In marketing psychological services, the I/O psychologist realistically appraises the chances of meeting the client's goal(s) and informs the client of the degree of success that can be anticipated. Since the user may or may not possess sophistication in psychological methods and applications, the limitations are stated in terms that are comprehensible to the user

In presenting statements of reasonable anticipation, the I/O psychologist attempts to be accurate in all regards. This guideline also applies to statements of personal competency and of the competency and experience of the psychological service unit that the I/O psychologist represents. Statements and materials do not make claims or suggest benefits that are not supportable by scientifically acceptable evidence. Since the I/O psychologist may stand to gain financially through the recommendation of a given product or service, particular sensitivity to such issues is essential to avoid compromise of professional responsibilities and objectives.

2.5 *Providers of I/O psychological services do not seek to gain competitive advantage through the use of privileged information.*

INTERPRETATION. In the course of work with a user, I/O practitioners may become aware of the management practices, organizational structure, personnel policies, or financial structure of competing units. Since such information is usually revealed in a privileged context, it is not employed for competitive advantage. Similarly, practitioners may be called on to review the proposal of a competing unit. Information so gained is not used to gain competitive advantage.

2.6 *Providers of I/O psychological services who purchase the services of another psychologist provide a clear statement of the role of the purchaser.*

INTERPRETATION When an I/O psychological service unit purchases the services of another such unit, the purchasing unit states in advance whether it perceives its

30

role as that of a collaborator, a technical advisor, a scientific monitor, or an informed layperson. The purchaser clearly defines its anticipated role, specifies the extent to which it wishes to be involved in various aspects of program planning and work definition, and describes how differences of opinion on technical and scientific matters are to be resolved. Members of the staff of both the unit purchasing services and the unit providing services are made fully aware of the various role definitions. Deferring all major project decisions to the purchaser is not necessarily considered appropriate in scientific development.

2.7 *Providers of I/O psychological services establish a system to protect confidentiality of their records.*

INTERPRETATION: I/O psychologists are responsible for maintaining the confidentiality of information about users of services, whether obtained by themselves or by those they supervise. All persons supervised by I/O psychologists, including nonprofessional personnel and students, who have access to records of psychological services are required to maintain this confidentiality as a condition of employment.

The I/O psychologist does not release confidential information, except with the written consent of the user directly involved or the user's legal representative. Even after the consent for release has been obtained, the I/O psychologist clearly identifies such information as confidential to the recipient of the information. If directed otherwise by statute or regulations with the force of law or by court order, the psychologist seeks a resolution to the conflict that is both ethically and legally feasible and appropriate.

Users are informed in advance of any limits in the setting for maintenance of confidentiality of psychological information.

When the user intends to waive confidentiality, the psychologist discusses the implications of releasing psychological information and assists the user in limiting disclosure only to information required by the present circumstances.

Raw psychological data (e.g., test protocols, interview notes, or questionnaire returns) in which a user is identified are released only with the written consent of the user or the user's legal representative and released only to a person recognized by the I/O psychologist as qualified and competent to use the data. (Note: The user may be an individual receiving career counseling, in which case individual confidentiality must be maintained, or the user may be an organization, in which case individual data may be shared with others within the organization. When individual information is to be shared with others, e.g., managers, the individual supplying the information is made aware of how this information is to be used.)

Any use made of psychological reports, records, or data for research or training purposes is consistent with this Guideline. Additionally, providers of I/O psychological services comply with statutory confidentiality requirements and those embodied in the American Psychological Association's *Ethical Principles of Psychologists* (APA, 1981).

Providers of I/O psychological services remain sensitive to both the benefits and the possible misuse of information regarding individuals that is stored in computerized data banks. Providers use their influence to ensure that such information is used in a socially responsible manner.

Guideline 3
ACCOUNTABILITY

Evaluating I/O Psychological Services

3.1 *The professional activities of providers of I/O psychological services are guided primarily by the principle of promoting human welfare.*

INTERPRETATION: I/O psychologists do not withhold services to a potential client on the basis of race, color, religion, sex, age, handicap, or national origin. Recognition is given, however, to the following considerations: the professional right of I/O psychologists to limit their practice to avoid potential conflict of interest (e.g., as between union and management, plaintiff and defendant, or business competitors); the right and responsibility of psychologists to withhold a procedure when it is not validly applicable; the right and responsibility of I/O psychologists to withhold evaluative, diagnostic, or change procedures or other services where they might be ineffective or detrimental to the achievement of goals and fulfillment of needs of individuals or organizations.

I/O psychologists who find that psychological services are being provided in a manner that is discriminatory or exploitative to users and/or contrary to these Guidelines or to state or federal statutes take appropriate corrective action, which may include the refusal to provide services. When conflicts of interest arise, the I/O psychologist is guided in the resolution of differences by the principles set forth by the American Psychological Association in the *Ethical Principles of Psychologists* (APA, 1981) and the "Guidelines for Conditions of Employment of Psychologists" (APA, 1972).

3.2 *There are periodic, systematic, and effective evaluations of psychological services.*

INTERPRETATION: Regular assessment of progress in achieving goals and meeting needs is provided in all I/O psychological service units. Such assessment includes both the validation of psychological services designed to predict outcomes and the evaluation of psychological services designed to induce organizational or individual change. This evaluation includes consideration of the effectiveness of I/O psychological services relative to

31

costs in terms of use of time and money and the availability of professional and support personnel

Evaluation of the efficiency and effectiveness of the I/O psychological service delivery system is conducted internally and, when possible, under independent auspices as well.

It is clearly explained to the user that evaluation of services is a necessary part of providing I/O psychological services and that the cost of such evaluation is justified as part of the cost of services.

FOOTNOTES

[1] See *Ethical Principles of Psychologists* (APA, 1981).

[2] See *Principles for the Validation and Use of Personnel Selection Procedures* (APA Division of Industrial and Organizational Psychology, 1980).

[3] The following two categories of persons who met the criteria indicated below on or before the adoption of these Specialty Guidelines on January 31, 1980, shall also be considered professional I/O psychologists: Category 1—persons who on or before September 4, 1974, (a) completed a master's degree from a program primarily psychological in content at a regionally accredited university, (b) completed 5 post-master's years of appropriate education, training, and experience in providing I/O psychological services as defined herein in the Definitions section, including a minimum of 2 years in an organizational setting, and (c) received a license or certificate in the state in which they practiced, conferred by a state board of psychological examiners. Category 2—persons who completed (a) a doctoral degree from a program primarily psychological in content at a regionally accredited university and (b) 3 postdoctoral years of appropriate education, training, and experience in providing I/O services as defined herein in the Definitions section, including a minimum of 1 year in an organizational setting.

REFERENCES

American Psychological Association. Guidelines for conditions of employment of psychologists. *American Psychologist*, 1972, *27*, 331–334.

American Psychological Association. *Standards for educational and psychological tests*. Washington, D.C.: Author, 1974. (a)

American Psychological Association. *Standards for providers of psychological services*. Washington, D.C.: Author, 1974. (b)

American Psychological Association. *Standards for providers of psychological services* (Rev. ed.). Washington, D.C.: Author, 1977.

American Psychological Association, Division of Industrial and Organizational Psychology. *Principles for the validation and use of personnel selection procedures* (2nd ed.). Berkeley, Calif.: Author, 1980. (Copies may be ordered from Lewis E. Albright, Kaiser Aluminum & Chemical Corporation, 300 Lakeside Drive—Room KB 2140, Oakland, California 94643.)

American Psychological Association. *Ethical principles of psychologists* (Rev. ed.). Washington, D.C.: Author, 1981.

Specialty Guidelines for the Delivery of Services by School Psychologists

The Specialty Guidelines that follow are based on the generic *Standards for Providers of Psychological Services* originally adopted by the American Psychological Association (APA) in September 1974 and revised in January 1977 (APA, 1974b, 1977b). Together with the generic *Standards*, these Specialty Guidelines state the official policy of the Association regarding delivery of services by school psychologists. Admission to the practice of psychology is regulated by state statute. It is the position of the Association that licensing be based on generic, and not on specialty, qualifications. Specialty guidelines serve the additional purpose of providing potential users and other interested groups with essential information about particular services available from the several specialties in professional psychology.

Professional psychology specialties have evolved from generic practice in psychology and are supported by university training programs. There are now at least four recognized professional specialties—clinical, counseling, school, and industrial/organizational psychology.

The knowledge base in each of these specialty areas has increased, refining the state of the art to the point that a set of uniform specialty guidelines is now possible and desirable. The present Guidelines are intended to educate the public, the profession, and other interested parties regarding specialty professional practices. They are also intended to facilitate the continued systematic development of the profession.

The content of each Specialty Guideline reflects a consensus of university faculty and public and private practitioners regarding the knowledge base, services provided, problems addressed, and clients served.

Traditionally, all learned disciplines have treated the designation of specialty practice as a reflection of preparation in greater depth in a particular subject matter, together with a voluntary limiting of focus to a more restricted area of practice by the professional. Lack of specialty designation does not preclude general providers of psychological services from using the methods or dealing with the populations of any specialty, except insofar as psychologists voluntarily refrain from providing services they are not trained to render. It is the intent of these Guidelines, however, that after the grandparenting period, psychologists not put themselves forward as *specialists* in a given area of practice unless they meet the qualifications noted in the Guidelines (see Definitions). Therefore, these Guidelines are meant to apply only to those psychologists who wish to be designated as *school psychologists*. They do not apply to other psychologists.

These Guidelines represent the profession's best judgment of the conditions, credentials, and experience that contribute to competent professional practice. The APA strongly encourages, and plans to participate in, efforts to identify professional practitioner behaviors and job functions and to validate the relation between these and desired client outcomes. Thus, future revisions of these Guidelines will increasingly reflect the results of such efforts.

These Guidelines follow the format and, wherever applicable, the wording of the generic *Standards*.[1] (Note: Footnotes appear at the end of the Specialty Guidelines. See pp. 679–681.) The intent of these Guidelines is to improve the quality, effectiveness, and accessibility of psychological services. They are meant to provide guidance to providers, users, and sanctioners regarding the best judgment of the profession on these matters. Although the Specialty Guidelines have been derived from and are consistent with the generic *Standards*, they may be used as a separate document. *Standards for Providers of Psychological Services* (APA, 1977b), however, shall remain the basic policy statement and shall take precedence where there are questions of interpretation.

Professional psychology in general and school psychology in particular have had a long and difficult history of attempts to establish criteria for determining guidelines for the delivery of services. In school psychology, state departments of education have traditionally had a strong influence on the content of programs required for certification and on minimum competency levels for practice, leading to wide variations in requirements among the many states. These national Guidelines will reduce confusion, clarify important dimensions of specialty practice, and provide a common basis for peer review of school psychologists' performance.

The Committee on Professional Standards established by the APA in January 1980 is charged with keeping the generic *Standards* and the Specialty Guidelines respon-

---

These Specialty Guidelines were prepared through the cooperative efforts of the APA Committee on Standards for Providers of Psychological Services (COSPOPS) and the APA Professional Affairs Committee of the Division of School Psychology (Division 16) Jack I. Bardon and Nadine M. Lambert served as the school psychology representatives of COSPOPS, and Arthur Centor and Richard Kilburg were the Central Office liaisons to the committee. Durand F. Jacobs served as chair of COSPOPS, and Walter B. Pryzwansky chaired the Division 16 committee. Drafts of the school psychology Guidelines were reviewed and commented on by members of the Executive Committee of Division 16, representatives of the National Association of School Psychologists, state departments of education, consultants in school psychology, and many professional school psychologists in training programs and in practice in the schools

sive to the needs of the public and the profession. It is also charged with continually reviewing, modifying, and extending them progressively as the profession and the science of psychology develop new knowledge, improved methods, and additional modes of psychological services.

The Specialty Guidelines for the Delivery of Services by School Psychologists have been established by the APA as a means of self-regulation to protect the public interest. They guide the specialty practice of school psychology by specifying important areas of quality assurance and performance that contribute to the goal of facilitating more effective human functioning.

Principles and Implications of the Specialty Guidelines

These Specialty Guidelines have emerged from and reaffirm the same basic principles that guided the development of the generic *Standards for Providers of Psychological Services* (APA, 1977b):

1. These Guidelines recognize that admission to the practice of school psychology is regulated by state statute.

2. It is the intention of the APA that the generic *Standards* provide appropriate guidelines for statutory licensing of psychologists. In addition, although it is the position of the APA that licensing be generic and not in specialty areas, these Specialty Guidelines in school psychology should provide an authoritative reference for use in credentialing specialty providers of school psychological services by such groups as divisions of the APA and state associations and by boards and agencies that find such criteria useful for quality assurance.

3. A uniform set of Specialty Guidelines governs school psychological service functions offered by school psychologists, regardless of setting or source of remuneration. All school psychologists in professional practice recognize and are responsive to a uniform set of Specialty Guidelines, just as they are guided by a common code of ethics.

4. School psychology Guidelines establish clearly articulated levels of training and experience that are consistent with, and appropriate to, the functions performed. School psychological services provided by persons who do not meet the APA qualifications for a professional school psychologist (see Definitions) are to be supervised by a professional school psychologist. Final responsibility and accountability for services provided rest with professional school psychologists.

5. A uniform set of Specialty Guidelines governs the quality of services to all users of school psychological services in both the private and the public sectors. Those receiving school psychological services are protected by the same kinds of safeguards, irrespective of sector; these include constitutional guarantees, statutory regulation, peer review, consultation, record review, and staff supervision.

6. These Guidelines, while assuring the user of the school psychologist's accountability for the nature and quality of services specified in this document, do not preclude the school psychologist from using new methods or developing innovative procedures for the delivery of school psychological services.

These Specialty Guidelines for school psychology have broad implications both for users of school psychological services and for providers of such services:

1. Guidelines for school psychological services provide a foundation for mutual understanding between provider and user and facilitate more effective evaluation of services provided and outcomes achieved.

2. Guidelines for school psychological services are essential for uniformity of regulation by state departments of education and other regulatory or legislative agencies concerned with the provision of school psychological services. In addition, they provide the basis for state approval of training programs and for the development of accreditation procedures for schools and other facilities providing school psychological services.

3. Guidelines give specific content to the profession's concept of ethical practice as it applies to the functions of school psychologists.

4. Guidelines for school psychological services have significant impact on tomorrow's education and training models for both professional and support personnel in school psychology.

5. Guidelines for the provision of school psychological services influence the determination of acceptable structure, budgeting, and staffing patterns in schools and other facilities using these services.

6. Guidelines for school psychological services require continual review and revision.

The Specialty Guidelines presented here are intended to improve the quality and the delivery of school psychological services by specifying criteria for key aspects of the service setting. Some school settings may require additional and/or more stringent criteria for specific areas of service delivery.

Systematically applied, these Guidelines serve to establish a more effective and consistent basis for evaluating the performance of individual service providers as well as to guide the organization of school psychological service units.

Definitions

Providers of school psychological services refers to two categories of persons who provide school psychological services:

A. Professional school psychologists.[2,3] Professional school psychologists have a doctoral degree from a regionally accredited university or professional school providing an organized, sequential school psychology program in a department of psychology in a university or college, in an appropriate department of a school of education or other similar administrative organization, or in a unit of a professional school. School psychology programs that are accredited by the American Psychological Association are recognized as meeting the definition of a school psychology program. School psychology programs that are not accredited by the American Psychological Association meet the definition of a school psychology program if they satisfy the following criteria:

1. The program is primarily psychological in nature and stands as a recognizable, coherent organizational entity within the institution.

2. The program provides an integrated, organized sequence of study.

3. The program has an identifiable body of students who are matriculated in that program for a degree.

4. There is a clear authority with primary responsibility for the core and specialty areas, whether or not the program cuts across administrative lines.

5. There is an identifiable psychology faculty, and a psychologist is responsible for the program.

Patterns of education and training in school psychology[4] are consistent with the functions to be performed and the services to be provided, in accordance with the ages, populations, and problems found in the various schools and other settings in which school psychologists are employed. The program of study includes a core of academic experience, both didactic and experiential, in basic areas of psychology, includes education related to the practice of the specialty, and provides training in assessment, intervention, consultation, research, program development, and supervision, with special emphasis on school-related problems or school settings.[5]

Professional school psychologists who wish to represent themselves as proficient in specific applications of school psychology that are not already part of their training are required to have further academic training and supervised experience in those areas of practice.

B. All other persons who offer school psychological services under the supervision of a school psychologist. Although there may be variations in the titles and job descriptions of such persons, they are not called school psychologists. Their functions may be indicated by use of the adjective *psychological* preceding the noun.

1. A *specialist in school psychology* has successfully completed at least 2 years of graduate education in school psychology and a training program that includes at least 1,000 hours of experience supervised by a professional school psychologist, of which at least 500 hours must be in school settings. A specialist in school psychology provides psychological services under the supervision of a professional school psychologist.[6]

2. Titles for others who provide school psychological services under the supervision of a professional school psychologist may include *school psychological examiner, school psychological technician, school psychological assistant, school psychometrist,* or *school psychometric assistant.*

School psychological services refers to one or more of the following services offered to clients involved in educational settings, from preschool through higher edu-

cation, for the protection and promotion of mental health and the facilitation of learning:[7]

A. Psychological and psychoeducational evaluation and assessment of the school functioning of children and young persons. Procedures include screening, psychological and educational tests (particularly individual psychological tests of intellectual functioning, cognitive development, affective behavior, and neuropsychological status), interviews, observation, and behavioral evaluations, with explicit regard for the context and setting in which the professional judgments based on assessment, diagnosis, and evaluation will be used.

B. Interventions to facilitate the functioning of individuals or groups, with concern for how schooling influences and is influenced by their cognitive, conative, affective, and social development. Such interventions may include, but are not limited to, recommending, planning, and evaluating special education services; psychoeducational therapy; counseling; affective educational programs; and training programs to improve coping skills.[8]

C. Interventions to facilitate the educational services and child care functions of school personnel, parents, and community agencies. Such interventions may include, but are not limited to, in-service school-personnel education programs, parent education programs, and parent counseling.

D. Consultation and collaboration with school personnel and/or parents concerning specific school-related problems of students and the professional problems of staff. Such services may include, but are not limited to, assistance with the planning of educational programs from a psychological perspective; consultation with teachers and other school personnel to enhance their understanding of the needs of particular pupils; modification of classroom instructional programs to facilitate children's learning; promotion of a positive climate for learning and teaching; assistance to parents to enable them to contribute to their children's development and school adjustment; and other staff development activities.

E. Program development services to individual schools, to school administrative systems, and to community agencies in such areas as needs assessment and evaluation of regular and special education programs; liaison with community, state, and federal agencies concerning the mental health and educational needs of children; coordination, administration, and planning of specialized educational programs; the generation, collection, organization, and dissemination of information from psychological research and theory to educate staff and parents.

F. Supervision of school psychological services (see Guideline 1.2, Interpretation).

A *school psychological service unit* is the functional unit through which school psychological services are provided; any such unit has at least one professional school psychologist associated with it:

A. Such a unit provides school psychological services to individuals, a school system, a district, a community agency, or a corporation, or to a consortium of school systems, districts, community agencies, or corporations that contract together to employ providers of school psychological services. A school psychological service unit is composed of one or more professional school psychologists and, in most instances, supporting psychological services staff.

B. A school psychological service unit may operate as an independent professional service to schools or as a functional component of an administrative organizational unit, such as a state department of education, a public or private school system, or a community mental health agency.

C. One or more professional school psychologists providing school psychological services in an interdisciplinary or a multidisciplinary setting constitute a school psychological service unit.

D. A school psychological service unit may also be one or more professional psychologists offering services in private practice, in a school psychological consulting firm, or in a college- or university-based facility or program that contracts to offer school psychological services to individuals, groups, school systems, districts, or corporations.

Users of school psychological services include:

A. Direct users or recipients of school psychological services, such as pupils, instructional and administrative school staff members, and parents.

B. Public and private institutions, facilities, or organizations receiving school psychological services, such as boards of education of public or private schools, mental health facilities, and other community agencies and educational institutions for handicapped or exceptional children.

C. Third-party purchasers—those who pay for the delivery of services but who are not the recipients of services.

D. Sanctioners—such as those who have a legitimate concern with the accessibility, timeliness, efficacy, and standards of quality attending the provision of school psychological services. Sanctioners may include members of the user's family, the court, the probation officer, the school administrator, the employer, the facility director, and so on. Sanctioners may also include various governmental, peer review, and accreditation bodies concerned with the assurance of quality.

Guideline 1
PROVIDERS

1.1 *Each school psychological service unit offering school psychological services has available at least one professional school psychologist and as many additional professional school psychologists and support personnel as are necessary to assure the adequacy and quality of services offered.*

INTERPRETATION The intent of this Guideline is that one or more providers of psychological services in any school psychological service unit meet the levels of training and experience of the professional school psychologist specified in the preceding definitions.

When a professional school psychologist is not available on a full-time basis to provide school psychological services, the school district obtains the services of a professional school psychologist on a regular part-time basis. Yearly contracts are desirable to ensure continuity of services during a school year. The school psychologist so retained directs the psychological services, supervises the psychological services provided by support personnel, and participates sufficiently to be able to assess the need for services, review the content of services provided, and assume professional responsibility and accountability for them. A professional school psychologist supervises no more than the equivalent of 15 full-time specialists in school psychology and/or other school psychological personnel.

Districts that do not have easy access to professional school psychologists because of geographic considerations, or because professional school psychologists do not live or work in the area employ at least one full-time specialist in school psychology and as many more support personnel as are necessary to assure the adequacy and quality of services. The following strategies may be considered to acquire the necessary supervisory services from a professional school psychologist:

A. Employment by a county, region, consortium of schools, or state department of education of full-time supervisory personnel in school psychology who meet appropriate levels of training and experience, as specified in the definitions, to visit school districts regularly for supervision of psychological services staff.

B. Employment of professional school psychologists who engage in independent practice for the purpose of providing supervision to school district psychological services staff.

C. Arrangements with nearby school districts that employ professional school psychologists for part-time employment of such personnel on a contract basis specifically for the purpose of supervision as described in Guideline 1.

The school psychologist directing the school psychological service unit, whether on a full- or part-time basis, is responsible for determining and justifying appropriate ratios of school psychologists to users, to specialists in school psychology, and to support personnel, in order to ensure proper scope, accessibility, and quality of services provided in that setting. The school psychologist reports to the appropriate school district representatives any findings regarding the need to modify psychological services or staffing patterns to assure the adequacy and quality of services offered.

1.2 *Providers of school psychological services who do not meet the requirements for the professional school psychologist are supervised directly by a professional school psychologist who assumes professional responsibility and accountability for the services provided. The level and extent of supervision may vary from task to task so long as the supervising psychologist retains a sufficiently close supervisory relationship to meet this Guideline. Special proficiency training or supervision may be provided by a professional psychologist of another specialty or by a professional from another discipline whose competency in the given area has been demonstrated.*"

INTERPRETATION: Professional responsibility and accountability for the services provided require that the supervisor review reports and test protocols; review and discuss intervention strategies, plans, and outcomes; maintain a comprehensive view of the school's procedures and special concerns; and have sufficient opportunity to discuss discrepancies among the views of the supervisor, the supervised, and other school personnel on any problem or issue. In order to meet this Guideline, an appropriate number of hours per week are devoted to direct face-to-face supervision of each full-time school psychological service staff member. In no event is this supervision less than one hour per week for each staff member. The more comprehensive the psychological services are, the more supervision is needed. A plan or formula for relating increasing amounts of supervisory time to the complexity of professional responsibilities is to be developed. The amount and nature of supervision is specified in writing to all parties concerned.

1.3 Wherever a school psychological service unit exists, a professional school psychologist is responsible for planning, directing, and reviewing the provision of school psychological services.

INTERPRETATION: A school psychologist coordinates the activities of the school psychological service unit with other professionals, administrators, and community groups, both within and outside the school. This school psychologist, who may be the director, coordinator, or supervisor of the school psychological service unit, has related responsibilities including, but not limited to, recruiting qualified staff, directing training and research activities of the service, maintaining a high level of professional and ethical practice, and ensuring that staff members function only within the areas of their competency.

To facilitate the effectiveness of services by raising the level of staff sensitivity and professional skills, the psychologist designated as director is responsible for participating in the selection of staff and support personnel whose qualifications are directly relevant to the needs and characteristics of the users served.

In the event that a professional school psychologist is employed by the school psychological service unit on a basis that affords him or her insufficient time to carry out full responsibility for coordinating or directing the unit, a specialist in school psychology is designated as

director or coordinator of the school psychological services and is supervised by a professional school psychologist employed on a part-time basis, for a minimum of 2 hours per week.

1.4 When functioning as part of an organizational setting, professional school psychologists bring their backgrounds and skills to bear on the goals of the organization, whenever appropriate, by participating in the planning and development of overall services.

INTERPRETATION: Professional school psychologists participate in the maintenance of high professional standards by serving as representatives on, or consultants to, committees and boards concerned with service delivery, especially when such committees deal with special education, pupil personnel services, mental health aspects of schooling, or other services that use or involve school psychological knowledge and skills.

As appropriate to the setting, school psychologists' activities may include active participation, as voting and as office-holding members, on the facility's executive, planning, and evaluation boards and committees.

1.5 School psychologists maintain current knowledge of scientific and professional developments to preserve and enhance their professional competence.

INTERPRETATION: Methods through which knowledge of scientific and professional developments may be gained include, but are not limited to, (a) the reading or preparation of scientific and professional publications and other materials, (b) attendance at workshops and presentations at meetings and conventions, (c) participation in on-the-job staff development programs, and (d) other forms of continuing education. The school psychologist and staff have available reference material and journals related to the provision of school psychological services. School psychologists are prepared to show evidence periodically that they are staying abreast of current knowledge in the field of school psychology and are also keeping their certification and licensing credentials up-to-date.

1.6 School psychologists limit their practice to their demonstrated areas of professional competence.

INTERPRETATION: School psychological services are offered in accordance with the providers' areas of competence as defined by verifiable training and experience. When extending services beyond the range of their usual practice, school psychologists obtain pertinent training or appropriate professional supervision. Such training or supervision is consistent with the extension of functions performed and services provided. An extension of services may involve a change in the theoretical orientation of the practitioner, in the techniques used, in the client age group (e.g., children, adolescents, or parents), or in the kinds of problems addressed (e.g., mental retardation, neurological impairment. learning disabilities. family relationships).

1.7 *Psychologists who wish to qualify as school psychologists meet the same requirements with respect to subject matter and professional skills that apply to doctoral training in school psychology.*[10]

INTERPRETATION: Education of psychologists to qualify them for specialty practice in school psychology is under the auspices of a department in a regionally accredited university or of a professional school that offers the doctoral degree in school psychology, through campus- and/or field-based arrangements. Such education .. ..individualized, with due credit being given for relevant course work and other requirements that have previously been satisfied. In addition to the doctoral-level education specified above. appropriate doctoral-level training is required. An internship or experience in a school setting is not adequate preparation for becoming a school psychologist when prior education has not been in that area. Fulfillment of such an individualized training program is attested to by the awarding of a certificate by the supervising department or professional school that indicates the successful completion of preparation in school psychology.

1.8 *Professional school psychologists are encouraged to develop innovative theories and procedures and to provide appropriate theoretical and/or empirical support for their innovations.*

INTERPRETATION: A specialty of a profession rooted in science intends continually to explore, study, and conduct research with a view to developing and verifying new and improved methods of serving the school population in ways that can be documented.

Guideline 2
PROGRAMS

2.1 *Composition and organization of a school psychological service unit:*

2.1.1 *The composition and programs of a school psychological service unit are responsive to the needs of the school population that is served.*

INTERPRETATION: A school psychological service unit is structured so as to facilitate effective and economical delivery of services. For example, a school psychological service unit serving predominantly low-income, ethnic, or racial minority children has a staffing pattern and service programs that are adapted to the linguistic, experiential, and attitudinal characteristics of the users. Appropriate types of assessment materials and norm ref-

erence groups are utilized in the practice of school psychology.

2.1.2 *A description of the organization of the school psychological service unit and its lines of responsibility and accountability for the delivery of school psychological services is available in written form to instructional and administrative staff of the unit and to parents, students, and members of the community.*

INTERPRETATION: The description includes lines of responsibility, supervisory relationships. and the level and extent of accountability for each person who provides school psychological services.

2.1.3 *A school psychological service unit includes sufficient numbers of professional and support personnel to achieve its goals, objectives, and purposes.*

INTERPRETATION: A school psychological service unit includes one or more professional school psychologists, specialists in school psychology, and other psychological services support personnel. When a professional school psychologist is not available to provide services on a full- or part-time basis, the school psychological services are conducted by a specialist in school psychology, supervised by a professional school psychologist (see Guideline 1.2).

The work load and diversity of school psychological services required and the specific goals and objectives of the setting determine the numbers and qualifications of professional and support personnel in the school psychological service unit. For example, the extent to which services involve case study, direct intervention, and/or consultation will be significant in any service plan. Case study frequently involves teacher and/or parent conferences, observations of pupils, and a multi-assessment review, including student interviews. Similarly, the target populations for services affect the range of services that can be offered. One school psychologist, or one specialist in school psychology under supervision, for every 2,000 pupils is considered appropriate.[11]

Where shortages in personnel exist, so that school psychological services cannot be rendered in a professional manner, the director of the school psychological service unit informs the supervisor/administrator of the service about the implications of the shortage and initiates action to remedy the situation. When this fails, the director appropriately modifies the scope or work load of the unit to maintain the quality of services rendered.

2.2 *Policies:*

2.2.1 *When the school psychological service unit is composed of more than one person or is a component of a larger organization, a written statement of its objectives and scope of services is developed, maintained, and reviewed.*

INTERPRETATION: The school psychological service unit reviews its objectives and scope of services annually and revises them as necessary to ensure that the school psychological services offered are consistent with staff competencies and current psychological knowledge and practice. This statement is discussed with staff, reviewed by the appropriate administrators, distributed to instructional and administrative staff and school board members, and when appropriate, made available to parents, students, and members of the community upon request.

2.2.2 *All providers within a school psychological service unit support the legal and civil rights of the users.*[12]

INTERPRETATION: Providers of school psychological services safeguard the interests of school personnel, students, and parents with regard to personal, legal, and civil rights. They are continually sensitive to the issue of confidentiality of information, the short-term and long-term impacts of their decisions and recommendations, and other matters pertaining to individual, legal, and civil rights. Concerns regarding the safeguarding of individual rights of school personnel, students, and parents include, but are not limited to, due-process rights of parents and children, problems of self-incrimination in judicial proceedings, involuntary commitment to hospitals, child abuse, freedom of choice, protection of minors or legal incompetents, discriminatory practices in identification and placement, recommendations for special education provisions, and adjudication of domestic relations disputes in divorce and custodial proceedings. Providers of school psychological services take affirmative action by making themselves available to local committees, review boards, and similar advisory groups established to safeguard the human, civil, and legal rights of children and parents.

2.2.3 *All providers within a school psychological service unit are familiar with and adhere to the American Psychological Association's Standards for Providers of Psychological Services, Ethical Principles of Psychologists, Standards for Educational and Psychological Tests, Ethical Principles in the Conduct of Research With Human Participants, and other official policy statements relevant to standards for professional services issued by the Association.*

INTERPRETATION: A copy of each of these documents is maintained by providers of school psychological services and is available upon request to all school personnel and officials, parents, members of the community, and where applicable, students and other sanctioners.

2.2.4 *All providers within a school psychological service unit conform to relevant statutes established by federal, state, and local governments.*

INTERPRETATION: All providers of school psychological services are familiar with and conform to appropriate statutes regulating the practice of psychology. They also are informed about state department of education requirements and other agency regulations that have the force of law and that relate to the delivery of school psychological services (e.g., certification of, eligibility for, and placement in, special education programs). In addition, all providers are cognizant that federal agencies such as the Department of Education and the Department of Health and Human Services have policy statements regarding psychological services. Providers of school psychological services are familiar as well with other statutes and regulations, including those addressed to the civil and legal rights of users (e.g., Public Law 94-142, The Education for All Handicapped Children Act of 1975), that are pertinent to their scope of practice.

It is the responsibility of the American Psychological Association to maintain files of those federal policies, statutes, and regulations relating to this section and to assist its members in obtaining them. The state psychological associations, school psychological associations, and state licensing boards periodically publish and distribute appropriate state statutes and regulations.

2.2.5 *All providers within a school psychological service unit inform themselves about and use the network of human services in their communities in order to link users with relevant services and resources.*

INTERPRETATION School psychologists and support staff are sensitive to the broader context of human needs. In recognizing the matrix of personal and societal problems, providers make available to clients information regarding human services such as legal aid societies, social services, health resources like mental health centers, private practitioners, and educational and recreational facilities. School psychological staff formulate and maintain a file of such resources for reference. The specific information provided is such that users can easily make contact with the services and freedom of choice can be honored. Providers of school psychological services refer to such community resources and, when indicated, actively intervene on behalf of the users. School psychologists seek opportunities to serve on boards of community agencies in order to represent the needs of the school population in the community.

2.2.6 *In the delivery of school psychological services, providers maintain a cooperative relationship with colleagues and co-workers in the best interest of the users.*

INTERPRETATION: School psychologists recognize the areas of special competence of other psychologists and of other professionals in the school and in the community for either consultation or referral purposes (e.g., school social workers, speech therapists, remedial reading teachers, special education teachers, pediatricians, neurologists, and public health nurses). Providers of school psychological services make appropriate use of other professional, research, technical, and administrative resources whenever these serve the best interests of the school staff, children, and parents and establish and maintain cooperative and/or collaborative arrangements with such other resources as required to meet the needs of users.

2.3 Procedures:

2.3.1 A school psychological service unit follows a set of procedural guidelines for the delivery of school psychological services.

INTERPRETATION: The school psychological service staff is prepared to provide a statement of procedural guidelines in written form in terms that can be understood by school staff, parents, school board members, interested members of the community, and when appropriate, students and other sanctioners. The statement describes the current methods, forms, case study and assessment procedures, estimated time lines, interventions, and evaluation techniques being used to achieve the objectives and goals for school psychological services.

This statement is communicated to school staff and personnel, school board members, parents, and when appropriate, students or other sanctioners through whatever means are feasible, including in-service activities, conferences, oral presentations, and dissemination of written materials.

The school psychological service unit provides for the annual review of its procedures for the delivery of school psychological services.

2.3.2 Providers of school psychological services develop plans appropriate to the providers' professional practices and to the problems presented by the users. There is a mutually acceptable understanding between providers and school staff, parents, and students or responsible agents regarding the goals and the delivery of services.

INTERPRETATION: The school psychological service unit notifies the school unit in writing of the plan that is adopted for use and resolves any points of difference. The plan includes written consent of guardians of students and, when appropriate, consent of students for the services provided. Similarly, the nature of the assessment tools that are to be used and the reasons for their inclusion are spelled out. The objectives of intervention(s) of a psychological nature as well as the procedures for implementing the intervention(s) are specified. An estimate of time is noted where appropriate. Parents and/or students are made aware of the various decisions that can be made as a result of the service(s), participate in accounting for decisions that are made, and are informed of how appeals may be instituted.

2.3.3 Accurate, current, and pertinent documentation of essential school psychological services provided is maintained.

INTERPRETATION: Records kept of psychological services may include, but are not limited to, identifying data, dates of services, names of providers of services, types of services, and significant actions taken. These records

are maintained separately from the child's cumulative record folder. Once a case study is completed and/or an intervention begun, records are reviewed and updated at least monthly.

2.3.4 Each school psychological services unit follows an established record retention and disposition policy.

INTERPRETATION: The policy on maintenance and review of psychological records (including the length of time that records not already part of school records are to be kept) is developed by the local school psychological service unit. This policy is consistent with existing federal and state statutes and regulations.

2.3.5 Providers of school psychological services maintain a system to protect confidentiality of their records.

INTERPRETATION: School psychologists are responsible for maintaining the confidentiality of information about users of services, from whatever source derived. All persons supervised by school psychologists, including nonprofessional personnel and students, who have access to records of psychological services maintain this confidentiality as a condition of employment. All appropriate staff receive training regarding the confidentiality of records.

Users are informed in advance of any limits for maintenance of confidentiality of psychological information. Procedures for obtaining informed consent are developed by the school psychological service unit. Written informed consent is obtained to conduct assessment or to carry out psychological intervention services. Informing users of the manner in which requests for information will be handled and of the school personnel who will share the results is part of the process of obtaining consent.

The school psychologist conforms to current laws and regulations with respect to the release of confidential information. As a general rule, however, the school psychologist does not release confidential information, except with the written consent of the parent or, where appropriate, the student directly involved or his or her legal representative. Even after consent for release has been obtained, the school psychologist clearly identifies such information as confidential to the recipient of the information. When there is a conflict with a statute, with regulations with the force of law, or with a court order, the school psychologist seeks a resolution to the conflict that is both ethically and legally feasible and appropriate.

Providers of school psychological services ensure that psychological reports which will become part of the school records are reviewed carefully so that confidentiality of pupils and parents is protected. When the guardian or student intends to waive confidentiality, the school psychologist discusses the implications of releasing psychological information and assists the user in limiting disclosure to only that information required by the present circumstance.

Raw psychological data (e.g., test protocols, counseling or interview notes, or questionnaires) in which a user is identified are released only with the written consent of the user or his or her legal representative, or by court order when such material is not covered by legal confidentiality, and are released only to a person recognized by the school psychologist as competent to use the data.

Any use made of psychological reports, records, or data for research or training purposes is consistent with this Guideline. Additionally, providers of school psychological services comply with statutory confidentiality requirements and those embodied in the American Psychological Association's *Ethical Principles of Psychologists* (APA, 1981).

Providers of school psychological services remain sensitive to both the benefits and the possible misuse of information regarding individuals that is stored in large computerized data banks. Providers use their influence to ensure that such information is managed in a socially responsible manner.

Guideline 3
ACCOUNTABILITY

3.1 *The promotion of human welfare is the primary principle guiding the professional activity of the school psychologist and the school psychological service unit.*

INTERPRETATION: School psychological services staff provide services to school staff members, students, and parents in a manner that is considerate and effective.

School psychologists make their services readily accessible to users in a manner that facilitates the users' freedom of choice. Parents, students, and other users are made aware that psychological services may be available through other public or private sources, and relevant information for exercising such options is provided upon request.

School psychologists are mindful of their accountability to the administration, to the school board, and to the general public, provided that appropriate steps are taken to protect the confidentiality of the service relationship. In the pursuit of their professional activities, they aid in the conservation of human, material, and financial resources.

The school psychological service unit does not withhold services to children or parents on the basis of the users' race, color, religion, gender, sexual orientation, age, or national origin. Recognition is given, however, to the following considerations: (a) the professional right of school psychologists, at the time of their employment, to state that they wish to limit their services to a specific category of users (e.g., elementary school children, exceptional children, adolescents), noting their reasons so

that employers can make decisions regarding their employment, assignment of their duties, and so on; (b) the right and responsibility of school psychologists to withhold an assessment procedure when not validly applicable; (c) the right and responsibility of school psychologists to withhold evaluative, psychotherapeutic, counseling, or other services in specific instances in which their own limitations or client characteristics might impair the effectiveness of the relationship; and (d) the obligation of school psychologists to seek to ameliorate through peer review, consultation, or other personal therapeutic procedures those factors that inhibit the provision of services to particular users. In such instances, it is incumbent on school psychologists to advise clients about appropriate alternative services. When appropriate services are not available, school psychologists inform the school district administration and/or other sanctioners of the unmet needs of clients. In all instances, school psychologists make available information, and provide opportunity to participate in decisions, concerning such issues as initiation, termination, continuation, modification, and evaluation of psychological services. These Guidelines are also made available upon request.

Accurate and full information is made available to prospective individual or organizational users regarding the qualifications of providers, the nature and extent of services offered, and where appropriate, the financial costs as well as the benefits and possible risks of the proposed services.

Professional school psychologists offering services for a fee inform users of their payment policies, if applicable, and of their willingness to assist in obtaining reimbursement when such services have been contracted for as an external resource.

3.2 *School psychologists pursue their activities as members of the independent, autonomous profession of psychology.*[13]

INTERPRETATION: School psychologists are aware of the implications of their activities for the profession of psychology as a whole. They seek to eliminate discriminatory practices instituted for self-serving purposes that are not in the interest of the users (e.g., arbitrary requirements for referral and supervision by another profession) and to discourage misuse of psychological concepts and tools (e.g., use of psychological instruments for special education placement by school personnel or others who lack relevant and adequate education and training). School psychologists are cognizant of their responsibilities for the development of the profession and for the improvement of schools. They participate where possible in the training and career development of students and other providers; they participate as appropriate in the training of school administrators, teachers, and paraprofessionals; and they integrate, and supervise the implementation of, their contributions within the structure established for delivering school psychological services. Where appropriate, they facilitate the development of, and participate in, professional standards review mechanisms.

School psychologists seek to work with other professionals in a cooperative manner for the good of the users and the benefit of the general public. School psychologists associated with special education or mental health teams or with multidisciplinary settings support the principle that members of each participating profession have equal rights and opportunities to share all privileges and responsibilities of full membership in the educational or human service activities or facilities and to administer service programs in their respective areas of competence. (Refer also to Guideline 2.2.5, Interpretation.)

3.3 *There are periodic, systematic, and effective evaluations of school psychological services.*

INTERPRETATION: When the psychological service unit representing school psychology is a component of a larger organization (e.g., school system, county or state regional district, state department of education), regular evaluation of progress in achieving goals is provided for in the service delivery plan, including consideration of the effectiveness of school psychological services relative to costs in terms of use of time and money and the availability of professional and support personnel.

Evaluation of the school psychological service delivery system is conducted internally and, when possible, under independent auspices as well. This evaluation includes an assessment of effectiveness (to determine what the service unit accomplished), efficiency (to determine the costs of providing the services), continuity (to ensure that the services are appropriately linked to other educational services), availability (to determine the appropriateness of staffing ratios), accessibility (to ensure that the services are readily available to members of the school population), and adequacy (to determine whether the services meet the identified needs of the school population).

It is highly desirable that there be a periodic reexamination of review mechanisms to ensure that these attempts at public safeguards are effective and cost efficient and do not place unnecessary encumbrances on the providers or impose unnecessary expenses on users or sanctioners for services rendered.

3.4 *School psychologists are accountable for all aspects of the services they provide and are responsive to those concerned with these services.*

INTERPRETATION: In recognizing their responsibilities to users, sanctioners, and other providers, and where appropriate and consistent with the users' legal rights and privileged communications, school psychologists make available information about, and provide opportunity to participate in, decisions concerning such issues as initiation, termination, continuation, modification, and evaluation of school psychological services.

Guideline 4
ENVIRONMENT

4.1 *Providers of psychological services promote development in the school setting of a physical, organizational, and social environment that facilitates optimal human functioning.*

INTERPRETATION: Federal, state, and local requirements for safety, health, and sanitation are observed.

As providers of services, school psychologists are concerned with the environment of their service units, especially as it affects the quality of service, but also as it impinges on human functioning in the school. Attention is given to the privacy and comfort of school staff, students, and parents. Parent and staff interviews are conducted in a professional atmosphere, with the option for private conferences available. Students are seen under conditions that maximize their privacy and enhance the possibility for meaningful intervention; for example, they should have the opportunity to leave their classroom inconspicuously and should be free from interruptions when meeting with the psychologist. Physical arrangements and organizational policies and procedures are conducive to the human dignity, self-respect, and optimal functioning of school staff, students, and parents and to the effective delivery of service.

FOOTNOTES

[1] The footnotes appended to these Specialty Guidelines represent an attempt to provide a coherent context of earlier APA policy statements and other documents regarding professional practice. The Guidelines extend these previous policy statements where necessary to reflect current concerns of the public and the profession.

[2] There are three categories of individuals who do not meet the definition of *professional school psychologist* but who can be considered professional school psychologists if they meet certain criteria.

The following two categories of professional psychologists who met the criteria indicated below on or before the adoption of these Specialty Guidelines on January 31, 1980, are considered professional school psychologists: Category 1—those who completed (a) a doctoral degree program primarily psychological in content, but not in school psychology, at a regionally accredited university or professional school and (b) 3 postdoctoral years of appropriate education, training, and experience in providing school psychological services as defined herein, including a minimum of 1,200 hours in school settings; Category 2—those who on or before September 4, 1974, (a) completed a master's degree from a program primarily psychological in content at a regionally accredited university or professional school and (b) held a license or certificate in the state in which they practiced, conferred by a state board of psychological examiners, or the endorsement of a state psychological association through voluntary certification, and who, in addition, prior to January 31, 1980, (c) obtained 5 post-master's years of appropriate education, training, and experience in providing school psychological services as defined herein, including a minimum of 2,400 hours in school settings.

After January 31, 1980, professional psychologists who wish

to be recognized as professional school psychologists are referred to Guideline 1.7.

The APA Council of Representatives passed a "Resolution on the Master's-Level Issue" in January 1977 containing the following statement, which influenced the development of a third category of professional school psychologists:

The title "Professional Psychologist" has been used so widely and by persons with such a wide variety of training and experience that it does not provide the information the public deserves.

As a consequence, the APA takes the position and makes it a part of its policy that the use of the title "Professional Psychologist," and its variations such as "Clinical Psychologist," "Counseling Psychologist," "School Psychologist," and "Industrial Psychologist" are reserved for those who have completed a Doctoral Training Program in Psychology in a university, college, or professional school of psychology that is APA or regionally accredited. In order to meet this standard, a transition period will be acknowledged for the use of the title "School Psychologist," so that ways may be sought to increase opportunities for doctoral training and to improve the level of educational codes pertaining to the title. (Conger, 1977, p. 426)

For the purpose of transition, then, there is still another category of persons who can be considered professional school psychologists for practice in elementary and secondary schools. Category 3 consists of persons who meet the following criteria on or before, but not beyond, January 31, 1985: (a) a master's or higher degree, requiring at least 2 years of full-time graduate study in school psychology, from a regionally accredited university or professional school; (b) at least 3 additional years of training and experience in school psychological services, including a minimum of 1,200 hours in school settings; and (c) a license or certificate conferred by a state board of psychological examiners or a state educational agency for practice in elementary or secondary schools.

Preparation equivalent to that described in Category 3 entitles an individual to use the title *professional school psychologist* in school practice, but it does not exempt the individual from meeting the requirements of licensure or other requirements for which a doctoral degree is prerequisite.

[3] A professional school psychologist who is licensed by a state or District of Columbia board of examiners of psychology for the independent practice of psychology and who has 2 years of supervised (or equivalent) experience in health services, of which at least 1 year is postdoctoral, may be listed as a "Health Service Provider in Psychology" in the *National Register of Health Service Providers in Psychology:*

A Health Service Provider in Psychology is defined as a psychologist, certified/licensed at the independent practice level in his/her state, who is duly trained and experienced in the delivery of direct, preventive, assessment and therapeutic intervention services to individuals whose growth, adjustment, or functioning is actually impaired or is demonstrably at high risk of impairment. (Council for the National Register of Health Service Providers in Psychology, 1980, p. xi)

[4] The areas of knowledge and training that are a part of the educational program for all professional psychologists have been presented in two APA documents, *Education and Credentialing in Psychology II* (APA, 1977a) and *Criteria for Accreditation of Doctoral Training Programs and Internships in Professional Psychology* (APA, 1979). There is consistency in the presentation of core areas in the education and training of all professional psychologists. The description of education and training in these Guidelines is based primarily on the document *Education and Credentialing in Psychology II.* It is intended to indicate broad areas of required curriculum, with the ex-

pectation that training programs will undoubtedly want to interpret the specific content of these areas in different ways depending on the nature, philosophy, and intent of the programs.

[5] Although specialty education and training guidelines have not yet been developed and approved by APA, the following description of education and training components of school psychology programs represents a consensus regarding specialty training in school psychology at this time.

The *education* of school psychologists encompasses the equivalent of at least 3 years of full-time graduate academic study. While instructional formats and course titles' may vary from program to program, each program has didactic and experiential instruction (a) in scientific and professional areas common to all professional psychology programs, such as ethics and standards, research design and methodology, statistics, and psychometric methods, and (b) in such substantive areas as the biological bases of behavior, the cognitive and affective bases of behavior, the social, cultural, ethnic, and sex role bases of behavior, and individual differences. Course work includes social and philosophical bases of education, curriculum theory and practice, etiology of learning and behavior disorders, exceptional children, and special education. Organization theory and administrative practice should also be included in the program. This list is not intended to dictate specific courses or a sequence of instruction. It is the responsibility of programs to determine how these areas are organized and presented to students. Variations in educational format are to be expected.

The *training* of school psychologists includes practicum and field experience in conjunction with the educational program. In addition, the program includes a supervised internship experience beyond practicum and field work, equivalent to at least 1 academic school year, but in no event fewer than 1,200 hours, in schools or in a combination of schools and community agencies and centers, with at least 600 hours of the internship in the school setting. An appropriate number of hours per week should be devoted to direct face-to-face supervision of each intern. In no event is there less than 1 hour per week of direct supervision. Overall professional supervision is provided by a professional school psychologist. However, supervision in specific procedures and techniques may be provided by others, with the agreement of the supervising professional psychologist and the supervisee. The training experiences provided and the competencies developed occur in settings in which there are opportunities to work with children, teachers, and parents and to supervise others providing psychological services to children.

[6] In order to implement these Specialty Guidelines, it will be necessary to determine in each state which non-doctoral-level school psychologists certified by the state department of education are eligible to be considered professional school psychologists for practice in elementary and secondary schools. A national register of all professional school psychologists and specialists in school psychology would be a useful and efficient means by which to inform the public of the available school psychological services personnel.

[7] Functions and activities of school psychologists relating to the teaching of psychology, the writing or editing of scholarly or scientific manuscripts, and the conduct of scientific research do not fall within the purview of these Guidelines.

[8] Nothing in these Guidelines precludes the school psychologist from being trained beyond the areas described herein (e.g., in psychotherapy for children, adolescents, and their families in relation to school-related functioning and problems) and, therefore, from providing services on the basis of this training to clients as appropriate.

[9] In some states, a supervisor's certificate is required in order to use the title *supervisor* in the public schools. Supervision of providers of psychological services by a professional school psy-

chologist does not mean that the school psychologist is thereby authorized or entitled to offer supervision to other school personnel. Supervision by the school psychologist is confined to those areas appropriate to his or her training and educational background and is viewed as part of the school psychologist's professional responsibilities and duties.

The following guideline for supervision has been written by the Executive Committee of the Division of School Psychology:

In addition to being a professional school psychologist, the person who supervises school psychological services and/or school psychological personnel shall have the following qualifications: broad understanding of diagnostic assessment, consultation, programming, and other intervention strategies; skills in supervision; the ability to empathize with supervisees; and commitment to continuing education. The supervising school psychologist also shall have had the equivalent of at least 2 years of satisfactory full-time, on-the-job experience as a school psychologist practicing directly in the school or dealing with school-related problems in independent practice.

[10] This Guideline follows closely the statement regarding "Policy on Training for Psychologists Wishing to Change Their Specialty" adopted by the APA Council of Representatives in January 1976. Included therein was the implementing provision that "this policy statement shall be incorporated in the guidelines of the Committee on Accreditation so that appropriate sanctions can be brought to bear on university and internship training programs that violate [it]" (Conger, 1976, p. 424).

[11] Two surveys of school psychological practice provide a rationale for the specification of this Guideline (Farling & Hoedt, 1971; Kicklighter, 1976). The median ratios of psychologists to pupils were 1 to 9,000 in 1966 and 1 to 4,000 in 1974. Those responding to Kicklighter's survey projected that the ratio of psychologists to pupils would be 1 to 2,500 in 1980. These data were collected before the passage of Public Law 94-142, the Education for All Handicapped Children Act of 1975. The regulations for implementing this act require extensive identification, assessment, and evaluation services to children, and it is reasonable in 1981 to set an acceptable ratio of psychologists to pupils at 1 to 2,000.

[12] See also Ethical Principles of Psychologists (APA, 1981), especially Principles 5 (Confidentiality), 6 (Welfare of the Consumer), and 9 (Research With Human Participants), and Ethical Principles in the Conduct of Research With Human Participants (APA, 1973). Also, in 1978 Division 17 approved in principle a statement on "Principles for Counseling and Psychotherapy With Women," which was designed to protect the interests of female users of counseling psychological services.

[13] Support for the principle of the independence of psychology as a profession is found in the following:

As a member of an autonomous profession, a psychologist rejects limitations upon his [or her] freedom of thought and action other than those imposed by his [or her] moral, legal, and social responsibilities. The Association is always prepared to provide appropriate assistance to any responsible member who becomes subjected to unreasonable limitations upon his [or her] opportunity to function as a practitioner, teacher, researcher, administrator, or consultant. The Association is always prepared to cooperate with any responsible profes-

sional organization in opposing any unreasonable limitations on the professional functions of the members of that organization.

This insistence upon professional autonomy has been upheld over the years by the affirmative actions of the courts and other public and private bodies in support of the right of the psychologist—and other professionals—to pursue those functions for which he [or she] is trained and qualified to perform. (APA, 1968, p. 9)

Organized psychology has the responsibility to define and develop its own profession, consistent with the general canons of science and with the public welfare.

Psychologists recognize that other professions and other groups will, from time to time, seek to define the roles and responsibilities of psychologists. The APA opposes such developments on the same principle that it is opposed to the psychological profession taking positions which would define the work and scope of responsibility of other duly recognized professions. (APA, 1972, p. 333)

REFERENCES

American Psychological Association. Psychology as a profession. Washington, D.C.: Author, 1968.

American Psychological Association. Guidelines for conditions of employment of psychologists. American Psychologist, 1972, 27, 331–334.

American Psychological Association. Ethical principles in the conduct of research with human participants. Washington, D.C.: Author, 1973.

American Psychological Association. Standards for educational and psychological tests. Washington, D.C.: Author, 1974. (a)

American Psychological Association. Standards for providers of psychological services. Washington, D.C.: Author, 1974. (b)

American Psychological Association. Education and credentialing in psychology II. Report of a meeting, June 4–5, 1977. Washington, D.C.: Author, 1977. (a)

American Psychological Association. Standards for providers of psychological services (Rev. ed.). Washington, D.C.: Author, 1977. (b)

American Psychological Association. Criteria for accreditation of doctoral training programs and internships in professional psychology. Washington, D.C.: Author, 1979 (amended 1980).

American Psychological Association. Ethical principles of psychologists (Rev. ed.). Washington, D.C.: Author, 1981.

Conger, J. J. Proceedings of the American Psychological Association, Incorporated, for the year 1975: Minutes of the annual meeting of the Council of Representatives. American Psychologist, 1976, 31, 406–434.

Conger, J. J. Proceedings of the American Psychological Association, Incorporated, for the year 1976: Minutes of the annual meeting of the Council of Representatives. American Psychologist, 1977, 32, 408–438.

Council for the National Register of Health Service Providers in Psychology. National register of health service providers in psychology. Washington, D.C.: Author, 1980.

Farling, W. H., & Hoedt, K. C. National survey of school psychologists. Washington, D.C.: Department of Health, Education, and Welfare, 1971.

Kicklighter, R. H. School psychology in the U.S.: A quantitative survey. Journal of School Psychology, 1976, 14, 151–156.

Appendix F
Code of Ethics of the National Association of Social Workers*

---

*Reprinted with permission, from The National Association of Social Workers, Inc., Silver Spring, Md.

Preamble

This code is intended to serve as a guide to the everyday conduct of members of the social work profession and as a basis for the adjudication of issues in ethics when the conduct of social workers is alleged to deviate from the standards expressed or implied in this code. It represents standards of ethical behavior for social workers in professional relationships with those served, with colleagues, with employers, with other individuals and professions, and with the community and society as a whole. It also embodies standards of ethical behavior governing individual conduct to the extent that such conduct is associated with an individual's status and identity as a social worker.

This code is based on the fundamental values of the social work profession that include the worth, dignity, and uniqueness of all persons as well as their rights and opportunities. It is also based on the nature of social work, which fosters conditions that promote these values.

In subscribing to and abiding by this code, the social worker is expected to view ethical responsibility in as inclusive a context as each situation demands and within which ethical judgement is required. The social worker is expected to take into consideration all the principles in this code that have a bearing upon any situation in which ethical judgement is to be exercised and professional intervention or conduct is planned. The course of action that the social worker chooses is expected to be consistent with the spirit as well as the letter of this code.

In itself, this code does not represent a set of rules that will prescribe all the behaviors of social workers in all the complexities of professional life. Rather, it offers general principles to guide conduct, and the judicious appraisal of conduct, in situations that have ethical implications. It provides the basis for making judgements about ethical actions before and after they occur. Frequently, the particular situation determines the ethical principles that apply and the manner of their application. In such cases, not only the particular ethical principles are taken into immediate consideration, but also the entire code and its spirit. Specific applications of ethical principles must be judged within the context in which they are being considered. Ethical behavior in a given situation must satisfy not only the judgement of the individual social worker, but also the judgement of an unbiased jury of professional peers.

iii

This code should not be used as an instrument to deprive any social worker of the opportunity or freedom to practice with complete professional integrity; nor should any disciplinary action be taken on the basis of this code without maximum provision for safeguarding the rights of the social worker affected.

The ethical behavior of social workers results not from edict, but from a personal commitment of the individual. This code is offered to affirm the will and zeal of all social workers to be ethical and to act ethically in all that they do as social workers.

The following codified ethical principles should guide social workers in the various roles and relationships and at the various levels of responsibility in which they function professionally. These principles also serve as a basis for the adjudication by the National Association of Social Workers of issues in ethics.

In subscribing to this code, social workers are required to cooperate in its implementation and abide by any disciplinary rulings based on it. They should also take adequate measures to discourage, prevent, expose, and correct the unethical conduct of colleagues. Finally, social workers should be equally ready to defend and assist colleagues unjustly charged with unethical conduct.

Summary of Major Principles

I. The Social Worker's Conduct and Comportment as a Social Worker

A. Propriety. The Social worker should maintain high standards of personal conduct in the capacity or identity as social worker.

B. Competence and Professional Development. The social worker should strive to become and remain proficient in professional practice and the performance of professional functions.

C. Service. The social worker should regard as primary the service obligation of the social work profession.

D. Integrity. The social worker should act in accordance with the highest standards of professional integrity.

E. Scholarship and Research. The social worker engaged in study and research should be guided by the conventions of scholarly inquiry.

II. The Social Worker's Ethical Responsibility to Clients

F. Primacy of Clients' Interests. The social worker's primary responsibility is to clients.

G. Rights and Prerogatives of Clients. The social worker should make every effort to foster maximum self-determination on the part of clients.

H. Confidentiality and Privacy. The social worker should respect the privacy of clients and hold in confidence all information obtained in the course of professional service.

I. Fees. When setting fees, the social worker should ensure that they are fair, reasonable, considerate, and commensurate with the service performed and with due regard for the clients' ability to pay.

III. The Social Worker's Ethical Responsibility to Colleagues

J. Respect, Fairness, and Courtesy. The social worker should treat colleagues with respect, courtesy, fairness, and good faith.

K. Dealing with Colleagues' Clients. The social worker has the responsibility to relate to the clients of colleagues with full professional consideration.

IV. The Social Worker's Ethical Responsibility to Employers and Employing Organizations

    L. Commitments to Employing Organizations. The social worker should adhere to commitments made to the employing organizations.

V. The Social Worker's Ethical Responsibility to the Social Work Profession

    M. Maintaining the Integrity of the Profession. The social worker should uphold and advance the values, ethics, knowledge, and mission of the profession.

    N. Community Service. The social worker should assist the profession in making social services available to the general public.

    O. Development of Knowledge. The social worker should take responsibility for identifying, developing, and fully utilizing knowledge for professional practice.

VI. The Social Worker's Ethical Responsibility to Society

    P. Promoting the General Welfare. The social worker should promote the general welfare of society.

2

The NASW Code of Ethics

I. The Social Worker's Conduct and Comportment as a Social Worker

    A. Propriety—The Social worker should maintain high standards of personal conduct in the capacity or identity as social worker.

    1. The private conduct of the social worker is a personal matter to the same degree as is any other person's, except when such conduct compromises the fulfillment of professional responsibilities.

    2. The social worker should not participate in, condone, or be associated with dishonesty, fraud, deceit, or misrepresentation.

    3. The social worker should distinguish clearly between statements and actions made as a private individual and as a representative of the social work profession or an organization or group.

    B. Competence and Professional Development—The social worker should strive to become and remain proficient in professional practice and the performance of professional functions.

    1. The social worker should accept responsibility or employment only on the basis of existing competence or the intention to acquire the necessary competence.

    2. The social worker should not misrepresent professional qualifications, education, experience, or affiliations.

    C. Service —The social worker should regard as primary the service obligation of the social work profession.

    1. The social worker should retain ultimate responsibility for the quality and extent of the service that individual assumes, assigns, or performs.

    2. The social worker should act to prevent practices that are inhumane or discriminatory against any person or group of persons.

    D. Integrity —The social worker should act in accordance with the highest standards of professional integrity and impartiality.

    1. The social worker should be alert to and resist the influences and pressures that interfere with the exercise of professional discretion and impartial judgement required for the performance of professional functions.

    2. The social worker should not exploit professional relationships for personal gain.

3

E. Scholarship and Research — The social worker engaged in study and research should be guided by the conventions of scholarly inquiry.

1. The social worker engaged in research should consider carefully its possible consequences for human beings.

2. The social worker engaged in research should ascertain that the consent of participants in the research is voluntary and informed, without any implied deprivation or penalty for refusal to participate, and with due regard for participants' privacy and dignity.

3. The social worker engaged in research should protect participants from unwarranted physical or mental discomfort, distress, harm, danger, or deprivation.

4. The social worker who engages in the evaluation of services or cases should discuss them only for the professional purposes and only with persons directly and professionally concerned with them.

5. Information obtained about participants in research should be treated as confidential.

6. The social worker should take credit only for work actually done in connection with scholarly and research endeavors and credit contributions made by others.

II. The Social Worker's Ethical Responsibility to Clients

F. Primacy of Clients' Interests—The social worker's primary responsibility is to clients.

1. The social worker should serve clients with devotion, loyalty, determination, and the maximum application of professional skill and competence.

2. The social worker should not exploit relationships with clients for personal advantage, or solicit the clients of one's agency for private practice.

3. The social worker should not practice, condone, facilitate or collaborate with any form of discrimination on the basis of race, color, sex, sexual orientation, age, religion, national origin, marital status, political belief, mental or physical handicap, or any other preference or personal characteristic, condition or status.

4. The social worker should avoid relationships or commitments that conflict with the interests of clients.

5. The social worker should under no circumstances engage in sexual activities with clients.

6. The social worker should provide clients with accurate and complete information regarding the extent and nature of the services available to them.

7. The social worker should apprise clients of their risks, rights, opportunities, and obligations associated with social service to them.

8. The social worker should seek advice and counsel of colleagues and supervisors whenever such consultation is in the best interest of clients.

9. The social worker should terminate service to clients, and professional relationships with them, when such service and relationships are no longer required or no longer serve the clients' needs or interests.

10. The social worker should withdraw services precipitously only under unusual circumstances, giving careful consideration to all factors in the situation and taking care, to minimize possible adverse effects.

11. The social worker who anticipates the termination or interruption of service to clients should notify clients promptly and seek the transfer, referral, or continuation of service in relation to the clients' needs and preferences.

G. Rights and Prerogatives of Clients—The social worker should make every effort to foster maximum self-determination on the part of clients.

1. When the social worker must act on behalf of a client who has been adjudged legally incompetent, the social worker should safeguard the interests and rights of that client.

2. When another individual has been legally authorized to act in behalf of a client, the social worker should deal with that person always with the client's best interest in mind.

3. The social worker should not engage in any action that violates or diminishes the civil or legal rights of clients.

H. Confidentiality and Privacy — The social worker should respect the privacy of clients and hold in confidence all information obtained in the course of professional service.

1. The social worker should share with others confidences revealed by clients, without their

consent, only for compelling professional reasons.

2. The social worker should inform clients fully about the limits of confidentiality in a given situation, the purposes for which information is obtained, and how it may be used.

3. The social worker should afford clients reasonable access to any official social work records concerning them.

4. When providing clients with access to records, the social worker should take due care to protect the confidences of others contained in those records.

5. The social worker should obtain informed consent of clients before taping, recording, or permitting third party observation of their activities.

I. Fees —When setting fees, the social worker should ensure that they are fair, reasonable, considerate, and commensurate with the service performed and with due regard for the clients' ability to pay.

1. The social worker should not divide a fee or accept or give anything of value for receiving or making a referral.

III. The Social Worker's Ethical Responsibility to Colleagues

J. Respect, Fairness, and Courtesy —The social worker should treat colleagues with respect courtesy, fairness, and good faith.

1. The social worker should cooperate with colleagues to promote professional interests and concerns.

2. The social worker should respect confidences shared by colleagues in the course of their professional relationships and transactions.

3. The social worker should create and maintain conditions of practice that facilitate ethical and competent professional performance by colleagues.

4. The social worker should treat with respect, and represent accurately and fairly, the qualifications, views, and findings of colleagues and use appropriate channels to express judgements on these matters.

5. The social worker who replaces or is replaced by a colleague in professional practice should act with consideration for the interest, character, and reputation of that colleague.

6. The social worker should not exploit a dispute between a colleague and employers to obtain

6

a position or otherwise advance the social worker's interest.

7. The social worker should seek arbitration or mediation when conflicts with colleagues require resolution for compelling professional reasons.

8. The social worker should extend to colleagues of other professions the same respect and cooperation that is extended to social work colleagues.

9. The social worker who serves as an employer, supervisor, or mentor to colleagues should make orderly and explicit arrangements regarding the conditions of their continuing professional relationship.

10. The social worker who has the responsibility for employing and evaluating the performance of other staff members, should fulfill such responsibility in a fair, considerate, and equitable manner, on the basis of clearly enunciated criteria.

11. The social worker who has the responsibility for evaluating the performance of employees, supervisees, or students should share evaluations with them.

K. Dealing with Colleagues' Clients —The social worker has the responsibility to relate to the clients of colleagues with full professional consideration.

1. The social worker should not solicit the clients of colleagues.

2. The social worker should not assume professional responsibility for the clients of another agency or a colleague without appropriate communication with that agency or colleague.

3. The social worker who serves the clients of colleagues, during a temporary absence or emergency, should serve those clients with the same consideration as that afforded any client.

IV. The Social Worker's Ethical Responsibility to Employers and Employing Organizations

L. Commitments to Employing Organization ——The social worker should adhere to commitments made to the employing organization.

1. The social worker should work to improve the employing agency's policies and procedures, and the efficiency and effectiveness of its services.

7

2. The social worker should not accept employ-ment or arrange student field placements in an organization which is currently under public sanction by NASW for violating person-nel standards, or imposing limitations on or penalties for professional actions on behalf of clients.

3. The social worker should act to prevent and eliminate discrimination in the employing organization's work assignments and in its employment policies and practices.

4. The social worker should use with scrupulous regard, and only for the purpose for which they are intended, the resources of the employing organization.

V. The Social Worker's Ethical Responsibility to the Social Work Profession

M. Maintaining the Integrity of the Profes-sion—The social worker should uphold and advance the values, ethics, knowledge, and mission of the profession.

1. The social worker should protect and enhance the dignity and integrity of the profession and should be responsible and vigorous in discus-sion and criticism of the profession.

2. The social worker should take action through appropriate channels against unethical con-duct by any other member of the profession.

3. The social worker should act to prevent the unauthorized and unqualified practice of social work.

4. The social worker should make no misrepre-sentation in advertising as to qualifica-tions, competence, service, or results to be achieved.

N. Community Service—The social worker should assist the profession in making social services available to the general public.

1. The social worker should contribute time and professional expertise to activities that pro-mote respect for the utility, the integrity, and the competence of the social work profession.

2. The social worker should support the formula-tion, development, enactment and implemen-tation of social policies of concern to the profession.

O. Development of Knowledge—The social worker should take responsibility for iden-tifying, developing, and fully utilizing knowledge for professional practice.

1. The social worker should base practice upon recognized knowledge relevant to social work.

2. The social worker should critically examine, and keep current with emerging knowledge relevant to social work.

3. The social worker should contribute to the knowledge base of social work and share research knowledge and practice wisdom with colleagues.

VI. The Social Worker's Ethical Responsibility to Society

P. Promoting the General Welfare—The social worker should promote the general welfare of society.

1. The social worker should act to prevent and eliminate discrimination against any person or group on the basis of race, color, sex, sexual orientation, age, religion, national origin, marital status, political belief, mental or physical handicap, or any other preference or personal characteristic, condition, or status.

2. The social worker should act to ensure that all persons have access to the resources, ser-vices, and opportunities which they require.

3. The social worker should act to expand choice and opportunity for all persons, with special regard for disadvantaged or oppressed groups and persons.

4. The social worker should promote conditions that encourage respect for the diversity of cultures which constitute American society.

5. The social worker should provide appropriate professional services in public emergencies.

6. The social worker should advocate changes in policy and legislation to improve social condi-tions and to promote social justice.

7. The social worker should encourage informed participation by the public in shaping social policies and institutions.

NASW Policy Statements

PROFESSIONAL STANDARDS

1. Code of Ethics

2. Standards for Social Work Personnel Practices

4. NASW Standards for the Classification of Social Work Practice

5. Standards for the Regulation of Social Work practice

10. Standards for Continuing Professional Education

PRACTICE STANDARDS

6. Standards for Social Work in Health Care Settings

7. Standards for Social Work Services in Schools

8. Standards for Social Work Practice in Child Protection

9. Standards for Social Work Services in Long Term Care Facilities.

About NASW

The National Association of Social Workers (NASW) is the largest organization of professional social workers in the world, with members in 55 chapters throughout the United States and in the Virgin Islands, Puerto Rico, and Europe. Founded in 1955 from a merger of seven predecessor social work organizations, NASW's primary functions include professional development, establishing professional standards of social work practice, advancing sound social policies, and membership services. Membership in NASW is open to all professional social workers. For the 1980s, NASW has established major priorities in five crucial areas: (1) securing adequate public and private financing for human services, (2) gaining public recognition and legal regulation for the social work profession, (3) combatting discrimination, (4) promoting political and legislative activity, and (5) continuing education. The Academy of Certified Social Workers (ACSW) is an administrative unit. For further information, write NASW, 7981 Eastern Avenue, Silver Spring, Maryland 20910.

For information on obtaining copies, write:
Publication Sales
NASW
The NASW Building
7981 Eastern Avenue
Silver Spring, MD 20910

Appendix G
The Principles of Medical Ethics*
With Annotations Especially
Applicable to Psychiatry

In 1973, the American Psychiatric Association published the first edition of the PRINCIPLES OF MEDICAL ETHICS WITH ANNOTATIONS ESPECIALLY APPLICABLE TO PSYCHIATRY. Subsequently, revisions were published as the Board of Trustees and the Assembly approved additional annotations. In July of 1980, the American Medical Association approved a new version of the Principles of Medical Ethics (the first revision since 1957) and the APA Ethics Committee[1] incorporated many of its annotations into the new Principles, which resulted in the 1981 edition.

FOREWORD

All PHYSICIANS should practice in accordance with the medical code of ethics set forth in the Principles of Medical Ethics of the American Medical Association. An up-to-date expression and elaboration of these statements is found in the *Opinions and Reports of the Judicial Council* of the American Medical Association.[2] Psychiatrists are strongly advised to be familiar with these documents.[3]

---

*American Psychiatric Association, *The Principles of Medical Ethics With Annotations Especially Applicable to Psychiatry.* 1987, American Psychiatric Association. Reprinted with permission.

[1]The committee included Herbert Klemmer, M.D., Chairperson, Miltrades Zaphiropoulos, M.D., Ewald Busse, M.D., John R. Saunders, M.D., Robert McDevitt, M.D., and J. Brand Brickman, M.D. William P. Camp, M.D., and Robert A. Moore, M.D., serve as consultants to the APA Ethics Committee.

[2]Opinions and Reports of the Judicial Council Chicago, American Medical Association, 1981.

[3]Chapter 8, Section I of the By-Laws of the American Psychiatric Association states, "All members of the American Psychiatric Association shall be bound by the ethical code of the medical profession, specifically defined in the *Principles of Medical Ethics* of the American Medical Association." In interpreting the APA Constitution and By-Laws, it is the opinion of the Board of Trustees that inactive status in no way removes a physician member from responsibility to abide by the *Principles of Medical Ethics.*

However, these general guidelines have sometimes been difficult to interpret for psychiatry, so further annotations to the basic principles are offered in this document. While psychiatrists have the same goals as all physicians, there are special ethical problems in psychiatric practice that differ in coloring and degree from ethical problems in other branches of medical practice, even though the basic principles are the same. The annotations are not designed as absolutes and will be revised from time to time so as to be applicable to current practices and problems.

Following are the AMA Principles of Medical Ethics, printed in their entirety, and then each principle printed separately along with an annotation especially applicable to psychiatry.

PRINCIPLES OF MEDICAL ETHICS, AMERICAN MEDICAL ASSOCIATION

PREAMBLE

The medical profession has long subscribed to a body of ethical statements developed primarily for the benefit of the patient. As a member of this profession, a physician must recognize responsibility not only to patients, but also to society, to other health professionals, and to self. The following Principles, adopted by the American Medical Association, are not laws, but standards of conduct which define the essentials of honorable behavior for the physician.

SECTION 1

A physician shall be dedicated to providing competent medical service with compassion and respect for human dignity.

SECTION 2

A physician shall deal honestly with patients and colleagues, and strive to expose those physicians deficient in character or competence, or who engage in fraud or deception.

SECTION 3

A physician shall respect the law and also recognize a responsibility to seek changes in those requirements which are contrary to the best interests of the patient.

SECTION 4

A physician shall respect the rights of patients, of colleagues, and of other health professionals, and shall safeguard patient confidences within the constraints of the law.

SECTION 5

A physician shall continue to study, apply, and advance scientific knowledge, make relevant information available to patients, colleagues, and the public, obtain consultation, and use the talents of other health professionals when indicated.

SECTION 6

A physician shall, in the provision of appropriate patient care, except in emergencies, be free to choose whom to serve, with whom to associate, and the environment in which to provide medical services.

SECTION 7

A physician shall recognize a responsibility to participate in activities contributing to an improved community.

PRINCIPLES WITH ANNOTATIONS

Following are each of the AMA Principles of Medical Ethics printed separately along with annotations especially applicable to psychiatry.

PREAMBLE

The medical professional has long subscribed to a body of ethical statements developed primarily for the benefit of the patient. As a member of this profession, a physician must recognize responsibility not only to patients, but also to society, to other health professionals, and to self. The following Principles, adopted by the American Medical Association, are not laws, but standards of conduct which define the essentials of honorable behavior for the physician.[4]

---

[4]Statements in italics are taken directly from the American Medical Association's Principles of Medical Ethics.

SECTION 1

A physician shall be dedicated to providing competent medical service with compassion and respect for human dignity.

1. The patient may place his/her trust in his/her psychiatrist knowing that the psychiatrist's ethics and professional responsibilities preclude him/her gratifying his/her own needs by exploiting the patient. This becomes particularly important because of the essentially private, highly personal, and sometimes intensely emotional nature of the relationship established with the psychiatrist.

2. A psychiatrist should not be a party to any type of policy that excludes, segregates, or demeans the dignity of any patient because of ethnic origin, race, sex, creed, age, socioeconomic status, or sexual orientation.

3. In accord with the requirements of law and accepted medical practice, it is ethical for a physician to submit his/her work to peer review and to the ultimate authority of the medical staff executive body and the hospital administration and its governing body. In case of dispute, the ethical psychiatrist has the following steps available:

   a. Seek appeal from the medical staff decision to a joint conference committee, including members of the medical staff executive committee and the executive committee of the governing board. At this appeal, the ethical psychiatrist could request that outside opinions be considered.

   b. Appeal to the governing body itself.

   c. Appeal to state agencies regulating licensure of hospitals if, in the particular state, they concern themselves with matters of professional competency and quality of care.

   d. Attempt to educate colleagues through development of research projects and data and presentations at professional meetings and in professional journals.

   e. Seek redress in local courts, perhaps through an enjoining injunction against the governing body.

f. Public education as carried out by an ethical psychiatrist would not utilize appeals based solely upon emotion, but would be presented in a professional way and without any potential exploitation of patients through testimonials.

4. A psychiatrist should not be a participant in a legally authorized execution.

SECTION 2

A physician shall deal honestly with patients and colleagues, and strive to expose those physicians deficient in character or competence, or who engage in fraud or deception.

1. The requirement that the physician conduct himself with propriety in his/her profession and in all the actions of his/her life is especially important in the case of the psychiatrist because the patient tends to model his/her behavior after that of his/her therapist by identification. Further, the necessary intensity of the therapeutic relationship may tend to activate sexual and other needs and fantasies on the part of both patient and therapist, while weakening the objectivity necessary for control. Sexual activity with a patient is unethical.

2. The psychiatrist should diligently guard against exploiting information furnished by the patient and should not use the unique position of power afforded him/her by the psychotherapeutic situation to influence the patient in any way not directly relevant to the treatment goals.

3. A psychiatrist who regularly practices outside his/her area of professional competence should be considered unethical. Determination of professional competence would be made by peer review boards or other appropriate bodies.

4. Special consideration should be given to those psychiatrists who, because of mental illness, jeopardize the welfare of their patients and their own reputations and practices. It is ethical, even encouraged, for another psychiatrist to intercede in such situations.

5. Psychiatric services, like all medical services, are dispensed in the context of a contractual arrangement between the patient and the treating physician. The provisions of the contractual arrangement, which are binding on the physician as well as on the patient, should be explicitly established.

6. It is ethical for the psychiatrist to make a charge for a missed appointment when this falls within the terms of the specific contractual agreement with the patient. Charging for a missed appointment or for one not cancelled 24 hours in advance need not, in itself, be considered unethical if a patient is fully advised that the physician will make such a charge. The practice, however, should be resorted to infrequently and always with the utmost consideration of the patient and his/her circumstances.

7. An arrangement in which a psychiatrist provides supervision or administration to other physicians or nonmedical persons for a percentage of their fees or gross income is not acceptable; this would constitute fee-splitting. In a team of practitioners, or a multidisciplinary team, it is ethical for the psychiatrist to receive income for administration, research, education, or consultation. This should be based upon a mutually agreed upon and set fee or salary, open to renegotiation when a change in the time demand occurs. (See also Section 5, Annotations 2, 3, and 4.)

8. When a member has been found to have behaved unethically by the American Psychiatric Association or one of its constituent district branches, there should not be automatic reporting to the local authorities responsible for medical licensure, but the decision to report should be decided upon the merits of the case.

SECTION 3

A physician shall respect the law and also recognize a responsibility to seek changes in those requirements which are contrary to the best interests of the patient.

1. It would seem self-evident that a psychiatrist who is a lawbreaker might be ethically unsuited to practice his/her profession. When such illegal activities bear directly upon his/her practice, this would obviously be the case. However, in other instances, illegal activities such as those concerning the right to protest social injustices might not bear on either the image of the psychiatrist or the ability of the specific psychiatrist to treat his/her patient ethically and well. While no committee or board could offer prior assurance that any illegal activity would not be considered unethical, it is conceivable that an individual could violate a law without being guilty of professionally unethical behavior. Physicians lose no right of citizenship on entry into the profession of medicine.

2. Where not specifically prohibited by local laws governing medical practice, the practice of acupuncture by a psychiatrist is not unethical per se. The psychiatrist should have professional competence in the use of acupuncture. Or, if he/she is supervising the use of acupuncture by nonmedical individuals, he/she should provide proper medical supervision. (See also Section 5, Annotations 3 and 4.)

SECTION 4

A physician shall respect the rights of patients, of colleagues, and of other health professionals, and shall safeguard patient confidences within the constraints of the law.

1. Psychiatric records, including even the identification of a person as a patient, must be protected with extreme care. Confidentiality is essential to psychiatric treatment. This is based in part on the special nature of psychiatric therapy as well as on the traditional ethical relationship between physician and patient. Growing concern regarding the civil rights of patients and the possible adverse effects of computerization, duplication equipment, and data banks makes the dissemination of confidential information an increasing hazard. Because of the sensitive and private nature of the information with which the psychiatrist deals, he/she must be circumspect in the information that he/she chooses to

disclose to others about a patient. The welfare of the patient must be a continuing consideration.

2. A psychiatrist may release confidential information only with the authorization of the patient or under proper legal compulsion. The continuing duty of the psychiatrist to protect the patient includes fully apprising him/her of the connotations of waiving the privilege of privacy. This may become an issue when the patient is being investigated by a government agency, is applying for a position, or is involved in legal action. The same principles apply to the release of information concerning treatment to medical departments of government agencies, business organizations, labor unions, and insurance companies. Information gained in confidence about patients seen in student health services should not be released without the student's explicit permission.

3. Clinical and other materials used in teaching and writing must be adequately disguised in order to preserve the anonymity of the individuals involved.

4. The ethical responsibility of maintaining confidentiality holds equally for the consultations in which the patient may not have been present and in which the consultee was not a physician. In such instances, the physician consultant should alert the consultee to his/her duty of confidentiality.

5. Ethically the psychiatrist may disclose only that information which is relevant to a given situation. He/she should avoid offering speculation as fact. Sensitive information such as an individual's sexual orientation or fantasy material is usually unnecessary.

6. Psychiatrists are often asked to examine individuals for security purposes, to determine suitability for various jobs, and to determine legal competence. The psychiatrist must fully describe the nature and purpose and lack of confidentiality of the examination to the examinee at the beginning of the examination.

7. Careful judgment must be exercised by the psychiatrist in order to include, when appropriate, the parents or guardian in the treatment of a minor. At the same time

the psychiatrist must assure the minor proper confidentiality.

8. Psychiatrists at times may find it necessary, in order to protect the patient or the community from imminent danger, to reveal confidential information disclosed by the patient.

9. When the psychiatrist is ordered by the court to reveal the confidences entrusted to him/her by patients he/she may comply or he/she may ethically hold the right to dissent within the framework of the law. When the psychiatrist is in doubt, the right of the patient to confidentiality and, by extension, to unimpaired treatment, should be given priority. The psychiatrist should reserve the right to raise the question of adequate need for disclosure. In the event that the necessity for legal disclosure is demonstrated by the court, the psychiatrist may request the right to disclosure of only that information which is relevant to the legal question at hand.

10. With regard for the person's dignity and privacy and with truly informed consent, it is ethical to present a patient to a scientific gathering, if the confidentiality of the presentation is understood and accepted by the audience.

11. It is ethical to present a patient or former patient to a public gathering or to the news media only if that patient is fully informed of enduring loss of confidentiality, is competent, and consents in writing without coercion.

12. When involved in funded research, the ethical psychiatrist will advise human subjects of the funding source, retain his/her freedom to reveal data and results, and follow all appropriate and current guidelines relative to human subject protection.

13. Ethical considerations in medical practice preclude the psychiatric evaluation of any adult charged with criminal acts prior to access to, or availability of, legal counsel. The only exception is the rendering of care to the person for the sole purpose of medical treatment.

SECTION 5

A physician shall continue to study, apply, and advance scientific knowledge, make relevant information available to patients, colleagues, and the public, obtain consultation, and use the talents of other health professionals when indicated.

1. Psychiatrists are responsible for their own continuing education and should be mindful of the fact that theirs must be a lifetime of learning.

2. In the practice of his/her specialty, the psychiatrist consults, associates, collaborates, or integrates his/her work with that of many professionals, including psychologists, psychometricians, social workers, alcoholism counselors, marriage counselors, public health nurses, etc. Furthermore, the nature of modern psychiatric practice extends his/her contacts to such people as teachers, juvenile and adult probation officers, attorneys, welfare workers, agency volunteers, and neighborhood aides. In referring patients for treatment, counseling, or rehabilitation to any of these practitioners, the psychiatrist should ensure that the allied professional or paraprofessional with whom he/she is dealing is a recognized member of his/her own discipline and is competent to carry out the therapeutic task required. The psychiatrist should have the same attitude toward members of the medical professional to whom he/she refers patients. Whenever he/she has reason to doubt the training, skill, or ethical qualifications of the allied professional, the psychiatrist should not refer cases to him/her.

3. When the psychiatrist assumes a collaborative or supervisory role with another mental health worker, he/she must expend sufficient time to assure that proper care is given. It is contrary to the interests of the patient and to patient care if he/she allows himself/herself to be used as a figurehead.

4. In relationships between psychiatrists and practicing licensed psychologists, the physician should not delegate to the psychologist or, in fact, to any nonmedical person any matter requiring the exercise of professional medical judgment.

5. The psychiatrist should agree to the request of a patient for consultation or to such a request from the family of an incompetent or minor patient. The psychiatrist may suggest possible consultants, but the patient or family should be given free choice of the consultant. If the psychiatrist disapproves of the professional qualifications of the consultant or if there is a difference of opinion that the primary therapist cannot resolve, he/she may, after suitable notice, withdraw from the case. If this disagreement occurs within an institution or agency framework, the differences should be resolved by the mediation or arbitration of higher professional authority within the institution

SECTION 6

A physician shall, in the provision of appropriate patient care, except in emergencies, be free to choose whom to serve, with whom to associate, and the environment in which to provide medical services.

1. Physicians generally agree that the doctor-patient relationship is such a vital factor in effective treatment of the patient that preservation of optimal conditions for development of a sound working relationship between a doctor and his/her patient should take precedence over all other considerations. Professional courtesy may lead to poor psychiatric care for physicians and their families because of embarrassment over the lack of a complete give-and-take contract.

SECTION 7

A physician shall recognize a responsibility to participate in activities contributing to an improved community.

1. Psychiatrists should foster the cooperation of those legitimately concerned with the medical, psychological, social, and legal aspects of mental health and illness. Psychiatrists are encouraged to serve society by advising and consulting with the executive, legislative, and judiciary branches of the government. A psychiatrist should clarify whether he/she speaks as an individual or as a representative of an organization. Furthermore,

psychiatrists should avoid cloaking their public statements with the authority of the profession (e.g., "Psychiatrists know that . . .").

2. Psychiatrists may interpret and share with the public their expertise in the various psychosocial issues that may affect mental health and illness. Psychiatrists should always be mindful of their separate roles as dedicated citizens and as experts in psychological medicine.

3. On occasion psychiatrists are asked for an opinion about an individual who is in the light of public attention, or who has disclosed information about himself/herself through public media. It is unethical for a psychiatrist to offer a professional opinion unless he/she has conducted an examination and has been granted proper authorization for such a statement.

4. The psychiatrist may permit his/her certification to be used for the involuntary treatment of any person only following his/her personal examination of that person. To do so, he/she must find that the person, because of mental illness, cannot form a judgment as to what is in his/her own best interests and that, without such treatment, substantial impairment is likely to occur to the person or others.

Appendix H
Dos and Don'ts in Handling Your Client

Dos

1. Attempt mediation before litigation.

2. Help your client understand that two parents living apart will not see their child(ren) as much as two parents living together.

3. Help your client understand that two individuals living apart will have more expenses than two individuals living together.

4. Realize that time with the child(ren) and financial support are two separate areas and that one has no legal effect on the other.

5. Recognize the fact that, in the traditional situation, the mother is going to think the father has too much disposable income, and the father is going to think the mother has too much time with the child(ren).

6. Help your client consider a joint custody arrangement versus a sole custody arrangement.

7. Help your client consider sharing holidays as opposed to alternating holidays.

8. Encourage your client not to move any more often than necessary.

9. Encourage your client to be sensitive to the child(ren)'s needs as well as his or her own.

10. Encourage your client to plan and consult with the other parent in advance for time with the child(ren).

11. Encourage your client to observe time schedules with the child(ren) strictly. The tardy parent should phone, leaving word as to the reason for the lateness and estimated new time.

12. Encourage your client to be flexible with regard to visitation times with the other parent.

13. Encourage your client to do whatever is necessary to resolve the angry feelings toward the ex-spouse.

14. Present a united front on the handling of any problems with the child(ren).

15. Encourage your client not to allow the child(ren) to have too much decision-making power.

16. Encourage your client to take the child(ren) to a therapist if the psychological adjustment appears too problematic.

17. Encourage your client to tell the child(ren) as often as necessary that he or she is still loved and that he or she is not getting divorced from the parents.

18. Encourage your client to provide the child(ren) with an emotional environment in which he or she is free to continue to love the other parent and to spend time with that parent.

19. Encourage good feelings from the child(ren) about the other parent and his or her extended family.

20. Encourage the child(ren) to remember the other parent on special occasions, allowing him or her to telephone on a reasonable basis (the time and length of the phone calls to be in accordance with family rules).

21. Encourage your client to use discretion as to the time and frequency of phone calls to the child(ren).

22. Encourage your client to recognize the fact that child(ren) will feel powerless and helpless.

23. Encourage your client to recognize the fact that child(ren) will feel insecure and may exhibit regressive behaviors.

24. Encourage your client to provide appropriate models for the child(ren).

25. Encourage your client to provide the child(ren) with the opportunity to see where the other parent is going to live after moving out of the house.

26. Encourage the parents to put their differences aside long enough to attend school conferences together.

27. Recognize the right of the parents to consult with school officials concerning the child(ren)'s welfare and education status, and the right to inspect and receive student records, if state law allows.

28. Recognize the right of the parents to receive, or have forwarded promptly from the appropriate parent or school, copies of all school reports, calendar of school events, and notices of parent-teacher conferences and school programs.

29. Recognize the right of the parents to be notified in case of the child(ren)'s "serious illness."

30. Recognize the right of the parents to authorize emergency medical, surgical, hospital, dental, institutional, or psychiatric care.

31. Recognize the right of the parents to inspect and receive the child(ren)'s medical and dental records and the right to consult with any treating physician or dentist of the child(ren).

32. Encourage your client to tell the child(ren) the separation is going to take place before it takes place. The client and the other parent should do this together.

33. Encourage your client to recognize the fact that child(ren) do need more contact with the same-sex parent during adolescence.

34. Encourage your client to allow grandparents to continue to have contact with the child(ren).

35. Encourage your client to communicate with the other parent openly, honestly, and regularly to avoid misunderstandings which are harmful to the child(ren).

36. Encourage your client to plan together with the other parent, rather than through the child(ren).

37. Help the parents understand that the most maladjusted children are those of parents who are still fighting five years after the marital rupture.

Don'ts

1. Do not allow your client to agree to any type of alternating 50/50 arrangement.

2. Do not allow overnight visitations for infants.

3. Do not let your client allow the child(ren) to feel guilty for the divorce process.

4. Do not allow your client to let latency-age child(ren) (especially 9 to 12 years of age) choose not to go on visitation with the former spouse.

5. Do not allow your client to let teenage child(ren) become too parental.

6. Do not let your client allow the child(ren) to exhibit too much acting-out behavior as part of feeling sorry for the fact that the parents are going through a divorce.

7. Do not let the client take sides or take issue with decisions or actions made by the other parent, especially in front of the child(ren).

8. Do not allow your client to get the child(ren) caught in the middle of arranging visitations.

9. Do not allow your client to communicate with the other parent through the child(ren).

10. Do not allow your client to fight, argue, or degrade the other parent in the presence of the child(ren).

11. Do not allow your client to plan visitations with the child(ren) and arrive late or not come at all.

12. Do not allow your client to withhold time with the other parent as a punishment to the child(ren) or the other parent.

13. Do not allow your client to badmouth the other parent to the child(ren).

14. Do not allow your client to discuss any of the financial aspects of the divorce process (support, maintenance, arrearages) with the child(ren).

15. Do not let your client always believe what the child(ren) says about the other parent.

16. Do not allow your client to use the child(ren) as a pawn to express anger toward the other parent.

17. Do not allow your client to overburden the child(ren) by requiring too much responsibility for growing up.

18. Do not allow your client to overburden the child(ren) by requiring too much responsibility for maintaining the psychological functioning of the parent.

19. Do not allow your client to overburden the child(ren) by making the child(ren) the center of focus of argument between the parents.

20. Do not require the child(ren) to spend any more time than necessary with a parent who is out of touch with reality (psychotic).

21. Do not allow your client to split the child(ren) up, if at all possible.

22. Do not allow your client to introduce the child(ren) to every new relationship the client has developed until there is some meaning to the relationship.

23. Do not let the client allow the child(ren) to observe sexually intimate behavior between the client and a partner.

24. Do not allow your client to let the child(ren) sleep in the same room when the client is engaging in sexually intimate behavior.

25. Do not allow the client to let the child(ren), at any time, sleep in the same bed with the client, except for occasional, unusual circumstances.

Appendix I
Research Terms*

analysis of variance (ANOVA): A widely used statistical procedure for determining the significance of differences obtained on an experimental variable studied under two or more conditions. Differences are commonly assigned to three aspects: the individual differences among the subjects or patients studied, group differences, however classified (e.g., by sex), and differences according to the various treatments to which they have been assigned. The method can assess both the main effects of a variable and its interaction with other variables that have been studied simultaneously.

concordance: In genetic studies, the similarity in a twin pair with respect to the presence or absence of a disease or trait.

control: The term is used in three contexts: (1) the process of keeping the relevant conditions of an experiment constant, (2) causing an *independent variable* to vary in a specified and known manner, and (3) using a spontaneously occurring and discoverable fact as a check or standard of comparison to evaluate the facts obtained after the manipulation of the independent variable.

control group: In the ideal case, a group of subjects matched as closely as possible to an experimental group of subjects on all relevant aspects and exposed to the same treatments except the independent variable under investigation.

correlation: The extent to which two measures vary together, or a measure of the strength of the relationship between two variables. It is usually expressed by a coefficient which varies between +1.0, perfect agreement, and -1.0, a perfect inverse relationship. A correlation coefficient of 0.0 would mean a perfectly random relationship. The correlation coefficient signifies the degree to which knowledge of one score

*From American Psychiatric Association, "Table of Research Terms," *American Psychiatric Glossary, Sixth Edition.* Copyright 1988, American Psychiatric Press. Selected terms reprinted with permission.

or variable can predict the score on the other variable. A high correlation between two variables does not necessarily indicate a causal relationship between them: the correlation may follow because each of the variables is highly related to a third yet unmeasured factor.

double-blind: A study in which a number of treatments, usually one or more drugs and a placebo, are compared in such a way that neither the patient nor the persons directly involved in the treatment know which preparation is being administered.

experimental design: The logical framework of an experiment which maximizes the probability of obtaining or detecting real effects and minimizes the likelihood of ambiguities regarding the significance of the experimentally observed differences.

experimental study designs

  case control: An investigation in which groups of individuals are selected in terms of whether they do (cases) or do not (controls) have the disorder, the etiology of which is being studied.

  cross sectional: Study in which measurements are made in different samples at the same point in time.

  independent group: Different treatments are given to different groups; for example, comparing an untreated group with a treated group. Methodologically very sound, but often requires large samples if there is much variability between individuals.

  longitudinal: Study in which observations on the same individuals are made at two or more different points in time. Most cohort and case-control studies are longitudinal.

experimenter bias: Experimenter expectations that are inadvertently communicated to patients or subjects. Such expectations may influence experimental findings.

external validity: The applicability of the generalizations that may be made from the experimental findings beyond the occasion with those specific subjects, experimental conditions, experimenters, or measurements.

intervening variable: Something intervening between an antecedent circumstance and its consequence, modifying the relation between the two. For example, appetite can be an intervening variable determining whether or not a given food will be eaten. The intervening variable may be inferred rather than empirically detected.

mean: The arithmetic average of a set of observations; the sum of scores divided by the number of scores.

median: The middle value in a set of values that have been arranged in order from highest to lowest.

mode: The most frequently occurring observation in a set of observations.

non-parametric tests of significance: When data do not satisfy certain statistical assumptions, such as being normally distributed, other specialized statistical procedures which do not require assumptions of normality must be employed. These methods are often based upon an analysis of ranks rather than on the distribution of the actual scores themselves. Widely used examples are the chi-square, Spearman rank order correlation, median, and Mann-Whitney U tests.

null hypothesis: Testing the null hypothesis requires a computation to determine the limits within which two groups may differ in their results, e.g., an *experimental* and a *control group*—even though if the experiment were often repeated or the groups were larger no difference would be found. The probability of the obtained difference being found if no true difference existed is commonly expressed as a p-value, e.g., $p < .05$ that the null hypothesis is true.

operational definition: The meaning of a concept when it is translated into terms amenable to systematic observation and measurement, e.g., temperature defined by a thermometer reading under standard conditions.

parameter: Any quantitative value that a variable can take.

parametric study: One which examines the effects on a *dependent variable* of variations, usually across a broad range, in the values of the *independent variable*.

parametric tests of significance: Tests based on the assumption that the form of the distribution of the observations is known, usually a so-called normal distribution. Widely used tests based on such an assumption include analysis of variance, t-tests, and Pearsonian correlation coefficients.

placebo: In psychopharmacology, a pill which contains no pharmacologically active ingredient.

population: A statistical concept that refers to all individuals or instances that theoretically could be available for study or measurement. Statistical inference involves generalizing from the observation of some specified sample to the population.

practice effects: The modification in task performances as a result of repeated trials or training in the task.

predictor variable: The test or other form of performance which is used to predict the person's status on a *criterion variable*. For example, scores on the Scholastic Aptitude Test might be used to predict the criterion "finishing college within the top 33% of graduating class." Scores on the Scholastic Aptitude Test would be predictor scores.

q-sort: A personality assessment technique in which the subject (or someone who observes him) indicates the degree to which a standardized set of descriptive statements actually describes the subject. The term reflects the "sorting" procedures occasionally used with this technique.

random sample: A group of subjects selected in such a way that each member of the population from which the sample is derived has an equal or known chance (probability) of being chosen for the sample.

reliability: The extent to which the same test or procedure will yield the same result either over time or with different observers. The most commonly reported reliabilities are (1) test-retest reliability—the correlation between the first and second test of a number of subjects; (2) the split-half reliability—the correlation within a single test of two similar parts of the test; and (3) interrater reliability—the agreement between different individuals scoring the same procedure or observations.

significance level: The arbitrarily selected probability level for rejecting the *null hypothesis*, commonly .05 or .01.

significant differences: When statistical tests show that a given difference is not likely to have occurred by chance. In many behavioral studies, the likelihood of an event occurring less frequently than 1 in 20 times (p<.05) is considered the minimal acceptable significance level. The determination that a given difference between two groups is significant can merely serve to identify the likelihood that it was not a chance event. In no way does this prove that the demonstrated systematic difference is necessarily due to the reasons hypothesized by an investigator. Systematic factors not considered by the investigator can sometimes be responsible for significant differences.

standard deviation (SD): A mathematical measure of the dispersion or spread of scores clustered about the *mean*. In any distribution which approximates the normal curve in form, about 65% of the measurements will lie within one SD of the mean, and about 95% will lie within two SDs of the mean.

statistical inference: The process of using a limited sample of data to infer something about a larger population of potentially obtainable data which has not been observed.

test of significance: A comparison of the observed probability of an event with the predicted probability which is based on calculations deduced from statistical chance distributions of such events.

type I error: The error which is made when the *null hypothesis* is true, but as the result of the *test of significance* is rejected or declared false.

type II error: The error which is made when the *null hypothesis* is false, but due to the results of the *test of significance* is not rejected or declared false.

variable: Any characteristic in an experiment which may assume different values.

independent variable: The variable under the experimenter's control.

dependent variable: That aspect of the subject which is measured after the manipulation of the *independent variable* and assumed to vary as a function of the independent variable.

variance: The square of the *standard deviation*. Used in analysis of variance.

Appendix J
Glossary*

abnormal: In psychological terms, any mental or behavioral activity that deviates from culturally or scientifically determined norms.

abstinence: Voluntarily denying oneself some kind of gratification; in the area of alcohol or drug dependence, being without the substance on which the subject is dependent. The abstinence syndrome is equivalent to withdrawal symptoms and its appearance suggests the presence of physiologic dependence or addiction.

addiction: Dependence on a chemical substance to the extent that a physiologic and/or psychologic need is established. This may be manifested by any combination of the following symptoms: tolerance, preoccupation with obtaining and using the substance, use of the substance despite anticipation of probable adverse consequences, repeated efforts to cut down or control substance use, and withdrawal symptoms when the substance is unavailable or not used.

affect, flat: Absence or near absence of any signs of affective expression.

affective disorder: Disorder in which mood change or disturbance is the primary manifestation.

agitated depression: A severe major depressive disorder in which psychomotor agitation is prominent; formerly known as involutional melancholia.

anorexia nervosa: A disorder marked by severe and prolonged refusal to eat, with severe weight loss, amenorrhea or impotence, disturbance of body image, and an intense fear of becoming obese. Most frequently encountered in girls and young women. May be associated with bulimia.

---

*American Psychiatric Association, *American Psychiatric Glossary*, *Sixth Edition*. Copyright 1988, American Psychiatric Press. Selected terms reprinted with permission.

anxiety: Apprehension, tension, or uneasiness from anticipation of danger, the source of which is largely unknown or unrecognized. Primarily of intrapsychic origin, indistinction to fear, which is the emotional response to a consciously recognized and usually external threat or danger. May be regarded as pathologic when it interferes with effectiveness in living, achievement of desired goals or satisfaction, or reasonable emotional comfort.

apperception: Perception as modified and enhanced by one's own emotions, memories, and biases.

attention deficit disorder (ADD): A DSM-III-R category for a childhood disorder characterized by developmentally inappropriate short attention span, poor concentration, and frequent hyperactivity.

autism: A pervasive developmental disorder caused by a physical disorder of the brain appearing during the first three years of life. Symptoms include disturbances in physical, social, and language skills; abnormal responses to sensations; and abnormal ways of relating to people, objects, and events.

behavior therapy: A mode of treatment that focuses on modifying observable and, at least in principle, quantifiable behavior by means of systematic manipulation of the environment and behavioral variables thought to be functionally related to the behavior. Some behavior therapy techniques are operant conditioning, shaping, token economy, systematic desensitization, aversion therapy, and flooding.

bipolar disorder: A mood disorder in which there are episodes of both mania and depression; formerly called manic depressive psychosis, circular or mixed type. A mild form of bipolar disorder is sometimes labeled cyclothymic disorder. Bipolar disorder may be subdivided into manic, depressed, or mixed types on the basis of currently presenting symptoms.

bulimia: Episodic eating binges or excessive intake of food or fluid, generally beyond voluntary control. Characteristics are self-induced vomiting and purging following eating, which is of the binge-eating variety. The resulting loss of

body fluids and electrolytes may lead to severe disturbances such as EKG abnormalities and tetany. Sometimes
seen as a symptom in anorexia nervosa.

cognition: A general term encompassing all the various
modes of knowing and reasoning.

concrete thinking: Thinking characterized by immediate
experience, rather than abstractions. Seen in persons who
have never developed the ability to generalize.

decompensation: The deterioration of existing defenses, leading to an exacerbation of pathologic behavior.

defense mechanism: Unconscious intrapsychic processes
serving to provide relief from emotional conflict and anxiety. Conscious efforts are frequently made for the same reasons, but true defense mechanisms are unconscious.

delusion: A false belief firmly held despite incontrovertible
and obvious proof or evidence to the contrary. Further, the
belief is not one ordinarily accepted by other members of
the person's culture or subculture.

denial: A defense mechanism, operating unconsciously, used
to resolve emotional conflict and allay anxiety by disavow-
ing thoughts, feelings, wishes, needs, or external reality
factors that are consciously intolerable.

developmental disorder: A handicap or impairment originating before the age of 18 which may be expected to continue indefinitely and which constitutes a substantial
impairment. The disability may be attributable to mental
retardation, cerebral palsy, epilepsy, or other neurologic
conditions and may include autism.

disorientation: Loss of awareness of the position of the self in
relation to space, time, or other persons; confusion.

drug dependence: Habituation to, abuse of, and/or addiction
to a chemical substance. Largely because of psychologic
craving, the life of the drug-dependent person revolves
around the need for the specific effect of one or more chemical agents on mood or state of consciousness. The term thus

includes not only the addiction (which emphasizes the physiologic dependence), but also drug abuse (where the pathologic craving for drugs seems unrelated to physical dependence). Examples: alcohol, opiates, synthetic analgesics with morphine-like effects, barbiturates, other hypnotics, sedatives and some antianxiety agents, cocaine, psychostimulants, marijuana, and psychotomimetic drugs.

hallucination: A sensory perception in the absence of an actual external stimulus. May occur in any of the senses.

hyperactivity: In DSM-III-R, called an attention deficit disorder (ADD); excessive motor activity, generally purposeful. It is frequently, but not necessarily, associated with internal tension or a neurologic disorder. Usually, the movements are more rapid than customary for the person.

inappropriate affect: A display of emotion that is out of harmony with reality.

magical thinking: A conviction that thinking equates with doing. Occurs in dreams in children, in primitive people, and in patients under a variety of conditions. Characterized by lack of realistic relationship between cause and effect.

narcissism (narcism): Self-love as opposed to object-love (love of another person). In psychoanalytic theory, cathexis (investment) of the psychic representation of the self with libido (sexual interest and energy). An excess interferes with relations with others. To be distinguished from egotism, which carries the connotation of self-centeredness, selfishness, and conceit. Egotism is but one expression of narcissism.

phobia: An obsessive, persistent, unrealistic, intense fear of an object or situation. The fear is believed to arise through a process of displacing an internal (unconscious) conflict to an external object symbolically related to the conflict.

posttraumatic stress disorder: Disorder developing after experiencing a psychologically distressing event. It is characterized by reexperiencing the event and by overresponsiveness to, or involvement with, stimuli that recall the event. Also called "Vietnam vet's disease." Depression, startle reactions, flashback phenomena, and dissociative episodes are present.

projection: A defense mechanism, operating unconsciously, in which what is emotionally unacceptable in the self is unconsciously rejected and attributed (projected) to others.

reality testing: The ability to evaluate the external world objectively and to differentiate adequately between it and the internal world. Falsification of reality, as with massive denial or projection, indicates a severe disturbance of ego functioning and/or the perceptual and memory processes upon which it is partly based.

regression: Partial or symbolic return to more infantile patterns of reacting or thinking. Manifested in a wide variety of circumstances such as normal sleep, play, physical illness, and in many mental disorders.

repression: A defense mechanism, operating unconsciously, that banishes unacceptable ideas, fantasies, affects, or impulses from consciousness or that keeps out of consciousness what has never been conscious. Although not subject to voluntary recall, the repressed material may emerge in disguised form. Often confused with the conscious mechanism of suppression.

secondary gain: The external gain derived from any illness, such as personal attention and service, monetary gains, disability benefits, and release from unpleasant responsibility.

separation anxiety: The fear and apprehension noted in infants when removed from the mother (or surrogate mother) or when approached by strangers. Most marked from sixth to tenth month. In later life, similar reactions may be caused by separation from significant persons or familiar surroundings.

symptom: A specific manifestation of a patient's condition indicative of an abnormal physical or mental state; a subjective perception of illness.

syndrome: A configuration of symptoms that occur together and constitute a recognizable condition.

unconscious: That part of the mind or mental functioning of which the content is only rarely subject to awareness. It is a repository for data that have never been conscious (primary repression) or that may have become conscious briefly and later repressed (secondary repression).

References

Abidin, R.A. *Parenting Stress Index*. 2d ed. Charlottesville, Va.: Pediatric Psychology Press, 1986.

Academy of Certified Social Workers. *Mark of Professional Excellence*. Silver Spring, Md.: National Association of Social Workers, undated.

Ackerman, Marc J. "Child Sexual Abuse: Bona Fide or Fabricated?" *American Journal of Family Law* 1 (1987): 181–85.

Ackerman, Marc J. "Recent Psychological Research on the Effect of Divorce on Children." *Wisconsin Journal of Family Law* 4 (1984): 29–31.

Ackerman, Marc J., and Schoendorf, Kathleen. *The Ackerman-Schoendorf Parent Evaluation for Custody Tests (ASPECT)*. Los Angeles: Western Psychological Services, in press.

Ackerman, Robert J. *Children of Alcoholics: A Guidebook for Educators, Therapists, and Parents*. 2d ed. Holmes Beach, Fla.: Learning Publications, 1983.

Aiken, Lewis. *Psychological Testing and Assessment*. 5th ed. Newton, Mass.: Allyn & Bacon, 1985.

American Psychiatric Association. *Diagnostic and Statistical Manual of Mental Disorders, Third Edition, Revised*. Washington, D.C.: American Psychiatric Association, 1987.

American Psychological Association. "Casebook for Providers of Psychological Services." *American Psychologist* 39 (1984): 663–68.

American Psychological Association. "Ethical Principles of Psychologists." *American Psychologist* 36 (1981): 633–38.

American Psychological Association. "General Guidelines for Providers of Psychological Services." *American Psychologist* 42 (1987): 1–12.

American Psychological Association. "Specialty Guidelines for the Delivery of Services." *American Psychologist* 36 (1981): 640–81.

Anastasi, Anne. *Psychological Testing.* 5th ed. New York: MacMillan, 1982.

Anastasi, Anne. *Psychological Testing.* 6th ed. New York: MacMillan, 1988.

Anderson, T.W., and Sclove, Stanley L. *An Introduction to DTE Statistical Analysis of Data.* Boston: Houghton Mifflin, 1978.

Anthony, N.C. "Comparison of Client Standard, Exaggerated and Matching MMPI Profiles." *Journal of Consulting and Clinical Psychology* 36 (1971): 100–03.

Atkinson, L., Quarrington, B., Alp, I.E., and Cyr, J. "Rorschach Validity: An Empirical Approach to the Literature." *Journal of Clinical Psychology* 42 (1986): 360–62.

Bales, J. "APA Rebuts Criticism of Clinician Witnesses." *APA Monitor* 19 (1988): 17.

Barland, T.H. "The Role of the Guardian ad Litem as Viewed by the Judiciary." Wisconsin State Bar Spring Convention, 1983.

Barnard, C.P. and Jenson, G. "Child Custody Evaluations: A Rational Process for an Emotion-laden Event." *The American Journal of Family Therapy* 12 (1984): 61–67.

Barron, F. "An Ego Strength Scale Which Predicts Response to Psychotherapy." *Journal of Consulting Psychology* 17 (1953): 327–33.

Bazelon, D. "Veils, Values and Social Responsibility." *American Psychologist* 37 (1982): 115–21.

Beck, S.J., Beck, A.G., Levitt, Eugene E., and Molish, Herman B. *Rorschach's Test.* 3d ed. New York: Grune & Stratton, 1961.

Bellak, Leopold. *T.A.T., C.A.T. and S.A.T. in Clinical Use.* 4th ed. Orlando, Fla.: Grune & Stratton, 1986.

Bellak, Leopold and Bellak, Sonya. *Children's Apperception Test.* Larchmont, N.Y.: C.P.S., Inc., 1949.

Belsky, J., Robins, J., and Gamble, W. "The Determinants of Parental Competence: Toward a Theory." In *Beyond the Dyad,* edited by M. Lewis. New York: Plenum Press, 1984.

Berkman, C.F. "Child Psychiatry and the Law." *Journal of the Academy of Child Psychiatry* 23 (1984): 708–12.

Berkowitz, Alan, and Perkins, H. Wesley. "Personality Characteristics of Children of Alcoholics." *Journal of Consulting and Clinical Psychology* 56 (1988): 206–09.

Berman, A. "The Expert at Trial: Personality Persuades." *Family Advocate* 9 (1986): 11–12.

Bernstein, Lewis, Ph.D. *Psychological Testing: II. The Rorschach Test.* Reprinted from the Journal Children's Asthma Research Institute and Hospital 1 (1961).

Blau, T. *The Psychologist as Expert Witness.* New York: Wiley, 1984.

Bolton, F.G., and Bolton, S.R. *A Guide for Clinical and Legal Practitioners, Working with the Violent Family.* Troy, N.Y.: Sage Publishers, 1987.

Bradway, K.P., Thompson, C.W., and Cravens, R.B. "Preschool I.Q.'s After 25 Years." *Journal of Educational Psychology* 49 (1958): 278–81.

Bresee, Patricia, Stearns, Jeffrey, Bess, Bruce, and Pecker, Leslie. "Allegations of Child Sexual Abuse in Child Custody Disputes: A Therapeutic Assessment Model." *American Journal of Orthopsychiatry* 56 (1986): 550–59.

Bricklin, B. *Bricklin Perceptual Scales.* Furlong, Penn.: Village Publishing, 1984.

Bronfenbrenner, U. *The Ecology of Human Development: Experiments by Nature and Design.* Cambridge, Mass.: Harvard University Press, 1979.

Buck, J., and Hammer, E.F. *Advances in the House-Tree-Person Technique: Variations in Applications.* Los Angeles: Western Psychological Services, 1969.

Burns, R.C., and Kaufman, S.H. *Kinetic Family Drawings (KFD): An Introduction to Understanding Children Through Kinetic Drawings.* New York: Brunner-Mazel, 1970.

Butcher, J. MMPI-2 Briefing Session. Chicago: Department of Professional Development and Conference Services, September 1989.

Butcher, J., and Graham, J. MMPI Workshop. Minneapolis, June, 1987.

Butcher, James N., and Graham, John R. "Clinical Applications of the MMPI." 23rd Annual Seminar. Oconomowoc, Wis., April 1988.

Caldwell, A. "Families of MMPI Code Types." Paper presented at the 12th Annual Symposium on the MMPI. Tampa, Fla., 1977.

Caldwell, Alex, and O'Hare, Christopher. *A Handbook of MMPI Personality Types*. Santa Monica, Cal.: Clinical Psychology Services, 1986.

Campbell, Robert Jean. *Psychiatric Dictionary*. 5th ed. New York: Oxford University Press, 1981.

Carkhauff, R.R., Barnette, L., and McCall, J.N. *The Counselor's Handbook: Scale and Profile Interpretations of the MMPI*. Urbana, Ill.: R.W. Parkinson, 1965.

Carlson, Kenneth A. *Carlson Psychological Survey*. Port Huron, Mich.: Research Psychologists Press, 1982.

Carr, A.C. "Psychological Testing of Personality." In H. Kaplan and B. Sadock, *Comprehensive Textbook of Psychiatry/IV*, 514–35. Baltimore: Williams & Wilkins, 1985.

Carson, R. "Interpretative Manual to the MMPI." *MMPI: Research Developments and Clinical Applications*. New York: McGraw Hill, 1969, 279–96.

Carson, R. "MMPI Profile Interpretation." Paper read at the 7th Annual Symposium on the MMPI, Mexico City, 1972.

Chasin, R., and Gruenebaum, H. "A Model for Evaluation in Custody Disputes." *The American Journal of Family Therapy* 9 (1981): 43–47.

Clements, Colleen D., and Ciccone, J. Richard. "Ethics and Expert Witnesses: The Troubled Role of Psychiatrists in Court." *Bulletin American Academy Psychiatry Law* 12 (1984): 127–36.

Code of Ethics. Silver Spring, Md.: National Association of Social Workers, 1980.

Colligan, R.C., Osborn, D., Swenson, Wm., and Offord, K.P. "Development of Contemporary Norms." *Journal of Clinical Psychology* 40 (1984): 100–07.

Cooke, M.K., and Kiesler, D.J. "Prediction of College Students Who Later Require Personal Counseling." *Journal of Counseling Psychology* 14 (1967): 346–49.

Cosden, Merith. Rotter Incomplete Sentences Blank, Julian B. Rotter. Cleveland, Ohio: The Psychological Corp. In D. Keyser & R. Sweetland, *Test Critiques*. Kansas City, Mo.: Test Corporations of America 2 (1984): 653–60.

Cottle, W.C. *The MMPI: A Review*. Lawrence, Kan.: University of Kansas Press, 1953.

Craig, R. "A Comparison of MMPI Profiles of Heroin Addicts Based on Multiple Methods of Classification." *Journal of Personality Assessment* 48 (1984): 115–29.

Cuadra, C. A. "A Psychometric Investigation of Control Factors and Psychological Adjustment." Doctoral Diss., University of California, 1953.

Dahlstrom, W. Grant, Welsh, George Schlager, and Dahlstrom, Leona E. *An MMPI Handbook*. Vol. I, Clinical Interpretation (A Revised Ed.) & Vol. II. Minneapolis: University of Minnesota Press, 1982.

Dana, R.H. "Rorschach." In O. Buros, *The Eighth Mental Measurements Yearbook*, 1040–42. Highland Park, N.J.: Gryphon Press, 1978.

Derdeyn, A., Levy, A., Looney, J., Schetky, D., Westman, J., Scott, E., and Spurlock, J. *Child Custody Consultation, Report of the Task Force on Clinical Assessment in Child Custody*. Washington, D.C.: American Psychiatric Association, 1981.

deYoung, Mary. "A Conceptual Model for Judging the Truthfulness of a Young Child's Allegation of Sexual Abuse." *American Journal of Orthopsychiatry* 56 (1986): 550–59.

Diagnostic and Statistical Manual of Mental Disorders, Third Edition, Revised. Washington, D.C.: American Psychiatric Association, 1987.

diLeo, J. *Children's Drawings as Diagnostic Aids*. New York: Brunner-Mazel, 1973.

Drake, L.E., and Oetting, E.R. *An MMPI Codebook for Counselors*. Minneapolis: University of Minnesota Press, 1959.

Dubinsky, Susan, Gamble, Dorothy J., and Rodgers, Martha. "A Literature Review of Subtle Obvious Items on the MMPI." *Journal of Personality Assessment* 49 (1985): 62–68.

Duckworth, Jane, and Anderson, Wayne. *MMPI Interpretation Manual for Counselors and Clinicians*. 3d ed. Muncie, Ind.: Accelerated Development, 1986.

Eckenrode, J., Powers, J., Doris, J., Munsch, J., and Bolger, N. "Substantiation of Child Abuse and Neglect Reports." *Journal of Consulting and Clinical Psychology* 6 (1988): 9–16.

Ellison, Edythe. "Issues Concerning Parental Harmony and Children's Psychosocial Adjustment." *American Journal of Orthopsychiatry* 53 (1983): 73–79.

Ellison Good-King, Patricia, and Brantner, John P. *A Practical Guide to the MMPI*. Minneapolis: University of Minnesota Press, 1974.

Erikson, E. *Childhood and Society*. New York: W.W. Norton, 1963.

Erikson, Steve. Divorce Mediation Workshop, Wisconsin Psychological Association. Fall, 1984.

"Ethical Principles of Psychologists." *American Psychologist* 36 (1981): 633–38.

Exner, J.E., Jr. *A Rorschach Workbook for The Comprehensive System*. 2d ed. Bayville, N.Y.: Rorschach Workshops, 1985.

Exner, J.E., Jr. "Problems with Brief Rorschach Protocols." *Journal of Personality Assessment* 52 (1988): 640–47.

Exner, J.E., Jr. "Searching for Projection in the Rorschach." *Journal of Personality Assessment* 53 (1989): 520–36.

Exner, J.E., Jr., and Clark, B. *The Rorschach-Clinical Diagnosis of Mental Disorders*. New York: Plenum Press, 1978.

Exner, J.E., Jr., and Exner, D.E. "How Clinicians Use the Rorschach." *Journal of Personality Assessment* 36 (1972): 403–08.

Exner, John E., Jr., Thomas, Eugene A., and Mason, Barbara. "Children's Rorschachs: Description and Prediction." *Journal of Personality Assessment* 49 (1985): 13–20.

Finkelhor, David. "The Sexual Abuse of Children: Current Research Reviewed." *Psychiatric Annals* 17 (1987): 233–41.

Fowler, R., and Matarazzo, J. In J. Bales, "APA Rebuts Criticism of Clinician Witnesses." *APA Monitor* 19 (1988): 17.

Frances, A.J., Widiger, T.A., and Pincus, H.A. "The Development of DSM-IV." *Archives of General Psychiatry* 46 (1989): 373–75.

Franke, Linda B. *Growing Up Divorced*. New York: Linden Press/Simon & Schuster, 1983.

Gallucci, Nicholas T. "The Influence of the Elevated F Scales on the Validity of Adolescent MMPI Profiles." *Journal of Personality Assessment* 51 (1987): 133–39.

Gallucci, N., Kay, D. and Thornby, J. "Sensitivity of Eleven Substance Abuse Scales from the MMPI to Change in Clinical Status." *Psychology of Addictive Behaviors* 3 (1989): 29–33.

Garbarino, James, Guttmann, Edna, and Seeley, Janice. *The Psychologically Battered Child*. San Francisco: Jossey-Bass, 1987.

Gardner, Richard A., M.D. *Family Evaluation and Child Custody Litigation*. Cresskill, N.J.: Creative Therapeutics, 1982.

Gardner, Richard. "Issues in Child and Adolescent Therapy in Divorce." 5th Annual Intervention for the Child and Family at Risk Workshop, Milwaukee, Wis.: April, 1986.

Gardner, R.A. *Psychotherapy with Children of Divorce.* New York: Jason Aronson, 1976.

"General Guidelines for Providers of Psychological Services." *American Psychologist* 42 (1987).

Givelber, F. "The Parent-Child Relationship and the Development of Self-Esteem." In J. Mack and S. Ablon (eds.) *The Development and Sustenance of Self-Esteem in Children,* 163–67. New York: International Universities Press, 1983.

Gold, Erica. "Long-term Effects of Sexual Victimization in Childhood: An Attributional Approach." *Journal of Consulting and Clinical Psychology* 54 (1986): 471–75.

Goldberg, L.R. "Diagnosticians vs. Diagnostic Signs: The Diagnosis of Psychosis vs. Neurosis for the MMPI." *Psychological Monographs* 79 (1965): Whole Number 602.

Golding, S., Grisso, T., and Shapiro, D. Working Draft: "Specialty Guidelines for Forensic Psychologists" (6/89 revision). Division of Psychology and the Law. Washington, D.C.: American Psychological Association, 1989.

Goldstein, J.A., Freud, Ann, and Solnit, A.J. *Beyond the Best Interests of the Child.* New York: Free Press, 1973.

Goldzband, M. *Custody Cases and Expert Witnesses, A Manual for Attorneys.* New York: Harcourt Brace Jovanovich, 1980.

Good, P., and Brantner, J. *A Practical Guide to the MMPI.* Minneapolis: University of Minnesota, 1974.

Goodenough, F. *Measurement of Intelligence by Drawings.* New York: Harcourt, Brace and World, 1926.

Goodman, G. S., and Aman, C. "Children's Use of Anatomically Correct Dolls To Report An Event." Paper presented at the meeting of the Society for Research In Child Development. Baltimore, Md., April 1987. In G. Melton and S. Limber, "Psychologists Involvement In Cases of Maltreatment: Limits of Role and Expertise." *American Psychologist* 44 (1989): 1225–33.

Gough, H.G. "Simulated Patterns of the MMPI." *Journal of Abnormal and Social Psychology* 42 (1947): 215–25.

Gough, H.G. "Studies of Social Intolerance: III Relationship of the PR Scale to Other Variables." *Journal of Social Psychology* 33 (1951): 257–62.

Gough, H.G. "A Short Social Status Inventory." *Journal of Educational Psychology* 40 (1949): 52–56.

Gough, H.G. "A Dimension of Social Status: II Relationship of the St Scale to Other Variables." *American Sociological Review* 13 (1948): 534–37.

Gough, H.G., McClosky, H. and Meehl, P.E. "A Personality Scale of Dominance." *Journal of Abnormal and Social Psychology* 46 (1951): 360–66.

Graham, John R. *The MMPI: A Practical Guide*. 2d ed. New York: Oxford University Press, 1987.

Graham, John R., and Lilly, Ries. *Psychological Testing*. Englewood Cliffs, N.J.: Prentice-Hall, 1984.

Graham, John, and McCord, Gary. "Interpretation of Moderately Elevated MMPI Scores for Normal Subjects." *Journal of Personality Assessment* 49 (1985): 477–84.

Graham, John R., and Strenger, Virginia E. "MMPI Characteristics of Alcoholics: A Review." *Journal of Consulting and Clinical Psychology* 56 (1988): 197–205.

Greenberg, E., and Rappaport, J. "Children's Competence and Desire to Participate in Custody Decision-Making." Paper presented at the meeting of the American Psychological Association, Toronto, Canada, August 1984.

Greene, Roger L. *The MMPI: An Interpretive Manual*. New York: Grune & Stratton, 1980.

Grinspoon, L., and Bakalar, J. "Substance Use Disorders." In A. Nicholi, Jr. (ed.) *The New Harvard Guide to Psychiatry*. Boston: Harvard University Press, 1988.

Guidubaldi, J., Cleminshaw, H., Perry, J., Nastasi, B., and Adams, B. "Longitudinal Effects of Divorce on Children: A Report from the NASPKSU Nationwide Study." Paper presented at the meeting of the American Psychological Association, Toronto, Canada, August 1984.

Gynther, M. "The Clinical Utility of the "Invalid" MMPI F Scores." *Journal of Consulting Psychology* 25 (1961): 540–42.

Gynther, M. "White Norms and Black MMPI's: A Prescription for Discrimination?" *Psychological Bulletin* 78 (1972): 386–402.

Haier, Richard, Rieder, Ronald, Khouri, Filippe, and Buschbaum, Monte. "Extreme MMPI Scores and The Research and Diagnostic Criteria." *Archives of General Psychology* 36 (1979): 528–34.

Hall, Gordon, Majuro, Roland, Vitaliano, Peter, and Proctor, William. "The Utility of the MMPI with Men Who Have Sexually Assaulted Children." *Journal of Consulting and Clinical Psychology* 54 (1986): 493–96.

Hammer, E.F. *The Clinical Application of Projective Drawings.* Springfield, Ill.: C.C. Thomas, 1958.

Hanvik, L.J. "MMPI Profiles in Patients with Low Back Pain." *Journal of Consulting Psychology* 15 (1951): 350–53.

Harris, D. *Children's Drawings As Measures Intellectual Maturity.* New York: Harcourt, Brace and World, 1963.

Harris, R.E., and Lingoes, J.C. "Subscales for the MMPI: An Aid to Profile Interpretation." Unpublished manuscript, University of California, 1955.

Hathaway, S.R. "Scales 5 (Masculinity-Femininity) 6 (Paranoia) and 8 (Schizophrenia)." In G. Welsh and W. Dahlstrom (eds.) *Basic Readings in the MMPI in Psychology and Medicine.* Minneapolis: University Press, 1986.

Hathaway, S.R., and McKinley, J.C. "A Multiphasic Personality Schedule (Minnesota: III) The Measurement of Symptomatic Depression. *Journal of Psychology* 14 (1942): 73–84.

Hedlund, James L., and Vieweg, Bruce W. "The Michigan Alcoholism Screening Test (MAST): A Comprehensive Review." *Journal of Operational Psychiatry* 15 (1984): 55–64.

Herman, Judith, Russell, Diana, and Trocki, Karen. Long-term Effects of Incestuous Abuse in Childhood." *American Journal of Psychiatry* 143 (1986): 1293–96.

Hershorn, Michael, and Rosenbaum, Alan. "Children of Marital Violence: A Closer Look at the Unintended Victims." *American Journal of Orthopsychiatry* 52 (1985): 260–66.

Hetherington, E.M. "Divorce: A Child's Perspective." *American Psychologist* 34 (1979): 851–58.

Hetherington, E.M., Cox, M., and Cox, R. "The Aftermath of Divorce." In J. Stevens and M. Matthews (eds.) *Mother-Child, Father-Child Relations*. Washington, D.C.: National Association for the Education of Young Children, 1978.

Hetherington, E.M., and Furstenberg, F.F. "Sounding the Alarm." *READINGS: A Journal of Reviews and Commentary in Mental Health* 4 (1989): 4–8.

Hibbs, B.J., Kobas, J.C., and Gonzalez, J. "Affects of Ethnicity, Sex and Age on MMPI Profiles." *Psychological Reports* 45 (1979): 591–97.

Hokanson, J.E., and Calden, G. "Negro-White Differences on the MMPI." *Journal of Clinical Psychology* 16 (1960): 32–33.

Howell, R.J., and Toepke, K.E. "Summary of the Child Custody Laws for the Fifty States." *The American Journal of Family Therapy* 12 (1984): 56–60.

Hursley, John, Hanson, Carl, and Parker, Kevin. "A Summary of the Reliability & Stability of MMPI Scores." *Journal of Clinical Psychology* 44 (1988): 44–46.

Ilfeld, Frederic, Ilfeld, Holly, and Alexander, John. "Does Joint Custody Work? A First Look At Outcome Data of Relitigation." *American Journal of Psychiatry* 139 (1982): 62–66.

International Classification of Diseases. See *Manual of the International Statistical Classification of Diseases, Injuries, and Causes of Death, Clinical Modification, ICD-9-CM*.

Isaacs, Marla Beth, Montavo, Braulio, and Abelsohn, David. *The Difficult Divorce–Therapy for Children and Families.* New York: Basic Books, 1986.

Jacobs, John. "Divorce and Child Custody Resolution: Conflicting Legal and Psychological Paradigms." *American Journal of Psychiatry* 143 (1986): 190–97.

Jacobson, George R. *The Alcoholisms: Detection, Assessment, and Diagnosis.* New York: Human Sciences Press, 1976.

Johnston, Janet, Campbell, Linda, and Tall, Mary. "Impasses to the Resolution of Custody and Visitation Disputes." *American Journal of Orthopsychiatry* 55 (1985): 112–29.

Jurjevick, R.M. "Short Interval Test/Retest of the MMPI, CPI Cornell, Index and Symptom Checklist." *Journal of General Psychology* 74 (1966): 201–06.

Kaplan, Harold I., and Sadock, Benjamin J. (eds.) *Comprehensive Textbook of Psychiatry/IV.* Williams & Wilkins, 1985.

Karras, D., and Berry, K. "Custody Evaluations: A Critical Review." *Professional Psychology: Research and Practice* 16 (1985): 76–85.

Katz, Mitchel, Hampton, Robert, Newberger, Eli, Bowles, Roy, and Snyder, Jane. "Returning Children Home, Clinical Decision-Making in Cases of Child Abuse and Neglect." *American Journal of Orthopsychiatry* 56 (1986): 253–62.

Kaufman, Alan, and Kaufman, Nadeen. *Kaufman Assessment Battery for Children: Administration and Scoring Manual.* Circle Pines, Minn.: American Guidance Service, 1983.

Kaufman, Alan, and Kaufman, Nadeen. *Kaufman Assessment Battery for Children: Interpretative Manual.* Circle Pines, Minn.: American Guidance Service, 1983.

Kaufman, A.S. "Factor Analysis of the WISC-R at 11 Age Levels Between 6 and 16 Years." *Journal of Consulting and Clinical Psychology* 43 (1975): 135–47.

Kaufman, A.S. *Intelligence Testing with the WISC-R.* New York: Wiley, 1979.

Keilin, W.G., and Bloom, L.J. "Child Custody Evaluation Practices: A Survey of Experienced Professionals." *Professional Psychology: Research and Practice* 17 (1986): 338–46.

Keith-Spiegel, Patricia, and Koocher, Gerald P. *Ethics in Psychology: Professional Standards and Cases.* New York: Random House, 1985.

Kelly, Joan, and Wallerstein, Judith. "Part-time Parent, Part-time Child: Visiting After Divorce." *Journal of Clinical Psychology* (Summer 1987) 51–54. In L. Franke, *Growing Up Divorced.* New York: Linden Press/Simon Schuster, 1983.

Kestenbaum, Clarise J., and Williams, Daniel T. *Handbook of Clinical Assessment of Children and Adolescents.* Vol. 1 & 2. New York: University Press, 1988.

Klerman, G. "Classification and DSM-III-R." In A. Nicholi, *The New Harvard Guide to Psychiatry.* Cambridge, Mass.: Harvard University Press, 1988.

Klopfer, Bruno, Ainsworth, Mary, Klopfer, Walter, and Holt, Robert. *Developments in the Rorschach Technique.* Vol. 1, *Technique and Theory.* New York: Harcourt, Brace and World, 1954.

Klopfer, B., and Kelley, D.M. *The Rorschach Technique.* Yonkers, N.Y.: World Book, 1942.

Kluft, Richard. "Incest and Adult Psychopathology: An Overview and A Study of the 'Sitting Duck Syndrome.'" Philadelphia: The Institute of the Pennsylvania Hospital, 1988.

Knapp, Samuel, and Vandecreek, Leon. "Psychotherapy and Privileged Communications in Child Custody Cases." *Professional Psychology: Research and Practice* 16 (1985): 398–407.

Koppitz, E. "Emotional Indictors in Human Figure Drawings of Shy and Aggressive Children." *Journal of Clinical Psychology* 22 (1966): 466–69.

Korchin, Sheldon, J. *Modern Clinical Psychology, Principles of Intervention in the Clinic and Community.* New York: Basic Books, 1976.

Kunce, J., and Anderson, W. "Normalizing the MMPI." *Journal of Clinical Psychology* 32 (1976): 776–80.

Kunce, J., and Anderson, W. "Perspectives on Uses of the MMPI and Non-Psychiatric Settings." In P. McReynolds and G. Chelune (eds.) *Advances in Psychological Assessment.* San Francisco: Jossey-Bass, 1984.

Kurdek, L. "An Integrative Perspective on Children's Divorce Adjustment." *American Psychologist* 36 (1981): 856–66.

Kurdek, L.A., and Berg, B. "Correlates of Children's Adjustment to Their Parents' Divorces." In L. Kurdek (ed.), *Children and Divorce, New Decisions for Child Development.* San Francisco: Jossey-Bass, 1983.

Kurdek, L., Blisk, D., and Siesky A. "Correlates of Children's Long Term Adjustment to Their Parents' Divorce." *Developmental Psychology* 17 (1981): 565–79.

Lachar, D. *The MMPI: Clinical Assessment and Automative Interpretation.* Los Angeles: Western Psychological Services, 1974.

Lamb, Sharon. "Treating Sexually Abused Children: Issues of Blame and Responsibility." *American Journal of Orthopsychiatry* 56 (1986): 303–07.

Lanyon, R.I. "Psychological Assessment Procedures in Court-related Settings." *Professional Psychology: Research and Practice* 17 (1986): 260–68.

Lerner, Howard, and Lerner, Paul M. "Rorschach Inkblot Test." In D. Keyser and R. Sweetland, *Test Critiques.* Kansas City, Mo.: Test Corporation of America 4 (1984): 523–52.

Lewis, Dorothy Otnow. "Adult Antisocial Behavior and Criminality." In H. Kaplan and B. Sadock, *Comprehensive Textbook of Psychiatry/IV*, 1865–70. Baltimore: Williams & Wilkins, 1985.

Lowenstein, J., and Koopman, E.J. "A Comparison of the Self-Esteem Between Boys Living with Single Parent Mothers and Single Parent Fathers." *Journal of Divorce* 2 (1979): 195.

Lowery, C.R. "Child Custody Decisions in Divorce Proceedings: A Survey of Judges." *Professional Psychology* 12 (1981): 492–98.

Lowery, C.R. "The Wisdom of Solomon." *Law and Human Behavior* 8 (1984): 371–80.

Lowery, C.R. "Parents and Divorce: Identifying the Support Network for Decisions About Custody." *The American Journal of Family Therapy* 12 (1984): 26–32.

Lubin, Bernard, Larsen, Reed M., and Matarazzo, Joseph D. "Patterns of Psychological Test Usage in the United States: 1935-1982." *American Psychologist* 39 (1984): 451–54

Lundy, Allan. "Testing Conditions and TAT Validity: Meta-analysis of the Literature Through 1983." Paper presented at the meeting of the American Psychological Association, Toronto, August 1984.

Lundy, Allan. "The Reliability of the Thematic Apperception Test." *Journal of Personality Assessment* 49 (1985): 141–45.

Lundy, Allan. "Instructional Set and Thematic Apperception Test Validity." *Journal of Personality Assessment* 52 (1988): 309–20.

Lytle-Vieira, J. "Kramer vs. Kramer Revisited: The Social Work Role in Child Custody Cases." *Social Work* 32 (1987): 5–10.

MacAndrew, C. "The Differentiation of Male Alcoholic Outpatients from Non-alcoholic Psychiatric Outpatients by Using the MMPI." *Quarterly Journal of Studies in Alcohol* 26 (1965): 238–46.

Maccoby, Eleanor E. *Social Development: Psychological Growth and the Parent-Child Relationship.* New York: Harcourt Brace Jovanovich, 1980.

Mack, John E., and Ablon, Steven L. *The Development and Sustenance of Self-Esteem in Childhood.* New York: International Universities Press, 1983.

Majuro, R., Kahn, T., Vitaliano, P., Wagner, B., and Zegree, J. "Anger, Hostility and Depression in Domestically Violent Versus Generally Assaultive Men and Nonviolent Control Subjects." *Journal of Consulting and Clinical Psychology* 6 (1988): 17–23.

Manual of the International Statistical Classification of Diseases, Injuries, and Causes of Death, Clinical Modification, ICD-9-CM. 9th ed. Ann Arbor, Mich.: Commission on Professional and Hospital Activities, 1977.

Mara, Barbara. "Child Sexual Abuse." A Workshop Presented at the Southeastern Psychological Association Convention, Orlando, Fla., March 1986.

McCarthy, Dorothea. *Manual for the McCarthy Scales of Children's Abilities.* New York: The Psychological Corporation, 1972.

McDermott, J.F., Wem-Shing, Tseng, Char, W.I., and Fukunaga, M.A. *Child Custody Decision-Making.* New York: American Academy of Child Psychiatry, 1978.

McDonald, R., and Bynther, M. "MMPI Differences Associated with Sex, Race and Class and Two Adolescent Samples." *Journal of Consulting Psychology* 27 (1963): 112–16.

McKinney, Barbara, and Peterson, Rolf A. "Parenting Stress Index." In D. Keyser and R. Sweetland, *Test Critiques.* Kansas City, Mo.: Test Corporations of America 1 (1984): 504–05.

Megargee, E.I., Cook, P.E., and Mendelsohn, G.A. "Development and Validation of an MMPI Scale of Assaultiveness and Over-Controlled Individuals." *Journal of Abnormal Psychology* 72 (1967): 519–28.

Meissner, W. "Theories of Personality and Psychopathology: Classical Psychoanalysis." In H. Kaplan and B. Sadock, *Comprehensive Textbook of Psychiatry/IV,* 337–418. Baltimore: Williams & Wilkins, 1985.

Melton, G.B., and Limber, S. "Psychologists Involvement in Cases of Maltreatment: Limits of Role and Expertise." *American Psychologist* 44 (1989): 1225–33.

Melton, Gary B., Petrila, John, Poythress, Norman G., and Slobogin, Christopher. *Psychological Evaluations for the Courts: A Handbook for Mental Health Professionals and Lawyers.* New York: Guilford Press, 1987.

Mental Disability Law Reporter American Bar Association 7 (March-April 1983): 110–12.

Mitchell, James V., Jr. (ed.). *The Ninth Mental Measurements Yearbook.* Lincoln, Neb.: The Buros Institute of Mental Measurements, 1985.

Mitler, C., Wertz, C., and Counts, S. "Racial Differences on the MMPI." *Journal of Clinical Psychology* 17 (1961): 140–59.

Morey, L., Roberts, W., and Penk, W. "MMPI Alcoholic Subtypes: Replication and Validity of the 2-7-8-4 Subtype." *Journal of Abnormal Psychology* 96 (1987): 164–66.

Morgan, C.D., and Murray, H.A. "A Method for Investigating Fantasies: The Thematic Apperception Test." *Archives of Neurology and Psychiatry* 34 (1935): 289–306.

Murray, H.A., and the Staff of the Harvard Psychology Clinic. *Explorations in Personality.* New York: Oxford University Press, 1938.

Murray, H.A., and the Staff of the Harvard Psychology Clinic. *Thematic Apperception Test Manual.* Cambridge, Mass.: Harvard University, 1943.

NASW Standards for the Practice of Clinical Social Work. Silver Spring, Md.: National Association of Social Workers, 1984.

National Register of Health Service Providers in Psychology. Washington, D.C.: Council for the National Register of Health Service Providers in Psychology, 1987 ed.

Navran, L. "A Rationally Derived MMPI Scale to Measure Dependence." *Journal of Consulting Psychology* 18 (1954): 192.

Neal, J.H. "Children's Understanding of Their Parents' Divorces." In L. Kurdek (ed.), *Children and Divorce, New Directions for Child Development.* San Francisco: Jossey-Bass, 1983.

Nelson, S.E. "The Development of an Indirect Objection Measure, A Social Status and Relationship to Certain Psychiatric Syndromes." Doctoral Diss., University of Minnesota, 1952.

Newmark, Charles S. *Major Psychological Assessment Instruments*. Newton, Mass.: Allyn & Bacon, 1985.

Newsweek Magazine. December 8, 1986.

Nissenbaum, G. "The Expert at Trial: Tests Tell All." *Family Advocate* 9 (1986): 14–19.

Nichols, W.C. "Therapeutic Needs of Children in Family System Reorganization." *Journal of Divorce* 7 (1984): 23–43.

Ogdon, Donald P. *Psychodiagnotics and Personality Assessment: A Handbook*. Los Angeles: Western Psychological Services, 1977.

Ogdon, Donald P. *Psychodiagnostics and Personality Assessment: A Handbook*. 2d ed. Los Angeles: Western Psychological Services, 1984.

Otto, R., and Hall, J. "The Utility of the Michigan Alcoholism Screening Test in the Detection of Alcoholics and Problem Drinkers." *Journal of Personality Assessment* 52 (1988): 499–505.

Patterson, G., DeBaryshe, B., and Ramsey, E. "Developmental Perspective on Antisocial Behavior." *American Psychologist* 44 (1989): 329–35.

Pearlman, M. "Social Class Membership and Test Taking Attitude." Master's Thesis, University of Chicago, 1950.

Pearson, John, and Swenson, Wendell. *A User's Guide to the Mayo Clinic Automated MMPI Program*. New York: The Psychological Corporation, 1967.

Peterson, Rolf A. In O.K. Buros, *The Eighth Mental Measurements Yearbook*, 1042–45. Highland Park, N.J.: Gryphon Press, 1978.

Phillips, Leslie, and Smith, Joseph G. *Rorschach Interpretation: Advanced Technique*. New York: Grune & Stratton, 1953.

Pope, Kenneth S. "Clinical and Legal Issues in Assessing and Treating the Violent Patient." *The Independent Practitioner* (1986): 16–21.

"Precursors of Affective III May Be Detectable in Infants 12-15 Months." *Clinical Psychiatry News* 15 (1987): 1.

Preng, Kathryn W., and Clopton, James R. "Application of the MacAndrew Alcoholism Scale to Alcoholics with Psychiatric Diagnosis." *Journal of Personality Assessment* 50 (1986): 113–22.

The Psychological Corporation. *1987 Catalog: Tests, Products and Services for Psychological Assessment.* New York: Harcourt Brace Jovanovich, 1987.

Roseby, V. "A Custody Evaluation Model for Pre-School Children." Paper presented at the meeting of the American Psychological Association, Toronto, Canada, August 1984.

Rosen, R. "Some Crucial Issues Concerning Children of Divorce." *Journal of Divorce* 3 (1979): 19–26.

Rotter, J., and Rafferty, J. *Manual, The Rotter Incomplete Sentences Blank.* Cleveland: The Psychological Corporation, 1950.

Ryan, R. "Thematic Apperception Test." In D. Keyser and R. Sweetland, *Test Critiques.* Kansas City, Mo.: Test Corporation of America 2 (1984): 799–814.

Sack, Stephen Mitchell. *The Complete Legal Guide to Marriage, Divorce, Custody, and Living Together.* New York: McGraw-Hill, 1987.

Santrock, J., and Warshak, R. "Father Custody and Social Development in Boys and Girls." *Journal of Social Issues* 35 (1979): 112.

Sattler, J. *Assessments of Children's Intelligence and Special Abilities.* 2d ed. Boston: Allyn & Bacon, 1982.

Sattler, Jerome M. *Assessment of Children.* 3d ed. San Diego: Jerome Sattler, 1988.

Schenkenberg, T., Gottfredson, D., and Christensen, P. "Age Differences in the MMPI Scale Scores from 1189 Psychiatric Patients." *Journal of Clinical Psychology* 40 (1984): 1420–26.

Schwartz, L.L. *The Effects of Divorce on Children at Different Ages: A Descriptive Study.* ERIC, ED. 1985, 261–67.

Scott, Ronald, and Stone, David. "MMPI Measures of Psychological Disturbance in Adolescent and Adult Victims of Father-Daughter Incest." *Journal of Clinical Psychology* 42 (1986): 251–59.

Scott, Ronald, and Stone, David. "MMPI Profile Constellations in Incest Families." *Journal of Consulting and Clinical Psychology* 54 (1986): 364–68.

Serkownek, K. *Subscales for Scales 5 and 0 of the MMPI.* Unpublished Manuscript, 1975.

Shiller, Virginia. "Joint versus Maternal Custody for Families with Latency Age Boys: Parent Characteristics and Child Adjustment." *American Journal of Orthopsychiatry* 56 (1986): 486–89.

Shuman, Daniel W. *Psychiatric and Psychological Evidence.* Colorado Springs: Shepard's/McGraw-Hill, 1986.

Siegel, M. "Cognitive and Projective Test Assessment." In C. Kestenbaum and D. Williams (eds.), *Handbook of Clinical Assessment of Children and Adolescents,* 359–84. New York: New York University Press, 1988.

Skafte, D. *Child Custody Evaluations: A Practical Guide.* Beverly Hills, Cal.: Sage, 1985.

Smith, J. *Medical Malpractice Psychiatric Care.* Colorado Springs: Shepard's/McGraw-Hill, 1986.

Specialty Guidelines for the Delivery of Services. Washington, D.C.: American Psychological Association, 1981.

Spence, Janet T., Cotton, John W., Underwood, Benton J., and Duncan, Carl P. *Elementary Statistics.* 4th ed. Englewood Cliffs, N.J.: Prentice-Hall, 1983.

Spitzer, R., and Williams, J. "Classification of Mental Disorders." In H. Kaplan and B. Sadock, *Comprehensive Textbook of Psychiatry/IV,* 591–613. 4th ed. Baltimore: Williams & Wilkins, 1985.

Sprinthall, Richard C. *Basic Statistical Analysis.* 2d ed. Englewood Cliffs, N.J.: Prentice-Hall, 1987.

Sprock, J., and Blashfield, R. "Classification and Nosology." In M. Hersen, A. Kazdin, and A. Bellack, *The Clinical Psychology Handbook,* 289–307. New York: Pergamon, 1983.

Standards for Educational and Psychological Testing. Washington, D.C.: American Psychological Association, 1985.

Stein, K.B. "The TSC Scales: The Outcome of a Cluster Analysis of the 550 MMPI Items." In P. McReynolds (ed.), *Advances in Psychological Assessment* Vol. I. Palo Alto: Science and Behavior Books, 1968.

Stein, M.I. "Thematic Apperception Test and Related Methods." In B. Wolman (ed.), *Clinical Diagnosis of Mental Disorders,* 179–235. New York: Plenum Press, 1978.

Steinman, Susan. "The Experience of Children in a Joint Custody Arrangement: A Report of a Study." *American Journal of Orthopsychiatry* 51 (1981): 403–14.

Stolberg, A.L., and Anker, J.M. "Cognitive and Behavioral Changes in Children Resulting from Parental Divorce and Consequent Environmental Changes." *Journal of Divorce* 7 (1984): 23–40.

Stolberg, A.L., and Cullen, P.M. "Preventive Interventions for Families of Divorce: The Divorce Adjustment Project." In L. Kurdek (ed.), *Children and Divorce: New Directions for Child Development.* San Francisco: Jossey-Bass, 1983.

Stone, Evelyn M. *American Psychiatric Glossary.* Washington, D.C.: American Psychiatric Press, 1988.

Stromberg, Clifford D., Haggarty, D.J., Leibenluft, R.F., McMillian, M.H., Mishkin, B., Rubin, B.L., and Trilling, H.R. *The Psychologist's Legal Handbook.* Washington, D.C.: The Council for the National Register of Health Service Providers in Psychology, 1988.

Swanson, Lisa, and Baiggio, Mary Kay. "Therapeutic Perspectives on Father-Daughter Incest." *American Journal of Psychiatry* 142 (1985): 667–74.

Swartz, Jon D. "Thematic Apperception Test." In O. Buros, *The Eighth Mental Measurements Yearbook,* 1127–30. Highland Park, N.J.: Gryphon Press/Highland Press, 1978.

Tarasoff v. The Regents of the University of California, 551 P.2d 334 (Cal. 1983).

Thompson, R.A. "The Father's Case in Child Custody Disputes."
In M. Lamb and A. Sagi (eds.), *Fatherhood and Family
Policy*. Hillsdale, N.J.: Lawrence Erlbaum, 1983.

Thorndike, Robert L., Hagen, Elizabeth P., and Sattler, Jerome
M. *Stanford-Binet Intelligence Scale: 4th Ed.: Guide for
Administering and Scoring*. Chicago: Riverside
Publishing, 1986.

Thorndike, Robert L., Hagen, Elizabeth P., and Sattler, Jerome
M. *Stanford-Binet Intelligence Scale: 4th Ed.: Technical
Manual*. Chicago: Riverside Publishing, 1986.

Tischler, G. "Evaluation of DSM-III." In H. Kaplan and B.
Sadock, *Comprehensive Textbook of Psychiatry/IV*,
617–21. 4th ed. Baltimore: Williams & Wilkins, 1985.

Tritell, Susan. "Diagnostic and Therapeutic Uses of Drawings
of Children Who Have Been Sexually Abused, A Review
of the Literature." Doctoral Diss., Wisconsin School of
Professional Psychology, 1988.

Tromboli, R., and Kilgore, R. "A Psychodynamic Approach to
MMPI Interpretation." *Journal of Personality
Assessment* 47 (1983): 614–26.

Wagner, Edwin E., Alexander, Ralph A., Roos, Gary, and Adair,
Holiday. "Optimum Split-Half Reliabilities for the
Rorschach: Projective Techniques Are More Reliable
Than We Think." *Journal of Personality Assessment* 50
(1986): 107–12.

Wallerstein, J.S. "Children of Divorce: The Psychological Tasks
of the Child." *American Journal of Orthopsychiatry* 53
(1983): 230–45.

Wallerstein, Judith. "Children of Divorce: Preliminary Report
of a Ten-Year Follow-up of Older Children and
Adolescents." *Journal of the American Academy of
Child Psychiatry* 24 (1985): 545–53.

Wallerstein, Judith. Cape Cod Institute. Greenwich, Conn.:
Institute for Psychological Study, 1986.

Wallerstein, Judith. "Children of Divorce: Report of a Ten-Year
Follow-up of Early Latency Age Children." *American
Journal of Orthopsychiatry* 57 (1987): 199–211.

Wallerstein, J., and Blakeslee, S. *Second Chances.* New York: Ticknor & Fields, 1989.

Wallerstein, Judith, and Corbin, Shauna. "Father-Child Relationships After Divorce: Child Support and Educational Opportunity." *Family Law Quarterly* 20 (1986): 109–28.

Wallerstein, J.S., and Kelly, J.B. *Surviving the Break-up: How Children and Parents Cope with Divorce.* New York: Basic Books, 1980.

Warshak, R.A., and Santrock, J.W. "The Impact of Divorce in Father-Custody and Mother-Custody Homes: The Child's Perspective." In L. Kurdak (ed.), *Children and Divorce: New Directions for Child Development.* San Francisco: Jossey-Bass, 1983.

Watkins, C., and Campbell, V. "Personality Assessment and Counseling Psychology." *Journal of Personality Assessment* 53 (1989): 296–307.

Watson, Robert I., Jr. "The Sentence Completion Method." In B. Wolman (ed.), *Clinical Diagnosis of Mental Disorders: A Handbook,* 255–79. New York: Plenum Press, 1978.

Wechsler, David. *Manual for the Pre-school and Primary Scale of Intelligence.* New York: Psychological Corporation, 1967.

Wechsler, David. *Manual for the Wechsler Intelligence Scale for Children-Revised.* New York: Psychological Corporation, 1974.

Wechsler, David. *The Measurement and Appraisal of Adult Intelligence.* 4th ed. Baltimore: Williams & Wilkins, 1958.

Wechsler, David. *Wechsler Adult Intelligence Scale-Revised.* New York: Psychological Corporation, 1981.

Weithorn, L. "Psychological Consultation in Divorce Custody Litigation." In L. Weithorn (ed.), *Psychology and Child Custody Determinations.* Lincoln, Neb.: University of Nebraska Press, 1987.

Weithorn, L., and Grisso, T. "Psychological Evaluations in Divorce Custody: Problems, Principles, Procedures." In L. Weithorn (ed.), *Psychology and Child Custody Determinations*. Lincoln, Neb.: University of Nebraska Press, 1987.

Weithorn, Lois A., (ed.). "Psychology and Child Custody Determinations Knowledge." *Roles and Expertise*. Lincoln, Neb.: University of Nebraska Press, 1987.

Well, Robert, Bogat, G. Anne, and Davidson, William S., II. "The Assessment of Child Abuse Potential and the Prevention of Child Abuse and Neglect: A Policy Analysis." *American Journal of Community Psychology*, in press.

Whiting, L. Personal communication. December 20, 1988.

Whiting, L. *State Comparison of Laws Regulating Social Work*. Silver Spring, Md.: National Association of Social Workers, 1988.

Wiggins, Elizabeth, and Brandt, Jason. "The Detection of Simulated Amnesia." *Law and Human Behavior* 2 (1988): 57–78.

Wiggins, J.S., Goldberg, L.R., and Applebom, M. "MMPI Content Scales: Interpretive Norms and Correlations with Other Scales." *Journal of Consulting and Clinical Psychology* 37 (1971): 403–10.

Wiener, E.M. "Subtle and Obvious Keys for the MMPI." *Journal of Consulting Psychology* 12 (1984): 164–70.

Williams, H.L. "Development of a Causality Scale for the MMPI." *Journal of Clinical Psychology* 8 (1952): 293–97.

Wohl, A., and Kaufman, B. *Silent Screams and Hidden Cries: An Interpretation of Art Work by Children from Violent Homes*. New York: Brunner/Mazel, 1985.

Woititz, J. "Adult Children of Alcoholics." In *The Medical Psychotherapist* 5 (1989): 9.

Wolfe, David, Edwards, Betty, Manion, Ian, and Koverola, Catherine. "Early Intervention for Parents at Risk of Child Abuse and Neglect: A Preliminary Investigation." *Journal of Consulting and Clinical Psychology* 6 (1988): 40–47.

Wolman, Benjamin. *Clinical Diagnosis of Mental Disorders: A Handbook*. New York: Plenum Press, 1978.

Ziskin, Jay. *Coping with Psychiatric and Psychological Testimony*. 3d ed. Venice, Cal.: Law & Psychology Press, 1981.

Ziskin, J. "Use of the MMPI in Forensic Settings." In J. Butcher, G. Dahlstrom, M. Gynther, and W. Schofield (eds.), *Clinical Notes on the MMPI*. Minneapolis: National Computer Systems 9, 1981.

Index